TECHNOLOGY-DRIVEN SUPPLY CHAIN MANAGEMENT IN INDUSTRIAL 4.0 ERA

Resilience, Responsiveness and Reliability

TECHNOLOGY-DRIVEN SUPPLY CHAIN MANAGEMENT IN INDUSTRIAL 4.0 ERA

Resilience, Responsiveness and Reliability

Editors

Bin Shen
Donghua University, China

Ciwei Dong
Zhongnan University of Economics and Law, China

Chi To Ng
The Hong Kong Polytechnic University, Hong Kong

World Scientific

NEW JERSEY • LONDON • SINGAPORE • GENEVA • BEIJING • SHANGHAI • TAIPEI • CHENNAI

Published by

World Scientific Publishing Co. Pte. Ltd.
5 Toh Tuck Link, Singapore 596224
USA office: 27 Warren Street, Suite 401-402, Hackensack, NJ 07601
UK office: 57 Shelton Street, Covent Garden, London WC2H 9HE

Library of Congress Control Number: 2025005538

British Library Cataloguing-in-Publication Data
A catalogue record for this book is available from the British Library.

TECHNOLOGY-DRIVEN SUPPLY CHAIN MANAGEMENT IN INDUSTRIAL 4.0 ERA
Resilience, Responsiveness and Reliability

ISBN 978-981-98-1170-0 (hardcover)
ISBN 978-981-98-0858-8 (ebook for institutions)
ISBN 978-981-98-1171-7 (ebook for individuals)

For any available supplementary material, please visit
https://www.worldscientific.com/worldscibooks/10.1142/14235#t=suppl

Desk Editors: Soundararajan Raghuraman/Pui Yee Lum

Typeset by Stallion Press
Email: enquiries@stallionpress.com

https://doi.org/10.1142/9789819808588_fmatter

Preface

Industry 4.0 has profoundly impacted the global economy in recent decades. With its rapid development, automated and intelligent production using Cyber–Physical Systems and the Internet of Things (IoT) has been realized through the digitalization of industrial value chains and has transformed the approaches to managing supply chains. This book — *Technology-Driven Supply Chain Management in the Industrial 4.0 Era: Resilience, Responsiveness, and Reliability* — delves into the heart of this revolution. It explores how advanced technologies are reshaping the supply chain landscape and enabling organizations to achieve unprecedented levels of efficiency, agility, and robustness.

In this book, we examine how technology-driven supply chain systems and networks can affect resilience, responsiveness, and reliability in the Industrial 4.0 era. This book is a testament to the power of technology in driving supply chain excellence. It serves as a valuable resource for professionals, academics, and students alike, offering insights into the latest trends, case studies, and best practices in the field. We have brought together a diverse group of experts who share their knowledge and experiences, providing a 360-degree view of the challenges and opportunities that lie ahead.

As we step into the future, the supply chain has evolved from a mere operational function to a strategic asset. It is the lifeline of any organization, and its management is critical to success in a competitive marketplace. The pages that follow are not just a compilation of theories but a practical guide to navigate the complexities of the modern supply chain, equipped with the transformative tools and technologies of Industry 4.0.

We invite you to join us on this exploration of technology-driven supply chain management, where every page promises to unlock new insights and strategies for building a supply chain that is not only efficient but also adaptable, intelligent, and future-proof. If you have any queries or suggestions for the book, feel free to contact Ciwei Dong at dongciwei@zuel.edu.cn.

Bin Shen, Ciwei Dong, and Chi To Ng
January 31, 2025

https://doi.org/10.1142/9789819808588_fmatter

About the Editors

Bin Shen is Professor and Vice Dean at Glorious Sun School of Business and Management, Donghua University, Shanghai. He was a Humboldt Fellow in Germany. His research interests focus on supply chain management, digitalization, and ESG. His work has appeared in *Production and Operations Management, Journal of Business Ethics, Decision Science Journal, European Journal of Operational Research, International Journal of Production Economics*, and *Transportation Research Part E — Logistics and Transportation Review*, among others. He is the associate editor of *Transportation Research Part E — Logistics and Transportation Review* and the senior editor of *Electronic Commerce Research and Applications.*

Ciwei Dong is Professor at the School of Business Administration, Zhongnan University of Economics and Law, China. His research interests are in supply chain management, sustainable operations, technology and operations management, etc. His work has appeared in *Asia-Pacific Journal of Operational Research, Production and Operations Management, European Journal of Operational Research, International Journal of Production Economics, Transportation Research Part E — Logistics and Transportation Review*, and *Annals of Operations Research*, among others.

Chi To Ng is Professor at the Department of Logistics and Maritime Studies, The Hong Kong Polytechnic University. He obtained his Ph.D. from The Chinese University of Hong Kong. His research interests include optimization, supply chain management, operations management, scheduling, and healthcare management. He has published over 170 papers in prestigious international journals, such as *Production and Operations Management*, *Naval Research Logistics*, *IEEE Transactions on Automatic Control*, *Operations Research Letters*, *European Journal of Operational Research*, *International Journal of Production Economics*, and *Computers and Operations Research.*

https://doi.org/10.1142/9789819808588_fmatter

Contents

https://doi.org/10.1142/9789819808588_fmatter

Introduction

Bin Shen, Ciwei Dong, and Chi To Ng

Technology is a key driver in the transformation of the business landscape. In recent years, cutting-edge innovations like blockchain, sophisticated robotics, 3D printing, automated identification technologies, the Internet of Things (IoT), machine learning, and artificial intelligence have been popularly adopted in supply chain management. These innovations can not only improve business performance but also enhance supply chain resilience, responsiveness, and reliability. (The definitions of resilience, responsiveness, and reliability are shown in Table 1.) It has been recognized that the new technologies adopted in supply chains can help achieve unparalleled ability for precise measurement, tracking, and transparency.

Integrating innovative technologies makes supply chains more resilient, responsive, and reliable. Advanced technologies are pivotal in enhancing supply chain performance. They enable tighter control over manufacturing processes, develop more efficient inventory management, and foster greater collaboration among

Table 1. Definitions of resilience, responsiveness, and reliability.

Term	Definitions
Resilience	It refers to the ability of a supply chain to withstand and recover from disruptions. In an era where global events can ripple through supply chains with unprecedented speed, the importance of building resilient systems cannot be overstated. This book will examine the technologies and strategies that enable supply chains to absorb shocks and continue to function effectively.
Responsiveness	It refers to the capacity to adapt quickly to changes in demand and supply. With the rise of e-commerce, consumer expectations for rapid delivery and customization have skyrocketed. We will discuss how technology-driven supply chains can sense and react to these changes in real time, ensuring customer satisfaction and competitive advantage.
Reliability	It is the cornerstone of trust in any supply chain. It encompasses the consistent delivery of products and services as promised. In the Industrial 4.0 era, reliability is not just about meeting expectations but also about exceeding them through the seamless integration of technology into every aspect of the supply chain.

supply chain partners. Additionally, they boost the efficiency of order tracking and delivery, enable swift responses to market changes, and allow for more precise demand forecasting. Leveraging cutting-edge technologies like blockchain and IoT, supply chain participants can share demand-and-supply information transparently, reducing information asymmetry. This transparency facilitates closer collaboration through shared insights, thereby enhancing overall channel performance. A case in point is the automotive industry, which has extensively adopted IoT and blockchain to achieve transparency and visibility in information flow.

Automatic identification technologies, such as Radio-Frequency Identification (RFID), offer transparency in inventory levels, enhance inventory management, and provide the technological foundation for rapid responses. The food industry, for example, has embraced RFID to maintain visible inventory levels and improve supply chain transparency and visibility. This is particularly crucial in the food sector due to the perishable nature of its products, where access to data on inventory quantities and locations is essential.

Additive manufacturing and advanced robotics also play a significant role in increasing productivity and streamlining production processes. Additive manufacturing, which includes 3D printing, is transforming the manufacturing and retail sectors by enhancing supply chain efficiency and enabling customization to meet consumer demands. The healthcare and jewelry industries have been among the early adopters of 3D printing technology.

Table 2. Examples of advanced technologies and their values in supply chain management.

Values of advanced technologies in supply chain management	List of relevant advanced technologies	Supply chain impacts
Increased control over production	Advanced robotics, additive manufacturing, the Internet of Things, and artificial intelligence	Improving resilience
Better inventory management	Automatic identification, the Internet of Things, machine learning, and artificial intelligence	Improving resilience
Increased collaboration between supply chain partners	Blockchain, automatic identification, and the Internet of Things	Improving reliability
More effective order tracking and delivery	Automatic identification and the Internet of Things	Improving responsiveness
Quick response	Advanced robotics, additive manufacturing, automatic identification, the Internet of Things, and machine learning	Improving responsiveness
Increased supply chain transparency	Blockchain, automatic identification, and the Internet of Things	Improving reliability
Demand forecasting	Automatic identification, the Internet of Things, machine learning, and artificial intelligence	Improving responsiveness

In the retail sector, information technology is now being used to generate vast datasets on consumer preferences. Recent studies have shown that machine learning and artificial intelligence are poised to make significant contributions by providing more accurate market demand forecasts. These technologies are set to revolutionize how businesses understand and respond to consumer behavior.

In this book, we will cover 10 chapters on technology-driven supply chain management in Industry 4.0. We aim to help supply chain executives progressively overhaul their strategic approaches and embrace cutting-edge technological advancements (Table 2). The findings can provide managerial insights into new initiatives to improve the supply chain resilience, responsiveness, and reliability of organizations that are confronted with numerous decisions to balance potential benefits against the challenges they may encounter.

https://doi.org/10.1142/9789819808588_fmatter

Acknowledgments

This book was partially funded by the Key Program of the National Social Science Foundation of China (Grant No. 23AZD030) and the National Natural Science Foundation of China (Grant No. 72271050, 72371248).

https://doi.org/10.1142/9789819808588_0001

Chapter 1

Operational Research for Technology-Driven Supply Chains in the Industry 4.0 Era: Recent Development and Future Studies†

Suyuan Luo

College of Economics and College of Management
Shenzhen University, 3688 Nanhai Avenue
Nanshan District, Shenzhen 518006, P. R. China
suyuanluo@126.com

Tsan-Ming Choi*

Business Division, Institute of Textiles and Clothing
The Hong Kong Polytechnic University
Hung Hom, Kowloon, Hong Kong
jason.choi@polyu.edu.hk

Today, supply chain operations have entered the Industry 4.0 era. Technologies, such as blockchain, big-data, artificial intelligence, additive manufacturing and cloud-computing, are all hot topics. Motivated by their importance, in this paper, we conduct a review of the closely related literature in the well-established mainstream operational research (OR) journals. From our research, we first examine the OR literature on Industry 4.0 related studies. Then we classify the technology-operations-related literature into three major categories, namely, information technologies for supply chain operations, technologies for sustainable operations, and technologies for production operations. Various less popular areas on technology-driven operations in supply chains, namely, technology licensing and outsourcing (TLO), online data, and risk, finance and security (RFS), are also examined. From the reviews, we identify the major research gaps. After that, we establish a future research agenda. We believed that this paper lays the foundation for further OR studies on technology-driven supply chain management in the Industry 4.0 era.

Keywords: Industry 4.0; technology-driven supply chain operations; operational research (OR); research agenda; literature review.

*Corresponding author.
†To cite this article, please refer to its earlier version published in the Asia-Pacific Journal of Operational Research, Vol. 39, No. 1, (February 2022), DOI: 10.1142/S0217595920400217. Reprinted with permission from World Scientific Publishing Co. Pte. Ltd.

1. Introduction

1.1. *Background*

Manufacturing and service operations have entered the digital age. Blockchain (Babich and Hilary, 2020; Choi and Luo, 2019; Choi *et al.*, 2019), big data analytics (Shen and Chan, 2017; Choi, 2018; Nguyen *et al.*, 2018), Internet of Things (IoTs), artificial intelligence (AI) (Luo *et al.*, 2019; Akter *et al.*, 2020), cloud computing (Tsai *et al.*, 2013; Manuel, 2015), additive manufacturing (Song and Zhang, 2020; Arbabian and Wagner, 2020), cyber-systems, human–machine interactions (Ding *et al.*, 2020), etc., are all hot terminologies (or "buzzwords") that can be seen in both the industry and the operational research (OR) literature. In fact, Industry 4.0 (Tang and Veelenturf, 2019; Abdul-Hamid *et al.*, 2020) can be described in a laymen term as the fourth industrial revolution in which supply chain operations and industrial manufacturing are all highly automatic and supported by technologies such as robotics, AI, IoTs, etc. Industry 4.0 is commonly regarded as an extension of Industry 3.0 in which computerization is achieved.[a] Major and popular cases of successful industrial development in the Industry 4.0 era include auto-mobile manufacturing using flexible cell manufacturing,[b] battery production for "electric vehicles"[c] and intelligent future factory using AI.[d] Even though it is argued that not all companies and industries are ready,[e] it is commonly believed that most business operations would be affected and moved towards the Industry 4.0 era. For instance, flexible manufacturing systems (Lin *et al.*, 2018) and smart factory models would be more and more common.

See Table 1 for some technologies which are widely applied in Industry 3.0 and Industry 4.0. Figure 1 further shows the respective technological transitions from Industry 3.0 to Industry 4.0.[f] For more details of manufacturing operations in the Industry 4.0 era, refer to the technical report by Deloitte.[g]

In manufacturing engineering, several prior studies have been conducted to reveal insights regarding how different technologies (such as blockchains technology (Choi, 2019), decision support systems (Wang *et al.*, 2019) and robotics) play a role

[a] https://www.forbes.com/sites/bernardmarr/2018/09/02/what-is-industry-4-0-heres-a-super-easy-explanation-for-anyone/#13efaba29788 (accessed 23 July 2020).
[b] https://www.bcg.com/publications/2018/flexible-cell-manufacturing-revolutionize-carmaking (accessed 1 August 2020).
[c] https://www.bcg.com/publications/2018/future-battery-production-electric-vehicles (accessed 1 August 2020).
[d] https://www.bcg.com/publications/2018/artificial-intelligence-factory-future (accessed 1 August 2020).
[e] https://www2.deloitte.com/us/en/insights/deloitte-review/issue-22/industry-4-0-technology-manufacturing-revolution.html (accessed 1 August 2020).
[f] Note that there are many more related technologies, see the following URL For nine technologies that are related to industrial production in the Industry 4.0 era: https://www.bcg.com/capabilities/operations/embracing-industry-4.0-rediscovering-growth (accessed 1 August 2020).
[g] https://www2.deloitte.com/content/dam/Deloitte/ch/Documents/manufacturing/ch-en-manufacturing-industry-4-0-24102014.pdf (accessed 1 August 2020).

Table 1. Common technologies being utilized in operations in Industry 4.0/Industry 3.0.

Technologies	In Industry 4.0 or Industry 3.0
ERP systems	Industry 3.0
Internt based EDI	Industry 3.0
Robots	Industry 3.0 ("Common" machines/robots) Industry 4.0 (Smart robotics)
Cloud computing	Industry 3.0 and Industry 4.0
Blockchain technology	Industry 4.0
IoTs	Industry 4.0
AI	Industry 4.0
Additive manufacturing (3D printing)	Industry 4.0

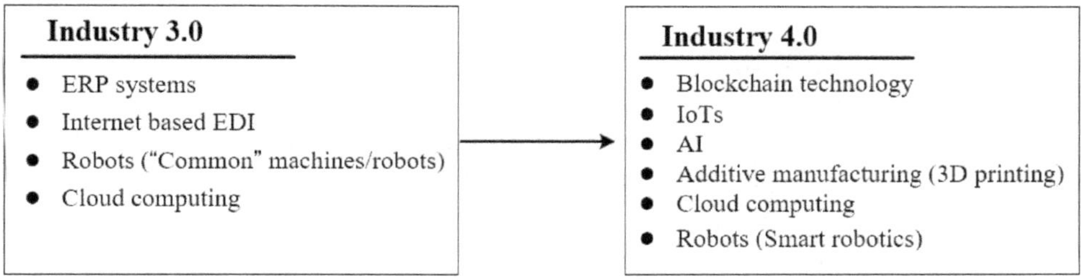

Fig. 1. Transitions of the major technologies for supply chain operations from Industry 3.0 to Industry 4.0.

in industrial applications. In production research, many analyses have been carried out to highlight how data (such as real time data) could be best utilized to enhance production efficiency. In OR, many scattered studies are examining different facets of Industry 4.0 and the associated technology-driven supply chains. However, there is a lack of a consolidated view of the current state-of-the-arts studies in the area.

Motivated by the importance of Industry 4.0 and the related challenges in the corresponding technology-driven supply chain operations, we develop this paper with a goal of reviewing the current OR literature and uncovering the most highly relevant studies in the area. This will lay the foundation for further studies in the area.

1.2. *Methodology, contribution statement, and paper's structure*

In this paper, we aim to identify the most relevant studies in mainstream OR literature. We do not aim to be exhaustive. Instead, we focus on relevance and quality. As a result, we conducted a title word searching in Google Scholar. We focus on the well-established leading OR journals such as *Annals of Operations Research*, *Asia-Pacific Journal of Operational Research*, *Computers and Operations Research*, *European Journal of Operational Research*, *International Transactions in Operational Research*, *Journal of the Operational Research Society*, *OR Spectrum*, *Operations*

Research, and *Operations Research Letters*. We first search for the title word of "Industry 4.0". Then, we search for the title words including both "technology" and "supply chain". After that, we further expand the searching with "technology" only while we conduct a content analysis one by one. Finally, we identify the set of 31 papers. Then, we supplement the searching results with our own acquaintance of the field. From all the collected articles, we proceed to conduct the classifications as well as digestions of the content. The details will be reported in the subsequent sections.

As a remark, for the classification schemes, we basically follow the searching outcomes and put the related works together. To be specific, "Industry 4.0" is naturally a group. Then, information technologies for supply chain operations, technologies for sustainable operations, and technologies for production operations become the other important classified areas for examination.[h]

To the best of our knowledge, this is the first study focusing on reviewing prior OR studies on research related to technology-driven supply chain operations in the Industry 4.0 era. Both research gaps and future research agenda are proposed. The findings would provide hence a good reference value to both the industrialists and academics.

The rest of this paper is arranged as follows. Section 2 shows the review of OR studies in the industry 4.0 related papers. Section 3 is devoted to the examination of operations studies in technology-driven supply chains. Section 4 presents the

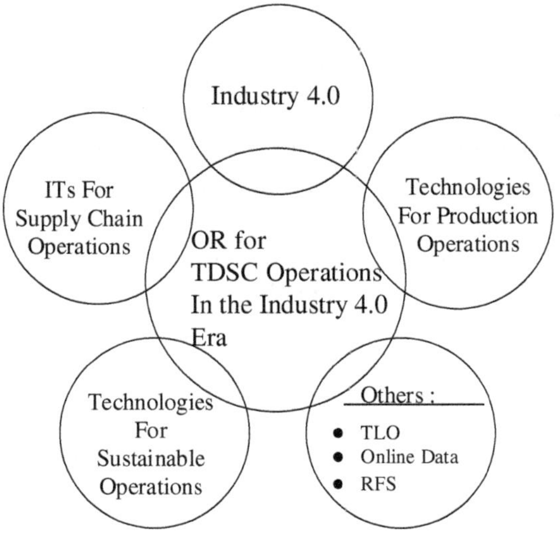

Fig. 2. Classifications of the reviewed papers. (P.S.: TDSC: Technology-driven supply chain).

[h]Note that a paper may fall into more than one classified area. In this case, we would put the paper in the area which is deemed as the most relevant one.

Table 2. The list of OR journals in which the reviewed papers are selected and the corresponding numbers of papers referenced in this paper.

Journals	Numbers
Annals of Operations Research	12
Asia-Pacific Journal of Operational Research	6
Computers and Operations Research	7
European Journal of Operational Research	22
International Transactions in Operational Research	4
Journal of the Operational Research Society	4
Operations Research	5
Operations Research Letters	1
OR Spectrum	1

research gaps. Section 5 introduces the future research agenda. Section 6 concludes this paper with a discussion of limitations.

To better present classifications of the reviewed literature, we prepare Fig. 2 in which the five major scopes of studies are depicted. Table 2 also shows the number of OR papers we made reference to in this paper. From Table 2, we can see that *European Journal of Operational Research*, and *Annals of Operations Research* are the two OR journals in which most related papers are referenced. Then, *Asia-Pacific Journal of Operational Research*, and *Computers and Operations Research* follow. All these four OR journals are hence very important outlets publishing research in technology-driven supply chain operations.

2. Operations Issues in Industry 4.0

In the Industry 4.0 era, human–machine interactions are critical. In the OR literature, Schlüter *et al.* (2016) examine supply chains in the steel industry. The authors present a system in which real-data can be collected to help identify operational risk proactively. Lin *et al.* (2019) empirically explore the critical factors associated with Industry 4.0. Using the data from the Chinese production sector, the authors reveal the influences of how these critical factors affect corporate profitability. They also interestingly highlight that the sponsors from the government may not be as significant as conventional wisdom might have predicted. Fragapane *et al.* (2020) study the intralogistics operations in manufacturing systems. The authors explore the machine scheduling problems associated with the use of robotics. They demonstrate the benefits that can be created by the use of "autonomous mobile robots". Ghaleb *et al.* (2020) study manufacturing operations challenges with the use of Industry 4.0's technologies. The authors discuss the impacts of stochastic "job arrivals" and "machine breakdowns". The key aspect that the authors highlight is the use of "real-time information" and how it improves production scheduling. Based on the classic "flexible job-shop scheduling problem", the authors propose an improved optimal decision with the use of real-time available information.

Motivated by the importance of sustainability, de Sousa Jabbour *et al.* (2018) consider both the circular economy concept and Industry 4.0 together. The authors review the related literature. Then, they establish a new proposal for further studies. They also depict an insightful roadmap for operations in the circular economy. After that, Liu and De Giovanni (2019) analytically investigate the channel coordination challenges in Industry 4.0. The authors focus on highlighting how various technologies, such as additive manufacturing and auto-robots, can be used to reduce emissions and wastages of materials. The authors uncover that with "green process innovation", Pareto optimality can be achieved. Most recently, Abdul-Hamid *et al.* (2020) conduct an industry-based study and uncover how Industry 4.0 affects sustainable supply chain operations (i.e., the "circular economy). The authors focus on

Table 3. Summary of the reviewed OR papers in Industry 4.0.

Papers	Analytical	Empirical	Conceptual	Key features	Key insights/ findings
Schlüter *et al.* (2016)	X			Real data empirical analyses	A proactive risk identification scheme is developed.
Lin *et al.* (2019)		X		Real data empirical analyses	Critical factors for Chinese manufacturers in the Industry 4.0 era.
Fragapane *et al.* (2020)	X			Scheduling optimization	Autonomous mobile robots-based scheduling schemes are developed.
Ghaleb *et al.* (2020)	X			Scheduling optimization	How real time data can be used to enhance production scheduling.
de Sousa Jabbour *et al.* (2018)			X	Literature review based analyses	A framework for Industry 4.0 in the circular economy.
Liu and De Giovanni (2019)	X			Pareto optimality analyses	Coordination of green process innovation in supply chains with Industry 4.0 technologies.
Abdul-Hamid *et al.* (2020)		X		Real data empirical analyses	Identify the key factors to achieve circular economy in the Industry 4.0 era.

the Malaysian "palm oil industry". The authors apply the "fuzzy Delphi method" to analyze the collected data. They identify various critical issues that are crucial and fundamental for achieving the circular economy in Industry 4.0 era.

Table 3 shows a summary of the literature reviewed in the scope of "operations issues in Industry 4.0".

Note that an important aspect of Industry 4.0 is the deployment of big data analytics and related tools (Zhang *et al.*, 2018). For instance, Kaur and Singh (2018) propose the use of big data to reduce emissions for purchasing and sourcing problems in the Industry 4.0 era. The authors build standard optimization models and develop heuristic algorithms to solve the problem. Zhan and Tan (2020) develop how big data can be employed to improve supply chain profitability. The authors establish a new analytical framework. As the area is huge, interested readers can refer to various related reviews or discussion papers. For example, regarding the use of big data for "simulation optimization", please refer to Xu *et al.* (2015). For demand forecast updates with the use of data, see Shen and Chan (2017). We refer readers to Choi *et al.* (2018), Nguyen *et al.* (2018) and Galetsi and Katsaliaki (2019) for a comprehensive discussion of the use of big data for supply chain operations.

3. Technology and Supply Chain Operations

3.1. *Information technologies for supply chain operations*

For technology-driven supply chains, the "radio frequency identification (RFID) technology" is probably the most commonly explored IT device. In the OR literature, Sari (2010) studies the performance of adopting RFID with the consideration of a four-level supply system. The author explores when it is advantageous to adopt RFID technology. The author finds the cooperation degree plays a critical role. Tao *et al.* (2020) discuss the management of inventory related to RFID technology via conducting a game-theoretic analysis. The authors discover that both the manufacturer and dealer would tend to pay the "RDIF tag cost" according to the sharing rate.

Other than RFID, telecommunication and blockchain technology are also important. In the earlier date, Çanakoğlu and Bilgiç (2007) theoretically study the telecommunication industry facing random demand. The authors take the "profit-sharing contract" and "coordinating quantity discount contract" into consideration. Then, they analytically examine the optimal decision for the input for the technology and the network volume. Zheng *et al.* (2020) examine the blockchain technology that supported the contracting mechanism. The authors highlight how intelligent contracting can be implemented using blockchain. Most recently, Fan *et al.* (2020) analytically explore whether it is beneficial to apply blockchain in business operations. The authors focus on examining consumer preferences towards product provenance information. They theoretically uncover when it is wise to adopt this advanced important technology. The authors also examine supply chain

Table 4. Summary of the reviewed OR papers in Information technologies.

Papers	Analytical	Empirical	Conceptual	Key features	Key insights/ findings
Fan *et al.* (2020)	X			Game theory	Obtain the conditions to utilize blockchain technology with concern of traceability customers.
Sari (2010)	X		X	Game theory	The use of RFID technology brings benefits when the cooperation degree between players increases.
Tao *et al.* (2020)	X			Game theory	Both the manufacturer and dealer tend to pay the "RDIF tag cost" according to the sharing rate.
Çanakoğlu and Bilgiç (2007)	X			Optimization	Derive the optimal decision for the input for the technology and the network volume.

coordination challenges and comment on the conditions under which the revenue sharing contract can help coordinate the channel. Other important studies related to blockchain have also been published such as the use of blockchain for on-demand platform service operations for risk attitude identification (Choi *et al.*, 2020) and the study on the use of blockchain to replace banking services (Choi, 2020).

Table 4 shows a summary of the literature reviewed in the scope of "information technologies for supply chain operations".

3.2. *Technologies for sustainable operations*

Sustainability is critical in supply chain operations nowadays (Shen, 2014; Shen *et al.*, 2014; Chan *et al.*, 2017). In the OR literature, Han *et al.* (2017) investigate the balance between revenue and green responsibility. They consider a "polyethylene terephthalate (PET) bottles" firm as a real-world case. Then, they examine the performance of the "weight reduction" strategy. Feng *et al.* (2017) focus their attention on the two-level reverse supply system with Stackelberg model. They compare the performance of "dual-recycling channel" and "single-channel counterparts" and identify that the former one is preferred. They also numerically examine the impact of customer's preferences. Li *et al.* (2019) explore the influence from the "secondary market". They theoretically develop a dual-period model and derive a dynamic pricing strategy. Their analytical results show that OEMs tend to provide a well-designed menu to properly entice all players to take part in the re-manufacturing program. Sun *et al.* (2020) concern the power sustainable operations in China, which involves power firms and grid companies. The authors uncover the distinct regional disparity about the sustainable effect and technology of China. Then, they propose some managerial insights empirically from both government and enterprise levels. Hong *et al.* (2017) study different licensing ways in remanufacturing operations with the use of technologies. The authors analytically evaluate the optimal mode between fixed fee and royalty. They demonstrate the fixed-fee is the critical factor in identifying the better licensing method. Saberi *et al.* (2018) discuss the fund input of the environment protection technology associated with a multi-level model. The authors establish a "modified projection" method and conduct several numerical experiments to test the implications derived from the optimal environment investment. Wu and Kao (2018) study the interactions in the remanufacturing industry-related technology improvement. Their study includes an "original equipment manufacturer (OEM)" and an "independent remanufacturer (IR)". In addition, the authors propose and compare the optimal revenue under two collaborative methods, including the "technology licensing" method and the "R&D joint venture" scheme. Turken *et al.* (2020) present a study on the investment in an "end-of-pipe and green technology" with three critical emission rules. The authors determine the optimal decisions under different scenarios. The authors interestingly find out that the situation which can generate the best local transportation emissions performance has an adverse effect on the global level (i.e., not globally optimal). Bi *et al.* (2017) consider customers with environmental awareness when the government participates in sponsoring companies. The authors derive the firms' decision and government's selection under two cases. The authors find critical elements that affect the government's optimal decision. Then, Fang and Ma (2019) take the "heterogeneous agents" and stochastic price into account to examine the "carbon emission trading" strategy. The authors illustrate the significant effect of the proposed strategy by conducting various numerical analyses. They further advocate that the government should play a role in encouraging technology adoption. Ma *et al.* (2009) consider the risk attitude of agents in the green supply chain. The authors obtain rational decisions under different cooperation scenarios between agents. The authors also argue that eco-friendly problems can be well-tackled by implementing a random carbon taxation scheme.

Table 5 shows a concise summary of the OR literature reviewed in "technologies for sustainable operations".

3.3. *Technologies for production operations*

Production is a critical link in supply chain systems and also a classic topic in the OR literature. Over the past decades, various OR studies involving technologies and production have been published (Hottenrott and Grunow, 2019). For instance, Li and Tirupati (1994) investigate the optimal decision on technologies mix with the

Table 5. Summary of the reviewed OR papers in technologies for sustainable operations.

Papers	Analytical	Empirical	Conceptual	Key features	Key insights/findings
Han *et al.* (2017)	X			Optimization	Weight reduction generates high cost efficiency and environmental benefits under the carbon emission rule.
Sun *et al.* (2020)		X		Real data empirical analyses	Uncover the distinct regional disparity about the sustainable effect and technology of China.
Hong *et al.* (2017)	X			Game theory	Demonstrate that the fixed-fee is the critical factor in identifying the better licensing method.
Saberi *et al.* (2018)	X			Optimization and numerical analyses	Establish a "modified projection" method and conduct numerical experiments to test the implication of the environment investment.
Wu and Kao (2018)	X			Revenue management	Obtain the optimal revenue under two collaborative methods.
Turken *et al.* (2020)	X			Optimization	Uncover that the best local transportation emissions performance has an opposite effect on the "global level" performance.
Bi *et al.* (2017)	X			Optimization	Identify the key factors affecting government's subsidy program.
Fang and Ma (2019)	X			Optimization and computational tests	Highlight the impacts of "heterogeneous agents" and "stochastic price" on the optimal "carbon emission trading" policy.
Ma *et al.* (2009)	X			Game theory	Get the rationally optimal decisions under different cooperation between agents.

consideration of both specialization and flexibility. The authors utilize mathematical programming as a means to help lower the production cost. They prove that the method has good performance in acquiring acceptable output. Verter and Dincer (1992) point out a key point that production tactics play an important role for companies with global operations. The authors carefully check the related literature. Then, they conclude that a comprehensive consideration of three critical factors improve the performance of multi-national enterprises. Kleindorfer and Partovi (1990) explore the selection of technology based on the "Ackoffs process". The authors propose a model to assess the performance of technologies. They not only consider the cost minimization alone, but also propose a more holistic framework for real-world applications. Boonman *et al.* (2015) investigate the "strategic capacity investment" decision related to the flexible and particular designed manufacturing technique. They discuss the benefits of both strategies and reveal the conditions in which companies prefer one strategy to the other. They also interestingly find that the incumbent company would always choose the flexible strategy. Aydin and Parker (2018) study the developed technology in a competitive situation. They mainly take the innovation demand and revenue of the technology into consideration. By comparing, they point out the effects of "technological potential" on supplier's profit. Then, they provide suggestions to participants including governments on the optimal strategies for technology deployment. In Pereira (2004), the author empirically explores the effects of "information systems and technology (IST)" of the banking department in Portuguese. His research findings show that the IST and labor could form a useful combination. Podinovski *et al.* (2018) explore a nonparametric method to evaluate the performance of operations with various component technologies. The authors employ an improved "multiple hybrid returns-to-scale (MHRS) technology" and examine its performance. They proved the effectiveness of the proposed method with simulated data scientifically.

Table 6 shows a summary of the literature reviewed in the scope of "technologies for production operations".

3.4. *Others*

The OR literature has also examined various topics related to technology-driven supply chain operations. We present the core studies in three areas as follows.

3.4.1. *Technology licensing and outsourcing (TLO)*

Technology licensing and outsourcing are two important aspects that are timely and critical. In the literature, Zhang *et al.* (2018) study "strategic technology licensing" with the consideration of a supply chain system with one "original equipment manufacturer" and one "contract manufacturer". The authors derive the optimal decisions on product licensing and pricing. They prove that the "probability distribution" of the random technology performance is crucial as the optimal licensing decision heavily relies on it. Wu (2018) explores the "technology licensing"

Table 6. Summary of the reviewed OR papers in technologies for production operations.

Papers	Analytical	Empirical	Conceptual	Key features	Key insights/findings
Li and Tirupati (1994)	X			Mathematical programming based analyses	Build the mathematical programming based method to evaluate the performance of technology mix.
Verter and Dincer (1992)			X	Literature review based analyses	Identify the critical factors which can improve the performance for multi-national enterprises.
Kleindorfer and Partovi (1990)	X			Optimization	Propose a general selecting method of production technology.
Boonman *et al.* (2015)	X			Optimization	Companies prefer the dedicated technological solutions under some cases while only the incumbent choose the flexible strategy for production operations.
Aydin and Parker (2018)	X			Consumer-driven models	Identify how technologies' development is affected by various consumer market factors.
Pereira (2004)		X		Real data empirical analyses	Observe the impacts of "information systems and technology (IST)" on the banking department in Portugal.
Podinovski *et al.* (2018)		X		Simulated data and nonparametric methodology	Propose a nonparametric method to evaluate the performance in a manufacturing system.

problem in the supply chain with the competition. The authors model the problem as a "dynamic duopoly" in which two firms, called the "innovating firm" and the "non-innovating firm" compete. They analytically find that the myopic behavior of the competing companies would bring harm in terms of yielding a "low innovation level" and a keener degree of competition. Research and developments are always important for technology licensing and outsourcing. Kim and Lim (2015) explore the impacts of outsourcing research and developments in supply chain operations. The authors consider the case in which the supply chain is "innovation-driven". The authors interestingly reveal that in establishing a research and development campaign, having more participating suppliers is beneficial.

3.4.2. *Online data*

Nowadays, e-commerce is well-established and all kinds of businesses operate online (Wu *et al.*, 2019; Xu *et al.*, 2020; Zhang and Choi, 2020). With the advancement of e-commerce and Internet technologies, sellers can dynamically choose the best market segments or even consumers to serve. Motivated by this fact, Elmachtoub and Levi (2016) conduct an OR study in a supply-chain context. The authors consider the case when "online customers arrive sequentially" over a certain period. Then, the authors develop a decision rule on whether to accept or reject the customer. Luo *et al.* (2019) develop a new "AI-trader" model with online stock data. The authors discuss the proposed methodology for business operations. Li *et al.* (2019) investigate the crowd sourcing challenge in an online-offline supply chain system. The authors incorporate the online reviews into the crowd sourcing mechanism, which affects the product design.

3.4.3. *Risk, finance and security (RFS)*

Supply chains face risk (Sun *et al.*, 2020) and security issues. In the literature, Lee *et al.* (2011) analyze how investing in ITs can help improve security for supply chains. The authors studied incentive alignment schemes that can optimize and coordinate supply chain security. The authors interestingly show that if the security issues are sufficiently significant, supply chain members may vote for not investing in technologies. Demand prediction-related technologies (DPTs) are always important in supply chain systems to reduce demand risk. Yuan and Zhu (2016) explore how DPTs affect the information distortion problem (i.e., the bullwhip effect) in the supply chain. The authors compared different DPTs related models by conducting simulation-based experiments. Omrani *et al.* (2017) conduct a data envelopment analysis (DEA) for a supply network problem facing data uncertainty. The authors consider an uncertain and risky environment in which data involves a high degree of stochasticity. They hence derive "a scenario-based robust optimization approach" to help. A computational analysis is conducted to demonstrate how the

Table 7. Summary of the reviewed OR papers in Sec. 3.4.

Scopes	Papers	Analytical	Empirical	Conceptual	Key features	Key insights/findings
Technology licensing and outsourcing	Zhang *et al.* (2018)	X			Optimization	Highlight that the "probability distribution" of the random technology performance is critical.
	Wu (2018)	X			Optimization	Reveal that the myopic behavior of the competing companies would bring harms in terms of yielding a "low innovation level".
	Kim and Lim (2015)	X			Game theory	Show that in establishing a research and development campaign, having more participating suppliers is beneficial.
Online data	Elmachtoub and Levi (2016)	X			Optimization	Establish a decision rule on whether to accept or reject the customer is developed.
	Li *et al.* (2019)	X			Optimization	Propose how online reviews can be incorporated into the crowd sourcing mechanism to achieve the optimal product design.
Risk, Finance and Security	Lee *et al.* (2011)	X			Game theory	Derive the incentive alignment schemes to coordinate the supply chain with IT security issues.
	Yuan and Zhu (2016)	X			Optimization	Indicate how DPTs can be used to fight the bullwhip effect .
	Omrani *et al.* (2017)	X			Stochastic optimization	Propose a "scenario-based robust optimization approach" to combat the data uncertainty challenges.
	Dye *et al.* (2017)	X			Revenue management	Establish an "optimal dynamic pricing and preservation technology investment" model.
	Reza-Gharehbagh *et al.* (2020)	X			Optimization	Explore when the online P-2-P financing scheme should be adopted.

proposed approach and model can be applied. Handling items which would deteriorate over time, Dye *et al.* (2017) propose an optimal revenue management policy with the considerations of "reference price effects". The authors establish an "optimal dynamic pricing and preservation technology investment" model using standard OR technique.

In supply chain finance, Reza-Gharehbagh *et al.* (2020) study the innovative online P-2-P ("peer-to-peer") scheme for acquiring capitals in the supply chain context. The authors focus on the small-and-medium enterprises. They analytically examine how a money-constrained small-and-medium firm chooses the financing option in the presence of a P-2-P online financial platform. Formulating the problem as a Stackelberg game, insights are generated into the equilibria with the use of the online P-2-P financing schemes.

Table 7 shows a brief summary of the literature examined in Sec. 3.4.

4. Research Gaps

From Secs. 2 and 3, we have examined the literature related to OR studies on Industry 4.0 and technology-driven supply chain operations. However, we can also see many areas are under-explored, and hence many research gaps are present. We discuss them as follows.

Industry 4.0: In the current OR studies focusing on Industry 4.0, many studies are conceptual in nature. Some studies are either exploratory in nature or just adopt computational approaches to generate some insights. As such, theoretical research is largely missing. This is also related to the high complexity associated with supply chain systems in the Industry 4.0 era. Moreover, in addition to big data analytics, OR studies with respect to many other technological devices and tools are relatively under-explored. Thus, this opens up another avenue for further studies.

Information technologies (ITs) for supply chain operations: ITs are critical and RFID is an IT device that has been widely explored. Robotics (machine scheduling), cloud (Xu *et al.*, 2015; Aydin *et al.*, 2020) and mobile computing are rather well-examined in the literature. However, additive manufacturing, AI, blockchain technology, and IoTs are relatively under-explored. Studies on the coordination among these IT solutions and the proper deployment of them in real-world operations are all missing in the OR literature.

Technologies for sustainable operations: Sustainable and green supply chain operations in the Industry 4.0 era would require the implementation of many technological solutions. Current studies focus on theoretical analyses based on prior research with the assumption of various popular functional forms (e.g., quadratic cost function for technology investment). Empirical research and real-world case studies are relatively under-explored.

Technologies for production operations: Machine schedule and production optimization are well-studied in the OR literature. However, some paradigm shifts of methodologies would be needed in the Industry 4.0 era. For example, real-time information updating and data-driven optimization are critically important but are relatively under-examined in the current literature.

Technology licensing and outsourcing: Technology supply chains, such as those focusing on research and developments, are important. However, only a few OR studies focus on exploring them. This is an under-explored area. Moreover, the current literature lacks sufficient real-world empirical cases on technology licensing and outsourcing to support the theoretical models and results.

Online data: With the advance of the Internet and mobile computing, data such as those from social media, platforms (Choi *et al.*, 2020) as well as e-commerce supply chains (Shen *et al.*, 2020), would play a crucial role. Many areas are under-explored. Moreover, innovative business models such as crowdfunding, crowd sourcing, etc. are all currently under-studied.

Risk, finance and security: OR studies in Industry 4.0 should also touch some topics such as risk. Risk includes operational risk (e.g., demand risk (Shen *et al.*, 2020)), systems security-related risk (e.g., cyber-security) as well as financial risk (e.g., exchange rate or supply chain finance). Some studies are reported by far from sufficient.

5. Future Research Agenda

From the reviews conducted above, a few important areas are identified to be important for further studies. We now discuss them one by one as follows.

More theoretical research for Industry 4.0: As we can see from the reviewed papers and the research gaps that we have discussed in Sec. 4, most current OR studies on Industry 4.0 are either conceptual based or highly exploratory in nature. To establish a solid theory in OR, we need to have mathematically proven and analytically derived closed-form results. More related studies should hence be developed. In the literature, Liu and De Giovanni (2019), Li *et al.* (2019) and Fragapane *et al.* (2020) are good examples and references.

Information technologies for supply chain operations: As uncovered in Sec. 4, additive manufacturing (i.e., 3D printing), AI, blockchain technology, and IoTs are some important IT solutions which are currently under-explored. Further studies should be conducted. More importantly, most OR studies on IT solutions mainly focus on exploring them in isolation. However, in practice, these IT solutions are usually deployed together. As a consequence, the coordination among these IT solutions, the optimal combination as well as the proper deployment of them for real-world operations deserve deeper explorations. Studies such as Cai *et al.* (2020) and Choi *et al.* (2020), which combine platform technologies and blockchain together could be the references for this proposed further study area.

More empirical research for technology investment and sustainable operations: The current studies on technology investment and sustainable operations assume specific functional forms for the sake of analytical tractability. However, more empirical evidence is needed to ensure these assumed functional forms are valid. Moreover, more empirical real case based research should be conducted to further highlight the real world values of the theoretical results. See de Sousa Jabbour *et al.* (2018) for some examples.

Technologies for production operations: In the Industry 4.0 era, technologies are much more advanced and demanding. Some innovative OR methodologies should be proposed and used. To be specific, as we proposed in Sec. 4, real-time information updating and the related production optimization decision-supporting tools are both crucial areas that should be investigated in future OR studies. Araz *et al.* (2020) and Choi *et al.* (2018) discuss and review many related studies that can act as an excellent reference for future studies in this direction.

Online data: Innovative business operational models, such as crowdfunding, crowd sourcing, etc. are interesting and important. The use of data from social media platforms is also critical (Singh *et al.*, 2018). Many concepts and behavioral patterns such as social influences (Chen *et al.*, 2019) should be considered. The current OR literature only touches the surface of these areas. To have a better understanding, much more innovative models and solution tools should be proposed and examined. Chen *et al.* (2015) and Chen *et al.* (2019) are both good examples to support further studies with the use of online data such as those from social media platforms.

Risk, finance and security: Operations with the use of new technologies in the Industry 4.0 era are highly risky. The risk comes from uncertainties, systems security as well as the financial requirements. More OR studies on topics such as supply chain risk management (Araz *et al.*, 2020), cyber-security, and supply chain cash flow management are all very important. More analytical and empirical studies on these topics should be conducted in the future. Choi (2020), which studies cryptocurrency, is one of the examples related to this stream of future research.

Multi-methodological research: Most recent OR studies related to Industry 4.0 and technology-driven supply chains focus on the adoption of one single research methodology. For example, a study can be analytical in nature and derives results by mathematics with many assumptions of functional forms. This is common but far from perfect because, in the Industry 4.0 era, many "norms" and "practices" are no longer valid. As such, we need to validate the findings by empirical cases and real practices based data. There are various examples of "multi-methodological research" (see Choi *et al.*, 2016; Chiu *et al.*, 2019; Li *et al.*, 2019; Guo *et al.*, 2020. More OR studies utilizing the multi-methodological research approach should be conducted for technology-driven supply chain operations in the Industry 4.0 era.

Roles of specific technologies: There are studies on blockchain technology (Chod *et al.*, 2018), RFID, big data (Fisher and Raman, 2018; Guha and Kumar,

2018; Schoenherr and Speier-Pero, 2015) analytics, etc. For instance, blockchain is known to be helpful with supply chain transparency (Sodhi and Tang, 2018) and product provenance information disclosure. However, more details should be included because most current studies assume these technological tools as standard "resources". For future research, the key is on capturing the core and unique features of these technologies in the analytical models. Chod *et al.* (2020) which combine the analytical signaling theory and blockchain coding in real application development is an outstanding reference for research in this proposed direction.

Data-driven supply chain operations: Traditional OR models have assumptions on, e.g., the distributions of random variables. However, in technology-driven supply chains, such as the big data supply chains, optimal decisions are driven directly by data (e.g., real time decision making). As a result, the "data-driven operations" would require another modeling approach to conduct the analysis. More research of this type should be conducted in the future. Here, both "methodologies" and "applications" of data-driven OR studies for supply chain operations should be carried out. Ban and Rudin (2019) is an excellent example to show data-driven supply chain operations studies. Zhao *et al.* (2020) is another reference to indicate how practical application tools can be developed based on data-driven models for vehicle routing.

6. Conclusion

6.1. *Summary and concluding remarks*

Today, in the Industry 4.0 era, technologies, such as blockchain technology, big-data analytics, artificial intelligence (AI) and data mining, Internet-of-Things (IoTs), and cloud-computing (Helo *et al.*, 2019), are all hot topics in supply chain operations. Motivated by their importance, in this paper, we have conducted a selected review of the related literature in the well-established mainstream leading operational research (OR) journals.

From our research, we have first examined the OR literature on Industry 4.0. We have found that most publications are conceptual. Then, we have explored technology-operations-related literature. We have classified the related studies into three major categories, namely, information technologies for supply chain operations, technologies for sustainable operations, and technologies for production operations. From the careful reviews, we have further identified various major research gaps. After that, we have established a future research agenda that would provide important guidance to researchers on the promising areas for further studies.

To the best of our knowledge, this paper is the first in the area which highlights the current state-of-the-arts OR literature in technology-driven supply chain operations in the Industry 4.0 era. We strongly believe that the derived results would be precious to both practitioners and academicians in OR. It also helps lay the foundation for further studies in the future.

6.2. *Limitations*

This is a selected review with the focal point on the most relevant OR papers published in the mainstream OR journals. We do not aim to exhaustively examine the vast literature and include all OR journals. Thus, many related studies will be missing in this review. Moreover, when we search the papers and conduct the filtering, personal bias and subjectivity would be present and hence we have to admit the respective limitations.

Acknowledgments

Suyuan Luo acknowledges the support from the Ministry of Education in China (MOE) Project of Humanities and Social Sciences (Grant Number: 20YJC630092), the National Natural Science Foundation of China [No. 71991461] and Guangdong Province Soft Science Research Project [No. 2019A101002074]. Tsan-Ming Choi's research is partially supported by The Hong Kong Polytechnic University (Project ID: P0009613). The authors sincerely thank the guest editor for his kind invitation for us to develop this paper. They also express their hearty thanks to three reviewers for their important comments which help us improve this paper a lot.

References

Abdul-Hamid, AQ, MH Ali, ML Tseng, S Lan and M Kumar (2020). Impeding challenges on industry 4.0 in circular economy: Palm oil industry in Malaysia. *Computers & Operations Research*, 123, 105052.

Akter, S, K Michael, MR Uddin, G McCarthy and M Rahman (2020). Transforming business using digital innovations: The application of AI, blockchain, cloud and data analytics. *Annals of Operations Research*, doi:https://doi.org/10.1007/s10479-020-03620-w.

Araz, O, TM Choi, S Salman and D Olson (2020). Role of analytics for operational risk management in the era of big data. *Decision Sciences*, doi:https://doi.org/10.1111/deci.12451.

Arbabian, ME and MR Wagner (2020). The impact of 3D printing on manufacturer–retailer supply chains. *European Journal of Operational Research*, 285(2), 538–552.

Aydin, A and RP Parker (2018). Innovation and technology diffusion in competitive supply chains. *European Journal of Operational Research*, 265(3), 1102–1114.

Aydin, N, İ Muter and SI Birbil (2020). Multi-objective temporal bin packing problem: An application in cloud computing. *Computers & Operations Research*, 121, 104959.

Babich, V and G Hilary (2020). OM Forum — Distributed ledgers and operations: What operations management researchers should know about blockchain technology. *Manufacturing & Service Operations Management*, 22(2), 223–240.

Ban, GY and C Rudin (2019). The big data newsvendor: Practical insights from machine learning. *Operations Research*, 67(1), 90–108.

Besbes, O, Y Gur and A Zeevi (2016). Optimization in online content recommendation services: Beyond click-through rates. *Manufacturing & Service Operations Management*, 18(1), 15–33.

Bi, G, M Jin, L Ling and F Yang (2017). Environmental subsidy and the choice of green technology in the presence of green consumers. *Annals of Operations Research*, 255(1–2), 547–568.

Boonman, HJ, V Hagspiel and PM Kort (2015). Dedicated versus product flexible production technology: Strategic capacity investment choice. *European Journal of Operational Research*, 244(1), 141–152.

Cai, YJ, TM Choi and J Zhang (2020). Platform supported supply chain operations in the blockchain era: Supply contracting and moral hazards. *Decision Sciences*, https://doi.org/10.1111/deci.12475.

Çanakoğlu, E and T Bilgiç (2007). Analysis of a two-stage telecommunication supply chain with technology dependent demand. *European Journal of Operational Research*, 177(2), 995–1012.

Chan, HL, B Shen and Y Cai (2017). Quick response strategy with cleaner technology in a supply chain: Coordination and win-win situation analysis. *International Journal of Production Research*, 56(10), 3397–3408.

Chen, Z-Y, Z-P Fan and M Sun (2015). Behavior-aware user response modeling in social media: Learning from diverse heterogeneous data. *European Journal of Operational Research*, 241(2), 422–434.

Chen, Z-Y, Z-P Fan and M Sun (2019). Individual-level social influence identification in social media: A learning-simulation coordinated method. *European Journal of Operational Research*, 273(3), 1005–1015.

Chiu, CH, HL Chan and TM Choi (2019). Risk minimizing price-rebate-return contracts in supply chains with ordering and pricing decisions: A multimethodological analysis. *IEEE Transactions on Engineering Management*, 67(2), 466–482.

Chod, J, N Trichakis, G Tsoukalas, H Aspegren and M Weber (2018). Blockchain and the value of operational transparency for supply chain finance. Working paper, Mack Institute for Innovation Management, Boston College. 25 Nov.

Choi, TM (2018). Incorporating social media observations and bounded rationality into fashion quick response supply chains in the big data era. *Transportation Research Part E: Logistics and Transportation Review*, 114, 386–397.

Choi, TM (2019). Blockchain-technology-supported platforms for diamond authentication and certification in luxury supply chains. *Transportation Research Part E: Logistics and Transportation Review*, 128, 17–29.

Choi, TM (2020). Creating all-win by blockchain technology in supply chains: Impacts of agents' risk attitudes towards cryptocurrency. *Journal of the Operational Research Society*, https://doi.org/10.1080/01605682.2020.1800419.

Choi, TM and S Luo (2019). Data quality challenges for sustainable fashion supply chain operations in emerging markets: Roles of blockchain, government sponsors and environment taxes. *Transportation Research Part E: Logistics and Transportation Review*, 131, 139–152.

Choi, TM, TCE Cheng and X Zhao (2016). Multi-methodological research in operations management. *Production and Operations Management*, 25(3), 379–389.

Choi, TM, S Guo, N Liu and X Shi (2020). Optimal pricing in on-demand-service-platform-operations with hired agents and risk-sensitive customers in the blockchain era. *European Journal of Operational Research*, 284(3), 1031–1042.

Choi, TM, SW Wallace and Y Wang (2018). Big data analytics in operations management. *Production and Operations Management*, 27(10), 1868–1883.

Choi, TM, X Wen, X Sun and SH Chung (2019). The mean-variance approach for global supply chain risk analysis with air logistics in the blockchain technology era. *Transportation Research Part E: Logistics and Transportation Review*, 127, 178–191.

de Sousa Jabbour, ABL, CJC Jabbour, M Godinho Filho and D Roubaud (2018). Industry 4.0 and the circular economy: A proposed research agenda and original roadmap for sustainable operations. *Annals of Operations Research*, 270(1–2), 273–286.

Ding, X, TM Choi and Y Tian (2020). HRI: Hierarchic radio imaging-based device-free localization. *IEEE Transactions on Systems, Man, and Cybernetics: Systems*, https://doi.org/10.1109/TSMC.2020.2997018.

Dye, CY, CT Yang and CC Wu (2017). Joint dynamic pricing and preservation technology investment for an integrated supply chain with reference price effects. *Journal of the Operational Research Society*, https://doi.org/10.1057/s41274-017-0247-y.

Elmachtoub, AN and R Levi (2016). Supply chain management with online customer selection. *Operations Research*, 64(2), 458–473.

Fan, ZP, XY Wu and BB Cao (2020). Considering the traceability awareness of consumers: Should the supply chain adopt the blockchain technology? *Annals of Operations Research*, https://doi.org/10.1007/s10479-020-03729-y.

Fang, C and T Ma (2019). Technology adoption with carbon emission trading mechanism: modeling with heterogeneous agents and uncertain carbon price. *Annals of Operations Research*, https://doi.org/10.1007/s10479-019-03297-w.

Feng, L, K Govindan and C Li (2017). Strategic planning: Design and coordination for dual-recycling channel reverse supply chain considering consumer behavior. *European Journal of Operational Research*, 260(2), 601–612.

Fisher, M and A Raman (2018). Using data and big data in retailing. *Production and Operations Management*, 27(9), 1665–1669.

Fragapane, G, D Ivanov, M Peron, F Sgarbossa and JO Strandhagen (2020). Increasing flexibility and productivity in industry 4.0 production networks with autonomous mobile robots and smart intralogistics. *Annals of Operations Research*, https://doi.org/10.1007/s10479-020-03526-7.

Galetsi, P and K Katsaliaki (2019). A review of the literature on big data analytics in healthcare. *Journal of the Operational Research Society*, https://doi.org/10.1080/01605682.2019.1630328.

Ghaleb, M, H Zolfagharinia and S Taghipour (2020). Real-time production scheduling in the Industry-4.0 context: Addressing uncertainties in job arrivals and machines breakdowns. *Computers & Operations Research*, 123, 105031.

Guha, S and S Kumar (2018). Emergence of big data research in operations management, information systems, and healthcare: Past contributions and future roadmap. *Production and Operations Management*, 27(9), 1724–1735.

Guo, S, TM Choi and B Shen (2020). Green product development under competition: A study of the fashion apparel industry. *European Journal of Operational Research*, 280(2), 523–538.

Han, S, Y Jiang, L Zhao, SC Leung and Z Luo (2017). Weight reduction technology and supply chain network design under carbon emission restriction. *Annals of Operations Research*, 290, 567–590.

Helo, P, D Phuong and Y Hao (2019). Cloud manufacturing–scheduling as a service for sheet metal manufacturing. *Computers & Operations Research*, 110, 208–219.

Hong, X, K Govindan, L Xu and P Du (2017). Quantity and collection decisions in a closed-loop supply chain with technology licensing. *European Journal of Operational Research*, 256(3), 820–829.

Hottenrott, A and M Grunow (2019). Flexible layouts for the mixed-model assembly of heterogeneous vehicles. *OR Spectrum*, 41, 943–979.

Kaur, H and SP Singh (2018). Heuristic modeling for sustainable procurement and logistics in a supply chain using big data. *Computers & Operations Research*, 98, 301–321.

Kim, KK and MK Lim (2015). R&D outsourcing in an innovation-driven supply chain. *Operations Research Letters*, 43(1), 20–25.

Kleindorfer, PR and FY Partovi (1990). Integrating manufacturing strategy and technology choice. *European Journal of Operational Research*, 47(2), 214–224.
Li, G, L Li, TM Choi and SP Sethi (2019). Green supply chain management in Chinese firms: Innovative measures and the moderating role of quick response technology. *Journal of Operations Management*, https://doi.org/10.1002/joom.1061.
Li, J, Y Yu and C Liu (2019). Product design crowd sourcing in a dual-channel supply chain: Joint reviews from manufacturer and consumers. International Transactions in Operational Research, https://doi.org/10.1111/itor.12749.
Li, S and D Tirupati (1994). Dynamic capacity expansion problem with multiple products: Technology selection and timing of capacity additions. *Operations Research*, 42(5), 958–976.
Li, Y, L Feng, K Govindan and F Xu (2019). Effects of a secondary market on original equipment manufactures' pricing, trade-in remanufacturing, and entry decisions. *European Journal of Operational Research*, 279(3), 751–766.
Lin, B, W Wu and M Song (2019). Industry 4.0: Driving factors and impacts on firm's performance: An empirical study on China's manufacturing industry. *Annals of Operations Research*, https://doi.org/10.1007/s10479-019-03433-6.
Lin, JT, CC Chiu, E Huang and HM Chen (2018). A multi-fidelity model approach for simultaneous scheduling of machines and vehicles in flexible manufacturing systems. *Asia-Pacific Journal of Operational Research*, 35(1), 1850005.
Liu, B and P De Giovanni (2019). Green process innovation through Industry 4.0 technologies and supply chain coordination. *Annals of Operations Research*, https://doi.org/10.1007/s10479-019-03498-3.
Luo, S, X Lin and Z Zheng (2019). A novel CNN-DDPG based AI-trader: Performance and roles in business operations. *Transportation Research Part E: Logistics and Transportation Review*, 131, 68–79.
Ma, T, A Grubler and Y Nakamori (2009). Modeling technology adoptions for sustainable development under increasing returns, uncertainty, and heterogeneous agents. *European Journal of Operational Research*, 195(1), 296–306.
Manuel, P (2015). A trust model of cloud computing based on quality of service. *Annals of Operations Research*, 233(1), 281–292.
Nguyen, T, ZHOU Li, V Spiegler, P Ieromonachou and Y Lin (2018). Big data analytics in supply chain management: A state-of-the-art literature review. *Computers & Operations Research*, 98, 254–264.
Omrani, H, F Adabi and N Adabi (2017). Designing an efficient supply chain network with uncertain data: A robust optimization — data envelopment analysis approach. *Journal of the Operational Research Society*, 68(7), 816–828.
Pereira, MJ (2004). Impacts of information systems and technology on productivity and competitiveness of the Portuguese banking sector: An empirical study. *International Transactions in Operational Research*, 11(1), 43–62.
Podinovski, VV, OB Olesen and CS Sarrico (2018). Nonparametric production technologies with multiple component processes. *Operations Research*, 66(1), 282–300.
Reza-Gharehbagh, R, A Hafezalkotob, S Asian, A Makui and AN Zhang (2020). Peer-to-peer financing choice of SME entrepreneurs in the re-emergence of supply chain localization. *International Transactions in Operational Research*, 27(5), 2534–2558.
Saberi, S, JM Cruz, J Sarkis and A Nagurney (2018). A competitive multiperiod supply chain network model with freight carriers and green technology investment option. *European Journal of Operational Research*, 266(3), 934–949.
Sari, K (2010). Exploring the impacts of radio frequency identification (RFID) technology on supply chain performance. *European Journal of Operational Research*, 207(1), 174–183.

Schlüter, F, P Sprenger, A Spyridakos and L Vryzidis (2016). Migration framework for decentralized and proactive risk identification in a steel supply chain via Industry 4.0 technologies. In *Conference Proceedings of the 5th International Symposium and 27th National Conference on Operational Research*, Athens, pp. 85–91.

Schoenherr, T and C Speier-Pero (2015). Data science, predictive analytics, and big data in supply chain management: Current state and future potential. *Journal of Business Logistics*, 36(1), 120–132.

Shen, B (2014). Sustainable fashion supply chain: Lessons from H&M. *Sustainability*, 6(9), 6236–6249.

Shen, B and HL Chan (2017). Forecast information sharing for managing supply chains in the big data era: Recent development and future research. *Asia-Pacific Journal of Operational Research*, 34(1), 1740001.

Shen, B, T Zhang, X Xu, HL Chan and TM Choi (2020). Pre-ordering in luxury fashion: Will additional demand information bring negative effects to the retailer? *Decision Sciences* (in press).

Shen, B, JH Zheng, PS Chow and KY Chow (2014). Perception of fashion sustainability in online community. *The Journal of the Textile Institute*, 105(9), 971–979.

Singh, A, N Shukla and N Mishra (2018). Social media data analytics to improve supply chain management in food industries. *Transportation Research Part E: Logistics and Transportation Review*, 114, 398–415.

Sodhi, MS and CS Tang (2019). Research opportunities in supply chain transparency. *Production and Operations Management*, 28(12), 2946–2959.

Song, JS and Y Zhang (2020). Stock or print? Impact of 3-D printing on spare parts logistics. *Management Science*, 66(9), 3860–3878.

Sun, J, G Li and MK Lim (2020). China's power supply chain sustainability: An analysis of performance and technology gap. *Annals of Operations Research*, https://doi.org/10.1007/s10479-020-03682-w.

Sun, X, SH Chung, TM Choi, JB Sheu and HL Ma (2020). Combating lead-time uncertainty in global supply chain's shipment-assignment: Is it wise to be risk-averse? *Transportation Research Part B: Methodological*, 138, 406–434.

Tang, CS and LP Veelenturf (2019). The strategic role of logistics in the industry 4.0 era. *Transportation Research Part E: Logistics and Transportation Review*, 129, 1–11.

Tao, F, K Lai, YY Wang and T Fan (2020). Determinant on RFID technology investment for dominant retailer subject to inventory misplacement. *International Transactions in Operational Research*, 27(2), 1058–1079.

Tsai, JT, JC Fang and JH Chou (2013). Optimized task scheduling and resource allocation on cloud computing environment using improved differential evolution algorithm. *Computers & Operations Research*, 40(12), 3045–3055.

Turken, N, J Carrillo and V Verter (2020). Strategic supply chain decisions under environmental regulations: When to invest in end-of-pipe and green technology. *European Journal of Operational Research*, 283(2), 601–613.

Verter, V and MC Dincer (1992). An integrated evaluation of facility location, capacity acquisition, and technology selection for designing global manufacturing strategies. *European Journal of Operational Research*, 60(1), 1–18.

Wang, X, TM Choi, Z Li and S Shao (2019). An effective local search algorithm for the multidepot cumulative capacitated vehicle routing problem. *IEEE Transactions on Systems, Man, and Cybernetics: Systems*, https://doi.org/10.1109/TSMC.2019.2938298.

Wu, CH (2018). Price competition and technology licensing in a dynamic duopoly. *European Journal of Operational Research*, 267(2), 570–584.

Wu, CH and YJ Kao (2018). Cooperation regarding technology development in a closed-loop supply chain. *European Journal of Operational Research*, 267(2), 523–539.
Wu, D, TM Choi and X Yue (2019). Emerging issues in multi-channel operations management in the O2O era. *International Journal of Production Economics*, 215, 1–2.
Xu, J, E Huang, CH Chen and LH Lee (2015). Simulation optimization: A review and exploration in the new era of cloud computing and big data. *Asia-Pacific Journal of Operational Research*, 32(3), 1550019.
Xu, L, J Wei, TM Choi and W Wang (2020). Managing online channel and optimization in supply chain systems with different channel leaderships. *IEEE Transactions on Systems, Man, and Cybernetics: Systems*, https://doi.org/10.1109/TSMC.2020.2966252.
Yuan, XG and N Zhu (2016). Bullwhip effect analysis in two-level supply chain distribution network using different demand forecasting technology. *Asia-Pacific Journal of Operational Research*, 33(3), 1650016.
Zhan, Y and KH Tan (2020). An analytic infrastructure for harvesting big data to enhance supply chain performance. *European Journal of Operational Research*, 281(3), 559–574.
Zhang, Q, J Zhang, G Zaccour and W Tang (2018). Strategic technology licensing in a supply chain. *European Journal of Operational Research*, 267(1), 162–175.
Zhang, T and TM Choi (2020). Optimal consumer sales tax policies for online-offline retail operations with consumer returns. *Naval Research Logistics*, https://doi.org/10.1002/nav.21935.
Zhao, Q, C Zhou and G Pedrielli (2020). A decision support system for data-driven driver-experience augmented vehicle routing problem. *Asia-Pacific Journal of Operational Research*, https://doi.org/10.1142/S0217595920500189.
Zheng, K, Z Zhang and J Gauthier (2020). Blockchain-based intelligent contract for factoring business in supply chains. *Annals of Operations Research*, https://doi.org/10.1007/s10479-020-03601-z.

Biography

Suyuan Luo received her PhD from Shanghai University of Finance and Economics in 2019. During her PhD study, she visited the University of Washington (Seattle). She is now working at Shenzhen University. She has published research papers in journals such as *Transportation Research Part E, IEEE Access, Journal of Cleaner Production, and Information Systems and e-Business Management.* Her research interests include e-commerce, big data analytics, cybersecurity and data mining.

Tsan-Ming Choi is currently a Full Professor at the Hong Kong Polytechnic University. He has authored/edited 16 books and published over 200 papers in Web of Science indexed journals. He is serving as the co-editor-in-chief of *Transportation Research Part E*, a department editor of *IEEE Transactions on Engineering Management*, a senior editor of *Production and Operations Management*, and *Decision Support Systems*, and an associate editor of *Decision Sciences*, *IEEE Transactions on Systems, Man and Cybernetics — Systems*, and *Information Sciences.* He is currently a member of the engineering panel of the Research Grants Council (Hong Kong).

https://doi.org/10.1142/9789819808588_0002

Chapter 2

Price and Product Quality Decisions for a Two-Echelon Supply Chain in the Blockchain Era†

Zhongmiao Sun

Glorious Sun School of Business and Management
Donghua University, 1882 Yan'an West Road
Shanghai, P. R. China
2805894616@qq.com

Qi Xu*

Glorious Sun School of Business and Management
Donghua University, 1882 Yan'an West Road
Shanghai, P. R. China
xuqi@dhu.edu.cn

Baoli Shi

Glorious Sun School of Business and Management
Donghua University, 1882 Yan'an West Road
Shanghai, P. R. China
shibaoli2017@163.com

Frequent problems of counterfeiting have spawned consumer demands to monitor the entire supply chain. The application of blockchain technology with anti-counterfeiting and traceability can improve the reliability and authenticity of product information and eliminate consumer doubts about product quality. Furthermore, based on the transparency of blockchain technology, brand suppliers can independently obtain the market demand information through information sharing. This paper introduces a consumer suspicion coefficient to illustrate the application of blockchain technology in the supply chain. Considering product authenticity verification and information sharing, we study the optimal pricing and product quality decisions in a two-level supply chain under the following three scenarios: (1) no blockchain technology, a traditional supply chain, and no information sharing (case *TN*); (2) no blockchain technology but a traditional supply chain with information sharing (case *TS*); and (3) a supply chain based on blockchain technology (case *BT*). We find that when the consumer suspicion coefficient increases, consumers will have limited faith in the authenticity of the product, which will affect the retailer's optimal decision and profit. By comparing the equilibrium results of several cases, we also find that demand information sharing by the retailer may not achieve a win-win outcome in a decentralized channel in the absence of blockchain technology.

*Corresponding author.
†To cite this article, please refer to its earlier version published in the Asia-Pacific Journal of Operational Research, Vol. 39, No. 1, (February 2022), DOI: 10.1142/S0217595921400169.

Under demand information sharing based on blockchain technology, however, if the consumer suspicion coefficient exceeds a certain threshold, the brand supplier and retailer can achieve a win–win outcome. In addition, the extended models reveal that in a centralized supply chain, regardless of the state of market demand, blockchain technology can always improve product quality and retail price and optimize supply chain profit.

Keywords: Pricing; quality; demand information sharing; consumer suspicion coefficient; product authenticity.

1. Introduction

The industry 4.0 era offers many advanced technologies such as blockchain, advanced robotics, additive manufacturing and the Internet of Things (Olsen and Tomlin, 2020). Among them, blockchain-enabled supply chain management has recently received considerable attention (Choi, 2019; Choi *et al.*, 2020a,b; Shen *et al.*, 2020). It plays an important role in product traceability and supply chain transparency (Wang *et al.*, 2020). Supply chains have become more complicated than ever before and include many suppliers, manufacturers, warehouses, entities and online sales channels, and it is generally difficult for them to share information in real time. Each chain node generally uses its own supply chain system and upstream and downstream parties to share key information, resulting in low efficiency of the supply chain and supply-demand imbalance. In addition, even if the chain nodes use a unified supply chain information system, it is difficult to guarantee the authenticity and transparency of information sharing without the support of blockchain technology. Existing evidence shows that some companies are seeking to use blockchain technology to improve the transparency of products in the supply chain and realize the sharing of upstream and downstream information. For example, Tmall Luxury Pavilion achieves full link fidelity traceability of luxury goods through blockchain technology, thus attracting 50 top luxury brand suppliers to support the service, including Valentino, Givenchy, and DKNY.[a] In addition, the well-known Provenance Platform provides blockchain technology support for more than 200 retailers, including the famous Danish designer brand Martine Jarlgaard.[b] However, the application of blockchain in supply chains and retail markets remains in its infancy (Wamba *et al.*, 2020), and not all firms will adopt blockchain technology. Although large companies such as Wal-Mart, Target and Starbucks have pioneered the use of this technology,[c] the widespread adoption of blockchain in supply chains continues to face major obstacles such as adjustments in decisions, conflicts of interest, and complexity. In addition, the advantages of blockchain are very prominent, but the disadvantages sometimes coexist with the advantages such as low transaction efficiency, no privacy and high energy consumption.

Moreover, with the continuous increase in consumption levels, the quality and authenticity of products have attracted particular attention from consumers, and

[a]https://www.sohu.com/a/227973197_99972249 (accessed on 5 September 2020).
[b]https://www.provenance.org/case-studies (accessed on 5 September 2020).
[c]http://www.86eye.com/63249.html (accessed on 20 January 2021).

blockchain technology provides guarantees for the traceability and authenticity of supply chain products. Although the existing literature has considered the advantages of blockchain technology in product authenticity verification (e.g., Choi, 2019), there are few studies on product quality decisions in a blockchain technology-based supply chain. Moreover, there is even less research on demand information sharing through blockchain technology in supply chain management from the perspective of model-driven technology. In this paper, we are motivated by the problem of adopting blockchain technology for product authenticity verification and demand information sharing in supply chain management. Consequently, our research focuses on the following questions: (1) In a traditional supply chain without blockchain technology, how do asymmetric demand information and consumers' suspicion of product authenticity affect the decisions and profits of supply chain members? (2) How does the application of blockchain technology affect the pricing and quality decisions of supply chain members? (3) Compared with the traditional supply chain, can the sharing of demand information through blockchain technology achieve a win–win outcome? (4) In a supply chain with a centralized channel, how does blockchain technology affect the joint decisions of supply chain members and profits?

To answer these questions, we construct stylized Stackelberg models in a two-echelon supply chain, which comprises a brand supplier (he) and a retailer (she). The brand supplier first sets the wholesale price and product quality, and then the retailer determines the retail price. We mainly consider three cases: the retailer does not share demand information in a traditional supply chain without blockchain technology, the retailer shares demand information in a traditional supply chain without blockchain technology, and a blockchain technology-based supply chain model. We assume that consumers are skeptical about the authenticity of the brand product. Note that for the traditional supply chain, if the retailer does not share demand information, the brand supplier only knows the probability of the market demand state, that is, the information between them is asymmetric. In addition, we also construct two extended models based on a centralized channel: one is the traditional centralized supply chain model, and the other is the blockchain technology-based centralized supply chain model. We thus derive the supply chain members' joint decisions in the centralized channel and analyze the effect of blockchain technology.

To the best of our knowledge, this paper is the first to consider both product authenticity verification and demand information sharing under blockchain technology in supply chain management and the resulting pricing and product quality decisions. The main contributions of this research are twofold. First, although there has been substantial valuable research on the demand information sharing problem (e.g., Cui *et al.*, 2015; Guan *et al.*, 2020; Yu *et al.*, 2020), few studies have considered consumers' suspicions regarding product authenticity and explored demand information sharing in a blockchain technology-based supply chain. Therefore, we propose several game-theoretic models and derive the equilibrium results in different cases. We find that the retailer's optimal retail price, the brand supplier's optimal wholesale price and optimal quality, and their profits all decrease with the consumer suspicion coefficient. In addition, demand information sharing by the retailer may not achieve a win-win outcome in a traditional supply chain. Specifically, when market demand is low, the retailer is better off and the brand supplier is worse off under demand information sharing. In contrast, when market demand is high, the brand supplier is better off and the retailer is worse off under demand information sharing. Second, we compare and analyze the equilibrium results in different cases. In particular, we find that the performance of demand information sharing based on blockchain technology differs from that of demand information sharing by the retailer in traditional supply chains. Under demand information sharing based on blockchain technology, the brand supplier and retailer can achieve a win–win outcome when the consumer suspicion coefficient exceeds a certain threshold. In addition, when blockchain technology is implemented in a centralized supply chain, the product quality and profit of the supply chain can be improved.

The remainder of this paper is organized as follows. In Sec. 2, we present a review of the related literature. The problem description is given in Sec. 3. In Sec. 4, we conduct the model analysis. The effects of blockchain technology are presented in Sec. 5. Section 6 analyzes the extended models. Section 7 contains our conclusions and suggestions for future research. All proofs are placed in Appendix A.

2. Literature Review

Our study is primarily connected to three research streams in the literature: blockchain technology, demand information sharing, and pricing and product quality in supply chains.

2.1. *Blockchain technology*

Increasing attention is being paid to blockchain technology in supply chain management (Choi *et al.*, 2020a; Shen *et al.*, 2020). Blockchain is a peer-to-peer distributed network, which is non-tamperable, open and transparent, and decentralized (Bashir, 2017). Some literature highlights the advantages of blockchain technology in logistics and supply chain (Kshetri, 2018; Aste *et al.*, 2017; Hughes *et al.*, 2019). Aste *et al.* (2017) analyzed the impact of blockchain technology on society and industry and reported that blockchain technology can increase cooperation between supply chain members. Biswas *et al.* (2017) proposed a wine supply chain traceability system based on blockchain technology in which every transaction is recorded as a block in the chain and visible to relevant participants. They found that blockchain technology can enhance the trust of customers, thanks to the traceability of products throughout the supply chain. Chen (2018) showed that blockchain technology can support the prevention of product fraud and counterfeit goods throughout the supply chain, which has the positive effects of reducing costs and improving efficiency. The above literature ignores network modeling in the functional implementation of blockchain technology. Recently, Wang *et al.* (2020) further used novel blockchain technology to address the information gaps in construction industries. They detailed the transaction flows of a blockchain-based information management model and achieved visualization of the framework. Vaio and Varriale (2020) indicated that it is necessary to investigate the airport industry and pay attention to the main impact of blockchain technology on OM from the perspective of sustainability. Although these studies have reported that the adoption of blockchain technology can present numerous benefits for supply chain management, there are still few studies on the practical application of blockchain technology from a model-driven perspective. Therefore, some scholars focus on studying the use of blockchain technology in supply chain management by constructing stylized theoretic analysis models. For example, Choi (2019) considered the application of blockchain technology in the luxury supply chain, established a traditional retail model, a blockchain technology-supported platform sales model, and a traditional retail model supported by the blockchain technology platform and reported the optimal decisions for the supply chain in different cases. They also analyzed the value of blockchain technology in diamond authentication and identification and found that the shopping convenience provided by traditional retailers is the key factor in determining which mode is optimal. Shen *et al.* (2020) explored the value of blockchain in the supply chain for disclosing the quality of second-hand products, and they found that with the support of blockchain, horizontal integration is more helpful for increasing the total profit of the supply chain. In addition, Choi *et al.* (2020a) assumed that blockchain technology can disclose product information, constructed a duopoly model of two leasing service platforms, analyzed the equilibrium strategy for product information disclosure between platforms, and discussed the impact of product information disclosure supported by blockchain technology on consumer surplus and sellers' interests. Related studies also include Shi and Choi (2019) and Choi *et al.* (2020b), among others. However, unlike all of these works, this paper not only considers authenticity verification using blockchain technology but also considers the sharing of demand information. We also analyze the effects of the application of blockchain technology on pricing and product quality decisions.

2.2. *Demand information sharing*

Our study is also related to demand information sharing in supply chain management. There is a growing literature focused on the impact of demand information sharing on system performance. For example, Lee *et al.* (2000) sought to address how to quantify the benefits of initiatives that enable more demand information sharing in a two-level supply chain composed of a retailer and a manufacturer, and they demonstrated that demand information sharing can lower supply chain inventory levels and costs more than not sharing. Cui *et al.* (2015) proved the effectiveness of information sharing by comparing three levels of upstream inventory information sharing and showed that the positive value of information sharing comes from effectively improving the accuracy of forecasting. Jiang *et al.* (2016)

focused on information sharing in a distribution channel where the manufacturer possesses better demand forecast information than the downstream retailer. They proposed three information sharing models, including no information sharing, voluntary information sharing, and mandatory information sharing, and found that under the voluntary and compulsory sharing models, more accurate prediction is beneficial to both companies, but in the no-sharing model, it may damage the two companies. Sun *et al.* (2019) considered the relationship between manufacturer intrusion and cost reduction decisions under asymmetric or symmetric demand information. They found that when and only if the direct marketing channel is relatively effective will encroachment behavior cause manufacturers to invest more money to reduce costs. The above literature concluded that demand information sharing can generally improve the benefits of the supply chain system.

In addition, some scholars have further considered demand information sharing in competitive environments. For example, Cheng and Wu (2005) considered a two-echelon supply chain with multiple competing retailers and evaluated the impact of demand information sharing on inventory and costs. Their results show that demand information sharing has a positive effect, and with the improvement of the information sharing level, the inventory level and expected cost of manufacturers decrease. Ha and Tong (2008) considered contract and information sharing in two competitive supply chains; they assumed that each supply chain consists of a manufacturer and a retailer, and the two supply chains are the same, except that they may have different investment costs of information sharing. They emphasized the importance of contract type as the driving factor of the value of information sharing and the role of information sharing capacity as the source of competitive advantage in supply chain competition. Guan *et al.* (2020) also explored the issue of demand information sharing in two competing supply chains and found that information sharing can benefit supply chains if manufacturers are efficient at service investment. Related studies also include Shang *et al.* (2015) and Ha *et al.* (2017). However, this paper considers consumers' suspicions about product authenticity and explores demand information sharing based on blockchain technology, which was not covered by the related studies cited above.

2.3. *Pricing and product quality*

A number of studies have investigated optimal pricing and product quality decisions (Rao and Monroe, 1989; Feng and Xie, 2007; Peterson and Jolibert, 2015). In particular, product quality is a critical concern in supply chain management (Lejarza and Balde, 2020). Some research focuses on the authenticity of products. Qian (2011) identified the heterogeneous effect of entering counterfeit products on the sales of third-grade genuine products and found that counterfeit products have both advertising effects on brands and substitution effects on genuine products, and the former effect persists for several years. Stevenson and Busby (2015) analyzed the strategies adopted by product counterfeiters when using legitimate supply chains, discussed the impact of counterfeiting on competing resources, and proposed countermeasures to improve the resilience of the supply chain to counterfeiting threats. Cho *et al.* (2015) compared two types of counterfeiting, including fraudulent counterfeiting through infiltrating legitimate (but accomplice) dealers and nonfraudulent counterfeiting through illegal channels, and studied the impact of anti-fraud strategies on brand companies, counterfeiters and consumers. They found that by improving quality, brand companies can increase their expected profits, while non-deceptive counterfeiters can only steal a trivial amount of brand value. Recently, some scholars have been interested in joint price and product quality decisions. Li and Qi (2020) studied a company's pricing and product quality decisions from the perspective of expected utility theory. They assumed that the company was concerned about demand risk due to the uncertainty of customer value and found that when price and quality are all the only decision variables, the optimal price decreases as the degree of risk aversion increases, while the optimal quality increases with the degree of risk aversion. Ye and Yang (2020) assumed that a company would sell its products to strategic consumers who were sensitive to both price and quality. They proposed four equilibrium strategies, including simultaneously reducing costs and degrading quality, only reducing costs, simultaneously increasing prices and upgrading quality, and simultaneously reducing costs and upgrading quality. They suggested that companies should carefully examine the cost structure when making price and quality level decisions. Related studies also include Chenavaz *et al.* (2020) and Bertini *et al.* (2020). However, most of these studies did not consider the impact of the application of blockchain technology on product quality. We compare the supply chain members' optimal pricing and product quality decisions in a traditional supply chain with those in a blockchain technology-based supply chain and analyze the effects of the consumers' distrust of product quality on the optimal decisions and profits of the supply chain members.

3. Problem Description and Assumptions

Consider a two-echelon supply chain consisting of a brand supplier (he) and a retailer (she). The brand supplier produces brand product (e.g., a luxury bag) with quality q and wholesales the brand product to the retailer (e.g., a brick-and-mortar store) at wholesale price w. The retailer then sells the brand product to the end consumer with unit retail price p. We assume that the unit production cost of the brand supplier is m, and the corresponding product quality cost function is represented as $C(q) = q^2/2$, which is also adopted by Li *et al.* (2019). The economic interpretation of this cost assumption has two aspects: (1) It satisfies $C(0) = 0$ and $dC(q)/dq > 0$, which indicates that the product quality cost $C(q)$ of the brand supplier increases in brand product quality q. (2) It also satisfies $d^2C(q)/dq^2 > 0$, which implies an increasing marginal cost invested by the brand supplier to improve brand product quality.

In reality, when consumers doubt the authenticity of a product, this is often reflected as distrust in the quality of the product. Therefore, following Choi (2019), we introduce a suspicion coefficient for product authenticity to express consumers' skepticism regarding product quality. Let $(1-k)\cdot q$ denote the product quality perceived by consumers, where $k\cdot \in [0,1]$ denotes the coefficient of consumers' suspicion of product authenticity (hereafter, consumer suspicion coefficient). The greater k is, the more consumers distrust the authenticity of the product. Referring to previous research (e.g., Yao and Liu, 2005; Li *et al.*, 2019), we assume the following linear market demand function:

$$D = a - p + b(1-k)q, \tag{1}$$

where market demand is affected by two factors: the retailer price p and the product quality perceived by consumers $(1-k)\cdot q$. In addition, $b\cdot \in [0,1]$ denotes the measure of the responsiveness of the brand product's market demand to its own retail price. The demand intercept a is the primary demand for the brand product. There are two states of demand $a = \{a_h, a_l\}$, where a_h indicates high market demand and a_l indicates low market demand (i.e., $a_l < a_h$) (Zhang *et al.*, 2019). Since the retailer is closer to its own market terminal, the retailer can obtain more accurate market demand information than suppliers. We assume that the demand known by the retailer is a_i $(i = h,\ l)$. Usually, in a decentralized supply chain system, the brand suppliers do not know the exact demand of the market; they only know the probability distribution of demand. Let λ denote the probability of demand a_h, and the corresponding $1-\lambda$ represents the probability of demand a_l. Briefly, considering the privacy of demand information, the demand state a_i is the retailer's private information, but λ is public information.

In addition, this paper assumes that there is a Stackelberg game between the brand supplier and the retailer, where the brand supplier acts as the Stackelberg leader and the retailer acts as the Stackelberg follower (Zhu, 2015; Zhao *et al.*, 2020). In the decision-making process, the brand supplier first makes his wholesale price and product quality decisions, and the retailer then sets her retail price maximize her profit.

In a traditional supply chain without blockchain technology, as illustrated in Fig. 1, with the advantage of being close to the front end of the market, the retailer can acquire accurate market demand information, while the brand supplier only obtains market demand information through sharing by the retailer (Zhou *et al.*, 2017; Guan *et al.*, 2020). Otherwise, the brand supplier will have to make decisions

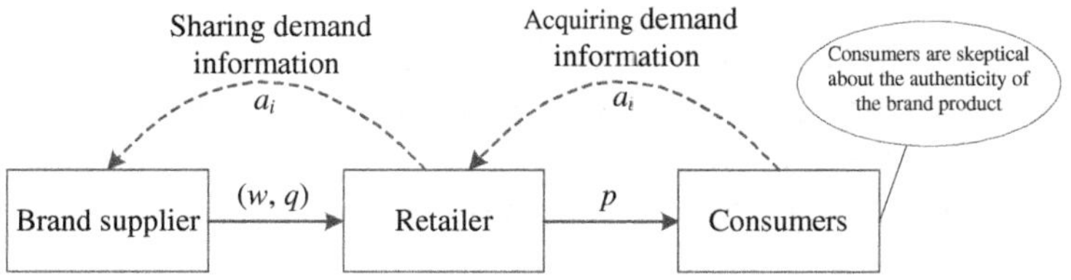

Fig. 1. Traditional supply chain model.

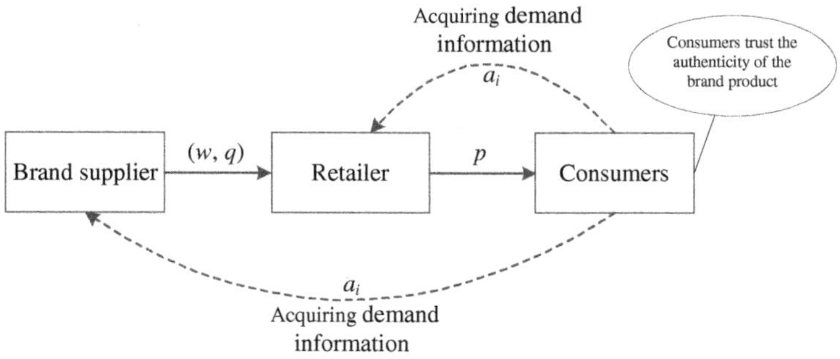

Fig. 2. Blockchain technology-based supply chain model.

based on the probability of market demand states. In addition, due to consumers' distrust of product quality (the material of the bag, the production process, etc.), consumers are skeptical about the authenticity of the brand product (i.e., $k \neq 0$).

In the blockchain technology-based supply chain, as illustrated in Fig. 2, we consider how the blockchain concept and technology are embodied in the supply chain in two respects: (1) Product authenticity verification, which is attributed to the traceability of blockchain technology. Evidence from the blockchain technology-based wine supply chain, which enables all participants (including consumers) can verify the overall process, including raw materials, transport and storage conditions, processing, distribution, and sales (Biswas *et al.*, 2017). Another example is diamond authentication and certification in luxury supply chains (Choi, 2019). This application eliminates consumers' doubts about product authenticity; thus, the consumer suspicion coefficient $k = 0$. (2) Information sharing, which is attributed to the decentralized and transparent nature of blockchain technology. Evidence is accumulating that the blockchain network enables the creation of an irrefutable record of data and real-time information sharing among various participants (Wang *et al.*, 2020). Therefore, all supply chain members can capture and manipulate customer data and employ these data to acquire market demand information.

Without loss of generality, we follow Choi (2019) and Choi *et al.* (2020b) to assume the cost of blockchain technology is 0. The reason is that the fixed cost of blockchain technology is substantial but it is viewed as a sunk cost, which is omitted in real supply chain operations afterwards. Also, the unit cost of blockchain technology is very small and can be ignored.

4. Model Analysis

This section discusses the supply chain members' optimal decisions and profits in three cases. For the traditional supply chain without blockchain technology, we consider two cases in which the retailer does or does not share demand information with the brand supplier. The third case is the blockchain technology-based supply chain model, which is different from the first two cases because blockchain technology not only realizes the sharing of demand information but also realizes authenticity verification of brand products. We also analyze the equilibrium solutions of the brand supplier and the retailer in the three cases. For convenience, we use *TN*, *TS*, and *BT* to denote the case of no information sharing under the traditional supply chain, the case of information sharing under the traditional supply chain, and the case of the blockchain technology-based supply chain, respectively.

4.1. *Traditional supply chain models*

4.1.1. *No information sharing (TN)*

We first study the situation where the retailer does not share demand information with the brand supplier in a traditional supply chain. In this situation, the market demand information held by the brand supplier and the retailer is asymmetric. The retailer can accurately acquire the market demand state $a_i = a_h$ or a_l, so she will determine the retail price p_i^{TN} based on different market demand states. However, the brand supplier only knows that the probability of the high market demand state is λ and that of the low market demand state is $(1-\lambda)$. He will set the wholesale price w^{TN} and product quality q^{TN} based on the public information (i.e., λ). Correspondingly, the demand function D_i^{TN} of the retailer under market demand state i can be expressed as follows:

$$D_i^{TN} = a_i - p_i^{TN} + b(1-k)q^{TN}. \tag{2}$$

Moreover, the profit functions of the brand supplier and the retailer are as follows:

$$\pi_s^{TN} = \max_{w^{TN},q^{TN}} \left[\lambda(w^{TN}-m)D_h^{TN} + (1-\lambda)(w^{TN}-m)D_l^{TN} - \frac{1}{2}q^{TN^2}\right], \tag{3}$$

$$\pi_{ri}^{TN} = \max_{p_i^{TN}} [(p_i^{TN} - w^{TN})D_i^{TN}], \quad i = h, l. \tag{4}$$

For given w^{TN} and q^{TN}, the optimal retail price p_i^{TN} for retailer under market demand state i, where $i = h$, l, is

$$p_i^{TN}(w^{TN}, q^{TN}) = \frac{1}{2}(a_i + b(1-k)q^{TN} + w^{TN}). \tag{5}$$

Substituting Eq. (5) into Eq. (2) yields the demand D_i^{TN} at the retailer's optimal retail price (for given w^{TN} and q^{TN})

$$D_i^{TN}(w^{TN}, q^{TN}) = \frac{1}{2}(a_i + b(1-k)q^{TN} - w^{TN}). \tag{6}$$

With Eq. (6), we can rewrite the profit function of the brand supplier as follows:

$$\pi_s^{TN} = \max_{w^{TN},q^{TN}} \left[\frac{1}{2}(w^{TN}-m)(u + xq^{TN} - w^{TN}) - \frac{1}{2}q^{TN^2}\right], \tag{7}$$

where $x = b(1-k)$, $u = \lambda a_h + (1-\lambda)a_l$.

According to the first-order partial derivatives of π_s^{TN} with respect to w^{TN} and q^{TN}, it is easy to obtain the optimal wholesale price w^{TN*} and the optimal product quality q^{TN*}. Consequently, we can derive the optimal profits of the brand supplier and the retailer based on their optimal decisions. We summarize the results in Lemma 1.

Lemma 1. *In case TN, at the Stackelberg equilibrium, the optimal decisions and profits of the brand supplier and the retailer are as follows:*

$$p_i^{TN^*} = \frac{a_i}{2} + \frac{u(x^2+2)}{2(4-x^2)} + \frac{m(1-x^2)}{(4-x^2)},$$

$$w^{TN^*} = \frac{(2u + m(2-x^2))}{(4-x^2)},$$

$$q^{TN^*} = \frac{x(u-m)}{(4-x^2)}, \quad \pi_s^{TN^*} = \frac{(u-m)^2}{2(4-x^2)},$$

$$\pi_{ri}^{TN^*} = \left(\frac{a_i(4-x^2) - u(2-x^2) - 2m}{2(4-x^2)}\right)^2,$$

where $i = h,\ l;\ x = b(1-k),\ u = \lambda a_h + (1-\lambda)a_l$.

From Lemma 1, we have the supply chain members' optimal decisions and profits, and the following proposition is provided.

Proposition 1. *In case TN, effects of the parameters* λ, k *and* m *are as follows:*

(i) $\frac{\partial p_i^{TN^*}}{\partial \lambda} > 0,\ \frac{\partial w^{TN^*}}{\partial \lambda} > 0,\ \frac{\partial q^{TN^*}}{\partial \lambda} > 0;$
(ii) $\frac{\partial p_i^{TN^*}}{\partial k} < 0,\ \frac{\partial w^{TN^*}}{\partial k} < 0,\ \frac{\partial q^{TN^*}}{\partial k} < 0;$
(iii) $\frac{\partial p_i^{TN^*}}{\partial m} > 0,\ \frac{\partial w^{TN^*}}{\partial m} > 0,\ \frac{\partial q^{TN^*}}{\partial m} < 0;$
(iv) $\frac{\partial \pi_s^{TN^*}}{\partial \lambda} > 0,\ \frac{\partial \pi_s^{TN^*}}{\partial k} < 0,\ \frac{\partial \pi_s^{TN^*}}{\partial m} < 0;$
(v) $\frac{\partial \pi_{ri}^{TN^*}}{\partial \lambda} < 0,\ \frac{\partial \pi_{ri}^{TN^*}}{\partial k} < 0,\ \frac{\partial \pi_{ri}^{TN^*}}{\partial m} < 0.$

Proposition 1 reveals that the probability λ of the high market demand state (i.e., $a_i = a_h$) positively affects the brand supplier's wholesale price and quality and retailer's retail price. This indicates that when the retailer is reluctant to share demand information, both the brand supplier and the retailer will be affected by the asymmetry of demand information. The higher the probability that the brand supplier believes that the market is in a state of high demand, the more motivated he is to improve the wholesale price and quality of the brand product, and accordingly, the retailer will increase the retail price. However, the consumer suspicion coefficient k negatively affects the supply chain members' optimal decisions. This is because the consumers' doubts about the authenticity of the brand product reduce the retailer's demand, and the brand supplier and the retailer will have to reduce the wholesale price and retail price to encourage consumers to buy. Moreover, the result implies that consumer suspicion is detrimental to brand product quality. The reason is that consumers in reality are usually perceptual, and they may not trust the quality of brand products, which makes brand suppliers unwilling to make more efforts to improve product quality. In addition, Proposition 1(iii) shows that the brand supplier's wholesale price and the retailer's retail price both increase with the unit production cost m, while the quality of the brand product decreases. The explanation is straightforward and in line with reality.

Moreover, Propositions 1(iv) and (v) describe the effects of the parameters λ, k and m on the supply chain members' profits. The results show that the brand supplier's profit increases with the probability λ of the high market demand state, while regardless of the state of market demand, the retailer's profit decreases. The reason is that the increase in λ encourages the brand supplier to increase his wholesale price, which is disadvantageous to the retailer in any market demand state. The results also show that the brand supplier and the retailer's profits are both decreasing with the consumer suspicion coefficient k and the unit production cost m, which implies that consumers' doubts about the authenticity of the brand product are detrimental to all supply chain members.

In general, when a certain brand product is more likely to be counterfeited, the greater the degree of consumer suspicion of the brand product, the lower the quality and price of the brand product, and the less the profit of the supply chain members. Finally, there may be low-cost and inferior brand products in the market.

4.1.2. *Information sharing (TS)*

This section considers the scenario in which the retailer shares demand information with the brand supplier. As we all know, many problems in the supply chain can be attributed to the problem of information asymmetry among enterprises in the chain, and the most typical one is "bullwhip effect". Under this background, some supply chain upstream and downstream enterprises improve their operation through information sharing strategy. For example, the famous Absolut Company shares demand-related information with their immediate suppliers. In detail, with the advantage of being close to the market terminals, retailers can predict the market demand states relatively accurately through the historical sales and order records of products, the pre-sale period sales in promotion activities, or the online click stream of customers, and share the demand information with suppliers. In this scenario, the market demand information held by the brand supplier and the retailer is symmetric. Here, the retailer can determine her retail price p_i^{TS} based on different market demand states, and the brand supplier can also set his wholesale price w_i^{TS} and product quality q_i^{TS} based on different market demand states. The profit functions of the brand supplier and retailer are provided based on the demand functions D_i^{TS} of the different market demand states, which are defined as follows:

$$\pi_{si}^{TS} = \max_{w_i^{TS}, q_i^{TS}} \left[(w_i^{TS} - m)(a_i - p_i^{TS} + b(1-k)q_i^{TS}) - \frac{1}{2} q_i^{TS^2} \right], \tag{8}$$

$$\pi_{ri}^{TS} = \max_{p_i^{TS}} [(p_i^{TS} - w_i^{TS})(a_i - p_i^{TS} + b(1-k)q_i^{TS})], \tag{9}$$

where $i = h, l$.

By Eq. (9), the retailer's optimal retail price satisfies the following:

$$p_i^{TS}(w_i^{TS}, q_i^{TS}) = \frac{1}{2}(a_i + b(1-k)q_i^{TS} + w_i^{TS}). \tag{10}$$

According to the first-order partial derivatives of π_{si}^{TS} with respect to w_i^{TS} and q_i^{TS}, we can derive the brand supplier's optimal decisions as follows:

$$w_i^{TS}(q_i^{TS}) = \frac{1}{2}(a_i + xq_i^{TS} + m), \tag{11}$$

$$q_i^{TS}(w_i^{TS}) = \frac{x}{2}(w_i^{TS} - m). \tag{12}$$

By combining Eqs. (11) and (12), we can obtain w_i^{TS*} and q_i^{TS*}. By plugging them into Eq. (10), we can obtain p_i^{TS*}. Consequently, we can derive the brand supplier and retailer's optimal profits based on their optimal decisions, which are summarized in Lemma 2.

Lemma 2. *In case TS, at the Stackelberg equilibrium, the optimal decisions and profits of the brand supplier and the retailer are as follows:*

$$p_i^{TS^*} = \frac{3a_i + m(1-x^2)}{(4-x^2)},$$

$$w_i^{TS^*} = \frac{(2a_i + m(2-x^2))}{(4-x^2)},$$

$$q_i^{TS^*} = \frac{x(a_i - m)}{(4-x^2)},$$

$$\pi_{si}^{TS^*} = \frac{(a_i - m)^2}{2(4-x^2)},$$

$$\pi_{ri}^{TS^*} = \left(\frac{a_i - m}{4-x^2}\right)^2.$$

where $i = h, l$; $x = b(1-k)$.

Compared with case *TN*, the following proposition reveals whether demand information sharing in the traditional supply chain can change the influences of the consumer suspicion coefficient k and other related parameters on the decisions and profits of supply chain members. According to the supply chain members' optimal decisions and profits in Lemma 2, we obtain Proposition 2.

Proposition 2. *In case TS, the effects of the parameters λ, k and m are as follows:*

(i) $\frac{\partial p_i^{TS^*}}{\partial \lambda} = 0$, $\frac{\partial w_i^{TS^*}}{\partial \lambda} = 0$, $\frac{\partial q_i^{TS^*}}{\partial \lambda} = 0$;
(ii) $\frac{\partial p_i^{TS^*}}{\partial k} < 0$, $\frac{\partial w_i^{TS^*}}{\partial k} < 0$, $\frac{\partial q_i^{TS^*}}{\partial k} < 0$;
(iii) $\frac{\partial p_i^{TS^*}}{\partial m} > 0$, $\frac{\partial w_i^{TS^*}}{\partial m} > 0$, $\frac{\partial q_i^{TS^*}}{\partial m} < 0$;

(iv) $\frac{\partial \pi_{s_i}^{TS*}}{\partial \lambda} = 0$, $\frac{\partial \pi_{s_i}^{TS*}}{\partial k} < 0$, $\frac{\partial \pi_{s_i}^{TS*}}{\partial m} < 0$;
(v) $\frac{\partial \pi_{ri}^{TS*}}{\partial \lambda} = 0$, $\frac{\partial \pi_{ri}^{TS*}}{\partial k} < 0$, $\frac{\partial \pi_{ri}^{TS*}}{\partial m} < 0$.

In the traditional supply chain without blockchain technology, if the retailer is willing to share the market demand information, the brand supplier can eliminate the uncertainty of market demand. Thus, his optimal decisions and profits are naturally independent of the probability λ of the market demand state. Accordingly, the retailer only needs to make the optimal response based on the brand supplier's decisions under market demand state i, and her optimal decisions and profits are also independent of the probability λ. In addition, Proposition 2 shows that in case *TS*, the effects of the consumer suspicion coefficient k and the unit production cost m on the chain members' optimal decisions and profits are the same as in case *TN*. This indicates that the retailer's demand information sharing cannot improve the impact of consumers' doubts regarding product authenticity. This is because the demand information sharing strategy among supply chain members only improves the information asymmetry between brand supplier and retailer, and affects the optimal decision-making of supply chain members, but it does not change consumers' cognition of product quality, and fails to provide consumers with the function of product traceability.

4.2. *Blockchain technology-based supply chain model (BT)*

Having explored the traditional supply chain models, we now consider case *BT* in which the brand supplier or (and) retailer implement(s) blockchain technology in the supply chain. As described in Fig. 2, blockchain technology has two main functions for the brand supplier and retailer: product authenticity verification and market demand information sharing. The former function means that all production details of the brand product are clearly displayed and can always be verified with the support of blockchain technology, which eliminates consumers' doubts about the authenticity of the product, and thus the parameter $k = 0$. The latter function implies that because blockchain technology makes the supply chain transparent, each member of the supply chain can obtain market demand information. Relative to traditional technology (e.g., RFID), blockchain offers unique value in supply chain management. For example, blockchain guarantees that product information cannot be tampered with, which can be used to identify counterfeit products, thereby affecting the credibility of product quality information for consumers. Additionally, brand suppliers can independently obtain market demand information through blockchain, which avoids delay and error in information sharing between supply chain members.

In this case, the demand function D_i^{BT} of the brand product under market demand state i can be represented as follows:

$$D_i^{BT} = a_i - p_i^{BT} + bq_i^{BT}. \tag{13}$$

The profit functions of the brand supplier and retailer are as follows:

$$\pi_{si}^{BT} = \max_{w_i^{BT}, q_i^{BT}} \left[(w_i^{BT} - m)(a_i - p_i^{BT} + bq_i^{BT}) - \frac{1}{2} q_i^{BT^2} \right], \tag{14}$$

$$\pi_{ri}^{BT} = \max_{p_i^{BT}} [(p_i^{BT} - w_i^{BT})(a_i - p_i^{BT} + bq_i^{BT})], \tag{15}$$

where $i = h, l$.

First, the retailer's optimal decision satisfies the following:

$$p_i^{BT}(w_i^{BT}, q_i^{BT}) = \frac{1}{2}(a_i + bq_i^{BT} + w_i^{BT}). \tag{16}$$

Accordingly, the brand supplier and retailer's optimal decisions and profits can be summarized in Lemma 3.

Lemma 3. *In case BT, at the Stackelberg equilibrium, the optimal decisions and profits of the brand supplier and the retailer are as follows:*

$$p_i^{BT^*} = \frac{3a_i + m(1 - b^2)}{(4 - b^2)},$$

$$w_i^{TS^*} = \frac{(2a_i + m(2 - b^2))}{(4 - b^2)},$$

$$q_i^{BT^*} = \frac{b(a_i - m)}{(4 - b^2)},$$

$$\pi_{si}^{BT^*} = \frac{(a_i - m)^2}{2(4 - b^2)},$$

$$\pi_{ri}^{BT^*} = \left(\frac{a_i - m}{4 - b^2} \right)^2,$$

where $i = h, l$.

Compared with cases *TN* and *TS*, the following proposition specifies how the parameters λ, k and m affect the supply chain members' equilibrium pricing and profit decisions in case BT.

Proposition 3. *In case BT, the effects of the parameters* λ, k *and* m *are as follows:*

(i) $\frac{\partial p_i^{BT^*}}{\partial \lambda} = 0, \frac{\partial w_i^{BT^*}}{\partial \lambda} = 0, \frac{\partial q_i^{BT^*}}{\partial \lambda} = 0;$
(ii) $\frac{\partial p_i^{BT^*}}{\partial k} = 0, \frac{\partial w_i^{BT^*}}{\partial k} = 0, \frac{\partial q_i^{BT^*}}{\partial k} = 0;$
(iii) $\frac{\partial p_i^{BT^*}}{\partial m} > 0, \frac{\partial w_i^{BT^*}}{\partial m} > 0, \frac{\partial q_i^{BT^*}}{\partial m} < 0;$
(iv) $\frac{\partial \pi_{si}^{BT^*}}{\partial \lambda} = 0, \frac{\partial \pi_{si}^{BT^*}}{\partial k} = 0, \frac{\partial \pi_{si}^{BT^*}}{\partial m} < 0;$
(v) $\frac{\partial \pi_{ri}^{BT^*}}{\partial \lambda} = 0, \frac{\partial \pi_{ri}^{BT^*}}{\partial k} = 0, \frac{\partial \pi_{ri}^{BT^*}}{\partial m} < 0.$

Proposition 3 shows that with the support of blockchain technology, the probability λ of the market demand state and the consumer suspicion coefficient k have no effects on the supply chain members' optimal decisions and profits. This reveals that blockchain technology realizes the functions of product authenticity verification and demand information sharing. The reason is that the traceability of blockchain technology ensures the quality of products purchased by consumers, and the transparency of blockchain technology provides information sharing for supply chain members. In addition, the effect of the unit production cost m on the supply chain members' optimal decisions and profits is the same as in cases *TN* and *TS*. This implies that even with the support of blockchain technology, an increase in the unit production cost m is unfavorable to supply chain members.

5. Effects of Blockchain Technology

In the preceding section, we derived the brand supplier and retailer's optimal decisions and profits in three different cases. In this section, we compare the three cases to study the effects of blockchain technology on the supply chain members. We focus on the following questions. For different market demand states, how does the implementation of blockchain technology change the optimal decision of each member in the traditional supply chain? Is blockchain technology beneficial to all members?

Proposition 4. *Effects of blockchain technology on the chain members' optimal decisions*:

(i) *When* $a_i = a_h$, $p_h^{BT^*} > p_h^{TS^*} > p_h^{TN^*}$, $w_h^{BT^*} > w_h^{TS^*} > w^{TN^*}$, $q_h^{BT^*} > q_h^{TS^*} > q^{TN^*}$;

(ii) *When*

$$a_i = a_l, \begin{cases} \text{if } 0k < k_{th1}, & \text{then } p_l^{TS^*} < p_l^{BT^*} < p_l^{TN^*} \\ \text{if } k_{th1} \leq k < 1, & \text{then } p_l^{TS^*} < p_l^{TN^*} \leq p_l^{BT^*} \end{cases};$$

$$\begin{cases} \text{if } 0 < k < k_{th2}, & \text{then } w_l^{TS^*} < w_l^{BT^*} < w^{TN^*} \\ \text{if } k_{th2} \leq k < 1, & \text{then } w_l^{TS^*} < w^{TN^*} \leq w_l^{BT^*} \end{cases},$$

$$\begin{cases} \text{if } 0 < k < k_{th3}, & \text{then } q_l^{TS^*} < q_l^{BT^*} < q^{TN^*} \\ \text{if } k_{th3} \leq k < 1, & \text{then } q_l^{TS^*} < q^{TN^*} \leq q_l^{BT^*} \end{cases};$$

where $k_{th1} = 1 - \frac{1}{b}\sqrt{\frac{4a_l(2+b^2)+2b^2(u-3m)-8u}{a_l(2+b^2)+u(4-b^2)-6m}}$, $k_{th2} = 1 - \frac{1}{b}\sqrt{\frac{4(a_l-u)+b^2(u-m)}{a_l-m}}$, k_{th3} *is the unique root of the equation* $-b(a_l - m)x^2 - (u - m)(4 - b^2)x + 4b(a_l - m) = 0$, *and* $x = b(1 - k)$.

Proposition 4 compares the optimal decisions of the brand supplier and retailer in the three cases *TN*, *TS* and *BT*. To facilitate analysis and understanding, we present the results of Proposition 4 in Figs. 3–5. We first compare cases *TN* and *TS*

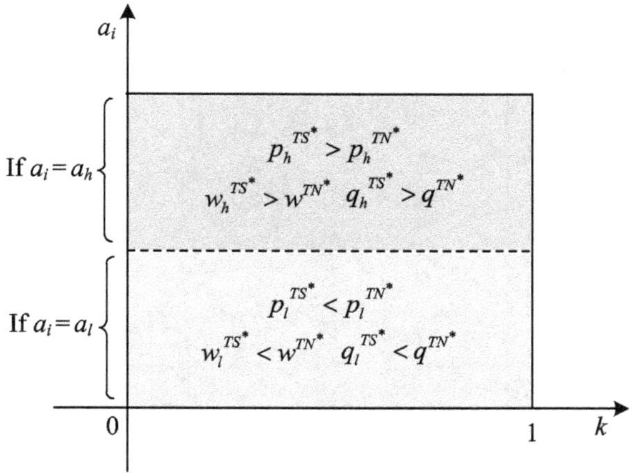

Fig. 3. Comparisons of the supply chain members' optimal decisions in cases *TN* and *TS*.

(see Fig. 3). Figure 3 shows that if the market demand state is high, the retailer's optimal retail price and the brand supplier's optimal wholesale price and optimal quality in case *TS* are all higher than those in case *TN*, but if the market demand state is low, the result is the opposite. This indicates that demand information sharing by the retailer will lead to consistent changes in the optimal decisions of supply chain members, and this change is related to the market demand state. In the high demand state, the retailer's demand information sharing will encourage brand supplier to actively improve product quality, and the wholesale price and sales price of products will also increase. The reason is that when the real market demand is optimistic, the improvement of product quality can attract more consumer demand, and the increase of price can increase the marginal revenue of enterprises, thus bringing additional profits. On the contrary, when the brand supplier gets that the market demand state is low, the pessimistic market demand will make him choose to reduce product quality to save costs and avoid losses. Accordingly, the wholesale price and sales price of products will decrease to stimulate market demand.

Figure 4 compares cases *BT* and *TN* and shows that only when the market demand state is low and the consumer suspicion coefficient k is small, the retailer's optimal retail price, the brand supplier's optimal wholesale price and optimal quality in case *BT* all be lower than those in case *TN*; otherwise, the result is the opposite. Obviously, this result is different from that in Fig. 3. This is because compared to case *TN*, blockchain technology not only realizes demand information sharing but also realizes product authenticity verification. If the consumer suspicion coefficient is large (i.e., $k \geqq \max\{k_{th1}, k_{th2}, k_{th3}\}$), the implementation of blockchain technology can greatly improve consumers' trust in product quality and increase consumers' motivation to purchase. Here, even if the market demand state is low, the supply chain members are still willing to improve product quality and prices to obtain additional profits. However, if the consumer suspicion coefficient is small

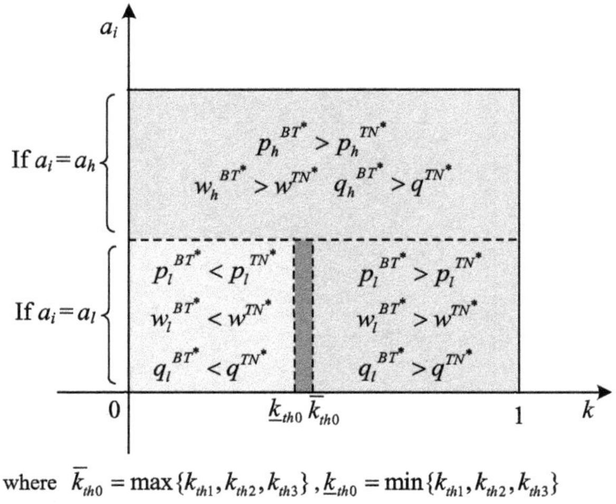

Fig. 4. Comparisons of the supply chain members' optimal decisions in cases BT and TN.

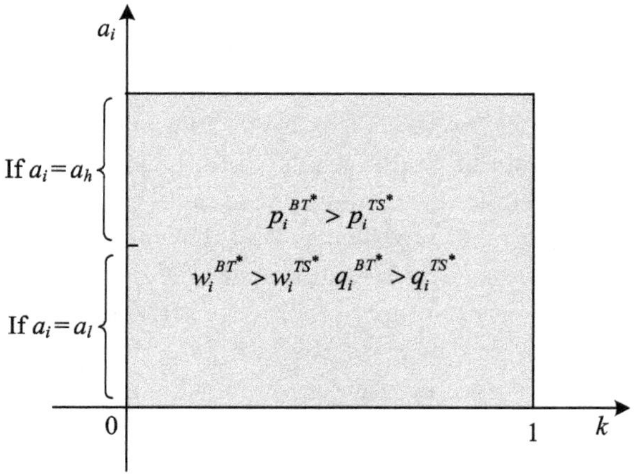

Fig. 5. Comparisons of the chain members' optimal decisions in cases BT and TS.

(i.e., $k \leqq \min\{k_{th1}, k_{th2}, k_{th3}\}$) in the low market demand state, the implementation of blockchain technology may not be conducive to improving product quality. The reason is that consumers (such as loyal customers and fans) have enough trust in the brand product quality without blockchain technology, and the implementation of blockchain technology is insufficient to change the pessimistic market demand. Similar explanation of Fig. 3 in the low market demand state can be applied to here. Accordingly, supply chain members are unwilling to increase product quality and prices.

Compared with case TS, blockchain technology further realizes product authenticity verification. Figure 5 shows that regardless of the state of market demand, the optimal decisions of the brand supplier and retailer in case BT are all higher than those in case TS. This indicates that blockchain technology can help improve product quality by eliminating consumers' doubts about the authenticity of the brand product, and it will also encourage supply chain members to increase product prices. The reasons are as follows: the implementation of blockchain technology can help consumers verify the authenticity of products through traceability, which increases consumers' trust in product quality. Thus, the brand supplier has the motivation to improve product quality to attract more customers to purchase. In equilibrium, the increase in consumer demand will naturally prompt supply chain members to increase product prices to optimize their profits.

Proposition 5. *Effects of blockchain technology on the chain members' profits*:

(i) *When* $a_i = a_h$, $\pi_s^{TN^*} < \pi_{sh}^{TS^*} < \pi_{sh}^{BT^*}$,

$$\begin{cases} \text{if } 0 < k < k_{th4}, & \text{then } \pi_{rh}^{TS^*} < \pi_{rh}^{BT^*} < \pi_{rh}^{TN^*} \\ \text{if } k_{th4} \le k < 1, & \text{then } \pi_{rh}^{TS^*} < \pi_{rh}^{TN^*} \le \pi_{rh}^{BT^*} \end{cases};$$

(ii) *When* $a_i = a_l$,

$$\begin{cases} \text{if } 0 < k < k_{th5}, & \text{then } \pi_{sl}^{TS^*} < \pi_{sl}^{BT^*} < \pi_s^{TN^*} \\ \text{if } k_{th5} \le k < 1, & \text{then } \pi_{sl}^{TS^*} < \pi_s^{TN^*} \le \pi_{sl}^{BT^*} \end{cases}, \quad \pi_{rl}^{TN^*} < \pi_{rl}^{TS^*} < \pi_{rl}^{BT^*};$$

where $k_{th4} = 1 - \frac{1}{b}\sqrt{\frac{b^2(a_h-m)-(4-b^2)(a_h-u)}{(a_h-m)-2(4-b^2)(a_h-u)}}$, $k_{th5} = 1 - \frac{1}{b}\sqrt{4 - \frac{(u-m)^2(4-b^2)}{(a_l-m)^2}}$.

Proposition 5 compares the brand supplier and retailer's optimal profits in the three cases TN, TS and BT. Similarly, we present the results of Proposition 5 in Figs. 6–8.

The comparison of cases TN and TS is shown in Fig. 6. The result shows that when the market demand is high, the brand supplier's profit is higher in TS than

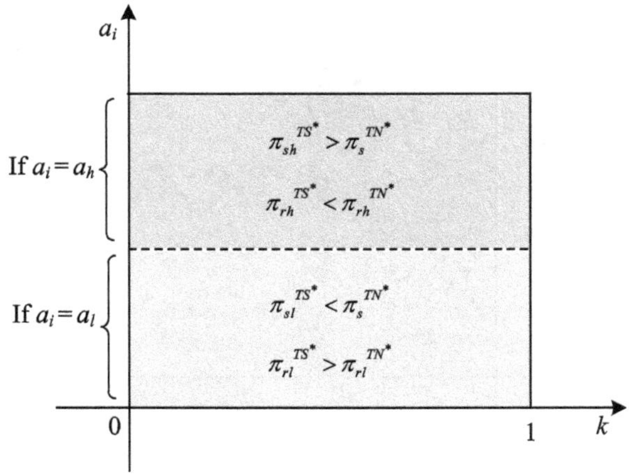

Fig. 6. Comparisons of supply chain members' profits in TN and TS.

in *TN*, while the retailer's profit is lower in *TS* than in *TN*. In contrast, when the market demand state is low, the profit of the brand supplier is lower in *TS* than in *TN*, while the profit of the retailer is higher in *TS* than in *TN*. This indicates that the retailer's demand information sharing is not necessarily beneficial to both sides. When market demand is high, demand information sharing is beneficial for the brand supplier but detrimental to the retailer. The reason is that when the brand supplier obtains market demand information, he can determine that the market demand state is high and increase the wholesale price of the product, which is unfavorable to the retailer. However, when market demand is low, the retailer is better off but the brand supplier is worse off with demand information sharing. This is because after obtaining the market demand information, the brand supplier determines that market demand is low and reduces the wholesale price, which is beneficial to the retailer. Based on the above results, we can discuss that the retailer's demand information sharing strategy under different market demand states cannot achieve a win-win situation for supply chain members. At the same time, under the retailer's active information sharing mechanism, she may share false demand information or selectively share demand information in order to pursue her own interests.

Figure 7 shows the comparison of the supply chain members' profits in cases *BT* and *TN*. There are three different regions in Fig. 7; if the consumer suspicion coefficient k is small (i.e., $k \leqq \min\{k_{th4}, k_{th5}\}$), the profit relationship of each member between *BT* and *TN* (note the two areas on the left in Fig. 7) is the same as that between *TS* and *TN* (see Fig. 6). However, if the consumer suspicion coefficient k is large (i.e., $k \geqq \max\{k_{th4}, k_{th5}\}$), regardless of the state of market demand, the brand supplier and the retailer's profits in case *BT* case are both higher than in case *TN*, which is different from the results in Fig. 6. This conclusion indicates that implementing blockchain technology in the supply chain may lead to a win-win outcome

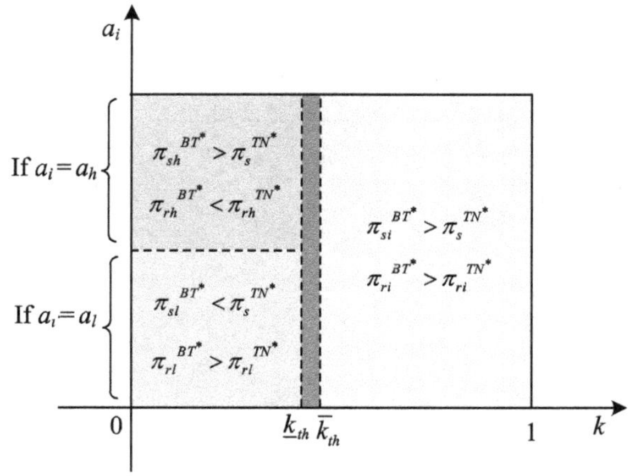

where $\bar{k}_{th} = \max\{k_{th4}, k_{th5}\}$, $\underline{k}_{th} = \min\{k_{th4}, k_{th5}\}$

Fig. 7. Comparisons of supply chain members' profits in *BT* and *TN*.

(see the area on the right in Fig. 7), which depends on the consumer suspicion coefficient. If the consumer suspicion coefficient is relatively large, the implementation of blockchain technology is more likely to be beneficial to both sides. Compared with Fig. 6, blockchain technology is conducive to the sharing of demand information in the supply chain. The reason is that blockchain technology has further verified the authenticity of the brand product, stimulated consumer demand, and increased the profits of supply chain members, thereby compensating for the lack of demand information sharing in the traditional supply chain (that is, it is only beneficial to one party). Overall, for the traditional supply chain with no demand information sharing strategy, the brand supplier and retailer can decide whether to invest in blockchain technology according to the possibility of brand products being counterfeited. In other words, when consumers think that the brand products are less likely to be counterfeited, that is, the product quality is more reliable, consumers trust the brand products, and supply chain members do not need to invest in blockchain technology. On the contrary, when consumers think that the brand products are more likely to be counterfeited, that is, consumers are more suspicious of the quality of the brand products, it is necessary to invest in blockchain technology.

Figure 8 compares cases *BT* and *TS*, which shows that regardless of the state of market demand and the consumer suspicion coefficient, the brand supplier and retailer's profits in case *BT* are both higher than those in case *TS*. This indicates that blockchain technology stimulates an increase in market demand by eliminating consumer suspicion about product authenticity, which is beneficial for both the brand supplier and the retailer. Therefore, for the traditional supply chain with demand information sharing strategy, the brand supplier and retailer do not care about the market demand states, they are always willing to actively implement blockchain technology to increase their profits.

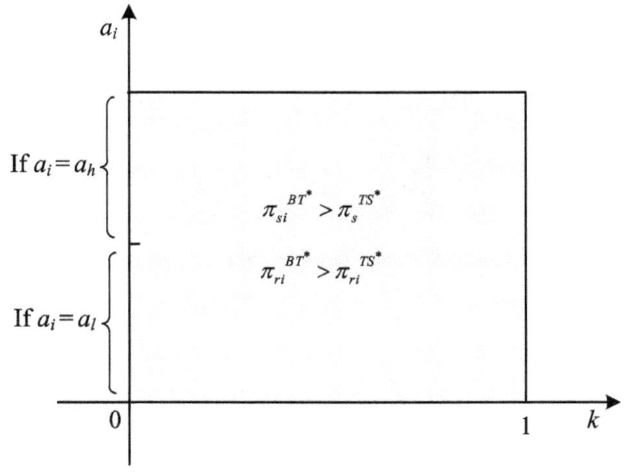

Fig. 8. Comparisons of the chain members' profits in *BT* and *TS*.

6. Extended Models

In Secs. 4 and 5, we analyzed and compared the supply chain members' optimal decisions and profits in three cases. However, the previous section focused on decentralized channels, and one natural proposal is to further analyze the effect of blockchain technology on the supply chain under centralized channels. In this section, we will study how the brand supplier and the retailer can make joint decisions under the traditional centralized supply chain and the blockchain technology-based centralized supply chain and the effect of blockchain technology on the centralized supply chain. Note that for the centralized channels, the brand supplier and the retailer have a cooperative relationship with the goal of maximizing the total profit of the supply chain. At this time, they will make joint decisions based on the actual market demand states (i.e., $a_i = a_h$ or a_l).

First, for the traditional centralized supply chain (TC), the brand supplier and the retailer jointly determine the retail price p_i^{TC} and quality q_i^{TC} of the brand product to maximize the total profit of the supply chain. The supply chain profit function based on the demand function D_i^{TC} in the different market demand states is as follows:

$$\pi_{\text{sci}}^{TC} = \max_{p_i^{TC}, q_i^{TC}} \left[(p_i^{TC} - m) \times (a_i - b(1-k)p_i^{TC} + bq_i^{TC}) - \frac{1}{2} q_i^{TC^2} \right], \quad i = h, l. \tag{17}$$

By solving Eq. (17), we can derive the optimal joint decisions of the supply chain members and the supply chain profit, namely, Lemma 4.

Lemma 4. *In case TC, the brand supplier and retailer's optimal joint decisions and the supply chain profit are as follows:*

$$p_i^{TC^*} = \frac{a_i + m(1-x^2)}{(2-x^2)}, \quad q_i^{TC^*} = \frac{x(a_i - m)}{(2-x^2)},$$

$$\pi_{\text{sci}}^{TC^*} = \frac{(a_i - m)^2}{2(2-x^2)}, \quad \textit{where } i = h, l; x = b(1-k).$$

For the blockchain technology-based centralized supply chain (BC), the supply chain profit function under different market demand states can be expressed as follows:

$$\pi_{\text{sci}}^{BC} = \max_{p_i^{BC}, q_i^{BC}} \left[(p_i^{BC} - m)(a_i - bp_i^{BC} + bq_i^{BC}) - \frac{1}{2} q_i^{BC^2} \right]. \tag{18}$$

Similarly, by solving Eq. (18), we can derive Lemma 5.

Lemma 5. *In case BC, the brand supplier and retailer's optimal joint decisions and the supply chain profit are as follows*:

$$p_i^{BC^*} = \frac{a_i + m(1-b^2)}{(2-b^2)}, \quad q_i^{BC^*} = \frac{b(a_i - m)}{(2-b^2)},$$

$$\pi_{\text{sci}}^{BC^*} = \frac{(a_i - m)^2}{2(2-b^2)}, \quad \textit{where } i = h, l.$$

By comparing the results in Lemmas 4 and 5, we derive the following proposition.

Proposition 6. *The effects of blockchain technology under a centralized supply chain*: $p_i^{BC^*} > p_i^{TC^*}$, $q_i^{BC^*} > q_i^{TC^*}$, $\pi_{\text{sci}}^{BC^*} > q_{\text{sci}}^{TC^*}$.

Proposition 6 shows that for a centralized supply chain, regardless of the state of market demand, the optimal retail price, the optimal quality and the supply chain profit in case *BC* are all larger than those in case *TC*. In the centralized supply chain, there is a partnership between the brand supplier and the retailer. It is natural that the information between them is symmetric. Under the traditional centralized supply chain (*TC*), the chain members will suffer from the loss of demand due to the consumers' doubts about the authenticity of the brand product. However, when the supply chain members implement blockchain technology, consumer demand in the centralized supply chain will increase, and the brand supplier and retailer will take advantage of this to improve product quality and retail price to obtain additional profit. Therefore, for the traditional centralized supply chain based on contractual cooperation, it is always advantageous for brand supplier and retailer to jointly introduce blockchain technology. At the same time, from another perspective, it also shows that for brand suppliers with direct sales channels, it is always advantageous to implement blockchain technology alone. The reason is that the brand supplier under the direct selling model is similar to a single centralized supply chain.

7. Conclusion

This paper considers product authenticity verification and demand information sharing using blockchain technology in supply chain management, and we study pricing and product quality decisions in a two-echelon supply chain, which comprises a brand supplier and a retailer. This research first analyzes the traditional supply chain without blockchain technology, which includes two cases: the retailer does or does not share demand information. Thereafter, the blockchain technology-based supply chain model is further considered. By comparing equilibrium results in different cases, this study analyzes the effects of blockchain technology on the optimal decisions and profits of chain members. In addition, we investigate the joint decisions of the supply chain members under a centralized supply chain and analyze the effects of blockchain technology.

From our study, the main conclusions and insights are as follows:

(1) The research results of the impact of asymmetric demand information have several implications for decision makers of the traditional supply chain to improve their operations. First, the result suggests that when the probability of high market demand increases, the brand supplier should improve product quality and wholesale price, and the retailer should increase retail price. Second, the increase of the probability of high market demand is beneficial to the brand supplier, but interestingly it is bad for the retailer. Third, we find that the supply chain members' optimal decisions and profits both decrease with the consumer suspicion coefficient, which proves that consumers' suspicion of the authenticity of brand products (e.g., luxury goods) is unfavorable to the traditional supply chain enterprises (e.g., Givenchy).

(2) This paper provides some insights for the managers of traditional supply chain enterprises who will (may) implement blockchain technology. By comparing the equilibrium results between cases BT and TN, the result suggests that after the implementation of blockchain technology, if the market demand state is high, the brand supplier and the retailer should improve the product quality, wholesale price and retail price. If the market demand state is low, their optimal decisions may increase or decrease, which depends on consumers' suspicion coefficient. More specifically, when the consumer suspicion coefficient is large, managers should still improve the optimal decisions, while when the consumer suspicion coefficient is small, managers should appropriately reduce the optimal decisions. In addition, by comparing the equilibrium results between cases BT and TS, we find that after the implementation of blockchain technology, the result suggests that regardless of the state of market demand, managers should improve the optimal quality of products, wholesale price and sales price, which can improve the profitability of the supply chain.

(3) This study provides some managerial insights for the demand information sharing in traditional supply chains in the era of blockchain technology. For a traditional supply chain without blockchain technology, the retailer can benefit from the demand information sharing only when market demand is low, whereas the brand supplier can benefit from it only when market demand is high. Therefore, in a traditional supply chain, demand information sharing strategy by the retailer does not achieve a win–win outcome. However, under demand information sharing based on blockchain technology, when the consumer suspicion coefficient is greater than a certain threshold, regardless of the market demand state, demand information sharing through blockchain technology is always beneficial to both sides and can achieve a win–win outcome.

(4) We obtain some managerial implications for managers of the traditional centralized supply chain based on coordination contracts to implement blockchain technology. The result suggests that after the implementation of blockchain technology, managers should increase the product quality and retail price, and

the profit of the supply chain will be improved. In addition, this result is also applicable to brand suppliers with direct marketing channels, which is similar to the operation of a centralized supply chain.

Our work has some limitations and can be extended in several ways. First, we only consider a single-channel supply chain. Further studies could consider the case of a dual-channel supply chain. Second, we assume that consumers are homogeneous, and from a utility perspective, it would be interesting to consider heterogeneous consumers. Third, further research could consider the implementation of blockchain technology with different levels of power in the channel structure.

Appendix A. All Proofs

Proof of Lemma 1. It is straightforward to derive that $\pi_{ri}^{TN}$is concave in p_i^{TN} (P.S.: $\partial^2\pi_{ri}^{TN}/\partial p_i^{TN^2} < 0$). In addition, the Hessian Matrix H^{TN} of in terms of w^{TN} and q^{TN} is obtained through Eq. (7). That is,

$$H^{TN} = \begin{bmatrix} \dfrac{\partial^2\pi_s^{TN}}{\partial w^{TN^2}} & \dfrac{\partial^2\pi_s^{TN}}{\partial w^{TN}\partial q^{TN}} \\ \dfrac{\partial^2\pi_s^{TN}}{\partial q^{TN}\partial w^{TN}} & \dfrac{\partial^2\pi_s^{TN}}{\partial q^{TN^2}} \end{bmatrix} = \begin{bmatrix} -1 & x/2 \\ x/2 & -1 \end{bmatrix}.$$

Thus, we can obtain $|H_1^{TN}| < 0$ and $|H_2^{TN}| = \frac{1}{4}(4 - x^2) > 0$, and the brand supplier's profit function is a joint concave function with respect to w^{TN} and q^{TN}. According to Eq. (7), the first-order partial derivatives of π_s^{TN} with regard to w^{TN} and q^{TN} are as follows:

$$\begin{cases} \dfrac{\partial\pi_s^{TN}}{\partial w^{TN}} = \dfrac{1}{2}(u + m + xq) - w, \\ \dfrac{\partial\pi_s^{TN}}{\partial q^{TN}} = \dfrac{1}{2}x(w - m) - q. \end{cases} \tag{A.1}$$

According to first-order conditions (A.1), we can get w^{TN^*} and q^{TN^*}. Put them into Eq. (5), we can get $p_i^{TN^*}$. Then, π_s^{TN*} and $\pi_{ri}^{TN^*}$ can be obtained by substituting w^{TN^*}, q^{TN^*} and $p_i^{TN^*}$ into Eqs. (3) and (4). □

Proof of Proposition 1. According to Lemma 1, the first-order partial derivatives of $p_i^{TN^*}$ with respect to the parameters λ, k and m are as follows:

$$\begin{cases} \dfrac{\partial p_i^{TN^*}}{\partial\lambda} = \dfrac{(a_h - a_l)(x^2 + 2)}{2(4 - x^2)} > 0, \\ \dfrac{\partial p_i^{TN^*}}{\partial k} = \dfrac{-6bx(u - m)}{(4 - x^2)^2} < 0, \\ \dfrac{\partial p_i^{TN^*}}{\partial m} = \dfrac{(1 - x^2)}{(4 - x^2)} > 0. \end{cases} \tag{A.2}$$

Similarly, we can respectively judge whether the first-order partial derivatives of w^{TN*}, q^{TN*}, π_{ri}^{TN*} and π_s^{TN*} with respect to parameters λ, k and m are positive or negative. Thus, Proposition 1 can be derived. □

Proof of Lemma 2. By analyzing the retailer's profit function Eq. (9), π_{ri}^{TS} is strictly concave with respect to p_i^{TN} because $\partial^2\pi_{ri}^{TS}/\partial p_i^{TS^2} < 0$. Also, by substituting Eq. (10) into Eq. (8), the Hessian Matrix H_i^{TS} in terms of w_i^{TS} and q_i^{TS} under market demand state i is

$$H_i^{TS} = \begin{bmatrix} \dfrac{\partial^2\pi_{si}^{TS}}{\partial w_i^{TS^2}} & \dfrac{\partial^2\pi_{si}^{TS}}{\partial w_i^{TS}\partial q_i^{TS}} \\ \dfrac{\partial^2\pi_{si}^{TS}}{\partial q_i^{TS}\partial w_i^{TS}} & \dfrac{\partial^2\pi_{si}^{TS}}{\partial q_i^{TS^2}} \end{bmatrix} = \begin{bmatrix} -1 & x/2 \\ x/2 & -1 \end{bmatrix}.$$

Given that $0 < x = b(1-k) < 1$, we have $|H_{i1}^{TS}| < 0$ and $|H_{i2}^{TS}| = \frac{1}{4}(4-x^2) > 0$. Thus, the brand supplier's optimal profit function is a joint concave function with respect to w_i^{TS} and q_i^{TS}. Next, similar to the proofs of Lemma 1 and thus omitted. □

Proof of Proposition 2. According to the optimal solutions in Lemma 2, we can directly observe that the optimal decisions and profits of the chain members are independent with the parameter λ.

Furthermore, similar to the proof of Proposition 1, we can respectively judge whether the first-order partial derivatives of p_i^{TS*}, w_i^{TS*}, q_i^{TS*}, π_{ri}^{TS*} and π_{si}^{TS*} with respect to parameters k and m are positive or negative, and then we compare the above results with Proposition 1. Thus, Proposition 2 can be obtained. □

Proof of Lemma 3. By Eq. (15), we can obtain $\partial^2\pi_{ri}^{BT}/\partial p_i^{BT^2} = -2$. Also, we plug Eq. (16) into Eq. (14), and the Hessian Matrix H_i^{BT} in terms of w_i^{BT} and q_i^{BT} under market demand state i is

$$H^{BT} = \begin{bmatrix} \dfrac{\partial^2\pi_{si}^{BT}}{\partial w_i^{BT^2}} & \dfrac{\partial^2\pi_{si}^{BT}}{\partial w_i^{BT}\partial q_i^{BT}} \\ \dfrac{\partial^2\pi_{si}^{BT}}{\partial q_i^{BT}\partial w_i^{BT}} & \dfrac{\partial^2\pi_{si}^{BT}}{\partial q_i^{BT^2}} \end{bmatrix} = \begin{bmatrix} -1 & b/2 \\ b/2 & -1 \end{bmatrix}.$$

Given that $0 < b < 1$, we have $|H_{i1}^{BT}| < 0$ and $|H_{i2}^{BT}| = \frac{1}{4}(4-b^2) > 0$. Then, the brand supplier's optimal payoff is strictly concave with respect to w_i^{BT} and q_i^{BT}. Next, similar to the proofs of Lemmas 1 and 3 can be easily derived. □

Proof of Proposition 3. According to the optimal solutions in Lemma 3, we can directly observe that the optimal decisions and profits of the chain members are independent with the parameters λ and k.

Furthermore, similar to the proof of Proposition 1, we can, respectively, judge whether the first-order partial derivatives of p_i^{BT*}, w_i^{BT*}, q_i^{BT*}, π_{ri}^{BT*} and π_s^{BT*}

with respect to parameters m are positive or negative, and then we compare the above results with Propositions 1 and 2. Thus, Proposition 3 can be obtained. □

Proof of Proposition 4. According to Lemmas 1–3, (i) By comparing the optimal decision of each member in the *TN* and *TS* cases, the following calculations can be made for $p_i^{TS} - p_i^{TN}$, $w_i^{TS} - w^{TN}$ and $q_i^{TS} - q^{TN}$, respectively:

$$\begin{cases} p_i^{TS} - p_i^{TN} = \dfrac{(x^2+2)(a_i-u)}{2(4-x^2)}, \\ w_i^{TS} - w^{TN} = \dfrac{2(a_i-u)}{(4-x^2)}, \\ q_i^{TS} - q^{TN} = \dfrac{x(a_i-u)}{(4-x^2)}. \end{cases} \tag{A.3}$$

By Eq. (A.3), we know that if $a_i = a_h$, then $a_h > u$, and $p_h^{TS} > p_h^{TN}$, $w_h^{TS} > w^{TN}$, $q_h^{TS} > q^{TN}$; if $a_i = a_l$, then $a_l < u$, and $p_l^{TS} < p_h^{TN}$, $w_l^{TS} < w^{TN}$, $q_l^{TS} < q^{TN}$.

(ii) By comparing the optimal decision of each member in the *BT* and *TN* cases, if $a_i = a_h$, we can get $p_h^{BT} > p_h^{TN}$, $w_h^{BT} > w^{TN}$, $q_h^{BT} > q^{TN}$; if $a_i = a_l$, we can obtain that

$$\begin{cases} \text{if } 0 < k < k_{th1}, & \text{then } p_l^{BT} < p^{TN} \\ \text{if } k_{th1} \le k < 1, & \text{then } p_l^{BT} \ge p^{TN} \end{cases}, \quad \begin{cases} \text{if } 0 < k < k_{th2}, & \text{then } w_l^{BT} < w^{TN} \\ \text{if } k_{th2} \le k < 1, & \text{then } w_l^{BT} \ge w^{TN} \end{cases},$$

$$\begin{cases} \text{if } 0 < k < k_{th3}, & \text{then } q_l^{BT} < q^{TN} \\ \text{if } k_{th3} \le k < 1, & \text{then } q_l^{BT} \ge q^{TN} \end{cases}.$$

(iii) By comparing the optimal decision of each member in the *BT* and *TS* cases, we can derive that $p_i^{BT} > p_i^{TS}$, $w_i^{BT} > w_i^{TS}$ and $q_i^{BT} > q_i^{TS} (i = h, l)$. □

Therefore, by combining the results of (i), (ii), (iii) above, we can get Proposition 4.

Proof of Proposition 5. According to Lemmas 1–3, (i) By comparing the profit of each member in the *TN* and *TS* cases, the following calculations can be made for $\pi_{si}^{TS} - \pi_s^{TN}$ and $\pi_{ri}^{TS} - \pi_{ri}^{TN}$, respectively:

$$\begin{cases} \pi_{si}^{TS} - \pi_s^{TN} = \dfrac{((a_i-m)+(u-m))(a_i-u)}{2(4-x^2)}, \\ \pi_{ri}^{TS} - \pi_{ri}^{TN} = \left(\dfrac{a_i(6-x^2)-u(2-x^2)-4m}{2(4-x^2)}\right)\left(\dfrac{-(2-x^2)(a_i-u)}{2(4-x^2)}\right). \end{cases} \tag{A.4}$$

By Eq. (A.4), we know that if $a_i = a_h$, then $a_h > u$, and $\pi_{si}^{TS} > \pi_s^{TN}$, $\pi_{ri}^{TS} < \pi_{ri}^{TN}$; if $a_i = a_l$, then $a_l < u$, and $\pi_{si}^{TS} < \pi_s^{TN}$, $\pi_{ri}^{TS} > \pi_{ri}^{TN}$.

(ii) By comparing the profit of each member in the BT and TN cases, if $a_i = a_h$, we can get $\pi_{sh}^{BT^*} > \pi_s^{TN^*}$ and

$$\begin{cases} \text{if } 0 < k < k_{th4}, & \text{then } \pi_{rh}^{BT^*} < \pi_{rh}^{TN^*} \\ \text{if } k_{th4} \le k < 1, & \text{then } \pi_{rh}^{BT^*} \ge \pi_{rh}^{TN^*} \end{cases};$$

if $a_i = a_l$, we can derive that

$$\begin{cases} \text{if } 0 < k < k_{th5}, & \text{then } \pi_{sl}^{BT^*} < \pi_s^{TN^*} \\ \text{if } k_{th5} \le k < 1, & \text{then } \pi_{sl}^{BT^*} \ge \pi_s^{TN^*} \end{cases}$$

and $\pi_{rl}^{BT^*} > \pi_{rl}^{TN^*}$.

(iii) By comparing the profit of each member in the BT and TS cases, we can derive that $\pi_{si}^{BT^*} > \pi_{si}^{TS^*}$ and $\pi_{ri}^{BT^*} > \pi_{ri}^{TS^*} (i = h, l)$. □

Therefore, by combining the results of (i), (ii), (iii) above, we can get Proposition 5.

Proof of Lemma 4. According to Eq. (17), the first-order partial derivatives of π_{sci}^{TC} with regard to p_i^{TC} and q_i^{TC} are as follows:

$$\begin{cases} \dfrac{\partial \pi_{\text{sci}}^{TC}}{\partial p_i^{TC}} = (p_i^{TC} - m)x - q_i^{TC}, \\ \dfrac{\partial \pi_{\text{sci}}^{TC}}{\partial q_i^{TC}} = (a_i - p_i + xq_i^{TC}) - (p_i - m). \end{cases} \tag{A.5}$$

By Eq. (A.5), we can get $p_i^{TC^*}$ and $q_i^{TC^*}$, then put them into π_{sci}^{TC}, we can get π_{sci}^{TC*}. □

Proof of Lemma 5. According to Eq. (18), the first-order partial derivatives of π_{sci}^{BC} with regard to p_i^{BC} and q_i^{BC} are as follows:

$$\begin{cases} \dfrac{\partial \pi_{\text{sci}}^{BC}}{\partial p_i^{BC}} = (p_i^{BC} - m)b - q_i^{BC}, \\ \dfrac{\partial \pi_{\text{sci}}^{BC}}{\partial q_i^{BC}} = (a_i - p_i + bq_i^{BC}) - (p_i - m). \end{cases} \tag{A.6}$$

By Eq. (A.6), we can get $p_i^{BC^*}$ and $q_i^{BC^*}$, then put them into π_{sci}^{BC}, we can get $\pi_{\text{sci}}^{BC^*}$. □

Proof of Proposition 6. By comparing the optimal solutions between Lemmas 4 and 5, one can easily derive the result. □

Acknowledgments

The authors are grateful to the Editor and anonymous referees for their very valuable comments and suggestions. This research was supported by the National Natural Science Foundation of China (Grant No. 71572033, 71832001), and the Fundamental Research Funds for the Central Universities and Graduate Student Innovation Fund of Donghua University (Grant No. CUSF-DH-D-2021062 and CUSF-DHU-223201900089).

References

Aste, T, P Tasca and TD Matteo (2017). Blockchain technologies: The foreseeable impact on society and industry. *Computer*, 50(9), 18–28.

Biswas, K, V Muthukkumarasamy and WL Tan (2017). Blockchain based wine supply chain traceability system. *Future Technologies Conference*, Vancouver, BC, Canada, pp. 1–7.

Bertini, M, D Halbheer and O Koenigsberg (2020). Price and quality decisions by self-serving managers. *International Journal of Research in Marketing*, 37(2), 236–257.

Bashir, I (2017). *Mastering Blockchain*. Birmingham: Packt Publishing.

Choi, TM (2019). Blockchain-technology-supported platforms for diamond authentication and certification in luxury supply chains. *Transportation Research Part E: Logistics and Transportation Review*, 128, 17–29.

Choi, TM, LP Feng and R Li (2020a). Information disclosure structure in supply chains with rental service platforms in the blockchain technology era. *International Journal of Production Economics*, 221(3), 107473.

Choi, TM, S Guo, N Liu and XT Shi (2020b). Optimal pricing in on-demand-service-platform-operations with hired agents and risk-sensitive customers in the blockchain era. *European Journal of Operational Research*, 284, 1031–1042.

Cui, R, G Allon, A Bassamboo and JV Mieghem (2015). Information sharing in supply chains: An empirical and theoretical valuation. *Management Science*, 61(11), 2803–2824.

Chen, RY (2018). A traceability chain algorithm for artificial neural networks using T–S fuzzy cognitive maps in blockchain. *Future Generation Computer Systems*, 80, 198–210.

Cheng, TCE and YN Wu (2005). The impact of information sharing in a two-level supply chain with multiple retailers. *Journal of the Operational Research Society*, 56(10), 1159–1165.

Cho, SH, X Fang and S Tayur (2015). Combating strategic counterfeiters in licit and illicit supply chains. *Manufacturing and Service Operations Management*, 17(3), 273–289.

Chenavaz, RY, G Feichtinger, RF Hartl and PM Kort (2020). Modeling the impact of product quality on dynamic pricing and advertising policies. *European Journal of Operational Research*, 284, 990–1001.

Feng, J and J Xie (2007). Performance-based advertising: Price and advertising as signals of product quality. *Social Science Electronic Publishing*, 23(3), 1030–1041.

Guan, ZL, XM Zhang, MS Zhou and YR Dan (2020). Demand information sharing in competing supply chains with manufacturer-provided service. *International Journal of Production Economics*, 220, 107450.

Hughes, L, YK Dwivedi, SK Misra, NP Rana, V Raghavan and V Akella (2019). Blockchain research, practice and policy: Applications, benefits, limitations, emerging research themes and research agenda. *International Journal of Information Management*, 49, 114–129.

Ha, AY and S Tong (2008). Contracting and information sharing under supply chain competition. *Management Science*, 54, 701–715.

Ha, AY, Q Tian and S Tong (2017). Information sharing in competing supply chains with production cost reduction. *Manufacturing and Service Operations Management*, 19, 246–262.

Jiang, B, L Tian, Y Xu and F Zhang (2016). To share or not to share: Demand forecast sharing in a distribution channel. *Marketing Science*, 35(5), 800–809.

Kshetri, N (2018). Blockchain's roles in meeting key supply chain management objectives. *International Journal of Information Management*, 39(4), 80–89.

Li, G, L Li and J Sun (2019). Pricing and service effort strategy in a dual-channel supply chain with showrooming effect. *Transportation Research Part E: Logistics and Transportation Review*, 126, 32–48.

Lee, HL, KC So and CS Tang (2000). The value of information sharing in a two-level supply chain. *Management Science*, 46(5), 626–643.

Lejarza, F and M Balde (2020). Closed-loop optimal operational planning of supply chains with fast product quality dynamics.*Computers and Chemical Engineering*, 132, 106594.

Li, X and XT Qi (2019). On pricing and quality decisions with risk aversion. *Omega*, 13, 102118.

Olsen, TL and B Tomlin (2020). Industry 4.0: Opportunities and challenges for operations management. *Manufacturing and Service Operations Management*, 22(1), 113–122.

Peterson, RA and AJ Jolibert (2015). A cross national investigation of price and brand as determinant of perceived product quality. *Journal of Applied Psychology*, 61(4), 533–536.

Qian, Y (2011). Counterfeiters: Foes or friends? How do counterfeits affect different product quality tiers? Northwestern University–Kellogg School of Management, Working Paper.

Rao, AR and KB Monroe (1989). The effect of price, brand name, and store name on buyers' perceptions of product quality an integrative review. *Journal of Marketing Research*, 26(3), 351–357.

Shi, X and TM Choi (2019). Enhancing food safety by using blockchain technologies. The Hong Kong Polytechnic University, Working Paper.

Shen, B, XY Xu and Q Yuan (2020). Selling secondhand products through an online platform with blockchain. *Transportation Research Part E: Logistics and Transportation Review*, 142, 102066.

Sandeep, S and K Manjunath (2017). Performance modeling of a two-echelon supply chain under different levels of upstream inventory information sharing. *Computers & Operations Research*, 77, 210–225.

Sun, X, W Tang, J Chen, S Li and J Zhang (2019). Manufacturer encroachment with production cost reduction under asymmetric information. *Transportation Research Part E: Logistics and Transportation Review*, 128, 191–211.

Shang, W, AY Ha and S Tong (2015). Information sharing in a supply chain with a common retailer. *Management Science*, 62, 245–263.

Stevenson, M and J Busby (2015). An exploratory analysis of counterfeiting strategies: Towards counterfeit-resilient supply chains. *International Journal of Operations & Production Management*, 35(1), 110–144.

Vaio, AD and L Varriale (2020). Blockchain technology in supply chain management for sustainable performance: Evidence from the airport industry. *International Journal of Information Management*, 52(6), 102014.

Wamba, SF, MM Queiroz and L Trinchera (2020). Dynamics between blockchain adoption determinants and supply chain performance: An empirical investigation. *International Journal of Production Economics*, 229, 107791.

Wang, ZJ, TY Wang, H Hu, J Gong, X Ren and QY Xiao (2020). Blockchain-based framework for improving supply chain traceability and information sharing in precast construction. *Automation in Construction*, 111, 103063.

Yu, YG, SJ Zhou and Y Shi (2020). Information sharing or not across the supply chain: The role of carbon emission reduction. *Transportation Research Part E: Logistics and Transportation Review*, 137, 101915.

Yao, DQ and JJ Liu (2005). Competitive pricing of mixed retail and e-tail distribution channels. *Omega*, 33(3), 235–247.

Ye, TF and HQ Yang (2020). Price and quality management with strategic consumers: Whether to introduce a high or low product variant. *Applied Mathematics and Computation*, 386, 125541.

Zhang, S, B Dan and M Zhou (2019). After-sale service deployment and information sharing in a supply chain under demand uncertainty. *European Journal of Operational Research*, 279(2), 351–363.

Zhao, J, YM Zhou, ZH Cao and J Min (2020). The shelf space and pricing strategies for a retailer-dominated supply chain with consignment based revenue sharing contracts. *European Journal of Operational Research*, 280(3), 926–939.

Zhu, SX (2015). Integration of capacity, pricing, and lead-time decisions in a decentralized supply chain. *International Journal of Production Economics*, 164, 14–23.

Zhou, M, B Dan, S Ma and X Zhang (2017). Supply chain coordination with information sharing: The informational advantage of GPOs. *European Journal of Operational Research*, 256(3), 785–802.

Biography

Zhongmiao Sun is a PhD student of Glorious Sun School of Business and Management at the Donghua University, majoring in management science and engineering. His recent research interests include operations management in sharing economy and supply chain management.

Qi Xu is a PhD supervisor, Professor of Glorious Sun School of Business and Management at the Donghua University. She is mainly interested in research of operations management, e-commerce and supply chain management, etc. She has supervised many MS and PhD students in these areas. She has published more than 100 of articles in the famous international and domestic journals, such as International Journal of Production Economics, International Journal of Production Research, Annals of Operations Research, and International Transactions in Operational Research.

Baoli Shi is a PhD student of Glorious Sun School of Business and Management at the Donghua University, majoring in management science and engineering. Her areas of expertise include pre-sale decision and supply chain management of fashion clothing.

https://doi.org/10.1142/9789819808588_0003

Chapter 3

Cooperative Decision Making of Supply Chain Members of Shipping Logistics Services Under the Background of Blockchain†

Yujing Chen

Department of Institute of Logistics
Science Engineering, Shanghai Maritime University
Shanghai 201306, P. R. China
345440378@qq.com

Bin Yang*

Department of Institute of Logistics
Science Engineering Shanghai Maritime University
Shanghai 201306, P. R. China
binyang@shmtu.edu.cn

The supply chain of shipping logistics services is an important branch of logistics service supply chain. To ensure the effective operation of the supply chain and to solve problems such as asymmetric information, difficult data quality assurance, and uncontrollable transportation in shipping logistics services, blockchain technology are proposed to reduce information interaction problems. In view of the factors of information sharing and customers' sensitivity to information quality, a tripartite evolutionary game model with the shipping company, the port and the freight forwarder as the research objects was established, and the cooperative decision making of node companies was discussed before and after the application of blockchain technology. Theoretical derivation and data analysis show that ports and freight forwarder in the supply chain of shipping logistics services dominated by shipping companies are less affected by information sharing and customers' sensitivity to information quality. With the increase in the application of blockchain technology, when customers have lower expectations for information quality, shipping companies are more willing to cooperate actively. The willingness to cooperate actively between ports and shipping companies is increasing faster than when blockchain technology is not used. Therefore, shipping companies should encourage the active use of blockchain technology to reduce the degree of information sharing between ports and freight forwarder and the influences of customer expectations on shipping companies.

Keywords: Blockchain; shipping logistics services; information sharing; customers' sensitivity.

*Corresponding author.
†To cite this article, please refer to its earlier version published in the Asia-Pacific Journal of Operational Research, Vol. 39, No. 1, (February 2022), DOI: 10.1142/S0217595921400182. Reprinted with permission from World Scientific Publishing Co. Pte. Ltd.

1. Introduction

1.1. *Background and motivation*

As the competition in the shipping market continues to intensify, meeting the needs of customers with integrated supply chain services is difficult for traditional single transportation services. Ports, shipping companies, logistics companies, and other service chain companies have begun to actively seek cooperation to develop supply chains of shipping logistics services. The supply chain of shipping logistics services is based on shipping logistics. It integrates ports, logistics companies, shipping companies, and government regulatory agencies through information technology to control and manage the logistics, capital flow, and information flow in the entire service supply chain. In this manner, customers are provided with integrated services, thereby achieving the functional logistics network structure optimization of shipping logistics systems.

However, the content of shipping logistics service is diverse with many intermediate links. In the actual transport connection process, the cooperation problems such as information asymmetry, lack of cooperation and coordination mechanism, and unreasonable income distribution occur, which reduce the overall performance of the supply chain of shipping logistics services. Uncertain logistics demand, uncontrollable transport process, and unstable service quality occur in the supply chain of shipping logistics services, which make the cooperation between supply chain members more prominent. They also increase the complexity of solving enterprise cooperation problems in the supply chain and affect the smoothness of supply chain connection.

Our research background is mainly for maritime transportation in shipping logistics services. The key node companies that provide maritime logistics transportation services for the shipping logistics service supply chain are shipping companies, ports and freight forwarders. There is a relationship between service and being served, choice and being chosen, division of labor and cooperation, and coexistence of interests. They complete maritime logistics and transportation services through information exchange. In order to ensure their interests and privacy, the true transportation information will be concealed by the node companies. It will lead to some cooperation issues such as information asymmetry between the three parties.

With the advent of the big data era, blockchain technology has been gradually applied to the global logistics of the maritime shipping supply chain to enhance efficiency through the digitalization of maritime shipping records (Chung-Shan, 2019). Such as, Maersk Group, which has the world's largest container fleet, announced a partnership with IBM to jointly establish the TradeLens platform and use blockchain technology to organize global trade. The TradeLens platform uses blockchain technology in digitizing the entire supply chain to help manage and track tens of millions of containers around the world and uses blockchain technology to simplify the operation of the entire global shipping ecosystem. Blockchain is not the only solution to realize information sharing, management and tracking of goods.

For example, the Internet of Things can also provide help, but it cannot be trusted by customers because it is easy to tamper with the information. The construction of the supply chain of shipping logistics services using blockchain technology is still in the initial stage of development. Thus, studying the cooperative decision making of node enterprises is necessary, which provides theoretical support for the development of shipping logistics.

1.2. *Research questions and contributions*

We study the effect of the competition and cooperation decision of the shipping logistics service supply chain node enterprises, when blockchain is used. We take the supply chain which is consisted by the shipping company, the port and the freight forwarder into consideration. Then a system dynamics model of tripartite evolutionary game is developed to analyze the strategy interaction of the supply chain node enterprises and simulate the corresponding evolution process. Based on the background of the shipping logistics service supply chain with the blockchain, we considered the effects of the quality of information sharing and customers' sensitivity to information quality on the decision making of node enterprises. In terms of supply chain structure, we have considered two situations: (1) a traditional shipping logistics service supply chain dominated by shipping companies; (2) a decentralized shipping logistics service supply chain using blockchain technology.

Our research questions are as follows. (1) What are the competition and cooperation decisions of traditional logistics service supply chain node enterprises when considering information sharing and changes in customer sensitivity? (2) Does the application of blockchain technology affect the cooperative decision-making of node enterprises? (3) Before and after the application of the blockchain, what the impact of the information sharing between node companies and the change of customers' sensitivity to information quality have on the node companies?

To the best of our knowledge, this paper is the first analytical study exploring the impact brought by blockchain technology on the co-competition decision of shipping logistics service supply chain node enterprises. From a theoretical perspective, we study the impact of blockchain technology on corporate decision-making in the shipping logistics service supply chain, and put forward corresponding management recommendations by analyzing these results.

2. Literature Review

There are many related researches on information sharing, information quality, and cooperation mechanisms in the logistics service supply chain, but there are few specific documents on shipping logistics services. At present, shipping companies, freight forwarders and ports as the research object in the literature and ports are mostly researched on the shipping logistics service supply chain. There is less research on the supply chain with shipping companies as the main research object. With the impact of economic globalization, node enterprises are no longer operating independently and alone in the past. The competition, cooperation and coordination in the shipping field have attracted the attention of scholars.

2.1. *Co-opetition relation of shipping logistics service supply chain*

The existing academic research on the decision of competition and cooperation attracted the attention of scholars, most of which focused on profit, service capacity and social welfare. Lee *et al.* (2014) explored the competition game among shipping carriers, land carriers and port companies, and proved through example analysis that the profits brought by cooperation are not necessarily greater than competition. Wang *et al.* (2014) proposed a non-cooperative game model to analyze the shipping competition between two shipping companies in an emerging liner container shipping market. Xu *et al.* (2015) studied the problem of empty container dispatch between freight forwarder and carriers in the shipping supply chain under cooperative and non-cooperative conditions and analyzed the competition and cooperation between freight forwarder. Song *et al.* (2016) designed a non-cooperative game model and studied a transshipment transportation system involving two ports and a shipping company from the perspective of transportation chain.

In addition, the cooperative supply chain is divided into horizontal alliances and vertical alliances. Some scholars have studied the value of the horizontal alliance of two competing carriers in the environment of maritime service competition, and used revenue sharing and service cost allocation contracts to coordinate the maritime transport chain (Liu and Wang, 2015). In the vertical alliance, the research mostly focuses on shipping companies and freight forwarders. Li *et al.* (2015) took the vertical transportation system composed of a shipping company and two freight forwarders as the research object, and studied the service capacity sharing and competition and cooperation relationship between the two freight forwarders. In the existing literature, the research on most of the competition and cooperation relations of shipping logistics service supply chain focuses on profit, coordination, etc. We use evolutionary game theory to construct a game model, and analyze the cooperation enthusiasm of node companies in the shipping logistics service supply chain based on different influencing factors.

2.2. *Information sharing and the quality of information*

Our study is related to the research on supply chain in the presence of information. In the service supply chain, information sharing is the focus of scholars' attention, mostly focusing on the information asymmetry between cost, market demand and forecast. The existing academic research is on the information asymmetry and information sharing, most of which focused on transshipment time, transportation cost, and cooperation contract. Sternberg (2014) studied the issue of information sharing between shipping companies and road transporters, and pointed out that the lack of information communication between the participants has led to a longer turnaround time for the hub. Ruina (2021) studied the contract between freight forwarders and carriers under asymmetric information, and pointed out the impact of information asymmetry on transportation costs. Information quality is considered to be fundamentally related to the degree to which information system products convey meaning (DeLone *et al.*, 1992). Throughout the supply chain, the quality of information is usually shared between manufacturers and retailers (Ghosh and Galbreth, 2013). Guan (2015) pointed out that the information quality decision of the manufacturer affects the income and decision-making of retailers and consumers. Markopoulos (2018) pointed out that the way consumers obtain quality information is not only from manufacturers, but also from outside sources. Although consumers can obtain certain information, the quality of information is controlled by manufacturers and retailers, and the quality of information obtained by consumers cannot be guaranteed. Therefore, the sensitivity of customers to information quality is an influencing factor to be discussed in our study. In the existing academic, there is no research based on information asymmetry to discuss shipping logistics service competition and cooperation decision. Based on the degree of information sharing and the sensitivity of customers to information quality, we have discussed the evolution of competition and cooperation on the node enterprises of the shipping logistics service supply chain.

2.3. *The application of blockchain technology in the supply chain*

In this study, we propose to use blockchain technology to solve the problem of information asymmetry. There are many theoretical studies on blockchain technology. We will focus on blockchain research on supply chain information sharing, process architecture, and member cooperation. Wang *et al.* (2020) constructed a blockchain-based information management framework to realize supply chain information sharing management, real-time scheduling control and information traceability. Hackius *et al.* (2020) established a transparent and unchanging information-sharing mechanism through blockchain technology to reduce the conventional needs for collaboration. Many scholars studied the influence of blockchain technology on the cooperation mechanism in the supply chain and the cooperation relationship between supply chain members. Anssen *et al.* (2017) studied the influence of blockchain technology on government organizations and processes and used blockchain applications to ensure management processes. Biswas *et al.* (2017) used blockchain technology to improve the cooperative relationship between stakeholders and the traceability of products. Aste *et al.* (2017) investigated the use of blockchain technology to increase cooperation among members, which reduced the cost of members and increased the efficiency of the supply chain. Baharmand *et al.* (2019) established partnerships with logistics service providers in the supply chain through blockchain-based smart contracts to improve the effectiveness and efficiency of logistics services. Kim *et al.* (2019) studied and investigated how the use of blockchain in supply chain activities affects (increases or decreases) the efficiency and growth of supply chain partnerships, thereby affecting supply chain performance results.

There is a foundation for the practical application of blockchain technology in shipping, but there is still little theoretical knowledge. Yang (2019) evaluated the influence of blockchain technology on maritime supply chain and reported the development direction of maritime digitalization based on blockchain. Based on the two influencing factors of information sharing and customers' sensitivity to information quality, we compares the competition and cooperation decisions of shipping logistics service supply chain node enterprises before and after the application of blockchain technology.

3. Problem Description and Model Development

3.1. *Model assumptions*

Three players, namely shipping company, port and freight forwarder, are assumed to be involved in the game process in the supply chain of shipping logistics services. Each node enterprise is bounded rationally economic people, that is, each party does not have a predictive ability, takes the existing strategy as a condition, and takes actions or decisions in accordance with past customary behavior or experience. In terms of strategy selection, the best strategy of each node enterprise is slowly found in the game process. Thus, the stable equilibrium solution of the evolutionary game is not the result of a one-time selection.

To simplify the problem, only two pure strategies before and after the use of the blockchain by node companies are considered. The shipping company adopts an active cooperation strategy $B_1$and a passive cooperation strategy B_2. After the blockchain is used, the shipping company adopts an active cooperation strategy to encourage ports and freight forwarder to join the blockchain. The port adopts the active cooperation strategy G_1 and the passive strategy G_2. After the blockchain is used, the active cooperation is represented by participating in the blockchain. Similarly, the freight forwarder adopt an active cooperation strategy H_1 and a passive strategy H_2. After the blockchain is used, active cooperation is manifested as a participation in the blockchain. Decision tree of the node enterprise's strategies is shown in Fig. 1.

3.2. *Modeling assumptions*

3.2.1. *Parameter assumptions without blockchain technology*

(1) The shipping company

The basic income of shipping company transportation is r_s. The information sharing degree of the shipping company is q_1. When information is shared, whether the information is completely correct cannot be guaranteed. At the same time, α denotes customers' sensitivity to the information quality. Information quality refers to the information used by the shipping company when sharing information. μ_1 and μ_2 are the information qualities when the information provided by the port and the freight forwarder are used.

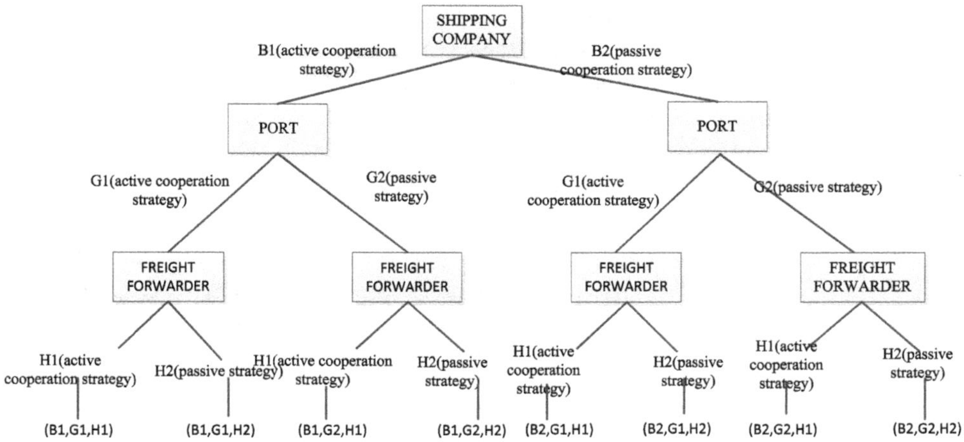

Fig. 1. The structure tree of tripartite game.

The cost of information exchange between the shipping company and port and freight forwarder is k_1 and k_2. c_1 indicates the shipping cost of the shipping company. Shipping companies will encourage ports and shipping companies to cooperate actively and provide subsidies to ports and freight forwarders. When the port is actively cooperating, the amount of subsidy by the shipping company to the port is m_1. It obtains the incentive income when both parties share information as $\theta_1 q_1$ while obtaining the source income from information quality as $\alpha\mu_1$. If the port chooses to cooperate negatively, the degree of port information sharing will decrease and the information quality of the shipping company will decrease μ_3. The shipping company's lost income is $\alpha\mu_3$. The freight forwarder chooses to cooperate actively, and the shipping company subsidizes the freight forwarder as m_2, and it obtains the incentive income when both parties share information as $\theta_2 q_2$. The source of income from information quality is $\alpha\mu_2$. If the freight forwarder chooses to cooperate passively, then the information sharing degree of the freight forwarder will decrease, the information quality of the shipping company will be reduced μ_4, and the shipping company's loss of revenue will be $\alpha\mu_4$. If the shipping company chooses to cooperate passively and does not share information, then the shipping company's loss of income is g_1.

(2) The port

The basic income of the port is r_p, and q_2 is the degree of port information sharing. When no blockchain consortium exists, u_5 and u_6 indicate the information quality when the information provided by the shipping company and the freight forwarder is used, respectively. The cost of information exchange between the port and the shipping company and freight forwarder is k_3, k_4; and the port maintenance cost is c_2. When the shipping company actively cooperates, the transaction fee of m_3 can be reduced. The incentive income of the port when the two parties share information is $\theta_3 q_2$, and the passenger income brought by the information quality is $\alpha\mu_4$. If the shipping company cooperates passively, then the information quality of the port will be reduced by μ_7, and the port will lose passenger revenue $\alpha\mu_7$. Freight forwarder chooses to cooperate actively. Both parties can reduce or exempt the transaction cost as m_4. The port's incentive income when both parties share information is $\theta_4 q_2$, and the source income from information quality is $\alpha\mu_5$. If the negative cooperation of freight forwarder will cause the decline of information quality, then the information quality of the port will be reduced by μ_8, and the port's loss of income will be $\alpha\mu_8$. If the port chooses to cooperate negatively, that is, the port is not sharing information, then the port loses its income is g_2.

(3) The freight forwarder

The basic income of freight forwarder is r_h. q_3 is the information sharing degree of freight forwarder. When blockchain alliance does not exist, μ_9 and μ_{10} are the information qualities when using the information provided by the shipping company and by the port, respectively. The cost of information exchange with the shipping company and the port is k_5 and k_6. Platform maintenance cost is c_3. If the shipping company actively cooperates, then the transaction fee m_5 can be reduced. When the freight forwarder obtains information sharing between the two parties, the incentive income is $\theta_5 q_3$, and the customer source income brought by the information quality is $\alpha\mu_9$. If the shipping company causes a decline in the quality of information, then the information quality of the freight forwarder is reduced by μ_{11}, and the loss of the freight forwarder is $\alpha\mu_{11}$. If the port chooses to cooperate actively, then the incentive income of the freight forwarder when both parties share information is $\theta_6 q_3$, and the passenger source income brought by the information quality is $\alpha\mu_{10}$. If the port causes a decline in information quality, then the information quality of the freight forwarder decreases by μ_{12}, and the loss of the freight forwarder is $\alpha\mu_{12}$. If the freight forwarder chooses to cooperate passively and chooses not to share information, then the freight forwarder loses revenue g_3.

In order to make it easier to read, we prepared a table about parameters (Table 1).

3.2.2. *Parameter assumptions with blockchain technology*

Assuming that the shipping company is the leader in the supply chain of shipping logistics services, the three members must reach an alliance agreement to improve the operation of the entire supply chain, increase revenue, and encourage members to join the blockchain alliance chain.

(1) The shipping company

The shipping company chooses to encourage blockchain technology. The use of blockchain in the supply chain is t, and the technology cost is γt^2. That is, after the supply chain uses the blockchain, the degree of information sharing and the use of information quality by the three parties are the same. The customers' sensitivity to

Table 1. Variables and parameters for the supply chain of shipping logistics services without blockchain technology.

Symbols	Notes
r_i, $i = s, p, h$	The basic income of the node enterprise, s means shipping company, p means port, h means freight forwarder.
q_j, $j = 1, 2, 3$	The information sharing degree of the node enterprise, 1 means shipping company, 2 means port, 3 means freight forwarder.
k	The cost of information exchange between node enterprises
μ	The quality of information obtained by node enterprises during information exchange.
θ	Unit incentive income obtained by sharing information among node enterprises.
g_j, $j = 1, 2, 3$	Loss of gains when node companies cooperate negatively.
α	Customers' sensitivity to the information quality.
m_1, m_2	Subsidies given by shipping companies when they actively cooperate with port and freight forwarder.
m_3, m_4, m_5	When the node enterprise chooses to cooperate actively, the two parties reduce the transaction cost.

information quality is $\alpha_1 t$, and false transaction does not exist. The port actively cooperating and participating in the blockchain are represented. The funds that the shipping company encourages to the port are $m_6 (m_6 > m_1)$. The incentive income of the shipping company's information sharing is $\theta_7 t$. The passenger source income brought by the improvement of its information quality is $\alpha_1 \mu_t$, which reduces the cost of information exchange (tk_t). When the freight forwarder actively cooperate, the reward for the shipping company to encourage participation in the blockchain is $m_7 (m_7 > m_2)$. The incentive income obtained by the shipping company when sharing information is $\theta_8 t$, and the passenger source benefits from the improvement of information quality ($\alpha_1 \mu_t$). The shipping company will also reduce the cost of information exchange to tk_2. If the port and freight forwarder cooperate negatively, then the use of blockchain will be reduced. That is, the use of blockchain will be reduced to t_1 while decreasing the degree of information sharing. The shipping company's revenue will decrease by $\alpha_1 \mu_{t1}$. If the shipping company cooperates passively, then it will be punished by the alliance chain of $g_5 + g_6$.

(2) The port

When the port chooses to join the blockchain technology, the maintenance cost of the blockchain is εt^2. The shipping company encourages the blockchain, and the incentive benefit of port information sharing is $\theta_9 t$, which reduces the information interaction cost of both parties (tk_3); and the passenger source benefit brought by the improvement of information quality is $\alpha_1 t$. When the freight forwarder actively cooperate and the port obtains an incentive income $\theta_{10} t$, its information interaction cost is reduced by tk_4 and the passenger source income brought by the improvement of information quality is $\alpha_1 \mu_t$. If the shipping company cooperates negatively, it will reduce the maintenance of the blockchain, the degree of using the blockchain will decrease t_2, the degree of information sharing will decrease, and the port revenue

Table 2. Variables and parameters for the supply chain of shipping logistics services with blockchain.

Symbols	Notes
t	The degree of information sharing and the use of information quality.
γt^2, εt^2, δt^2	The cost of node enterprises to maintain the blockchain platform, γ, ε and δ respectively, represent the sensitivity of the shipping company, port, and freight forwarder to the degree of blockchain use.
μ_t	When actively joining the blockchain platform, the information quality of the node enterprise.
t_1	The negative cooperation of port or freight forwarder reduces the use of blockchain in the supply chain.
t_2	The negative cooperation of the shipping company reduces the use of blockchain in the supply chain.
g_j, $j = 4, 5, 6$	Node companies are punished by the alliance chain when they cooperate negatively. 4 represents the shipping company, 5 represents the port, and 6 represents the freight forwarder.
α_1	The customer's sensitivity to information quality under the use of blockchain.
m_j, $j = 6, 7$	The shipping company encourages port and freight forwarder to join the incentive subsidies given by blockchain. 6 represents the port and 7 represents the freight forwarder.

Table 3. Payment matrix without blockchain technology.

Game strategics	Income (shipping company, port, freight forwarder)		
B$_1$, G$_1$, H$_1$	$r_s - k_1 - k_2 - c_1 - m_1 - m_2 + \theta_1 q_1 + \theta_2 q_1 + \alpha\mu_1 + \alpha\mu_2 + m_5 + m_3$	$r_p - k_3 - k_4 - c_2 + m_1 + m_3 + m_4 + \theta_3 q_2 + \theta_4 q_2 + \alpha\mu_4 + \alpha\mu_5$	$r_h - k_5 - k_6 - c_3 + m_5 + m_4 + m_2 + \theta_5 q_3 + \alpha\mu_9 + \theta_6 q_3 + \alpha\mu_{10}$
B$_1$, G$_1$, H$_2$	$r_s - k_1 - k_2 - c_1 - m_1 + m_2 + \theta_1 q_1 + \alpha\mu_1 - \alpha\mu_4 - m_5 + m_3$	$r_p - k_3 - k_4 - c_2 + m_1 + m_3 - m_4 + \theta_3 q_2 + \alpha\mu_4 - \alpha\mu_8$	$r_h - k_5 - k_6 - c_3 - m_5 - m_4 - g_3 - m_2$
B$_1$, G$_2$, H$_1$	$r_s - k_1 - k_2 - c_1 + m_1 - m_2 + \theta_2 q_1 + \alpha\mu_2 - \alpha\mu_3 + m_5 - m_3$	$r_p - k_3 - k_4 - c_2 - m_1 - m_3 - m_4 - g_2$	$r_h - k_5 - k_6 - c_3 + m_5 - m_4 + m_2 + \theta_5 q_3 + \alpha\mu_9 - \alpha\mu_{12}$
B$_1$, G$_2$, H$_2$	$r_s - k_1 - k_2 - c_1 - m_1 - m_2 - \alpha\mu_3 - \alpha\mu_4 - m_5 - m_3$	$r_p - k_3 - k_4 - c_2 - m_1 - m_3 - m_4 - g_2 - \alpha\mu_8$	$r_h - k_5 - k_6 - c_3 - m_5 - m_4 - g_3 - m_2 - \alpha\mu_{12}$
B$_2$, G$_1$, H$_1$	$r_s - k_1 - k_2 - c_1 + m_1 + m_2 - m_5 - m_3 - g_1$	$r_p - k_3 - k_4 - c_2 + m_1 - m_3 + m_4 + \theta_4 q_2 - \alpha\mu_7 + \alpha\mu_5$	$r_h - k_5 - k_6 - c_3 - m_5 + m_4 - m_2 + \theta_6 q_3 + \alpha\mu_{10} - \alpha\mu_{11}$
B$_2$, G$_1$, H$_2$	$r_s - k_1 - k_2 - c_1 + m_1 + m_2 - \alpha\mu_3 - m_5 - m_3 - \alpha\mu_4 - g_1$	$r_p - k_3 - k_4 - c_2 - m_1 - m_3 - m_4 - \alpha\mu_7 - \alpha\mu_8$	$r_h - k_5 - k_6 - c_3 - m_5 - m_4 - g_3 - m_2 - \alpha\mu_{11}$
B$_2$, G$_2$, H$_1$	$r_s - k_1 - k_2 - c_1 + m_1 + m_2 - m_5 - m_3 - g_1 - \alpha\mu_3$	$r_p - k_3 - k_4 - c_2 - m_1 - m_3 - m_4 - g_2 - \alpha\mu_7$	$r_h - k_5 - k_6 - c_3 - m_5 - m_4 - m_2 + \alpha\mu_{11} - \alpha\mu_{12}$
B$_2$, G$_2$, H$_2$	$r_s - k_1 - k_2 - c_1 + m_1 + m_2 - m_5 - m_3 - g_1 - \alpha\mu_4 - \alpha\mu_3$	$r_p - k_3 - k_4 - c_2 - m_1 - m_3 - m_4 - g_2 - \alpha\mu_7 - \alpha\mu_8$	$r_h - k_5 - k_6 - c_3 - m_5 - m_4 - g_3 - m_2 - \alpha\mu_{11} - \alpha\mu_{12}$

will decrease by $\alpha_1\mu_{t2}$. If the degree of passive cooperative use of blockchain by the freight forwarder decreases t_2, then the degree of information sharing decreases, and port revenue decreases by $\alpha_1\mu_{t1}$. If the port cooperates negatively, it will be punished by the alliance chain $g_4 + g_6$.

(3) The freight forwarder

When the freight forwarder joins the blockchain technology, the maintenance cost of the blockchain is δt^2. When the shipping company encourages the blockchain, the incentive income obtained by the freight forwarder is $\theta_{11}t$, and the information interaction cost reduces by tk_5. When the port actively cooperates, the incentive income obtained by freight forwarder is $\theta_{12}t$ and the cost of information interaction

Table 4. Payment matrix with blockchain technology.

Game strategics	Income (shipping company, port, freight forwarder)		
B1, G1, H1	$r_s - k_1 - k_2 - c_1 - \gamma t^2 - m_6 - m_7 + \theta_7 t + \theta_8 t + 2\alpha_1\mu_t + tk_2 + tk_1 + m_5 + m_3$	$r_p - k_3 - k_4 - c_2 - \varepsilon t^2 + m_3 + m_4 + \theta_9 t + \theta_{10} t + tk_3 + tk_4 + 2\alpha_1\mu_t + m_6$	$r_h - k_5 - k_6 - c_3 - \delta t^2 + \theta_{11} t + \theta_{12} t + tk_5 + tk_6 + m_7 + m_5 + m_4$
B1, G1, H2	$r_s - k_1 - k_2 - c_1 - \gamma t^2 - m_6 + m_3 + \theta_7 t + \alpha_1\mu_t - \alpha_1\mu_{t_1} + tk_1 - m_5 + g_4$	$r_p - k_3 - k_4 - c_2 - \varepsilon t^2 + m_3 - m_4 + \theta_9 t + tk_3 + \alpha_1\mu_t - \alpha_1\mu_{t_1} + m_6 + g_5$	$r_h - k_5 - k_6 - c_3 - \delta t^2 - g_4 - g_5 - m_5 - m_4 - m_7$
B1, G2, H1	$r_s - k_1 - k_2 - c_1 - \gamma t^2 + m_6 - m_7 + \theta_8 t + \alpha_1\mu_t - \alpha_1\mu_{t_1} + tk_2 + m_5 - m_3 + g_4$	$r_p - k_3 - k_4 - c_2 - \varepsilon t^2 - m_3 - m_4 - m_6 - g_4 - g_6$	$r_h - k_5 - k_6 - c_3 - \delta t^2 + \theta_{11} t + tk_5 + m_7 + m_5 - m_4 + g_6 - \alpha_1\mu_{t_1}$
B1, G2, H2	$r_s - k_1 - k_2 - c_1 - \gamma t^2 + m_6 + m_7 - 2\alpha_1\mu_{t_1} - m_5 - m_3 + 2g_4 + g_5 + g_6$	$r_p - k_3 - k_4 - c_2 - \varepsilon t^2 - m_3 - m_4 - m_6 - g_4 - g_6 - \alpha_1\mu_{t_1} + g_5$	$r_h - k_5 - k_6 - c_3 - \delta t^2 - g_4 - g_5 - m_5 - m_4 - m_7 - \alpha_1\mu_{t_1} + g_6$
B2, G1, H1	$r_s - k_1 - k_2 - c_1 - \gamma t^2 + m_6 + m_7 - m_5 - m_3 - g_5 - g_6$	$r_p - k_3 - k_4 - c_2 - \varepsilon t^2 - m_3 + m_4 + \theta_{10} t + tk_4 + \alpha_1\mu_t - \alpha_1\mu_{t_2} - m_6 + g_5$	$r_h - k_5 - k_6 - c_3 - \delta t^2 + \theta_{12} t + tk_6 - m_7 - m_5 + m_4 + g_6 - \alpha_1\mu_{t_2}$
B2, G1, H2	$r_s - k_1 - k_2 - c_1 - \gamma t^2 + m_6 + m_7 - m_5 - m_3 - g_5 - g_6 + g_4 - \alpha_1\mu_{t_1}$	$r_p - k_3 - k_4 - c_2 - \varepsilon t^2 - m_3 - m_4 - \alpha_1\mu_{t_1} - \alpha_1\mu_{t_2} - m_6 + 2g_5$	$r_h - k_5 - k_6 - c_3 - \delta t^2 - g_4 + g_6 - g_5 - m_5 - m_4 - m_7 - \alpha_1\mu_{t_2}$
B2, G2, H1	$r_s - k_1 - k_2 - c_1 - \gamma t^2 + m_6 + m_7 - m_5 - m_3 - g_5 + g_4 - \alpha_1\mu_{t_1} - g_6$	$r_p - k_3 - k_4 - c_2 - \varepsilon t^2 - m_3 - m_4 - m_6 - g_4 - g_6 + g_5 - \alpha_1\mu_{t_2}$	$r_h - k_5 - k_6 - c_3 - \delta t^2 - m_7 - m_5 - m_4 + 2g_6 - \alpha_1\mu_{t_2} - \alpha_1\mu_{t_1}$
B2, G2, H2	$r_s - k_1 - k_2 - c_1 - \gamma t^2 + m_6 + m_7 - m_5 - m_3 + 2g_4 - 2\alpha_1\mu_{t_1} - g_5 - g_6$	$r_p - k_3 - k_4 - c_2 - \varepsilon t^2 - m_3 - m_4 - m_6 + 2g_5 - \alpha_1 t_2 - \alpha_1\mu_{t_1} - g_4 - g_6$	$r_h - k_5 - k_6 - c_3 - \delta t^2 + 2g_6 - m_5 - m_4 - m_7 - \alpha_1\mu_{t_1} - \alpha_1\mu_{t_2} - g_4 - g_5$

is reduced by tk_6. If the degree of negative cooperation information sharing of the shipping company declines, freight forwarder' revenue will decrease by $\alpha_1\mu_{t2}$. If the port's passive cooperative use of blockchain is reduced to t_1, then the degree of information sharing will decrease and freight forwarder' revenue will decrease by $\alpha_1\mu_{t1}$. If the freight forwarder cooperates passively, that is, it does not participate in the blockchain technology, the loss of income is $g_4 + g_5$.

In order to make it easier to read, we have made a table about parameters (Table 2).

3.3. *Payoff matrix*

3.3.1. *Payment matrix without blockchain technology*

According to both assumptions and model variables, we can obtain the payment matrix without blockchain technology, as listed in Table 3.

3.3.2. *Payment matrix with blockchain technology*

According to both assumptions and model variables, we can obtain the payment matrix without blockchain technology, as listed in Table 4.

4. Solving Evolutionary Stability Strategy and Analyzing Strategies Based on Reality

4.1. *Pay off function without blockchain*

Assuming that the shipping company adopts an active cooperation strategy and the probability of actively cooperating with the port and freight forwarder is φ, the probability of adopting a passive cooperation strategy is $1 - \varphi$. The probability of active cooperation among the port, shipping company, and freight forwarder is λ, and the probability of passive cooperation strategy is $1-\lambda$. The probability of active cooperation of the freight forwarder ρ, and the probability of adopting a passive cooperation model is $1 - \rho$.

According to Table 1, the value function of all game players without blockchain who can be obtained under strategies is as follows:

When the shipping company choose B_1, the value function is

$$\begin{aligned}E_{S1} = {} & \lambda\rho(r_s - k_1 - k_2 - c_1 - m_1 - m_2 + \theta_1 q_1 + \theta_2 q_1 + \alpha\mu_1 + \alpha\mu_2 + m_5 + m_3)\\ & + \lambda(1-\rho)(r_s - k_1 - k_2 - c_1 - m_1 + m_2 + \theta_1 q_1 + \alpha\mu_1 - \alpha\mu_4 - m_5 + m_3)\\ & + (1-\lambda)\rho(r_s - k_1 - k_2 - c_1 + m_1 - m_2 + \theta_2 q_1 + \alpha\mu_2 - \alpha\mu_3 + m_5 - m_3)\\ & + (1-\lambda)(1-\rho)(r_s - k_1 - k_2 - c_1 - m_1 - m_2 - \alpha\mu_3 - \alpha\mu_4 - m_5 - m_3).\end{aligned} \tag{1}$$

When the shipping company choose B_2, the value function is

$$\begin{aligned}E_{s2} &= \lambda\rho(r_s - k_1 - k_2 - c_1 + m_1 + m_2 - m_5 - m_3 - g_1)\\&\quad + \lambda(1-\rho)(r_s - k_1 - k_2 - c_1 + m_1 + m_2 - \alpha\mu_3 - m_5 - m_3 - \alpha\mu_4 - g_1)\\&\quad + (1-\lambda)\rho(r_s - k_1 - k_2 - c_1 + m_1 + m_2 - m_5 - m_3 - g_1 - \alpha\mu_3)\\&\quad + (1-\lambda)(1-\rho)(r_s - k_1 - k_2 - c_1 + m_1 + m_2 - m_5 - m_3 - g_1\\&\quad - \alpha\mu_4 - \alpha\mu_3).\end{aligned} \tag{2}$$

Mixed strategy value functions of the shipping company are

$$E_S = \varphi E_{S1} + (1-\varphi)E_{S2} \tag{3}$$

When the port chooses G_1, the value function is

$$\begin{aligned}E_{P1} &= \varphi\rho(r_p - k_3 - k_4 - c_2 + m_1 + m_3 + m_4 + \theta_3 q_2 + \theta_4 q_2 + \alpha\mu_4 + \alpha\mu_5)\\&\quad + \varphi(1-\rho)(r_p - k_3 - k_4 - c_2 + m_1 + m_3 - m_4 + \theta_3 q_2 + \alpha\mu_4 - \alpha\mu_8)\\&\quad + (1-\varphi)\rho(r_p - k_3 - k_4 - c_2 + m_1 - m_3 + m_4 + \theta_4 q_2 - \alpha\mu_7 + \alpha\mu_5)\\&\quad + (1-\varphi)(1-\rho)(r_p - k_3 - k_4 - c_2 - m_1 - m_3 - m_4 - \alpha\mu_7 - \alpha\mu_8).\end{aligned} \tag{4}$$

When the port choose G_2, the value function is

$$\begin{aligned}E_{P2} &= \varphi\rho(r_p - k_3 - k_4 - c_2 - m_1 - m_3 - m_4 - g_2)\\&\quad + \varphi(1-\rho)(r_p - k_3 - k_4 - c_2 - m_1 - m_3 - m_4 - g_2 - \alpha\mu_8)\\&\quad + (1-\varphi)\rho(r_p - k_3 - k_4 - c_2 - m_1 - m_3 - m_4 - g_2 - \alpha\mu_7)\\&\quad + (1-\varphi)(1-\rho)(r_p - k_3 - k_4 - c_2 - m_1 - m_3 - m_4 - g_2\\&\quad - \alpha\mu_7 - \alpha\mu_8).\end{aligned} \tag{5}$$

Mixed strategy value functions of the port are

$$E_P = \lambda E_{P1} + (1-\lambda)E_{P2} \tag{6}$$

When the freight forwarder chooses H_1, the value function is

$$\begin{aligned}E_{f1} &= \varphi\lambda(r_h - k_5 - k_6 - c_3 + m_5 + m_4 + m_2 + \theta_5 q_3 + \alpha\mu_9 + \theta_6 q_3 + \alpha\mu_{10})\\&\quad + \varphi(1-\lambda)(r_h - k_5 - k_6 - c_3 + m_5 - m_4 + m_2 + \theta_5 q_3 + \alpha\mu_9 - \alpha\mu_{12})\\&\quad + (1-\varphi)\lambda(r_h - k_5 - k_6 - c_3 - m_5 + m_4 - m_2 + \theta_6 q_3 + \alpha\mu_{10} - \alpha\mu_{11})\\&\quad + (1-\varphi)(1-\lambda)(r_h - k_5 - k_6 - c_3 - m_5 - m_4 - m_2 + \alpha\mu_{11} - \alpha\mu_{12}).\end{aligned} \tag{7}$$

When the freight forwarder chooses H_2, the value function is

$$\begin{aligned}E_{f2} &= \varphi\lambda(r_h - k_5 - k_6 - c_3 - m_5 - m_4 - g_3 - m_2)\\ &\quad + \varphi(1-\lambda)(r_h - k_5 - k_6 - c_3 - m_5 - m_4 - g_3 - m_2 - \alpha\mu_{12})\\ &\quad + (1-\varphi)\lambda(r_h - k_5 - k_6 - c_3 - m_5 - m_4 - g_3 - m_2 - \alpha\mu_{11})\\ &\quad + (1-\varphi)(1-\lambda)(r_h - k_5 - k_6 - c_3 - m_5 - m_4 - g_3 - m_2\\ &\quad - \alpha\mu_{11} - \alpha\mu_{12}). \qquad (8)\end{aligned}$$

Mixed strategy value functions of the freight forwarder are

$$E_f = \lambda E_{f1} + (1-\lambda)E_{f2}. \qquad (9)$$

The evolutionary stability strategy of replication dynamics equation in the shipping company, the port and the freight forwarder is solved, respectively.

The evolutionary replication dynamics equation of the shipping company is

$$\begin{aligned}f(\varphi) &= \varphi(E_{S1} - E_S)\\ &= \varphi(1-\varphi)(g_1 - 2m_1 - 2m_2 + \lambda(2m_2 - g_1 + 2m_3 + \alpha\mu_1 + \alpha\mu_3 + \theta_1 q_1)\\ &\quad + \rho(2m_1 + 2m_5 + \alpha\mu_2 + \theta_2 q_1) + \lambda\rho(g_1 - 2m_1 - 2m_2 - \alpha\mu_3)). \qquad (10)\end{aligned}$$

In the same way, the evolutionary replication dynamics equation of the port is

$$\begin{aligned}f(\lambda) &= \lambda(1-\lambda)(g2 + \varphi(2m_1 + 2m_3 + \alpha\mu_4 + \theta_3 q_2)\\ &\quad + \rho(2m_1 + 2m_4 + \alpha\mu_5 + \theta_4 q_2) - 2\varphi m_1\rho). \qquad (11)\end{aligned}$$

The evolutionary replication dynamics equation of the freight forwarder is

$$\begin{aligned}f(\rho) &= \rho(1-\rho)(g_3 + 2\alpha\mu_{11} + \varphi(2m_2 + 2m_5 + \alpha\mu_9 - 2\alpha\mu_{11} + \theta_5 q_3)\\ &\quad + \lambda(2m_4 + \alpha\mu_{10} - 2\alpha\mu_{11} + \theta_6 q_3) + 2\alpha\varphi\lambda\mu_{11}). \qquad (12)\end{aligned}$$

4.2. *Pay off function with blockchain*

According to Table 2, the value function of all game players without blockchain who can be obtained under strategies is as follows:

When the shipping company chooses B_1, the value function is

$$\begin{aligned}E_{s1}^{BC} &= \lambda\rho(r_s - k_1 - k_2 - c_1 - \gamma t^2 - m_6 - m_7 + \theta_7 t + \theta_8 t + 2\alpha_1\mu_t\\ &\quad + tk_2 + tk_1 + m_5 + m_3) + \lambda(1-\rho)(r_s - k_1 - k_2 - c_1 - \gamma t^2 - m_6\\ &\quad + m_3 + \theta_7 t + \alpha_1\mu_t - \alpha_1\mu_{t_1} + tk_1 - m_5 + g_4) + (1-\lambda)\rho(r_s - k_1 - k_2\end{aligned}$$

$$- c_1 - \gamma t^2 + m_6 - m_7 + \theta_8 t + \alpha_1\mu_t + tk_2 - \alpha_1\mu_{t_1} + tk_2 + m_5 - m_3 + g_4)$$
$$+ (1-\lambda)(1-\rho)(r_s - k_1 - k_2 - c_1 - \gamma t^2 + m_6 + m_7 - 2\alpha_1\mu_{t_1}$$
$$- m_5 - m_3 + 2g_4 + g_5 + g_6). \tag{13}$$

When the shipping company chooses B_2, the value function is

$$E_{s2}^{BC} = \lambda\rho(r_s - k_1 - k_2 - c_1 - \gamma t^2 + m_6 + m_7 - m_5 - m_3 - g_5 - g_6)$$
$$+ \lambda(1-\rho)(r_s - k_1 - k_2 - c_1 - \gamma t^2 + m_6 + m_7 - m_5 - m_3 - g_5 - g_6$$
$$+ g_4 - \alpha_1\mu_{t_1}) + (1-\lambda)\rho(r_s - k_1 - k_2 - c_1 - \gamma t^2 + m_6 + m_7 - m_5$$
$$- m_3 - g_5 + g_4 - \alpha_1\mu_{t_1} - g_6)$$
$$+ (1-\lambda)(1-\rho)(r_s - k_1 - k_2 - c_1 - \gamma t^2 + m_6 + m_7 - m_5 - m_3$$
$$+ 2g_4 - 2\alpha_1\mu_{t_1} - g_6 - g_5). \tag{14}$$

Mixed strategy value functions of the shipping company are

$$E_S^{BC} = \varphi E_{S1}^{BC} + (1-\varphi)E_{S2}^{BC}. \tag{15}$$

When the port chooses G_1, the value function is

$$E_{p1}^{BC} = \varphi\rho(r_p - k_3 - k_4 - c_2 - \varepsilon t^2 + m_3 + m_4 + \theta_9 t + \theta_{10} t + tk_3 + tk_4$$
$$+ 2\alpha_1\mu_t + m_6) + \varphi(1-\rho)(r_p - k_3 - k_4 - c_2 - \varepsilon t^2 + m_3 - m_4 + \theta_9 t + tk_3$$
$$+ \alpha_1\mu_t - \alpha_1\mu_{t_1} + m_6 + g_5) + (1-\varphi)\rho(r_p - k_3 - k_4 - c_2 - \varepsilon t^2 - m_3$$
$$+ m_4 + \theta_{10} t + tk_4 + \alpha_1\mu_t - \alpha_1\mu_{t_2} + g_5 - m_6) + (1-\varphi)(1-\rho)(r_p - k_3$$
$$- k_4 - c_2 - \varepsilon t^2 - m_3 - m_4 - m_6 - \alpha_1\mu_{t_1} - \alpha_1\mu_{t_2} + 2g_5). \tag{16}$$

When the port chooses G_2, the value function is

$$E_{p2}^{BC} = \varphi\rho(r_p - k_3 - k_4 - c_2 - \varepsilon t^2 - m_3 - m_4 - g_4 - g_6 - m_6) + \varphi(1-\rho)(r_p - k_3$$
$$- k_4 - c_2 - \varepsilon t^2 - m_3 - m_4 - m_6 - g_4 - g_6 - \alpha_1\mu_{t_1} + g_5) + (1-\varphi)$$
$$\times \rho(r_p - k_3 - k_4 - c_2 - \varepsilon t^2 - m_3 - m_4 - m_6 - g_4 - g_6 + g_5 - \alpha_1\mu_{t_2})$$
$$+ (1-\varphi)(1-\rho)(r_p - k_3 - k_4 - c_2 - \varepsilon t^2 - m_3 - m_4 - m_6 + 2g_5 - \alpha_1\mu_{t_2}$$
$$- \alpha_1\mu_{t_1} - g_4 - g_6). \tag{17}$$

Mixed strategy value functions of the port is

$$E_p^{BC} = \lambda E_{p1}^{BC} + (1-\lambda)E_{p2}^{BC}. \tag{18}$$

When the freight forwarder chooses H_1, the value function is

$$\begin{aligned}E_{f1}^{BC} &= \varphi\lambda(r_h - k_5 - k_6 - c_3 - \delta t^2 + \theta_{11}t + \theta_{12}t + tk_5 + tk_6 + m_7 + m_5 + m_4)\\ &\quad + \varphi(1-\lambda)(r_h - k_5 - k_6 - c_3 - \delta t^2 + \theta_{11}t + tk_5 + m_7 + m_5 - m_4 + g_6\\ &\quad - \alpha_1\mu_{t_1}) + (1-\varphi)\lambda(r_h - k_5 - k_6 - c_3 - \delta t^2 + \theta_{12}t + tk_6 - m_5 + m_4\\ &\quad - m_7 + g_6 - \alpha_1\mu_{t_2}) + (1-\varphi)(1-\lambda)(r_h - k_5 - k_6 - c_3 - \delta t^2 - m_5\\ &\quad - m_4 - m_7 + 2g_6 - \alpha_1\mu_{t_2} - \alpha_1\mu_{t_1}).\end{aligned} \tag{19}$$

When the freight forwarder chooses H_2, the value function is

$$\begin{aligned}E_{f2}^{BC} &= \varphi\lambda(r_h - k_5 - k_6 - c_3 - \delta t^2 - g_4 - g_5 - m_5 - m_4 - m_7) + \varphi(1-\lambda)\\ &\quad \times (r_h - k_5 - k_6 - c_3 - \delta t^2 - g_4 - g_5 + g_6 - m_5 - m_4 - m_7 - \alpha_1\mu_{t_1})\\ &\quad + (1-\varphi)\lambda(r_h - k_5 - k_6 - c_3 - \delta t^2 - g_5 - m_5 - m_4 - m_7 - \alpha_1\mu_{t_2}\\ &\quad - g_4 + g_6) + (1-\varphi)(1-\lambda)(r_h - k_5 - k_6 - c_3 - \delta t^2 + 2g_6 - m_5 - m_4 - m_7\\ &\quad - \alpha_1\mu_{t_1} - \alpha_1\mu_{t_2} - g_5 - g_4).\end{aligned} \tag{20}$$

Mixed strategy value functions of the freight forwarder are

$$E_f^{BC} = \lambda E_{f1}^{BC} + (1-\lambda)E_{f2}^{BC}. \tag{21}$$

In the same way, the evolutionary replication dynamics equation of the shipping company is

$$\begin{aligned}f^{BC}(\varphi) &= \varphi(E_{S1}^{BC} - E_S^{BC}) = \varphi(1-\varphi)(g_5 + g_6 + \lambda(2m_3 - 2m_6 - m_7\\ &\quad + \alpha_1\mu_t + \theta_7 t + k_1 t) + \rho(-g_6 + 2m_5 - 2m_7 + \alpha_1\mu_t + 2\theta_8 t + k_2 t)\\ &\quad + \lambda\rho(g_6 + m_7 - \theta_8 t));\end{aligned} \tag{22}$$

The evolutionary replication dynamics equation of the port is

$$\begin{aligned}f^{BC}(\lambda) &= \lambda(1-\lambda)(\varphi(g_4 + g_5 + g_6 + 2m_3 + 2m_6 + \alpha_1\mu_t + k_3 t + \theta_9 t)\\ &\quad + \rho(g_4 + g_6\rho + 2m_4\rho + \alpha_1\mu_t + \theta_{10}t + k_4 t) - \varphi\rho(g_4 + g_5 + g_6)).\end{aligned} \tag{23}$$

The evolutionary replication dynamics equation of the freight forwarder is

$$\begin{aligned}f^{BC}(\rho) &= \rho(1-\rho)(\varphi(g_4 + g_5 + g_6 + 2m_5 + 2m_7 + \theta_{11}t + k_5 t)\\ &\quad + \lambda(g_6 + 2m_4 + \theta_{12}t + k_6 t) - 2\varphi\lambda g_6).\end{aligned} \tag{24}$$

4.3. *Solving evolutionary stability strategy based on replication dynamic equation*

The local stability of the Jacobian matrix is used to obtain the evolutionary stability strategy of the differential equation system. When the equilibrium point satisfies all the eigenvalues of the Jacobian matrix with nonpositive values, the stability strategy is selected. The Jacobian matrix here is shown in Appendices A and B.

Assuming that no blockchain exists, let formulas (10)–(12) be equal to zero; then, we can obtain the equilibrium points: $T_1(0,0,0)$, $T_2(0,0,1)$, $T_3(0,1,0)$, $T_4(0,1,1)$, $T_5(1,0,0)$, $T_6(1,0,1)$, $T_7(1,1,0)$, and $T_8(1,1,1)$. Bring the equilibrium point into the Jacobian matrix and obtain the corresponding eigenvalues. Table 3 is the value of $\mathrm{Det}^{BC}J$ and $\mathrm{Tr}^{BC}J$ without blockchain and Table 4 is the corresponding eigenvalue without blockchain. These are shown in Appendix A.3.

If the matrix satisfies the condition $\mathrm{Det}J > 0$, $\mathrm{Tr}J < 0$, the equilibrium point is evolutionary stable strategy (ESS). Further analysis is performed to determine the positive and negative conditions of DetJ and Tr, and are divided into three stable strategies as follows:

(1) If $g_1 - g_2 - g_3 - 4m_1 - 2m_2 - 4m_4 - \alpha\mu_5 - \alpha\mu_{10} - \theta_4 q_2 - \theta_6 q_3 < 0$, and its absolute value is greater than $2m_5 + \alpha\mu_1 + \alpha\mu_2 + \theta_1 q_1 + \theta_2 q_1 + 2m_3$, then $T_4(0,\ 1,\ 1)$ is the ESS.

(2) If$g_2 - g_1 - g_3 - 4m_5 - \alpha\mu_2 - \alpha\mu_9 - \theta_2 q_1 - \theta_5 q_3 <$, and its absolute value is greater than $2m_1+2m_3+2m_4+\alpha\mu_4+\alpha\mu_5+\theta_3 q_2+\theta_4 q_2$, then $T_6(1,\ 0,\ 1)$ is the ESS.

(3) If $g_1 - 2m_1 - 2m_2 + 2m_3 + 2m_5 + \alpha\mu_1 + \alpha\mu_2 + \theta_1 q_1 + \theta_2 q_1 <$, then $T_6(1,\ 1,\ 1)$ is the ESS. If other points cannot meet the requirements of Det > 0, Tr < 0, then they are unbalanced points.

In combination with the analysis of eigenvalue results, further assumptions are made based on the above analysis. Two main cases are as follows:

Situation 1. Assume $g_1 - 2m_1 - 2m_2 + 2m_3 + \alpha\mu_1 + 2m_5 + \alpha\mu_2 + \theta_1 q_1 + \theta_2 q_1 <$, $g_2 + 2m_1 + 2m_4 + \alpha\mu_5 + \theta_4 q_2 > 0$, and $g_3 + 2m_4 + \alpha\mu_{10} + \theta_6 q_3 > 0$. That is, when the shipping company chooses not to cooperate, the profit and punishment are greater than the profit brought by cooperation. The eigenvalues of the Jacobian matrix corresponding to the equilibrium point $T_4(0,1,1)$ are all nonpositive, with a corresponding evolution strategy of passive cooperation, active cooperation, and active cooperation (Table 4).

Situation 2. Assume $g_1 - 2m_1 - 2m_2 + 2m_3 + \alpha\mu_1 + 2m_5 + \alpha\mu_2 + \theta_1 q_1 + \theta_2 q_1 >$, $g_2+2m_1+2m_4+\alpha\mu_5+\theta_4 q_2 > 0$, and $g_3+2m_4+\alpha\mu_{10}+\theta_6 q_3 > 0$. That is, the profit and penalty when the shipping company chooses the willingness to cooperate are greater than the profit brought by the cooperation. The eigenvalues of the Jacobian matrix corresponding to the equilibrium point $T_4(1,1,1)$ are all nonpositive, with a corresponding evolution strategy of active cooperation, active cooperation, and active cooperation (Table 4).

In the same vein, we consider using the blockchain to bring the equilibrium point into the Jacobian matrix and obtain the corresponding eigenvalues (Tables D.1 and D.2 are shown in Appendix D).

Table D.1 is analyzed as follows:

Situation 1. Assume $g_5+g_6+2m_3+2m_5-2m_6-2m_7+2\alpha_1 t+\theta_7 t+\theta_8 t+k_1 t+k_2 t<0$ and $2m_4-4m_3-2g_6-2\alpha_1 t-\theta_7 t-\theta_9 t-k_1 t-k_3 t+\theta_{11} t+\theta_{12} t+k_5 t+k_6 t+2m_5+3m_7<0$. When the equilibrium point is $T_8(1,1,1)$, with $\mathrm{Det}J>0$, $\mathrm{Tr}<0$, $T_8(1,1,1)$ is the stable point.

Situation 2. Assume $g_5+g_6+2m_3+2m_5-2m_6-2m_7+2\alpha_1 t+\theta_7 t+\theta_8 t+k_1 t+k_2 t>$ and $2m_4-4m_3-2g_6-2\alpha_1 t-\theta_7 t-\theta_9 t-k_1 t-k_3 t+\theta_{11} t+\theta_{12} t+k_5 t+k_6 t+2m_5+3m_7<$. When the equilibrium point is $T_4(0,1,1)$, $T_6(1,0,1)$ and $T_7(1,1,0)$ are the stable points.

In combination with the eigenvalue matrix, when the equilibrium points are $T_6(1,0,1)$ and $T_7(1,1,0)$, the ESS conditions are not met. Therefore, when Situation 2 is met,$T_4(0,1,1)$ is only the stable point that meets the requirements.

5. Numerical Analysis

Using MATLAB software, the evolution of the strategy of shipping company, port and freight forwarder. This paper gives the following assumptions for the initial values of the parameters.

$$r_s=150,\quad c_1=3,\quad \mu_1=10,\quad \mu_2=10,\quad \mu_3=7,\quad \mu_4=7,\quad \theta_1=3,$$

$$\theta_2=3,\quad k_1=3,\quad k_2=4,$$

$$r_p=100,\quad k_3=3,\quad k_4=4,\quad c_2=2,\quad \mu_5=10,\quad \mu_6=10,\quad \mu_7=7,\quad \mu_8=7,$$

$$\theta_4=3,\quad \theta_3=3,$$

$$r_h=40,\quad k_5=4,\quad k_6=4,\quad c_3=1,\quad \mu_9=10,\quad \mu_{10}=10,\quad \mu_{11}=6,\quad \mu_{12}=6,$$

$$\theta_5=2,\quad \theta_6=2.$$

5.1. *Supply chain of shipping logistics services without blockchain technology*

5.1.1. *Effects of changes in shipping company subsidies on partnership evolution*

The effect of subsidy policy on the cooperation choices of various companies is investigated from the perspective of the shipping company. Assume that the remaining parameters are as follows:

$$g_1=20,\quad g_2=20,\quad g_3=30,\quad q_1=q_2=q_3=0.5,\quad \alpha=0.5,$$

$$m_3=5,\quad m_4=5,\quad m_5=10.$$

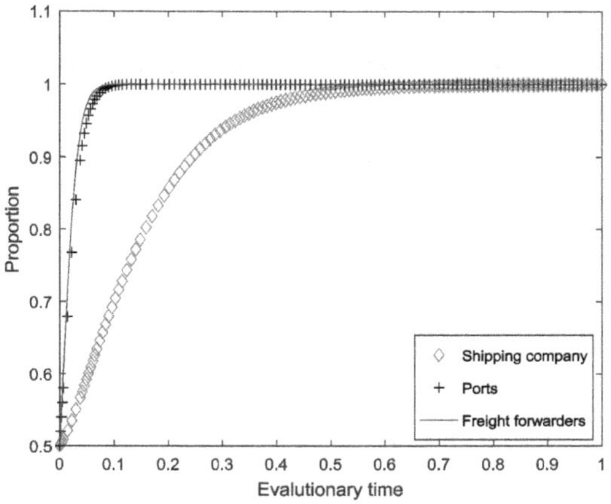

Fig. 2. The evolution result of the node enterprise under the small subsidy of the shipping company.

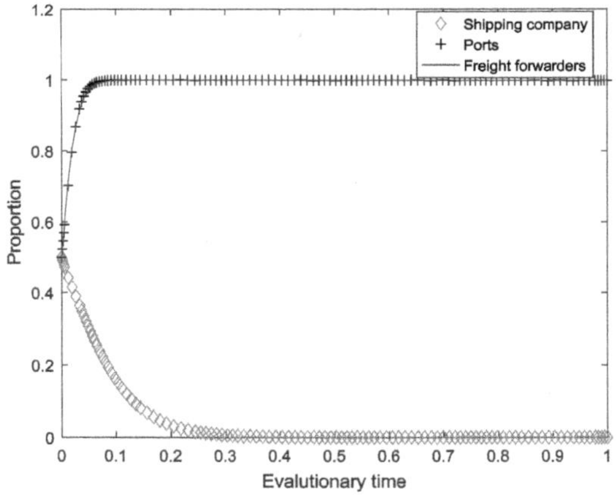

Fig. 3. The evolution result of the node enterprise under the high subsidy of the shipping company.

First, we consider the small subsidy of the shipping company. The amount of the small subsidy is the same as the transaction price of the port and freight forwarder, that is, $m_1 = 15$, $m_2 = 15$. Figure 2 shows the evolution result of the node enterprise under the small subsidy of the shipping company. From the figure, with the encouragement of subsidy policies, λ, ρ converges to 1 over time; that is, the port and freight forwarder will eventually choose to cooperate actively. As the subsidy party, the shipping company shows that φ converges to 1. That is, the shipping company chooses to actively cooperate in the case of small subsidies. In comparison with the port and freight forwarder, the rate of φ converging to 1 is significantly less than those of λ and ρ. The speed of convergence is 1. The shipping company provides high subsidies, that is, when $m_1 = 20$, $m_2 = 20$ the evolution result of the node enterprise is shown in Fig. 3. From the figure, when the shipping company

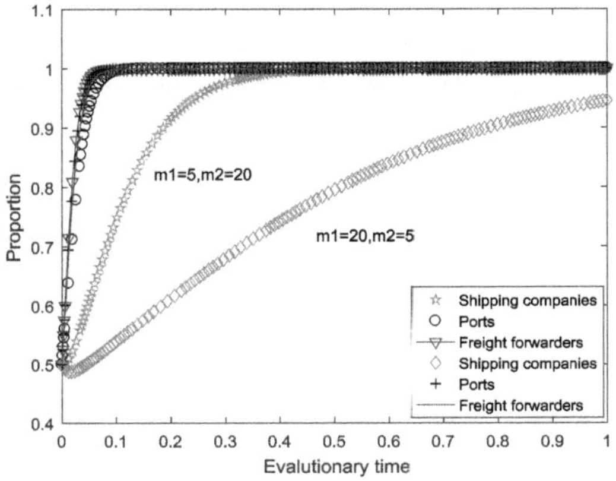

Fig. 4. The evolution results of the node enterprises under different degrees of subsidies by the shipping company.

provide high subsidies, λ and ρ converge to 1. That is, the port and the freight forwarder will eventually choose to cooperate actively, and the speed of convergence is higher than the speed of small subsidies. Moreover, φ converges to 0; that is, the shipping company chooses passive cooperation in the case of small subsidies.

Figure 4 shows the evolution results of node enterprises considering the different subsidies of the shipping company to the port and the freight forwarder. The two main cases are as follows. When the shipping company provide high subsidies to the port and small subsidies to freight forwarder, that is, when $m_1 = 20$, $m_2 = 5$, the evolution result of node enterprises is shown in Fig. 4 λ and ρ converge to 1; that is, the port and the freight forwarder will eventually choose to cooperate actively. As the subsidy party, the shipping company shows that φ converges to 1. That is, the shipping company chooses to cooperate actively when subsidizing the port. When the shipping company provides small subsidies to the port and high subsidies to the freight forwarder, that is, when $m_1 = 5$, $m_2 = 20$, the evolution result of node enterprises is shown in Fig. 4. λ and ρ converge to 1; that is, the port and the freight forwarder will eventually choose to cooperate actively. As the subsidy party, the shipping company converges to 1. That is, the shipping company chooses to cooperate actively when subsidizing the port. However, in the case of (0, 0, 1), φ gradually converges to 0 and then slowly converges to 1 as time goes by. We compare the two cases shown in Fig. 4. Although φ has converged to 1, when the shipping company subsidizes the freight forwarder more and the port is subsidized for a small amount, the convergence speed of φ is significantly lower than when the shipping company subsidizes the port more.

The simulation results show that as long as shipping company subsidize the port and the freight forwarder, the port and the freight forwarder are willing to actively cooperate. The subsidy will not have a great impact on the port and the freight forwarder, but it will affect the enthusiasm of the shipping company for cooperation.

When the shipping company provide high subsidies to the freight forwarder, their willingness to cooperate will be less than when they provide high subsidies to the port. This is because the freight forwarder mainly provides logistics solutions and customer needs. When the shipping company provides subsidies, the freight forwarder can be obtained. However, for the shipping company, the profit cannot be much at the beginning. As time goes by, the shipping company's willingness to cooperate gradually increases. The port mainly provides port services for the shipping company, which can bring more profits to the shipping company. Therefore, the willingness of the shipping company to actively cooperate increased rapidly.

5.1.2. *Effect of the degree of information sharing on the evolution of cooperative relations*

We investigate the influence of the degree of information sharing of node companies on the evolution of cooperation. First, we consider the evolution of cooperation between the shipping company under different information sharing levels. When $q_1 = 0.2$, the degree of information sharing of shipping company is low. Given that the degree of information sharing affects the profit loss of the enterprise, we assume $g_1 = 30$, $g_2 = 10$, $g_3 = 15$, $q_2 = q_3 = 0.5$, $\alpha = 0.5$, $m_1 = 20$, $m_2 = 20$, $m_3 = m_4 = m_5 = 5$ for the remaining parameters. From the Fig. 5, the shipping company suffers greater loss when its degree of information sharing is low. The transaction costs between node companies will decrease, and λ and ρ converge to 1. That is, the port and the freight forwarder will eventually choose to actively cooperate. Moreover, φ converges to 1; that is, when the shipping company conducts information sharing at a low level, it chooses to actively cooperate.

When $q_1 = 0.7$, the shipping company has a high degree of information sharing. We assume $g_1 = 12$, $g_2 = 10$, $g_3 = 15$, $q_2 = q_3 = 0.5$, $\alpha = 0.5$ for the remaining parameters. The evolution result at this time is shown in Fig. 5(2). When the information sharing degree of the shipping company is high, λ and ρ converge to 1. That is, the port and freight forwarder will eventually choose to cooperate actively. Moreover, φ converges to 1; that is, when the shipping company is carrying out

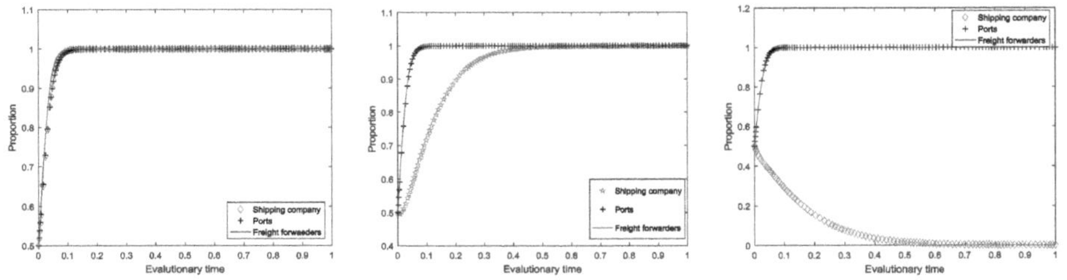

(1) (2) (3)

Fig. 5. The evolution result of enterprise cooperation under different information sharing levels of the shipping company.

information sharing at a low level, it chooses to cooperate actively. However, in comparison with the lower information sharing degree, the convergence speed of φ is significantly slower.

When $q_1 = 0.8$, the shipping company has a high degree of information sharing ($g_1 = 10$, $g_2 = 10$, $g_3 = 15$, $q_2 = q_3 = 0.5$, $\alpha = 0.5$). The evolution result is shown in Fig. 5(3). At this time, λ and ρ converge to 1; that is, the port and freight forwarder will eventually choose to cooperate actively. However, φ converges to 0; that is, the shipping company chooses to cooperate negatively when sharing information to a high degree. These calculation results show that providing subsidies and information sharing by the shipping company has little effect on the willingness of the port and the freight forwarder to cooperate actively. When the degree of information sharing is higher, the willingness of the shipping company to choose active cooperation gradually decreases.

Then, we consider the evolution of cooperation between enterprises under different information sharing levels in the port. When $q_2 = 0.2$, the degree of information sharing of the shipping company is low. Given that the degree of information sharing affects the profit loss of the enterprise, we assume $g_1 = 10$, $g_2 = 30$, $g_3 = 10$, $q_1 = q_3 = 0.5$, $\alpha = 0.5$, $m_1 = 20$, $m_2 = 20$, $m_3 = m_4 = m_5 = 5$. The evolution result is shown in Fig. 6(1). The lower the port's information sharing degree is, the greater the loss g_2 will be. λ and ρ converge to 1; that is, the port and the freight forwarder will eventually choose to actively cooperate. Moreover, φ converges to 0.4, which indicates that the shipping company is more willing to cooperate passively when the degree of port information sharing is low.

When $q_2 = 0.5$, the port's information sharing degree is high, and the remaining parameters are assumed as $g_1 = g_2 = 10$, $g_3 = 15$, $q_1 = q_3 = 0.5$, $\alpha = 0.5$, $m_1 = 20$, $m_2 = 20$, $m_3 = m_4 = m_5 = 10$. The evolution result is shown in Fig. 6(2). When the information sharing degree of the shipping company is high, λ and ρconverge to 1. That is, the port and the freight forwarder will eventually choose to cooperate actively. φ gradually converges to 0.7, which implies that the shipping company's willingness to cooperate actively improves.

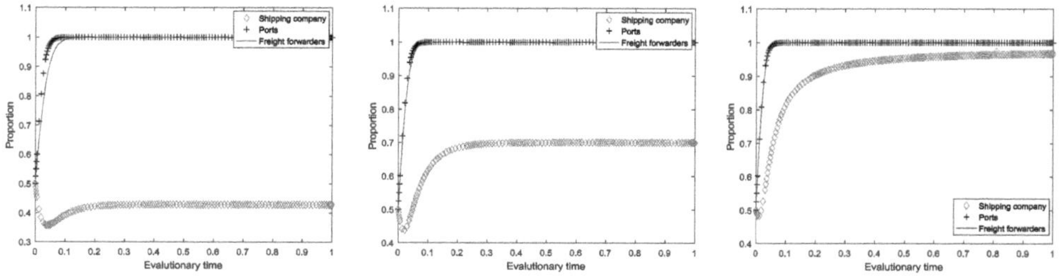

(1) (2) (3)

Fig. 6. The evolution results of enterprises' cooperation under different information sharing levels in the port.

When $q_2 = 0.8$, the port's information sharing degree is high, and the remaining parameters are assumed as $g_1 = 10$, $g_2 = 5$, $g_3 = 15$, $q_1 = q_3 = 0.5$, $\alpha = 0.5$, $m_1 = 20$, $m_2 = 20$, $m_3 = m_4 = m_5 = 15$. The evolution result is shown in Fig. 6(3). λ and ρ converge to 1; that is, the port and freight forwarder will eventually choose to cooperate actively. Moreover, φ converges to 1, which indicates that the shipping company has the strongest willingness to cooperate actively when the port is sharing information at a high level. The calculation results show that the degree of the port information sharing affects the willingness of the shipping company to cooperate actively but has little effect on the willingness of the freight forwarder. When the port's information sharing degree is higher, the shipping company's willingness to choose active cooperation gradually tends to 1. If the port's information sharing degree is lower, then the shipping company's willingness to choose passive cooperation is higher.

We consider the evolution of cooperation between companies under different information sharing levels of the freight forwarder and that between enterprises under different information sharing levels in ports. When $q_3 = 0.2$, the degree of information sharing of the freight forwarder is low. At the same time, given that the degree of information sharing affects the profit loss of the enterprise, the remaining parameters are assumed $g_1 = 10$, $g_2 = 10$, $g_3 = 30$, $q_1 = q_2 = 0.5$, $\alpha = 0.5$, $m_1 = 20$, $m_2 = 20$, $m_3 = m_4 = m_5 = 5$. The evolution result is shown in Fig. 7(1). The lower the information sharing degree of freight forwarder is, the greater the loss will be. λ and ρ converge to 1; that is, the port and shipping company will eventually choose to cooperate actively. Moreover, φ converges to 0.4, which indicates that the shipping company is in Fig. 7(1). When the information sharing of freight forwarder is low, it chooses to cooperate passively.

When $q_3 = 0.5$, the information sharing degree of freight forwarder is high, and the remaining parameters are assumed $g_1 = g_2 = 10$, $g_3 = 15$, $q_1 = q_2 = 0.5$, $\alpha = 0.5$, $m_1 = 20$, $m_2 = 20$, $m_3 = m_4 = m_5 = 10$. The evolution result is shown in Fig. 7(2). When the information sharing degree of the freight forwarder is high, λ and ρ converge to 1. That is, the port and the freight forwarder will eventually

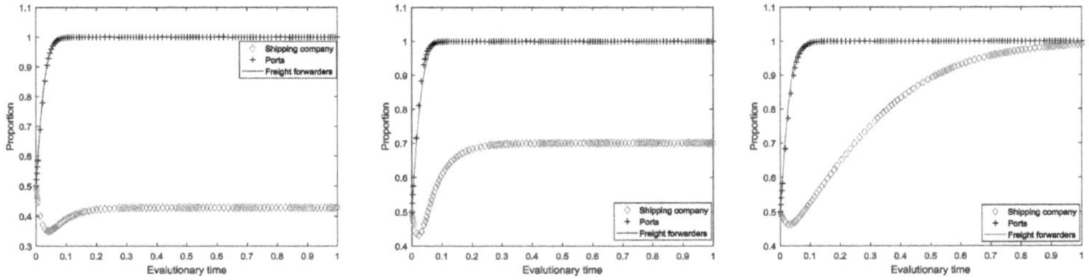

(1) (2) (3)

Fig. 7. The evolution result of enterprise cooperation under different information sharing levels of the shipping company.

choose to cooperate actively. Moreover, φ gradually converges to 0.7, which implies the shipping company's willingness to cooperate actively.

When $q_3 = 0.8$, the information sharing degree of freight forwarder is high, and the remaining parameters are assumed $g_1 = 10$, $g_2 = 10$, $g_3 = 5$, $q_1 = q_3 = 0.5$, $\alpha = 0.5$, $m_1 = 20$, $m_2 = 20$, $m_3 = m_4 = m_5 = 15$. The evolution result is shown in Fig. 7(3). λ and ρ converge to 1; that is, the port and freight forwarder will eventually choose to cooperate actively. Moreover, φ converges to 1; that is, the shipping company has the strongest willingness to cooperate actively when sharing information at a high level. The calculation results show that the level of information sharing of freight forwarder affects the willingness of the shipping company to cooperate actively but has little effect on the willingness of the port. When the information sharing degree of the port is higher, the willingness of the shipping company to choose active cooperation gradually tends to 1. If the information sharing degree of freight forwarder is lower, then the willingness of the shipping company to choose passive cooperation is higher.

As shown in Figs. 4–6, the information sharing process of node companies has little effect on the willingness of freight forwarder and port to cooperate, whereas the degree of information sharing between freight forwards and port has a greater influence on shipping companies' willingness to cooperate. When the level of information sharing is high, the shipping company's willingness to cooperate actively increases. When the level of information sharing is low, the shipping company has a high willingness to cooperate negatively at the beginning and is less willing to cooperate actively over time.

5.1.3. *Influence of customers' sensitivity to information quality on partnership evolution*

We investigate the effect of customers' sensitivity to information quality on partnership evolution. Given that different degrees of information sharing affect the quality of information, the different degrees of information sharing are analyzed simultaneously, and the evolution result is shown in Fig. 8. First, we assume that $\alpha = 0.2$. When $q_1 = q_2 = q_3 = 0.8$, the evolution result is shown in Fig. 8(1). λ and ρ converge to 1; that is, the port will eventually choose to cooperate actively. Moreover, converges to 0.9; that is, the shipping company is more willing to cooperate actively when sharing of information is at a high level. When $q_1 = q_2 = q_3 = 0.2$, the evolution result is shown in Fig. 8(2). λ and ρ converge to 1; that is, the port will eventually choose to actively cooperate. Moreover, converges to 0.7; that is, when the shipping company is sharing information at a high level, its willingness to actively cooperate is low but strong.

Second, we assume that $\alpha = 0.5$. When $q_1 = q_2 = q_3 = 0.8$, the evolution result is shown in Fig. 8(3). λ and ρ converge to 1; that is, the port and freight forwarder will eventually choose to actively cooperate. Moreover, converges to 0; that is, the shipping company's willingness to cooperate negatively is strongest when sharing

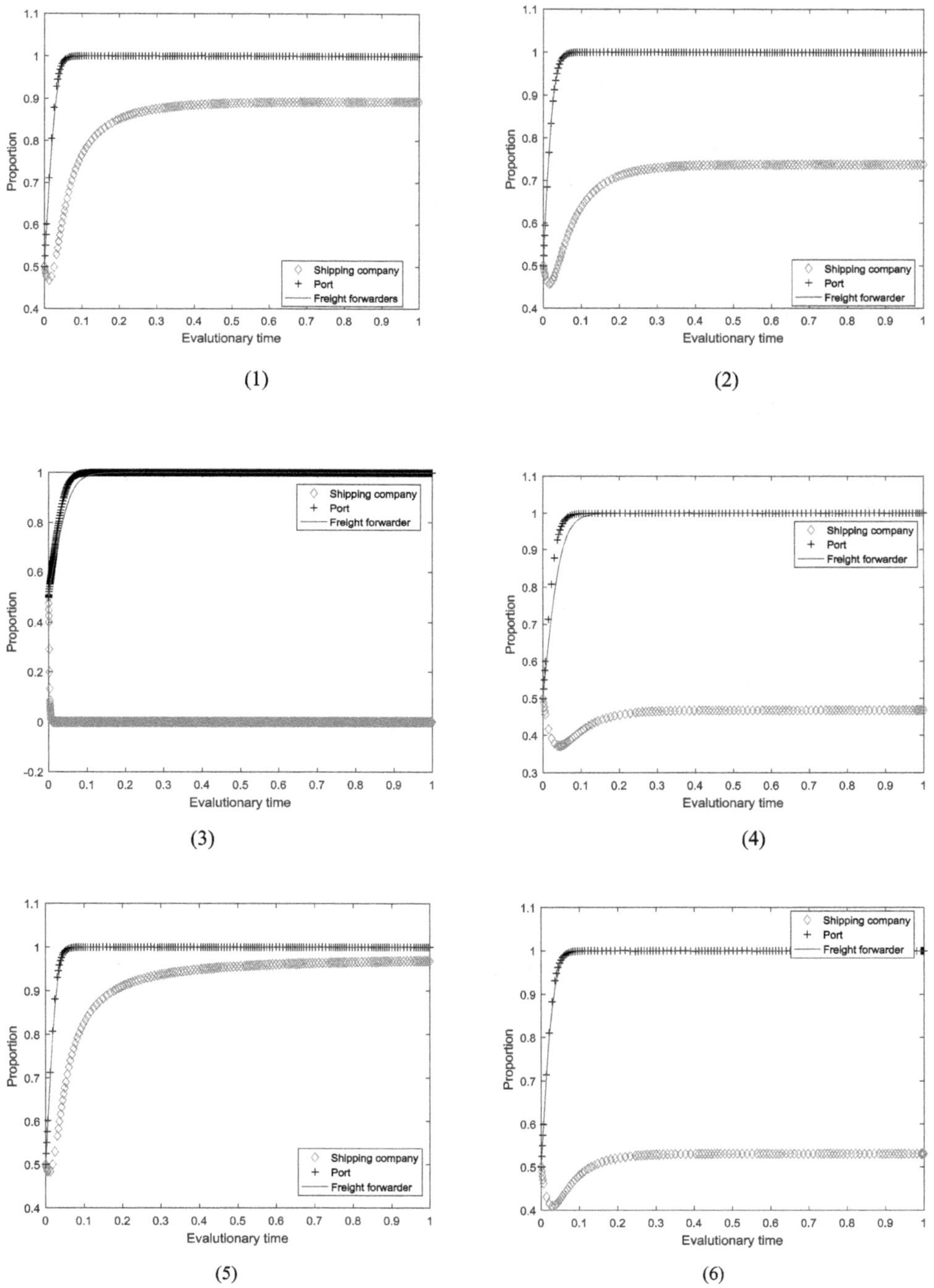

Fig. 8. Customers' sensitivity to information quality and partnership evolution.

information at a high level. When $q_1 = q_2 = q_3 = 0.2$, the evolution result is shown in Fig. 8(4). λ and ρ converge to 1; that is, the port and freight forwarder will eventually choose to actively cooperate. Furthermore, converges to 0.4; that is, the shipping company passively cooperates when sharing information at a high level.

Third, we assume that $\alpha = 0.8$. When $q_1 = q_2 = q_3 = 0.8$, the evolution result is shown in Fig. 8(5). λ and ρ converge to 1; that is, the port and freight forwarder will eventually choose to cooperate actively. In addition, converges to 1; that is, the shipping company is efficient when sharing information and has a strong willingness to cooperate actively. When $q_1 = q_2 = q_3 = 0.2$, the evolution result is shown in Fig. 7(6). λ and ρ converge to 1; that is, the port and freight forwarder will eventually choose to cooperate actively. Moreover, converges to 0.5; that is, the shipping company is less willing to cooperate when they share information efficiently.

As shown in Figs. 8(1)–8(6), when customers are more sensitive to information quality, the degree of information sharing increases and node companies are more willing to choose active cooperation. When customers' sensitivity to information quality is low, the degree of information sharing increases. Moreover, the willingness of the port and the freight forwarder to cooperate actively increases, whereas the willingness of the shipping company to cooperate actively decreases. When the customers' sensitivity to information quality is approximately 0.5, the shipping company's willingness to cooperate actively is 0. Especially when the information sharing level is high, the shipping company's willingness to choose negative cooperation is the strongest, because the customer requires information quality. When it is lower, the degree of information sharing is higher and the profit obtained by the shipping company after high subsidies is far less than the profit when information sharing is low; thus, they will choose passive cooperation.

5.2. *Supply chain of shipping logistics services under the application of blockchain*

Assuming that the model parameters under the blockchain application are

$$m_6 = 10, \quad m_7 = 10, \quad \theta_7 = 2, \quad \theta_8 = 2, \quad \theta_9 = 2, \quad \theta_{10} = 2, \quad \theta_{11} = 2,$$

$$\theta_{12} = 2, \quad g_4 = 10, \quad g_5 = 10, \quad g_6 = 15, \quad \varepsilon = \delta = \gamma = 1.$$

5.2.1. *Influence of the degree of information sharing on the evolution of cooperative relations*

First, we consider the evolution of cooperation between shipping companies under different information sharing levels. When $t = 0.8$, $\mu_t = 0.8$, $\mu_{t_1} = \mu_{t_2} = 0.2$ (Fig. 9(1)), λ and ρ converge to 1; that is, the port and freight forwarder will eventually choose to actively cooperate. Moreover, converges to 1; that is, the shipping company has a strong willingness to cooperate actively when sharing information. When $t = 0.5$, $\mu_t = 0.5$, $\mu_{t_1} = \mu_{t_2} = 0.2$ (Fig. 9(2)), λ and ρ converge to 1; that is,

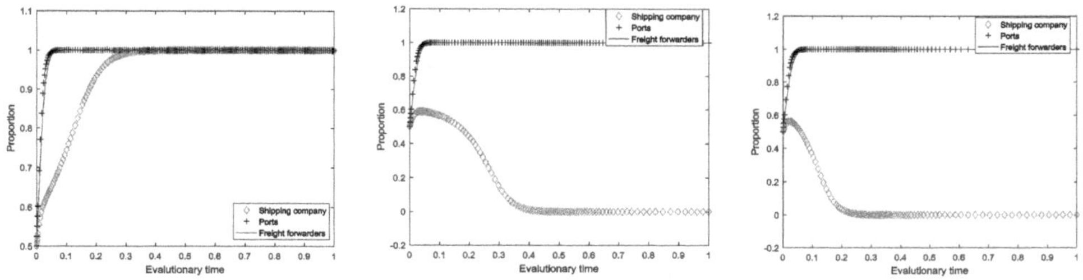

(1) (2) (3)

Fig. 9. Customers' sensitivity to information quality and partnership evolution.

the port and freight forwarder will eventually choose to cooperate actively. In addition, converges to 0; that is, the shipping company has a strong willingness to cooperate negatively when sharing information. When $t = 0.2$, $\mu_t = 0.2$, $\mu_{t_1} = \mu_{t_2} = 0.2$ (Fig. 9(3)), λ and ρ converge to 1; that is, the port and freight forwarder will eventually choose to cooperate actively. Moreover, converges to 0; that is, the shipping company has a strong willingness to cooperate negatively when sharing information.

As shown in Fig. 9, under the premise that the customers' sensitivity to information quality remains unchanged, only the influence of information sharing on cooperative relationship is considered. Regardless of whether the degree of information sharing is high or low, it has little effect on the willingness of the port and the freight forwarder to cooperate, but has a greater effect on the shipping company. Then, the shipping company will gradually increase their willingness to cooperate as the degree of information sharing increases.

5.2.2. *Influence of customers' sensitivity to information quality on partnership evolution*

We investigate the influence of customers' sensitivity to information quality on partnership evolution. First, we consider $\alpha_1 = 0.2$, $t = 0.8$, $\mu_t = 0.8$, $\mu_{t_1} = \mu_{t_2} = 0.2$. As shown in Fig. 10(1), λ and ρ converge to 1; that is, the port and freight forwarder will eventually choose to actively cooperate. In addition, φ converges to 1; that is, when the degree of quality sensitivity is low and the degree of information sharing is high, the shipping company's willingness to actively cooperate is strong. When $\alpha_1 = 0.8$, $t = 0.8$, $\mu_t = 0.8$, $\mu_{t_1} = \mu_{t_2} = 0.2$ (Fig. 10(2)), λ and ρ converge to 1; that is, the port and freight forwarder will eventually choose to cooperate actively. At this time, φ converges to 0; that is, the shipping company is more sensitive to the quality of information. When it is low and when the degree of information sharing is high, its willingness to actively cooperate is low. From the two figures, when λ converges to 1 faster than ρ converges to 1, customers have higher requirements for information quality; however, for the shipping company, when customers have low information quality requirements, the implementation of high-level information

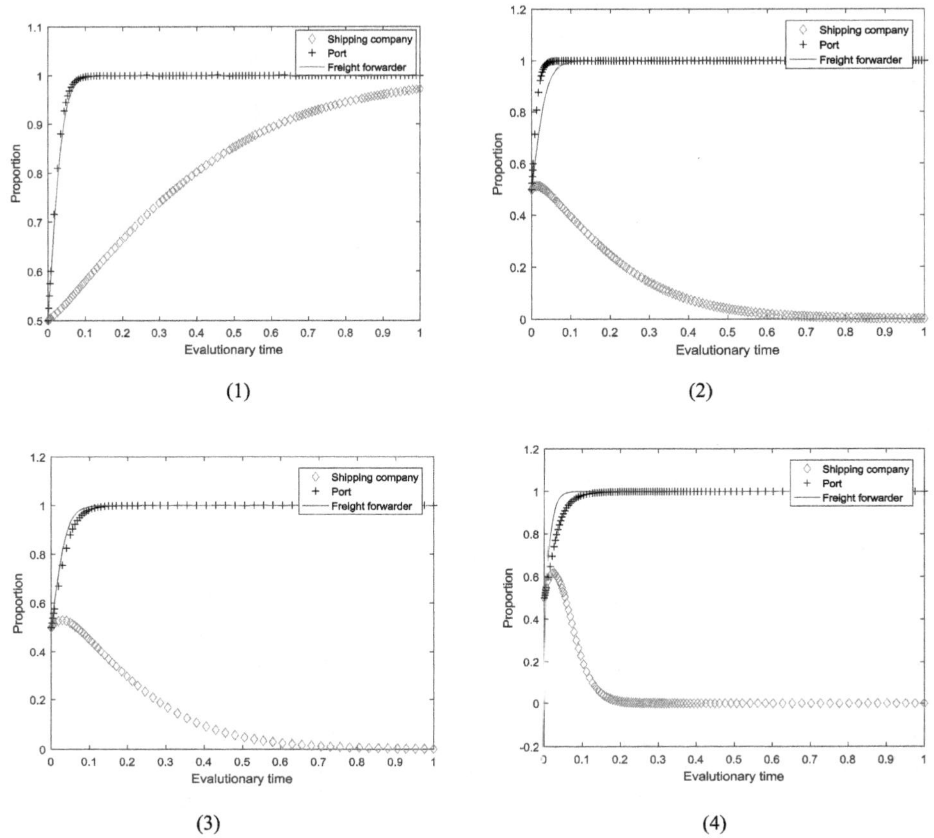

Fig. 10. Customers' sensitivity to information quality and partnership evolution.

sharing is more attractive to customers. The higher the customer requirements are, the lower the willingness of the shipping company to actively cooperate will be.

When $\alpha_1 = 0.2$, $t = 0.5$, $\mu_t = 0.5$, $\mu_{t_1} = \mu_{t_2} = 0.2$ (Fig. 10(3)), λ and ρ converge to 1; that is, the port and the freight forwarder will eventually choose to actively cooperate. In addition, φconverges to 0; that is, when the shipping company's sensitivity to the quality of information is low and when the degree of information sharing is high, its willingness to actively cooperate is strong. When $\alpha_1 = 0.8$, $t = 0.5$, $\mu_t = 0.5$, $\mu_{t_1} = \mu_{t_2} = 0.2$ (Fig. 10(4)) λ and ρ converge to 1; that is, the port and freight forwarder will eventually choose to actively cooperate. At this time, φconverges to 0; that is, the shipping company is more sensitive to the quality of the information. When it is low and when the degree of information sharing is high, its willingness to actively cooperate is low. From the two figures, the speed at which ρ converges to 1 is faster than the speed at which λ converges to 1 indicates that the customers have higher requirements for information quality. However, for the shipping company, when the customers' requirements for information quality are low, the implementation is high. The level of information sharing is more attractive to customers. However, the higher the customer requirements are, the lower the willingness of the shipping company to actively cooperate will be. By comparing Figs. 10(2) and 10(4), we find that when the customers have high requirements for information quality, the speed of φ converging to 0 when the information sharing degree and information quality are high is lower than the speed when the information sharing degree is low. That is, the shipping company's negative willingness to cooperate will decrease with the degree of information sharing and information quality.

5.3. *The impact of reward and punishment strategies on node companies*

We keep other parameters unchanged, the degree of information sharing and the sensitivity of customers to information quality are $t = 0.8$, $\alpha_1 = 0.8$. We analyze different incentive and punishment strategies. When $m_6 = m_7 = 5$, the penalty is $g_4 = g_5 = g_6 = 5$. As shown in Fig. 11(1), λ and ρ converge to 1. But with the evolution of longer, λ and ρ converge to 0. In addition, φconverges to 0. That is, the port and the freight forwarder will eventually choose to actively cooperate in the early stage of blockchain investment, the shipping company is more sensitive to this strategy. When $g_4 = g_5 = g_6 = 20$, λ and ρ converge to 1, that is, the port and the freight forwarder will eventually choose to actively cooperate.

When $m_6 = m_7 = 20$, the penalty is $g_4 = g_5 = g_6 = 5$ (Fig. 10(3)), or the penalty is $g_4 = g_5 = g_6 = 20$(Fig. 11(3)) λ and ρ converge to 1 andφconverges to 0. That is, he port and the freight forwarder will eventually choose to actively cooperate, but the shipping company is affected by the incentive policy, and its willingness to actively cooperate is weak.

As can be seen from the figure, when the incentive is large, the cooperative decision of the port and the freight forwarder is not affected by the penalty strategy. When the incentive is small, the freight forwarder and the port are affected by the penalty strategy. When the penalty is more, the freight forwarder and port are more constrained, and they are more willing to cooperate. Similarly, for shipping companies, the greater the cost of incentives, the greater the willingness of shipping companies to cooperate.

Compare with Sec. 5.1.1, when using the blockchain technology, the shipping company's incentive strategy will lead to its low willingness to cooperate. When the supply chain without blockchain, the incentive policies and punishment strategies of the shipping company has little impact on the freight forwarder and the port. When customers are more sensitive to information quality, lower penalties will lead to a decline in the willingness of the freight forwarder and the port to actively cooperate. When the shipping company takes the multi-subsidy policy and no punishment, the stronger the willingness of the freight forwarder and the port to cooperate actively. This shows that the punishment strategy can promote the willingness of the freight forwarder and the port to cooperate actively. In order to

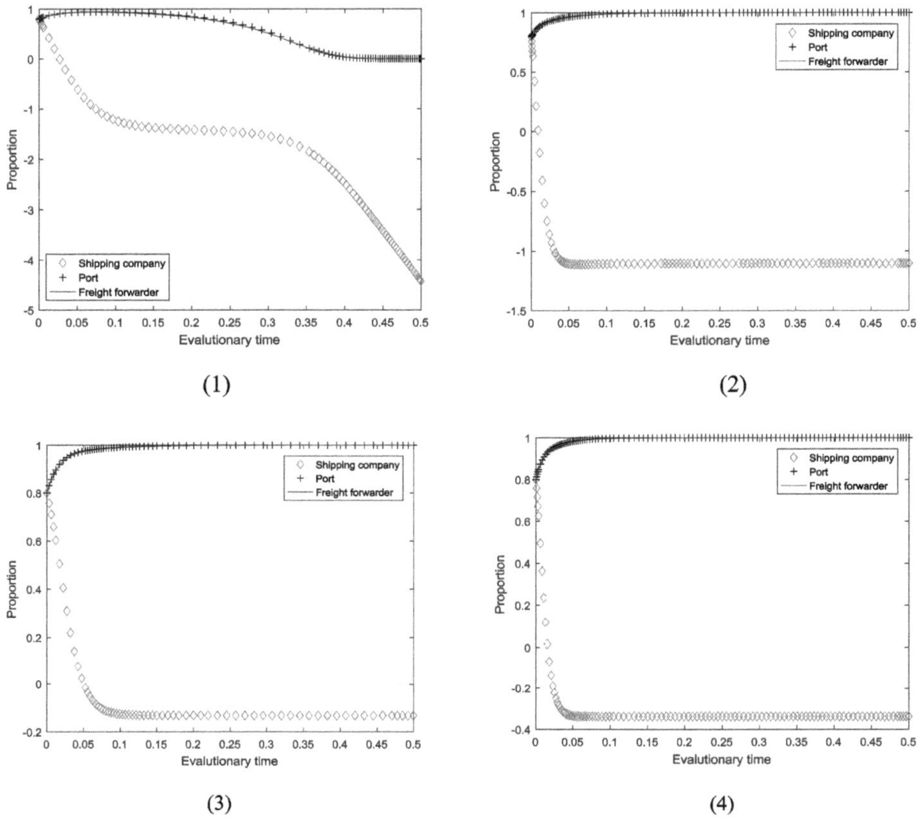

Fig. 11. Cooperative decision-making of node enterprises under different rewards and punishments.

promote information technology and improve customer satisfaction, the shipping company should establish a reward and punishment mechanism to maintain cooperative decision-making between the freight forwarder and the port.

6. Conclusions and Management Implication

6.1. *Main conclusion*

The supply chain of shipping logistics services led by the shipping company is the research object in this study. A tripartite game model is designed from the perspective of blockchain technology application. This study investigates and analyzes the influence of the degree of information sharing and customers' sensitivity to information quality on the relationship and evolution path. Numerical simulation is conducted to verify the results. Finally, the following conclusions are drawn:

(1) On the basis of theoretical analysis and data simulation, as long as shipping companies subsidize ports and freight forwarders, the willingness of ports and

freight forwarder to actively cooperate will increase. The degree of information sharing between ports and freight forwarder affect the willingness of shipping companies to actively cooperate. The higher the degree of information sharing between ports and freight forwarder is, the more willing shipping companies will be to actively cooperate. The customers' requirements for information quality affect the willingness of the node companies to cooperate. The shipping company's willingness to actively cooperate increases with the degree of information sharing (how low or high the customers' requirements for information quality are). At an intermediate value, as the degree of information sharing increases, shipping companies' willingness to actively cooperate decreases more and more. After the application of blockchain technology, the higher the degree of information sharing is in the case that customers have higher requirements for information quality, the lower the shipping company's willingness to cooperate actively will be. Moreover, the speed of port's willingness to cooperate actively increases, whereas that of freight forwarder' willingness to cooperate actively decreases.

(2) Blockchain technology changes the way of information sharing, such that the information sharing of all node companies is at a unified level. The decision of shipping companies will be less affected by ports and freight forwarder, and the willingness to cooperate will increase with the improvement of the unified sharing level. In addition, blockchain technology can ensure that the information uploaded by enterprises is accurate and cannot be tampered with. When the information quality is guaranteed and the degree of information sharing is high, shipping companies are willing to actively cooperate.

(3) Shipping companies are more sensitive to the extent to which blockchain is used. Moreover, when ports and freight forwarder consider customer requirements for information quality, they will be affected by blockchain technology, and the willingness to cooperate with ports and freight forwarder will increase faster than in unused areas. Blockchain technology is fast. Therefore, shipping companies should invest in blockchain technology and encourage ports and freight forwarder to join in a blockchain alliance.

6.2. *Management implication*

In order to accurately give the shipping company some management insights, we first clarify the composition of the shipping company's payoff in the game. When the shipping company chooses B1, the shipping company will pay the input cost of blockchain technology, while gaining extra benefit for the investment. In order to clarify the information sharing and the information quality by the port and the freight forwarder, the investment cost of the shipping company needs to be pay attention to. If there is an incorrect information by the port and the freight forwarder, some of consumers will be lost. The port and the freight forwarder will pay penalty to the shipping company. It can be known that the shipping company's payoff will be affected by decisions of consumers and the information quality.

(1) In the early stage of alliance chain development, the shipping company should increase cost investment in blockchain. Since all three parties have invested in the blockchain at the initial stage of investment, for the port and the freight forwarder, especially freight forwarders, the input costs are too high. Their benefits will be lower than when the blockchain is not used. In order to ensure the continuous development of the service supply chain, providing incentive strategies by the shipping company for ports and freight forwarders.

(2) An effective supervision mechanism can be develop by the shipping company. When customers have lower requirements for information quality, the degree of information sharing by the port and the freight forwarder will be reduce. This will lead to a decrease in the efficiency of the entire supply chain. The degree of information sharing between the port and the freight forwarder will affect shipping company's profits and willingness to cooperate, thereby reducing the service quality of the entire service supply chain and affecting market demand. Therefore, the shipping company should formulate a reasonable reward and punishment mechanism to effectively supervise the degree of information sharing and information quality between the port and the freight forwarder.

Appendix A. The Jacobian Matrix

$$J = \begin{bmatrix} \frac{\partial f(\varphi)}{\partial \varphi} & \frac{\partial f(\varphi)}{\partial \lambda} & \frac{\partial f(\varphi)}{\partial \rho} \\ \frac{\partial f(\lambda)}{\partial \varphi} & \frac{\partial f(\lambda)}{\partial \lambda} & \frac{\partial f(\lambda)}{\partial \rho} \\ \frac{\partial f(\rho)}{\partial \varphi} & \frac{\partial f(\rho)}{\partial \lambda} & \frac{\partial f(\rho)}{\partial \rho} \end{bmatrix} = \begin{bmatrix} F_{11} & F_{12} & F_{13} \\ F_{21} & F_{22} & F_{23} \\ F_{31} & F_{32} & F_{33} \end{bmatrix}$$

$$J^{BC} = \begin{bmatrix} \frac{\partial f^{BC}(\varphi)}{\partial \varphi} & \frac{\partial f^{BC}(\varphi)}{\partial \lambda} & \frac{\partial f^{BC}(\varphi)}{\partial \rho} \\ \frac{\partial f^{BC}(\lambda)}{\partial \varphi} & \frac{\partial f^{BC}(\lambda)}{\partial \lambda} & \frac{\partial f^{BC}(\lambda)}{\partial \rho} \\ \frac{\partial f^{BC}(\rho)}{\partial \varphi} & \frac{\partial f^{BC}(\rho)}{\partial \lambda} & \frac{\partial f^{BC}(\rho)}{\partial \rho} \end{bmatrix} = \begin{bmatrix} F_{11}^{BC} & F_{12}^{BC} & F_{13}^{BC} \\ F_{21}^{BC} & F_{22}^{BC} & F_{23}^{BC} \\ F_{31}^{BC} & F_{32}^{BC} & F_{33}^{BC} \end{bmatrix}.$$

$$\begin{aligned} F_{11} = {} & (1-2\varphi)(g_1 - 2m_1 - 2m_2 + \lambda(-g_1 + 2m_2 + 2m_3 + a\mu_1 + \alpha\mu_3 + \theta_1 q_1) \\ & + \rho(2m_1 + 2m_5 + \alpha\mu_2 + \theta_2 q_1) + \lambda\rho(g_1 - 2m_1 - 2m_2 - \alpha\mu_3)) \end{aligned}$$

$$\begin{aligned} F_{12} = {} & \varphi(1-\varphi)(2m_2 - g_1 + 2m_3 + \alpha\mu_1 + \alpha\mu_3 + \theta_1 q_1 + g_1\rho \\ & - 2m_1\rho - 2m_2\rho - \alpha\mu_3\rho) \end{aligned}$$

$$F_{13} = \varphi(1-\varphi)(2m_1 + 2m_5 + \alpha\mu_2 + g_1\lambda + \theta_2 q_1 - 2\lambda m_1 - 2\lambda m_2 - \alpha\lambda\mu_3)$$

$$F_{21} = \lambda(1-\lambda)(2m_1 + 2m_3 + \alpha\mu_4 + \theta_3 q_2 - 2m_1\rho)$$

$$F_{22} = (1-2\lambda)(g_2 + \varphi(2m_1 + 2m_3 + \alpha\mu_4 + \theta_3 q_2) + \rho(2m_1 + 2m_4 + \alpha\mu_5 + \theta_4 q_2) - 2\varphi\rho m_1)$$

$$F_{23} = \lambda(1-\lambda)(2m_1 + 2m_4 + \alpha\mu_5 - 2\varphi m_1 + \theta_4 q_2)$$

$$F_{31} = \rho(1-\rho)(2m_2 + 2m_5 + \alpha\mu_9 - 2\alpha\mu_{11} + \theta_5 q_3 + 2\alpha\lambda\mu_{11})$$

$$F_{32} = \rho(1-\rho)(2m_4 + \alpha\mu_{10} - 2\alpha\mu_{11} + \theta_6 q_3 + 2\alpha\varphi\mu_{11})$$

$$F_{33} = (1-2\rho)(g_3 + 2\alpha\mu_{11} + \varphi(2m_2 + 2m_5 + \alpha\mu_9 - 2\alpha\mu_{11} + \theta_5 q_3) + \lambda(2m_4 + \alpha\mu_{10} - 2\alpha\mu_{11} + \theta_6 q_3) + 2\alpha\varphi\lambda\mu_{11})$$

$$F_{11}^{BC} = (1-2\varphi)(2g_5 + 2g_6 + \lambda(-g_5 - g_6 + 2m_3 - 2m_6 - m_7 + \alpha_1\mu_t + \theta_7 t + k_1 t) + \rho(-g_5 - g_6 + 2m_5 - 2m_7 + \alpha_1\mu_t + 2\theta_8 t + k_2 t) + \lambda\rho(g_5 + g_6 + m_7 - \theta_8 t))$$

$$F_{12}^{BC} = \varphi(1-\varphi)(2m_3 - g_6 - g_5 - 2m_6 - m_7 + \alpha_1\mu_t + \theta_7 t + g_5\rho + g_6\rho + k_1 t + m_7\rho - \theta_8\rho t)$$

$$F_{13}^{BC} = \varphi(1-\varphi)(2m_5 - g_6 - g_5 - 2m_7 + g_5\lambda + g_6\lambda + a_1\mu_t + 2\theta_8 t + \lambda m_7 + k_2 t - \theta_8\lambda t)$$

$$F_{21}^{BC} = \lambda(1-\lambda)(2m_3 + 2m_6 + \alpha_1\mu_t + \theta_9 t + k_3 t)$$

$$F_{22}^{BC} = (1-2\lambda)(g_4 + g_6 + \varphi(2m_3 + 2m_6 + \alpha_1 t + \theta_9 t + k_3 t) + \rho(2m_4 + \alpha_1\mu_t + \theta_{10} t + k_4 t))$$

$$F_{23}^{BC} = \lambda(1-\lambda)(2m_4 + \alpha_1\mu_t + \theta_{10} t + k_4 t)$$

$$F_{31}^{BC} = \rho(1-\rho)(2m_5 + 2m_7 + \theta_{11} t + k_5 t)$$

$$F_{32}^{BC} = \rho(1-\rho)(2m_4 + \theta_{12} t + k_6 t)$$

$$F_{33}^{BC} = (1-2\rho)(g_4 + g_5 + \varphi(2m_5 + 2m_7 + \theta_{11} t + k_5 t) + \lambda(2m_4 + \theta_{12} t + k_6 t)).$$

Appendix B. DetJ and Tr of the Jacobian Matrix Respectively

$$\mathrm{Det}J = \varphi(\lambda(2\rho-1)(\lambda-1)AG - \lambda\rho(\lambda-1)(\rho-1)DC)(\varphi-1) \times (H + g_1\rho - 2m_1\rho - 2m_2\rho - \alpha\mu_3\rho)$$

$$
\begin{aligned}
&- (2\varphi - 1)((2\lambda - 1)(2\rho - 1)EA - \lambda\rho(\lambda - 1)(\rho - 1)BD) \\
&\times (g_1 - 2m_1 - 2m_2 + \lambda H + \rho F) + \varphi(\varphi - 1)(\rho(2\lambda - 1)(\rho - 1) \\
&\times CE - \lambda\rho(\lambda - 1)(\rho - 1)BG)F
\end{aligned}
$$

$$
\begin{aligned}
A &= g_3 + 2\alpha\mu_{11} + 2\varphi m_2 + 2\varphi m_5 + 2\lambda m_4 + \alpha\varphi\mu_9 - 2\alpha\varphi\mu_{11} + \alpha\lambda\mu_{10} \\
&\quad - 2\alpha\lambda\mu_{11} + \theta_5\varphi q_3 + \theta_6\lambda q_3 + 2\alpha\varphi\lambda\mu_{11} \\
B &= 2m_4 + \alpha\mu_{10} - 2\alpha\mu_{11} + \theta_6 q_3 + 2\alpha\varphi\mu_{11} \\
C &= 2m_2 + 2m_5 + \alpha\mu_9 - 2\alpha\mu_{11} + \theta_5 q_3 + 2\alpha\lambda\mu_{11} \\
D &= 2m_1 + 2m_4 + \alpha\mu_5 - 2\varphi m_1 + \theta_4 q_2 \\
E &= g_2 + 2\varphi m_1 + 2\varphi m_3 + 2m_1\rho + 2m_4\rho \\
&\quad + \alpha\varphi\mu_4 + \theta_3\varphi q_2 + a\mu_5\rho - 2\varphi m_1\rho + \theta_4 q_2\rho \\
F &= 2m_1 + 2m_5 + a\mu_2 + g_1\lambda + \theta_2 q_1 - 2\lambda m_1 - 2\lambda m_2 - \alpha\lambda\mu_3 \\
G &= 2m_1 + 2m_3 + \alpha\mu_4 + \theta_3 q_2 - 2m_1\rho \\
H &= 2m_2 - g_1 + 2m_3 + \alpha\mu_1 + \alpha\mu_3 + \theta_1 q_1 \\
\operatorname{Tr} J &= -(2\varphi - 1)(g_1 - 2m_1 - 2m_2 + \lambda H + \rho F) - (2\lambda - 1)E - (2\rho - 1)A \\
\operatorname{Det} J^{BC} &= \varphi(\lambda(2\rho - 1)(\lambda - 1)D_1B_1 - \lambda\rho(\lambda - 1)(\rho - 1)E_1(2m_4 + \alpha_1\mu_t + \theta_{10}t + k_4t)) \\
&\quad (\varphi - 1)G_1 - (2\varphi - 1)((2\lambda - 1)(2\rho - 1)(g_4 + g_5 + \varphi E_1 + \lambda F_1)A_1 \\
&\quad - \lambda\rho(\lambda - 1)(\rho - 1)F_1(2m_4 + \alpha_1\mu_t + \theta_{10}t + k_4t))C_1 + \varphi(\rho(2\lambda - 1)(\rho - 1) \\
&\quad E_1A_1 - \lambda\rho(\lambda - 1)(\rho - 1)F_1D_1)(\varphi - 1)(H_1 + g_5\lambda + g_6\lambda + \lambda m_7 - \theta_8\lambda t) \\
TrJ^{BC} &= -(2\lambda - 1)A_1 - (2\varphi - 1)C_1 - (2\rho - 1)B_1 \\
A_1 &= g_4 + g_6 + 2\varphi m_3 + 2\varphi m_6 + 2m_4\rho + \alpha_1\varphi\mu_t + \theta_9\varphi t + \varphi k_3 t + \alpha_1\rho t \\
&\quad + \theta_{10}\rho t + k_4\rho t \\
B_1 &= g_4 + g_5 + 2\varphi m_5 + 2\varphi m_7 + 2\lambda m_4 + \theta_{11}\varphi t + \theta_{12}\lambda t + \varphi k_5 t + k_6\lambda t \\
C_1 &= 2g_5 + 2g_6 + \lambda G_1 + \rho H_1, \\
D_1 &= 2m_3 + 2m_6 + \alpha_1\mu_t + \theta_9 t + k_3 t \\
E_1 &= 2m_5 + 2m_7 + \theta_{11}t + k_5 t, \\
F_1 &= 2m_4 + \theta_{12}t + k_6 t
\end{aligned}
$$

$$G_1 = 2m_3 - g_5 - g_6 - 2m_6 - m_7 + \alpha_1\mu_t + \theta_7 t + k_1 t + g_5\rho + g_6\rho + m_7\rho - \theta_8\rho t$$

$$H_1 = 2m_5 - g_5 - g_6 - 2m_7 + \alpha_1 t + 2\theta_8 t + k_2 t.$$

Appendix C.

Table C.1. Values of DetBC J and TrBC J without blockchain.

Equilibrium points	Det J	+/−	Tr J	+/−
$T_1(0,0,0)$	$-g_2(g_3+2\alpha\mu_{11})(2m_1-g_1+2m_2)$	−	$g_1+g_2+g_3-2m_1-2m_2 +2\alpha\mu_{11}$	+
$T_2(0,0,1)$	$-(g_3+2\alpha\mu_{11})(g_1-2m_2+2m_5 +\alpha\mu_2+\theta_2 q_1)(g_2+2m_1+2m_4 +\alpha\mu_5+\theta_4 q_2)$	−	$g_1+g_2-g_3+2m_1 -2m_2+2m_4+2m_5 +\alpha\mu_2+\alpha\mu_5 -2\alpha\mu_{11}+\theta_2 q_1 +\theta_4 q_2$	+
$T_3(0,1,0)$	$-g_2(g_3+2m_4+\alpha\mu_{10}+\theta_6 q_3)(2m_3-2m_1+\alpha\mu_1+\alpha\mu_3+\theta_1 q_1)$	−	$g_3-g_2-2m_1+2m_3+2m_4 +\alpha\mu_1+\alpha\mu_3+\alpha\mu_{10} +\theta_1 q_1+\theta_6 q_3$	+
$T_4(0,1,1)$	$(g_3+2m_4+\alpha\mu_{10}+\theta_6 q_3)(g_2+2m_1+2m_4+\alpha\mu_5+\theta_4 q_2)(g_1-2m_1-2m_2+2m_3+2m_5 +\alpha\mu_1+\alpha\mu_2+\theta_1 q_1+\theta_2 q_1)$	+	$g_1-g_2-g_3-4m_1 -2m_2-4m_4-\alpha\mu_5 -\alpha\mu_{10}-\theta_4 q_2 -\theta_6 q_3+2m_5 +\alpha\mu_1+\alpha\mu_2 +\theta_1 q_1+\theta_2 q_1 +2m_3$	+/−
$T_5(1,0,0)$	$(2m_1+2m_2-g_1)(g_2+2m_1+2m_3 +\alpha\mu_4+\theta_3 q2)(g_3+2m_2+2m_5 +\alpha\mu_9+\theta_5 q_3)$	+	$g_2-g_1+g_3+4m_1+4m_2 +2m_3+2m_5+\alpha\mu_4 +\alpha\mu_9+\theta_3 q_2+\theta_5 q_3$	+
$T_6(1,0,1)$	$(g_1-2m_2+2m_5+\alpha\mu_2+\theta_2 q_1)(g_3+2m_2+2m_5+\alpha\mu_9+\theta_5 q_3)(g_2+2m_1+2m_3+2m_4 +\alpha\mu_4+\alpha\mu_5+\theta_3 q_2+\theta_4 q_2)$	+	$g_2-g_1-g_3-4m_5 -\alpha\mu_2-\alpha\mu_9 -\theta_2 q_1-\theta_5 q_3 +2m_1+2m_3+2m_4 +\alpha\mu_4+\alpha\mu_5+\theta_3 q_2 +\theta_4 q_2$	+/−
$T_7(1,1,0)$	$(2m_3-2m_1+\alpha\mu_1+\alpha\mu_3+\theta_1 q_1)(g_2+2m_1+2m_3+\alpha\mu_4+\theta_3 q_2)(g_3+2m_2+2m_4+2m_5+\alpha\mu_9 +\alpha\mu_{10}+\theta_5 q_3+\theta_6 q_3)$	+	$g_3-g_2+2m_2-4m_3 -\alpha\mu_1-\alpha\mu_3 -\alpha\mu_4-\theta_1 q_1 -\theta_3 q_2+2m_4 +2m_5+\alpha\mu_9+\alpha\mu_{10} +\theta_5 q_3+\theta_6 q_3$	+
$T_8(1,1,1)$	$-(g_2+2m_1+2m_3+2m_4 +\alpha\mu_4+\alpha\mu_5 +\theta_3 q_2+\theta_4 q_2) \times(g_3+2m_2+2m_4+2m_5 +\alpha\mu_9+\alpha\mu_{10}+\theta_5 q_3 +\theta_6 q_3)(g_1-2m_1 -2m_2+2m_3+2m_5+\alpha\mu_1 +\alpha\mu_2+\theta_1 q_1 +\theta_2 q_1)$	+/−	$-g_1-g_2-g_3-4m_3-4m_4 -4m_5-\alpha\mu_1-\alpha\mu_2 -\alpha\mu_4-\alpha\mu_5 -\alpha\mu_9-\alpha\mu_{10} -\theta_1 q_1-\theta_2 q_1 -\theta_3 q_2-\theta_4 q_2 -\theta_5 q_3-\theta_6 q_3$	−

Table C.2. Corresponding eigenvalues without blockchain.

Equilibrium points	Eigenvalues β_1	Eigenvalues β_2	Eigenvalues β_3
$T_1(0,0,0)$	$g_1 - 2m_1 - 2m_2$	g_2	$g_3 + 2\alpha\mu_{11}$
$T_2(0,0,1)$	$g_1 - 2m_2 + 2m_5 + \alpha\mu_2 + \theta_2 q_1$	$g_2 + 2m_1 + 2m_4 + \alpha\mu_5 + \theta_4 q_2$	$-(g_3 + 2\alpha\mu_{11})$
$T_3(0,1,0)$	$-2m_1 + 2m_3 + a\mu_1 + \alpha\mu_3 + \theta_1 q_1$	$-g_2$	$g_3 + 2m_4 + \alpha\mu_{10} + \theta_6 q_3$
$T_4(0,1,1)$	$g_1 - 2m_1 - 2m_2 + 2m_3 + a\mu_1 + \theta_1 q_1 + 2m_5 + \alpha\mu_2 + \theta_2 q_1$	$-(g_2 + 2m_1 + 2m_4 + \alpha\mu_5 + \theta_4 q_2)$	$-(g_3 + 2m_4 + \alpha\mu_{10} + \theta_6 q_3)$
$T_5(1,0,0)$	$-(g_1 - 2m_1 - 2m_2)$	$g_2 + 2m_1 + 2m_3 + \alpha\mu_4 + \theta_3 q_2$	$g_3 + 2m_2 + 2m_5 + \alpha\mu_9 + \theta_5 q_3$
$T_6(1,0,1)$	$-(g_1 - 2m_2 + 2m_5 + \alpha\mu_2 + \theta_2 q_1)$	$g_2 + 2m_1 + 2m_3 + \alpha\mu_4 + \theta_3 q_2 + 2m_4 + \alpha\mu_5 + \theta_4 q_2$	$-(g_3 + 2m_2 + 2m_5 + \alpha\mu_9 + \theta_5 q_3)$
$T_7(1,1,0)$	$-(-2m_1 + 2m_3 + a\mu_1 + \alpha\mu_3 + \theta_1 q_1)$	$-(g_2 + 2m_1 + 2m_3 + \alpha\mu_4 + \theta_3 q_2)$	$g_3 + 2m_2 + 2m_5 + \alpha\mu_9 - 2\alpha\mu_{11} + \theta_5 q_3 + 2m_4 + \alpha\mu_{10} + \theta_6 q_3$
$T_8(1,1,1)$	$-(g_1 - 2m_1 - 2m_2 + 2m_3 + a\mu_1 + \theta_1 q_1 + 2m_5 + \alpha\mu_2 + \theta_2 q_1)$	$-(g_2 + 2m_1 + 2m_3 + \alpha\mu_4 + \theta_3 q_2 + 2m_4 + \alpha\mu_5 + \theta_4 q_2)$	$-(g_3 + 2m_2 + 2m_5 + \alpha\mu_9 + \theta_5 q_3 + 2m_4 + \alpha\mu_{10} + \theta_6 q_3)$

Appendix D. Tables D.1 and D.2

Table D.1. Values of DetBC J and TrBC J with blockchain.

Equilibrium points	Det^{BC} J	+/−	Tr^{BC} J	+/−
$T_1(0,0,0)$	$(g_4+g_5)(g_4+g_6)(2g_5+2g_6)$	+	$2g_4+3g_5+3g_6$	+
$T_2(0,0,1)$	$-(g_4+g_5)(g_4+g_6+2m_4+\alpha_1\mu_t+\theta_{10}t+k_4t)(g_5+g_6+2m_5-2m_7+\alpha_1\mu_t+2\theta_8t+k_2t)$	+/−	$2g_6+2m_4+2m-2m_7+2\alpha_1\mu_t+2\theta_8t+\theta_{10}t+k_2t+k_4t$	+
$T_3(0,1,0)$	$-(g_4+g_6)(g_4+g_5+2m_4+\theta_{12}t+k_6t)(g_5+g6+2m_3-2m_6-m_7+\alpha_1\mu_t+\theta_7t+k_1t)$	−	$2g_5+2m_3+2m_4-2m_6-m_7+\alpha_1\mu_t+\theta_7t+\theta_{12}t+k_1t+k_6t$	+
$T_4(0,1,1)$	$(g_4+g_5+2m_4+\theta_{12}t+k_6t)(g_4+g_6+2m_4+\alpha_1\mu_t+\theta_{10}t+k_4t)(g_5+g_6+2m_3+2m_5-2m_6-2m_7+2\alpha_1\mu_t+\theta_7t+\theta_8t+k_1t+k_2t)$	+/−	$2m_3-2g_4-4m_4+2m_5-2m_6-2m_7-k_4t-k_6t-\theta_{10}t-\theta_{12}t+\alpha_1\mu_t+\theta_7t+\theta_8t+k_1t+k_2t$	+/−
$T_5(1,0,0)$	$-(2g_5+2g_6)(g_4+g_5+2m_5+2m_7+\theta_{11}t+k_5t)(g_4+g_6+2m_3+2m_6+\alpha_1\mu_t+\theta_9t+k_3t)$	−	$2g_4-g_5-g_6+2m_3+2m_5+2m_6+2m_7+\alpha_1\mu_t+\theta_9t+\theta_{11}t+k_3t+k_5t$	+
$T_6(1,0,1)$	$(g_4+g_5+2m_5+2m_7+\theta_{11}t+k_5t)(g_5+g_6+2m_5-2m_7+\alpha_1\mu_t+2\theta_8t+k_2t)(g_4+g_6+2m_3+2m_4+2m6+2\alpha_1\mu_t+\theta_9t+\theta_{10}t+k_3t+k_4t)$	+/−	$2m_3-2g_5-4m_5-2\theta_8t-\theta_{11}t-k_2t-k_5t+2m_6+2m_4+\alpha_1\mu_t+\theta_9t+\theta_{10}t+k_3t+k_4t$	+/−
$T_7(1,1,0)$	$(g_4+g_6+2m_3+2m_6+\alpha_1\mu_t+\theta_9t+k_3t)(g_5+g_6+2m_3-2m_6-m_7+\alpha_1\mu_t+\theta_7t+k_1t)(g_4+g_5+2m_4+2m_5+2m_7+\theta_{11}t+\theta_{12}t+k_5t+k_6t)$	+/−	$2m_4-4m_3-2g_6-2\alpha_1\mu_t-\theta_7t-\theta_9t-k_1t-k_3t+\theta_{11}t+\theta_{12}t+k_5t+k_6t+2m_5+3m_7$	+/−
$T_8(1,1,1)$	$-(g_4+g_5+2m_4+2m_5+2m_7+\theta_{11}t+\theta_{12}t+k_5t+k_6t)(g_4+g_6+2m_3+2m_4+2m_6+2\alpha_1\mu_t+\theta_9t+\theta_{10}t+k_3t+k_4t)(g_5+g_6+2m_3+2m_5-2m_6-2m_7+2\alpha_1\mu_t+\theta_7t+\theta_8t+k_1t+k_2t)$	+/−	$-g_1-g_2-g_3-4m_3-4m_4-4m_5-\alpha\mu_1-\alpha\mu_2-\alpha\mu_4-\alpha\mu_5-\alpha\mu_9-\alpha\mu_{10}-\theta_1q_1-\theta_2q_1-\theta_3q_2-\theta_4q_2-\theta_5q_3-\theta_6q_3$	−

Table D.2. Corresponding eigenvalues with blockchain.

Equilibrium points	Eigenvalues β_1^{BC}	Eigenvalues β_2^{BC}	Eigenvalues β_3^{BC}
$T_1(0,0,0)$	$2g_5+2g_6$	g_4+g_6	g_4+g_5
$T_2(0,0,1)$	$g_5+g_6+2m_5-2m_7+\alpha_1 t+2\theta_8 t+k_2 t$	$g_4+g_6+2m_4+\alpha_1 t+\theta_{10}t+k_4 t$	$-(g_4+g_5)$
$T_3(0,1,0)$	$g_5+g_6+2m_3-2m_6-m_7+\alpha_1 t+\theta_7 t+k_1 t$	$-(g_4+g_6)$	$g_4+g_5+2m_4+\theta_{12}t+k_6 t$
$T_4(0,1,1)$	$2m_3-2m_6-2m_7+2\alpha_1 t+\theta_7 t+k_1 t+2m_5+\theta_8 t+k_2 t+g_5+g_6$	$-(g_4+g_6+2m_4+\alpha_1 t+\theta_{10}t+k_4 t)$	$-(g_4+g_5+2m_4+\theta_{12}t+k_6 t)$
$T_5(1,0,0)$	$-2g_5-2g_6$	$g_4+g_6+2m_3+2m_6+\alpha_1 t+\theta_9 t+k_3 t$	$g_4+g_5+2m_5+2m_7+\theta_{11}t+k_5 t$
$T_6(1,0,1)$	$-(g_5+g_6+2m_5-2m_7+\alpha_1 t+2\theta_8 t+k_2 t)$	$g_4+g_6+2m_3+2m_6+2\alpha_1 t+\theta_9 t+k_3 t+2m_4+\theta_{10}t+k_4 t$	$-(g_4+g_5+2m_5+2m_7+\theta_{11}t+k_5 t)$
$T_7(1,1,0)$	$-(g_5+g_6+2m_3-2m_6-m_7+\alpha_1 t+\theta_7 t+k_1 t)$	$-(g_4+g_6+2m_3+2m_6+\alpha_1 t+\theta_9 t+k_3 t)$	$g_4+g_5+2m_5+2m_7+\theta_{11}t+k_5 t+2m_4+\theta_{12}t+k_6 t$
$T_8(1,1,1)$	$-(2m_3-2m_6+2\alpha_1 t+\theta_7 t+k_1 t+g_5+g_6+2m_5-2m_7+\theta_8 t+k_2 t)$	$-(g_4+g_6+2m_3+2m_6+2\alpha_1 t+\theta_9 t+k_3 t+2m_4+\theta_{10}t+k_4 t)$	$-(g_4+g_5+2m_5+2m_7+\theta_{11}t+k_5 t+2m_4+\theta_{12}t+k_6 t)$

References

Aste, T, P Tasca and T Di Matteo (2017). Blockchain technologies: The foreseeable impact on society and industry. *Computer*, 50(9), 18–28.

Baharmand, H and T Comes (2019). Leveraging partnerships with logistics service providers in humanitarian supply chains by blockchain-based smart contracts. *IFAC Papers On Line*, 52(13): 12–17.

Biswas, K, V Muthukkumarasamy and WL Tan (2017). Blockchain based wine supply chain traceability system. In *Future Technologies Conf.*, November, Vancouver, BC, Canada.

DeLone, WH and ER McLean (1992). McLean information systems success: The quest for the dependent variable. *Information Systems Research*, 3(1), 60–95.

Ghosh, B and MR Galbreth (2013). The impact of consumer attentiveness and search costs on firm quality disclosure: A competitive analysis. *Management Science* 59(11), 2604–2621.

Guan, X. and YJ Chen (2015). Hierarchical quality disclosure in a supply chain with cost heterogeneity. *Decision Support System* 76, 63–75.

Hackius, N and M Petersen (2020). Translating high hopes into tangible benefits: How incumbents in supply chain and logistics approach blockchain, *IEEE ACESS*, 8, 34993–35003.

Kim, J-S and N Shin (2019). The impact of blockchain technology application on supply chain partnership and performance. *Sustainability*, 11, 61–81.

Lee, HS, M Boile, S Theofain and S Choo (2014). Game theoretical models of the cooperative carrier behavior. *Ksce Journal of Civil Engineering*, 18, 1528–1538.

Li, L and RQ Zhang (2015). Cooperation through capacity sharing between competing forwarders. *Transport Research Part E: Logistic and Transportation Review*, 75, 11–131.

Liu, JG and J Wang (2019). Carrier alliance incentive analysis and coordination in a maritime transport chain based on service competition. *Transport Research Part E: Logistic and Transportation Review*, 128, 333–355.

Markopoulos, MP and K Hosanagar (2018). A model of product design and information disclosure investments. *Management Science*, 64(2), 739–759.

Olnes, S, J Ubacht and M Janssen (2017). Blockchain in government: Benefits and implications of distributed ledger technology for information sharing. *Government Information Quarterly*, 34, 355–364.

Song, DP, A Lyons and D Li *et al.* (2016). Modeling port competition from a transport chain perspective. *Transportation Research Part E: Logistics and Transportation*, 87, 75–96.

Sternberg, H, G Prockl and J Holmström (2014). The efficiency potential of ICT in Haulier operations. *Computers in Industry*, 65(8), 1161.

Wang, H, Q Meng and XN Zhang (2014) Game-theoretica models for competition analysis in a new emerging liner container shipping market. *Transportation Research Part B: Methodological*, 70, 201–227.

Wang, Z, T Wang, H Hu, J Gong, X En and Q Xiao (2020). Blockchain-based framework for improving supply chain traceability and information sharing in precast construction. *Automation in Construction*, 111, 103063.

Yang, C-S (2019). Maritime shipping digitalization: Blockchain-based technology applications, future improvements, and intention to use. *Transportation Research Part E: Logistics and Transportation Review*, 131, 108–117.

Yang, R, M Yu, C-Y Lee and Y Du (2021). Contracting in ocean transportation with empty container repositioning under asymmetric information. *Transportation Research Part E*, 145, 102173.

Xu, L, K Govindan and X Bu *et al.* (2015). Pricing and balancing of the sea-cargo service chain with empty equipment repositioning. *Computers & Operations Research*, 54, 286–294.

Biography

Yujing Chen is a PhD student of Shanghai Maritime University. Her research interests include non-car operating common carrier, service supply chain and shipping logistics.

Bin Yang has been working as a Professor of the Logistics Research Center at the Shanghai Maritime University. His main research tops are logistics industry and function planning, metropolitan logistics, smart logistics, green logistics.

https://doi.org/10.1142/9789819808588_0004

Chapter 4

When and How Should Cross-Border Platforms Manage Blockchain Technology in the Presence of Purchasing Agents?[†]

Xiutian Shi
School of Economics and Management
Nanjing University of Science and Technology
Nanjing 210094, P. R. China
xtshi@njust.edu.cn

Shuning Yao
School of Economics and Management
Nanjing University of Science and Technology
Nanjing 210094, P. R. China
shuning.yao@njust.edu.cn

Yizhong Ma*
School of Economics and Management
Nanjing University of Science and Technology
Nanjing 210094, P. R. China
**yzma-2004@163.com*

Copycat issues and unreliable purchasing agents have challenged cross-border consumption and hurt the brands and online platforms significantly. We explicate a setting in which a platform orders from a brand, then sells and competes with the purchasing agents in an overseas market. Worried about the copycat issues, consumers undertake risk when purchasing from both platforms and agents. The blockchain adoption may help release this uncertainty by purchasing from a platform. We show the values and impacts of this new technology on the platform, brand and consumers. It is interesting to observe that the platform does not always have incentive to adopt blockchain, even if it is costless. In the presence of blockchain, we show that the revenue sharing, two-part tariff and profit sharing contracts can achieve supply chain coordination, but the cost sharing contract fails to do so. In the extended models, we discuss what will happen when the brand decides domestic retail price and the platform links optional information nodes to blockchain.

Keywords: Pricing; platform operations; blockchain; purchasing agents; copycat.

*Corresponding author.
[†]To cite this article, please refer to its earlier version published in the Asia-Pacific Journal of Operational Research, Vol. 39, No. 1, (February 2022), DOI: 10.1142/S0217595921400200. Reprinted with permission from World Scientific Publishing Co. Pte. Ltd.

1. Introduction

In recent decades, the significant growth of cross-border consumption supported by brands' overseas strategy and online platform operations has been accompanied by a prevalence of copycat issues such as pirated and counterfeited goods (Wiedmann *et al.*, 2012). According to the shopping survey published by China Consumers Association (CCA) in 2017, many foreign goods, such as Estee Lauder ANR Eye cream, sold online are counterfeit. Some famous cross-border platforms, Kaola.com used to be affiliated to NetEase Inc., JD.Com and related shops on Taobao.com underwent grilling for selling suspected counterfeit goods in the report (Liao, 2018). A related significant irritant for foreign brands is their infringement. Hurt by the above-mentioned scandals, Estee Lauder sued Kaola.com and demanded $178,447 in damages (Week in China, 2019).

Against this backdrop, some administrations of market supervision, such as the Federal Trade Commission in the U.S. and the Trading Standards Institute in the U.K., have launched network transaction monitoring platforms to weed out counterfeit products in e-commerce (Ledger Insights, 2019). Under this pressure, cross-border online platforms make great efforts in confirming the subject products are genuine by providing clear and reliable authentic certifications. Unfortunately, the situation is not all roses. The conflicts arisen with famous brands have dealt a blow to these cross-border platforms' reputation among international suppliers and consumers. In addition, though some giant platforms do offer reliable products, the copycat issues still exist due to employees'/consumers' moral hazard problem in the logistics/returns process. From the Organisation for Economic Cooperation and Development (OECD), pirated goods worth $509 billion were seized and stealthily substitute during the logistic process in 2016, representing 3.3% of global trade (Week in China, 2019).

Moreover, the concept of shopping via a "Daigou", which refers to personal shoppers and freelance retail consultants, who buy products from country and sell to another one as purchasing agents, is booming all over the world (BBC News, 2016). Some of the purchasing agents are credible and play a role as an unauthorized distribution channel to sell the branded products only. While some of them are unreliable and have incentives to sell copycat products for extravagant profits (Progress Asia, 2019). The existence of purchasing agents raises challenges about trust to the consumers, who are more confused about the products and difficult to believe that the goods are genuine. Interestingly, brands hold ambiguous attitude toward the gray feature of purchasing agents (Autrey *et al.*, 2015). On the one hand, the unreliable agents make the brand's reputation suffer from copycat issues in the overseas market. On the other hand, the credible agents help the brand develop and serve overseas markets without operating stores. In addition, the legality of unauthorized channels represented by credible agents makes brands unable to combat with legal means, which renders the existence of purchasing agents to be a predominate challenge in operations (Autrey *et al.*, 2014). This observation in the real world makes cross-border platforms' operations with self-verifiability more difficult and challenging, as they have to make more efforts to prove the authenticity and foster consumers' trust.

Literature and industrial practice have suggested that technologies such as BarCode, Radio Frequency Identification (RFID) and big data may release great values in solving the trust and moral hazard problems (Lee and Ozer, 2007; Choi *et al.*, 2018; Luo and Choi, 2020). After years of development of information technologies in supply chain management, with the advance of blockchain technology, authentication and certification can solve the platforms' copycat problem and distinguish themselves from unreliable purchasing agents (Choi, 2019). Unlike the manufacturers who have strong incentive to make copycat and pursuit extravagant profit (Gao *et al.*, 2016), online platforms such as JD.com and TMall from Alibaba have their own anti-counterfeit supply system for product authentication (Ledger Insights, 2019). For instance, the blockchain-based Zhiyi supply chain owned by JD.com now tracks 60,000 products through blockchain technology. However, adopting the new technologies usually incurs substantial costs in building the block and related system. Hence, platforms have to search the trade-off between the values and costs from blockchain adoption.

Based on the aforementioned observations, this paper contributes to the online cross-border platforms' operations and the debate on the role of blockchain technology. We build a stylized analytical model to explore the following major research questions:

(1) What is a platform's optimal pricing decision with and without implementing blockchain, when facing the existence of purchasing agents?
(2) When will the implementation of blockchain benefit the platform? What are the values of blockchain to the brand and consumers?
(3) How should a platform manage the adoption of blockchain? Does signing contracts help? What is the impact of blockchain adoption on the supply chain coordination?
(4) How robust are the results when considering (a) the endogenous retail price in the domestic market, (b) the option of driving purchasing agents out of market, and (c) information disclosure decision?

We explicate a setting in which a platform orders from a brand, then sells and competes with the purchasing agents in an overseas market. Consumers buy a product based on the comparison between purchasing from the platform and agents. Worried about the copycat issues, consumers undertake risk when purchasing from both parties and thus perceive a discounted valuation. Blockchain adoption helps release this uncertainty but occurs a fixed cost.

By exploring the answers to the research questions under the above novel model, we theoretically derive in analytical closed-forms several critical insights. The major findings are summarized as follows. After deriving the optimal wholesale price and retail price for the brand and platform with/without blockchain, we show the values and impacts of this new technology on the platform, brand and consumers. Surprisingly, the platform does not always have incentive to adopt blockchain, even if it is costless. In addition, the value of blockchain is not always positive for the brand and consumers either, as the double marginalization amplifies after consumers' worries are released by the blockchain adoption.

As the fixed cost for blockchain technology is substantial, we check the supply chain coordination with blockchain, which may increase the platform's incentive to adopt it, under different contracts. We show that the revenue sharing, two-part tariff and profit sharing contracts can achieve coordination with the blockchain adoption, but the cost sharing contract fails to do so.

In extensions, we discuss what will happen when the brand decides domestic retail price and whether it has incentive to drive the purchasing agents out of the market. Moreover, we also show the impact of purchasing agents on the performances of both the brand and platform. Eventually, we investigate the platform's information disclosure problem and discuss how many information nodes should be linked to blockchain.

The remainder of this paper is as follows. We establish the basic models with/without blockchain in Sec. 2. We investigate when the platform has incentive to adopt blockchain and discuss all-win situations in Sec. 3. In Sec. 4, we investigate the supply chain coordination in the presence of blockchain under some widely observed contracts. For robustness checking and insights discussion, we explore various extensions in Sec. 5. Section 6 concludes the paper with remarks. All mathematical proofs are presented in Appendix A.

1.1. *Literature review*

Our paper contributes to three streams of literature on operations and supply chain management. The first stream studies the operations problems with the consideration of counterfeits and copycats issues. The second stream investigates the issues on platform operations and blockchain application. The third one relates with supply chain coordination and commonly adopted contracts.

The extant literature on counterfeits and copycats issues has focused on the demand, economic impact, incumbents' defensive strategies. Examples can be observed by Wilcox *et al.* (2009), Qian (2014), Gao *et al.* (2016), Sharif and Nazir (2017) and Gao *et al.* (2017). Debate has been raised that the policies that deter copycats may or may not improve social welfare. Focused on the counterfeits issue, Zhang *et al.* (2012) investigate the effects of counterfeits on genuine products' price. Cho *et al.* (2015) investigate the effects of counterfeit types (i.e., deceptive or non-deceptive) on the effectiveness of anti-counterfeiting strategies. Zhang and Zhang (2015) explore how to utilize the supply chain structures to combat the deceptive counterfeits. Li *et al.* (2016a) investigate the competition between a bandit supply chain and a legal mainstream firm selling similar products and show that the bandit supply chain may spur the branded firm's performance. Besides the counterfeits issues, we also investigate the impact of unauthorized selling channels where the brands products are traded (Li *et al.*, 2016b). Ahmadi and Yang (2000) show that price discrimination may be the motivation for firms to purchase from markets with low prices and resell in the high-priced one. Xiao *et al.* (2011) further consider that the unauthorized selling channel may be managed by firms or individuals. Wang *et al.* (2020) conduct a comprehensive review on counterfeiting and unauthorized channels in supply chains. They highlight that platform related operations, business intelligence and data analytics are critical for future studies in the area.

Unlike the literature focuses on the brands' and manufacturers' strategies facing counterfeits and copycats issues, we argue that cross-border platforms have strong incentive to sell reliable product with authentication for reputation in the long term. Hence, our paper is related to the literature on non-deceptive firms that differentiate themselves from deceptive counterfeits. Green and Smith (2002) provide an in-depth description of how a firm address the threat of counterfeits, facing unwary consumers. Zhang and Zhang (2015) consider the above problem with consideration of consumers' uninformed purchasing behaviors. Unlike the existing literature, we suggest that the platform should consider adopting blockchain technology to deal with the copycats issues and compete with purchasing agents. With the advancement of blockchain technology, Choi (2019) shows that platforms may utilize blockchain to win consumers' trust with certification and differentiate themselves from copycats. Galvez *et al.* (2018) examine the use of blockchain technology in retailing and food industry. Babich and Hilary (2020) highlight the adoption of blockchain for operations management, including topics such as supply chain risk management and use of information. Dai (2018) explores a platform operations problem for resource-competing users with the use of blockchain technology. Choi *et al.* (2019) review the literature and propose the use of blockchain technology in global supply chains with air logistics. More recently, Cai *et al.* (2020) investigate the platform supported supply chain operations with blockchain consideration and discuss the moral hazards. Choi *et al.* (2020) comprehensively review operations management with blockchain technologies in the industry 4.0 era and beyond. In our work, we attempt to explore the supply chain coordination in the presence of blockchain adoption.

The supply chain coordination is widely investigated in literature. As it is well-known that the wholesale price contracts cannot coordinate the traditional supply chain, we discuss whether the platform has stronger incentive to adopt blockchain under different contracts. For a comprehensive review of coordination under supply chain contracts, please refer to Cachon (2003) for details. In our work, we examine the impact of the blockchain adoption on the cost/revenue sharing contract (Cachon and Lariviere, 2005), the two-part tariff and profit-sharing contracts (Wei and Choi, 2010; Shi *et al.*, 2020), which are all prevalent contracts. We have shown that in the presence of blockchain, contracts that have been commonly adopted cannot always achieve supply chain coordination.

2. Modeling

Consider a brand (he) manages and satisfies the local demand himself at a retail price p_l in the domestic market. Note that the domestic demand is composed of domestic consumers, who buy product for themselves, and purchasing agents, who resell the product to the overseas market at a price p_a per unit, where $p_a = p_l + m$ and m represents the profit margin or so called premium earned by the agent. Based on the observations in the real world, the value of m is relatively low because agents usually get benefits from alternative sourcing such as tax incentives. If there is no alternative channel to choose, overseas consumers have to buy products from the agents. As some of the purchasing agents have incentives to sell copycat products for extravagant profits, it hurts the brand's reputation in the overseas market. We consider two types of purchasing agents, namely credible and unreliable, to capture this feature in the market. Without loss of generality, the credible agents, who take the proportion α of the total number, always order from the brand and sell genuine products, where $\alpha \in [0, 1]$. The rest of them (i.e., $1 - \alpha$) are unreliable agents, who sell copycat only and make no contribution to the brand. The brand (consumer) cannot detect the consumers' (agents') type from their purchasing (selling) behaviors (Autrey *et al.*, 2014; Wang *et al.*, 2020).

For easy reference, the notation used in the basic model is listed in Table 1. In order to investigate the brand's overseas marketing strategy, we study a setting, under which the brand sells through an additional international online platform (she). We assume that the brand is a leader and the platform is a follower in the supply chain. This power structure has been implemented by famous brands such as Louis Vuitton (LV). Initially, the two firms' relationship is governed by a wholesale price contract, under which the platform orders a product at a wholesale price w and sells it to the overseas market at a retail price p_o. We assume that $p_o \geq p_l$. In order to focus on the relationship between the brand and platform and the selling issues in the overseas market, we assume the retail price in the domestic market

Table 1. Summary of notation.

Notation	Meaning
p_l	Brand's retail price in the domestic market
w	Wholesale price
p_a	Agents' selling price in the overseas market
p_o	Platform's selling price in the overseas market
α	The proportion of the credible agents who make contribution to the brand
m	The agents profit margin
v	Consumer's initial valuation of the product
δ_o	Valuation discount by purchasing from the platform
δ_a	Valuation discount by purchasing from the agents
T_b	The fixed cost of blockchain adoption
π_o	The platform's profit
π_b	The brand's profit
CS	Consumer surplus

(i.e., p_l) is exogenous and the agents' profit margin (m) is zero first, but consider a endogenous domestic retail price and a positive profit margin for the agents as an extension. Focused on the operations of the brand and platform in the overseas market, we omit the domestic demand for simplification. An overseas consumer can exclusively buy a product from either the purchasing agent or the platform.

2.1. *Without blockchain*

We normalize the market size to 1 and assume that an overseas consumer weighs the retail price and product valuation before making purchase decisions. We use a random variable v, which is uniformly distributed (i.e., $v \sim$ Unif(0,1)), to capture the consumer's heterogeneous initial valuation of the product. Facing uncertainties, such as quality and copycat issues due to sourcing from unreliable firms, an overseas consumer undertakes the risk by purchasing from both parties and thus perceives a discounted valuation (Yoo and Lee, 2011). We denote the consumer's discounted valuation as $\delta_a v$ and $\delta_o v$, when purchasing from the agent and platform, respectively. Being aware of the existence of unreliable agents, consumers usually bear more risk to purchase from agents on behalf of themselves. Therefore, we assume that $0 < \delta_a < \delta_o < 1$. The utilities of purchasing from the agent and platform are, $u_a(v) = \delta_a v - p_a$ and $u_o(v) = \delta_o v - p_o$, respectively. The consumer buys a product based on the comparison of u_a and u_o when receiving a non-negative utility. Then, the demands to the agents and platform without blockchain are $D_a = \text{Prob}\{u_a(v) \geq u_o^+(v)\}$ and $D_o = \text{Prob}\{u_o(v) \geq u_a^+(v)\}$, respectively.

With the above assumptions and description of demand, we have the profit functions for the brand and online platform without blockchain as follows:

- The brand's profit function is

$$\pi_b^N(w) = wD_o^N + \alpha p_l D_a^N. \tag{1}$$

- The online platform's profit function is

$$\pi_o^N(p_o) = (p_o - w)D_o^N. \tag{2}$$

Acting as the leader, the brand moves first and decides the wholesale price to maximize his profit. It is followed by the online platform determines the overseas retail price in response to the given wholesale price.

2.2. *With blockchain*

In order to win the consumers' trust, some online platforms, such as Amazon, Tmall.com and JD.com, adopt blockchain technology to show the procurement traceability and anti-counterfeiting features. After reviewing the product information about source of procurement, customs clearance and warehouse logistics, the consumers' purchasing uncertainty is completely released with the platform's blockchain adoption (i.e., $\delta_o = 1$). Then, the utility and demand of purchasing from the platform with blockchain become, $\bar{u}_o(v) = v - p_o$ and $\bar{D}_o = \text{Prob}\{\bar{u}_o(v) \geq u_a^+(v)\}$, respectively. Accordingly, the demand to the agents is denoted as D_a^B with blockchain, where $D_a^B = \text{Prob}\{u_a^+(v) \geq \bar{u}_o(v)\}$. Note that the blockchain is not a free lunch. A fixed cost T_b is incurred for system setup, maintenance and server hosting.

After blockchain adoption, the profit functions of the brand and online platform are given in the following, respectively:

- The brand's profit function is

$$\pi_b^B(w) = wD_o^B + \alpha p_l D_a^B. \tag{3}$$

- The online platform's profit function is

$$\pi_o^B(p_o) = (p_o - w)D_o^B - T_b. \tag{4}$$

The operations decision sequence is as the same as that in the absence of blockchain.

3. Analyses

We solve the problem from backward. For a notational purpose, we denote the gap of discount factors between purchasing from the platform and agent as $\Delta\delta = \delta_o - \delta_a$. Especially, $\Delta\delta = 1 - \delta_a$ with blockchain. As the profit functions in the absence and presence of blockchain are concave, we can derive the optimal retail and wholesale prices by solving the respective first order conditions. The optimal decisions and related performances are summarized in Lemma 1.

Lemma 1. *The optimal decisions and profits with and without blockchain are listed in Table 2. The blockchain adoption increases both the optimal retail price and wholesale price at the same time (i.e., $p_o^B > p_o^N$ and $w^B > w^N$).*

One important result from Lemma 1 is that the adoption of blockchain increases the optimal retail and wholesale prices simultaneously. One reason supporting this finding is the fact that the consumers' product uncertainty is released by the traceability and visibility due to the blockchain adoption. It implies that the consumers

Table 2. Optimal decisions and profits with and without blockchain.

	Without blockchain	With blockchain
Optimal retail price	$p_o^N = \frac{3}{4}\Delta\delta + \frac{3+\alpha}{4}p_l$	$p_o^B = \frac{3}{4}(1-\delta_a) + \frac{3+\alpha}{4}p_l$
Optimal wholesale price	$w^N = \frac{1}{2}\Delta\delta + \frac{1+\alpha}{2}p_l$	$w^B = \frac{1}{2}(1-\delta_a) + \frac{1+\alpha}{2}p_l$
Optimal profit of the platform	$\Pi_o^N = \frac{1}{16}\Delta\delta(1 + \frac{1-\alpha}{\Delta\delta}p_l)^2$	$\Pi_o^B = \frac{1}{16}(1-\delta_a)(1 + \frac{1-\alpha}{1-\delta_a}p_l)^2 - T_b$
Optimal profit of the brand	$\Pi_b^N = \frac{1}{8}\Delta\delta(1 + \frac{1-\alpha}{\Delta\delta}p_l)^2 + \alpha p_l - \frac{\alpha p_l^2}{\delta_a}$	$\Pi_b^B = \frac{1}{8}(1-\delta_a)(1 + \frac{1-\alpha}{1-\delta_a}p_l)^2 + \alpha p_l - \frac{\alpha p_l^2}{\delta_a}$

essentially undertake a part of the blockchain adoption cost to reduce their uncertainty about the purchasing risk. In addition, this result also hints that the double marginalization amplifies after adopting the blockchain technology. Next, we will investigate the platform's incentive to adopt blockchain and measure the value of blockchain from the perspectives of the brand, consumers and supply chain.

From Table 2, we can measure the value of blockchain for the brand and platform by comparing the optimal profits under cases with and without blockchain. We define $\Delta\Pi_b^{\mathrm{BN}} = \Pi_b^B - \Pi_b^N$ and $\Delta\Pi_o^{\mathrm{BN}} = \Pi_o^B - \Pi_o^N$ to represent the values of blockchain for the brand and online platform, respectively. Based on Table 2, we can easily show the expressions of $\Delta\Pi_b^{\mathrm{BN}}$ and $\Delta\Pi_o^{\mathrm{BN}}$ as follows:

$$\Delta\Pi_b^{\mathrm{BN}} = \frac{(1-\delta_o)B}{8}, \tag{5}$$

$$\Delta\Pi_o^{\mathrm{BN}} = \frac{(1-\delta_o)B}{16} - T_b, \tag{6}$$

where $B = 1 - \frac{(1-\alpha)^2 p_l^2}{(1-\delta_a)(\delta_o-\delta_a)}$.

Next, we check the impact of blockchain on the consumers by conducting analysis on consumer surplus under cases with and without blockchain adoption. We define CS^N and CS^B as the consumer surplus without/with blockchain as follows:

$$\begin{aligned} \mathrm{CS}^N &= \int_{\frac{p_l}{\delta_a}}^{\frac{p_o^N - p_l}{\Delta\delta}} (\delta_a v - p_l)dv + \int_{\frac{p_o^N - p_l}{\Delta\delta}}^{1} (\delta_o v - p_o^N)dv, \\ \mathrm{CS}^B &= \int_{\frac{p_l}{\delta_a}}^{\frac{p_o^B - p_l}{1-\delta_a}} (\delta_a v - p_a)dv + \int_{\frac{p_o^B - p_l}{1-\delta_a}}^{1} (v - p_o^B)dv. \end{aligned} \tag{7}$$

Comparing between the cases with and without blockchain, we can derive the value of blockchain from the consumers' perspective. Define $\Delta\mathrm{CS}^{\mathrm{BN}} = \mathrm{CS}^B - \mathrm{CS}^N$ to capture the impact of blockchain adoption on the consumer surplus, we have

$$\Delta\mathrm{CS}^{\mathrm{BN}} = \frac{1}{32}(1-\delta_o)B - \frac{9}{16}(1-\alpha)p_l. \tag{8}$$

From Eqs. (5), (6) and (8), the values of blockchain for the brand, online platform and consumer surplus depend on the critical parameter B. We have the following proposition as a preliminary for measuring the values of blockchain.

Proposition 1. *When* $\delta_o < \delta_a + \frac{(1-\alpha)^2 p_l^2}{1-\delta_a}$, (a) *the online platform has no incentive to adopt blockchain, even if it is costless* (*i.e.*, $T_b = 0$), (b) *the values of blockchain are negative to the brand and consumers.*

Proposition 1 is important and anti-intuitive. It spotlights the condition, under which adopting blockchain hurts the brand, platform and consumers at the same time. Interestingly, when the valuation discount to consumers by purchasing from the platform without blockchain is low (i.e., $\delta_o < \delta_a + \frac{(1-\alpha)^2 p_l^2}{1-\delta_a}$ or equivalently

$B < 0$), the platform prefers to not adopt blockchain to release consumers' purchasing uncertainties, even if it costs nothing. Under the same condition, both the brand and consumers dislike the blockchain adoption. The paradox results can be explained by the double marginalization of the supply chain. When the valuation discount by purchasing from online platform is relatively large (i.e., $\delta_o \geq \delta_a + \frac{(1-\alpha)^2 p_l^2}{1-\delta_a}$), adopting blockchain technology benefits the platform and brand by reducing consumers' worry about copycat issues. On the contrary, when the valuation discount is sufficiently low, the retail price and wholesale price increase, because the blockchain adoption aggravates double marginalization, which reduces the demand and overwhelms the benefit from releasing consumers' purchasing uncertainty eventually.

In addition, the condition in Proposition 1 is more likely to be satisfied, if δ_a and p_l increase. It implies that adopting blockchain is more likely to hurt the brand, platform and consumers with relatively large δ_a and high p_l. Moreover, as the proportion of credible agents (i.e., α) increases, it blunts the incentive of adopting blockchain as well. It shows that when a high proportion of agents are credible, both the brand and consumers have no need for the anti-counterfeit technology provided by blockchain adoption. Then, the platform has no incentive to adopt blockchain technology, even if it is costless.

Next, we investigate when the online platform has incentive to adopt blockchain and related impacts on the brand and consumers, on the premise of the existence of potential value by doing so (i.e., $B \geq 0$). We have the following proposition.

Proposition 2. *When* $B \geq 0$, (a) *the online platform has incentive to adopt blockchain, if and only if* $B \geq \frac{16T_b}{(1-\delta_o)}$; (b) *the brand always gets benefits from the blockchain adoption*; (c) *the consumers get benefits from blockchain if and only if* $B \geq \frac{18(1-\alpha)p_l}{1-\delta_a}$.

Proposition 2 implies that as long as the fixed cost of blockchain adoption is not too high, the platform has incentive to adopt this technology, which always benefits the brand. In addition, the consumers start to gain benefits from the blockchain adoption when the value of B is large enough. Proposition 2 is very important, as it shows that an all-win situation is achieved with blockchain adoption, when $B \geq \max\{\frac{16T_b}{1-\delta_o}, \frac{18(1-\alpha)p_l}{1-\delta_a}\}$. From the first part of Proposition 2, the condition that spurs the platform to adopt blockchain is more likely to hold, as α and T_b decrease or p_l increases. It implies that in order to pursue the consumers' trust and advantages in price competition, the online platform has a strong incentive to adopt blockchain, when only a small proportion of the agents are credible or the local retail price is high enough. This result well explains the observation in the real world. As suspected counterfeit or copycat goods are often detected in maquillage and fashion industries, the retail price of which is usually high, platforms, such as JD.Com and Kaola.com, invest in blockchain technology for these products with priority.

Then, we establish and compare the values of blockchain for the platform, brand and consumers in the following corollary. Note that the comparison is conducted based on the assumption that the all-win situation is achieved (i.e., $B \geq \max\{\frac{16T_b}{1-\delta_o}, \frac{18(1-\alpha)p_l}{1-\delta_a}\}$), otherwise, the result is trivial as blockchain hurts one or two members in the supply chain.

Corollary 1. *When the all-win situation is achieved,* (a) $\Delta\Pi_B^{\mathrm{BN}} > \Delta\mathrm{CS}^{\mathrm{BN}} > \Delta\Pi_o^{\mathrm{BN}} > 0$, *if* $\frac{(1-\delta_o)B}{16} \geq T_b > \frac{(1-\delta_o)B}{32} + \frac{9(1-\alpha)p_l}{16}$; (b) $\Delta\Pi_B^{\mathrm{BN}} > \Delta\Pi_o^{\mathrm{BN}} > \Delta\mathrm{CS}^{\mathrm{BN}} > 0$, *if* $T_b \leq \frac{(1-\delta_o)B}{32} + \frac{9(1-\alpha)p_l}{16}$.

Corollary 1 shows that the brand seizes the most of benefit from blockchain adoption, as it costs nothing to him. For the consumers, though Lemma 1 implies that they have to pay more in the presence of blockchain, the adoption of this technology still benefits them by improving the consumer surplus, when B, which increases in δ_o, is sufficiently large. In line with the industrial observations, the fixed cost of blockchain adoption, which is usually substantial, plays an important role in the comparison. When the cost of blockchain adoption is sufficiently high, the online platform obtains the least value by blockchain adoption among the three parties. From Propositions 1 and Corollary 1, adopting blockchain aggravates the double marginalization and the platform may gain the least benefit from doing so. The results drive us to investigate the supply chain coordination with the consideration of blockchain issues.

4. Supply Chain Coordination with Blockchain Adoption

In the previous sections, we have focused on a decentralized supply chain with/without blockchain adoption. In this section, we analyze a centralized supply chain, where the brand and online platform act as central planner, who decides the retail price in the overseas market only. We use superscript C to indicate the centralized scenario. The total supply chain profit is

$$\pi_{\mathrm{sc}} = p_o D_o^C + \alpha p_l D_a^C - T_b. \tag{9}$$

The optimal retail price and system profit are summarized in the following lemma.

Lemma 2. *In a centralized supply chain with blockchain adoption, the optimal retail price is* $p_o^C = \frac{1-\delta_a+(1+\alpha)p_l}{2}$ *and the optimal total profit of the supply chain is* $\Pi_{\mathrm{sc}}^C = \frac{(1-\delta_a)}{4}(1 + \frac{(1-\alpha)p_l}{1-\delta_a})^2 + \alpha p_l - \frac{\alpha p_l^2}{\delta_a} - T_b$.

Next, we compare the performances between the decentralized and centralized scenarios from the perspective of supply chain. Denote the total profit of the supply chain in the decentralized case with blockchain adoption as Π_{sc}^B. After comparing Π_{sc}^B and Π_{sc}^C, we have the following proposition.

Proposition 3. *The total supply chain profit in the centralized supply chain is greater than in the decentralized one with blockchain adoption (i.e.,* $\Pi_{\mathrm{sc}}^C > \Pi_{\mathrm{sc}}^B$*).*

From Proposition 3, it is valuable to further explore the supply chain coordination under different contracts. Next, we investigate cost sharing (CS), revenue sharing (RS), two-part tariff (TT) and profit sharing (PS) contracts to examine which one can achieve coordination. Note that all the contracts are widely observed in the industry and discussed by literature.

Under the cost sharing contract, the fixed cost for blockchain adoption is shared by the brand and platform. We assume that the brand shares with a proportion θ and the platform undertakes the rest of fixed cost $(1-\theta)T_b$, where $\theta \in [0,1]$. The profit functions of the brand and platform are presented as follows:

- The brand's profit function under a cost sharing contract is
$$\pi_b^{\text{CS}} = wD_o^B + \alpha p_l D_a^B - \theta T_b. \tag{10}$$
- The platform's profit function under a cost sharing contract is
$$\pi_o^{\text{CS}} = p_o D_o^B - wD_o^B - (1-\theta)T_b. \tag{11}$$

After checking the supply chain coordination under the cost sharing contract, we have the following proposition.

Proposition 4. *The supply chain with blockchain adoption fails to be coordinated under the cost sharing contract.*

This result is rather counter-intuitive, as we expect that cost sharing will strengthen the platform's incentive to adopt blockchain technology, which benefit the brand by reducing the overseas consumers' purchasing uncertainty. However, we find that the brand has to drop the wholesale price and bear a part of the fixed cost of blockchain adoption under this contract. The reduced profit margin and shared fixed cost may dominate the increase of overseas demand, which blunts the domestic demand as consumers switch from the purchasing agent to the online platform. As a result, the brand's profit is hurt by the cost sharing contract in the presence of blockchain.

Under the revenue sharing contract, we denote the revenue sharing portion as γ, where $\gamma \in [0,1]$. The revenue obtained from selling to the overseas market directly is shared by the brand and platform with proportions γ and $1-\gamma$, respectively. Then, the profit functions of the brand and platform are given in the follows:

- The brand's profit function under a revenue sharing contract is
$$\pi_b^{\text{RS}} = wD_o^B + \gamma p_o D_o^B + \alpha p_l D_a^B. \tag{12}$$
- The platform's profit function under a revenue sharing contract is
$$\pi_o^{\text{RS}} = (1-\gamma)p_o D_o^B - wD_o^B - T_b. \tag{13}$$

Regarding the supply chain coordination with blockchain adoption under RS contract, we obtain the following proposition.

Proposition 5. *Under a revenue sharing contract, the supply chain coordination can be achieved with the revenue sharing portion, retail price and wholesale price satisfy:* $\gamma^{\text{RS}} = \frac{3}{4}$, $p_o^{\text{RS}} = \frac{1-\delta_a}{2} + \frac{1+\alpha}{2}p_l$ *and* $w^{\text{RS}} = \frac{1}{4}\alpha p_l$.

This proposition indicates that a RS contract can coordinate the supply chain and achieve the Pareto improvement. Under this contract, both the brand and platform are able to increase profit in the presence of blockchain than that without signing this contract. Note that the brand has to reduce the wholesale price under this contract (i.e., $w^{\mathrm{RS}} < w^B$), at the same time, the platform drops the retail price (i.e., $p_o^{\mathrm{RS}} < p_o^B$), which drives more consumers to purchase without worrying about the copycat. Then, the incremental demand dominates the loss of profit margin and the revenue sharing scheme guarantees both firms' profit improvement as a result.

Under the two-part tariff contract, the platform has to pay a lump-sum payment F to the brand, besides the wholesale price. For TT, the profit functions of the brand and platform become as follows:

- The brand's profit function under a two-part tariff contract is

$$\pi_b^{\mathrm{TT}}(w) = wD_o^B + \alpha p_l D_a^B + F. \tag{14}$$

- The platform's profit function under a two-part tariff contract is

$$\pi_o^{\mathrm{TT}}(p_o) = (p_o - w)D_o^B - T_b - F. \tag{15}$$

Regarding the supply chain coordination under TT contract in the presence of blockchain, we obtain the following proposition.

Proposition 6. *Under a two-part tariff contract, the supply chain coordination can be achieved with the lump-sum payment, retail price and wholesale price satisfy:* $F^{\mathrm{TT}} = \frac{3}{16}(1-\delta_a)(1+\frac{1-\alpha}{1-\delta_a}p_l)^2$, $p_o^{\mathrm{TT}} = \frac{1-\delta_a}{2} + \frac{1+\alpha}{2}p_l$ *and* $w^{\mathrm{TT}} = \alpha p_l$.

Proposition 6 indicates that a two-part tariff contract can still coordinate the supply chain after adopting blockchain technology. Under this contract, the platform enjoys a lower wholesale price (i.e., $w^{\mathrm{TT}} < w^B$) and yields some profit margin by reducing the retail price $p_o^{\mathrm{TT}} < p_o^B$. However, the benefit of coordination is completely grabbed by the brand who acts as a leader and gains all the extra profit from the supply chain coordination by charging the lump-sum payment.

Under the profit-sharing contract, we consider a profit sharing portion ϕ. As the total supply chain profit with blockchain adoption is Π_{sc}^C, the brand gains ϕ of it and the platform obtains the remaining. The profit functions of the brand and platform are as follows:

- The brand's profit function under a profit-sharing contract is

$$\pi_b^{\mathrm{PS}} = \phi(p_o D_o^B + \alpha p_l D_a^B - T_b). \tag{16}$$

- The platform's profit function under a profit-sharing contract is

$$\pi_o^{\mathrm{PS}} = (1-\phi)(p_o D_o^B + \alpha p_l D_a^B - T_b). \tag{17}$$

We check the coordination of the supply chain under the PS contract in the following proposition.

Proposition 7. *A profit-sharing contract can achieve coordination of the supply chain, if and only if* $T_b < \frac{1}{16}(1-\delta_a)(1+\frac{1-\alpha}{1-\delta_a}p_l)^2$, *with a profit sharing portion* $\phi = \frac{\frac{3}{16}(1-\delta_a)(1+\frac{1-\alpha}{1-\delta_a}p_l)^2+\alpha p_l-\frac{\alpha}{\delta_a}p_l^2}{\frac{1}{4}(1-\delta_a)(1+\frac{1-\alpha}{1-\delta_a}p_l)^2+\alpha p_l-\frac{\alpha}{\delta_a}p_l^2-T_b}$.

As a special combination of revenue sharing and cost sharing contacts, the profit sharing contract can achieve coordination when the fixed cost of blockchain adoption is relatively low, which guarantees that the profit sharing portion locates in a reasonable range. When the fixed cost of blockchain exceeds the threshold in Proposition 7, the brand has no incentive to share the cost under this contract.

5. Extended Studies

In this section, we extend our baseline model by considering the following issues: endogenous retail price in the domestic market, the value of purchasing agents and partial information disclosure in the presence of blockchain. We would like to check the robustness of our results and discuss new managerial insights.

5.1. *Endogenous retail price in the domestic market*

In the basic model, we assume that the domestic retail price is given and the purchasing agents do not charge premium. In this section, we assume that the brand decides the local retail price to maximize his profit with positive premium m, which is exogenously given by the agent. Then, the retail price to a consumer who purchases from the agent becomes: $p_a = p_l + m$.

Firstly, we investigate the optimal pricing decision in the scenario without blockchain. After adopting all the optimal decisions without blockchain, given the local retail price p_l, the brand's profit becomes

$$\Pi_b^N(p_l) = \frac{\alpha^2 p_l^2}{8\Delta\delta} + \left(\frac{3\Delta\delta - p_a}{4\Delta\delta} - \frac{p_a}{\delta_a}\right)\alpha p_l + \frac{(\Delta\delta + p_a)^2}{8\Delta\delta}. \tag{18}$$

We denote the optimal retail price in the local market as p_l^N and have the following lemma.

Lemma 3. *The brand's optimal retail price in the local is*

$$p_l^N = \begin{cases} \dfrac{3(\delta_o - \delta_a + m)}{1-\alpha} & \text{if } m > \dfrac{3\Delta\delta\delta_a}{4\delta_o - 3\delta_a}; \\ \min\{\bar{p}_l^N, p_l^{N*}\} & \text{otherwise,} \end{cases}$$

where $\bar{p}_l^N = \frac{3m\delta_a + 3\Delta\delta\delta_a - 4m\delta_o}{4\delta_o - (3+\alpha)\delta_a}$, $p_l^{N*} = \frac{m[4\alpha\delta_o - (1+3\alpha)\delta_a] - (1+3\alpha)\Delta\delta\delta_a}{(1-\alpha)^2\delta_a - 8\alpha\Delta\delta}$.

Lemma 3 implies that the brand raises the price, which equals to the platform's retail price in the overseas market, to stop serving overseas consumers through agents, when the consumers' valuation discount by purchasing from agents is sufficiently low and the agent's profit margin is sufficiently high, Note that this condition is more likely to hold as δ_o decreases. This is because under the two conditions, the consumers have strong incentive to switch from the agent to the platform. Then, the brand prefers to let the platform be a monopoly in the overseas market. Otherwise, the brand will set the local price to the global optimal level, which decreases in the agent's profit margin m.

Next, we derive the brand's optimal domestic retail price in the presence of blockchain adoption. As the valuation uncertainty is completely released by purchasing from the platform in this case, the brand's profit function becomes

$$\Pi_b^B(p_l) = \frac{\alpha^2 p_l^2}{8(1-\delta_a)} + \left(\frac{3(1-\delta_a)-p_a}{4(1-\delta_a)} - \frac{p_a}{\delta_a}\right)\alpha p_l + \frac{(1-\delta_a+p_a)^2}{8(1-\delta_a)}. \tag{19}$$

Denoting the optimal retail price in the domestic market as p_l^B, we have the following lemma.

Lemma 4. *The brand's optimal retail price in the local is*

$$p_l^B = \begin{cases} \dfrac{3(1-\delta_a+m)}{1-\alpha} & \textit{if } m > \dfrac{3(1-\delta_a)\delta_a}{4-3\delta_a}; \\ \min\{\bar{p}_l^B, p_l^{B*}\} & \textit{otherwise,} \end{cases}$$

where $\bar{p}_l^B = \frac{3m\delta_a+3(1-\delta_a)\delta_a-4m}{4-(3+\alpha)\delta_a}$, $p_l^{B*} = \frac{m[4\alpha-(1+3\alpha)\delta_a]-(1+3\alpha)(1-\delta_a)\delta_a}{(1-\alpha)^2\delta_a-8\alpha(1-\delta_a)}$.

The managerial insights are similar to that in the case without blockchain. Note that the valuation discount (i.e., δ_a) and premium (i.e., m) from purchasing agents play important roles in the brand's optimal domestic retail price decision. Then, we conduct a numerical analysis to further illustrate the impact of δ_a on the optimal domestic price and performances from the perspectives of the brand, platform and consumers. In order to illustrate the difference between cases with exogenous and endogenous local retail prices, we also demonstrate the scenario with and without blockchain with an exogenous p_l as a benchmark.

For the values of parameters, we set $\alpha = 0.5$, $\delta_o = 0.8$, $m = 0.02$ and $T_b = 0.064$. In the case where the local retail price is exogenous, we let $p_l = 0.1$. As the valuation discount δ_a is a key parameter in this problem, we change it from 0 to 0.75. This setting well satisfies all the assumptions in our model.

First, we focus on the cases with and without blockchain adoption with endogenous local price. Figure 1 confirms that when the value of δ_a is relatively small, no one purchases from the agents due to a high domestic retail price. As δ_a increases, a consumer's incentive of purchasing from agents is getting strong. Then, the brand prefers to sell through the agents to obtain more demand by dropping the local retail price in the absence of blockchain. Unfortunately, the unreliable agents make no contribution to the brand and seize overseas demand from the platform and credible agents. As a result, the profit gaps between cases with and without blockchain adoption amplify for both firms, when the value of δ_a becomes sufficiently large. This amplification is strengthened by the impact of δ_a on local prices. It is interesting to observe that when δ_a is sufficiently large, the brand adopts a low local price

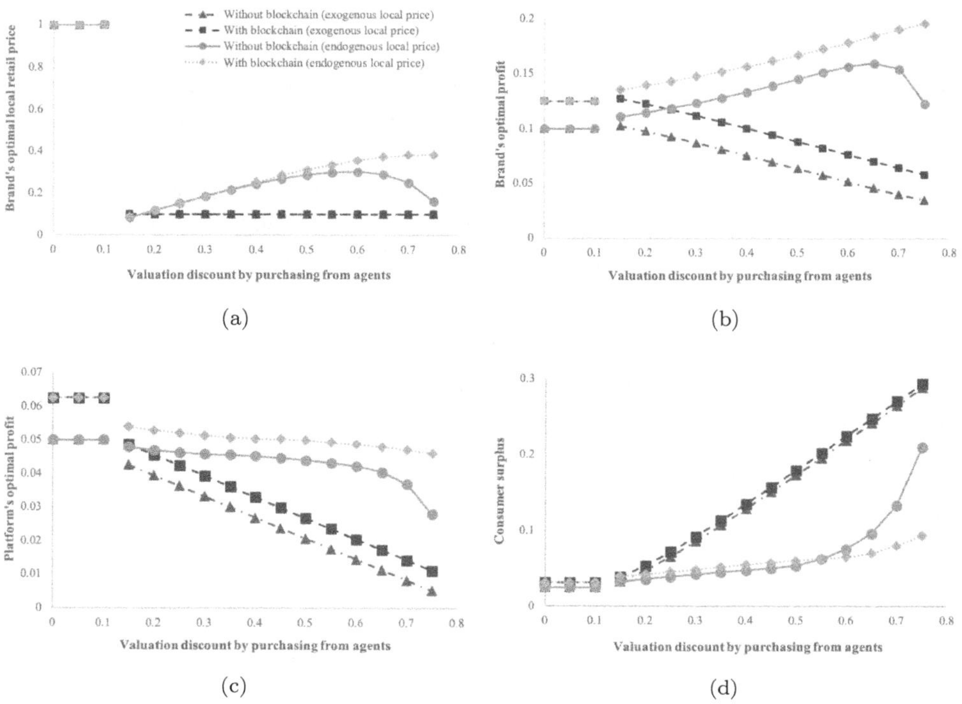

Fig. 1. Impact of δ_a with/without blockchain on (a) the optimal domestic price, (b) the brand's optimal profit, (c) the platform's optimal profit and (d) the consumer surplus in exogenous and endogenous local price cases.

to attract more demand to purchase from agents without blockchain adoption. This low local price policy in the absence of blockchain reduces the profits of both the brand and platform significantly. As a result, the value of blockchain increases in δ_a for both the brand and platform. A win–win situation is achieved for the brand and platform, after the adoption of blockchain with endogenous local retail price. However, an all-win situation is only available when the value of δ_a is relatively small, the consumer surplus is hurt by blockchain otherwise. This observation is reported by Fig. 1. Figure 1(a) implies that the brand always charges a higher local price with blockchain adoption compared with that in the absence of blockchain and the gap increases in δ_a. It is natural that the high retail price hurts the consumer surplus with blockchain.

In addition, Fig. 1 also shows the impact of endogenous local price on the firms' profits and consumer surplus. It hints that both firms' profits improve while the consumer surplus is hurt after adopting the endogenous local price with/without blockchain, respectively. Figure 1(b) further demonstrates the joint effect of endogenous local price and blockchain adoption for the brand. When δ_a is relatively large, the endogenous price benefits the brand more even in the absence of the blockchain adoption.

5.2. *The value of purchasing agents*

Previous analysis is based on the assumption that the purchasing agents always exist in the market. In this section, we investigate what will happen if the brand has an option to drive the agents out of the market by adjusting the domestic price. Based on the results in Sec. 5.1, the purchasing agents will leave, when the brand sets a sufficiently high retail price in the domestic market. Then, the profits of the brand and platform without/with blockchain adoption can be easily obtained by letting the agents' demand be $D_a = 0$. In addition, the optimal profits of the brand and platform without agent and blockchain are $\Pi_o^{N,A} = \frac{\delta_o}{16}$ and $\Pi_b^{N,A} = \frac{\delta_o}{8}$, respectively. By letting $\delta_o = 1$, the optimal profits for the brand and platform in the presence of blockchain, which are denoted as $\Pi_o^{B,A}$ and $\Pi_b^{B,A}$, can be obtained, respectively. Next, we conduct the numerical analysis to investigate the value of purchasing agents by illustrating the performances of the brand and platform with/without blockchain adoption, respectively.

For the values of parameters, we set $\alpha = 0.5$, $\delta_a = 0.2$ and $m = 0.15$. As the valuation discount δ_o plays an important role in this problem, we change δ_o from 0.3 to 1. This setting still satisfies the assumptions in our model. We compare the profits under scenarios with/without purchasing agents in the presence/absence of blockchain adoption for both the brand and platform, respectively.

Figure 2 demonstrates the joint effects of the blockchain and agent on the profits of the brand and platform, respectively. Figure 2(a) shows that the existence of purchasing agents hurts the brand in the absence of blockchain when δ_o is relatively low. It implies that when consumers have serious concerns about the copycat issues of the online platform, the brand has to depend on the agents to reach the overseas market. As a result, the brand's profit is hurt by the unreliable agents. Otherwise, the existence of agents benefits the brand with/without blockchain adoption. The value of agents originates from two aspects. Acting as a rival of the platform, the existence of agents make the platform keep a relatively low and competitive

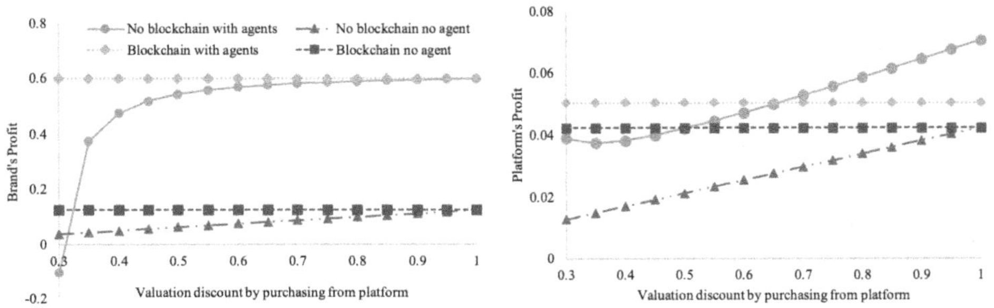

(a) (b)

Fig. 2. Joint effects of the blockchain and agent on (a) the brand's profit and (b) the platform's profit.

retail price, which spurs the overseas demand and benefits the brand eventually. In addition, the brand profits from the existence of purchasing agents who serve the price-sensitive consumers in the overseas market, even if some revenue is lost due to copycat issues.

Figure 2(b) also provides some interesting insights for the platform. Her competitors, the purchasing agents, improve her profit with/without blockchain adoption. This is because the existence of unreliable agents strengthens the brand's incentive to sell product through the platform by dropping the wholesale price. Moreover, when the valuation discount δ_o is relatively small, the platform prefers to adopt the blockchain and becomes the monopoly in the overseas market. On the contrary, the platform would rather to compete with the agents than adopting the blockchain, when δ_o is relatively large. This result implies that the purchasing agents and blockchain adoption are substitutes in attracting overseas consumers.

5.3. *Partial information disclosure*

In the real world, it is not always necessary for platforms to link all the information nodes to blockchain. For instance, KaoLa.com owned by Alibaba Group only links the customs clearance, logistic and transportation information to the blockchain. Since the sourcing information is not available from the blockchain, consumers still face risk, such as the copycat issues, from platform purchasing. To capture this feature, we consider $\bar{\delta}_o$ as the valuation discount, after the platform linking partial information to blockchain, where $\delta_o \leq \bar{\delta}_o \leq 1$. We also assume that the fixed cost for blockchain adoption, defined as $C(\bar{\delta}_o)$, is convex increasing in information disclosure $\bar{\delta}_o$. Here, we define $C(\bar{\delta}_o) = T_b\bar{\delta}_o^2$, where T_b is the cost coefficient, which is substantial and $T_b > \frac{(1-\alpha)^2 p_l^2}{(\bar{\delta}_o - \delta_a)^3}$.

Replacing δ_o with $\bar{\delta}_o$ in our model, the platform's profit with blockchain adoption becomes: $\Pi_o^B(\bar{\delta}_o) = \frac{1}{16}(\bar{\delta}_o - \delta_a)(1 + \frac{1-\alpha}{(\bar{\delta}_o - \delta_a)}p_l)^2 - T_b\bar{\delta}_o^2$. We can easily show that the platform's profit is concave in $\bar{\delta}_o$, which represents the number of information nodes linked to the blockchain by the platform. We have the following lemma.

Lemma 5. *An optimal number of information nodes denoted as $\bar{\delta}_o^*$ that satisfying $(1 - 32T_b\bar{\delta}_o^*)(\bar{\delta}_o^* - \delta_a)^2 = (1-\alpha)^2 p_l^2$ should be linked to blockchain.*

To investigate the platform's information disclosure problem vividly, we let $T_b = 0.8$, $\delta_o = 0.5$ and change $\bar{\delta}_o$ from 0.5 to 1. Viewing the scenario without blockchain as a benchmark, it is not always optimal for the platform to link all the information nodes to blockchain from Fig. 3, due to the substantial cost.

Adopting Lemma 5, we vary the value of δ_a from 0.15 to 0.45 and search the optimal amount of information disclosure first. Then, we check the profits of the brand and platform with/without blockchain in Fig. 4, when the platform has an option to decide the number of information nodes linked to blockchain.

Figure 4(a) shows that the value of blockchain is not very straightforward for the brand, when the platform links only some of information nodes to blockchain. When

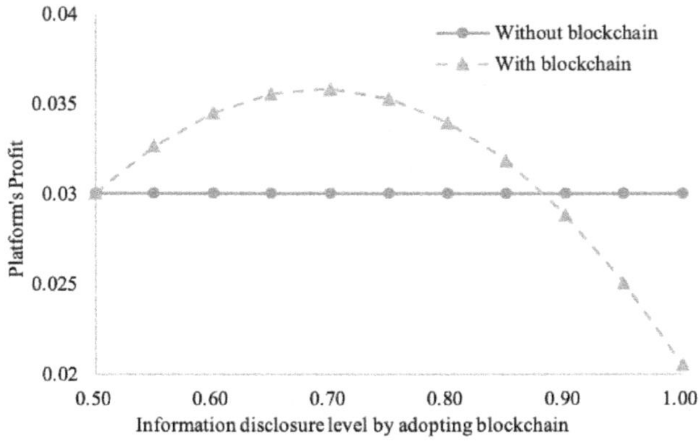

Fig. 3. The impact of information disclosure decision on the platform's profit.

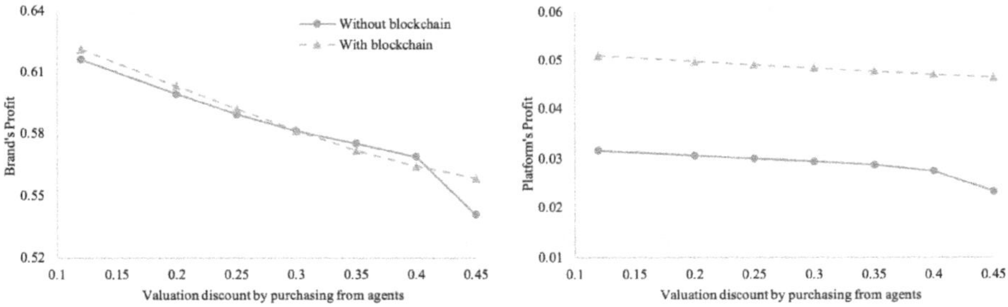

(a) (b)

Fig. 4. Impact of δ_a on (a) the brand's profit and (b) the platform's profit with information linking decisions.

δ_a is relatively small, the adoption of blockchain benefits the brand to attract more consumers to purchase with less concerns. As the value of δ_a becomes medium, the brand's profit is higher without blockchain. This is because the impact of blockchain on releasing consumers' uncertainty becomes less significant under this condition. However, when δ_a is sufficiently large, the platform has a stronger incentive to link more information to blockchain. As a result, the value of blockchain amplifies for both the brand and platform from Figs. 4(a) and 4(b).

6. Conclusion

6.1. *Concluding remarks*

Copycat issues have challenged cross-border consumption supported by brands' overseas strategy and online platforms' operations. The existence of purchasing agents, who can be divided into credible and unreliable groups, makes it more difficult for platforms to clarify business ethics and convince consumers with trust. Motivated by the real world challenge associated with the copycats and purchasing agents, we theoretically explore this problem based on a game model along a supply chain. We spotlight on whether the platform should adopt blockchain technology and how to manage it.

In the basic model, in which the platform and brand decide retail and wholesale prices, we have analytically proven that if the valuation discount to consumers by purchasing from platform is substantially low, implementing blockchain hurts the platform, drivers and consumers, even if it is costless. We also show the circumstance, under which all-win situation can be achieved after blockchain adoption.

Since the platform's incentive to adopt blockchain depends on the fixed cost for the adoption of the new technology, we try to investigate whether a cost sharing contract can achieve coordination and strengthen the above mentioned incentive. Unfortunately, the brand's profit drops so significantly that a cost sharing contract fails to achieve supply chain coordination in the presence of blockchain. On the contrary, some other widely adopted contracts, such as revenue sharing contract, two-part tariff contract and profit sharing contract, help the two firms reach coordination.

We also extend our baseline model by considering the following issues: endogenous retail price in the domestic market, the value of purchasing agents and partial information disclosure in the presence of blockchain. After the brand adopting an optimal domestic retail price, we show that blockchain still benefits the brand and platform by reducing consumers' purchasing uncertainty. However, consumer surplus drops due to the blockchain adoption, which raises retail price in the domestic market notably. We also show that the brand profits from the existence of purchasing agents who serve the price-sensitive consumers, even if some revenue is lost due to copycats. Eventually, we explore the value of blockchain when the platform has option to decide how many information nodes to link to blockchain.

6.2. *Future research*

In this study, we focus on the case that a platform is the only one who has incentives to adopt blockchain and gain trust from consumers. Whether the brand also has the motivation to adopt this new technology deserves explorations. For the purchasing agents, we do not consider about their pricing decisions so far. It is interesting to discuss whether the credible agents prefer to use pricing decision as a signal to differentiate themselves from the unreliable agents. These additional motivations for the strategies of brands and agents also represent interesting issues for the supply chain coordination with contract design.

Appendix A. Proofs

Proof of Lemma 1. Based on the assumption that $D_a > 0$, we have $\frac{p_a}{p_o} \leq \frac{\delta_a}{\delta_o}$. Then, after solving the indifferent point of utilities, the demands to the agent and platform without/with blockchain are summarized in Table A.1.

Table A.1. The demands to the agents and platform.

	Without blockchain	With blockchain
D_a	$\frac{p_o-p_a}{\Delta\delta}-\frac{p_a}{\delta_a}$	$\frac{p_o-p_a}{1-\delta_a}-\frac{p_a}{\delta_a}$
D_o	$1-\frac{p_o-p_a}{\Delta\delta}$	$1-\frac{p_o-p_a}{1-\delta_a}$

Next, we search the optimal decisions for the platform and brand without/with blockchain, respectively.

Case 1. Without blockchain.

Substituting the demands in Table A.1 into profit functions (1) and (2), we have $\pi_o^N=(p_o-w)(1-\frac{p_o-p_a}{\Delta\delta}), \pi_b^N=w(1-\frac{p_o-p_a}{\Delta\delta})+\alpha p_l(\frac{p_o-p_a}{\Delta\delta}-\frac{p_a}{\delta_a})$.

First, taking the first and second order derivatives of π_o with respect to p_o, yields the following:

$$\frac{\partial\pi_o^N}{\partial p_o}=\frac{-2}{\Delta\delta}p_o+\frac{p_a}{\Delta\delta}+1,\quad \frac{\partial^2\pi_o^N}{\partial p_o^2}=\frac{-2}{\Delta\delta}<0.$$

Thus, π_o is a concave in p_o. Solving the first-order condition with respect to p_o yields the optimal selling price of platform, given wholesale price w

$$p_o^*(w)=\frac{\Delta\delta+p_a+w}{2}.$$

The brand decides the optimal wholesale price based on the expectation of the platform's best response. After substituting $p_o^*(w)$ into π_b^N, we have

$$\pi_b^N=\frac{-1}{2\Delta\delta}w^2+\left(\frac{1}{2}+\frac{p_a}{2\Delta\delta}+\frac{\alpha p_l}{2\Delta\delta}\right)w+\alpha p_l\left(\frac{1}{2}-\frac{p_a}{2\Delta\delta}-\frac{p_a}{\delta_a}\right).$$

Checking the second-order derivative of π_b^N with respect to w, we have $\frac{\partial^2\pi_b^N}{\partial w^2}=\frac{-1}{\Delta\delta}<0$. Thus, $\pi_b^N(p_o|w)$ is a concave in w.

Based on the assumption that $p_a=p_l$, solving the first-order condition by letting $\frac{\partial\pi_b^N}{\partial w}=0$, we have

$$w^N=\frac{1}{2}\Delta\delta+\frac{1+\alpha}{2}p_l.$$

After simple calculation, we have

$$p_o^N=\frac{3}{4}\Delta\delta+\frac{3+\alpha}{4}p_l.$$

By substituting the optimal decisions into the profits of the platform and brand, respectively, we have

$$\Pi_o^N=\frac{1}{16}\Delta\delta\left(1+\frac{1-\alpha}{\Delta\delta}p_l\right)^2,\quad \Pi_b^N=\frac{1}{8}\Delta\delta\left(1+\frac{1-\alpha}{\Delta\delta}p_l\right)^2+\alpha p_l-\frac{\alpha p_l^2}{\delta_a}.$$

For the searching of optimal decisions in Case 2, it follows from Case 1.

Since $\delta_o \leq 1$, it is easy to find the blockchain adoption increases both the retail price and wholesale price at the same time, i.e., $p^N < p^B$ and $w^N < w^B$. □

Proof of Proposition 1. When $\Delta\Pi_o^{\text{BN}} = \frac{(1-\delta_o)B}{16} - T_b < 0$, the profit gap is negative, and thus the online platform has no incentive to adopt the blockchain. Especially, when $T_b = 0$, $\Delta\Pi_o^{\text{BN}} < 0$ if $B < 0$, which is equivalent to $\delta_o < \delta_a + \frac{(1-\alpha)^2 p_l^2}{1-\delta_a}$. Similarly, when $B < 0$, $\Delta\Pi_b^{\text{BN}} < 0$, $\Delta\Pi_o^{\text{BN}} < 0$ and $\Delta\text{CS}^{\text{BN}} < 0$ hold. Adopting blockchain hurts all parties' profit even the adoption is free (i.e., $T_b = 0$). □

Proof of Proposition 2. When $B > 0$, the online platform has incentive to adopt blockchain only if the profit gap is nonnegative (i.e., $\Delta\Pi_o^{\text{BN}} = \frac{(1-\delta_o)B}{16} - T_b \geq 0$). Then, we have: $T_b \leq \frac{(1-\delta_o)B}{16}$. Based on the definition of consumer surplus, $\Delta\text{CS}^{\text{BN}} = \frac{(1-\delta_o)B}{16} - \frac{9(1-\alpha)p_l}{16} \geq 0$, if and only if $B \geq \frac{18(1-\alpha)p_l}{1-\delta_a}$. □

Proof of Corollary 1. Based on the assumption that $B > 0$, $\Delta\Pi_b^{\text{BN}} - \Delta\Pi_o^{\text{BN}} = \frac{(1-\delta_o)B}{16} + T_b > 0$ and $\Delta\Pi_b^{\text{BN}} - \Delta\text{CS}^{\text{BN}} > 0$ hold naturally. Then, comparing $\Delta\Pi_o^{\text{BN}}$ with $\Delta\text{CS}^{\text{BN}}$, we have

$$\Delta\text{CS}^{\text{BN}} - \Delta\Pi_o^{\text{BN}} = -\frac{(1-\delta_o)B}{32} - \frac{9(1-\alpha)p_l}{d16} + T_b,$$

which increases in T_b and decreases in B. Then, we have $\Delta\Pi_B^{\text{BN}} > \Delta\text{CS}^{\text{BN}} > \Delta\Pi_o^{\text{BN}} > 0$, if $\frac{(1-\delta_o)B}{16} \geq T_b > \frac{(1-\delta_o)B}{32} + \frac{9(1-\alpha)p_l}{16}$; and $\Delta\Pi_B^{\text{BN}} > \Delta\Pi_o^{\text{BN}} > \Delta\text{CS}^{\text{BN}} > 0$, if $T_b \leq \frac{(1-\delta_o)B}{32} + \frac{9(1-\alpha)p_l}{16}$. □

Proof of Lemma 2. From (9), we have: $\pi_{\text{sc}} = p_o(1 - \frac{p_o - p_a}{1-\delta_a}) + \alpha p_l(\frac{p_o - p_a}{1-\delta_a} - \frac{p_a}{\delta_a}) - T_b$ with simple calculation. Taking the first- and second-order derivatives of π_{sc} with respect to p_o, we have

$$\frac{\partial \pi_{\text{sc}}}{\partial p_o} = \frac{-2}{1-\delta_a} p_o + \frac{p_a + \alpha p_l}{1-\delta_a} + 1,$$

$$\frac{\partial^2 \pi_{\text{sc}}}{\partial p_o^2} = \frac{-2}{1-\delta_a} < 0.$$

It implies that π_{sc} is concave in p_o. Based on the assumption that $p_a = p_l$, we have $p_o^C = \frac{1-\delta_a+(1+\alpha)p_l}{2}$, by letting $\frac{\partial \pi_{\text{sc}}}{\partial p_o} = 0$ and solving the first-order condition. After substituting p_o^C into (9), the optimal total profit of the supply chain (i.e., Π_{sc}^C) is obtained. □

Proof of Proposition 3. Based on the optimal profits of the platform and brand with blockchain adoption, we rewrite the decentralized supply chain profit with blockchain (i.e., Π_{sc}^B) as follows:

$$\Pi_{\text{sc}}^B = \frac{3}{16}(1-\delta_a)\left(1 + \frac{(1-\alpha)p_l}{1-\delta_a}\right)^2 + \alpha p_l - \frac{\alpha p_l^2}{\delta_a} - T_b.$$

Comparing the profits of centralized and decentralized supply chains we have: $\Pi_{\text{sc}}^{C} - \Pi_{\text{sc}}^{B} = \frac{1}{16}(1-\delta_a)(1+\frac{(1-\alpha)p_l}{1-\delta_a})^2 > 0$, which holds intuitively. □

Proof of Proposition 4. Taking the first and second derivatives of the platform's profit function under cost sharing contract (i.e., π_o^{CS}), with respect to p_o, we have

$$\frac{\partial \pi_o^{\text{CS}}}{\partial p_o} = -\frac{2}{1-\delta_a}p_o + \frac{1-\delta_a+p_a+w}{1-\delta_a},$$

$$\frac{\partial^2 \pi_o^{\text{CS}}}{\partial p_o^2} = -\frac{2}{1-\delta_a} < 0.$$

It shows that π_o^{CS} is concave in p_o. Letting $\frac{\partial \pi_o^{\text{CS}}}{\partial p_o} = 0$, we have $\frac{-2}{1-\delta_a}p_o + \frac{1-\delta_a+p_a+w}{1-\delta_a} = 0$. To achieve the supply chain coordination, we replace p_o with p_o^C obtained in the centralized case. Then, we have $w^{\text{CS}} = \alpha p_l$. We further check the profits of each supply chain member under the cost sharing contract with sharing ratio θ, by substituting p_o^C and w^{CS}, respectively:

$$\Pi_o^{\text{CS}}(\theta) = \frac{1}{4}(1-\delta_a)\left(1+\frac{1-\alpha}{1-\delta_a}p_l\right)^2 - (1-\theta)T_b,$$

$$\Pi_b^{\text{CS}}(\theta) = \alpha p_l - \frac{\alpha}{\delta_a}p_l^2 - \theta T_b.$$

Note that $\Pi_b^{\text{CS}}(\theta) < \frac{1}{8}(1-\delta_a)(1+\frac{1-\alpha}{1-\delta_a}p_l)^2 + \alpha p_l - \frac{\alpha p_l^2}{\delta_a} = \Pi_b^B$, even if $\theta = 0$. Then, the brand has no incentive to sign the cost sharing contract for blockchain adoption. The cost-sharing contract fails to coordinate the supply chain with blockchain adoption. □

Proof of Proposition 5. Taking the first and second derivatives of the platform's profit under the revenue sharing contract (i.e., π_o^{RS}), with respect to p_o, we have

$$\frac{\partial \pi_o^{\text{RS}}}{\partial p_o} = \frac{-2(1-\gamma)}{1-\delta_a}p_o + \frac{(1-\gamma)(1-\delta_a)+(1-\gamma)p_a+w}{1-\delta_a},$$

$$\frac{\partial^2 \pi_o^{\text{RS}}}{\partial p_o^2} = \frac{-2(1-\gamma)}{1-\delta_a} < 0.$$

Hence, π_o^{RS} is concave in p_o. Let $\frac{\partial \pi_o^{\text{RS}}}{\partial p_o} = 0$, we have $\frac{(1-\gamma)(1-\delta_a)+(1-\gamma)p_a+w}{1-\delta_a} + \frac{-2(1-\gamma)}{1-\delta_a}p_o^{\text{RS}} = 0$. Replacing p_o with p_o^C, we have $\frac{-2(1-\gamma)}{1-\delta_a} \cdot \frac{1-\delta_a+(1+\alpha)p_l}{2} + \frac{(1-\gamma)(1-\delta_a)+(1-\gamma)p_a+w}{1-\delta_a} = 0$ and $w^{\text{RS}} = (1-\gamma)\alpha p_l > 0$, which is acceptable for the brand. Then, we further check the profits of each supply chain member, by substituting p_o^C and w^{RS} into the profit functions of the platform and brand under the revenue sharing contract, respectively,

$$\Pi_o^{\text{RS}}(\gamma) = \frac{1}{4}(1-\gamma)(1-\delta_a)\left(1+\frac{1-\alpha}{1-\delta_a}p_l\right)^2 - T_b,$$

$$\Pi_b^{\text{RS}}(\gamma) = \frac{1}{4}\gamma(1-\delta_a)\left(1+\frac{1-\alpha}{1-\delta_a}p_l\right)^2 + \alpha p_l - \frac{\alpha}{\delta_a}p_l^2.$$

Finally, we compare the profits of the platform and brand under the revenue sharing contract with that in the decentralized supply chain case, respectively. As the brand is the leader of the supply chain, letting $\Pi_o^B = \Pi_o^{\text{RS}}(\gamma)$, we have $\gamma = \frac{3}{4}$ and $\Pi_b^B < \Pi_b^{\text{RS}}(\frac{3}{4})$. The supply chain can be coordinated under this contract with blockchain adoption. □

Proof of Proposition 6. Taking the first and second derivatives of the platform's profit under the two-part tariff contract (i.e., π_o^{TT}), with respect to p_o, we have

$$\frac{\partial \pi_o^{\text{TT}}}{\partial p_o} = -\frac{2}{1-\delta_a}p_o + \frac{1-\delta_a+p_l+w}{1-\delta_a}, \quad \frac{\partial^2 \pi_o^{\text{TT}}}{\partial p_o^2} = -\frac{2}{1-\delta_a} < 0.$$

It is shown that π_o^{TT} is concave in p_o. Letting $\frac{\partial \pi_o^{\text{TT}}}{\partial p_o} = 0$, we have $-\frac{2}{1-\delta_a}p_o^{\text{TT}} + \frac{1-\delta_a+p_l+w}{1-\delta_a} = 0$. To achieve the supply chain coordination, replace p_o^{TT} with p_o^C. Then, we have $\frac{-2}{1-\delta_a} \cdot \frac{1-\delta_a+(1+\alpha)p_l}{2} + \frac{1-\delta_a+p_l+w}{1-\delta_a} = 0$, and $w^{\text{TT}} = \alpha p_l > 0$. Next, further check the profit of each firm, by substituting p_o^C and w^{TT} into their profits under two-part tariff contract, given lump-sum fee F, respectively,

$$\Pi_o^{\text{TT}}(F) = \frac{1}{4}(1-\delta_a)\left(1+\frac{1-\alpha}{1-\delta_a}p_l\right)^2 - T_b - F, \quad \Pi_b^{\text{TT}}(F) = \alpha p_l - \frac{\alpha}{\delta_a}p_l^2 + F.$$

Finally, we compare the profits of the platform and brand under the two-part tariff contract with that in the decentralized supply chain case, respectively. As the brand is the leader of the supply chain, letting $\Pi_o^B = \Pi_o^{\text{TT}}(F)$, we have $F = \frac{3}{16}(1-\delta_a)(1+\frac{1-\alpha}{1-\delta_a}p_l)^2$ and $\Pi_b^B < \Pi_b^{\text{TT}}(F)$. The supply chain can be coordinated under this contract with blockchain adoption. □

Proof of Proposition 7. Taking the first and second derivatives of the platform's profit under the profit-sharing contract (i.e., π_o^{PS}), with respect to p_o, we have

$$\frac{\partial \pi_o^{\text{PS}}}{\partial p_o} = -\frac{2(1-\phi)}{1-\delta_a}p_o + (1-\phi)\left(1+\frac{1+\alpha}{1-\delta_a}p_l\right),$$

$$\frac{\partial^2 \pi_o^{\text{PS}}}{\partial p_o^2} = -\frac{2(1-\phi)}{1-\delta_a} < 0.$$

The above inequality shows that π_o^{PS} is concave in p_o. Letting $\frac{\partial \pi_o^{\text{PS}}}{\partial p_o} = 0$, we have $\frac{-2(1-\phi)}{1-\delta_a}p_o^{\text{PS}} + (1-\phi)(1+\frac{1+\alpha}{1-\delta_a}p_l) = 0$. To coordinate the supply chain, replacing p_o^{PS} with p_o^C, we have $\frac{-2(1-\phi)}{1-\delta_a} \cdot \frac{1-\delta_a+(1+\alpha)p_l}{2} + (1-\phi)(1+\frac{1+\alpha}{1-\delta_a}p_l) = 0$ and $w^{\text{PS}} = 0$. We then further check the profits of each supply chain member. Substituting p_o^C and w^{PS} into the profit sharing contract given profit sharing ratio ϕ, we have

$$\Pi_o^{\mathrm{PS}}(\phi) = \frac{1}{4}(1-\phi)(1-\delta_a)\left(1+\frac{1-\alpha}{1-\delta_a}p_l\right)^2 + (1-\phi)\left(\alpha p_l - \frac{\alpha}{\delta_a}p_l^2 - T_b\right),$$

$$\Pi_b^{\mathrm{PS}}(\phi) = \frac{1}{4}\phi(1-\delta_a)\left(1+\frac{1-\alpha}{1-\delta_a}p_l\right)^2 + \phi\left(\alpha p_l - \frac{\alpha}{\delta_a}p_l^2 - T_b\right).$$

Finally, we compare the profits of the platform and brand under the profit sharing contract with that in the decentralized supply chain case, respectively. As the platform is the follower of the supply chain, we have $\Pi_o^B = \Pi_o^{\mathrm{PS}}(\phi)$. Then, it is easy to show that $\Pi_b^B < \Pi_b^{\mathrm{PS}}(\phi)$ with $\phi = \frac{\frac{3}{16}(1-\delta_a)(1+\frac{1-\alpha}{1-\delta_a}p_l)^2+\alpha p_l-\frac{\alpha}{\delta_a}p_l^2}{\frac{1}{4}(1-\delta_a)(1+\frac{1-\alpha}{1-\delta_a}p_l)^2+\alpha p_l-\frac{\alpha}{\delta_a}p_l^2-T_b}$. Therefore, the supply chain can be coordinated with a specific ϕ. □

Proof of Lemma 3. Based on the assumption that $p_a = p_l + m$, we rewrite the optimal results without blockchain adoption as follows:

$$p_o^N = \frac{3}{4}\Delta\delta + \frac{3+\alpha}{4}p_l + \frac{3}{4}m,$$

$$w^N = \frac{1}{2}\Delta\delta + \frac{1+\alpha}{2}p_l + \frac{1}{2}m,$$

$$\pi_o^N = \frac{(1-\alpha)^2 p_l^2}{16\Delta\delta} + \left[\frac{(1-\alpha)m}{8\Delta\delta} + \frac{1-\alpha}{8}\right]p_l + \frac{m^2}{16\Delta\delta} + \frac{m}{8} + \frac{1}{16}\Delta\delta,$$

$$\pi_b^N = \left[\frac{(1-\alpha)^2}{8\Delta\delta} - \frac{\alpha}{\delta_a}\right]p_l^2 + \left(\frac{3\alpha+1}{4} - \frac{\alpha m}{4\Delta\delta} - \frac{\alpha m}{\delta_a} + \frac{m}{4\Delta\delta}\right)p_l$$
$$+ \frac{1}{8}\Delta\delta\left(1+\frac{m}{\Delta\delta}\right)^2.$$

In order to guarantee the non-negative demand, i.e., $D_a \geq 0$, we let $\frac{p_l+m}{p_o} \leq \frac{\delta_a}{\delta_o}$. Replacing p_o with p_o^N, we have: $p_l \leq \frac{3m\delta_a+3\Delta\delta\delta_a-4m\delta_o}{4\delta_o-(3+\alpha)\delta_a}$. Because $\delta_o > \delta_a$ and $\alpha < 1$, the denominator of the above right-hand side is positive. Then, we only focus on the molecule of the right-hand side. When $m > \frac{3\Delta\delta\delta_a}{4\delta_o-3\delta_a}$, the upper bound of p_l becomes negative, then the agent faces no demand. As $p_l^N \leq p_o^N$, then, we have $p_l^N = p_o^N = \frac{3(\Delta\delta+m)}{1-\alpha}$. When $m \leq \frac{3\Delta\delta\delta_a}{4\delta_o-3\delta_a}$, the right-hand side is positive. Then, we denote the upper bound of p_l as $\bar{p_l}^N$, where $\bar{p_l}^N = \frac{3m\delta_a+3\Delta\delta\delta_a-4m\delta_o}{4\delta_o-(3+\alpha)\delta_a}$.

Next, we derive the optimal retail price under this case. Taking the first and second derivatives of the brand's profit with respect to p_l, yields the following:

$$\frac{\partial \pi_b^N}{\partial p_l} = \left[\frac{(1-\alpha)^2}{4\Delta\delta} - \frac{2\alpha}{\delta_a}\right]p_l + \frac{3\alpha+1}{4} - \frac{\alpha m}{4\Delta\delta} - \frac{\alpha m}{\delta_a} + \frac{m}{4\Delta\delta},$$

$$\frac{\partial^2 \pi_b^N}{\partial p_l^2} = \frac{(1-\alpha)^2}{4\Delta\delta} - \frac{2\alpha}{\delta_a}.$$

When $\delta_o > (\frac{\alpha}{8} + \frac{1}{8\alpha} + \frac{3}{4})\delta_a$, we have $\frac{\partial^2 \pi_b^N}{\partial p_l^2} < 0$ and π_b^N is a concave in p_l. Solving the first order condition with respect to p_l, we have: $p_l^{N*} = \frac{m[4\alpha\delta_o-(1+3\alpha)\delta_a]-(1+3\alpha)\Delta\delta\delta_a}{(1-\alpha)^2\delta_a-8\alpha\Delta\delta}$. To guarantee that the optimal decision is feasible, we only need to show that $\frac{\alpha m\delta_a+4\alpha m\Delta\delta-m\delta_a-(1+3\alpha)\Delta\delta\delta_a}{4\Delta\delta\delta_a} \leq 0$ holds, which is equivalent to $m[\frac{4\alpha\delta_o}{(1+3\alpha)\delta_a} - 1] < \delta_o - \delta_a$. Note that the above condition always holds because $m \leq \frac{3\Delta\delta\delta_a}{4\delta_o-3\delta_a} < \frac{\Delta\delta\delta_a(1+3\alpha)}{4\alpha\delta_o-(1+3\alpha)\delta_a}$. Then, $p_l^{N*} > 0$ is valid in this case. As the upper bound of the local price is $\bar{p_l}^N$, then, the optimal local retail price is $p_l^N = \min\{\bar{p_l}^N, p_l^{N*}\}$ in this case.

When $\delta_o \leq (\frac{\alpha}{8} + \frac{1}{8\alpha} + \frac{3}{4})\delta_a$, we have $\frac{\partial^2 \pi_b^N}{\partial p_l^2} \geq 0$ and π_b^N is convex in p_l. Thus, the optimal solution is obtained at either 0 or $\bar{p_l}^N$. Let $\pi_{b1}^N = \pi_b^N(0)$ and $\pi_{b2}^N = \pi_b^N(\bar{p_l}^N)$, respectively, we have

$$\pi_{b1}^N = \frac{1}{8}\Delta\delta\Big(1 + \frac{m}{\Delta\delta}\Big)^2,$$

$$\pi_{b2}^N = \left[\frac{(1-\alpha)^2}{8\Delta\delta} - \frac{\alpha}{\delta_a}\right]\bar{p_l}^{N^2} + \left(\frac{3\alpha+1}{4} - \frac{\alpha m}{4\Delta\delta} - \frac{\alpha m}{\delta_a} + \frac{m}{4\Delta\delta}\right)\bar{p_l}^N + \frac{1}{8}\Delta\delta\Big(1 + \frac{m}{\Delta\delta}\Big)^2.$$

Then, comparing π_{b1}^N with π_{b2}^N, we have

$$\pi_{b2}^N - \pi_{b1}^N = \frac{1}{4}\bar{p_l}^N\left[\left(\frac{4(1-\alpha)^2}{8\Delta\delta} - \frac{\alpha}{\delta_a}\right)\bar{p_l}^N + 1 + 3\alpha + \frac{(1-\alpha)\delta_a - 4\alpha\Delta\delta}{\delta_a\Delta\delta}\right] > 0.$$

The above inequality holds because $\delta_o \leq (\frac{\alpha}{8} + \frac{1}{8\alpha} + \frac{3}{4})\delta_a$ and $\alpha < 1$. Thus, $p_l^N = p_l^{N*} = \bar{p_l}^N$, when $\delta_o \leq (\frac{\alpha}{8} + \frac{1}{8\alpha} + \frac{3}{4})\delta_a$. □

Proof of Lemma 4. The proof of Lemma 4 is similar to Lemma 3. □

Proof of Lemma 5. From $\Pi_o^B(\bar{\delta}_o) = \frac{1}{16}(\bar{\delta}_o - \delta_a)(1 + \frac{1-\alpha}{(\bar{\delta}_o-\delta_a)}p_l)^2 - T_b\bar{\delta}_o^2$, we have

$$\frac{\partial \Pi_o^B}{\partial \bar{\delta}_o} = \frac{-(1-\alpha)^2 p_l^2}{16(\bar{\delta}_o - \delta_a)^2} + \frac{1}{16} - 2T_b\bar{\delta}_o \quad \frac{\partial^2 \Pi_o^B}{\partial \bar{\delta}_o^2} = \frac{2(1-\alpha)^2 p_l^2}{(\bar{\delta}_o - \delta_a)^3} - 2T_b.$$

It implies that Π_o^B is concave in $\bar{\delta}_o$ when $T_b > \frac{(1-\alpha)^2 p_l^2}{(\bar{\delta}_o-\delta_a)^3}$.

Solving the first order condition with respect to $\bar{\delta}_o$, we get

$$(1 - 32T_b\bar{\delta}_o) = \frac{(1-\alpha)^2 p_l^2}{(\bar{\delta}_o - \delta_a)^2} \quad \left(T_b > \frac{(1-\alpha)^2 p_l^2}{(\bar{\delta}_o - \delta_a)^3}\right).$$ □

Acknowledgments

We sincerely thank the editors and three anonymous reviewers for their insightful, critical and constructive comments on this paper, especially during the time with COVID-19 virus. This paper is partially supported by National Natural Science Foundation of China [Grant Numbers 72071113 and 71931006], and NJUST Graduate Scientific Research Training of 'Thousands' Project.

References

Ahmadi, R and B Yang (2000). Parallel imports: Challenges from unauthorized distribution channels. *Marketing Science*, 19, 279–294.

Autrey, RL, F Bova and DA Soberman (2014). Organizational structure and gray markets. *Marketing Science*, 33, 849–870.

Autrey, RL, F Bova and DA Soberman (2015). When gray is good: Gray markets and market-creating investments. *Production and Operations Management*, 24, 547–559.

Babich, V and G Hilary (2020). Distributed ledgers and operations: What operations management researchers should know about blockchain technology. *Manufacturing & Service Operations Management*, 22, 223–240.

BBC News (2016). Shopping in Australia, while in China. *BBC News* (October 23), https://bbc.com/news/business-37584730.

Cachon, GP (2003). Supply chain coordination with contracts. In *Handbooks in Operations Research and Management Science: Supply Chain Management: Design, Coordination and Operation*, AG de Kok and SC Graves (eds.), pp. 229–340. Amsterdam.

Cachon, G and M Lariviere (2005). Supply chain coordination with revenue sharing contracts: Strengths and limitations. *Management Science*, 51, 30–44.

Cai, Y, TM Choi and J Zhang (2020). Platform supported supply chain operations in the blockchain era: Supply contracting and moral hazards. *Decision Sciences*, doi: 10.1111/deci.12475.

Chen, X, X Wang and H Chan (2017). Manufacturer and retailer coordination for environmental and economic competitiveness: A power perspective. *Transportation Research Part E: Logistics and Transportation Review*, 97, 268–281.

Cho, S, X Fang and T Sridhar (2015). Combating strategic counterfeits in licit and illicit supply chains. *Manufacturing & Service Operations Management*, 17, 273–289.

Choi, TM (2019). Blockchain-technology-supported platforms for diamond authentication and certification in luxury supply chains. *Transportation Research Part E: Logistics and Transportation Review*, 128, 17–29.

Choi, TM, S Kumar, VS Mookerjee and X Yue (2020). Disruptive technologies and operations management in the Industry 4.0 era and beyond. *Production and Operations Management*, forthcoming.

Choi, TM, SW Wallace and Y Wang (2018). Big data analytics in operations management. *Production and Operations Management*, 27, 1868–1883.

Choi, TM, X Wen, X Sun and SH Chung (2019). The mean-variance approach for global supply chain risk analysis with air logistics in the blockchain technology era. *Transportation Research Part E*, 127, 178–191.

Dai, W (2018). Platform modeling and scheduling game with multiple intelligent cloud-computing pools for big data. *Mathematical and Computer Modeling of Dynamical Systems*, 24, 506–552.

Galvez, JF, JC Mejuto and J Simal-Gandara (2018). Future challenges on the use of blockchain for food traceability analysis. *Trends in Analytical Chemistry*, 107, 222–232.

Gao, SY, WS Lim and CS Tang (2016). Entry of copycats of luxury brands. *Marketing Science*, 36, 272–289.

Gao, SY, WS Lim and C Tang (2017). The impact of the potential entry of copycats: Entry conditions, consumer welfare, and social welfare. *Decision Sciences*, 48, 594–624.

Green, RT and T Smith (2002). Countering brand counterfeiters. *Journal of International Marketing*, 10, 89–106.

Ledger Insights (2019). Chinas trade watchdogs use blockchain to tackle counterfeit products. *Ledger Insights*, https://www.ledgerinsights.com/china-blockchain-anti-counterfeit-ecommerce-trade-watchdog/.

Lee, HL and O Ozer (2007). Unlocking the value of RFID. *Production and Operations Management*, 16, 40–64.

Li, M, S Sethi and J Zhang (2016). Competing with bandit supply chains. *Annals of Operations Research*, 240, 617–640.

Li, H, S Zhu, N Cui and J Li (2016). Analysis of gray markets in differentiated duopoly. *International Journal of Production Research*, 54, 4008–4027.

Liao, S (2018). E-Commerce sites flog fake foreign wares. *Yicai Global*, https://www.yicaiglobal.com/news/e-commerce-sites-flog-fake-foreign-wares-china-consumer-agency-says.

Luo, S and TM Choi (2020). Operational research for technology-driven supply chains in the industry 4.0 era: Recent development and future studies. *Asia-Pacific Journal of Operational Research*, doi: 10.1142/S0217595920400217.

Plambeck, EL and TA Taylor (2005). Sell the plant? The impact of contract manufacturing on innovation, capacity, and profitability. *Management Science*, 51, 133–150.

Progress Asia (2019). Asia buys in to E-commerce. *Progress Asia*, https://www.progressasia.org/asia-buys-in-to-e-commerce/.

Qian, Y (2014). Brand management and strategies against counterfeits. *Journal of Economics & Management Strategy*, 23, 317–343.

Sharif, M and K Nazir (2017). The influence of intellectual property rights on poaching in manufacturing outsourcing. *Production and Operations Management*, 27, 531–552.

Shi, X, H Chan and C Dong (2020). Value of bargaining contract in a supply chain system with sustainability investment: An incentive analysis. *IEEE Transactions on Systems, Man, and Cybernetics: Systems*, 50, 1622–1634.

Wang, Y, J Lin and TM Choi (2020). Gray market and counterfeiting in supply chains: A review of the operations literature and implications to luxury industries. *Transportation Research Part E*, 133, 101823.

Week in China (2018). Name and shame, Estee Lauder distributor sues NetEases Kaola. *Week in China*, https://www.weekinchina.com/2019/03/name-and-shame-2/.

Wei, Y and TM Choi (2010). Mean-variance analysis of supply chains under wholesale pricing and profit sharing scheme. *European Journal of Operational Research*, 204, 255–262.

Wiedmann, KP, N Hennigs and C Klarmann (2012). Luxury consumption in the trade-off between genuine and counterfeit goods: What are the consumers underlying motives and value-based drivers? *Journal of Brand Management*, 19, 544–566.

Wilcox, K, HM Kim and S Sen (2009). Why do consumers buy copycat luxury brands? *Journal of Marketing Research*, 46, 247–259.

Xiao, Y, U Palekar and Y Liu (2011). Shades of gray: The impact of gray markets on authorized distribution channels. *Quantitative Marketing & Economics*, 9, 155–178.

Yoo, WS and E Lee (2011). Internet channel entry: A strategic analysis of mixed channel structures. *Marketing Science*, 30, 29–41.

Zhang, J, LJ Hong and RQ Zhang (2012). Fighting strategies in a market with counterfeits. *Annals of Operations Research*, 192, 49–66.

Zhang, J and RQ Zhang (2015). Supply chain structure in a market with deceptive counterfeits. *European Journal of Operational Research*, 240, 84–97.

Biography

Xiutian Shi received the PhD degree in management science and engineering from Nanjing University, Nanjing, China, in 2014. She is currently an Associate Professor with the School of Economics and Management, Nanjing University of Science and Technology, Nanjing. She has published research papers in journals, such as the *European Journal of Operational Research*, *International Journal of Production Economics*, *Transportation Research Part E*, and *IEEE Transactions on Systems, Man, and Cybernetics: Systems*. Her current research interests include game-theoretic modeling of supply chain management and marketing-operations interface.

Shuning Yao is currently an Undergraduate Student with the School of Economics and Management, Nanjing University of Science and Technology, Nanjing, China.

Yizhong Ma received the PhD degree in Control Science and Engineering from Northwestern Polytechnic University, China, in 2003. He is a Chair Professor in Management Science and Engineering of Nanjing University of Science and Technology, China. He has published more than 100 research papers in journals, such as the *IISE Transaction*, *European Journal of Operational Research*, *Reliability Engineering and System Safety*, *Quality and Reliability Engineering International*, *Computer and Industrial Engineering*, *Quality Engineering, and so on*. His research fields include quality management and quality engineering, Six Sigma management, supply chain quality management. His work is supported by the National Natural Science Foundation of China (Nos. 71931006 and 71871119).

https://doi.org/10.1142/9789819808588_0005

Chapter 5

The Incentive Study in the Blockchain Era: A Two-Period Strategic Inventory Game†

Jianheng Zhou
Glorious Sun School of Business and Management
Donghua University, Shanghai, P. R. China
zjh001@dhu.edu.cn

Qingying Li*
Glorious Sun School of Business and Management
Donghua University, Shanghai, P. R. China
liqingying@dhu.edu.cn

In this paper, we conduct an incentive study on the adoption of the blockchain technology in a two-period model with retailer's use of strategic inventory. Without the adoption of the blockchain technology, the retailer has private information regarding the market size. We investigate the retailer's voluntary signaling decisions via his pricing and strategic inventory decisions. We determine the retailer's equilibrium price and the manufacturer's optimal wholesale price. Both separating and pooling equilibria are discussed, and the unique lexicographically maximum sequential equilibrium is identified. With the adoption of the blockchain technology, there is no information asymmetric between the supply chain members. We find that the manufacturer has the incentive to adopt the blockchain technology when the demand uncertainty is moderate to high, and the retailer has the incentive to adopt the blockchain technology when the demand uncertainty is low or high. When the manufacturer and the retailer have a misalignment in the adoption of the technology, a central planner can help to achieve coordination.

Keywords: Blockchain technology; signaling; strategic inventory; supply chain management.

1. Introduction

Blockchain technology is an emerging technology and adopted by supply chain business patterners nowadays (Babich and Hilary, 2020). The technology can be effective if all the supply chain members participate and agree on its adoption. One

*Corresponding author.
†To cite this article, please refer to its earlier version published in the Asia-Pacific Journal of Operational Research, Vol. 39, No. 1, (February 2022), DOI: 10.1142/S0217595921400248. Reprinted with permission from World Scientific Publishing Co. Pte. Ltd.

important advantage of adopting the blockchain technology is to improve the information transparency among the supply chain members. For example, BMW and the manufacturer Daimler apply the blockchain technology so as to provide the information about car manufacturing and usage process (Pollock, 2020). The famous luxury brands Louis Vuitton and Gucci also implement the blockchain technology to identify products' authenticity and quality (Newbold, 2019). More examples can be found in, for example, Shen *et al.* (2020) and Choi *et al.* (2020). In practice, however, some supply chain members may benefit from the information advantages or disadvantages. Therefore, the adoption of the blockchain technology may not necessarily benefit all the members. In this study, we investigate the supply chain members' incentives on adopting the blockchain technology.

It is common that firms carry inventory to either maintain safety stocks or to handle demand and supply uncertainties (Zipkin, 2000). Besides the operational reasons, firms can also carry inventory for strategic reasons, e.g., to argue for a lower wholesale price. Celsa, a steel manufacturer in Spain, stores large piles of scrap metal inventory outside of its factory. It turns out that the company does not carry the inventory to maintain the safety stock. Rather, the company intensively displays the inventory to the local dealers, indicating that the company will only buy the material if the wholesale price is low (Aartinez-de-Albeniz and Simchi-Levi, 2013). Anand *et al.* (2008) investigate such kind of retailer's use of strategic inventory. They show that the retailer's use of strategic inventory can always benefit the manufacturer, but benefits the retailer itself only if the cost of carrying inventory is not high.

The above insight is obtained wherein the supply chain members are perfectly informed about the demand information, which can be achieved with the adoption of the blockchain technology. However, in practice, while an upstream manufacturer usually has limited knowledge of market demand, a downstream retailer, being closer to the market, has better knowledge of market demand (Li *et al.*, 2014; Li and Zhou, 2019). That is, without the adoption of the blockchain technology, the retailer has a superiority on the market size information. Would this kind of information superiority benefit the retailer? Does the retailer have the incentive to remove its information advantageous by adopting the blockchain technology? Also, from the manufacturer's perspective, does the manufacturer have the incentive to adopt blockchain technology to gain the retailer's private information on the market size? If they differ in their incentives, is it possible to have them achieve an agreement? To answer these questions, we propose this study.

We consider a supply chain consisting of one manufacturer and one retailer, which trade in two consecutive periods. There exists information asymmetry between the supply chain members, where the retailer has private information on the market size. We consider two scenarios. One is adopting the blockchain technology, wherein the information asymmetry can be resolved. The other is without adopting the blockchain technology, wherein the retailer retains its information privilege so that a signaling game arises. We compare the supply chain members' profit under the two scenarios and conduct the incentive study.

The remainder of this paper is organized as follows. Section 2 reviews the related literature and Sec. 3 introduces the model and the benchmark cases. Section 4 studies the case without adopting the blockchain technology, and Sec. 5 investigates the scenario with the adoption of the blockchain technology and conduct the comparison. Section 6 concludes the paper. All the proofs are relegated to the appendix.

2. Literature Review

Three streams of the literature are related to this study: the strategic inventory, signaling games in supply chain management, and the adoption of the blockchain technology in operations management. We then review the most related literature according to the three streams.

2.1. *Strategic inventory*

Anand *et al.* (2008) show that when a manufacturer and a retailer trade in two periods, the retailer is motivated to strategically hold spillovers in inventory even in the absence of demand uncertainty. Furthermore, the retailer's adoption of strategic inventory can mitigate the effects of double marginalization and benefit the supply chain. The retailer's use of strategic inventory is considered under various settings. Arya and Mittendorf (2013) add a rebate contract to the model of Anand *et al.* (2008) and find that consumer rebates tend to reduce the retailer's strategic inventory, thereby benefiting both the members and the consumers of a supply chain. Arya *et al.* (2015) also extend the work of Anand *et al.* (2008) by investigating the effects of strategic inventory in a centralized/decentralized supply chain with multiple retailers. Using a two-period supply chain model, Guan *et al.* (2019) investigate an integrated model to determine the relationship between the retailer's strategic inventory holding and the supplier's encroachment of the demand market in the second period. They show that the supplier and the retailer are either harmed by or benefitted by sequential and simultaneous games. Mantin and Jiang (2017) assume that carried inventories face quality deterioration in future demand markets, and show that this deterioration harms the retailer's performance. Moon *et al.* (2018) extend the strategic inventory model by assuming that the demand function depends on both the selling price and product investment efforts, which can be carried out by either the manufacturer or the retailer. They show that manufacturer's investment effort can prevent the retailer from carrying inventory and retailer-investment effort can achieve a win–win situation. Roy *et al.* (2019) investigate a case wherein the manufacturer has no visibility of the retailer's use of strategic inventory and show that the manufacturer may prefer not to monitor the retailer's inventory. Li *et al.* (2020) show that strategic inventory intensifies chain-to-chain competition and reduces the mitigation effects on double marginalization.

Dey *et al.* (2019) investigate the effect of strategic inventory on green product design issues (either development-intensive or marginal-cost-intensive products). The manufacturer's preferences under different game sequences are discussed.

In the above studies, demand information is assumed to be common knowledge. With the exception of Roy *et al.* (2019), the other studies are conducted under full information scenarios. In this study, we investigate the effects of strategic inventory in an asymmetric information setting. Specifically, we investigate the signaling game between the manufacturer and the retailer, wherein the retailer signals the market size information to the manufacturer.

2.2. *Signaling games under asymmetric information*

Cachon and Lariviere (2001) are among the first to analyze credible information-sharing in a vertical supply chain, wherein the downstream manufacturer has private information on market demand and has the incentive to signal the information to the upstream supplier. Different contracts for different types of manufacturers have been identified. Li *et al.* (2014) study the effect of supplier encroachment under asymmetric information wherein the reseller signals market size information to the supplier via his/her order quantity. They show that when the reseller distorts his/her order quantity downward to signal information, the double marginalization effect is amplified, which may lead to a lose–lose situation. Bakshi *et al.* (2015) investigate the effects of two kinds of after-sale service contracts wherein product reliability is known only to the vendor. They show that a performance-based contract motivates the vendor to signal information by increasing his/her investment in spare inventory, whereas a resource-based contract urges the vendor to focus on saving inventory costs by reducing investment. Jiang *et al.* (2016) investigate three information-sharing formats in a supply chain: no sharing, voluntary sharing, and mandatory sharing. Under the voluntary sharing scheme, the manufacturer uses different wholesale prices to signal market size information to the retailer. The supply chain members' performance is determined using the three information formats. Li and Zhou (2019) consider the signaling game in the capacity reservation between an integrated device manufacturer and a foundry, wherein the former either sources from the latter or carries out her own production, subject to their reserved capacities. Credible vertical information sharing has also been analyzed by Yan *et al.* (2019a) and Yan *et al.* (2019b). Signaling games also arise between horizontal competitors. For example, Anand and Goyal (2009) study two competing retailers sourcing from the same supplier, wherein the incumbent is informed and the new entrant is uninformed. Ye *et al.* (2013) state that competing firms signal private information on their production capacities through their production quantities.

In addition to the above credible information-sharing studies, many others compare system performance with and without information sharing; see, for example, Ha and Tong (2008), Jain and Sohoni (2015), Huang and Wang (2017), and Dong *et al.* (2018).

2.3. *Blockchain technology in operations management*

Babich and Hilary (2020) summarize the blockchain technology's key strengths and weaknesses, according to which they propose three research themes with respect to Operations Management. That is, information, automation, and tokenization. In this work, we study the blockchain technology regarding its information characteristic, and thus we review the related literature from this theme. Applying blockchain technology in supply chain management can help improve the transparency and mitigate the impact of information asymmetric.

According to the above discussion, the use of strategic inventories in an asymmetric information setting has received little attention in the literature. To the best of our knowledge, this paper is the first to investigate the effect of strategic inventories under the blockchain era. Choi and Luo (2019) study the usage of blockchain technology to improve the data quality, which may improve the social welfare but harm the supply chain performance. Thus, the government should provide subsidy or decrease the environmental tax to enhance the blockchain technology. Chod *et al.* (2020) study the financing benefits of adopting blockchain to improve the supply chain transparency. The firm can signal its fundamental quality to the lenders either through inventory transactions or through loan requests with or without blockchain technology, respectively. They show that the former leads to lower signaling cost and is more efficient. Cai *et al.* (2020) study the markdown sponsor contract in a two-period model, which faces the risk of moral hazards. They argue that the blockchain technology can be applied to revise the contract and mitigate the moral hazards. Blockchain technology can also provide more information about the products for the customers. Fan *et al.* (2020) discuss the possibility of supply chain members sharing the cost of blockchain technology so as to realize the traceability of the products. Choi (2019) consider a blockchain technology supported platform's choice between directly selling or providing authentication for diamonds. Shen *et al.* (2020) investigate whether a platform selling secondhand products shall adopt blockchain technology to improve the available information to customers.

3. Model and Preliminary Results

We consider a supply chain consisting of one manufacturer (she) and one retailer (he). The manufacturer and the retailer trade in two consecutive periods. In period t, where $t = 1, 2$, the retailer sources products from the manufacturer at a wholesale price w_t, sells the products to the market at a retail price p_t, and the realized demand is $d_t = a - p_t$, where a is the market size in each period. Since the downstream is closer to the demand market, we assume that the downstream retailer has better information about the potential demand market than the upstream manufacturer. This assumption is commonly adopted in the studies considering information asymmetric. The market size a can be either a high value a_H with probability β, or a low value a_L with probability $1 - \beta$, where $a_H > a_L$ and $0 \leq \beta \leq 1$. Define $\mu = \beta a_H + (1 - \beta)a_L$ as the mean of the market size and $\theta = a_H/a_L$ as the level of demand uncertainty. At the beginning of period 1, the retailer can observe signals from the demand market size and clearly infer the market type. However, the manufacturer relies only on her *ex-ante* beliefs. Without the blockchain technology, the demand information asymmetry is commonly observed in practice, and is widely investigated in the literature (see, e.g., Anand and Goyal (2009), Li *et al.* (2014), Jiang *et al.* (2016)). Nowadays, however, thanks to the quickly development of the blockchain technology, this information asymmetry can be removed. That is, if the blockchain technology is adopted, then the manufacturer can also learn the true demand size as the retailer. We assume the cost for adopting the blockchain technology is a constant. This assumption makes sense because the installation of the blockchain technology is independent of the selling process. Without loss of generality, we assume the cost is zero (more discussion is provided in Sec. 5).

As discussed in the introduction, the retailer may strategically hold inventory to seek for a lower future wholesale price. Let I be the units of inventories that the retailer's strategically carrying from period 1 to period 2. Note that in this study the demand in period 2 is deterministic. Thus, the retailer will carry proper units of inventories to avoid salvage at the end of period 2. Therefore, without loss of generality, we assume there is no salvage cost. If the retailer carries inventories, then he also has to pay the inventory holding cost of h per unit. When the retailer decides on his selling price in period 1, i.e., p_1, and the strategic inventory level I, he may intentionally distort his decision to signal market information to the manufacturer, who is aware of this. Therefore, a signaling game arises between the two members. We analyze the retailer's decisions so that the market size information can be truthfully signaled.

The event sequence is as follows. The retailer/manufacturer first decides whether to adopt the blockchain technology. The market size information, i.e., the distribution of the market size is common information to both of the supply chain members. Nature first chooses the true market size a_i, where $i = H, L$. The retailer observes the true market size a_i The manufacturer observed the market size a_i if the blockchain technology is adopted, and relies only on her *ex-ante* belief if the blockchain technology is not adopted. In period 1, the manufacturer first determines the wholesale price w_1 based on her belief on the market size. Then, the retailer determines the selling price p_1 and the inventory level I, and the demand in period 1 d_1 is realized. After observing the retailers' decisions, the manufacturer may update her belief on the market size. Then, period 2 starts. The manufacturer again first determines the wholesale price w_2 according to the updated belief on the market size, then the retailer determines the selling price p_2, and the demand in period 2 d_2 is realized at the end. We plot the event sequence in Fig. 1.

To investigate the retailer's pricing and inventory decisions in period 1, we first specify the supply chain members' best responses in period 2. We define $\Pi_t^{ij}(\cdot)$ and $\pi_t^{ij}(\cdot)$ as the manufacturer's profit and the retailer's profit, respectively, from period t to the end of the planning horizon given that the true market size is a_i and the manufacturer believes that the market size is a_j in period t, where $t = 1, 2$, and

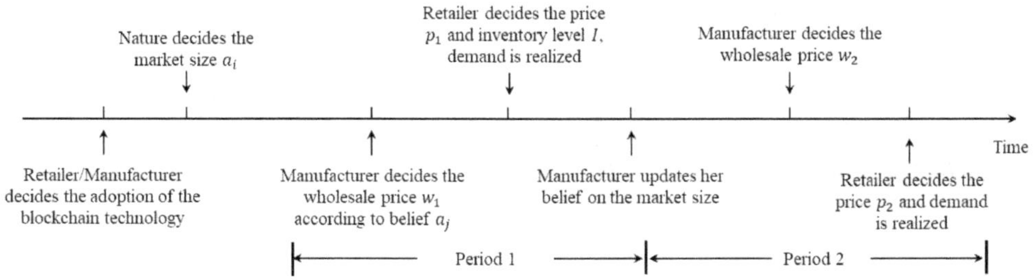

Fig. 1. Event sequence.

$i, j = H, L$. Note that $\Pi_t^{ij}(\cdot)$ may differ from the manufacturer's true profit because the manufacturer makes decisions according to the belief on the market size rather than the true market size. Note that we may have either $j = i$ or $j \neq i$ without the adoption of the blockchain technology, but we will have $j = i$ with the adoption of the blockchain technology. Here, we present the preliminary results without any restrictions on the relations between the two superscripts.

Both the members' profits in period 2 are affected by the retailer's inventory decision I in period 1. Given that in period 2 the manufacturer's wholesale price is w_2 and the retail price is p_2, we have

$$\pi_2^{ij}(w_2, p_2; I) = p_2(a_i - p_2) - w_2(a_i - p_2 - I)$$

and

$$\Pi_2^{ij}(w_2, p_2; I) = w_2(a_j - p_2 - I).$$

By maximizing the retailer's and the manufacturer's profits sequentially, we obtain the optimal decisions and profits in period 2 in the following lemma:

Lemma 1. *Suppose that the true market size is a_i, the manufacturer's belief is a_j (which the retailer is also aware of), where $i, j = H, L$, and the inventory in period 1 is I. The optimal decisions in period 2 are as follows:*

$$p_2^{ij}(I, w_2) = \frac{a_i + w_2}{2}, \quad p_2^{ij}(I) = \frac{2a_i + a_j - 2I}{4}, \quad w_2^j(I) = \frac{a_j}{2} - I,$$

and the corresponding profits are

$$\pi_2^{ij}(I) = \frac{1}{16}[(2a_i - a_j)^2 + 4I(2a_i + a_j - 3I)],$$

$$\Pi_2^{ij}(I) = \frac{1}{8}(3a_j - 2a_i - 2I)(a_j - 2I).$$

From the best responses in period 2 given in Lemma 1, we can subsequently discuss the manufacturer's and the retailer's profits in period 1. We define $\pi_1^{ij}(w_1, p_1, I)$ and $\Pi_1^{ij}(w_1, p_1, I)$ as the retailer's and the manufacturer's profit over the two periods, *respectively, given the manufacturer's wholesale price* w_1 *and his decisions* p_1 *and* I*. Then we have*

$$\pi_1^{ij}(p_1, w_1, I) = p_1(a_i - p_1) - w_1(a_i - p_1 + I) - hI + \pi_2^{ij}(I). \tag{1}$$

Regarding the manufacturer's profit, we have

$$\Pi_1^{ij}(p_1, w_1, I) = w_1(a_i - p_1 + I) + \Pi_2^{ij}(I)]. \tag{2}$$

Note that given the true market size a_i*, the manufacturer's belief in period 2 is* a_j *and her wholesale price is* w_1*, and the retailer's optimal joint decisions on* p_1 *and* I *are derived by maximizing* $\pi_1^{ij}(w_1, p_1, I)$*, given by (1). The retailer's decisions include the selling price* p_1 *and the strategic inventory level* I*. The following lemma shows that the two decisions can be determined independently.*

Lemma 2. *Suppose that the true market size is* a_i *and the manufacturer's belief is* a_j *(depending on the retailer's signal). The retailer's optimal joint decisions on the retail price and the strategic inventory level are given by*

$$I^*(w_1) = \frac{2a_i + a_j - 4w_1 - 4h}{6}, \quad p_1^*(w_1) = \frac{a_i + w_1}{2}.$$

Note that when $i = j$, the results in lemma 1 are simplified to the case in Anand *et al.* (2008). Both the inventory level and the selling price can be used to signal information to the manufacturer. In practical situation, the selling price is more easily observed by other supply chain members. Therefore, in this paper, we consider the case where the retailer signals information by using his selling price p_1. For simplicity, we omit the parameter I from the expression. We denote $\pi_1^{ij}(p_1, w_1)$

Table 1. Notations.

Notations	Description
a_i	The market size, $i = H, L$, $a_i = a_H$ with probability β and $a_i = a_L$ with probability 1-β
μ	The mean of the market size, $\mu = \beta a_H + (1-\beta)a_L$
θ	The demand uncertainty level, $\theta = a_H/a_L$
h	The unit inventory holding cost
d_t	The realized demand in period t, where $t = 1, 2$
p_t	The retailer's selling price in period t, where $t = 1, 2$
w_t	The manufacturer's wholesale price in period t, where $t = 1, 2$
Π_t^{ij}	The manufacturer's profit from period t to the end of the planning horizon, given that the true market size is a_i and the manufacturer believes that the market size is a_j in period t, where $t = 1, 2$, $i, j = H, L$
Π^B, Π^N	The manufacturer's optimal profit with (B) or without (N) the adoption of the blockchain technology
π_t^{ij}	The retailer's profit from period t to the end of the planning horizon, given that the true market size is a_i and the manufacturer believes that the market size is a_j in period t, where $t = 1, 2$, $i, j = H, L$
$\pi^B \pi^N$	The retailer's optimal profit with (B) or without (N) the adoption of the blockchain technology

as the retailer's profit over the two periods given that strategic inventory level is determined from Lemma 2. We have

$$\pi_1^{ij}(p_1, w_1) = \left[p_1(a_i - p_1) - w_1\left(a_i - p_1 + \frac{2a_i + a_j - 4w_1 - 4h}{6}\right)\right]$$
$$+ \frac{1}{12}(4a_i^2 - 2a_ia_j + a_j^2 - 4(h + \mathrm{w}_1)^2). \quad (3)$$

We subsequently analyze the retailer's signaling decisions in accordance with (3) rather than (1).

For ease of presentation, we summarize all of the notations in Table 1.

4. Without Blockchain Technology

In this section, we consider the case without adopting the blockchain technology, or equivalently, there exists information asymmetry on the market size information. The retailer can observe the true market size, but the manufacturer only has an *ex-ante* belief on the distribution of the market size. In this case, a signaling game arises between the two supply chain members (Li *et al.*, 2014; Jiang *et al.*, 2016; Li and Zhou, 2019). Recall that the manufacturer decides w_1 according to her *ex-ante* belief about market size, and subsequently updates her belief after observing the retailer's decisions in period 1. Using backward induction, we first analyze the retailer's signaling decisions and subsequently investigate the manufacturer's wholesale pricing decisions in period 1.

4.1. *The retailer's signaling decisions*

There are two mutually exclusive types of equilibria. The first is a separating equilibrium, wherein the retailer adopts different retail prices for different market sizes, and wherein the manufacturer can clearly infer market type from the retailer's pricing decisions. The second is a pooling equilibrium, wherein the retailer adopts the same retail price for both types of demand size, and wherein the manufacturer cannot update her prior beliefs. We discuss both equilibria in the following two subsections.

4.1.1. *Separating equilibrium*

We first consider separating equilibrium, wherein the retailers adopt different decisions while observing different market size information. Follow the literature about signaling game (Anand and Goyal, 2009; Li *et al.*, 2014), we say that the retailer is an i-type retailer if he observes market size a_i, and we adopt a threshold belief structure with a critical value $\hat{p}_1^s$. Specifically, in a separating equilibrium, the manufacturer believes that the market size is a_H when she observes a selling price $p_1 > \hat{p}_1^s$, and a_L when she observes a selling price $p_1 \leq \hat{p}_1^s$.

Note that in period 2, the manufacturer's wholesale price (given her belief that the market size is a_j) is $w_2 = \frac{a_j}{2} - I$; that is, the manufacturer offers a lower wholesale price if she believes that the market size is a_L. The retailer prefers a low wholesale price, which the manufacturer is aware of. Thus, a H-type retailer has the incentive to mimic, and a L-type retailer has the incentive to reveal. Therefore, a separating equilibrium can be attained by maximizing the retailer's profit $\pi_1^{ii}(p_1, w_1)$ within the domain of p_1 satisfying the following constraint:

$$\pi_1^{HL}(p_1, w_1) \leq \max_{p_1} \pi_1^{HH}(p_1, w_1),$$

wherein the right-hand side depicts the optimal profit that the H-type retailer can achieve when he signals the true market size information. This is the incentive compatibility constraint that assures the credibility of the retailer's signal. By maximizing $\pi_1^{ii}(p_1, w_1)$ subject to the above incentive compatibility constraint, we derive the following separating equilibrium results.

Proposition 1. *A separating equilibrium always exists. The L-type retailer adopts the retail price*

$$p_1^s(w_1; a_L) = \begin{cases} \dfrac{a_L + w_1}{2}, & \text{if } w_1 \leq \dfrac{9a_L(\theta - 1)}{8} - h, \\ \dfrac{a_L + w_1}{2} - \dfrac{\delta}{6}, & \text{if } w_1 > \dfrac{9a_L(\theta - 1)}{8} - h, \end{cases}$$

and the H-type retailer adopts the retail price $p_1^s(w_1; a_H) = \frac{a_H + w_1}{2}$,

$$\delta = \sqrt{6a_L(\theta - 1)(h + w_1)} - 3a_L(\theta - 1) > 0.$$

From Proposition 1, when the manufacturer's wholesale price is high, i.e., $w_1 > \frac{9a_L(\theta-1)}{8} - h$, the L-type retailer has to distort downward his retail price to signal the information. While costly separating is achieved here, costless separating can be achieved in other cases.

4.1.2. *Pooling equilibrium*

If the retailer adopts a pooling strategy, the manufacturer does not update her belief but retains her *ex-ante* belief about market size. We adopt a threshold belief structure with a critical value $\hat{p}_1^p$, which is commonly seen in the literature (Jiang *et al.*, 2016; Guo and Jiang, 2016; Jiang and Yang, 2018). Specifically, in a pooling equilibrium, the manufacturer believes that the market size is a_H if she observes a selling price $p_1 > \hat{p}_1^p$, and retains her *ex-ante* belief if she observes a selling price $p_1 \leq \hat{p}_1^p$.

Note that in a pooling equilibrium, the manufacturer chooses a wholesale price w_2 by maximizing her expected profit in period 2; that is,

$$\Pi_2^{ip}(I) = \beta \Pi_2^{iH}(I) + (1 - \beta)\Pi_2^{iL}(I),$$

where $\Pi_2^{ij}(I)$, $j = L, H$ is given in Lemma 1. Note that we use the superscript p to replace the manufacturer's belief j in the pooling equilibrium. We have $w_2^{ip} = \frac{\mu}{2} - I$.

Submitting the retailer's profit in the period, we have

$$\pi_1^{ip}(w_1, p_1) = p_1(a_i - p_1) - w_1(a_i - p_1 + I) - hI$$
$$+ \frac{1}{16}(4a_i^2 - 4a_i\mu + \mu^2 + 8a_iI + 4\mu I - 12I^2).$$

Unlike separating equilibrium, a pooling equilibrium may not always exist. We follow Anand and Goyal's (2008) logic to obtain the condition for a pooling equilibrium to exist. We can first show that the selling price maximizing $\pi_1^{ip}(w_1, p_1)$ is $\frac{a_i+w_1}{2}$, $i = H, L$. Thus, the H-type retailer wants pool if $p_1 \leq \frac{a_H+w_1}{2}$ and the L-type retailer wants to pool if $p_1 \leq \frac{a_L+w_1}{2}$. Therefore, if both types of retailers are willing to pool, the upper bound of the pooling equilibrium is $\min\{\frac{a_L+w_1}{2} \frac{a_H+w_1}{2}\} = \frac{a_L+w_1}{2}$. We also have an incentive compatibility constraint for the pooling equilibrium

$$\pi_1^{ip}(w_1, p_1) \geq \max_{p_1 > \bar{p}_1^p} \pi_1^{iH}(w_1, p_1), \quad i = L, H.$$

Following Anand and Goyal's (2008) logic, we obtain the following results regarding the pooling equilibrium.

Proposition 2. *If $\beta \leq \bar{\beta}(w_1)$, a pooling equilibrium exists, and both types of retailers pool at $p_1^p = \frac{a_L+w_1}{2}$, where*

$$\bar{\beta}(w_1) = \frac{4h + 4w_1 + 3(\theta - 1)a_L - 2\sqrt{4h^2 + 8hw_1 + 4w_1^2 + 9(\theta - 1)^2 a_L^2}}{3(\theta - 1)a_L}.$$

4.1.3. *Comparison of separating and pooling*

Propositions 1 and 2 show the retailer's separating and pooling equilibria. We observe that when $\beta \leq \bar{\beta}(w_1)$ both the equilibria exist; and when $\beta > \bar{\beta}(w_1)$, only the separating equilibrium exists. When there exist multiple equilibria, we need to refine the equilibria. There are different equilibrium refinement rules. The *intuitive criterion* is one of the commonly seen one, which has a possible drawback that it may sometimes rule out pooling due to logical incompleteness (Mailath *et al.*, 1993). Recently, many researchers adopt a *lexicographically maximum sequential equilibrium* (LMSE) outcome to overcome this issue and leads to an undefeated equilibrium (see, for example, Tian and Jiang (2017); Jiang *et al.* (2016); Guo and Jiang (2016); Li *et al.* (2020)). Here, we also apply the latter concept, which selects the most profitable outcome for the type that wants to reveal identity. Recall that in our model, the L-type retailer has the incentive to separate from the H-type retailer. Therefore, we refine the multiple equilibria by choosing the equilibrium the L-type retailer can achieve a higher profit.

By comparing the L-type retailer's profit under the two kinds of equilibria, we present the following proposition:

$$\bar{\beta}(w_1) = \frac{4h + 4w_1 - \sqrt{\frac{16(h+w_1)^2 - 3(\theta-1)}{(8h+8w_1+15(\theta-1)a_L - 4\sqrt{3}\sqrt{(\theta-1)a_L(8h+8w_1+3(\theta-1)a_L)})}}}{3(\theta-1)a_L}.$$

Proposition 3. *If $\beta < \bar{\beta}(w_1)$, the unique LMSE for the retailer is to pool, and if $\bar{\beta}(w_1) < \beta \leq \bar{\beta}(w_1)$, the unique LMSE for the retailer is to separate.*

Note that the two thresholds $\bar{\beta}(w_1)$ and $\bar{\beta}(w_1)$ also depend on the parameter θ, which represents uncertainty in market size. To further investigate the equilibrium versus the uncertainty, we rewrite the condition under which costly separating is attained, and obtain $\theta \leq \frac{9a_L+8h+8w_1}{9a_L}$. We depict the equilibrium cases in Fig. 2. When the demand uncertainty is high enough, say $\theta > \frac{9a_L+8h+8w_1}{9a_L}$, the L-type retailer cannot benefit from mimicking the H-type retailer due to the high cost of imitation. In this case, the retailer reaches a costless separation. When the demand uncertainty is moderate, say $\theta \leq \frac{9a_L+8h+8w_1}{9a_L}$, the L-type retailer has the incentive to mimic the H-type firm. From Propositions 1 and 2, a costly separating equilibrium always exists, and a pooling equilibrium exists only is $\beta \leq \bar{\beta}(w_1)$. Thus, when $\beta \leq \bar{\beta}(w_1)$ both costly separating and pooling are possible. Proposition 3 further shows that the H-type retailer can makes a higher profit under pooling if $\beta < \bar{\beta}(w_1)$. Therefore, as shown in Fig. 2, a separating equilibrium exists for any combination of parameters, and a pooling equilibrium exists in zones I and II. Furthermore, the unique LMSE is pooling in zone I and is costly separating in zone II.

4.2. *The manufacturer's optimal wholesale price*

In this section, we go backwards to the manufacturer's wholesale pricing decision given the retailer's unique LMSE retail price specified in Proposition 3. Recall that

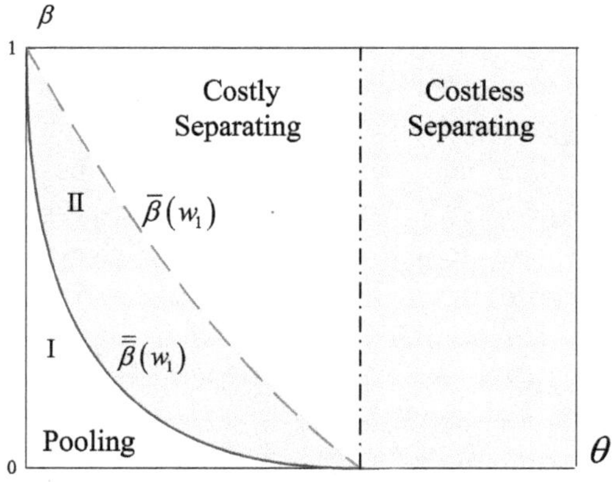

Fig. 2. The unique LMSE equilibrium under different system parameters.

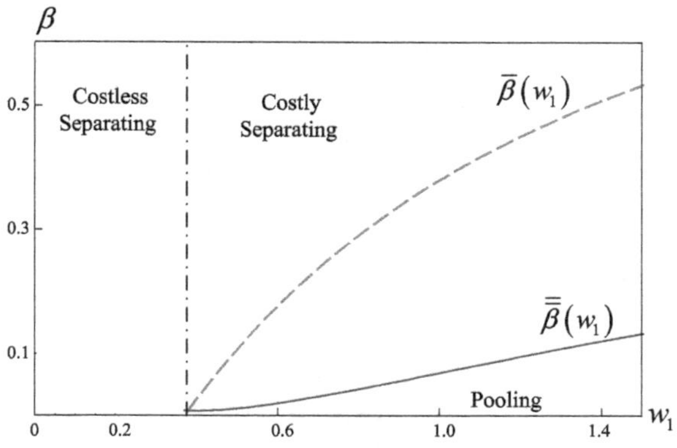

Fig. 3. The LMSE under different cases.

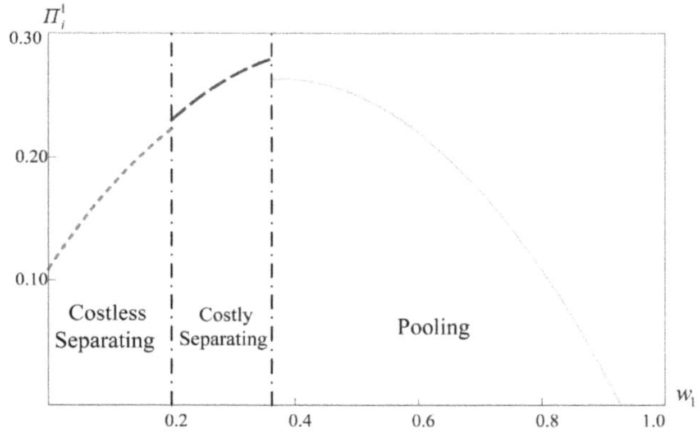

Fig. 4. The manufacturer's profit vs. the wholesale price w_1.

the retailer adopts a pooling equilibrium only if $\beta < \bar{\beta}(w_1)$, where the critical value $\bar{\beta}(w_1)$ depends on the wholesale price w_1. The complexity of the formulation of $\bar{\beta}(w_1)$ makes the theoretical analysis of the optimization of w_1 intractable. Therefore, in this section, we illustrate the equilibrium outcomes and the structural properties of the profit function $\Pi_1^i(w_1)$ given the retailer's optimal signaling price decision, by numerical examples.

In this numerical example, we set $a_L = 0.9, a_H = 1.5, \beta = 0.03, h = 0.3$. Figure 3 shows that the two thresholds $\bar{\beta}(w_1)$ and $\bar{\bar{\beta}}(w_1)$ increase in w_1. We observe that when w_1 is small, the retailer always achieves a costless separating. As w_1 increases, the retailer either adopts costly separating or pools. Specifically, when β is large, the retailer adopts costly separating, and when β is small, the retailer pools, which is consistent with the commonly held beliefs. If the probability of a large market size is very low, the effect of information asymmetry is also weak. Then, an L-type retailer has little incentive to separate.

By further fixing the value of β, we obtain the manufacturer's optimal profit versus the wholesale price w_1 (see Fig. 4). In this numerical example, we set $a_L = 0.9, a_H = 1.5, \beta = 0.02, h = 0.7$, the optimal wholesale price attained is $w_1 = 0.37$, wherein the retailer adopts costly separating. We conduct extensive numerical studies and find that an optimal solution is obtained by either separating or pooling.

5. With Blockchain Technology and Discussion

In the previous section, we analyzed the case without adopting the blockchain technology. In this section, we consider using the blockchain technology to remove the information asymmetry, and then compare the supply chain members' performance under the two scenarios. We use superscripts "B" and "N" to represent the cases with and without blockchain technology, respectively.

When the blockchain technology is adopted and the information asymmetry on the market size is removed, both the manufacturer and the retailer can observe the true market size, a_H or a_L, at beginning of the first period. The strategic inventory under the symmetric information scenario is investigated in Anand *et al.* (2008). In Anand *et al.* (2008), there is no uncertainty in the market size. In our case with the adoption of the blockchain technology, the uncertainty on the market size is resolved in stage 1a as illustrated in Table 1. Given the observed market size a_i, we let $\Pi^B(a_i)$ and $\pi^B(a_i)$ be the manufacturer and the retailer's profits, respectively, where the superscript "B" refers to the adoption of the "blockchain technology". Then from Anand *et al.* (2008), we have

$$\Pi^B(a_i) = \frac{155a_i^2 - 112a_ih + 304h^2}{1156b}, \quad \pi^B(a_i) = \frac{9a^2 - 4a_ih + 8h^2}{34b}.$$

Taking the expectation over the market size a_i, we have the manufacturer and the retailer's expected profits are

$$\Pi^B = \mathrm{E}_{a_i}[\Pi^B(a_i)], \quad \text{and} \quad \pi^B = \mathrm{E}_{a_i}[\pi^B(a_i)].$$

We also let $\Pi^B_{sc} = \Pi^B + \pi^B$ be the supply chain's total profit.

Without the adoption of the blockchain technology, the signaling game arises between the manufacturer and the retailer. We also let Π^N, π^N, and Π^N_{sc} be the manufacturer, the retailer, and the supply chain's profit in this case. Recall that the market size is a_H with probability β and a_L with probability $1-\beta$. Thus, the manufacturer's expected profit can be easily obtained by taking expectations over the profit under the two market sizes cases. The proof is straightforward and thus omitted.

Lemma 3. *Without the adoption of the blockchain technology, the manufacturer's expected profits are*

$$\Pi^N(w_1) = w_1\left[\frac{3\mu}{2} - (\beta \cdot p_1(w_1; a_H) + (1-\beta) \cdot p_1(w_1; a_L))\right] - \frac{(4w_1 - 1)(w_1 + h)}{6},$$

where $p_1(w_1; a_i)$ are given in Proposition 1, $i = H, L$.

Note that the profits in Lemma 3 is given in terms of w_1. This is because the optimal w_1 cannot be expressed in a closed from; see Sec. 4. Therefore, regarding the supply chain members' profits without the adoption of the blockchain technology, we conduct a numerical study.

We plot the supply chain members' profits in Fig. 5, where we use a red solid curve to depict the profits with the adoption of the blockchain technology, and we use a curve with dashes to depict the profits without the adoption of the blockchain technology. Figures 4(a)–4(c) show the profit for the manufacturer, retailer, and the supply chain, respectively.

In the numerical study, we set $\alpha_L = 0.8, h = 0.18, \beta = 0.4$, and we let θ vary in the interval $[1, +\infty]$. With this data setting, costly separating is the LMSE when $\theta < 1.74$, and costless separating is the LMSE, otherwise. Figure 5(a) shows the manufacturer's profit. We can observe that when the demand uncertainty θ is small, the manufacturer's profit is higher when the blockchain technology is not adopted, however, as θ increases, the manufacturer earns a higher profit when the blockchain technology is adopted. This implies that when the demand uncertainty is low, the manufacturer does not have the incentive to adopt the blockchain technology; however, when the demand uncertainty is high, the manufacturer will want to adopt the blockchain technology. This is easy to understand. Adopting the blockchain technology will help the manufacturer to obtain the retailer's private information on the market size. The value of this information increases as the demand uncertainty increases. Therefore, the manufacturer has a higher incentive to adopt the technology when the information has a higher value.

Figure 5(b) shows a different pattern regarding the retailer's profit. An interesting observation from Fig. 5(b) is that when a costless separating is achieved, the retailer's profit is not equal to but lower than that with the blockchain technology. In signaling games, when costless separating is attained, there is no cost for the one signaling the information so that there should no difference in the profit. Here, in our model, there exists difference in the retailer's profit at costless separating. This is because the manufacturer makes the wholesale price decision before the retailer's signaling decision. The manufacturer varies the wholesale price decisions under the two cases so that the retailer makes different profits even when the costless separating is attained. Figure 5(b) shows that the retailer has the incentive to adopt the blockchain technology only when the demand uncertainty is either low or high. Comparing the results in Figs. 5(a) and 5(b), we can see that when the demand uncertainty is low to moderate, the retailer and the manufacturer may have misalignment in adopting the blockchain technology, and when the demand uncertainty is high, they can both agree to the adoption of the blockchain technology.

When the manufacturer and the retailer cannot agree on the adoption of the blockchain technology, a natural question is whether a central planner can coordinate the two supply chain members? Figure 5(c) shows the possibility of the coordination, where the supply chain's total profit can be improved by adopting the blockchain technology when the demand uncertainty is moderate. Recall that

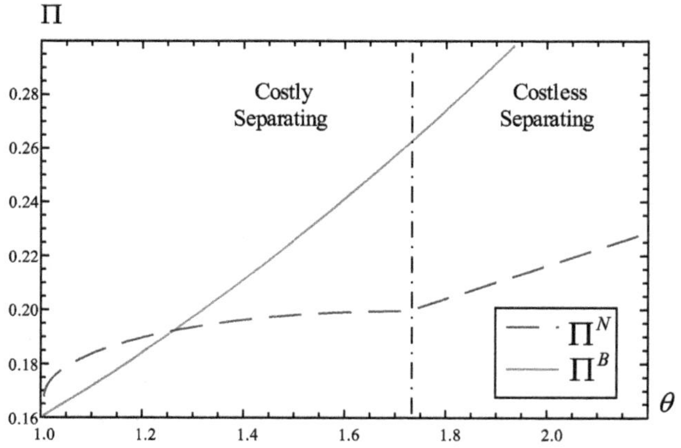

(a) Manufacturer's profit

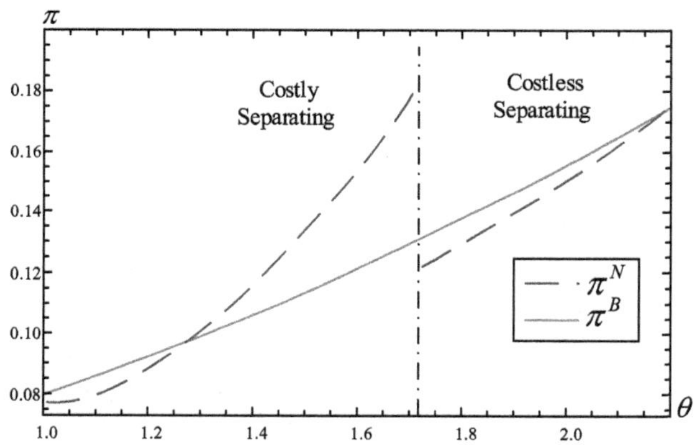

(b) Retailer's profit

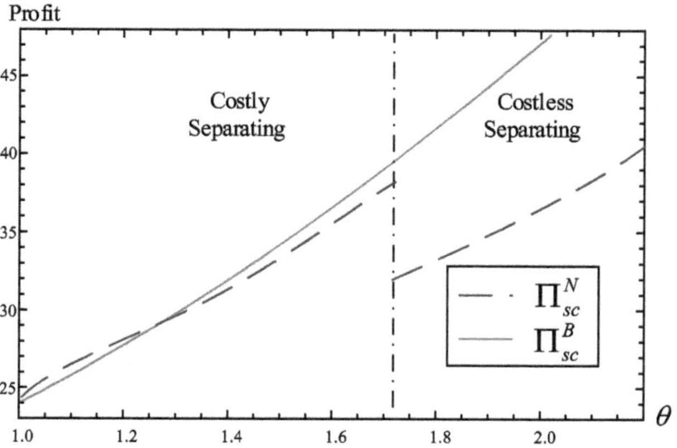

(c) Supply chain's total profit

Fig. 5. The supply chain members' profit with/without the blockchain technology.

we do not consider the cost for adopting the blockchain technology. It is interesting to observe that the adoption of blockchain is not always beneficial, even if it is costless. If the cost for the adoption of the blockchain technology is further included, the benefits from adopting the blockchain technology can be even more limited.

6. Conclusion

In this paper, we study supply chain members' incentives to adopt the blockchain technology in a two-period strategic inventory model. Without the blockchain technology, the retailer has private information about the market size, and signals the information via the retail price and the strategic inventory level in period 1. We derive both separating and pooling equilibria for the retailers and compare the two types of equilibria to determine the unique LMSE for the signaling game. When the blockchain technology is adopted, this kind of information asymmetry can be resolved. We numerically compare the supply chain members' profit under the two scenarios to investigate the incentives for the supply chain members to adopt the blockchain technology. We find that the manufacturer has the incentive to adopt the blockchain technology for a wide range of the demand uncertainty, but the retailer has the incentive for a smaller range. When they have misalignment on the incentive, a central planner may help to achieve this.

This paper has several limitations. First, focusing on the use of strategic inventory, we consider deterministic demand functions to eliminate the incentives of carrying inventory from the operational perspective. Future research may consider the joint effect of operational and strategic perspectives of carrying inventory. Second, we investigate only the retailer's signaling equilibria. Sophisticated contracts between the supply chain members could also be investigated.

Appendix A

Proof of Lemma 1. It suffices to derive the retailer and the manufacturer's optimal decisions. The retailer's profit in period 2 can be written as $\pi_2^{ij}(w_2, p_2; I) = p_2(a_i - p_2) - w_2(a_i - p_2 - I)$. It is easy to check the profit is concave in p_2. From the first order conditions (FOC), we have the retailer's optimal price is $p_2^{ij}(I, w_2) = \frac{a_i + w_2}{2}$. Consider manufacturer's wholesale price w_2. In the manufacturer's belief, the market size is a_j. Thus, the manufacturer will expect a retailing price $\frac{a_j + w_2}{2}$, Substituting the expected retail price to the manufacturer's profit function and applying FOC, we have $w_2^j(I) = \frac{a_j}{2} - I$. Lemma 1 proved by substituting the optimal decision to the corresponding profit functions. □

Proof of Lemma 2. The retailer's profit in period 1 can be written as

$$\pi_1^{ij}(p_1, w_1, I) = p_1(a_i - p_1) - w_1(a_i - p_1 + I) - hI + \pi_2^{ij}(I).$$

From the FOC condition, we have $I^*(w_1) = \frac{2a_i + a_j - 4w_1 - 4h}{6}$, $p_1(w_1) = \frac{a_i + w_1}{2}$. Substituting the two variables to $\pi_1^{ij}(w_1)$, we obtain Lemma 2. □

Proof of Proposition 1. First note that the H-type retailer has no incentive to mimic the L-type retailer's pricing if and only if

$$\pi_1^{HL}(p_1, w_1) \le \max_{p_1} \pi_1^{HH}(p_1, w_1),$$

from which we obtain $w_1 \le \frac{9a_L(\theta-1)}{8} - h$. Thus, if $w_1 > \frac{9a_L(\theta-1)}{8} - h$, then the H-type retailer has the inventive to mimic the L-type retailer pricing decision. Therefore, to achieve a separating equilibrium, the L-type retailer may need to distort his price to separate from the H-type retailer. Let $p_1^S(w_1; a_L)$ be a possible separating price. We have

$$\pi_1^{HL}(p_1^s, w_1) \le \max_{p_1} \pi_1^{HH}(p_1, w_1).$$

Expanding this condition, and for a pure strategy separating equilibrium to exist, $p_1^s(w_1; a_i), i = H, L$ must emerge as a simultaneous solution to the following constrained optimization program.

$$\begin{aligned}
&\max_{p_1} \pi_1^{LL}(p_1, w_1, I^*(w_1)) \\
&\quad = p_1(a_L - p_1) - w_1(a_L - p_1 + I^*(w_1)) - hI^*(w_1) \\
&\qquad + \frac{1}{16}(a_L^2 + 12a_L I^*(w_1) - 12I^*(w_1)^2) \\
&s.t. \quad (a_H - p_1)p_1 - w_1(a_H - p_1 + I^*(w_1)) - hI^*(w_1) + \pi_2^{HL}(I^*(w_1)) \\
&\quad \le \pi_1^{HH}(I^*(w_1)), \qquad \text{(A.1)}
\end{aligned}$$

where $I^*(w_1) = \frac{2a_i + a_j - 4w_1 - 4h}{6}$ and $\pi_1^{HH}(I) = \frac{6a_H^2 + 4h^2 + 8hw_1 + 7w_1^2 - 6a_H(h + 2w_1)}{12}$. Solving the above problem, we can obtain the threshold price as follows.

$$p_1^S(w_1; a_L) = \frac{1}{6}(3a_H + 3w_1 - \sqrt{6(a_H - a_L)(h + w_1)}).$$

Regarding the H-type retailer, since he can't mimic L-type retailer by adopting the same price $p_1^S(w_1; a_L)$, his optimal strategy is applying the optimal price under full information, i.e., $p_1^s(w_1; a_H) = \frac{a_H + w_1}{2}$. Proposition 1 is proved. □

Proof of Proposition 2. We first establish the optimal preferred pooling price in the first period, say p_{1p}^{*H} and p_{1p}^{*L} for the H-type retailer and L-type retailer respectively. Suppose there exists a pooling price p_{1p}. Upon observing this price, the manufacturer cannot separate the market size type and has to stick to her *ex-ante* belief, i.e., there is no updating on the market size. Thus, the wholesale price decision in period 2 is still based on his *ex-ante* belief, i.e., $w_2^S(a_j) = \frac{\mu}{2} - I$. It is easy to check that the retailer's best response selling price will be $p_2^S(w_2; a_i) = \frac{a_i + w_2}{2} = \frac{1}{4}(2a_i - 2I + \mu)$. Hence, the supply chain members' profit in period 2 can be obtained as follows.

$$\pi_2^{ip}(I) = \frac{1}{16}(4a_i^2 - 4a_i\mu + \mu^2 + 8a_iI + 4\mu I - 12I^2),$$

$$\Pi_2^{ip}(I) = \frac{1}{8}(\mu - 2I)(3\mu - 2a_i - 2I).$$

Then, we consider the retailer's profit in period 1. For the i-type retailer, where $i = HL$, the expected total profit is

$$\pi_1^{ip}(p_1; a_i) = p_1(a_i - p_1) - w_1(a_i - p_1 + I) - hI + \frac{1}{16}(4a_i^2 - 4a_i\mu + \mu^2 + 8a_iI + 4\mu I - 12I^2).$$

It is easy to check that the optimal price to maximizing the above profit function is $p_1^{ip} = \frac{a_i + w_1}{2}$. According to Anand and Goyal (2009), any pooling equilibrium must satisfy

$$p_1^p \le \min(p_{1p}^{*H}, p_{1p}^{*L}) = \frac{a_L + w_1}{2} := \bar{p}_1^p,$$

the right-hand side of which is the upper bound of the pooling equilibrium.

The H-type retailer prefers to pool if he can make a better profit with pooling rather than separating, i.e.,

$$p_1^p(a_H - p_1^p) - w_1(a_H - p_1^p + I) - hI + \frac{1}{16}(4a_H^2 - 4a_H\mu + \mu^2 + 8a_HI + 4I - 12I^2)$$
$$\ge \max_{p_1(w_1;a_H) > p_1^p} p_1(w_1; a_H)(a_H - p_1(w_1; a_H)) - w_1(a_H - p_1(w_1; a_H) + I) - hI + \frac{1}{16}(a_H^2 + 12a_HI - 12I^2).$$

Solving the above inequality, we obtain

$$p_1^p \ge \frac{1}{12}(6a_H + 6w_1 - \sqrt{3}\sqrt{3a_H^2 + 8a_Hh - 6a_H\mu - 8h\mu + 3\mu^2 + 8a_Hw_1 - 8\mu w_1}).$$

We apply the same logic to the L-type retailer and obtain that

$$p_1^p \ge \frac{1}{12}\left(6a_L + 6w_1 - \sqrt{3}\sqrt{\begin{matrix}3\mu^2 - 3a_H^2 + 6a_Ha_L - 6a_L\mu + 8a_Hh - 8h\mu \\ +8a_Hw_1 - 8\mu w_1\end{matrix}}\right).$$

To have the above two inequalities hold simultaneously, we define

$$\underline{p_1^p} = \frac{1}{12}(6a_H + 6w_1 - \sqrt{3}\sqrt{3a_H^2 + 8a_Hh - 6a_H\mu - 8h\mu + 3\mu^2 + 8a_Hw_1 - 8\mu w_1}).$$

Therefore, to support the existence of a pooling equilibrium, we shall have $\underline{p_1^p} < \bar{p}_1^p$, solving which we obtain

$$\beta \le \bar{\beta}(w_1) := \frac{1}{3(a_H - a_L)}(3a_H - 3a_L + 4h + 4w_1 - 2\sqrt{9a_H^2 - 18a_Ha_L + 9a_L^2 + 4(h + w_1)^2}).$$

Therefore, a pooling equilibrium exists if and only $\beta \leq \bar{\beta}(w_1)$. Proposition 2 is proved. □

Proof of Proposition 3. From Mailath *et al.* (1993), the LMSE selects the most profitable equilibrium for the type intends to reveal its identity. Therefore, in our model, we can compare the profit for the L-type retailer under the pooling and the separating equilibrium to determine the LMSE. Solving $\pi_1^p(w_1) \geq \pi_1^{LL}(w_1)$, we obtain

$$\beta \leq \frac{4h + 4w_1 - \sqrt{\frac{16(h+w_1)^2 - 3(\theta-1)}{(8h+8w_1+15(\theta-1)a_L - 4\sqrt{3}\sqrt{(\theta-1)a_L(8h+8w_1+3(\theta-1)a_L)})}}}{3(\theta-1)a_L} := \bar{\beta}(w_1).$$

Recall that a pooling equilibrium exists if $\beta \leq \bar{\beta}(w_1)$. Proposition 3 is thus proved. □

Acknowledgments

This research was supported in party by the National Natural Science Foundation of China (Grant Nos. 71872036, 71871052, 71832001 and 71501037) and the Fundamental Research Funds for the Central Universities (2232018H-07). The first author was also supported in part by the Humanities and Social Sciences Foundation of Ministry of Education of China (Grant No. 18YJA630153), and the Shanghai Social Science Foundation (Grant No. 2017BGL018). The second author was also supported in part by DHU Distinguished Young Professor Program.

References

Anand, K, R Anupindi and Y Bassok (2008). Strategic inventories in vertical contracts. *Management Science*, 54(10), 1792–1804.

Anand, KS and M Goyal (2009). Strategic information management under leakage in a supply chain. *Management Science*, 55(3), 438–452.

Arya, A, H Frimor and B Mittendorf (2015). Decentralized procurement in light of strategic inventories. *Management Science*, 61(3), 578–585.

Arya, A and B Mittendorf (2013). Managing strategic inventories via manufacturer-to-consumer rebates. *Management Science*, 59(4), 813–818.

Babich, V and G Hilary (2020). OM Forum — Distributed Ledgers and Operations: What Operations Management Researchers Should Know About Blockchain Technology. *Manufacturing & Service Operations Management*, 22(2), 223–240.

Bakshi, N, SH Kim and N Savva (2015). Signaling new product reliability with after-sales service contracts. *Management Science*, 61(8), 1812–1829.

Cachon, GP and MA Lariviere (2001). Contracting to assure supply: How to share demand forecasts in a supply chain. *Management science*, 47(5), 629–646.

Cai, YJ, TM Choi and J Zhang (2020). Platform supported supply chain operations in the blockchain era: Supply contracting and moral hazards. Decision Sciences, forthcoming.

Chod, J, N Trichakis, G Tsoukalas, H Aspegren and M Weber (2020). On the financing benefits of supply chain transparency and blockchain adoption. *Management Science*, 66(10), 4359–4349.

Choi, TM (2019). Blockchain-technology-supported platforms for diamond authentication and certification in luxury supply chains. *Transportation Research Part E: Logistics and Transportation Review*, 128, 17–29.

Choi, TM, L Feng and R Li (2020). Information disclosure structure in supply chains with rental service platforms in the blockchain technology era. *International Journal of Production Economics*, 221, 107473.

Choi, TM and S Luo (2019). Data quality challenges for sustainable fashion supply chain operations in emerging markets: Roles of blockchain, government sponsors and environment taxes. *Transportation Research Part E: Logistics and Transportation Review*, 131, 139–152.

Dey, K, S Roy and S Saha (2019). The impact of strategic inventory and procurement strategies on green product design in a two-period supply chain. *International Journal of Production Research*, 57(7), 1915–1948.

Dong, C, Y Yang and M Zhao (2018). Dynamic selling strategy for a firm under asymmetric information: Direct selling vs. agent selling. *International Journal of Production Economics*, 204, 204–213.

Fan, ZP, XY Wu and BB Cao (2020). Considering the traceability awareness of consumers: should the supply chain adopt the blockchain technology? *Annals of Operations Research*, forthcoming.

Guan, H, H Gurnani, X Geng and Y Luo (2019). Strategic inventory and supplier encroachment. *Manufacturing & Service Operations Management*, 21(3), 536–555.

Guo, X and B Jiang (2016). Signaling through price and quality to consumers with fairness concerns. *Journal of Marketing Research*, 53(6), 988–1000.

Ha, AY and S Tong (2008). Contracting and information sharing under supply chain competition. *Management Science*, 54(4), 701–715.

Huang, Y and Z Wang (2017). Information sharing in a closed-loop supply chain with technology licensing. *International Journal of Production Economics*, 191, 113–127.

Jain, A and M Sohoni (2015). Should firms conceal information when dealing with common suppliers? *Naval Research Logistics*, 62(1), 1–15.

Jiang, B, L Tian, Y Xu and F Zhang (2016). To share or not to share: Demand forecast sharing in a distribution channel. *Marketing Science*, 35(5), 800–809.

Li, Z, SM Gilbert and G Lai (2014). Supplier encroachment under asymmetric information. *Management science*, 60(2), 449–462.

Li, Q, H Ding, T Shi and Y Tang (2020). To share or not to share: The optimal advertising effort with asymmetric advertising effectiveness. *Annuals of Operations Research*, forthcoming.

Li, Q and J Zhou (2019). A horizontal capacity reservation game under asymmetric information. *International Journal of Production Research*, 57(4), 1103–1118.

Li, G, H Zheng, SP Sethi and X Guan (2020). Inducing downstream information sharing via manufacturer information acquisition and retailer subsidy. *Decision Sciences*, 51(3), 691–719.

Martinez de Albeniz, V and D Simchi-Levi (2013). Supplier-buyer negotiation games: Equilibrium conditions and supply chain efficiency. *Production and Operations Management*, 22, 397–409.

Mailath G, M Okuno-Fujiwara and A Postlewaite (1993). Belief-based refinements in signaling games. *Journal of Economic Theory*, 60(2), 241–276.

Mantin, B and L Jiang (2017). Strategic inventories with quality deterioration. *European Journal of Operational Research*, 258(1), 155–164.

Moon, I, K Dey and S Saha (2018). Strategic inventory: Manufacturer vs. retailer investment. *Transportation Research Part E: Logistics and Transportation Review*, 109, 63–82.

Newbold, A (2019). Louis Vuitton to launch first blockchain to help authenticate luxury goods. Vogue. May 17. https://www.vogue.co.uk/article/lvmhblockchain.

Pollock, D (2020). BMW opens its doors for mobility open blockchain initiative's first European colloquium. Forbes. https://www.forbes.com/sites/darrynpollock/2019/02/15/bmw-opens-its-doors-for-mobility-open-blockchain-initiatives-first-european-colloquium/#fb64dca7f1d4.

Roy, A, SM Gilbert and G Lai (2019). The implications of visibility on the use of strategic inventory in a supply chain. *Management Science*, 65(4), 1752–1767.

Shen, B, X Xu and Q Yuan (2020). Selling secondhand products through an online platform with blockchain. *Transportation Research Part E: Logistics and Transportation Review*, 142, 102066.

Tian, L and B Jiang (2017) Comment on "Strategic Information Management Under Leakage in a Supply Chain". *Management Science*, 63(12), 4258–4260.

Yan, Y, R Zhao and Y Lan (2019a). Moving sequence preference in coopetition outsourcing supply chain: Consensus or conflict. *International Journal of Production Economics*, 208, 221–240.

Yan, Y, R Zhao and T Xing (2019b). Strategic introduction of the marketplace channel under dual upstream disadvantages in sales efficiency and demand information. *European Journal of Operational Research*, 273(3), 968–982.

Ye, Q, I Duenyas and R Kapuscinski (2013). Should competing firms reveal their capacity? *Naval Research Logistics*, 60(1), 64–86.

Zhao, X, L Xue and F Zhang (2014). Outsourcing competition and information sharing with asymmetrically informed suppliers. *Production and Operations Management*, 23(10), 1706–1718.

Zipkin, PH (2000). *Foundations of Inventory Management.* Boston: McGraw-Hill.

Biography

Jianheng Zhou is a professor at the Glorious Sun School of Business and Management, Donghua University, China. She received her Ph.D. degree from Donghua University. Her research interests include supply chain management, operation management and supply chain optimization. She has published papers in *Decision Support Systems, European Journal of Operational Research, International Journal of Production Research, Electronic Commerce Research and Applications*, and many conference proceedings.

Qingying Li is a professor at the Glorious Sun School of Business and Management, Donghua University, China. She received her Ph.D. degree from the Hong Kong Polytechnic University. She has published her works in *Production and Operations Management, International Journal of Production Economics, International Journal of Production Research, Annals of Operations Research, Operations Research Letters*, etc. Her research interests include supply chain management, strategic queueing theory, and service operations management.

https://doi.org/10.1142/9789819808588_0006

Chapter 6

Cooperative Promotion of Cross-Market Firms Adopting 3D Printing Technology†

Ke Yan
School of Economics and Management
Beijing, Jiaotong University, Beijing
100044, P. R. China
17113147@bjtu.edu.cn

Guowei Hua*
School of Economics and Management
Beijing Jiaotong University, Beijing
100044, P. R. China
huagw@amss.ac.cn

T. C. E. Cheng
Faculty of Business
The Hong Kong Polytechnic University
Hong Kong, P. R. China
edwin.cheng@polyu.edu.hk

Traditionally, firms often run independent promotional activities to attract consumers and improve their competitiveness. With the rapid development of three-dimensional (3D) printing, also known as additive manufacturing, a growing number of firms in different markets cooperate to conduct cooperative promotion to meet consumer demand. Different from independent promotion, which means that firms promote their products through their individual promotional activities, when they carry out cooperative promotion, in addition to their individual promotional activities, they also carry out a series of cooperative promotional activities to promote their products. For such cross-market cooperation, it is of importance to consider the unit cost of production and the promotion cost to achieve competitive advantage and sustainability of the supply chain. We develop game-theoretic models to investigate the factors that make firms pursue cooperative promotion and how cooperative promotion affects their optimal decisions. We find that whether or not the firms join cooperative promotion mainly depends on the impacts of price, individual promotional activities, and cooperative promotional activities on demand, as well as the unit cost of production. Whether or not firms are willing to make more contribution to cooperative promotion depends on the difference between the efforts of individual promotional activities and cooperative promotional activities. In

*Corresponding author.
†To cite this article, please refer to its earlier version published in the Asia-Pacific Journal of Operational Research, Vol. 39, No. 1, (February 2022), DOI: 10.1142/S0217595921400285. Reprinted with permission from World Scientific Publishing Co. Pte. Ltd.

addition, as the consumer demand for the product increases, the firms will also increase their investments in cooperative and independent promotional activities. Moreover, as the unit cost of production and the impact of cooperative promotional activities on demand change, pursuing cooperative promotion is not necessarily more profitable than pursuing independent promotion.

Keywords: Industry 4.0; 3D printing; cooperative promotion; cross market; game theory.

1. Introduction

1.1. *Background and motivation*

Additive manufacturing, also known as three-dimensional (3D) printing, is an innovative technology for manufacturing (Sasson and Johnson, 2016). 3D printing is considered to be one of the core innovative technologies underpinning the rapid development of Industry 4.0 (Dilberoglu *et al.*, 2017). The overall market size of the global 3D printing industry reached US $119.6 billion in 2019, at a high growth rate of 29.9%. Meanwhile, with the rapid development of China's 3D printing market, the market size may exceed US$30 billion in 2020.

3D printing has existed for a long time, but with the continuous improvement in technology and reduction in cost, 3D printing has gradually become widespread among firms (Rayna and Striukova, 2016). Especially in the era of Industry 4.0, 3D printing is of great significance for intelligent production. German sports brand Adidas released its 3D printed running shoes Futurecraft3D, developed in collaboration with Belgian 3D printing company Materialise, in 2015. This innovative product has attracted considerable consumer attention. In view of the success of Adidas, 3D printing firm Prodways partnered with Nike to 3D print sneakers, while 3D printing firm Formlabs jointed hands with New Balance to produce 3D printed running shoes. Similarly, in the automobile industry, there are many cooperation efforts between auto manufacturers and 3D printing firms. For instance, car manufacturers Geely and Harvard cooperate with 3D printing firm Vistar, Audi partners with 3D Hubs, and Volvo works with Materialise to produce 3D printed automobile parts and components. In addition, there are abundant examples of such cross-market cooperation in various industries, such as aerospace, architecture, art, consumer goods etc. Such cooperations across firms in different markets not only promote the wide application of 3D printing, but also help each partnering firm expand beyond its own market and increase the exposure of its products to a wide range of customers through cross-market collaboration.

Under the siege of the COVID-19 pandemic, 3D printing helps solve the problem of shortage in medical supplies caused by disruption in the transport system. The United States, Italy, and other countries have applied 3D printing to produce ventilator parts and personal protective masks to solve the shortage problem of emergency medical supplies. In addition, 3D printing firms Prodways and 3D Hubs have cooperated with medical technology manufacturers to produce the key parts of medical devices and protective products. With the development and application of

3D printing in various industries, more and more manufacturers choose to partner with 3D printing firms to offer a wide variety of products. However, manufacturers will incur additional production cost in partnering with 3D printing firms to produce products. In addition, there are additional costs related to the advertisement, preferential treatment, and administrative measures that manufacturers take to attract more consumers. So, the impacts of production and promotional costs on cross-market collaboration is significant and need studying.

The above anecdotal evidence indicates that collaboration across firms serving different markets adopting 3D printing is an emerging issue that needs addressing. Although it is common in practice that cross-market firms adopting 3D printing cooperate in promoting their product/services, there are few studies on the cooperation of cross-market firms. The firms have no knowledge of how to craft their optimal operations under cooperation. Moreover, the potential theoretical implications of cooperation for firms are unknown. To fill the above gap, we study in this research the impacts of cooperative promotion of two cross-market firms that adopt 3D printing to produce products on their optimal decisions and the sustainable development of their supply chains. Specifically, we develop game-theoretic models to address the following questions: (1) Under what conditions should the firms pursue cooperative promotion? (2) How does the unit cost of production impact the cooperative promotion? (3) What are the impacts of cooperative promotion on the firms' optimal strategies?

1.2. *Main findings and contributions*

To answer the above research problems, we analyze both independent promotion and cooperative promotion. Under the independent promotion scheme, the two firms attract consumers through their own promotional activities independently, whereas under the cooperative promotion scheme, the two firms conduct a series of promotional activities together, in addition to their own independent promotional activities.

Our main findings are as follows: (1) Regardless of the promotion scheme that a firm adopts, successful cooperative promotion depends not only on the unit costs of production of the products, but also on the effects of the prices, and individual and cooperative promotion on demand. (2) When the effect of cooperative promotional activities on demand is greater than that of independent promotional activities, the firms are more willing to make more effort for cooperative promotional activities; otherwise, the firms prefer independent promotion. (3) As the consumer demands for the products rise, the firms are more willing to make more contribution to independent and cooperative promotional activities. (4) When the unit cost of production is relatively small, the firms can get more profits if they are less influenced by the cooperative promotional activities; otherwise, cooperative promotion will result in less profits for the involved firms. (5) When the unit cost of production is relatively large, whether the firms can earn more profits varies with changes in the effects of price and cooperative promotional activities on demand.

We make three contributions in this study as follows: (1) With the adoption of 3D printing, we analyze the cross-market firms' optimal strategies for cooperative promotion and their profitability. (2) Different from previous studies that mostly focus on cooperation between firms selling competitive and complementary products, we consider cooperation of cross-market firms, subject to the impacts of production and promotional costs. (3) Our findings help cross-market firms manage cooperative promotion more effectively and improve their profitability, furthering the sustainability of their respective supply chains.

We organize the rest of the paper as follows: In Sec. 2, we provide a brief review of the literature to identify the research gap and position our paper. In Sec. 3, we introduce the models and derive the Nash equilibrium solutions. In Sec. 4, we derive the findings on cooperative promotion of cross-market firms adopting 3D printing. Finally, in Sec. 5, we conclude the paper, discuss the managerial implications of the results, and suggest topics for future research.

2. Literature Review

The first application of 3D printing was documented in the 1990s. Due to the limitations of the nascent technology at that time, 3D printing was limited to the production of plastic models of objects (Rayna and Striukova, 2016). With the continuous development of the associated production and material technologies, 3D printing has been more and more widely used, and is no longer distant from consumers (Gosselin *et al.*, 2016).

Many studies have considered how 3D printing affects manufacturing and the supply chain (Rayna *et al.*, 2015; Berman, 2012; Mellor *et al.*, 2014; Liu *et al.*, 2014; Khajavi, 2014; Holmstrm *et al.*, 2016; Rogers *et al.*, 2014), e.g., reducing the inventory stock (Liu *et al.*, 2014), designing the supply chain configuration (Mellor *et al.*, 2014), changing the transport and logistics support functions (Boon and Van, 2018). Taking the design of mobile phone accessories for example, Beltagui *et al.* (2020) found that 3D printing can help enterprises overcome resource constraints, ultimately stimulating the growth of consumer demand, and continuously promoting the sustainable and innovative development of the supply chain. In addition, with the adoption of 3D printing, Weller *et al.* (2015) analyzed and summarized the four key criteria of manufacturing enterprises. Meanwhile, when the market is monopolistic or competitive, they studied how the firm can obtain higher profits by setting different prices for different types of products. With respect to the 3D printing platform, Rayna *et al.* (2015) analyzed how the platform impacts the co-creation activity and consumers through empirical research. Sun *et al.* (2020) investigated the pricing and optimal strategies of a 3D printing platform that provides consumers with standardized and personalized products, considering the product quality and labour cost. Meanwhile, when the platform pursues profit maximization and consumers pursue utility maximization, they compared the 3D printing platform's profits under the two scenarios where the platform has full pricing power and partial pricing power. Some other studies focus on finding the factors that affect the adoption of 3D printing. Schniederjans (2017) found that the individual characteristics of top management play a critical role in the adoption of 3D printing and the speed of adoption through a survey of 270 representatives of company executives. Chan *et al.* (2018) found that while 3D printing is becoming more well known and many firms in China are trying to capture the development opportunity, due to patent problems, 3D printing has not been well adopted and developed. Given this finding, they proposed that the patent platform and other methods be established in order to effectively solve the current dilemma.

Our study is also related to research on cooperative promotion. There is a large body of literature that focuses on different supply chain structures, cooperative mechanism settings, as well as presenting dynamic and static models to study cooperative promotion between manufacturers and retailers within the same supply chain (Aust and Buscher, 2014). Meanwhile, the papers on cooperative promotion can be divided into main two parts: a simple marketing channel involving a supplier and a retailer, and a complex marketing channel involving multiple manufacturers or multiple retailers (Jrgensen and Zaccour, 2014). As for research on the supply chain consisting of a supplier and a retailer, He *et al.* (2019) investigated supply chain coordination that can be achieved in the consumer electronics industry where the manufacturer offers different promotional subsidy rates to the retailer selling two generations of the product considering transfer payments. In the presence of demand uncertainty, Tsao (2015) studied how cooperative promotion affects the optimal decisions of the risk-neutral manufacturer and retailer. Meanwhile, there are many studies on the impacts of various factors in the supply chain on vertical cooperative promotion, e.g., considering the different power structures of supply chain members under a general demand function (Chaab and Rasti-Barzoki, 2016) and the negative impacts of some variables on demand (Ahmadi-Javid and Hoseinpour, 2012). Considering the competition among retailers, Wang *et al.* (2011) investigated the optimal decision-making of all the players and the optimal game structure to achieve channel coordination. The manufacturer would provide a promotional subsidy to the retailer to protect the profitability of the retailer and the supply chain with a positive threshold (He *et al.*, 2011). Moreover, several studies examine the impacts of cooperative promotion on the participants and supply chain from different perspectives, considering the negative impacts of promotional efforts on the manufacturers brand image (Huang *et al.*, 2018), consumers reference effect (Zhang *et al.*, 2013), different channel structures and decision sequences (Chutani and Sethi, 2018), the nonlinear dynamic system (Guo and Ma, 2018), organizational form (Bogetoft, 2021), and uncertain basic costs (Sarkar *et al.*, 2020). In addition to studying the optimal decisions on price, demand, promotional efforts, etc., Xiao *et al.* (2019) investigated the optimal ordering strategy of a retailer in a secondary supply chain where the manufacturer subsidizes the promotional spending of the retailer.

With intensifying competition in the market, more and more firms pursue horizontal cooperative promotion, not only limited to cooperation between the upstream and downstream parties within the same supply chain, so the related research is gradually increasing (Karray, 2011). Considering the threshold effect of advertising, which means that when the influence of advertising is below a certain value, advertising has a limited effect on raising consumer demand, Yu *et al.* (2021) investigated the effect of the threshold effect of advertising on the firms optimal decisions in the context of selling substitutable products under monopoly and duopoly situations. Considering how to choose the optimal partner for horizontal cooperative promotion, Karray and Sigu (2015) studied cooperation among three retailers where two of the retailers sell complementary products in that one retailer sells a complementary product and the other retailer sells an independent product. They found that the success of cooperation depends mainly on the degree of product complementarity, and the impacts of price, and independent and cooperative promotions on demand. The consumption-point programme has become common in the retailing industry, where retailers can attract more consumers by conducting horizontal cooperative promotion, and consumers can earn points after purchasing products and then use the points to offset part of the costs of the products purchased at other retailers. Moon *et al.* (2020) proposed a target rebate contract to address the cost spillover issue to increase the profits of retailers. Karray (2015) examined cooperative promotion of two supply chains that sell competing products with different channel structures, i.e., two decentralized structures where one is centralized and the other is decentralized. The manufacturers offer promotional subsidies to retailers while the latter pursue horizontal cooperative promotion simultaneously. When price competition is lower than promotional competition, the manufacturers would offer lower promotional subsidy rates to retailers, and the impacts of horizontal cooperative promotion on the participants profits depend mainly on the channel structure of the supply chain. Under the DC channel structure, horizontal cooperative promotion is beneficial to the manufacturers, but does not necessarily increase the retailers profits. So, choosing the right partner is critical for the success of cooperative promotion.

However, to the best of our knowledge, there is no study in the extant literature that analyzes the optimal strategies of cross-market firms that adopt 3D printing. Filling this research gap in the literature, we derive results that help cross-market firms better pursue cooperation and make optimal decisions. The firms can not only enhance their development through cooperation, but also attract more customers to sustain and grow their businesses. In sum, our study produces theoretically significant findings with insightful managerial implications that advance the research and practice of 3D printing.

3. The Model

Our research aims to help firms retain their existing consumers in a more effective way, while attracting more new consumers to buy their products through cooperation. We adopt a game-theoretical framework to analyze the pros and cons of pursuing cooperation with collaborating firms. We first introduce the notation used throughout the paper, before formulating the demand and profit functions of the firms under the independent and joint promotion schemes adopting 3D printing. We then derive the equilibrium solutions in Table 1, analyze their properties and discuss their managerial implications. We present the proofs of all the results in the Appendix A.

3.1. *The system*

With the application of 3D printing, we consider cooperation between two cross-market firms belonging to different supply chains, denoted as firm i ($i = 1, 2$). The two firms can choose to promote their products either independently or jointly. If cooperative promotion is adopted, firm i can not only stimulate the demand of its own consumers, but also attract the consumers of the other firm, so expanding the consumer group of its own product (Biswas, 2014). Because the firms are in different markets, there is no leader-follower relationship between them. When there is no cooperation between the two firms, they just promote their products independently by undertaking individual promotional activities, which we consider as the benchmark scenario, labeled as IP. Similarly, we label the scenario where the two firms adopt cooperative promotion to promote their products as CP. In the meantime, we use the superscript 0 to denote the decision variables under scenario IP so as to distinguish the decision variables under scenario CP.

We denote firm i's effort of independently promoting its product as a_i and its effort of undertaking cooperative promotional activities as b_i. We assume that the total number of consumers in the two markets is v and the ratio of splitting the market is α ($0 \leq \alpha \leq 1$). Thus, the numbers of basic customers of firms 1 and 2 are αv and $(1 - \alpha)v$, respectively. Following McGuire and Staelin (1983), and Choi (1991), we assume that consumers' demand for the product of cross-market firm i d_i is negatively proportional to the price of the product p_i. Also, firm i's product demand d_i increases with its effort of undertaking individual promotional activities a_i and its effort of undertaking joint promotional activities b_i (Karray, 2015; Karray and Sigu, 2015; Yu *et al.*, 2021). We also assume that the two firms' actions have symmetric effects, i.e., the effects of the prices on demand γ, the effects of the firms' efforts of undertaking independent promotional activities on demand ω, and the effect of the effort of undertaking joint promotional activities on demand θ are the same in each firm's demand function (see, e.g., Karray, 2011).

3.2. *Demand and profit functions*

We assume that the unit costs of production of the two products are c_i. Under scenario IP, i.e., each firm promotes its own product independently, the demands for the products of firms 1 and 2 are as follows:

$$d_1^0 = \alpha v - \gamma p_1^0 + \omega a_1^0, \tag{1}$$

$$d_2^0 = (1-\alpha)v - \gamma p_2^0 + \omega a_2^0. \tag{2}$$

Following the literature, we assume that the promotional cost is quadratic in the effort of undertaking the promotional activities (Chu, 1995; Karray, 2011). So a_i^2 and b_i^2 are the promotional costs of firm i with regard to its undertaking the individual and joint promotional activities, such as advertisement and administrative expenses, respectively. Thus, the two firms' profits under IP are as follows:

$$\pi_1^0 = (p_1^0 - c_1)(\alpha v - \gamma p_1^0 + \omega a_1^0) - (a_1^0)^2, \tag{3}$$

$$\pi_2^0 = (p_2^0 - c_2)\big((1-\alpha)v - \gamma p_2^0 + \omega a_2^0\big) - (a_2^0)^2. \tag{4}$$

With the application of 3D printing technology, the cross-market firms are no longer operating in their own markets. When two firms cooperate in promoting their products, firm is market will include not only its own customers but also the partner firms customers, which expand their target customer groups through cooperation. In other words, the populations of the basic customers for both firms are v. Meanwhile, the production cost of the 3D printed product is a factor that must be taken into account due to the influence of raw materials, processes, and other factors of 3D printing technology. So, we label the unit cost of production of the 3D printed product as c_3. Therefore, the profit function of firm i under CP is as follows:

$$\pi_i = (p_i - c_3)(v - \gamma p_i + \omega a_i + \theta(b_i + b_{3-i})) - a_i^2 - b_i^2, i = 1, 2. \tag{5}$$

In Eqs (3)–(5), the first terms are the firms' revenues, the second terms are the costs of conducting the independent promotional activities, and the third terms are the costs of undertaking the cooperative promotional activities. θ, γ, ω, and α are all positive, and α varies between 0 and 1.

3.3. *Equilibrium solutions*

Based on the developed model, we derive the equilibrium outcomes under IP and CP. The first model under IP is the benchmark scenario.

The two firms make decisions simultaneously to maximize their profits independently. We derive the Nash equilibrium solutions under IP and CP by solving the first-order conditions $\frac{\partial \pi_i^0}{\partial p_i^0} = \frac{\partial \pi_i^0}{\partial a_i^0} = 0$ and $\frac{\partial \pi_i}{\partial p_i} = \frac{\partial \pi_i}{\partial a_i} = \frac{\partial \pi_i}{\partial b_i} = 0$ to obtain the equilibrium solutions as shown in Table 1. Besides, to ensure the success of cooperation, all the results in both models must be positive, i.e., $p_i > 0$, $d_i > 0$, $a_i > 0$, $b_i > 0$, and $\pi_i > 0$.

Table 1. Equilibrium solutions.

IP	IP	CP
$p_1^0 = \frac{c_1(2\gamma-\omega^2)+2v\alpha}{4\gamma-\omega^2}$	$p_2^0 = \frac{c_2(2\gamma-\omega^2)+2v(1-\alpha)}{4\gamma-\omega^2}$	$p_i = \frac{c_3(2\gamma-\omega^2-2\theta^2)+2v}{4\gamma-\omega^2-2\theta^2}$
$a_1^0 = \frac{\omega(v\alpha-c_1\gamma)}{4\gamma-\omega^2}$	$a_2^0 = \frac{\omega\left(v(1-\alpha)-c_2\gamma\right)}{4\gamma-\omega^2}$	$a_i = \frac{\omega(v-c_3\gamma)}{4\gamma-\omega^2-2\theta^2}$
		$b_i = \frac{\theta(v-c_3\gamma)}{4\gamma-\omega^2-2\theta^2}$
$d_1^0 = \frac{2\gamma(v\alpha-c_1\gamma)}{4\gamma-\omega^2}$	$d_2^0 = \frac{2\gamma\left(v(1-\alpha)-c_2\gamma\right)}{4\gamma-\omega^2}$	$d_i = \frac{2\gamma(v-c_3\gamma)}{4\gamma-\omega^2-2\theta^2}$
$\pi_1^0 = \frac{(c_1\gamma-v\alpha)^2}{4\gamma-\omega^2}$	$\pi_2^0 = \frac{\left(c_2\gamma+v(\alpha-1)\right)^2}{4\gamma-\omega^2}$	$\pi_i = \frac{(v-c_3\gamma)^2(4\gamma-\omega^2-\theta^2)}{(4\gamma-\omega^2-2\theta^2)^2}$

4. Model Analysis and Comparison

Based on the equilibrium solutions obtained above, we first analyze the conditions under which cooperative promotion of the cross-market firms adopting 3D printing is more advantageous than non-cooperation. We then research the two firms' optimal decisions to examine the effects of cooperative promotion.

From the equilibrium solutions given in Table 1, we identify the necessary conditions for positive equilibrium solutions by solving the first-order conditions, and derive the conditions under which the firms will adopt cooperative promotion. Then, we analyze the obtained results to identify the conditions under which the two firms are willing to pursue cooperation.

Proposition 1. *The cross-market firms will pursue cooperative promotion when the following conditions are met*:

(1) $c_3 < \frac{v}{\gamma}$, *and* $\theta < \sqrt{\frac{4\gamma-\omega^2}{2}}$, *or*

(2) $c_3 > \frac{v}{\gamma}$, *and* $\sqrt{\frac{4\gamma-\omega^2}{2}} < \theta < \sqrt{4\gamma-\omega^2}$.

The result shows that whether the cross-market firms will pursue cooperative promotion not only depends on the unit cost of production, but also on the effects of the price, independent promotional activities, and cooperative promotional activities on demand. When two cross-market companies decide to use 3D printing technology to pursue cooperative promotion, it is important to make the optimal decisions based on changes in the unit production cost and the various factors that influence the success of cooperative promotion, even though cooperative promotion can attract more consumers. When the unit cost of production is relatively large, cooperative promotion would help increase consumer demand, so the firms can advertise new products made by 3D printing to increase their competitiveness. On the contrary, when the effect of cooperative promotion on demand is relatively small, the firms will not contribute much effort to cooperative promotion, leading to higher costs. Under the stated conditions, the two firms can maximize their profits while attracting more consumers to pursue supply chain sustainability by adopting cooperative promotion.

Proposition 2. *Analyzing the efforts of cooperative promotion and independent promotion under CP yields the following:*

(1) *Whether the firms are willing to expend more effort on cooperative promotion or independent promotion mainly depends on the effect of the promotional activities on demand.*
(2) *Changes in the firms contributions to independent promotional activities and cooperative promotional activities are consistent with consumers demands for the products.*

Given $b_i - a_i = \frac{(c_3\gamma - v)(\omega - \theta)}{4\gamma - \omega^2 - 2\theta^2}$, the firms willingness to conduct independent promotional activities or cooperative promotional activities is proportional to the difference in the effects of promotional activities on demand. Under CP, when the firms invest more in conducting cooperative promotional activities, they can attract more consumers and better promote the product. Conversely, they prefer to promote their products by conducting individual promotional activities to enhance competitiveness. Moreover, the results show that changes in b_i, a_i, and d_i are mainly related to $\frac{v - c_3\gamma}{4\gamma - \omega^2 - 2\theta^2}$. When the firms make more efforts for independent promotional activities and cooperative promotional activities, consumer demands for the products rise simultaneously, so increasing the influence of the 3D printed product and attracting more consumers. Eventually, a large number of customers are attracted to the firms in order to enjoy the innovative 3D printed product, increasing the likelihood that the consumers will consume the firms other products, conducive to the sustainable development of the supply chain. Similarly, when the firms spend less on cooperative promotional activities and independent promotional activities, consumer demand for the 3D printed product will decline.

Moreover, we compare the equilibrium solutions under the IP and CP scenarios to further analyze the impacts of cooperative promotion on the firms involved.

Proposition 3. *Concerning the effort of individual promotional activities, the firms contribution to individual promotional activities under CP is not necessarily higher than that under IP.*

Comparing the efforts for individual promotional activities under IP and CP, whether the firms adopting 3D printing technology will make more contributions mainly depends on the unit cost of production, market share ratio, as well as the effects of the price, independent promotional activities, and cooperative promotional activities on demand. For instance, when it is cheaper for the firm to produce its own product, but more expensive to produce the 3D printed product, while cooperative promotion has limited power to increase customer demand, the firm will invest more in individual promotion to better promote the product. When the effect of cooperative promotion on demand is relatively large, the firm will put more effort into cooperative promotion to attract more consumers. In real practice, the firms need to comprehensively weigh the various factors and to analyze the pros and cons, and reasonably allocate the expenses for individual promotional activities and cooperative promotional activities, so as to better promote the 3D printing product to obtain higher profits.

Proposition 4. *Comparing the profits of two firms under IP and CP yields the following*:

(1) *When the unit cost of production of the 3D printed product is relatively large, whether the two firms will be better off under CP depends on the effect of cooperative promotional activities on demand.*
(2) *When the unit cost of production of the 3D printed product is relatively small, whether the two firms will be better off under CP depends on the effect of price and cooperative promotional activities on demand.*

When the firms carry out cooperative promotion, with the effects of price and cooperative promotional activities on demand varying, the firms will not necessarily obtain higher profits than under IP. If the unit cost of production of the 3D printed product is relatively large, i.e., $c_3 > \frac{v}{\gamma}$, a greater effect of cooperative promotional activities will incur higher costs for the firms, so reducing the firms' profits. Conversely, participating in cooperative promotion will result in higher profits for the firms and contribute to the sustainability of the supply chain. In general, when the unit cost of production of the 3D printed product is relatively small, i.e., $c_3 < \frac{v}{\gamma}$, with a greater impact of cooperative promotional activities on demand, the firms will be more profitable by collaborating to promote the 3D printed product. Due to the effect of price on demand, the firms will earn higher profits by participating in cooperative promotion in certain intervals.

5. Numerical Studies

Since there are many parameters in our modelling framework, it is difficult to draw relevant conclusions from the analytical results directly. Therefore, we conducted numerical studies to more explicitly show the effect of horizontal cooperative promotion on the cooperation of cross-market firms adopting 3D printing technology.

The changes in profit differential are similar for both firms pursuing IP and CP, so we examine the change in profit of firm 1 to show the impact of cooperative promotion on profit. Assuming that $v = 60$, $c_1 = 20$, $\alpha = 0.6$, $\omega = 2$, and $\gamma = 2$, and dividing the feasible range of c_3 into two intervals $c_3 < \frac{v}{\gamma}$ and $c_3 > \frac{v}{\gamma}$ where $c_3 = 15$ and $c_3 = 40$, we show in Fig. 1 the impact of cooperative promotion.

As shown in Fig. 1, when the unit cost of producing the 3D printed product is relatively low, and if $t_2 < 0$, then cooperative promotion makes the firm gain more profit; if $t_2 > 0$, the firm's profit gradually increases as the impact of cooperative promotion on demand increases. On the other hand, when the cost of producing the 3D printed product is relatively large, the high expenses incurred from the promotional activities, the production cost of the product, etc., weaken cooperative promotions ability to generate more profit for the firm.

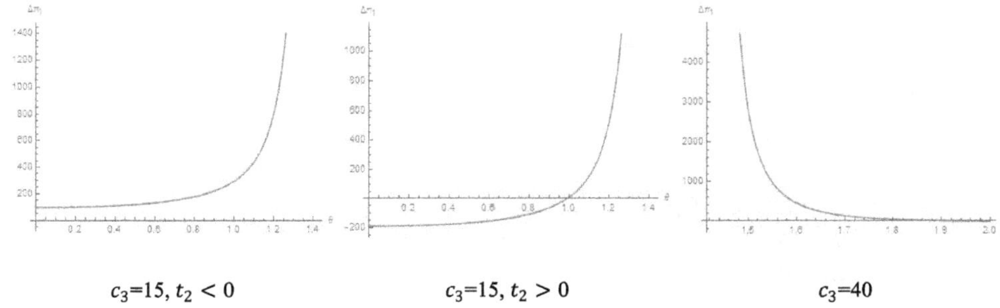

Fig. 1. Change in profit of firm 1.

6. Extended Model

In order to expand the scope of our research, we study the effect of the cost-sharing contract on the optimal decision-making of the cross-market firms.

Under CP, we assume that firm 1 shares a percentage δ ($0 \leq \delta \leq 1$) of the cost associated with the cooperative promotional activities, while firm 2 shares the remaining percentage $1 - \delta$ of the cost. The retailing price of the two firms are p_1 and p_2, respectively, so the profit functions are:

$$\pi_1 = (p_1 - \delta c_3)\big(v - \gamma p_1 + \omega a_1 + \theta(b_1 + b_2)\big) - a_1^2 - b_1^2, \tag{6}$$

$$\pi_2 = \big(p_2 - (1 - \delta)c_3\big)\big(v - \gamma p_2 + \omega a_2 + \theta(b_1 + b_2)\big) - a_2^2 - b_2^2. \tag{7}$$

Similarly, we examine the changes in profit of firm 1 under the cost-sharing contract between the IP and CP scenarios to explore the impact of cooperative promotion on the firm in the feasible intervals $c_3 < \frac{v}{\gamma}$ and $\theta < \sqrt{\frac{4\gamma-\omega^2}{2}}$, and $c_3 > \frac{v}{\gamma}$ and $\sqrt{\frac{4\gamma-\omega^2}{2}} < \theta < \sqrt{4\gamma - \omega^2}$.

As shown in Fig. 2, whether the firm can gain more profit by participating in cooperative promotion mainly depends on the market share, unit production cost, cost-sharing ratio, and the impacts of price, cooperative promotional activities, and

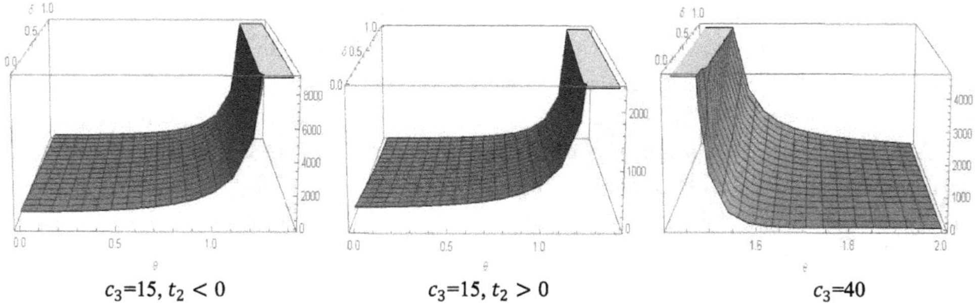

Fig. 2. Changes in profit of firm 1 under the cost-sharing contract.

individual promotional activities on demand. Similarly, when the cost of producing the 3D printed product is relatively large, the firms profit decreases with increasing impact of cooperative promotional activities because of the higher costs of the cooperative promotional activities, etc. In addition, the firm is not necessarily better off than that under IP.

7. Conclusions and Discussion

In the era of Industry 4.0, 3D printing as a revolutionary technology is rapidly driving the transformation of manufacturing to intelligence. Under the influence of 3D printing, more firms have started to cooperate with 3D printing firms to carry out cooperative promotion to attract consumers and enhance their competitiveness to cope with the fierce competition. Hence, cross-market firms have increasingly pursued cooperative promotion to produce 3D printed products. The firms seek not only to increase their own profits through cooperative promotion, but also attract more customers to enhance the sustainable development of their respective supply chains. In this context, we identify the factors that drive cross-market firms to participate in cooperative promotion, and examine the effects of cooperative promotion on the firms. We develop game-theoretic models to address our posed research questions. Our findings help managers make more rational decisions and pursue cooperative promotion more efficiently and effectively.

We find that the success of cooperative promotion not only depends on the unit cost of production of the 3D printed products, but also on the effects of the price, cooperative promotional activities, and individual promotional activities on demand. Under CP, when the effect of cooperative promotional activities on demand is higher than that of independent promotional activities, the firms are more likely to put more effort into cooperative promotional activities to better promote the 3D printed product and attract consumers. On the contrary, the firms are more willing to promote the 3D printed product and seek more sales opportunities through independent promotional activities. In addition, when the firms conduct cooperative promotion, more consumers are drawn to the 3D printed product as they spend more efforts on cooperative promotional activities and individual promotional activities. Therefore, the firms are able to attract more customers for their corresponding supply chains, which is conducive to sustainable development and fostering competitiveness. Similarly, when the firms reduce the effort of cooperative promotional activities and independent promotional activities, the demands for the products will decline. Moreover, when the unit cost of production of the 3D printed product is relatively large, as the effect of cooperative promotional activities on demand changes, cooperative promotion is not necessarily a good choice for the involved firms. If the firms are more influential in undertaking the cooperative promotional activities, the firms will increase their investments in cooperative promotional activities, so increasing the costs and making the firms less profitable than under IP. On the contrary, when the unit cost of production of the 3D printed products is relatively small, the firms are more profitable under CP when they are more influential in undertaking cooperative promotional activities.

In contrast to most of the literature on vertical cooperative promotion between the upstream and downstream parties within the same supply chain, we mainly analyze horizontal cooperation between two firms belonging to different supply chains. For instance, the existing research has studied how two firms selling competing products (Karray, 2015) and complementary products (Karray and Sigu, 2015) can effectively carry out cooperative promotional activities, and put forward relevant managerial suggestions for such firms. On the basis of existing research, the gradual adoption of 3D printing technology has led to an increasing number of cross-market firms adopting 3D printing technology to conduct cooperative promotion, which not only stimulates consumers desire to buy in their original market, but also attracts consumers from other markets to make purchases and achieve the purpose of increasing the consumer traffic. In addition, since 3D printing technology is still in the development stage, the unit production cost of the product is an important factor that needs to be considered. Therefore, we comprehensively analyze the mutual consumer attraction of firms in two different markets, while considering the impact of the unit production cost of the product on the cooperative promotional activities. We aim to provide firms with a full understanding of the circumstances under which such cooperation is feasible and the impacts of cooperative promotion on the optimal decisions of the players involved. In addition, our findings will help firms attract more consumers and improve their profits by pursuing cooperative promotion in actual practice, while promoting better application of 3D printing technology.

Future research could consider the risk attitudes of the players and the option contract in studying the profit distribution problem.

Appendix A

A.1. *Proof of Proposition* 1

We seek the optimal solutions for the corresponding variables by maximizing the profits of the two firms under IP and CP. First, the profit function of a firm has the maximum value when the Hessian matrix is negative definite. Then, according to the requirement that the relevant variables are positive, we derive the feasible conditions for CP. We denote the results under IP as p_i^0, a_i^0, d_i^0, and π_i^0, and those under CP as p_i, a_i, b_i, d_i, and π_i, with $i = 1, 2$.

A.1.1. *Equilibrium solutions under IP*

First, it is necessary for the Hessian matrix $\begin{bmatrix} -2\gamma & \omega \\ \omega & -2 \end{bmatrix}$ to be negative definite, so $\begin{cases} -2\gamma < 0 \\ 4\gamma - \omega^2 > 0 \end{cases}$ and we derive $\omega < 2\sqrt{\gamma}$. We solve the second-order conditions

$\frac{\partial \pi_i^0}{\partial p_i^0} = \frac{\partial \pi_i^0}{\partial a_i^0} = 0$, where

$$\pi_1^0 = (p_1^0 - c_1)(\alpha v - \gamma p_1^0 + \omega a_1^0) - (a_1^0)^2, \tag{A.1}$$

$$\pi_2^0 = (p_2^0 - c_2)\big((1-\alpha)v - \gamma p_2^0 + \omega a_2^0\big) - (a_2^0)^2. \tag{A.2}$$

to derive the equilibrium solutions in Table 1.

The other necessary conditions are $p_i^0 > 0$, $a_i^0 > 0$, $d_i^0 > 0$, and $\pi_i^0 > 0$, so $c_1 < \frac{v\alpha}{\gamma}$, and $c_2 < \frac{v(1-\alpha)}{\gamma}$.

A.1.2. *Equilibrium solutions under CP*

Similarly, it is necessary for the Hessian matrix

$$\begin{bmatrix} -2\gamma & \omega & \theta \\ \omega & -2 & 0 \\ \theta & 0 & -2 \end{bmatrix}$$

to be negative definite, so

$$\begin{cases} -2\gamma < 0 \\ 4\gamma - \omega^2 > 0 \\ -4\gamma + \omega^2 + \theta^2 < 0 \end{cases}$$

and we derive $\theta < \sqrt{4\gamma - \omega^2}$.

The other necessary conditions are $p_i > 0$, $a_i > 0$, $d_i > 0$, $b_i > 0$, and $\pi_i > 0$, so $c_3 < \frac{v}{\gamma}$, and $\theta < \sqrt{\frac{4\gamma-\omega^2}{2}}$ or $c_3 > \frac{v}{\gamma}$, and $\sqrt{\frac{4\gamma-\omega^2}{2}} < \theta < \sqrt{4\gamma - \omega^2}$.

A.2. *Proofs of Propositions 2*

When cooperative promotion is feasible, we here analyze the effects of cooperative promotion under CP in the following.

We first analysis the difference between the effort of cooperative promotional activities and individual promotional activities.

$$b_i - a_i = \frac{(c_3\gamma - v)(\omega - \theta)}{4\gamma - \omega^2 - 2\theta^2}. \tag{A.3}$$

We then analysis the relationship among the demand, and the effort of cooperative promotional activities and individual promotional activities.

$$b_i = \frac{\theta(v - c_3\gamma)}{4\gamma - \omega^2 - 2\theta^2}, \tag{A.4}$$

$$a_i = \frac{\omega(v - c_3\gamma)}{4\gamma - \omega^2 - 2\theta^2}, \tag{A.5}$$

$$d_i = \frac{2\gamma(v - c_3\gamma)}{4\gamma - \omega^2 - 2\theta^2}. \tag{A.6}$$

The changes of three variables are identical.

A.3. *Proof of Proposition* 3

We compare the efforts of individual promotional activities of two firms between IP and CP to discuss the effect of cooperative promotion on the two firms in the following. We first focus on the difference of the firm 1.

$$\Delta a_1 = \frac{2\omega\theta^2(v\alpha - c_1\gamma) - \omega(\omega^2 - 4\gamma)(c_1\gamma - c_3\gamma + v - v\alpha)}{(4\gamma - \omega^2)(4\gamma - \omega^2 - 2\theta^2)}. \tag{A.7}$$

The sign of the numerator of the above difference is uncertain, and the sign of the denominator is mainly affected by $4\gamma - \omega^2 - 2\theta^2$, so we discuss the numerator classification as shown below. The discriminate of $\omega(\omega^2 - 4\gamma)(c_1\gamma - c_3\gamma + v - v\alpha)$ equals to $\left((c_3 - c_1)\omega^2 + 4v(\alpha - 1)\right)^2 > 0$. We first study if $v\alpha - c_1\gamma > 0$.

(1) When $c_1 - c_3 > 0$, i.e., $c_1 > c_3$, and $c_1 < \frac{v\alpha}{\gamma}$, $c_3 > \frac{v}{\gamma}$ is impossible.

So when $c_3 < c_1 < \frac{v\alpha}{\gamma}$, $c_3 < \frac{v\alpha}{\gamma}$, and $\theta < \sqrt{\frac{4\gamma - \omega^2}{2}}$, $a_3 - a_1 > 0$.

(2) When $c_1 - c_3 < 0$, $\frac{v(\alpha-1)}{c_1 - c_3} < \frac{\omega^2}{4}$, i.e., $c_1 < \min\{c_3, \frac{v\alpha}{\gamma}\}$,

$$\frac{(\omega^2 - 4\gamma)(c_1\gamma - c_3\gamma + v - v\alpha)}{2v\alpha - 2c_1\gamma} - (4\gamma - \omega^2) = \frac{(\omega^2 - 4\gamma)(c_1\gamma + c_3\gamma - v - v\alpha)}{2c_1\gamma - 2v\alpha}.$$

If $v + v\alpha - c_3\gamma > 0$, $c_1\gamma + c_3\gamma - v - v\alpha > 0$, i.e., $c_3 < \frac{v + v\alpha}{\gamma}$ and $c_1 > \frac{v + v\alpha - c_3\gamma}{\gamma}$.

$$\frac{v + v\alpha - c_3\gamma}{\gamma} - \frac{v\alpha}{\gamma} = \frac{v - c_3\gamma}{\gamma},$$

$$\frac{v + v\alpha - c_3\gamma}{\gamma} - c_3 = \frac{v + v\alpha - 2c_3\gamma}{\gamma},$$

① $c_3 < \frac{v\alpha}{\gamma}$, i.e., $c_1 < c_3$,

$$\frac{v + v\alpha}{\gamma} - \frac{v}{\gamma} = \frac{v\alpha}{\gamma} > 0,$$

$$\frac{v + v\alpha}{\gamma} - \frac{v\alpha}{\gamma} = \frac{v}{\gamma} > 0,$$

$$\frac{v + v\alpha}{\gamma} - \frac{v + v\alpha}{2\gamma} = \frac{v + v\alpha}{2\gamma} > 0.$$

So this invalid.

② $c_3 > \frac{v\alpha}{\gamma}$, i.e., $\frac{v\alpha}{\gamma} < c_3 < \frac{v+v\alpha}{\gamma}$,

$$\frac{v + v\alpha}{2\gamma} - \frac{v}{\gamma} = \frac{v(\alpha - 1)}{2\gamma} < 0,$$

$$\frac{v + v\alpha}{2\gamma} - \frac{v\alpha}{\gamma} = \frac{v - v\alpha}{2\gamma} > 0.$$

$c_3 > \frac{v}{\gamma}$ is necessary, so $\frac{v}{\gamma} < c_3 < \frac{v+v\alpha}{\gamma}$.

So when $\frac{v+v\alpha-c_3\gamma}{\gamma} < c_1 < \frac{v\alpha}{\gamma}$, $\frac{v}{\gamma} < c_3 < \frac{v+v\alpha}{\gamma}$, $\sqrt{\frac{4\gamma-\omega^2}{2}} < \theta < \sqrt{4\gamma - \omega^2}$, $a_3 - a_1 > 0$.

If $v + v\alpha - c_3\gamma > 0$, $c_1\gamma + c_3\gamma - v - v\alpha < 0$, i.e., $c_3 < \frac{v+v\alpha}{\gamma}$ and $c_1 < \frac{v+v\alpha-c_3\gamma}{\gamma}$.

$$\frac{(\omega^2 - 4\gamma)(c_1\gamma - c_3\gamma + v - v\alpha)}{2v\alpha - 2c_1\gamma} - \frac{4\gamma - \omega^2}{2} = \frac{(\omega^2 - 4\gamma)(c_3\gamma - v)}{2c_1\gamma - 2v\alpha}.$$

① $c_3 < \frac{v\alpha}{\gamma}$, i.e., $c_1 < c_3$, when $c_3 < \frac{v+v\alpha}{2\gamma}$, $c_1 < c_3$ and when $\frac{v+v\alpha}{2\gamma} < c_3 < \frac{v+v\alpha}{\gamma}$, $c_1 < \frac{v+v\alpha-c_3\gamma}{\gamma}$.

So if $c_1 < c_3$, $c_3 < \frac{v+v\alpha}{2\gamma}$ or $c_1 < \frac{v+v\alpha-c_3\gamma}{\gamma}$, $\frac{v+v\alpha}{2\gamma} < c_3 < \frac{v}{\gamma}$, $\theta < \sqrt{\frac{(\omega^2-4\gamma)(c_1\gamma-c_3\gamma+v-v\alpha)}{2v\alpha-2c_1\gamma}}$, $a_3 - a_1 < 0$ and $\sqrt{\frac{(\omega^2-4\gamma)(c_1\gamma-c_3\gamma+v-v\alpha)}{2v\alpha-2c_1\gamma}} < \theta < \sqrt{\frac{4\gamma-\omega^2}{2}}$, $a_3 - a_1 > 0$. If $c_1 < \frac{v+v\alpha-c_3\gamma}{\gamma}$, $\frac{v}{\gamma} < c_3 < \frac{v+v\alpha}{\gamma}$, $\sqrt{\frac{4\gamma-\omega^2}{2}} < \theta < \sqrt{\frac{(\omega^2-4\gamma)(c_1\gamma-c_3\gamma+v-v\alpha)}{2v\alpha-2c_1\gamma}}$, $a_3 - a_1 > 0$ and $\sqrt{\frac{(\omega^2-4\gamma)(c_1\gamma-c_3\gamma+v-v\alpha)}{2v\alpha-2c_1\gamma}} < \theta < \sqrt{4\gamma - \omega^2}$, $a_3 - a_1 < 0$.

② $c_3 > \frac{v\alpha}{\gamma}$, i.e., $c_1 < \frac{v\alpha}{\gamma}$,

$$\frac{v + v\alpha}{\gamma} - \frac{v}{\gamma} = \frac{v\alpha}{\gamma} > 0,$$

$$\frac{v + v\alpha}{\gamma} - \frac{v\alpha}{\gamma} = \frac{v}{\gamma} > 0.$$

So if $c_1 < \frac{v\alpha}{\gamma}$, $\frac{v\alpha}{\gamma} < c_3 < \frac{v}{\gamma}$, $\theta < \sqrt{\frac{(\omega^2-4\gamma)(c_1\gamma-c_3\gamma+v-v\alpha)}{2v\alpha-2c_1\gamma}}$, $a_3 - a_1 < 0$ and $\sqrt{\frac{(\omega^2-4\gamma)(c_1\gamma-c_3\gamma+v-v\alpha)}{2v\alpha-2c_1\gamma}} < \theta < \sqrt{\frac{4\gamma-\omega^2}{2}}$, $a_3 - a_1 > 0$. If $c_1 < \frac{v+v\alpha-c_3\gamma}{\gamma}$,

$\frac{v}{\gamma} < c_3 < \frac{v+v\alpha}{\gamma}$, $\sqrt{\frac{4\gamma-\omega^2}{2}} < \theta < \sqrt{\frac{(\omega^2-4\gamma)(c_1\gamma-c_3\gamma+v-v\alpha)}{2v\alpha-2c_1\gamma}}$, $a_3 - a_1 > 0$ and $\sqrt{\frac{(\omega^2-4\gamma)(c_1\gamma-c_3\gamma+v-v\alpha)}{2v\alpha-2c_1\gamma}} < \theta < \sqrt{4\gamma-\omega^2}$, $a_3 - a_1 < 0$.

If $v+v\alpha-c_3\gamma < 0$, $c_1\gamma+c_3\gamma-v-v\alpha > 0$, i.e., $c_3 > \frac{v+v\alpha}{\gamma}$ and $c_1 < \min\{c_3, \frac{v\alpha}{\gamma}\}$.

① $c_3 < \frac{v\alpha}{\gamma}$, i.e., $c_1 < c_3$, and $c_3 > \frac{v+v\alpha}{\gamma}$ is necessary.

$$\frac{v+v\alpha}{\gamma}\frac{v\alpha}{\gamma} = \frac{v}{\gamma} > 0,$$

so it is invalid.

② $c_3 > \frac{v\alpha}{\gamma}$, i.e., $c_1 < \frac{v\alpha}{\gamma}$,

$$\frac{v+v\alpha}{\gamma}\frac{v\alpha}{\gamma} = \frac{v}{\gamma} > 0.$$

So when $c_1 < \frac{v\alpha}{\gamma}$, $c_3 > \frac{v\alpha}{\gamma}$, $\sqrt{\frac{4\gamma-\omega^2}{2}} < \theta < \sqrt{4\gamma-\omega}$, $a_3 - a_1 > 0$.

If $v + v\alpha - c_3\gamma < 0$, $c_1\gamma + c_3\gamma - v - v\alpha < 0$ is impossible.

(3) When $c_1 - c_3 < 0$, $\frac{v(\alpha-1)}{c_1-c_3} > \frac{\omega^2}{4}$, $\frac{\omega^2}{4} < \gamma < \frac{v(\alpha-1)}{c_1-c_3}$,

① $c_3 < \frac{v\alpha}{\gamma}$, i.e., $c_1 < c_3$,

$$\theta < \sqrt{\frac{4\gamma-\omega^2}{2}}, \quad a_3 - a_1 > 0.$$

② $c_3 > \frac{v\alpha}{\gamma}$, i.e., $c_1 < \frac{v\alpha}{\gamma}$,

$$\frac{v\alpha}{\gamma} < c_3 < \frac{v}{\gamma}, \quad \theta < \sqrt{\frac{4\gamma-\omega^2}{2}}, \quad a_3 - a_1 > 0 \quad \text{and} \quad c_3 > \frac{v}{\gamma},$$

$$\sqrt{\frac{4\gamma-\omega^2}{2}} < \theta < \sqrt{4\gamma-\omega^2}, \quad a_3 - a_1 < 0.$$

(4) When $c_1 - c_3 < 0$, $\frac{v(\alpha-1)}{c_1-c_3} > \frac{\omega^2}{4}$, $\gamma > \frac{v(\alpha-1)}{c_1-c_3}$,

$$\frac{(\omega^2-4\gamma)(c_1\gamma-c_3\gamma+v-v\alpha)}{2v\alpha-2c_1\gamma} - (4\gamma-\omega^2) = \frac{(\omega^2-4\gamma)(c_1\gamma+c_3\gamma-v-v\alpha)}{2c_1\gamma-2v\alpha}.$$

If $v + v\alpha - c_3\gamma > 0$, $c_1\gamma + c_3\gamma - v - v\alpha > 0$, i.e., $c_3 < \frac{v+v\alpha}{\gamma}$ and $c_1 > \frac{v+v\alpha-c_3\gamma}{\gamma}$.

$$\frac{v+v\alpha-c_3\gamma}{\gamma} - \frac{v\alpha}{\gamma} = \frac{v-c_3\gamma}{\gamma},$$

$$\frac{v+v\alpha-c_3\gamma}{\gamma} - c_3 = \frac{v+v\alpha-2c_3\gamma}{\gamma},$$

① $c_3 < \frac{v\alpha}{\gamma}$, i.e., $c_1 < c_3$,

$$\frac{v+v\alpha}{\gamma} - \frac{v}{\gamma} = \frac{v\alpha}{\gamma} > 0,$$

$$\frac{v+v\alpha}{\gamma} - \frac{v\alpha}{\gamma} = \frac{v}{\gamma} > 0,$$

$$\frac{v+v\alpha}{\gamma} - \frac{v+v\alpha}{2\gamma} = \frac{v+v\alpha}{2\gamma} > 0.$$

So this invalid.

② $c_3 > \frac{v\alpha}{\gamma}$, i.e., $\frac{v\alpha}{\gamma} < c_3 < \frac{v+v\alpha}{\gamma}$,

$$\frac{v+v\alpha}{2\gamma} - \frac{v}{\gamma} = \frac{v(\alpha-1)}{2\gamma} < 0,$$

$$\frac{v+v\alpha}{2\gamma} - \frac{v\alpha}{\gamma} = \frac{v-v\alpha}{2\gamma} > 0.$$

$c_3 > \frac{v}{\gamma}$ is necessary, so $\frac{v}{\gamma} < c_3 < \frac{v+v\alpha}{\gamma}$.

So when $\frac{v+v\alpha-c_3\gamma}{\gamma} < c_1 < \frac{v\alpha}{\gamma}$, $\frac{v}{\gamma} < c_3 < \frac{v+v\alpha}{\gamma}$, $\sqrt{\frac{4\gamma-\omega^2}{2}} < \theta < \sqrt{4\gamma-\omega^2}$, $a_3 - a_1 > 0$.

If $v + v\alpha - c_3\gamma > 0$, $c_1\gamma + c_3\gamma - v - v\alpha < 0$, i.e., $c_3 < \frac{v+v\alpha}{\gamma}$ and $c_1 < \frac{v+v\alpha-c_3\gamma}{\gamma}$.

$$\frac{(\omega^2-4\gamma)(c_1\gamma-c_3\gamma+v-v\alpha)}{2v\alpha-2c_1\gamma} - \frac{4\gamma-\omega^2}{2} = \frac{(\omega^2-4\gamma)(c_3\gamma-v)}{2c_1\gamma-2v\alpha}.$$

① $c_3 < \frac{v\alpha}{\gamma}$, i.e., $c_1 < c_3$,

when $c_3 < \frac{v+v\alpha}{2\gamma}$, $c_1 < c_3$ and when $\frac{v+v\alpha}{2\gamma} < c_3 < \frac{v+v\alpha}{\gamma}$, $c_1 < \frac{v+v\alpha-c_3\gamma}{\gamma}$.

So if $c_1 < c_3$, $c_3 < \frac{v+v\alpha}{2\gamma}$ or $c_1 < \frac{v+v\alpha-c_3\gamma}{\gamma}$, $\frac{v+v\alpha}{2\gamma} < c_3 < \frac{v}{\gamma}$, $\theta < \sqrt{\frac{(\omega^2-4\gamma)(c_1\gamma-c_3\gamma+v-v\alpha)}{2v\alpha-2c_1\gamma}}$, $a_3 - a_1 < 0$ and $\sqrt{\frac{(\omega^2-4\gamma)(c_1\gamma-c_3\gamma+v-v\alpha)}{2v\alpha-2c_1\gamma}} < \theta < \sqrt{\frac{4\gamma-\omega^2}{2}}$, $a_3 - a_1 > 0$. If $c_1 < \frac{v+v\alpha-c_3\gamma}{\gamma}$, $\frac{v}{\gamma} < c_3 < \frac{v+v\alpha}{\gamma}$, $\sqrt{\frac{4\gamma-\omega^2}{2}} < \theta < \sqrt{\frac{(\omega^2-4\gamma)(c_1\gamma-c_3\gamma+v-v\alpha)}{2v\alpha-2c_1\gamma}}$, $a_3-a_1 > 0$ and $\sqrt{\frac{(\omega^2-4\gamma)(c_1\gamma-c_3\gamma+v-v\alpha)}{2v\alpha-2c_1\gamma}} < \theta < \sqrt{4\gamma-\omega^2}$, $a_3 - a_1 < 0$.

② $c_3 > \frac{v\alpha}{\gamma}$, i.e., $c_1 < \frac{v\alpha}{\gamma}$,

$$\frac{v+v\alpha}{\gamma} - \frac{v}{\gamma} = \frac{v\alpha}{\gamma} > 0,$$

$$\frac{v+v\alpha}{\gamma} - \frac{v\alpha}{\gamma} = \frac{v}{\gamma} > 0.$$

So if $c_1 < \frac{v\alpha}{\gamma}$, $\frac{v\alpha}{\gamma} < c_3 < \frac{v}{\gamma}$, $\theta < \sqrt{\frac{(\omega^2-4\gamma)(c_1\gamma-c_3\gamma+v-v\alpha)}{2v\alpha-2c_1\gamma}}$, $a_3 - a_1 < 0$ and $\sqrt{\frac{(\omega^2-4\gamma)(c_1\gamma-c_3\gamma+v-v\alpha)}{2v\alpha-2c_1\gamma}} < \theta < \sqrt{\frac{4\gamma-\omega^2}{2}}$, $a_3 - a_1 > 0$. If $c_1 < \frac{v+v\alpha-c_3\gamma}{\gamma}$,

$\frac{v}{\gamma} < c_3 < \frac{v+v\alpha}{\gamma}$, $\sqrt{\frac{4\gamma-\omega^2}{2}} < \theta < \sqrt{\frac{(\omega^2-4\gamma)(c_1\gamma-c_3\gamma+v-v\alpha)}{2v\alpha-2c_1\gamma}}$, $a_3 - a_1 > 0$ and $\sqrt{\frac{(\omega^2-4\gamma)(c_1\gamma-c_3\gamma+v-v\alpha)}{2v\alpha-2c_1\gamma}} < \theta < \sqrt{4\gamma-\omega^2}$, $a_3 - a_1 < 0$.

If $v+v\alpha-c_3\gamma < 0$, $c_1\gamma+c_3\gamma-v-v\alpha > 0$, i.e., $c_3 > \frac{v+v\alpha}{\gamma}$ and $c_1 < \min\{c_3, \frac{v\alpha}{\gamma}\}$.

① $c_3 < \frac{v\alpha}{\gamma}$, i.e., $c_1 < c_3$, and $c_3 > \frac{v+v\alpha}{\gamma}$ is necessary.

$$\frac{v+v\alpha}{\gamma}\frac{v\alpha}{\gamma} = \frac{v}{\gamma} > 0,$$

so it is invalid.

② $c_3 > \frac{v\alpha}{\gamma}$, i.e., $c_1 < \frac{v\alpha}{\gamma}$,

$$\frac{v+v\alpha}{\gamma}\frac{v\alpha}{\gamma} = \frac{v}{\gamma} > 0.$$

So when $c_1 < \frac{v\alpha}{\gamma}$, $c_3 > \frac{v\alpha}{\gamma}$, $\sqrt{\frac{4\gamma-\omega^2}{2}} < \theta < \sqrt{4\gamma-\omega}$, $a_3 - a_1 > 0$.

If $v+v\alpha-c_3\gamma < 0$, $c_1\gamma+c_3\gamma-v-v\alpha < 0$ is impossible.

We then study the situation that if $v\alpha - c_1\gamma < 0$.

(1) When $c_1 - c_3 > 0$, i.e., $c_1 > \max\{c_3, \frac{v\alpha}{\gamma}\}$,

$$\frac{(\omega^2-4\gamma)(c_1\gamma-c_3\gamma+v-v\alpha)}{2v\alpha-2c_1\gamma} - (4\gamma-\omega^2) = \frac{(\omega^2-4\gamma)(c_1\gamma+c_3\gamma-v-v\alpha)}{2c_1\gamma-2v\alpha}.$$

If $v+v\alpha-c_3\gamma > 0$, $c_1\gamma+c_3\gamma-v-v\alpha < 0$, i.e., $c_3 < \frac{v+v\alpha}{\gamma}$ and $c_1 < \frac{v+v\alpha-c_3\gamma}{\gamma}$.

$$\frac{v+v\alpha-c_3\gamma}{\gamma} - \frac{v\alpha}{\gamma} = \frac{v-c_3\gamma}{\gamma},$$

$$\frac{v+v\alpha-c_3\gamma}{\gamma} - c_3 = \frac{v+v\alpha-2c_3\gamma}{\gamma}.$$

① $c_3 < \frac{v\alpha}{\gamma}$, i.e., $c_1 > \frac{v\alpha}{\gamma}\}$, $\frac{v+v\alpha-c_3\gamma}{\gamma} > \frac{v\alpha}{\gamma}$ is necessary, so $c_3 < \frac{v\alpha}{\gamma}$.

$$\frac{v}{\gamma} - \frac{v\alpha}{\gamma} = \frac{v(1-\alpha)}{\gamma} > 0,$$

$$\frac{v+v\alpha}{2\gamma} - \frac{v}{\gamma} = \frac{v(\alpha-1)}{2\gamma} < 0,$$

$$\frac{v+v\alpha}{2\gamma} - \frac{v\alpha}{\gamma} = \frac{v-v\alpha}{2\gamma} > 0.$$

So when $\frac{v\alpha}{\gamma} < c_1 < \frac{v+v\alpha-c_3\gamma}{\gamma}$, $c_3 < \frac{v\alpha}{\gamma}$, $\theta < \sqrt{\frac{4\gamma-\omega^2}{2}}$, $a_3 - a_1 > 0$.

② $c_3 > \frac{v\alpha}{\gamma}$, i.e., $c_1 > c_3$, $\frac{v+v\alpha-c_3\gamma}{\gamma} > c_3$ is necessary, so $c_3 < \frac{v+v\alpha}{2\gamma}$.

$$\frac{v+v\alpha}{2\gamma} - \frac{v}{\gamma} = \frac{v(\alpha-1)}{2\gamma} < 0,$$

$$\frac{v+v\alpha}{2\gamma} - \frac{v\alpha}{\gamma} = \frac{v-v\alpha}{2\gamma} > 0.$$

So when $c_3 < c_1 < \frac{v+v\alpha-c_3\gamma}{\gamma}$, $\frac{v\alpha}{\gamma} < c_3 < \frac{v+v\alpha}{2\gamma}$, $\theta < \sqrt{\frac{4\gamma-\omega^2}{2}}$, $a_3 - a_1 > 0$.

If $v + v\alpha - c_3\gamma > 0$, $c_1\gamma + c_3\gamma - v - v\alpha > 0$, i.e., $c_3 < \frac{v+v\alpha}{\gamma}$ and $c_1 > \frac{v+v\alpha-c_3\gamma}{\gamma}$.

① $c_3 < \frac{v\alpha}{\gamma}$, i.e., $c_1 > \frac{v\alpha}{\gamma}$, if $c_3 < \frac{v\alpha}{\gamma}$, $c_1 > \frac{v+v\alpha-c_3\gamma}{\gamma}$ and $c_3 > \frac{v\alpha}{\gamma}$, $c_1 > \frac{v\alpha}{\gamma}$.

$$\frac{v+v\alpha}{\gamma}\frac{v}{\gamma} > 0, \quad \frac{(\omega^2-4\gamma)(c_1\gamma - c_3\gamma + v - v\alpha)}{2v\alpha - 2c_1\gamma} - \frac{4\gamma-\omega^2}{2} = \frac{(\omega^2-4\gamma)(c_3\gamma - v)}{2c_1\gamma - 2v\alpha}.$$

So when $c_1 > \frac{v+v\alpha-c_3\gamma}{\gamma}$, $c_3 < \frac{v}{\gamma}$, $\theta < \sqrt{\frac{4\gamma-\omega^2}{2}}$, $a_3 - a_1 > 0$. When $\frac{v}{\gamma} < c_3 < \frac{v+v\alpha}{\gamma}$, $c_1 > \frac{v\alpha}{\gamma}$, $\sqrt{\frac{4\gamma-\omega^2}{2}} < \theta < \sqrt{\frac{(\omega^2-4\gamma)(c_1\gamma-c_3\gamma+v-v\alpha)}{2v\alpha-2c_1\gamma}}$, $a_3 - a_1 < 0$ and $\sqrt{\frac{(\omega^2-4\gamma)(c_1\gamma-c_3\gamma+v-v\alpha)}{2v\alpha-2c_1\gamma}} < \theta < \sqrt{4\gamma-\omega^2}$, $a_3 - a_1 > 0$.

② $c_3 > \frac{v\alpha}{\gamma}$, i.e., $c_1 > c_3$, if $c_3 < \frac{v+v\alpha}{2\gamma}$, $c_1 > \frac{v+v\alpha-2c_3\gamma}{\gamma}$ and $c_3 > \frac{v+v\alpha}{2\gamma}$, $c_1 > c_3$.

$$\frac{v+v\alpha}{2\gamma} - \frac{v}{\gamma} = \frac{v(\alpha-1)}{2\gamma} < 0,$$

$$\frac{v+v\alpha}{2\gamma} - \frac{v\alpha}{\gamma} = \frac{v-v\alpha}{2\gamma} > 0,$$

$$\frac{v+v\alpha}{2\gamma} - \frac{v+v\alpha}{\gamma} = \frac{-v-v\alpha}{2\gamma} < 0.$$

So when $c_1 > \frac{v+v\alpha-2c_3\gamma}{\gamma}$, $\frac{v\alpha}{\gamma} < c_3 < \frac{v+v\alpha}{2\gamma}$, $\theta < \sqrt{\frac{4\gamma-\omega^2}{2}}$, $a_3 - a_1 > 0$. When $c_1 > c_3$, $\frac{v+v\alpha}{2\gamma} < c_3 < \frac{v}{\gamma}$, $\theta < \sqrt{\frac{4\gamma-\omega^2}{2}}$, $a_3 - a_1 > 0$ and $\frac{v}{\gamma} < c_3 < \frac{v+v\alpha}{\gamma}$, $\sqrt{\frac{4\gamma-\omega^2}{2}} < \theta < \sqrt{4\gamma-\omega^2}$, $a_3 - a_1 > 0$.

If $v + v\alpha - c_3\gamma < 0$, $c_1\gamma + c_3\gamma - v - v\alpha > 0$, i.e., $c_3 > \frac{v\alpha+v}{\gamma}$, $c_1 > \max\{\frac{v\alpha}{\gamma}, c_3\}$

① $c_3 < \frac{v\alpha}{\gamma}$, i.e., $c_1 > \frac{v\alpha}{\gamma}$ this is invalid.

② $c_3 > \frac{v\alpha}{\gamma}$, i.e., $c_1 > c_3$,

$$\frac{(\omega^2-4\gamma)(c_1\gamma - c_3\gamma + v - v\alpha)}{2v\alpha - 2c_1\gamma} - \frac{4\gamma-\omega^2}{2} = \frac{(\omega^2-4\gamma)(c_3\gamma - v)}{2c_1\gamma - 2v\alpha}.$$

So when $c_1 > c_3$, when $c_3 > \frac{v\alpha+v}{\gamma}$, $\sqrt{\frac{4\gamma-\omega^2}{2}} < \theta < \sqrt{4\gamma-\omega^2}$, $a_3 - a_1 > 0$.

If $v + v\alpha - c_3\gamma < 0$, $c_1\gamma + c_3\gamma - v - v\alpha < 0$ is impossible.

(2) When $c_1 - c_3 < 0$, i.e., $c_1 > \frac{v\alpha}{\gamma}$, so $c_3 > \frac{v\alpha}{\gamma}$.

If $c_1 < c_3$, when $\frac{v\alpha}{\gamma} < c_3 < \frac{v}{\gamma}$, $\theta < \sqrt{\frac{4\gamma-\omega^2}{2}}$, $a_3 - a_1 < 0$ and when $c_3 > \frac{v}{\gamma}$, $\sqrt{\frac{4\gamma-\omega^2}{2}} < \theta < \sqrt{4\gamma - \omega^2}$, $a_3 - a_1 > 0$.

(3) When $c_1 - c_3 < 0$, $\frac{v(\alpha-1)}{c_1-c_3} > \frac{\omega^2}{4}$, $\frac{\omega^2}{4} < \gamma < \frac{v(\alpha-1)}{c_1-c_3}$,

$$\frac{(\omega^2 - 4\gamma)(c_1\gamma - c_3\gamma + v - v\alpha)}{2v\alpha - 2c_1\gamma} - (4\gamma - \omega^2) = \frac{(\omega^2 - 4\gamma)(c_1\gamma + c_3\gamma - v - v\alpha)}{2c_1\gamma - 2v\alpha}.$$

If $v + v\alpha - c_3\gamma > 0$, $c_1\gamma + c_3\gamma - v - v\alpha < 0$, i.e., $c_3 < \frac{v+v\alpha}{\gamma}$ and $c_1 < \frac{v+v\alpha-c_3\gamma}{\gamma}$.

$$\frac{v + v\alpha - c_3\gamma}{\gamma} - \frac{v\alpha}{\gamma} = \frac{v - c_3\gamma}{\gamma},$$

$$\frac{v + v\alpha - c_3\gamma}{\gamma} - c_3 = \frac{v + v\alpha - 2c_3\gamma}{\gamma}.$$

① $c_3 < \frac{v\alpha}{\gamma}$, i.e., $c_1 > \frac{v\alpha}{\gamma}\}$, $\frac{v+v\alpha-c_3\gamma}{\gamma} > \frac{v\alpha}{\gamma}$ is necessary, so $c_3 < \frac{v\alpha}{\gamma}$.

$$\frac{v}{\gamma} - \frac{v\alpha}{\gamma} = \frac{v(1-\alpha)}{\gamma} > 0,$$

$$\frac{v + v\alpha}{2\gamma} - \frac{v}{\gamma} = \frac{v(\alpha - 1)}{2\gamma} < 0,$$

$$\frac{v + v\alpha}{2\gamma} - \frac{v\alpha}{\gamma} = \frac{v - v\alpha}{2\gamma} > 0.$$

So when $\frac{v\alpha}{\gamma} < c_1 < \frac{v+v\alpha-c_3\gamma}{\gamma}$, $c_3 < \frac{v\alpha}{\gamma}$, $\theta < \sqrt{\frac{4\gamma-\omega^2}{2}}$, $a_3 - a_1 > 0$.

② $c_3 > \frac{v\alpha}{\gamma}$, i.e., $c_1 > c_3$, $\frac{v+v\alpha-c_3\gamma}{\gamma} > c_3$ is necessary, so $c_3 < \frac{v+v\alpha}{2\gamma}$.

$$\frac{v + v\alpha}{2\gamma} - \frac{v}{\gamma} = \frac{v(\alpha - 1)}{2\gamma} < 0,$$

$$\frac{v + v\alpha}{2\gamma} - \frac{v\alpha}{\gamma} = \frac{v - v\alpha}{2\gamma} > 0.$$

So when $c_3 < c_1 < \frac{v+v\alpha-c_3\gamma}{\gamma}$, $\frac{v\alpha}{\gamma} < c_3 < \frac{v+v\alpha}{2\gamma}$, $\theta < \sqrt{\frac{4\gamma-\omega^2}{2}}$, $a_3 - a_1 > 0$.

If $v + v\alpha - c_3\gamma > 0$, $c_1\gamma + c_3\gamma - v - v\alpha > 0$, i.e., $c_3 < \frac{v+v\alpha}{\gamma}$ and $c_1 > \frac{v+v\alpha-c_3\gamma}{\gamma}$.

① $c_3 < \frac{v\alpha}{\gamma}$, i.e., $c_1 > \frac{v\alpha}{\gamma}$, if $c_3 < \frac{v\alpha}{\gamma}$, $c_1 > \frac{v+v\alpha-c_3\gamma}{\gamma}$ and $c_3 > \frac{v\alpha}{\gamma}$, $c_1 > \frac{v\alpha}{\gamma}$.

$$\frac{v + v\alpha}{\gamma}\frac{v}{\gamma} > 0, \quad \frac{(\omega^2 - 4\gamma)(c_1\gamma - c_3\gamma + v - v\alpha)}{2v\alpha - 2c_1\gamma} - \frac{4\gamma - \omega^2}{2} = \frac{(\omega^2 - 4\gamma)(c_3\gamma - v)}{2c_1\gamma - 2v\alpha}.$$

So when $c_1 > \frac{v+v\alpha-c_3\gamma}{\gamma}$, $c_3 < \frac{v}{\gamma}$, $\theta < \sqrt{\frac{4\gamma-\omega^2}{2}}$, $a_3 - a_1 > 0$. When $\frac{v}{\gamma} < c_3 < \frac{v+v\alpha}{\gamma}$, $c_1 > \frac{v\alpha}{\gamma}$, $\sqrt{\frac{4\gamma-\omega^2}{2}} < \theta < \sqrt{\frac{(\omega^2-4\gamma)(c_1\gamma-c_3\gamma+v-v\alpha)}{2v\alpha-2c_1\gamma}}$, $a_3 - a_1 < 0$ and $\sqrt{\frac{(\omega^2-4\gamma)(c_1\gamma-c_3\gamma+v-v\alpha)}{2v\alpha-2c_1\gamma}} < \theta < \sqrt{4\gamma - \omega^2}$, $a_3 - a_1 > 0$.

② $c_3 > \frac{v\alpha}{\gamma}$, i.e., $c_1 > c_3$, if $c_3 < \frac{v+v\alpha}{2\gamma}$, $c_1 > \frac{v+v\alpha-2c_3\gamma}{\gamma}$ and $c_3 > \frac{v+v\alpha}{2\gamma}$, $c_1 > c_3$.

$$\frac{v+v\alpha}{2\gamma} - \frac{v}{\gamma} = \frac{v(\alpha-1)}{2\gamma} < 0,$$

$$\frac{v+v\alpha}{2\gamma} - \frac{v\alpha}{\gamma} = \frac{v-v\alpha}{2\gamma} > 0,$$

$$\frac{v+v\alpha}{2\gamma} - \frac{v+v\alpha}{\gamma} = \frac{-v-v\alpha}{2\gamma} < 0.$$

So when $c_1 > \frac{v+v\alpha-2c_3\gamma}{\gamma}$, $\frac{v\alpha}{\gamma} < c_3 < \frac{v+v\alpha}{2\gamma}$, $\theta < \sqrt{\frac{4\gamma-\omega^2}{2}}$, $a_3 - a_1 > 0$. When $c_1 > c_3$, $\frac{v+v\alpha}{2\gamma} < c_3 < \frac{v}{\gamma}$, $\theta < \sqrt{\frac{4\gamma-\omega^2}{2}}$, $a_3 - a_1 > 0$ and $\frac{v}{\gamma} < c_3 < \frac{v+v\alpha}{\gamma}$, $\sqrt{\frac{4\gamma-\omega^2}{2}} < \theta < \sqrt{4\gamma-\omega^2}$, $a_3 - a_1 > 0$.

If $v + v\alpha - c_3\gamma < 0$, $c_1\gamma + c_3\gamma - v - v\alpha > 0$, i.e., $c_3 > \frac{v\alpha+v}{\gamma}$, $c_1 > \max\{\frac{v\alpha}{\gamma}, c_3\}$.

① $c_3 < \frac{v\alpha}{\gamma}$, i.e., $c_1 > \frac{v\alpha}{\gamma}$ this is invalid.

② $c_3 > \frac{v\alpha}{\gamma}$, i.e., $c_1 > c_3$,

$$\frac{(\omega^2-4\gamma)(c_1\gamma - c_3\gamma + v - v\alpha)}{2v\alpha - 2c_1\gamma} - \frac{4\gamma-\omega^2}{2} = \frac{(\omega^2-4\gamma)(c_3\gamma - v)}{2c_1\gamma - 2v\alpha}.$$

So when $c_1 > c_3$, when $c_3 > \frac{v\alpha+v}{\gamma}$, $\sqrt{\frac{4\gamma-\omega^2}{2}} < \theta < \sqrt{4\gamma-\omega^2}$, $a_3 - a_1 > 0$.

If $v + v\alpha - c_3\gamma < 0$, $c_1\gamma + c_3\gamma - v - v\alpha < 0$ is impossible.

(4) When $c_1 - c_3 < 0$, $\frac{v(\alpha-1)}{c_1-c_3} > \frac{\omega^2}{4}$, $\gamma > \frac{v(\alpha-1)}{c_1-c_3}$, so $c_3 > \frac{v\alpha}{\gamma}$.

If $c_1 < c_3$, when $\frac{v\alpha}{\gamma} < c_3 < \frac{v}{\gamma}$, $\theta < \sqrt{\frac{4\gamma-\omega^2}{2}}$, $a_3 - a_1 < 0$ and when $c_3 > \frac{v}{\gamma}$, $\sqrt{\frac{4\gamma-\omega^2}{2}} < \theta < \sqrt{4\gamma-\omega^2}$, $a_3 - a_1 > 0$.

Analysis of difference of firm 2's effort of individual promotional activities is similar to that of firm 1.

A.4. *Proof of Proposition* 4

We compare the profits of two firms under IP and CP to further discuss the effect of cooperative promotion on the two firms separately in the following.

A.4.1. *For firm* 1

$$\Delta\pi_1 = \frac{-4(c_1\gamma - v\alpha)^2\theta^4 - (-4\gamma+\omega^2)^2\big(\gamma^2(c_1^2 - c_3^2) + 2\gamma v(c_3 - c_1\alpha) + v^2(\alpha^2-1)\big)}{(4\gamma-\omega^2)(4\gamma-\omega^2-2\theta^2)^2} + \frac{(4\gamma-\omega^2)\big(4\gamma^2(c_1^2-c_3^2) + 2\gamma v(c_3 - 4c_1\alpha) + v^2(4\alpha^2-1)\big)\theta^2}{(4\gamma-\omega^2)(4\gamma-\omega^2-2\theta^2)^2}. \tag{A.8}$$

Based on the proof of Proposition 1, $4\gamma - \omega^2 > 0$ and , so the denominator of $\Delta\pi_1$ must be greater than 0, hence we focus on analyzing the numerator, and we assume $t = \theta^2$ $(\theta < \sqrt{\frac{4\gamma-\omega^2}{2}}$, or $\sqrt{\frac{4\gamma-\omega^2}{2}} < \theta < \sqrt{4\gamma - \omega^2})$.

$$f(t) = -4(c_1\gamma - v\alpha)^2 t^2 - (-4\gamma + \omega^2)^2 \big(\gamma^2(c_1^2 - c_3^2) + 2\gamma v(c_3 - c_1\alpha) + v^2(\alpha^2 - 1)\big)$$
$$+ (4\gamma - \omega^2)\big(4\gamma^2(c_1^2 - c_3^2) + 2\gamma v(c_3 - 4c_1\alpha) + v^2(4\alpha^2 - 1)\big)t. \tag{A.9}$$

The discriminant of $f(t)$ equals $\Delta f(t) = (-c_3\gamma + v)^2(-4\gamma + \omega^2)^2\big((\gamma^2(8c_1^2 + c_3^2) - 2\gamma v(c_3 + 8c_1\alpha) + v^2(1 + 8\alpha^2)\big)$. We assume $\gamma^2(8c_1^2 + c_3^2) - 2\gamma v(c_3 + 8c_1\alpha) + v^2(1 + 8\alpha^2)$ is the function about γ, its $\Delta = -32v^2(c_1 - c_3\alpha)^2 < 0$, this part is always greater than 0, so there must be two intersections with the x-axis of $f(t)$. Its solutions are

$$t = \frac{\begin{array}{c}(4\gamma - \omega^2)\big(-\big(4\gamma^2(c_1^2 - c_3^2) + 2\gamma v(c_3 - 4c_1\alpha) + v^2(4\alpha^2 - 1)\big)\\ \pm (c_3\gamma - v)\sqrt{\gamma^2(8c_1^2 + c_3^2) - 2\gamma v(c_3 + 8c_1\alpha) + v^2(1 + 8\alpha^2)}\big)\end{array}}{-8(c_1\gamma - v\alpha)^2}.$$

The sign of t is uncertain, so we focus the numerator of t to analysis. We assume $f(\gamma) = -\big(4\gamma^2(c_1^2 - c_3^2) + 2\gamma v(c_3 - 4c_1\alpha) + v^2(4\alpha^2 - 1)\big)$, $\Delta f(\gamma) = 16v^2(c_1 - c_3\alpha)^2 > 0$, so it solutions are $\gamma_1 = \frac{v(2\alpha-1)}{2c_1-c_3}$, $\gamma_2 = \frac{v(1+2\alpha)}{2c_1+c_3}$, $\gamma_1 - \gamma_2 = \frac{-4v(c_1-c_3\alpha)}{(2c_1-c_3)(2c_1+c_3)}$. In addition, we assume $f(\gamma^*) = f(\gamma)^2 - (c_3\gamma - v)^2\big(\gamma^2(8c_1^2 + c_3^2) - 2\gamma v(c_3 + 8c_1\alpha) + v^2(1 + 8\alpha^2)\big) = 16(c_1\gamma - v\alpha)^2\big(\gamma^2(c_1^2 - c_3^2) + 2\gamma v(c_3 - c_1) + v^2(\alpha^2 - 1)\big)$, $\Delta\gamma^* = 4v^2(c_1 - c_3\alpha)^2 > 0$, so its solutions are $\gamma_1^* = \frac{v(\alpha-1)}{c_1-c_3}$, $\gamma_2^* = \frac{v(1+\alpha)}{c_1+c_3}$, $\gamma_1^* - \gamma_2^* = \frac{-2v(c_1-c_3\alpha)}{(c_1-c_3)(c_1+c_3)}$. According to the above analysis, we first analyze the sign of t along with $c_3\gamma - v > 0$, as well as we assume

$$t_1 = \frac{\begin{array}{c}(4\gamma - \omega^2)\big(-\big(4\gamma^2(c_1^2 - c_3^2) + 2\gamma v(c_3 - 4c_1\alpha) + v^2(4\alpha^2 - 1)\big)\\ + (c_3\gamma - v)\sqrt{\gamma^2(8c_1^2 + c_3^2) - 2\gamma v(c_3 + 8c_1\alpha) + v^2(1 + 8\alpha^2)}\big)\end{array}}{-8(c_1\gamma - v\alpha)^2},$$

the another solution is t_2, the classification is as follows:

(1) When $\alpha \le \frac{1}{2}$, $c_1 > \frac{c_3}{2}$, $\gamma \le \frac{v(1+2\alpha)}{2c_1+c_3}$, $f(\gamma) > 0$, but the sign of $f(\gamma^*)$ is uncertain, we need to classify.

① $c_1 > c_3$,

$$\frac{v(1 + 2\alpha)}{2c_1 + c_3} - \frac{v(1 + \alpha)}{c_1 + c_3} = \frac{-v(c_1 - c_3\alpha)}{(2c_1 + c_3)(c_1 + c_3)} < 0.$$

So when $\alpha \le \frac{1}{2}$, $c_1 > c_3$, $\gamma \le \frac{v(1+2\alpha)}{2c_1+c_3}$, $t_1 < 0$, $t_2 > 0$.

② $\alpha c_3 < c_1 < c_3$, i.e., $\frac{c_3}{2} < c_1 < c_3$,

$$\frac{v(\alpha-1)}{c_1-c_3} - \frac{v(1+2\alpha)}{2c_1+c_3} = \frac{-3v(c_1-c_3\alpha)}{(2c_1+c_3)(c_1-c_3)} > 0,$$

$$\frac{v(1+\alpha)}{c_1+c_3} - \frac{v(1+2\alpha)}{2c_1+c_3} = \frac{v(c_1-c_3\alpha)}{(2c_1+c_3)(c_1+c_3)} > 0.$$

So when $\alpha \le \frac{1}{2}$, $\frac{c_3}{2} < c_1 < c_3$, $\gamma \le \frac{v(1+2\alpha)}{2c_1+c_3}$, $t_1 < 0$, $t_2 > 0$.

③ $c_1 < \alpha c_3$, it is invalid.

(2) When $\alpha \le \frac{1}{2}$, $c_1 > \frac{c_3}{2}$, $\gamma > \frac{v(1+2\alpha)}{2c_1+c_3}$, $f(\gamma) < 0$, but the sign of $f(\gamma^*)$ is uncertain, we need to classify.

① $c_1 > c_3$,

$$\frac{v(1+2\alpha)}{2c_1+c_3} - \frac{v(1+\alpha)}{c_1+c_3} = \frac{-v(c_1-c_3\alpha)}{(2c_1+c_3)(c_1+c_3)} < 0.$$

So when $\alpha \le \frac{1}{2}$, $c_1 > c_3$, $\frac{v(1+2\alpha)}{2c_1+c_3} < \gamma \le \frac{v(1+\alpha)}{c_1+c_3}$, $t_1 < 0$, $t_2 > 0$. If $\gamma > \frac{v(1+\alpha)}{c_1+c_3}$, $t_1 > 0$, $t_2 > 0$, $t_2 > t_1$.

② $\alpha c_3 < c_1 < c_3$, i.e., $\frac{c_3}{2} < c_1 < c_3$,

$$\frac{v(\alpha-1)}{c_1-c_3} - \frac{v(1+2\alpha)}{2c_1+c_3} = \frac{-3v(c_1-c_3\alpha)}{(2c_1+c_3)(c_1-c_3)} > 0,$$

$$\frac{v(1+\alpha)}{c_1+c_3} - \frac{v(1+2\alpha)}{2c_1+c_3} = \frac{v(c_1-c_3\alpha)}{(2c_1+c_3)(c_1+c_3)} > 0.$$

So when $\alpha \le \frac{1}{2}$, $\frac{c_3}{2} < c_1 < c_3$, $\frac{v(1+2\alpha)}{2c_1+c_3} < \gamma \le \frac{v(1+\alpha)}{c_1+c_3}$, $t_1 < 0$, $t_2 > 0$. If $\frac{v(1+\alpha)}{c_1+c_3} < \gamma \le \frac{v(\alpha-1)}{c_1-c_3}$, $t_1 > 0$, $t_2 > 0$, $t_2 > t_1$. If $\gamma > \frac{v(\alpha-1)}{c_1-c_3}$, $t_1 < 0$, $t_2 > 0$.

③ $c_1 < \alpha c_3$, it is invalid.

(3) When $\alpha \le \frac{1}{2}$, $c_1 < \alpha c_3$, $\gamma \le \frac{v(2\alpha-1)}{2c_1-c_3}$, $f(\gamma) > 0$, but the sign of $f(\gamma^*)$ is uncertain, we need to classify.

① $c_1 > c_3$, it is invalid.

② $\alpha c_3 < c_1 < c_3$, it is invalid.

③ $c_1 < \alpha c_3$,

$$\frac{v(\alpha-1)}{c_1-c_3} - \frac{v(2\alpha-1)}{2c_1-c_3} = \frac{-v(c_1-c_3\alpha)}{(2c_1-c_3)(c_1-c_3)} > 0.$$

So when $\alpha \le \frac{1}{2}$, $c_1 < \alpha c_3$, $\gamma \le \frac{v(2\alpha-1)}{2c_1-c_3}$, $t_1 < 0$, $t_2 > 0$.

(4) When $\alpha \le \frac{1}{2}$, $c_1 < \alpha c_3$, $\frac{v(2\alpha-1)}{2c_1-c_3} < \gamma \le \frac{v(1+2\alpha)}{2c_1+c_3}$, $f(\gamma) < 0$, but the sign of $f(\gamma^*)$ is uncertain, we need to classify.

① $c_1 > c_3$, it is invalid.

② $\alpha c_3 < c_1 < c_3$, it is invalid.

③ $c_1 < \alpha c_3$,

$$\frac{v(\alpha-1)}{c_1-c_3} - \frac{v(2\alpha-1)}{2c_1-c_3} = \frac{-v(c_1-c_3\alpha)}{(2c_1-c_3)(c_1-c_3)} > 0,$$

$$\frac{v(\alpha-1)}{c_1-c_3} - \frac{v(1+2\alpha)}{2c_1+c_3} = \frac{-3v(c_1-c_3\alpha)}{(2c_1+c_3)(c_1-c_3)} < 0,$$

$$\frac{v(1+\alpha)}{c_1+c_3} - \frac{v(1+2\alpha)}{2c_1+c_3} = \frac{v(c_1-c_3\alpha)}{(2c_1+c_3)(c_1+c_3)} < 0.$$

So when $\alpha \le \frac{1}{2}$, $c_1 < \alpha c_3$, $\frac{v(2\alpha-1)}{2c_1-c_3} < \gamma \le \frac{v(\alpha-1)}{c_1-c_3}$, $t_1 < 0$, $t_2 > 0$. If $\frac{v(\alpha-1)}{c_1-c_3} < \gamma \le \frac{v(1+\alpha)}{c_1+c_3}$, $t_1 > 0$, $t_2 > 0$, $t_2 > t_1$. If $\frac{v(1+\alpha)}{c_1+c_3} < \gamma \le \frac{v(1+2\alpha)}{2c_1+c_3}$, $t_1 < 0$, $t_2 > 0$.

(5) When $\alpha \le \frac{1}{2}$, $c_1 < \alpha c_3$, $\gamma > \frac{v(1+2\alpha)}{2c_1+c_3}$, $f(\gamma) > 0$, but the sign of $f(\gamma^*)$ is uncertain, we need to classify.

① $c_1 > c_3$, it is invalid.

② $\alpha c_3 < c_1 < c_3$, it is invalid.

③ $c_1 < \alpha c_3$,

$$\frac{v(1+\alpha)}{c_1+c_3} - \frac{v(1+2\alpha)}{2c_1+c_3} = \frac{v(c_1-c_3\alpha)}{(2c_1+c_3)(c_1+c_3)} < 0.$$

So when $\alpha \le \frac{1}{2}$, $c_1 < \alpha c_3$, $\gamma > \frac{v(1+2\alpha)}{2c_1+c_3}$, $t_1 < 0$, $t_2 > 0$.

(6) When $\alpha \le \frac{1}{2}$, $\alpha c_3 < c_1 < \frac{c_3}{2}$, $\gamma \le \frac{v(1+2\alpha)}{2c_1+c_3}$, $f(\gamma) > 0$, but the sign of $f(\gamma^*)$ is uncertain, we need to classify.

① $c_1 > c_3$, it is invalid.

② $\alpha c_3 < c_1 < c_3$, i.e., $\alpha c_3 < c_1 < \frac{c_3}{2}$,

$$\frac{v(1+\alpha)}{c_1+c_3} - \frac{v(1+2\alpha)}{2c_1+c_3} = \frac{v(c_1-c_3\alpha)}{(2c_1+c_3)(c_1+c_3)} > 0.$$

So when $\alpha \le \frac{1}{2}$, $\alpha c_3 < c_1 < \frac{c_3}{2}$, $\gamma \le \frac{v(1+2\alpha)}{2c_1+c_3}$, $t_1 < 0$, $t_2 > 0$.

③ $c_1 < \alpha c_3$, it is invalid.

(7) When $\alpha \le \frac{1}{2}$, $\alpha c_3 < c_1 < \frac{c_3}{2}$, $\frac{v(1+2\alpha)}{2c_1+c_3} < \gamma \le \frac{v(2\alpha-1)}{2c_1-c_3}$, $f(\gamma) < 0$, but the sign of $f(\gamma^*)$ is uncertain, we need to classify.

① $c_1 > c_3$, it is invalid.

② $\alpha c_3 < c_1 < c_3$, i.e., $\alpha c_3 < c_1 < \frac{c_3}{2}$,

$$\frac{v(1+\alpha)}{c_1+c_3} - \frac{v(1+2\alpha)}{2c_1+c_3} = \frac{v(c_1-c_3\alpha)}{(2c_1+c_3)(c_1+c_3)} > 0,$$

$$\frac{v(1+\alpha)}{c_1+c_3} - \frac{v(2\alpha-1)}{2c_1-c_3} = \frac{3v(c_1-c_3\alpha)}{(2c_1-c_3)(c_1+c_3)} < 0,$$

$$\frac{v(\alpha-1)}{c_1-c_3} - \frac{v(2\alpha-1)}{2c_1-c_3} = \frac{-v(c_1-c_3\alpha)}{(2c_1-c_3)(c_1-c_3)} < 0.$$

So when $\alpha \leq \frac{1}{2}$, $\alpha c_3 < c_1 < \frac{c_3}{2}$, $\frac{v(1+2\alpha)}{2c_1+c_3} < \gamma \leq \frac{v(1+\alpha)}{c_1+c_3}$, $t_1 < 0$, $t_2 > 0$. If $\frac{v(1+\alpha)}{c_1+c_3} < \gamma \leq \frac{v(\alpha-1)}{c_1-c_3}$, $t_1 > 0$, $t_2 > 0$, $t_2 > t_1$. If $\frac{v(\alpha-1)}{c_1-c_3} < \gamma \leq \frac{v(2\alpha-1)}{2c_1-c_3}$, $t_1 < 0$, $t_2 > 0$.

③ $c_1 < \alpha c_3$, it is invalid.

(8) When $\alpha \leq \frac{1}{2}$, $\alpha c_3 < c_1 < \frac{c_3}{2}$, $\gamma > \frac{v(2\alpha-1)}{2c_1-c_3}$, $f(\gamma) > 0$, but the sign of $f(\gamma^*)$ is uncertain, we need to classify.

① $c_1 > c_3$, it is invalid.

② $\alpha c_3 < c_1 < c_3$, i.e., $\alpha c_3 < c_1 < \frac{c_3}{2}$,

$$\frac{v(\alpha-1)}{c_1-c_3} - \frac{v(2\alpha-1)}{2c_1-c_3} = \frac{-v(c_1-c_3\alpha)}{(2c_1-c_3)(c_1-c_3)} < 0.$$

So when $\alpha \leq \frac{1}{2}$, $\alpha c_3 < c_1 < \frac{c_3}{2}$, $\gamma > \frac{v(2\alpha-1)}{2c_1-c_3}$, $t_1 < 0$, $t_2 > 0$.

③ $c_1 < \alpha c_3$, it is invalid.

(9) When $\alpha > \frac{1}{2}$, $c_1 > \alpha c_3$, $\gamma \leq \frac{v(2\alpha-1)}{2c_1-c_3}$, $f(\gamma) < 0$, but the sign of $f(\gamma^*)$ is uncertain, we need to classify.

① $c_1 > c_3$,

$$\frac{v(1+\alpha)}{c_1+c_3} - \frac{v(2\alpha-1)}{2c_1-c_3} = \frac{3v(c_1-c_3\alpha)}{(2c_1-c_3)(c_1+c_3)} > 0.$$

So when $\alpha > \frac{1}{2}$, $c_1 > c_3$, $\gamma \leq \frac{v(2\alpha-1)}{2c_1-c_3}$, $t_1 < 0$, $t_2 > 0$.

② $\alpha c_3 < c_1 < c_3$,

$$\frac{v(1+\alpha)}{c_1+c_3} - \frac{v(2\alpha-1)}{2c_1-c_3} = \frac{3v(c_1-c_3\alpha)}{(2c_1-c_3)(c_1+c_3)} > 0.$$

So when $\alpha > \frac{1}{2}$, $\alpha c_3 < c_1 < c_3$, $\gamma \leq \frac{v(2\alpha-1)}{2c_1-c_3}$, $t_1 < 0$, $t_2 > 0$.

③ $c_1 < \alpha c_3$, it is invalid.

(10) When $\alpha > \frac{1}{2}$, $c_1 > \alpha c_3$, $\frac{v(2\alpha-1)}{2c_1-c_3} < \gamma \leq \frac{v(1+2\alpha)}{2c_1+c_3}$, $f(\gamma) > 0$, but the sign of $f(\gamma^*)$ is uncertain, we need to classify.

① $c_1 > c_3$,

$$\frac{v(1+\alpha)}{c_1+c_3} - \frac{v(2\alpha-1)}{2c_1-c_3} = \frac{3v(c_1-c_3\alpha)}{(2c_1-c_3)(c_1+c_3)} > 0,$$

$$\frac{v(1+\alpha)}{c_1+c_3} - \frac{v(1+2\alpha)}{2c_1+c_3} = \frac{v(c_1-c_3\alpha)}{(2c_1+c_3)(c_1+c_3)} > 0.$$

So when $\alpha > \frac{1}{2}$, $c_1 > c_3$, $\frac{v(2\alpha-1)}{2c_1-c_3} < \gamma \leq \frac{v(1+2\alpha)}{2c_1+c_3}$, $t_1 < 0$, $t_2 > 0$.

② $\alpha c_3 < c_1 < c_3$,

$$\frac{v(1+\alpha)}{c_1+c_3} - \frac{v(2\alpha-1)}{2c_1-c_3} = \frac{3v(c_1-c_3\alpha)}{(2c_1-c_3)(c_1+c_3)} > 0,$$

$$\frac{v(1+\alpha)}{c_1+c_3} - \frac{v(1+2\alpha)}{2c_1+c_3} = \frac{v(c_1-c_3\alpha)}{(2c_1+c_3)(c_1+c_3)} > 0.$$

So when $\alpha > \frac{1}{2}$, $\alpha c_3 < c_1 < c_3$, $\frac{v(2\alpha-1)}{2c_1-c_3} < \gamma \leq \frac{v(1+2\alpha)}{2c_1+c_3}$, $t_1 < 0$, $t_2 > 0$.

③ $c_1 < \alpha c_3$, it is invalid.

(11) When $\alpha > \frac{1}{2}$, $c_1 > \alpha c_3$, $\gamma > \frac{v(1+2\alpha)}{2c_1+c_3}$, $f(\gamma) < 0$, but the sign of $f(\gamma^*)$ is uncertain, we need to classify.

① $c_1 > c_3$,

$$\frac{v(1+\alpha)}{c_1+c_3} - \frac{v(1+2\alpha)}{2c_1+c_3} = \frac{v(c_1-c_3\alpha)}{(2c_1+c_3)(c_1+c_3)} > 0.$$

So when $\alpha > \frac{1}{2}$, $c_1 > c_3$, $\frac{v(1+2\alpha)}{2c_1+c_3} < \gamma \leq \frac{v(1+\alpha)}{c_1+c_3}$, $t_1 < 0$, $t_2 > 0$. If $\gamma > \frac{v(1+\alpha)}{c_1+c_3}$, $t_1 > 0$, $t_2 > 0$, $t_2 > t_1$.

② $\alpha c_3 < c_1 < c_3$,

$$\frac{v(1+\alpha)}{c_1+c_3} - \frac{v(1+2\alpha)}{2c_1+c_3} = \frac{v(c_1-c_3\alpha)}{(2c_1+c_3)(c_1+c_3)} > 0.$$

So when $\alpha > \frac{1}{2}$, $\alpha c_3 < c_1 < c_3$, $\frac{v(1+2\alpha)}{2c_1+c_3} < \gamma \leq \frac{v(1+\alpha)}{c_1+c_3}$, $t_1 < 0$, $t_2 > 0$. If $\frac{v(1+\alpha)}{c_1+c_3} < \gamma \leq \frac{v(\alpha-1)}{c_1-c_3}$, $t_1 > 0$, $t_2 > 0$, $t_2 > t_1$. If $\gamma > \frac{v(\alpha-1)}{c_1-c_3}$, $t_1 < 0$, $t_2 > 0$.

③ $c_1 < \alpha c_3$, it is invalid.

(12) When $\alpha > \frac{1}{2}$, $\frac{c_3}{2} < c_1 < \alpha c_3$, $\gamma \leq \frac{v(1+2\alpha)}{2c_1+c_3}$, $f(\gamma) < 0$, but the sign of $f(\gamma^*)$ is uncertain, we need to classify.

① $c_1 > c_3$, it is invalid.

② $\alpha c_3 < c_1 < c_3$, it is invalid.

③ $c_1 < \alpha c_3$, i.e., $\frac{c_3}{2} < c_1 < \alpha c_3$,

$$\frac{v(\alpha-1)}{c_1-c_3} - \frac{v(1+2\alpha)}{2c_1+c_3} = \frac{-3v(c_1-c_3\alpha)}{(2c_1+c_3)(c_1-c_3)} < 0,$$

$$\frac{v(1+\alpha)}{c_1+c_3} - \frac{v(1+2\alpha)}{2c_1+c_3} = \frac{v(c_1-c_3\alpha)}{(2c_1+c_3)(c_1+c_3)} < 0.$$

So when $\alpha > \frac{1}{2}$, $\frac{c_3}{2} < c_1 < \alpha c_3$, $\gamma \le \frac{v(\alpha-1)}{c_1-c_3}$, $t_1 < 0$, $t_2 > 0$. If $\frac{v(\alpha-1)}{c_1-c_3} < \gamma \le \frac{v(1+\alpha)}{c_1+c_3}$, $t_1 > 0$, $t_2 > 0$, $t_2 > t_1$. If $\frac{v(1+\alpha)}{c_1+c_3} < \gamma \le \frac{v(1+2\alpha)}{2c_1+c_3}$, $t_1 < 0$, $t_2 > 0$.

(13) When $\alpha > \frac{1}{2}$, $\frac{c_3}{2} < c_1 < \alpha c_3$, $\frac{v(1+2\alpha)}{2c_1+c_3} < \gamma \le \frac{v(2\alpha-1)}{2c_1-c_3}$, $f(\gamma) > 0$, but the sign of $f(\gamma^*)$ is uncertain, we need to classify.

① $c_1 > c_3$, it is invalid.

② $\alpha c_3 < c_1 < c_3$, it is invalid.

③ $c_1 < \alpha c_3$, i.e., $\frac{c_3}{2} < c_1 < \alpha c_3$,

$$\frac{v(\alpha-1)}{c_1-c_3} - \frac{v(1+2\alpha)}{2c_1+c_3} = \frac{-3v(c_1-c_3\alpha)}{(2c_1+c_3)(c_1-c_3)} < 0,$$

$$\frac{v(1+\alpha)}{c_1+c_3} - \frac{v(1+2\alpha)}{2c_1+c_3} = \frac{v(c_1-c_3\alpha)}{(2c_1+c_3)(c_1+c_3)} < 0.$$

So when $\alpha > \frac{1}{2}$, $\frac{c_3}{2} < c_1 < \alpha c_3$, $\frac{v(1+2\alpha)}{2c_1+c_3} < \gamma \le \frac{v(2\alpha-1)}{2c_1-c_3}$, $t_1 < 0$, $t_2 > 0$.

(14) When $\alpha > \frac{1}{2}$, $\frac{c_3}{2} < c_1 < \alpha c_3$, $\gamma > \frac{v(2\alpha-1)}{2c_1-c_3}$, $f(\gamma) < 0$, but the sign of $f(\gamma^*)$ is uncertain, we need to classify.

① $c_1 > c_3$, it is invalid.

② $\alpha c_3 < c_1 < c_3$, it is invalid.

③ $c_1 < \alpha c_3$, i.e., $\frac{c_3}{2} < c_1 < \alpha c_3$,

$$\frac{v(\alpha-1)}{c_1-c_3} - \frac{v(1+2\alpha)}{2c_1+c_3} = \frac{-3v(c_1-c_3\alpha)}{(2c_1+c_3)(c_1-c_3)} < 0,$$

$$\frac{v(1+\alpha)}{c_1+c_3} - \frac{v(1+2\alpha)}{2c_1+c_3} = \frac{v(c_1-c_3\alpha)}{(2c_1+c_3)(c_1+c_3)} < 0.$$

So when $\alpha > \frac{1}{2}$, $\frac{c_3}{2} < c_1 < \alpha c_3$, $\gamma > \frac{v(2\alpha-1)}{2c_1-c_3}$, $t_1 < 0$, $t_2 > 0$.

(15) When $\alpha > \frac{1}{2}$, $c_1 < \frac{c_3}{2}$, $\gamma \le \frac{v(1+2\alpha)}{2c_1+c_3}$, $f(\gamma) < 0$, but the sign of $f(\gamma^*)$ is uncertain, we need to classify.

① $c_1 > c_3$, it is invalid.

② $\alpha c_3 < c_1 < c_3$, it is invalid.

③ $c_1 < \alpha c_3$, i.e., $c_1 < \frac{c_3}{2}$,

$$\frac{v(\alpha-1)}{c_1-c_3} - \frac{v(1+2\alpha)}{2c_1+c_3} = \frac{-3v(c_1-c_3\alpha)}{(2c_1+c_3)(c_1-c_3)} < 0,$$

$$\frac{v(1+\alpha)}{c_1+c_3} - \frac{v(1+2\alpha)}{2c_1+c_3} = \frac{v(c_1-c_3\alpha)}{(2c_1+c_3)(c_1+c_3)} < 0.$$

So when $\alpha > \frac{1}{2}$, $c_1 < \frac{c_3}{2}$, $\gamma \le \frac{v(\alpha-1)}{c_1-c_3}$, $t_1 < 0$, $t_2 > 0$. If $\frac{v(\alpha-1)}{c_1-c_3} < \gamma \le \frac{v(1+\alpha)}{c_1+c_3}$, $t_1 > 0$, $t_2 > 0$, $t_2 > t_1$. If $\frac{v(1+\alpha)}{c_1+c_3} < \gamma \le \frac{v(1+2\alpha)}{2c_1+c_3}$, $t_1 < 0$, $t_2 > 0$.

(16) When $\alpha > \frac{1}{2}$, $c_1 < \frac{c_3}{2}$, $\gamma > \frac{v(1+2\alpha)}{2c_1+c_3}$, $f(\gamma) > 0$, but the sign of $f(\gamma^*)$ is uncertain, we need to classify.

① $c_1 > c_3$, it is invalid.

② $\alpha c_3 < c_1 < c_3$, it is invalid.

③ $c_1 < \alpha c_3$, i.e., $c_1 < \frac{c_3}{2}$,

$$\frac{v(\alpha-1)}{c_1-c_3} - \frac{v(1+2\alpha)}{2c_1+c_3} = \frac{-3v(c_1-c_3\alpha)}{(2c_1+c_3)(c_1-c_3)} < 0,$$

$$\frac{v(1+\alpha)}{c_1+c_3} - \frac{v(1+2\alpha)}{2c_1+c_3} = \frac{v(c_1-c_3\alpha)}{(2c_1+c_3)(c_1+c_3)} < 0.$$

So when $\alpha > \frac{1}{2}$, $c_1 < \frac{c_3}{2}$, $\gamma > \frac{v(1+2\alpha)}{2c_1+c_3}$, $t_1 < 0$, $t_2 > 0$.

All in all, based on the above analysis, we can conclude that when $c_3\gamma - v > 0$, $t_2 > t_1$ and $c_3\gamma - v < 0$, $t_2 < t_1$. Then we analysis how the difference of profit varies over the feasible interval. The difference of $t_1 - \frac{4\gamma-\omega^2}{2}$, $t_1 - (4\gamma-\omega^2)$, $t_2 - (4\gamma-\omega^2)$, and $t_2 - \frac{4\gamma-\omega^2}{2}$ are

$$\frac{\begin{array}{c}-(4\gamma-\omega^2)(v-c_3\gamma)^2 - (c_3\gamma-v)(4\gamma-\omega^2)\\ \times\sqrt{\gamma^2(8c_1^2+c_3^2)-2\gamma v(c_3+8c_1\alpha)+v^2(1+8\alpha^2)}\end{array}}{8(c_1\gamma-v\alpha)^2},$$

$$\times\frac{\begin{array}{c}(4\gamma-\omega^2)\big(-\big(\gamma^2(4c_1^2+c_3^2)-2\gamma v(c_3+4c_1\alpha)+v^2(1+4\alpha^2)\big)\\ -(c_3\gamma-v)\sqrt{\gamma^2(8c_1^2+c_3^2)-2\gamma v(c_3+8c_1\alpha)+v^2(1+8\alpha^2)}\big)\end{array}}{8(c_1\gamma-v\alpha)^2},$$

$$\times\frac{\begin{array}{c}(4\gamma-\omega^2)\big(-\big(\gamma^2(4c_1^2+c_3^2)-2\gamma v(c_3+4c_1\alpha)+v^2(1+4\alpha^2)\big)\\ +(c_3\gamma-v)\sqrt{\gamma^2(8c_1^2+c_3^2)-2\gamma v(c_3+8c_1\alpha)+v^2(1+8\alpha^2)}\big)\end{array}}{8(c_1\gamma-v\alpha)^2},$$

and

$$\frac{\begin{array}{c}-(4\gamma-\omega^2)(v-c_3\gamma)^2 + (c_3\gamma-v)(4\gamma-\omega^2)\\ \times\sqrt{\gamma^2(8c_1^2+c_3^2)-2\gamma v(c_3+8c_1\alpha)+v^2(1+8\alpha^2)}\end{array}}{8(c_1\gamma-v\alpha)^2}.$$

Similarly, we analysis the sign of above four differences, the denominators are always greater than 0, so we study the molecules. And we assume that $g(r) = \sqrt{\gamma^2(8c_1^2+c_3^2) - 2\gamma v(c_3+8c_1\alpha) + v^2(1+8\alpha^2)}$, $h(r) = \gamma^2(4c_1^2+c_3^2) - 2\gamma v(c_3 + 4c_1\alpha) + v^2(1+4\alpha^2)$.

(1) As for $t_1 - \frac{4\gamma-\omega^2}{2}$,

$$((4\gamma-\omega^2)(v-c_3\gamma)^2)^2 - g(r)^2(c_3\gamma-v)^2(4\gamma-\omega^2)^2$$
$$= -8(-c_3\gamma+v)^2(-4\gamma+\omega^2)^2(c_1\gamma-v\alpha)^2 < 0.$$

(2) As for $t_1-(4\gamma-\omega^2)$, The discriminant of $h(r)$ equals to $-16v^2(c_1-c_3\alpha)^2<0$, so $h(r)$ is always greater than 0.

$$\big(-(4\gamma-\omega^2)h(r)\big)^2 - (c_3\gamma-v)^2(4\gamma-\omega^2)^2g(r)^2 = 16(-4\gamma+\omega^2)^2(c_1\gamma-v\alpha)^4 > 0.$$

(3) As for $t_2 - \frac{4\gamma-\omega^2}{2}$,

$$(-(4\gamma-\omega^2)(v-c_3\gamma)^2)^2 - g(r)^2(c_3\gamma-v)^2(4\gamma-\omega^2)^2$$
$$= -8(-c_3\gamma+v)^2(-4\gamma+\omega^2)^2(c_1\gamma-v\alpha)^2 < 0.$$

(4) As for $t_2-(4\gamma-\omega^2)$,

The discriminant of $h(r)$ equals to $-16v^2(c_1-c_3\alpha)^2<0$, so $h(r)$ is always greater than 0.

$$\big(-(4\gamma-\omega^2)h(r)\big)^2 - (c_3\gamma-v)^2(4\gamma-\omega^2)^2g(r)^2 = 16(-4\gamma+\omega^2)^2(c_1\gamma-v\alpha)^4 > 0.$$

So we can conclude that when $c_3\gamma - v > 0$, if $\sqrt{\frac{4\gamma-\omega^2}{2}} < \theta \le \sqrt{t_2}$, $\Delta\pi_1 > 0$. If $\sqrt{t_2} < \theta \le \sqrt{4\gamma-\omega^2}$, $\Delta\pi_1 < 0$. When $c_3\gamma - v < 0$, if $t_2 < 0$, $\Delta\pi_1 > 0$. Under $t_2 > 0$, if $\theta \le \sqrt{t_2}$, $\Delta\pi_1 < 0$. If $\sqrt{t_2} < \theta \le \sqrt{\frac{4\gamma-\omega^2}{2}}$, $\Delta\pi_1 > 0$.

A.4.2. *For firm 2*

$$\Delta\pi_2 = \frac{(4\gamma-\omega^2)\big(4\gamma^2(c_2^2-c_3^2)+2\gamma v(c_3+4c_2(\alpha-1))+v^2(3-8\alpha+4\alpha^2)\big)\theta^2}{(4\gamma-\omega^2)(4\gamma-\omega^2-2\theta^2)^2}$$
$$+\frac{-(-4\gamma+\omega^2)^2\big(\gamma^2(c_2^2-c_3^2)+2\gamma v(c_3+c_2(\alpha-1))+v^2(\alpha-2)\alpha\big)}{(4\gamma-\omega^2)(4\gamma-\omega^2-2\theta^2)^2}$$
$$+\frac{-4\big(c_2\gamma+v(-1+\alpha)\big)^2\theta^4}{(4\gamma-\omega^2)(4\gamma-\omega^2-2\theta^2)^2}. \tag{A.10}$$

Based on the proof of Proposition 1, $4\gamma-\omega^2>0$, so the denominator of $\Delta\pi_2$ must be greater than 0, hence we focus on analyzing the numerator, and we assume $t=\theta^2$

$(\theta < \sqrt{\frac{4\gamma-\omega^2}{2}}$, or $\sqrt{\frac{4\gamma-\omega^2}{2}} < \theta < \sqrt{4\gamma - \omega^2})$.

$$\begin{aligned} f(t) = & -4t^2\big(c_2\gamma + v(\alpha-1)\big)^2 - (-4\gamma+\omega^2)^2\big(\gamma^2(c_2^2 - c_3^2) + 2\gamma v(c_3 + c_2(\alpha-1))\big) \\ & - (-4\gamma+\omega^2)^2(-v^2(\alpha-2)\alpha) + t(4\gamma-\omega^2)\big(2\gamma v(c_3 + 4c_2(\alpha-1)\big) \\ & + (4\gamma-\omega^2)(v^2(3-8\alpha+4\alpha^2))t + (4\gamma-\omega^2)\big(4\gamma^2(c_2^2-c_3^2)\big)t. \end{aligned} \tag{A.11}$$

The discriminant of $f(t)$ equals $\Delta f(t) = (-c_3\gamma+v)^2(-4\gamma+\omega^2)^2\big(\gamma^2(8c_2^2+c_3^2) + 2\gamma v(8c_2(\alpha-1) - c_3) + v^2(9+8\alpha^2-16\alpha)\big)$. Similarly, we assume $\gamma^2(8c_2^2+c_3^2) + 2\gamma v(8c_2(\alpha-1) - c_3) + v^2(9+8\alpha^2-16\alpha)$ is the function about γ, its discriminate $\Delta = -32v^2\big((c_2 + c_3(\alpha-1)\big)^2 < 0$, this part is always greater than 0, so there must be two intersections with the x axis of $f(t)$. Its solutions are

$$t = \frac{-(4\gamma-\omega^2)\big(4\gamma^2(c_2^2-c_3^2) + 2\gamma v(c_3+4c_2(\alpha-1)) + v^2(3-8\alpha+4\alpha^2)\big)}{-8\big(c_2\gamma+v(\alpha-1)\big)^2}$$

$$\pm \frac{\begin{array}{l}(4\gamma-\omega^2)(c_3\gamma - v) \\ \quad\times\sqrt{\gamma^2(8c_2^2+c_3^2) + 2\gamma v(-c_3+8c_2(\alpha-1)) + v^2(9-16\alpha+8\alpha^2)}\end{array}}{-8\big(c_2\gamma+v(\alpha-1)\big)^2}.$$

The sign of t is uncertain, so we focus the numerator of t to analysis. We assume $f(\gamma) = -\big(4\gamma^2(c_2^2-c_3^2) + 2\gamma v(c_3+4c_2(\alpha-1)) + v^2(3-8\alpha+4\alpha^2)\big)$, $\Delta f(\gamma) = 16v^2\big(c_2+c_3(\alpha-1)\big)^2 > 0$, so it solutions are $\gamma_1 = \frac{v(1-2\alpha)}{2c_2-c_3}$, $\gamma_2 = \frac{v(3-2\alpha)}{2c_2+c_3}$, $\gamma_1 - \gamma_2 = \frac{-4v\left(c_2+c_3(\alpha-1)\right)}{(2c_2-c_3)(2c_2+c_3)}$. In addition, we assume $f(\gamma^*) = f(\gamma)^2 - (c_3\gamma - v)^2\big(\gamma^2(8c_2^2+c_3^2) + 2\gamma v(-c_3+8c_2(\alpha-1)) + v^2(9-16\alpha+8\alpha^2)\big)$, $\Delta\gamma^* = 4v^2\big(c_2+c_3(\alpha-1)\big)^2 > 0$, so its solutions are $\gamma_1^* = \frac{-v\alpha}{c_2-c_3}$, $\gamma_2^* = \frac{v(2-\alpha)}{c_2+c_3}$, $\gamma_1^* - \gamma_2^* = \frac{-2v\left(c_2+c_3(\alpha-1)\right)}{(c_2-c_3)(c_2+c_3)}$. According to the above analysis, we first analyze the sign of t along with $c_3\gamma - v > 0$, as well as we assume

$$t_1 = \frac{-(4\gamma-\omega^2)\big(4\gamma^2(c_2^2-c_3^2) + 2\gamma v(c_3+4c_2(\alpha-1)) + v^2(3-8\alpha+4\alpha^2)\big)}{-8\big(c_2\gamma+v(\alpha-1)\big)^2}$$

$$+ \frac{\begin{array}{l}(4\gamma-\omega^2)(c_3\gamma - v) \\ \quad\times\sqrt{\gamma^2(8c_2^2+c_3^2) + 2\gamma v(-c_3+8c_2(\alpha-1)) + v^2(9-16\alpha+8\alpha^2)}\end{array}}{-8\big(c_2\gamma+v(\alpha-1)\big)^2},$$

the another solution is t_2, the classification is as follows:

(1) When $\alpha > \frac{1}{2}$, $c_2 > \frac{c_3}{2}$, $\gamma \leq \frac{v(3-2\alpha)}{2c_2+c_3}$, $f(\gamma) > 0$, but the sign of $f(\gamma^*)$ is uncertain, we need to classify.

① $c_2 > c_3$,

$$\frac{v(2-\alpha)}{c_2+c_3} - \frac{v(3-2\alpha)}{2c_2+c_3} = \frac{v\big(c_2+c_3(\alpha-1)\big)}{(2c_2+c_3)(c_2+c_3)} > 0.$$

So when $\alpha > \frac{1}{2}$, $c_2 > c_3$, $\gamma \le \frac{v(3-2\alpha)}{2c_2+c_3}$, $t_1 < 0$, $t_2 > 0$.

② $(1-\alpha)c_3 < c_2 < c_3$, i.e., $\frac{c_3}{2} < c_2 < c_3$,

$$\frac{v(2-\alpha)}{c_2+c_3} - \frac{v(3-2\alpha)}{2c_2+c_3} = \frac{v\big(c_2+c_3(\alpha-1)\big)}{(2c_2+c_3)(c_2+c_3)} > 0,$$

$$\frac{-v\alpha}{c_2-c_3} - \frac{v(3-2\alpha)}{2c_2+c_3} = \frac{-3v\big(c_2+c_3(\alpha-1)\big)}{(2c_2+c_3)(c_2-c_3)} > 0.$$

So when $\alpha > \frac{1}{2}$, $\frac{c_3}{2} < c_2 < c_3$, $\gamma \le \frac{v(3-2\alpha)}{2c_2+c_3}$, $t_1 < 0$, $t_2 > 0$.

③ $c_2 < (1-\alpha)c_3$, it is invalid.

(2) When $\alpha > \frac{1}{2}$, $c_2 > \frac{c_3}{2}$, $\gamma > \frac{v(3-2\alpha)}{2c_2+c_3}$, $f(\gamma) < 0$, but the sign of $f(\gamma^*)$ is uncertain, we need to classify.

① $c_2 > c_3$,

$$\frac{v(2-\alpha)}{c_2+c_3} - \frac{v(3-2\alpha)}{2c_2+c_3} = \frac{v\big(c_2+c_3(\alpha-1)\big)}{(2c_2+c_3)(c_2+c_3)} > 0.$$

So when $\alpha > \frac{1}{2}$, $c_2 > c_3$, $\frac{v(3-2\alpha)}{2c_2+c_3} < \gamma \le \frac{v(2-\alpha)}{c_2+c_3}$, $t_1 < 0$, $t_2 > 0$. If $\gamma > \frac{v(2-\alpha)}{c_2+c_3}$, $t_1 > 0$, $t_2 > 0$, $t_2 > t_1$.

② $(1-\alpha)c_3 < c_2 < c_3$, i.e., $\frac{c_3}{2} < c_2 < c_3$,

$$\frac{v(2-\alpha)}{c_2+c_3} - \frac{v(3-2\alpha)}{2c_2+c_3} = \frac{v\big(c_2+c_3(\alpha-1)\big)}{(2c_2+c_3)(c_2+c_3)} > 0,$$

$$\frac{-v\alpha}{c_2-c_3} - \frac{v(3-2\alpha)}{2c_2+c_3} = \frac{-3v\big(c_2+c_3(\alpha-1)\big)}{(2c_2+c_3)(c_2-c_3)} > 0.$$

So when $\alpha > \frac{1}{2}$, $\frac{c_3}{2} < c_2 < c_3$, $\frac{v(3-2\alpha)}{2c_2+c_3} < \gamma \le \frac{v(2-\alpha)}{c_2+c_3}$, $t_1 < 0$, $t_2 > 0$. If $\frac{v(2-\alpha)}{c_2+c_3} < \gamma \le \frac{-v\alpha}{c_2-c_3}$, $t_1 > 0$, $t_2 > 0$, $t_2 > t_1$. If $\gamma > \frac{-v\alpha}{c_2-c_3}$, $t_1 < 0$, $t_2 > 0$.

③ $c_2 < (1-\alpha)c_3$, it is invalid.

(3) When $\alpha \le \frac{1}{2}$, $c_2 > (1-\alpha)c_3$, $\gamma \le \frac{v(1-2\alpha)}{2c_2-c_3}$, $f(\gamma) < 0$, but the sign of $f(\gamma^*)$ is uncertain, we need to classify.

① $c_2 > c_3$,

$$\frac{v(2-\alpha)}{c_2+c_3} - \frac{v(1-2\alpha)}{2c_2-c_3} = \frac{3v\big(c_2+c_3(\alpha-1)\big)}{(2c_2-c_3)(c_2+c_3)} > 0.$$

So, when $\alpha \le \frac{1}{2}$, $c_2 > c_3$, $\gamma \le \frac{v(1-2\alpha)}{2c_2-c_3}$, $t_1 < 0$, $t_2 > 0$.

② $(1-\alpha)c_3 < c_2 < c_3$,

$$\frac{v(2-\alpha)}{c_2+c_3} - \frac{v(1-2\alpha)}{2c_2-c_3} = \frac{3v\big(c_2+c_3(\alpha-1)\big)}{(2c_2-c_3)(c_2+c_3)} > 0.$$

So, when $\alpha \leq \frac{1}{2}$, $(1-\alpha)c_3 < c_2 < c_3$, $\gamma \leq \frac{v(1-2\alpha)}{2c_2-c_3}$, $t_1 < 0$, $t_2 > 0$.

③ $c_2 < (1-\alpha)c_3$, it is invalid.

(4) When $\alpha < \frac{1}{2}$, $c_2 > (1-\alpha)c_3$, $\frac{v(1-2\alpha)}{2c_2-c_3} < \gamma \leq \frac{v(3-2\alpha)}{2c_2+c_3}$, $f(\gamma) > 0$, but the sign of $f(\gamma^*)$ is uncertain, we need to classify.

① $c_2 > c_3$,

$$\frac{v(2-\alpha)}{c_2+c_3} - \frac{v(1-2\alpha)}{2c_2-c_3} = \frac{3v\big(c_2+c_3(\alpha-1)\big)}{(2c_2-c_3)(c_2+c_3)} > 0,$$

$$\frac{v(2-\alpha)}{c_2+c_3} - \frac{v(3-2\alpha)}{2c_2+c_3} = \frac{v\big(c_2+c_3(\alpha-1)\big)}{(2c_2+c_3)(c_2+c_3)} > 0.$$

So, when $\alpha < \frac{1}{2}$, $c_2 > c_3$, $\frac{v(1-2\alpha)}{2c_2-c_3} < \gamma \leq \frac{v(3-2\alpha)}{2c_2+c_3}$, $t_1 < 0$, $t_2 > 0$.

② $(1-\alpha)c_3 < c_2 < c_3$,

$$\frac{v(2-\alpha)}{c_2+c_3} - \frac{v(1-2\alpha)}{2c_2-c_3} = \frac{3v\big(c_2+c_3(\alpha-1)\big)}{(2c_2-c_3)(c_2+c_3)} > 0,$$

$$\frac{v(2-\alpha)}{c_2+c_3} - \frac{v(3-2\alpha)}{2c_2+c_3} = \frac{v\big(c_2+c_3(\alpha-1)\big)}{(2c_2+c_3)(c_2+c_3)} > 0.$$

So, when $\alpha < \frac{1}{2}$, $(1-\alpha)c_3 < c_2 < c_3$, $\frac{v(1-2\alpha)}{2c_2-c_3} < \gamma \leq \frac{v(3-2\alpha)}{2c_2+c_3}$, $t_1 < 0$, $t_2 > 0$.

③ $c_2 < (1-\alpha)c_3$, it is invalid.

(5) When $\alpha \leq \frac{1}{2}$, $c_2 > (1-\alpha)c_3$, $\gamma > \frac{v(3-2\alpha)}{2c_2+c_3}$, $f(\gamma) < 0$, but the sign of $f(\gamma^*)$ is uncertain, we need to classify.

① $c_2 > c_3$,

$$\frac{v(2-\alpha)}{c_2+c_3} - \frac{v(3-2\alpha)}{2c_2+c_3} = \frac{v\big(c_2+c_3(\alpha-1)\big)}{(2c_2+c_3)(c_2+c_3)} > 0.$$

So, when $\alpha \leq \frac{1}{2}$, $c_2 > c_3$, $\frac{v(3-2\alpha)}{2c_2+c_3} < \gamma \leq \frac{v(2-\alpha)}{c_2+c_3}$, $t_1 < 0$, $t_2 > 0$. If $\gamma > \frac{v(2-\alpha)}{c_2+c_3}$, $t_1 > 0$, $t_2 > 0$, $t_2 > t_1$.

② $(1-\alpha)c_3 < c_2 < c_3$,

$$\frac{v(2-\alpha)}{c_2+c_3} - \frac{v(3-2\alpha)}{2c_2+c_3} = \frac{v\big(c_2+c_3(\alpha-1)\big)}{(2c_2+c_3)(c_2+c_3)} > 0.$$

So, when $\alpha \leq \frac{1}{2}$, $(1-\alpha)c_3 < c_2 < c_3$, $\frac{v(3-2\alpha)}{2c_2+c_3} < \gamma \leq \frac{v(2-\alpha)}{c_2+c_3}$, $t_1 < 0$, $t_2 > 0$. If $\frac{v(2-\alpha)}{c_2+c_3} < \gamma \leq \frac{-v\alpha}{c_2-c_3}$, $t_1 > 0$, $t_2 > 0$, $t_2 > t_1$. If $\gamma > \frac{-v\alpha}{c_2-c_3}$, $t_1 < 0$, $t_2 > 0$.

③ $c_2 < (1-\alpha)c_3$, it is invalid.

(6) When $\alpha \le \frac{1}{2}$, $\frac{c_3}{2} < c_2 < (1-\alpha)c_3$, $\gamma \le \frac{v(3-2\alpha)}{2c_2+c_3}$, $f(\gamma) < 0$, but the sign of $f(\gamma^*)$ is uncertain, we need to classify.

① $c_2 > c_3$, it is invalid.

② $(1-\alpha)c_3 < c_2 < c_3$, it is invalid.

③ $c_2 < (1-\alpha)c_3$, i.e., $\frac{c_3}{2} < c_2 < (1-\alpha)c_3$,

$$\frac{-v\alpha}{c_2 - c_3} - \frac{v(3-2\alpha)}{2c_2 + c_3} = \frac{-3v\big(c_2 + c_3(\alpha - 1)\big)}{(2c_2 + c_3)(c_2 - c_3)} < 0,$$

$$\frac{v(2-\alpha)}{c_2 + c_3} - \frac{v(3-2\alpha)}{2c_2 + c_3} = \frac{v\big(c_2 + c_3(\alpha - 1)\big)}{(2c_2 + c_3)(c_2 + c_3)} < 0.$$

So, when $\alpha \le \frac{1}{2}$, $\frac{c_3}{2} < c_2 < (1-\alpha)c_3$, $\gamma \le \frac{-v\alpha}{c_2-c_3}$, $t_1 < 0$, $t_2 > 0$. If $\frac{-v\alpha}{c_2-c_3} < \gamma \le \frac{v(2-\alpha)}{c_2+c_3}$, $t_1 > 0$, $t_2 > 0$, $t_2 > t_1$. If $\frac{v(2-\alpha)}{c_2+c_3} < \gamma \le \frac{v(3-2\alpha)}{2c_2+c_3}$, $t_1 < 0$, $t_2 > 0$.

(7) When $\alpha \le \frac{1}{2}$, $\frac{c_3}{2} < c_2 < (1-\alpha)c_3$, $\frac{v(3-2\alpha)}{2c_2+c_3} < \gamma \le \frac{v(1-2\alpha)}{2c_2-c_3}$, $f(\gamma) > 0$, but the sign of $f(\gamma^*)$ is uncertain, we need to classify.

① $c_2 > c_3$, it is invalid.

② $(1-\alpha)c_3 < c_2 < c_3$, it is invalid.

③ $c_2 < (1-\alpha)c_3$, i.e., $\frac{c_3}{2} < c_2 < (1-\alpha)c_3$,

$$\frac{-v\alpha}{c_2 - c_3} - \frac{v(3-2\alpha)}{2c_2 + c_3} = \frac{-3v\big(c_2 + c_3(\alpha - 1)\big)}{(2c_2 + c_3)(c_2 - c_3)} < 0,$$

$$\frac{v(2-\alpha)}{c_2 + c_3} - \frac{v(3-2\alpha)}{2c_2 + c_3} = \frac{v\big(c_2 + c_3(\alpha - 1)\big)}{(2c_2 + c_3)(c_2 + c_3)} < 0.$$

So, when $\alpha \le \frac{1}{2}$, $\frac{c_3}{2} < c_2 < (1-\alpha)c_3$, $\frac{v(3-2\alpha)}{2c_2+c_3} < \gamma \le \frac{v(1-2\alpha)}{2c_2-c_3}$, $t_1 < 0$, $t_2 > 0$.

(8) When $\alpha \le \frac{1}{2}$, $\frac{c_3}{2} < c_2 < (1-\alpha)c_3$, $\gamma > \frac{v(1-2\alpha)}{2c_2-c_3}$, $f(\gamma) < 0$, but the sign of $f(\gamma^*)$ is uncertain, we need to classify.

① $c_2 > c_3$, it is invalid.

② $(1-\alpha)c_3 < c_2 < c_3$, it is invalid.

③ $c_2 < (1-\alpha)c_3$, i.e., $\frac{c_3}{2} < c_2 < (1-\alpha)c_3$,

$$\frac{-v\alpha}{c_2 - c_3} - \frac{v(3-2\alpha)}{2c_2 + c_3} = \frac{-3v\big(c_2 + c_3(\alpha - 1)\big)}{(2c_2 + c_3)(c_2 - c_3)} < 0,$$

$$\frac{v(2-\alpha)}{c_2 + c_3} - \frac{v(3-2\alpha)}{2c_2 + c_3} = \frac{v\big(c_2 + c_3(\alpha - 1)\big)}{(2c_2 + c_3)(c_2 + c_3)} < 0.$$

So, when $\alpha \le \frac{1}{2}$, $\frac{c_3}{2} < c_2 < (1-\alpha)c_3$, $\gamma > \frac{v(1-2\alpha)}{2c_2-c_3}$, $t_1 < 0$, $t_2 > 0$.

(9) When $\alpha > \frac{1}{2}$, $(1-\alpha)c_3 < c_2 < \frac{c_3}{2}$, $\gamma \le \frac{v(3-2\alpha)}{2c_2+c_3}$, $f(\gamma) > 0$, but the sign of $f(\gamma^*)$ is uncertain, we need to classify.

① $c_2 > c_3$, it is invalid.

② $(1-\alpha)c_3 < c_2 < c_3$, i.e., $(1-\alpha)c_3 < c_2 < \frac{c_3}{2}$,

$$\frac{v(2-\alpha)}{c_2+c_3} - \frac{v(3-2\alpha)}{2c_2+c_3} = \frac{v\big(c_2+c_3(\alpha-1)\big)}{(2c_2+c_3)(c_2+c_3)} > 0.$$

So, when $\alpha > \frac{1}{2}$, $(1-\alpha)c_3 < c_2 < \frac{c_3}{2}$, $\gamma \le \frac{v(3-2\alpha)}{2c_2+c_3}$, $t_1 < 0$, $t_2 > 0$.

③ $c_2 < (1-\alpha)c_3$, it is invalid.

(10) When $\alpha > \frac{1}{2}$, $(1-\alpha)c_3 < c_2 < \frac{c_3}{2}$, $\frac{v(3-2\alpha)}{2c_2+c_3} < \gamma \le \frac{v(1-2\alpha)}{2c_2-c_3}$, $f(\gamma) < 0$, but the sign of $f(\gamma^*)$ is uncertain, we need to classify.

① $c_2 > c_3$, it is invalid.

② $(1-\alpha)c_3 < c_2 < c_3$, i.e., $(1-\alpha)c_3 < c_2 < \frac{c_3}{2}$,

$$\frac{v(2-\alpha)}{c_2+c_3} - \frac{v(3-2\alpha)}{2c_2+c_3} = \frac{v\big(c_2+c_3(\alpha-1)\big)}{(2c_2+c_3)(c_2+c_3)} > 0,$$

$$\frac{v(2-\alpha)}{c_2+c_3} - \frac{v(1-2\alpha)}{2c_2-c_3} = \frac{3v\big(c_2+c_3(\alpha-1)\big)}{(2c_2-c_3)(c_2+c_3)} < 0,$$

$$\frac{-v\alpha}{c_2-c_3} - \frac{v(1-2\alpha)}{2c_2-c_3} = \frac{-v\big(c_2+c_3(\alpha-1)\big)}{(2c_2-c_3)(c_2-c_3)} < 0.$$

So, when $\alpha > \frac{1}{2}$, $(1-\alpha)c_3 < c_2 < \frac{c_3}{2}$, $\frac{v(3-2\alpha)}{2c_2+c_3} < \gamma \le \frac{v(2-\alpha)}{c_2+c_3}$, $t_1 < 0$, $t_2 > 0$. If $\frac{v(2-\alpha)}{c_2+c_3} < \gamma \le \frac{-v\alpha}{c_2-c_3}$, $t_1 > 0$, $t_2 > 0$, $t_2 > t_1$. If $\frac{-v\alpha}{c_2-c_3} < \gamma \le \frac{v(1-2\alpha)}{2c_2-c_3}$, $t_1 < 0$, $t_2 > 0$.

③ $c_2 < (1-\alpha)c_3$, it is invalid.

(11) When $\alpha > \frac{1}{2}$, $(1-\alpha)c_3 < c_2 < \frac{c_3}{2}$, $\gamma > \frac{v(1-2\alpha)}{2c_2-c_3}$, $f(\gamma) < 0$, but the sign of $f(\gamma^*)$ is uncertain, we need to classify.

① $c_2 > c_3$, it is invalid.

② $(1-\alpha)c_3 < c_2 < c_3$, i.e., $(1-\alpha)c_3 < c_2 < \frac{c_3}{2}$,

$$\frac{-v\alpha}{c_2-c_3} - \frac{v(1-2\alpha)}{2c_2-c_3} = \frac{-v\big(c_2+c_3(\alpha-1)\big)}{(2c_2-c_3)(c_2-c_3)} < 0.$$

So, when $\alpha > \frac{1}{2}$, $(1-\alpha)c_3 < c_2 < \frac{c_3}{2}$, $\gamma > \frac{v(1-2\alpha)}{2c_2-c_3}$, $t_1 < 0$, $t_2 > 0$.

③ $c_2 < (1-\alpha)c_3$, it is invalid.

(12) When $\alpha > \frac{1}{2}$, $c_2 < (1-\alpha)c_3$, $\gamma \le \frac{v(1-2\alpha)}{2c_2-c_3}$, $f(\gamma) > 0$, but the sign of $f(\gamma^*)$ is uncertain, we need to classify.

① $c_2 > c_3$, it is invalid.

② $(1-\alpha)c_3 < c_2 < c_3$, it is invalid.

③ $c_2 < (1-\alpha)c_3$,

$$\frac{-v\alpha}{c_2 - c_3} - \frac{v(1-2\alpha)}{2c_2 - c_3} = \frac{-v\big(c_2 + c_3(\alpha - 1)\big)}{(2c_2 - c_3)(c_2 - c_3)} > 0.$$

So, when $\alpha > \frac{1}{2}$, $c_2 < (1-\alpha)c_3$, $\gamma \le \frac{v(1-2\alpha)}{2c_2 - c_3}$, $t_1 < 0$, $t_2 > 0$.

(13) When $\alpha > \frac{1}{2}$, $c_2 < (1-\alpha)c_3$, $\frac{v(1-2\alpha)}{2c_2-c_3} < \gamma \le \frac{v(3-2\alpha)}{2c_2+c_3}$, $f(\gamma) < 0$, but the sign of $f(\gamma^*)$ is uncertain, we need to classify.

① $c_2 > c_3$, it is invalid.

② $(1-\alpha)c_3 < c_2 < c_3$, it is invalid.

③ $c_2 < (1-\alpha)c_3$,

$$\frac{-v\alpha}{c_2 - c_3} - \frac{v(1-2\alpha)}{2c_2 - c_3} = \frac{-v\big(c_2 + c_3(\alpha - 1)\big)}{(2c_2 - c_3)(c_2 - c_3)} > 0,$$

$$\frac{v(2-\alpha)}{c_2 + c_3} - \frac{v(3-2\alpha)}{2c_2 + c_3} = \frac{-v\big(c_2 + c_3(\alpha - 1)\big)}{(2c_2 + c_3)(c_2 + c_3)} < 0.$$

So, when $\alpha > \frac{1}{2}$, $c_2 < (1-\alpha)c_3$, $\frac{v(1-2\alpha)}{2c_2-c_3} < \gamma \le \frac{-v\alpha}{c_2-c_3}$, $t_1 < 0$, $t_2 > 0$. If $\frac{-v\alpha}{c_2-c_3} < \gamma \le \frac{v(2-\alpha)}{c_2+c_3}$, $t_1 > 0$, $t_2 > 0$, $t_2 > t_1$. If $\frac{v(2-\alpha)}{c_2+c_3} < \gamma \le \frac{v(3-2\alpha)}{2c_2+c_3}$, $t_1 < 0$, $t_2 > 0$.

(14) When $\alpha > \frac{1}{2}$, $c_2 < (1-\alpha)c_3$, $\gamma > \frac{v(3-2\alpha)}{2c_2+c_3}$, $f(\gamma) > 0$, but the sign of $f(\gamma^*)$ is uncertain, we need to classify.

① $c_2 > c_3$, it is invalid.

② $(1-\alpha)c_3 < c_2 < c_3$, it is invalid.

③ $c_2 < (1-\alpha)c_3$,

$$\frac{-v\alpha}{c_2 - c_3} - \frac{v(1-2\alpha)}{2c_2 - c_3} = \frac{-v\big(c_2 + c_3(\alpha - 1)\big)}{(2c_2 - c_3)(c_2 - c_3)} > 0,$$

$$\frac{v(2-\alpha)}{c_2 + c_3} - \frac{v(3-2\alpha)}{2c_2 + c_3} = \frac{-v\big(c_2 + c_3(\alpha - 1)\big)}{(2c_2 + c_3)(c_2 + c_3)} < 0.$$

So, when $\alpha > \frac{1}{2}$, $c_2 < (1-\alpha)c_3$, $\gamma > \frac{v(3-2\alpha)}{2c_2+c_3}$, $t_1 < 0$, $t_2 > 0$.

(15) When $\alpha < \frac{1}{2}$, $c_2 < \frac{c_3}{2}$, $\gamma \le \frac{v(3-2\alpha)}{2c_2+c_3}$, $f(\gamma) < 0$, but the sign of $f(\gamma^*)$ is uncertain, we need to classify.

① $c_2 > c_3$, it is invalid.

② $(1-\alpha)c_3 < c_2 < c_3$, it is invalid.

③ $c_2 < (1-\alpha)c_3$, i.e., $c_2 < \frac{c_3}{2}$,

$$\frac{-v\alpha}{c_2 - c_3} - \frac{v(3-2\alpha)}{2c_2 + c_3} = \frac{-3v(c_2 + c_3(\alpha - 1))}{(2c_2 + c_3)(c_2 - c_3)} < 0,$$

$$\frac{v(2-\alpha)}{c_2 + c_3} - \frac{v(3-2\alpha)}{2c_2 + c_3} = \frac{-v(c_2 + c_3(\alpha - 1))}{(2c_2 + c_3)(c_2 + c_3)} < 0.$$

So, when $\alpha < \frac{1}{2}$, $c_2 < \frac{c_3}{2}$, $\gamma \leq \frac{-v\alpha}{c_2 - c_3}$, $t_1 < 0$, $t_2 > 0$. If $\frac{-v\alpha}{c_2-c_3} < \gamma \leq \frac{v(2-\alpha)}{c_2+c_3}$, $t_1 > 0$, $t_2 > 0$, $t_2 > t_1$. If $\frac{v(2-\alpha)}{c_2+c_3} < \gamma \leq \frac{v(3-2\alpha)}{2c_2+c_3}$, $t_1 < 0$, $t_2 > 0$.

(16) When $\alpha < \frac{1}{2}$, $c_2 < \frac{c_3}{2}$, $\gamma > \frac{v(3-2\alpha)}{2c_2+c_3}$, $f(\gamma) > 0$, but the sign of $f(\gamma^*)$ is uncertain, we need to classify.

① $c_2 > c_3$, it is invalid.

② $(1-\alpha)c_3 < c_2 < c_3$, it is invalid.

③ $c_2 < (1-\alpha)c_3$, i.e., $c_2 < \frac{c_3}{2}$,

$$\frac{-v\alpha}{c_2 - c_3} - \frac{v(3-2\alpha)}{2c_2 + c_3} = \frac{-3v(c_2 + c_3(\alpha - 1))}{(2c_2 + c_3)(c_2 - c_3)} < 0,$$

$$\frac{v(2-\alpha)}{c_2 + c_3} - \frac{v(3-2\alpha)}{2c_2 + c_3} = \frac{-v(c_2 + c_3(\alpha - 1))}{(2c_2 + c_3)(c_2 + c_3)} < 0.$$

So, when $\alpha < \frac{1}{2}$, $c_2 < \frac{c_3}{2}$, $\gamma > \frac{v(3-2\alpha)}{2c_2+c_3}$, $t_1 < 0$, $t_2 > 0$.

With regard to the profit of firm 2, we can draw a similar conclusion to that of firm 1, so we can conclude that when $c_3\gamma - v > 0$, if $\sqrt{\frac{4\gamma-\omega^2}{2}} < \theta \leq \sqrt{t_2}$, $\Delta\pi_2 > 0$. If $\sqrt{t_2} < \theta \leq \sqrt{4\gamma - \omega^2}$, $\Delta\pi_2 < 0$. When $c_3\gamma - v < 0$, if $t_2 < 0$, $\Delta\pi_2 > 0$. Under $t_2 > 0$, if $\theta \leq \sqrt{t_2}$, $\Delta\pi_2 < 0$. If $\sqrt{t_2} < \theta \leq \sqrt{\frac{4\gamma-\omega^2}{2}}$, $\Delta\pi_2 > 0$.

Acknowledgments

This research was supported by the National Natural Science Foundation of China (NSFC) under grant number 71831001 and Beijing Logistics Informatics Research Base.

References

Ahmadi-Javid, A, and P Hoseinpour (2012). On a cooperative advertising model for a supply chain with one manufacturer and one retailer. *European Journal of Operational Research*, 219(2), 458–466.

Aust, G and U Buscher (2014). Cooperative advertising models in supply chain management: A review. *European Journal of Operational Research*, 234(1), 1–14.

Beltagui, A, N Kunz and S Gold (2020). The role of 3D printing and open design on adoption of socially sustainable supply chain innovation. *International Journal of Production Economics*, 221, 107462.

Berman, B (2012). 3-D printing: The new industrial revolution. *Business Horizons*, 55(2), 155–162.

Bogetoft, P (2021). How upstream cooperatives limit downstream holdups. *Journal of Economic Behavior & Organization*, 181, 156–168.

Biswas, S (2014) *Relationship Marketing: Concepts, Theories and Cases*. PHI Learning Pvt. Ltd.

Boon, W and WB Van (2018). Influence of 3D printing on transport: A theory and experts judgment based conceptual model. *Transport Reviews*, 38(5), 556–575.

Ccidconsulting (2020). The global and Chinese 3D printing market status and development prospects in 2020. http://www.ccidconsulting.com/.

Chan, HK, J Griffin, JJ Lim, F Zeng and AS Chiu (2018). The impact of 3D Printing Technology on the supply chain: Manufacturing and legal perspectives. *International Journal of Production Economics*, 205, 156–162.

Chaab, J and M Rasti-Barzoki (2016). Cooperative advertising and pricing in a manufacturer-retailer supply chain with a general demand function: A game-theoretic approach. *Computers & Industrial Engineering*, 99, 112–123.

Choi, SC (1991). Price competition in a channel structure with a common retailer. *Marketing Science*, 10(4), 271–296.

Chu, W and PS Desai (1995). Channel coordination mechanisms for customer satisfaction. *Marketing Science*, 14(4), 343–359.

Chutani, A and SP Sethi (2018). Dynamic cooperative advertising under manufacturer and retailer level competition. *European Journal of Operational Research*, 268(2), 635–652.

Dilberoglu, UM, B Gharehpapagh, U Yaman and M Dolen (2017). The role of additive manufacturing in the era of industry 4.0. *Procedia Manufacturing*, 11, 545–554.

Guo, Z and J Ma (2018). Dynamics and implications on a cooperative advertising model in the supply chain. *Communications in Nonlinear Science and Numerical Simulation*, 64, 198–212.

Gosselin, C, R Duballet, P Roux, N Gaudillire, J Dirrenberger and P Morel (2016). Large-scale 3D printing of ultra-high performance concretea new processing route for architects and builders. *Materials & Design*, 100, 102–109.

He, X, A Krishnamoorthy, A Prasad and SP Sethi (2011). Retail competition and cooperative advertising. *Operations Research Letters*, 39(1), 11–16.

He, Y, H Wang, Q Guo and Q Xu (2019). Coordination through cooperative advertising in a two-period consumer electronics supply chain. *Journal of Retailing and Consumer Services*, 50, 179–188.

Holmstrm, J and J Partanen (2014). Digital manufacturing-driven transformations of service supply chains for complex products. *Supply Chain Management: An International Journal* 19(4), 421–430.

Huang, Z, J Nie and J Zhang (2018). Dynamic cooperative promotion models with competing retailers and negative promotional effects on brand image. *Computers & Industrial Engineering*, 118, 291–308.

Jrgensen, S and G Zaccour (2014). A survey of game-theoretic models of cooperative advertising. *European Journal of Operational Research*, 237(1), 1–14.

Karray, S (2011). Effectiveness of retail joint promotions under different channel structures. *European Journal of Operational Research*, 210(3), 745–751.

Karray, S (2015). Cooperative promotions in the distribution channel. *Omega*, 51, 49–58.

Karray, S and SP Sigu (2015). A game-theoretic model for co-promotions: Choosing a complementary versus an independent product ally. *Omega*, 54, 84–100.

Khajavi, SH, J Partanen and J Holmstrm (2014). Additive manufacturing in the spare parts supply chain. *Computers in Industry*, 65(1), 50–63.

Liu, P, SH Huang, A Mokasdar, H Zhou and L Hou (2014). The impact of additive manufacturing in the aircraft spare parts supply chain: Supply chain operation reference (scor) model based analysis. *Production Planning & Control*, 25(13–14), 1169–1181.

McGuire, TW and R Staelin (1983). An industry equilibrium analysis of downstream vertical integration. *Marketing Science*, 2(2), 161–191.

Mellor, S, L Hao and D Zhang (2014). Additive manufacturing: A framework for implementation. *International Journal of Production Economics*, 149, 194–201.

Moon, I, J Xu, X Feng and X Ruan (2020). Cooperative sales promotion with a point-sharing policy: Advantages and limitations. *Omega*, 94, 102038.

Prasad, A, R Venkatesh and V Mahajan (2010). Optimal bundling of technological products with network externality. *Marketing Science*, 56(12), 2224–2236.

Rayna, T and L Striukova (2016). From rapid prototyping to home fabrication: How 3D printing is changing business model innovation. *Technological Forecasting and Social Change*, 102, 214–224.

Rayna, T, L Striukova and J Darlington (2015). Co-creation and user innovation: The role of online 3D printing platforms. *Journal of Engineering and Technology Management*, 37, 90–102.

Rogers, H, N Baricz and KS Pawar (2016). 3D printing services: Classification, supply chain implications and research agenda. *International Journal of Physical Distribution & Logistics Management*, 46(10), 886–907.

Sarkar, B, M Omair and N Kim (2020). A cooperative advertising collaboration policy in supply chain management under uncertain conditions. *Applied Soft Computing*, 88, 105948.

Sasson, A and JC Johnson (2016). The 3D printing order: Variability, supercenters and supply chain reconfigurations. *International Journal of Physical Distribution Logistics Management*, 46(1), 82–94.

Sun, L, G Hua, TCE Cheng and Y Wang (2020). How to price 3D-printed products? Pricing strategy for 3D printing platforms. *International Journal of Production Economics*, 226, 107600.

Tsao, YC (2015). Cooperative promotion under demand uncertainty. *International Journal of Production Economics*, 167, 45–49.

Wang, SD, YW Zhou, J Min and YG Zhong (2011). Coordination of cooperative advertising models in a one-manufacturer two-retailer supply chain system. *Computers & Industrial Engineering*, 61(4), 1053–1071.

Weller, C, R Kleer and FT Piller (2015). Economic implications of 3D printing: Market structure models in light of additive manufacturing revisited. *International Journal of Production Economics*, 164, 43–56.

Xiao, D, YW Zhou, Y Zhong and W Xie (2019). Optimal cooperative advertising and ordering policies for a two-echelon supply chain. *Computers & Industrial Engineering*, 127, 511–519.

Yu, L, X He, J Zhang and C Xu (2021). Horizontal cooperative advertising with advertising threshold effects. *Omega*, 98, 102104.

Zhang, J, Q Gou, L Liang and Z Huang (2013). Supply chain coordination through cooperative advertising with reference price effect. *Omega*, 41(2), 345–353.

Biography

Ke Yan is currently studying for a doctorate in School of Economics and Management, Beijing Jiaotong University, as well as holds the bachelor degree in engineering and the master degree in management. He mainly studies the optimal operation decisions of supply chain under cross-market cooperation and smart logistic.

Guowei Hua is now a Professor and vice dean in School of Economics and Management, Beijing Jiaotong University. His expertise is to focus on the problems of supply chain management, facility location and operations management. He is the principal investigator of a major project of National Natural Science Foundation of China and gains the 2020 highly cited Chinese researchers of Elsevier. He has published some 50 articles on leading international journals and conferences.

T. C. E. Cheng is now a Professor in Department of Logistics and Maritime Studies, The Hong Kong Polytechnic University and the dean in Faculty of Business. His research covers a wide range of subjects, including the industrial and business applications of microcomputers, modelling and simulation of manufacturing systems, application of maximum entropy principle in reliability study and stochastic modelling and analysis of production and distribution systems etc. In 2020, the number of citations was 21,335 (excluding self-citations: 19,913) according to the ISI Web of Science.

https://doi.org/10.1142/9789819808588_0007

Chapter 7

Evolutionary Game Models of Cooperative Strategies in Blockchain-Enabled Container Transport Chains†

Zhi-Hua Hu*

Logistics Research Center, Shanghai Maritime University
Shanghai 201306, P. R. China
zhhu@shmtu.edu.cn

Ya-Jing Dong

Logistics Research Center, Shanghai Maritime University
Shanghai 201306, P. R. China
1374739298@qq.com

This paper describes the interaction between major and auxiliary container transport carriers (MCs and ACs) by using evolutionary game theory models, enabling them to cooperate and share information under sufficient penalties and incentives. The MCs are generally logistics service integrators, mega shipping companies, and port authorities, which affect the regulations and technology innovation much, while the ACs are rest carriers and logistics service providers. Evolutionary games are used to study the cooperative behavior between MCs and ACs in the shipping industry. As indicated by analytical studies, the cooperation between MCs and ACs will be invalid without introducing blockchain technology for adequate supervision. In peak season, an evolutionary equilibrium incurs between MCs and ACs under cooperation or non-cooperation behavior strategies. However, in off-seasons, the evolutionary equilibrium is unique in which both parties choose not to cooperate. When introducing blockchain technology for supervision, the carriers will cooperate in peak and off-seasons. Besides, through a simulation analysis of the established models, the results show that the introduction of blockchain technology can enable carriers to form cooperative alliances, resolve inefficient operations, and achieve a long-term stable equilibrium strategy. We can also apply the results for reference to the regional shipping industry.

Keywords: Container transportation chain; blockchain; evolutionary game; logistics management; evolutionary stable strategy (ESS).

1. Introduction

Ocean transportation plays a significant role in international trade and global supply chains, while container shipping is critical to the global product supply chain.

*Corresponding author.
†To cite this article, please refer to its earlier version published in the Asia-Pacific Journal of Operational Research, Vol. 39, No. 1, (February 2022), DOI: 10.1142/S0217595921400297. Reprinted with permission from World Scientific Publishing Co. Pte. Ltd.

The container transport chain contains many stakeholders, such as shippers and carriers, various operators, logistics, and various service providers. Due to the spatial distribution of logistics activities and facilities in container transportation, the container transport chain is a typical decentralized service with asymmetric information, leading to poor overall performances of the service chain (Deja *et al.*, 2019; Jiang *et al.*, 2015). As the most crucial transfer resource in container transportation, containers cannot be effectively positioned and shared without good cooperation, which leads to a waste of empty container resources and low overall profit of the whole supply chain. The most famous shipping companies and port authorities (e.g., Maersk and China COSCO Shipping Lines) have conducted demonstrative experiments to apply blockchain technologies for the secure bill of lading and information sharing. In a transport chain, from customers' view, the logistics service integrators will be in charge of the transportation and warehousing activities by integrating various logistics or other types of service providers. Here, we call a logistics service integrator or a mega service provider (e.g., port authorities and shipping companies) a major carrier (MC), and call an integrated service provider an auxiliary carrier (AC). The MCs may initialize the applications of blockchain technology. In a container transport chain, the MCs represent the mega shipping liners and port authorities, while the ACs are various service providers along the container transport chains. However, a single MC in the container transport chain contributing to the blockchain cannot make the technology available for all stakeholders. In this study, we investigate the evolutionary behaviors of cooperative and non-cooperative information sharing between the MC and AC in the container transport chain by considering the impacts of blockchain technology.

The container transport chains connect industries of various regions and countries in the world. However, due to economy, trade, legislation, culture, and political differences and barriers, the carriers and various service providers must sign and perform various contracts through information sharing mechanisms along a container transport chain. Information transparency is critical to establish confidential and credible container transport chains and improve cooperation among the chain's stakeholders. Various efficiency and security problems degrade the service levels and increase service costs. For example, the exchanges of information and bills will delay transportation and handling activities. The ocean bill of lading is an important document, and its transfer even incurs frauds. Blockchain is a potential technology to connect the distributed shipping services with secure information sharing mechanisms. In this study, blockchain is a typical representation of secure information sharing and transparency technology. In an ideal container transport chain, the carriers convey and acquire their business and operations information through blockchain. Each business and logistics activity will create a block as a secure information unit in the blockchain.

In the blockchain-based shared container model, the blockchain contract layer records the container conditions, rules, and related transport contracts. After being signed by all participants, the smart contract becomes a block in the blockchain data in the form of program code after the nodes in the blockchain application verify and validate it. The smart contract will predefine the container flow rules, the scenario that triggers the contract's execution (such as the end of the container land transport section, etc.), and the trigger rules in a specific scenario (case loss), etc. Blockchain monitors smart contracts' status in real-time, verifying external data to activate and execute contracts when the container's status changes. However, introducing blockchain incurs different sounds and reasons. The MC and AC will take cooperative and non-cooperative strategies responding to the application of blockchain technology. The successful application blockchain could achieve its benefits while it demands stakeholders of the container transport chain cooperatively joining the chain.

In this study, we describe the interactive relationship between two populations of carriers from evolutionary game theory, which enables carriers to cooperate with other carriers through sufficient penalty and incentive mechanisms. Comparing with the studies on container transport chains, shipping industries, and logistics chains, we focus on the secure information sharing and transparency technology applications in these scenarios. We investigate the blockchain as such a standard technology. The container transport chain is also a typical representative of global logistics and supply chains. We chose it because it is distributive and complicate in temporal and spatial dimensions. An application of emergent technology is an evolutionary process because various stakeholders will adopt it gradually and repeatedly. So, we use evolutionary game models to simulate this feature. In reality, it is implausible that the decision-maker is completely rational. Therefore, this paper introduces the evolutionary game into the container transport chain and assumes that the container transport subject is bounded rationality to study the cooperation between carrier groups. Traditional game theory describes what happens after the game is over but does not describe how it plays. Evolutionary games focus on the dynamic adjustment process of game decisions, find multiple Nash equilibria with solid reality, and then analyze the evolutionary stability strategy (ESS) that can last for a long time. An ESS is a strategy that other strategies cannot invade. In a container transport chain, the mega shipping companies and port authorities play significant roles in advancing technology innovation and applications. We introduce MC to describe this population of companies, while the rest related service providers are ACs.

In the rest of this paper, we first review the related studies in Sec. 2. Then, we describe the problem in Sec. 3. The evolutionary game models are devised and analyzed in Sec. 4, followed by numerical studies in Sec. 5. Finally, we discuss the implications and conclude the study in Sec. 6.

2. Related Studies

2.1. *Container transportation chain*

A container transport chain is a typical form of global logistics and supply chains when the transportation processes and facilities are focused. Different ocean bulk

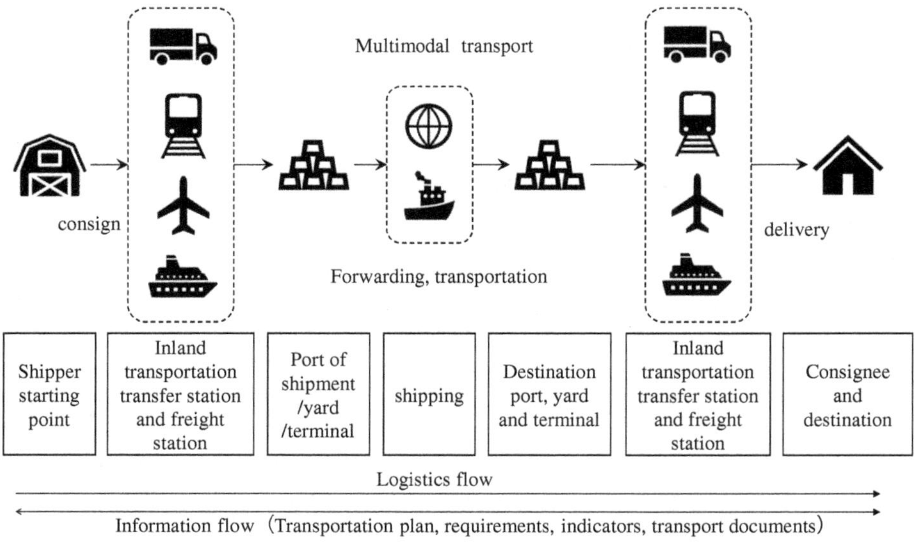

Fig. 1. Logistics and information flow in a container transport chain.

cargo transportation, containerized transportation generally serves the global product supply chains. So, container transport chains the distributive industries and contributes to the global economy and trade.

Figure 1 presents the processes of a container transport chain. Containerization encapsulates the products and hides the product details and features. In this aspect, it does not share the lifecycle of products. It indicates that the container transport chain consists of repeated processes. Moreover, Fig. 1 presents the logistics and information flow in a container transport chain. First, various transport activities and facilities are distributive, even in different countries. Second, in a container transport chain, the vessels and terminals are critical facilities operated by shipping companies and port authorities. Therefore, in this study, we take them as MCs, while other service providers are ACs. When we consider blockchain technology in a container transport chain, the political interactions between these two populations are critical for evolutionary behaviors.

Table 1 summarizes 13 pioneering studies on container transport chains in three dimensions. In the "topic" column, we can find the following keywords describing the research interests and focuses: hinterland, multimode/intermodal, container/containerization. Besides, traffic, sustainability, competition, and trade are also essential features considered. In the "stakeholders" column, some studies consider the system level stakeholders, while most studies consider the carriers in aspects of various transportation channels (road, rail, and waterway). Among these studies, the most popular methods applied include case study, empirical study, and review. Besides, some studies used mathematical programs, assessment methods, optimization algorithms, and behavior models to analyze or optimize container transport chains.

Table 1. Studies of container transport chains.

Study	Topics	Stakeholders	Methods
Parola and Sciomachen (2005)	Intermodal container transportation network	Port system	Simulation
Franc and Van der Horst (2010)	Hinterland transportation integration	Shipping lines Terminal operators	Empirical study
Frémont and Franc (2010)	Multimode transportation	Multimode carrier Road carrier	Case study
García *et al.* (2013)	Intermodal transportation	Truck, rail, and ocean carrier	Linear programming
Hilmola and Henttu (2015)	Transit traffic	Cross-border, transit, and rail carriers	Review, statistics, case study
Lam (2015)	Sustainable maritime supply chain	Shipping companies	Analytical network process, case study
Martínez-López *et al.* (2015)	Intermodal chain evaluation	Transportation systems	Empirical study
Song *et al.* (2016)	Port competition	Two ports	Non-cooperative game
Jeong *et al.* (2018)	Empty container management	Regional exporters and importers	Particle swarm optimization
Lee and Song (2017)	Ocean container transport	Ocean container carriers	Review
Lin (2019)	Containerized trade	Rail-based intermodal carriers	Empirical and case study
Lorenc and Kuźnar (2017)	Intermodal transport risk and costs	Intermodal carriers	Case study, simulation
Zhang and Zhu (2019)	Hinterland transportation chain	Shipping carriers	Discrete choice model

2.2. *Blockchain in container shipping studies*

The essence of blockchain is a trust mechanism that enables unfamiliar participants to build trust. Its core function is to ensure data integrity and reliability and reduce the trust cost required for business development without relying on the center or third-party institutions. The technical characteristics of blockchain can solve some fundamental problems existing in the container transport chain.

The researches on blockchain technology in the container shipping industry are generally theoretical. Most of them summarize the potential applications of blockchain technology in the container shipping industry and the challenges and implementation comments. In Table 2, we summarize ten studies that all emerge in the past two years. We investigated them in three aspects, corresponding to three columns in the table. First, these studies applied blockchain technology to obtain or advance the following functions of the container transport chain: smart contract, digital agreement, smart bill of lading, digitalization, secure booking, and administration. In the "stakeholders" column, we can see two study levels: carriers

Table 2. Studies of blockchains in the shipping industry.

Study	Blockchain features	Stakeholders	Methods
Hasan *et al.* (2019)	Smart contract	Sender and receiver	A
Jović *et al.* (2019)	Cryptocurrency and digital agreements	SC, logistics carriers	A
Yang (2019)	Shipping digitalization	SC	A
Nguyen *et al.* (2020)	Smart bill of lading	SC	A
Pu and Lam (2020)	Smart bill of lading	SC	A
Tan and Sundarakani (2020)	Freight booking	Freight carrier	C
Tsiulin *et al.* (2020)	Applications	SC, port operators	A
Bavassano *et al.* (2020)	Administration	Maritime sector	A
Papathanasiou *et al.* (2020)	Smart contract	SC	C
Zhou *et al.* (2020)	Applications	Maritime industry	C

Notes: A = Theoretical analysis, C = Case study, SC = Shipping carriers.

and operators at the operations and industrial levels. In this study, we consider two populations of carriers at the operations level. However, these two populations can represent the essential functions and chains of the whole shipping industry. In this third aspect, we investigated the research methods. In these ten studies, most conduct theoretical analysis, and three conduct case studies. To our knowledge, blockchain technology itself has been studied and tested by many famous companies in the shipping industry. However, we cannot find official declamations of successful and large-scale applications.

2.3. *Evolutionary games in transportation scenarios*

The evolutionary game theory focuses on the interaction among different populations. It is a valuable tool to analyze players' interactive mechanisms by establishing replicators' dynamics system (RDS). In actual economic activities, it is almost impossible for players to behave in a perfectly rational manner. The bounded rationality assumption of evolutionary game theory appears to have more practical significance concerning the perfect rationality of general game theory. The evolutionary games are usable in behavioral strategies and policy-making decisions of related stakeholders due to the advantages of evolutionary game theory.

In transportation scenarios, a transportation chain consists of many legs with generally dependent carriers and various service providers. These carriers and services interact with each other according to the business and process constraints. Considering them in groups or populations is rational because their logistics activities are distributive and cooperate to meet transportation demands. Table 3 summarizes a list of pioneering studies of evolutionary games in transportation scenarios with three aspects. In the "Issue" column, various topics in logistics and transportation occur. The evolutionary games are not limited in terms of topics and issues. The interacted populations and regulation are primary instruments in applications of evolutionary games. In transportation scenarios, logistics and

Table 3. Studies of evolutionary games in transportation scenarios.

Study	Issue	Population	Regulation
Abd *et al.* (2019)	Traffic assignment problem	Drivers	Pref
Feng *et al.* (2020)	Railway transportation safety	Railway administrator, LC, and the public	I&P
Ghannadpour and Zandiyeh (2020)	Cash-in-transit VRP	Robbers and cash carriers	Risk
Abd *et al.* (2019)	Traffic assignment problem	Drivers	Pref
Gu *et al.* (2017)	Low-carbon strategy	Government and highway LC	I&P
Hernández *et al.* (2018)	Carpool problem	Industry practitioners, the government, citizens	I&P
Lei and Gao (2018)	VRP	LC, passengers	I&P
Lei *et al.* (2020)	Ride-hailing regulation	LC, drivers, and passengers	I&P
Pu *et al.* (2020)	Online ride-hailing supervision	Passengers, drivers, and platform	I&P
Yi *et al.* (2020)	Responses to governance policies	Shippers, drivers, and platform	I&P
Zhang *et al.* (2020)	Sustainable transportation	Government, LC, and residents	I&P

Notes: I&P = Incentives and penalties; Pref = Preference (for checkpoints); Risk = (Transportation network) risk; VRP = Vehicle routing problem; LC = Logistics or transportation companies.

transportation companies are the primary players. Besides, some studies consider the government and the public simultaneously. In some specific studies, considering drivers and passengers introduces individual behaviors. The shipping or logistics platforms emerge as new players in the sharing economy. Incentives and penalties are primary regulation tools to affect the evolutionary processes. Besides, some studies formulate preferences and risks mediating evolutionary games.

2.4. *Summary*

This study contributes to three main streams of studies, as investigated above. First, the container transport chain is vital in global logistics and supply chains. In this study, we investigate its security and information sharing mechanisms considering blockchain technology. Although many scholars studied container transportation and various related operations, the container transport chain as a concept is widely used in the shipping industry and less used in academic literature. Service integration is a crucial characteristic, and so we use it to represent the coupled relations between service integrators and providers. Second, in this study, we take blockchain as a general instrument for information sharing, transparency, and security in transportation scenarios. As a technology, the blockchain is still in development. When its ecosystem can be acceptable by the industries, new technology sets and patterns will emerge. Third, considering stakeholders' characteristics along a container transport chain, we category the players into two populations representing the dominant players (mega shipping companies and port authorities) and general logistics service providers. We devised evolutionary game models between these two populations considering regulations. Besides, we study the impacts of blockchain-based supervision on the container transport chain, considering the peak and low seasons. It is an essential feature of the shipping industry that the market presents peak and low seasons.

3. Problem Description

3.1. *The problem*

Due to the long-distance characteristic of cross-country and cross-region transportation, the uncertainty and risk in the process of transportation and transfer are incredibly high. Therefore, in long-distance transportation, the container has been widely used in railway, highway, and waterway transportation due to its characteristics such as considerable strength, large volume, easy loading and unloading, and uniform specifications. Containerization and container transport has become the irresistible development direction and trend of domestic and international trade.

In the process of container transportation, a "door-to-door" container transport chain can be realized through the reasonable and efficient connection of different modes of transportation. In the specific operation, the transport contract is established between the container transport operator and the actual sub-carriers to form a cooperative relationship and realize efficient logistics services.

However, in practice, due to the imperfect construction of the inland collection and distribution system, different transportation modes and carriers operate independently without establishing an excellent cooperative partnership. Therefore, the coordinated container transport system has not been established, most of which are in the state of segmented transport, and lack coordination and overall development capacity. Simultaneously, there is no circulation of container information among each container's owners, many empty containers are forced to transfer in an invalid way, and container resources cannot be utilized efficiently. At this time through container resource sharing can effectively solve the problem of container resource waste. Through the cooperation between different carrier groups in the process of transportation, container sharing can be realized. Because blockchain technology advocates weak control, decentralization, autonomous mechanism, non-tampering, and coupling connection, it is complementary and highly consistent with the elemental form of sharing economy. So, blockchain technology can be used for adequate supervision, promote cooperation between carrier groups, and finally realize the efficient utilization of container resources. Figure 2 depicts a conceptual diagram considering the application of blockchain to the container transport chain.

In reality, it is improbable that the decision-maker is completely rational. Therefore, this paper introduces the evolutionary game into the container transport

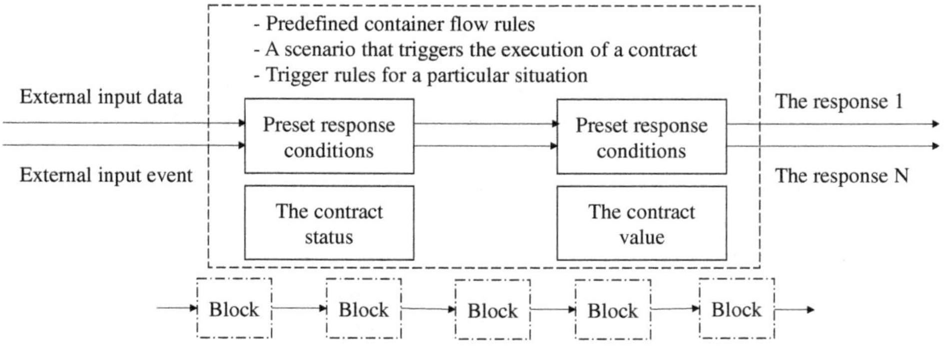

Fig. 2. Intelligent contract operation mechanism in container transport chain based on blockchain.

chain and assumes that the container transport subject is bounded rationality to study the cooperation between carrier groups. The evolutionary game replicative dynamic model proposed in the 1970s can not only predict the evolution process of bounded rational decision-maker's behavior, but also predict more accurate group equilibrium. Therefore, the replication dynamic model has been quoted by many scholars who study the evolutionary game of enterprises and add the random factor.

It is challenging to avoid speculative behavior in the enterprise group when the two carrier groups conduct alliance cooperation. For example, in order to reduce the cost of empty container storage at a particular stage, a carrier privately chooses to sublet the shared container to a third party; in order to solicit customers, maliciously interrupt the sharing and cooperation of container resources. The betrayal of one carrier will lead to the vicious retaliation of the other carrier, and the two groups will enter the vicious competition link, which will eventually lead to the loss of customers in the shipping area and the overall decline of the regional economy. The alliance cooperation between the MC and the AC based on the sharing of container resources in the peak and low seasons of shipping can promote the development of multimodal transport in container transportation and solve the problems of the imbalance between supply and demand of containers in the peak and low seasons of container shipping and the scramble for empty container resources caused by the imbalance of regional import and export.

3.2. *The notations*

In the following, MC is the carrier population representing the mega shipping companies and port authorities, which generally activate and support the blockchain in the container transport chain. The AC is the carrier population representing the rest carriers and service providers in the container transport chain. The variables and parameters used in the following sections are listed as follows.

Variables	
λ_1	Probability for MC to choose the "cooperate" strategy in peak seasons
$1-\lambda_1$	Probability for MC to choose the "non-cooperate" strategy in peak seasons
λ_2	Probability for AC to choose the "cooperate" strategy in peak seasons
$1-\lambda_2$	Probability for AC to choose the "non-cooperate" strategy in peak seasons
θ_1	Probability for MC to choose the "cooperate" strategy in off-seasons
$1-\theta_1$	Probability for MC to choose the "non-cooperate" strategy in off-seasons
θ_2	Probability for AC to choose the "cooperate" strategy in off-seasons
$1-\theta_2$	Probability for AC to choose the "non-cooperate" strategy in off-seasons.
Parameters	
π_1	MC profit in peak seasons when blockchain is not enabled
π_2	AC profit in peak seasons when blockchain is not enabled
v_1	MC profit in off-seasons when blockchain is not enabled
v_2	AC profit in off-seasons when blockchain is not enabled
C_h	Cost of non-cooperation in peak seasons
C_l	Cost of non-cooperation in off-seasons
a	AC credit penalty for non-cooperation when blockchain is enabled
b	MC credit penalty for non-cooperation when blockchain is enabled.

3.3. *Presumption*

(1) The MC population represents mega shipping companies and port authorities. So, they can obtain higher profits than the AC, namely, $\pi_1 > \pi_2 > 0$, $v_1 > v_2 > 0$.
(2) In peak seasons, due to the large volume of transportation, to better satisfy the logistics requirements, it is difficult for a single carrier to complete the transport task. In this case, the cooperation intention among the carriers is more significant than that in the off-seasons. So, we set $\lambda_1 > \theta_1, \lambda_2 > \theta_2$.
(3) In peak seasons, the profit of carriers is greater than that of the carriers in off-seasons, namely, $\pi_1 > v_1 > 0$, $\pi_2 > v_2 > 0$.
(4) In peak seasons, if both groups betray each other, the loss caused by malicious competition is more significant than that caused by malicious competition in off-seasons, namely, $C_h > C_l$. When one party betraying, there is no loss if the blockchain is not enabled, and the other party gains exclusive profit. When the blockchain is enabled, there is a credit loss, and one party can get credit compensation.
(5) From the perspective of long-term container supply chain operations, malicious competition in peak seasons will cause more significant losses than the carriers'

profits alone. We set $C_h > \pi_1 > \pi_2$. In the off-seasons, most of them are short-haul transportation tasks, which a single carrier population can also complete. In this case, the loss caused by malicious competition is less than the carriers' profit alone. Here, we set $v_1 > v_2 > C_l$.

4. Evolutionary Games Among Container Carriers

4.1. *Peak-season evolutionary games without blockchain*

Considering the limited rationality of MC and AC when the blockchain is not enabled, we formulate the payoff matrix of the evolutionary game between them in peak seasons in Table 4.

When the MC chooses to cooperate, the profit is $U^y_{OC^h}$. When the MC chooses to non-cooperate, the profit is $U^n_{OC^h}$. Then the average income of the MC in peak seasons is $\overline{U}_{OC^h}$.

$$U^y_{OC^h} = \lambda_2 \frac{\pi_1}{2},$$

$$U^n_{OC^h} = \lambda_2 \pi_1 + (1 - \lambda_2) \frac{\pi_1 - C_h}{2},$$

$$\overline{U}_{OC^h} = \lambda_1 U^y_{OC^h} + (1 - \lambda_1) U^n_{OC^h}.$$

When the AC chooses to cooperate, the profit is $U^y_{FC^h}$. When the AC chooses to non-cooperate, the profit is $U^n_{FC^h}$. Then the average income of the AC in peak seasons is $\overline{U}_{FC^h}$.

$$U^y_{FC^h} = \lambda_1 \frac{\pi_2}{2},$$

$$U^n_{FC^h} = \lambda_1 \pi_2 + (1 - \lambda_1) \frac{\pi_2 - C_h}{2},$$

$$\overline{U}_{FC^h} = \lambda_2 U^y_{FC} + (1 - \lambda_2) U^n_{FC^h}.$$

In the evolutionary game theory, the RDS is a dynamic differential equation that describes the frequency of a particular strategy used in a population. Therefore, the dynamic equation of "cooperate" chosen by MC and the dynamic equation of

Table 4. Payoff matrix between MC and AC in peak seasons.

Peak seasons		AC	
		Cooperate (λ_2)	Non-cooperate ($1 - \lambda_2$)
MC	Cooperate (λ_1)	$\frac{\pi_1}{2}, \frac{\pi_2}{2}$	$0, \pi_2$
	Non-cooperate ($1 - \lambda_1$)	$\pi_1, 0$	$\frac{\pi_1 - C_h}{2}, \frac{\pi_2 - C_h}{2}$

"cooperate" chosen by the AC are $\{F(\lambda_1), F(\lambda_2)\}$ as follows:

$$F(\lambda_1) = \frac{d\lambda_1}{dt} = \lambda_1(U^y_{OC^h} - \overline{U}_{OC^h}) = \frac{1}{2}(-1+\lambda_1)\lambda_1[\pi_1 + C_h(-1+\lambda_2)],$$

$$F(\lambda_2) = \frac{d\lambda_2}{dt} = \lambda_2(U^y_{FC^h} - \overline{U}_{FC^h}) = \frac{1}{2}[\pi_2 + C_h(-1+\lambda_1)](-1+\lambda_2)\lambda_2.$$

Proposition 1. *When* $\lambda_2 = \frac{(C_h-\pi_1)}{C_h}$, $F(\lambda_1)$ *is always* 0, *so all of these* λ_1 *are ESS*; *when* $\lambda_2 > \frac{(C_h-\pi_1)}{C_h}$, *then* $F'(0) < 0$, *so* $\lambda_1^* = 0$ *is ESS*; *when* $\lambda_2 < \frac{(C_h-\pi_1)}{C_h}$, *then* $F'(1) < 0$, *so* $\lambda_1^* = 1$ *is ESS.*

Proof. When the proportion of the AC choosing cooperation is higher than a specific value, the proportion of the MC choosing cooperation will gradually decrease to 0; on the contrary, when the proportion of the AC choosing cooperation is lower than this value, the proportion of the MC choosing cooperation will gradually increase to 1, as shown in Fig. 3. □

Proposition 2. *When* $\lambda_1 = \frac{(C_h-\pi_2)}{C_h}$, $F(\lambda_2)$ *is always* 0, *so all of these* λ_2 *are ESS*; *when* $\lambda_1 > \frac{(C_h-\pi_2)}{C_h}$, *then* $F'(0) < 0$, *so* $\lambda_2^* = 0$ *is ESS*; *when* $\lambda_1 < \frac{(C_h-\pi_2)}{C_h}$, *then* $F'(1) < 0$, *so* $\lambda_2^* = 1$ *is ESS.*

Proof. When the proportion of the MC choosing cooperation is higher than a specific value, the proportion of the AC choosing cooperation will gradually decrease to 0; on the contrary, when the proportion of the MC choosing cooperation is lower than this value, the proportion of the AC choosing cooperation will gradually increase to 1, as shown in Fig. 4. Comparing the values of MC and AC under a stable state, we can get $\lambda_2 < \lambda_1$. □

Proposition 3. *The equilibrium points (EPs) of the RDS are* $E_1 = (0,0)$, $E_2 = (0,1)$, $E_3 = (1,0)$, $E_4 = (1,1)$, $E_5 = (\lambda_1^0, \lambda_2^0)$, $\lambda_1^0 \in [0,1]$, $\lambda_2^0 \in [0,1]$, $\lambda_1^0 = 1 - \frac{\pi_2}{C_h}$, $\lambda_2^0 = 1 - \frac{\pi_1}{C_h}$.

Proof. We can obtain the EPs by solving $\{F(\lambda_1), F(\lambda_2)\}$. □

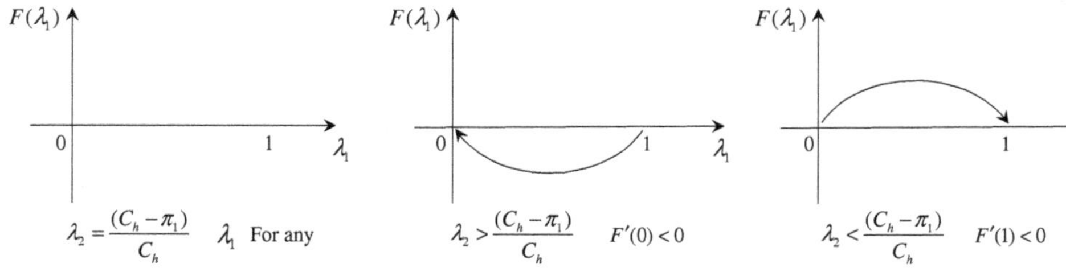

Fig. 3. Replication of dynamic phase diagrams for MC.

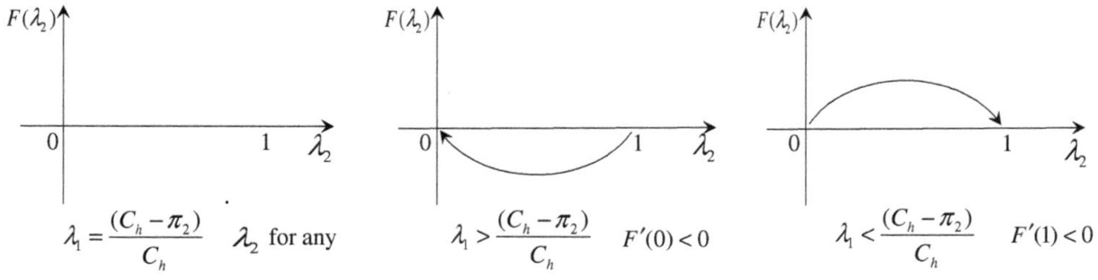

Fig. 4. Replication of dynamic phase diagrams for the AC.

Proposition 4. *In peak seasons, under bounded rationality, when the MC is superior to the AC, the ESSs of them will be categorized into two classes:* (1) *the MC chooses non-cooperate, while the AC chooses to cooperate;* (2) *the MC chooses to cooperate, while the AC chooses non-cooperate. Furthermore, the probability of the former ESS is greater than that of the latter.*

Proof. According to the stability analysis, if a proportion is known to be stable, then it is stable, and the proportion corresponds to ESS. If the trajectory starting from any small neighborhood of an EP of a dynamic system eventually evolves to this EP, the EP is locally asymptotically stable. Such a dynamic stable EP is the evolutionary EP. The stability of EPs can be analyzed using Jacobian matrices. The Jacobian matrix of the above replication dynamic system is as follows:

$$J = \begin{bmatrix} \dfrac{\partial F(\lambda_1)}{\partial \lambda_1} & \dfrac{\partial F(\lambda_1)}{\partial \lambda_2} \\ \dfrac{\partial F(\lambda_2)}{\partial \lambda_1} & \dfrac{\partial F(\lambda_2)}{\partial \lambda_2} \end{bmatrix} = \begin{bmatrix} a & b \\ c & d \end{bmatrix},$$

$$a = \frac{1}{2}(-1 + 2\lambda_1)[\pi_1 + C_h(-1 + \lambda_2)],$$

$$b = \frac{1}{2}C_h(-1 + \lambda_1)\lambda_1,$$

$$c = \frac{1}{2}C_h(-1 + \lambda_2)\lambda_2,$$

$$d = \frac{1}{2}(-1 + 2\lambda_2)[\pi_2 + C_h(-1 + \lambda_1)].$$ □

When the EP of the RDS satisfies the condition $\det J = \begin{vmatrix} a & b \\ c & d \end{vmatrix} = ad - bc > 0$, $\operatorname{tr} J = a + d < 0$, the EP is an ESS. When $\det J < 0$, the EP is a saddle point. To calculate the $\det J$ and $\operatorname{tr} J$ of the EP E_1, E_2, E_3, E_4, E_5, known from our hypothesis $C_h > \pi_1 > \pi_2 > 0$, then determine the sign. Table 5 presents the analytical results.

As presented in Fig. 5, in peak seasons, the ESSs of MC and AC are E_2 and E_3. To compare the pure strategic equilibrium achieved when both

Table 5. Stabilities of the evolutionary game between MC and AC in peak seasons.

EP	det J	tr J	State
E_1	$+$	$+$	Instability point
E_2	$+$	$-$	ESS
E_3	$+$	$-$	ESS
E_4	$+$	$+$	Instability point
E_5	$-$	0	Saddle point

Notes: "+" denotes greater than zero; "−" denotes less than zero; N denotes uncertainty.

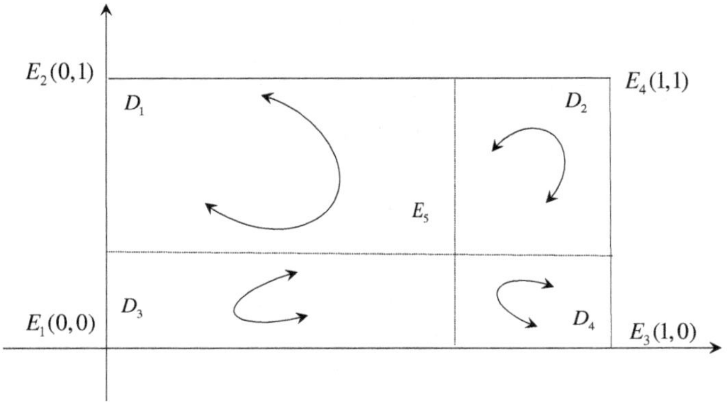

Fig. 5. The local stability of the evolutionary game between carrier groups in peak seasons.

MC and AC are perfectly rational, the two perfectly correspond to each other. E_5 is a saddle point. If the initial state of the MC and AC is presented in the region D_1, as a final evolutionary equilibrium, the MC will choose the betrayal strategy, while the AC will choose the strategy of cooperation. If the initial state of the MC and AC is presented in the region D_4, as a final evolutionary equilibrium, the AC will choose the betrayal strategy, while the MC will choose the strategy of cooperation. As can be seen from Fig. 5, $S_{D_1} = (1 - \frac{\pi_2}{C_h}) \times \frac{\pi_1}{C_h}$ and $S_{D_4} = (1 - \frac{\pi_1}{C_h}) \times \frac{\pi_2}{C_h}$. So, the area of the region D_1 is greater than D_4. When the initial state is present in the regions D_2 or D_3, the direction of evolution will be uncertain, but both carrier populations will eventually undergo continuous replication and evolution. In most cases, the ESS converges to E_2; in a few cases, the ESS converges to E_3.

4.2. *Off-season evolutionary games without blockchain*

Considering the limited rationality of MC and AC when the blockchain is not enabled, we formulate the payoff matrix of the evolutionary game between them in off-seasons in Table 6.

Table 6. Payoff matrix between MC and AC in off-seasons.

Off-season		AC	
		Cooperate (θ_2)	Non-cooperate ($1-\theta_2$)
MC	Cooperate (θ_1)	$\frac{v_1}{2}, \frac{v_2}{2}$	$0, v_2$
	Non-cooperate ($1-\theta_1$)	$v_1, 0$	$\frac{v_1 - C_l}{2}, \frac{v_2 - C_l}{2}$

When the MC groups choose to cooperate, the profit is $U^y_{OC^l}$. When the MC chooses to non-cooperate, the profit is $U^n_{OC^l}$. Then the average income of the MC in the off-season is $\overline{U}_{OC^l}$.

$$U^y_{OC^l} = \theta_2 \frac{v_1}{2},$$

$$U^n_{OC^l} = \theta_2 v_1 + (1-\theta_2)\frac{v_1 - C_l}{2},$$

$$\overline{U}_{OC^l} = \theta_1 U^y_{OC^l} + (1-\theta_1)U^n_{OC^l}.$$

When the AC chooses to cooperate, the profit is $U^y_{FC^l}$. When the AC choose to non-cooperate, the profit is $U^n_{FC^l}$. Then the average income of the AC in the off-season is $\overline{U}_{FC^l}$.

$$U^y_{FC^l} = \theta_1 \frac{v_2}{2},$$

$$U^n_{FC^l} = \theta_1 v_2 + (1-\theta_1)\frac{v_2 - C_l}{2},$$

$$\overline{U}_{FC^l} = \theta_2 U^y_{FC^l} + (1-\theta_2)U^n_{FC^l}.$$

The dynamic equations of "cooperate" chosen by MC and the dynamic equation of "cooperate" chosen by AC are $\{F(\theta_1), F(\theta_2)\}$ as follows:

$$F(\theta_1) = \frac{d\theta_1}{dt} = \theta_1\left(U^y_{OC^l} - \overline{U}_{OC^l}\right),$$

$$F(\theta_2) = \frac{d\theta_2}{dt} = \theta_2\left(U^y_{FC^l} - \overline{U}_{FC^l}\right).$$

Proposition 5. *Known from our hypothesis, $v_1 > v_2 > C_l$, $\theta_1, \theta_2 > 0$, when $\theta_2 > \frac{(C_l - v_1)}{C_l}$, $\theta_1^* = 0$ and $\theta_1^* = 1$ are stable states, but because of $\theta_2 > 0 > \frac{C_l - v_1}{C_l}$, then $F'(0) < 0$, $F'(1) > 0$, so only $\theta_1^* = 0$ is ESS.*

Proof. When the proportion of the AC choosing cooperation is higher than a specific value, the MC choosing cooperation will gradually decrease to 0, as shown in Fig. 6. □

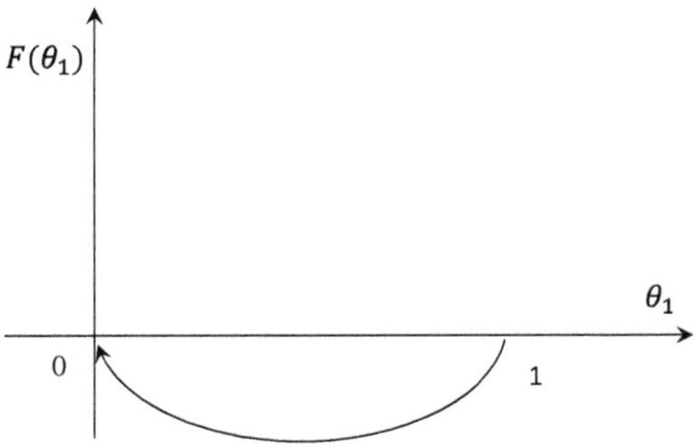

Fig. 6. Replication of dynamic phase diagrams for the MC.

Proposition 6. *By the same token, when* $\theta_1 > \frac{(C_l - v_2)}{C_l}$, $\theta_2^* = 0$ *and* $\theta_2^* = 1$ *are stable states, but because of* $\theta_1 > 0 > \frac{C_l - v_2}{C_l}$, *then* $F'(0) < 0$, $F'(1) > 0$, *so only* $\theta_2^* = 0$ *is ESS.*

Proof. When the proportion of the MC choosing cooperation is higher than a specific value, the proportion of the AC choosing cooperation will gradually decrease to 0, as shown in Fig. 7. □

Proposition 7. *The EPs of the RDS are* $E_1 = (0,0)$, $E_2 = (0,1)$, $E_3 = (1,0)$, $E_4 = (1,1)$, $E_5 = (\theta_1^0, \theta_2^0)$, $\theta_1^0 \in [0,1]$, $\theta_2^0 \in [0,1]$, $\theta_1^0 = 1 - \frac{v_2}{C_l}$, $\lambda_2^0 = 1 - \frac{v_1}{C_l}$.

Proof. We can obtain the EPs by solving $\{F(\theta_1), F(\theta_2)\}$. □

Proposition 8. *In off-seasons for shipping and under bounded rationality, when the MC is superior to the AC, there will be a unique evolutionary equilibrium between the MC and AC: the MC chooses to non-cooperate, and the AC chooses to non-cooperate.*

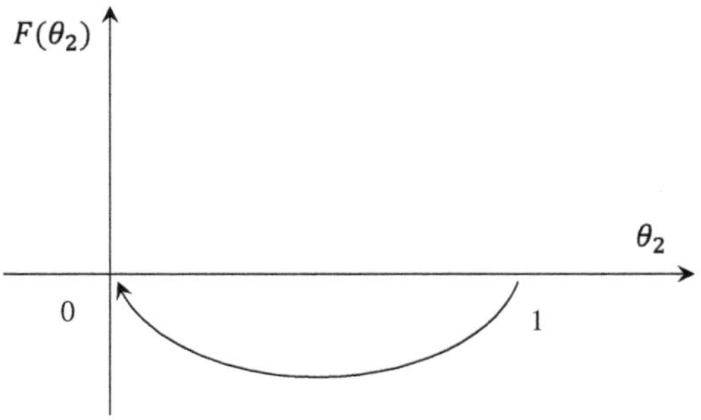

Fig. 7. Replication of dynamic phase diagrams for ACs.

Proof. The Jacobian matrix of the above replication dynamic system is as follows:

$$J = \begin{bmatrix} \dfrac{\partial F(\theta_1)}{\partial \theta_1} & \dfrac{\partial F(\theta_1)}{\partial \theta_2} \\ \dfrac{\partial F(\theta_2)}{\partial \theta_1} & \dfrac{\partial F(\theta_2)}{\partial \theta_2} \end{bmatrix} = \begin{bmatrix} a & b \\ c & d \end{bmatrix},$$

$$a = \frac{1}{2}(-1+2\theta_1)[v_1 + C_l(-1+\theta_2)],$$

$$b = \frac{1}{2}C_l(-1+\theta_1)\theta_1,$$

$$c = \frac{1}{2}C_l(-1+\theta_2)\theta_2,$$

$$d = \frac{1}{2}(-1+2\theta_2)[v_2 + C_l(-1+\theta_1)].$$ □

When the EP of the RDS satisfies the condition $\det J = \begin{vmatrix} a & b \\ c & d \end{vmatrix} = ad - bc > 0$, $\operatorname{tr} J = a + d < 0$, the EP is an ESS. When $\det J < 0$, the EP is a saddle point. To calculate the $\det J$ and $\operatorname{tr} J$ of the EP E_1, E_2, E_3, E_4, E_5, known from our hypothesis $v_1 > v_2 > C_l$, then determine the sign. Table 7 summarizes the above results.

As depicted in Fig. 8, in the off-season, E_1 is the ESS of the MC and AC. To compare the pure strategic equilibrium achieved when both carriers are perfectly rational, the two perfectly correspond to each other.

4.3. *Peak-season evolutionary games with blockchain*

When the blockchain is enabled, we formulate the payoff matrix of the evolutionary game between the MC and AC in peak seasons in Table 8.

When the MC chooses to cooperate, the profit is $\widetilde{U}^y_{OC^h}$. When the MC groups choose to non-cooperate, the profit is $\widetilde{U}^n_{OC^h}$. Then the average income of the MC

Table 7. Stabilities of the evolutionary game between MC and AC in off-seasons.

EP	$\det J$	$\operatorname{tr} J$	State
E_1	+	−	ESS
E_2	−	−	Saddle point
E_3	−	−	Saddle point
E_4	+	+	Instability point
E_5	−	0	Saddle point

Notes: "+" denotes greater than zero; "−" denotes less than zero; N denotes uncertainty.

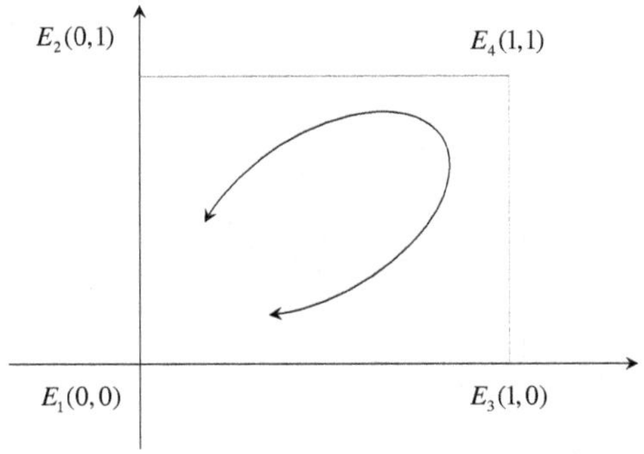

Fig. 8. The local stability of the evolutionary game between carrier groups in off-seasons.

Table 8. Payoff matrix impacted by blockchain in peak seasons.

Peak seasons		AC	
		Cooperate (λ_2)	Non-cooperate ($1-\lambda_2$)
MC	Cooperate (λ_1)	$\frac{\pi_1}{2}, \frac{\pi_2}{2}$	$a_h, \pi_2 - a_h$
	Non-cooperate ($1-\lambda_1$)	$\pi_1 - b_h, b_h$	$\frac{\pi_1 - C_h}{2}, \frac{\pi_2 - C_h}{2}$

in the peak season is $\overline{U}_{OC^h}$.

$$\widetilde{U}^y_{OC^h} = \lambda_2 \frac{\pi_1}{2} + (1-\lambda_2)a_h,$$

$$\widetilde{U}^n_{OC^h} = \lambda_2(\pi_1 - b_h) + (1-\lambda_2)\frac{\pi_1 - C_h}{2},$$

$$\overline{U}_{OC^h} = \lambda_1 U^y_{OC^h} + (1-\lambda_1)U^n_{OC^h}.$$

When the AC choose to cooperate, the profit is $\widetilde{U}^y_{FC^h}$. When the AC chooses to non-cooperate, the profit is $\widetilde{U}^n_{FC^h}$. Then the average income of the AC in peak seasons is $\overline{U}_{FC^h}$.

$$\widetilde{U}^y_{FC^h} = \lambda_1 \frac{\pi_2}{2} + (1-\lambda_1)b_h,$$

$$\widetilde{U}^n_{FC^h} = \lambda_1(\pi_2 - a_h) + (1-\lambda_1)\frac{\pi_2 - C_h}{2},$$

$$\overline{U}_{FC^h} = \lambda_2 U^y_{FC^h} + (1-\lambda_2)U^n_{FC^h}.$$

The dynamic equations of "cooperate" chosen by MC and the dynamic equation of "cooperate" chosen by AC are $\{\widehat{F(\lambda_1)}, \widehat{F(\lambda_2)}\}$ as follows:

$$\widehat{F(\lambda_1)} = \frac{d\lambda_1}{dt} = \lambda_1(\widetilde{U}^y_{OC^h} - \overline{U}_{OC^h}),$$

$$\widehat{F(\lambda_2)} = \frac{d\lambda_2}{dt} = \lambda_2(\widetilde{U}^y_{FC^h} - \overline{U}_{FC^h}).$$

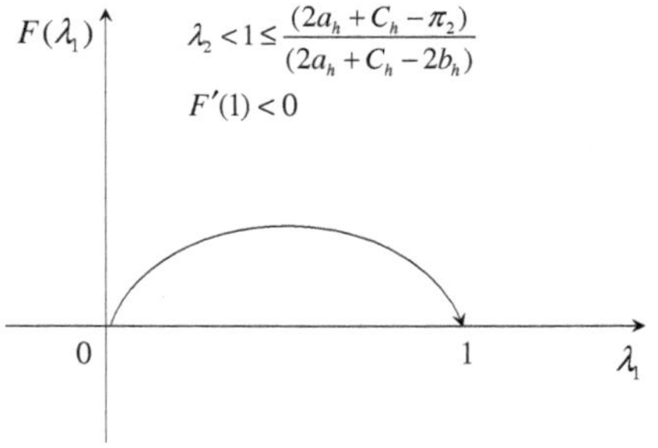

Fig. 9. Replication of dynamic phase diagrams for the MC.

Proposition 9. *When* $\lambda_2 < 1 \le \frac{(2a_h+C_h-\pi_2)}{(2a_h+C_h-2b_h)}$*, mean* $b_h \ge \frac{\pi_1}{2}$*,* $a_h \ge \frac{(\pi_1 - C_h)}{2}$*;* $\lambda_1^* = 0$ *and* $\lambda_1^* = 1$ *are stable states, but because of* $F'(0) > 0$*,* $F'(1) < 0$*, so only* $\hat{\lambda}_1^* = 1$ *is ESS.*

Proof. When the proportion of the AC choosing cooperation is lower than this value, the proportion of the MC choosing cooperation will gradually increase to 1, as shown in Fig. 9. □

Proposition 10. *When* $\lambda_1 < 1 \le \frac{(2b_h+C_h-\pi_2)}{(2b_h+C_h-2a_h)}$*, mean* $a_h \ge \frac{\pi_2}{2}$*,* $b_h \ge \frac{(\pi_2 - C_h)}{2}$*;* $\lambda_2^* = 0$ *and* $\lambda_2^* = 1$ *are stable states, but because of* $F'(0) > 0$*,* $F'(1) < 0$*, so only* $\lambda_2^* = 1$ *is ESS.*

Proof. When the proportion of the MC choosing cooperation is lower than this value, the proportion of the AC choosing cooperation will gradually increase to 1, as shown in Fig. 10. □

Proposition 11. *The EPs of the RDS are* $E_1 = (0,0)$*,* $E_2 = (0,1)$*,* $E_3 = (1,0)$*,* $E_4 = (1,1)$*,* $E_5 = (\overline{\lambda}_1^0, \overline{\lambda}_2^0)$*,* $\overline{\lambda}_1^0 \in [0,1]$*,* $\overline{\lambda}_2^0 \in [0,1]$*,* $\overline{\lambda}_1^0 = \frac{2b_h+C_h-\pi_2}{2b_h+C_h-2a_h}$*,* $\overline{\lambda}_2^0 = \frac{2b_h+C_h-\pi_2}{2a_h+C_h-2b_h}$*.*

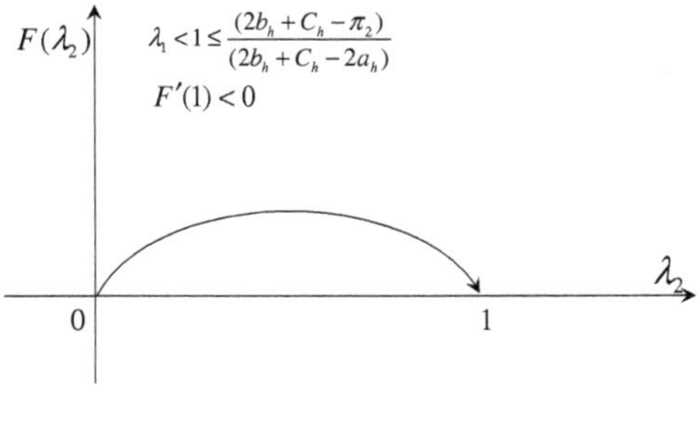

Fig. 10. Replication of dynamic phase diagrams for the AC.

Proof. We can obtain the EPs by solving $\{\widehat{F(\lambda_1)}, \widehat{F(\lambda_2)}\}$. □

Proposition 12. *When adopting the blockchain technology to conduct macro-control on the shipping market in this region, significant penalty parameters and compensation parameters should be selected separately according to the peak and low seasons of shipping, which will completely reverse the inefficient behaviors among carrier groups under the competition of shipping free market and accelerate the development of the regional economy of ports. In peak seasons and under limited rationality, when the MC is superior to the AC, and there is blockchain technology for supervision and control, guarantee* $b_h \geq \frac{\pi_1}{2}$, $a_h \geq \frac{\pi_2}{2}$. *Then, as the stable equilibrium, the MC and AC both choose to cooperate.*

Proof. The Jacobian matrix of the above replication dynamic system is as follows: When the EP of the RDS satisfies the condition $\det J = \left|\begin{smallmatrix} a & b \\ c & d \end{smallmatrix}\right| = ad - bc > 0, \operatorname{tr} J = a + d < 0$, the EP is an ESS. When $\det J < 0$, the EP is a saddle point. To calculate the $\det J$ and $\operatorname{tr} J$ of the EPs, E_1, E_2, E_3, E_4, E_5, known from our hypothesis $b_h \geq \frac{\pi_1}{2}, a_h \geq \frac{(\pi_1 - C_h)}{2}, a_h \geq \frac{\pi_2}{2}, b_h \geq \frac{(\pi_2 - C_h)}{2}$, then determine the sign. Table 9 summarizes the analytical results of the EPs.

$$J = \begin{bmatrix} \dfrac{\partial F(\lambda_1)}{\partial \lambda_1} & \dfrac{\partial F(\lambda_1)}{\partial \lambda_2} \\ \dfrac{\partial F(\lambda_2)}{\partial \lambda_1} & \dfrac{\partial F(\lambda_2)}{\partial \lambda_2} \end{bmatrix} = \begin{bmatrix} a & b \\ c & d \end{bmatrix},$$

$$a = \frac{1}{2}(-1 + 2\lambda_1)[-2a_h + \pi_1 + C_h(-1 + \lambda_2) + 2(a_h - b_h)\lambda_2],$$

$$b = \frac{1}{2}(2a_h - 2b_h + C_h)(-1 + \lambda_1)\lambda_1,$$

$$c = \frac{1}{2}(-2a_h + C_h + \pi_2 - b_h\pi_2 + 2b_h\pi_2\lambda_1)(-1 + \lambda_2)\lambda_2,$$

$$d = \frac{1}{2}(-1 + 2\lambda_2)[\pi_2 + C_h(-1 + \lambda_1) + (-2a_h + \pi_2 - b_h\pi_2)\lambda_1 + b_h\pi_2\lambda_1^2].$$ □

Table 9. EPs when blockchain is enabled in peak seasons.

EP	$\det J$	$\operatorname{tr} J$	State
E_1	+	+	Instability point
E_2	−	N	Saddle point
E_3	−	N	Saddle point
E_4	+	−	ESS
E_5	Meaningless		

Notes: "+" denotes greater than zero; "−" denotes less than zero; N denotes uncertainty.

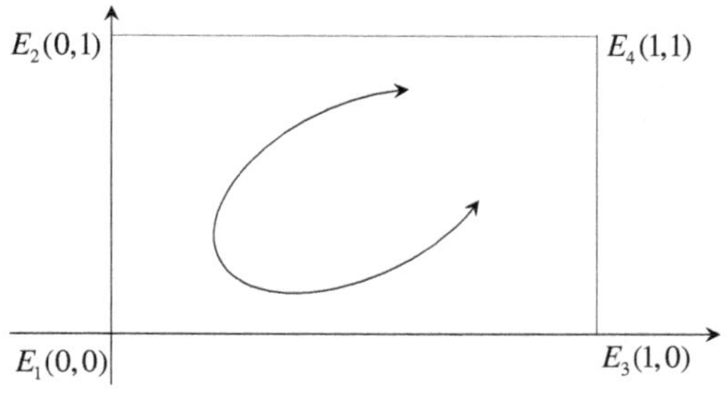

Fig. 11. The local stability of the evolutionary game between the MC and AC in peak seasons.

In peak seasons, $a_h > 0 > \frac{(\pi_1 - C_h)}{2}$, $b_h > 0 > \frac{(\pi_2 - C_h)}{2}$. Therefore, when referring to blockchain technology, the value range of parameters equivalent to controlling punishment and compensation is $b_h \geq \frac{\pi_1}{2}$, $a_h \geq \frac{\pi_2}{2}$. The local stability of the evolutionary game between the MC and AC is shown in Fig. 11.

4.4. *Off-season evolutionary games with blockchain*

When the blockchain is enabled, we formulate the payoff matrix of the evolutionary game between the MC and AC in off-seasons in Table 10.

When the MC chooses to cooperate, the profit is $\widetilde{U}^y_{OC^l}$. When the MC chooses to non-cooperate, the profit is $\widetilde{U}^n_{OC^l}$. Then the average income of the MC in the off-season is $\overline{U}_{OC^l}$.

$$\widetilde{U}^y_{OC^l} = \theta_2 \frac{v_1}{2} + (1-\theta_2) a_l,$$

$$\widetilde{U}^n_{OC^l} = \theta_2 (v_1 - b_l) + (1-\theta_2) \frac{v_1 - C_l}{2},$$

$$\overline{U}_{OC^l} = \theta_1 U^y_{OC^l} + (1-\theta_1) U^n_{OC^l}.$$

When the AC groups choose to cooperate, the profit is $\widetilde{U}^y_{FC^l}$. When the AC groups choose to non-cooperate, the profit is $\widetilde{U}^n_{FC^l}$. Then the average income of the

Table 10. Payoff matrix impacted by blockchain in off-seasons.

Off-season		AC	
		Cooperate (θ_2)	Non-cooperate ($1-\theta_2$)
MC	Cooperate (θ_1)	$\frac{v_1}{2}, \frac{v_2}{2}$	$a_l, v_2 - a_l$
	Non-cooperate ($1-\theta_1$)	$v_1 - b_l, b_l$	$\frac{v_1 - C_l}{2}, \frac{v_2 - C_l}{2}$

AC groups in the off-season is $\overline{U}_{FC^l}$.

$$\widetilde{U}^y_{FC^l} = \theta_1 \frac{v_2}{2} + (1-\theta_1) b_l,$$

$$\widetilde{U}^n_{FC^l} = \theta_1 (v_2 - a_l) + (1-\theta_1) \frac{v_2 - C_l}{2},$$

$$\overline{U}_{FC^l} = \theta_2 U^y_{FC^l} + (1-\theta_2) U^n_{FC^l}.$$

The dynamic equations of "cooperate" chosen by MC and the dynamic equation of "cooperate" chosen by AC are $\{\widehat{F(\theta_1)}, \widehat{F(\theta_2)}\}$.

$$\widehat{F(\theta_1)} = \frac{d\theta_1}{dt} = \theta_1 \big(\widetilde{U}^y_{OC^l} - \overline{U}_{OC^l}\big),$$

$$\widehat{F(\theta_2)} = \frac{d\theta_2}{dt} = \theta_2 \big(\widetilde{U}^y_{FC^l} - \overline{U}_{FC^l}\big).$$

Proposition 13. *When $\theta_2 < 1 \leq \frac{(2a_l + C_l - v_1)}{(2a_l + C_l - 2b_l)}$, mean $b_l \geq \frac{v_1}{2}$, $a_l \geq \frac{(v_1 - C_l)}{2}$; $\theta_1^* = 0$ and $\theta_1^* = 1$ are stable states, but because of $F'(0) > 0$, $F'(1) < 0$, so only $\theta_1^* = 1$ is ESS.*

Proof. When the proportion of the AC choosing cooperation is lower than this value, the proportion of the MC choosing cooperation will gradually increase to 1, as shown in Fig. 12. □

Proposition 14. *When $\theta_1 < 1 \leq \frac{(2b_l + C_l - v_2)}{(2b_l + C_l - 2a_l)}$, mean $a_l \geq \frac{v_2}{2}$, $b_l \geq \frac{(v_2 - C_l)}{2}$; $\theta_2^* = 0$ and $\theta_2^* = 1$ are stable states, but because of $F'(0) > 0$, $F'(1) < 0$, so only $\theta_2^* = 1$ is ESS.*

Proof. When the proportion of the MC choosing cooperation is lower than this value, the proportion of the AC choosing cooperation will gradually increase to 1, as shown in Fig. 13. □

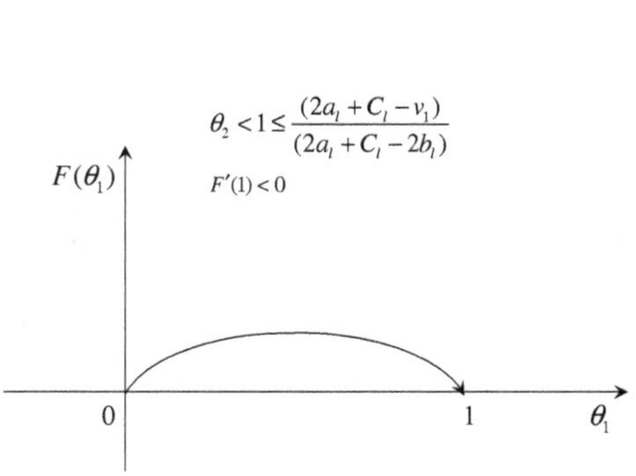

Fig. 12. Replication of dynamic phase diagrams for the MC in off-seasons.

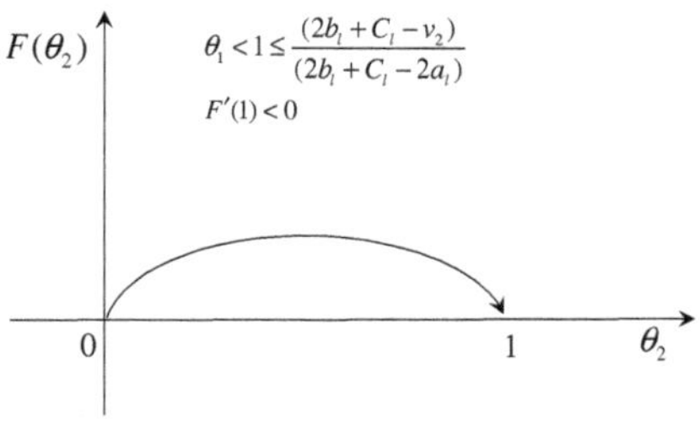

Fig. 13. Replication of dynamic phase diagrams for the AC in off-seasons.

Proposition 15. *The EPs of the RDS are* $E_1 = (0,0)$, $E_2 = (0,1)$, $E_3 = (1,0)$, $E_4 = (1,1)$, $E_5 = (\widehat{\theta}_1^0, \widehat{\theta}_2^0)$, $\widehat{\theta}_1^0 \in [0,1]$, $\widehat{\theta}_2^0 \in [0,1]$, $\widehat{\theta}_1^0 = \frac{2b_l + C_l - v_2}{2b_l + C_l - 2a_l}$, $\widehat{\theta}_2^0 = \frac{2a_l + C_l - v_1}{2a_l + C_l - 2b_l}$.

Proof. We can obtain the EPs by solving $\{\widehat{F(\theta_1)}, \widehat{F(\theta_2)}\}$. □

Proposition 16. *When adopting the blockchain technology to conduct macro-control on the shipping market in this region, significant penalty parameters and compensation parameters should be selected separately according to the peak and low seasons of shipping, which will completely reverse the inefficient behaviors among carrier groups under the competition of shipping free market and accelerate the development of the regional economy of ports. In peak seasons and under limited rationality, when the MC groups are superior to the AC, and there is blockchain technology for supervision and control, guarantee* $b_l \ge \frac{v_1}{2}$, $a_l \ge \frac{(v_1 - C_l)}{2}$, $a_l \ge \frac{v_2}{2}$, $b_l \ge \frac{(v_2 - C_l)}{2}$, *then the ESS of the MC and AC will be that they both choose cooperation.*

Proof. The Jacobian matrix of the above RDS is as follows:

$$J = \begin{bmatrix} \dfrac{\partial F(\theta_1)}{\partial \theta_1} & \dfrac{\partial F(\theta_1)}{\partial \theta_2} \\ \dfrac{\partial F(\theta_2)}{\partial \theta_1} & \dfrac{\partial F(\theta_2)}{\partial \theta_2} \end{bmatrix} = \begin{bmatrix} a & b \\ c & d \end{bmatrix},$$

$$a = \frac{1}{2}(-1 + 2\theta_1)[-2a_l + v_1 + C_l(-1 + \theta_2) + 2(a_l - b_l)],$$

$$b = \frac{1}{2}(2a_l - 2b_l + C_l)(-1 + \theta_1)\theta_1,$$

$$c = \frac{1}{2}(-2a_l + C_l + 2b_l)(-1 + \theta_2)\theta_2,$$

$$d = \frac{1}{2}(-1 + 2\theta_2)(v_2 + C_l(-1 + \theta_1) - 2[b_l + (a_l - b_l)\theta_1]).$$ □

When the EP of the RDS satisfies the condition $\det J = \begin{vmatrix} a & b \\ c & d \end{vmatrix} = ad - bc > 0$, $\operatorname{tr} J = a + d < 0$, the EP is an ESS. When $\det J < 0$, the EP is a saddle point. To

Table 11. EPs when blockchain is enabled in off-seasons.

EP	det J	tr J	State
E_1	+	+	Instability point
E_2	−	N	Saddle point
E_3	−	N	Saddle point
E_4	+	−	ESS
E_5	Meaningless		

Notes: "+" denotes greater than zero; "−" denotes less than zero; N denotes uncertainty.

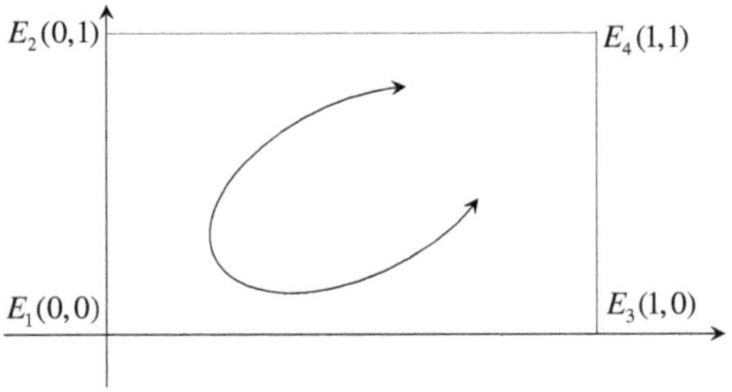

Fig. 14. The local stability of the evolutionary game between MC and AC in off-seasons.

calculate the det J and tr J of the EP E_1, E_2, E_3, E_4, E_5, known from our hypothesis $b_l \geq \frac{v_1}{2}$, $a_l \geq \frac{(v_1-C_l)}{2}$, $a_l \geq \frac{v_2}{2}$, $b_l \geq \frac{(v_2-C_l)}{2}$, then determine the sign. Table 11 summarizes the results analyzed above.

In off-seasons, $\frac{(v_1-C_l)}{2} > 0$, $\frac{(v_2-C_l)}{2} > 0$. Therefore, when referring to blockchain technology, the value range of parameters equivalent to controlling punishment and compensation is $b_l \geq \frac{v_1}{2}$, $a_l \geq \frac{(v_1-C_l)}{2}$, $a_l \geq \frac{v_2}{2}$, $b_l \geq \frac{(v_2-C_l)}{2}$. The local stability of the evolutionary game between carrier groups as is shown in Fig. 14.

5. Numerical Study

Suppose that within a container shipping area, the carriers (MC and AC) compete freely in the shipping market. In the peak season, long-distance container transportation demands are more; the MC is the dominant power in the market, and we set its profit to 10. In the off-seasons, there are more short-distance transportation demands, and the MC is still dominant in the market, while its profit is 6. In these two contexts, the profits obtained by the AC is 3. If the two parties (MC and AC) do not carry out practical cooperation and share container resources, customers' requirements cannot be met. However, at this time, short-distance transportation demands are more likely to rely on container transport chain cooperation, so the loss of both parties is lower than that of the two parties in peak seasons and lower than their operations cost. We set it to 2. In summary, we set the following parameters,

Table 12. Payoff matrix without blockchain in peak seasons.

Peak seasons Non-blockchain		AC	
		Cooperate (λ_2)	Non-cooperate ($1-\lambda_2$)
MC	Cooperate (λ_1)	$(5, 2)$	$(0, 4)$
	Non-cooperate ($1-\lambda_1$)	$(10, 0)$	$(-1, -4)$

Table 13. Payoff matrix without blockchain in off-seasons.

Off-seasons Non-blockchain		AC	
		Cooperate (θ_2)	Non-cooperate ($1-\theta_2$)
MC	Cooperate (θ_1)	$(3, 1.5)$	$(0, 3)$
	Non-cooperate ($1-\theta_1$)	$(6, 0)$	$(2, 0.5)$

$v_1 = 6$, $v_2 = 3$, $C_l = 2$. Tables 12 and 13 summarize the payoff matrix settings without blockchain in peak and off-seasons.

Using the data described above, we analyze the behavioral changes among carrier groups, and the data only need to reflect the income differences among carrier groups, without specific numerical calculation. Therefore, in the aspect of revenue, by considering the actual revenue distribution of the carrier group, the numerical value of the corresponding relationship is set for simulation analysis. The data does not come from the real world but is simulated from the real world.

If the two carrier populations (MC and AC) are entirely rational, there are two pure strategic equilibria in peak seasons: (long-term cooperation, mid-course betrayal), (mid-course betrayal, long-term cooperation); in off-seasons, there is a pure strategic equilibrium: (mid-stream betrayal, mid-stream betrayal).

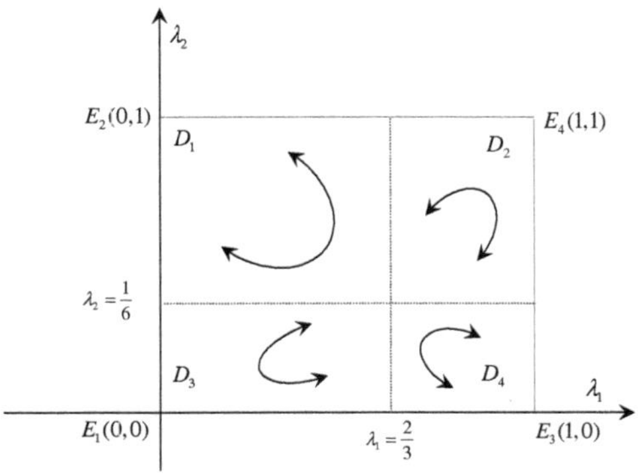

(a) Peak seasons

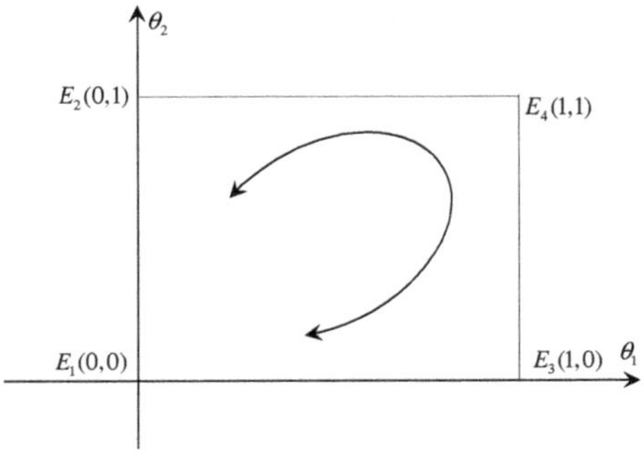

(b) Off-seasons

Fig. 15. Local stability of the evolutionary game between MC and AC.

Table 14. Payoff matrix impacted by blockchain in peak seasons.

Peak seasons Blockchain-enabled		AC	
		Cooperate (λ_2)	Non-cooperate ($1-\lambda_2$)
MC	Cooperate (λ_1)	$(5, 2)$	$(3, 1)$
	Non-cooperate ($1-\lambda_1$)	$(4, 6)$	$(-1, -4)$

Table 15. Payoff matrix impacted by blockchain in off-seasons.

Off-season Blockchain-enabled		AC	
		Cooperate (θ_2)	Non-cooperate ($1-\theta_2$)
MC	Cooperate (θ_1)	$(3, 1.5)$	$(2.5, 0.5)$
	Non-cooperate ($1-\theta_1$)	$(2, 4)$	$(2, 0.5)$

If the MC and AC are both bounded rational, the local stability of the evolutionary game between them is shown in Fig. 15. The evolutionary trends present that the two parties will non-cooperate.

When the blockchain technology is enabled, the carriers' revenue in this shipping area will no longer be the revenue under the free market competition, but the cooperation revenue is under control. Considering these judgments, we made the following assumptions: in peak season, $b_h \geq \frac{\pi_1}{2}$, $a_h \geq \frac{\pi_2}{2}$, and so $\pi_1 = 10$, $\pi_2 = 4$, $C_h = 12$, $a_h = 3, b_h = 6$; in off-seasons, $b_l \geq \frac{v_1}{2}, a_l \geq \frac{(v_1 - C_l)}{2}, a_l \geq \frac{v_2}{2}, b_l \geq \frac{(v_2 - C_l)}{2}$, and so $v_1 = 6$, $v_2 = 3$, $C_l = 2$, $a_l = 2.5$, $b_l = 4$. Considering enabled blockchain technology, we set the payoff matrices in peak and off-seasons in Tables 14 and 15 for the following experiments.

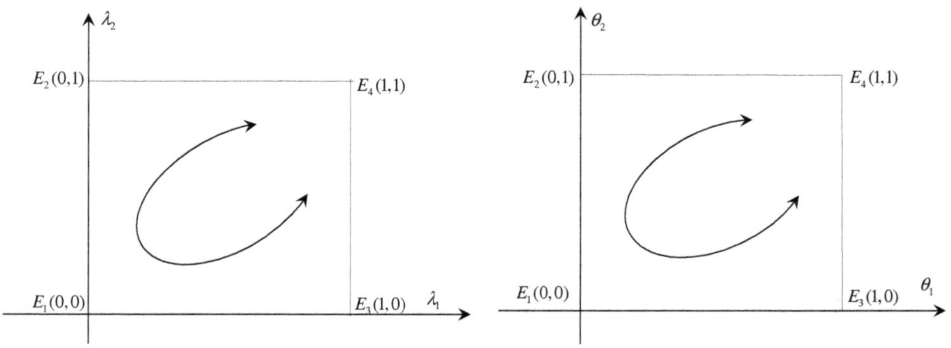

(a) Peak seasons (b) Off-seasons

Fig. 16. Local stability of the evolutionary game between MC and AC with enabled blockchain.

If the MC and AC are both perfectly rational, we can conclude that there is only a pure ESS in peak seasons or off-seasons: (cooperate, cooperate). Figure 16 depicts the evolutionary paths when the MC and AC are both bounded rational. By comparing these two paths, we conclude that when the dominant carriers control the cooperative behavior between the carrier populations, the two populations eventually evolve into an evolutionary equilibrium of complete cooperation, forming an efficient cooperative alliance, especially in the context of container transport chains.

6. Discussion and Conclusion

6.1. *Discussion*

(1) In peak seasons and blockchain is not enabled.
Considering whether the blockchain technology is not enabled in peak seasons, we analyze the MC and AC profits first, and then we devised the payoff matrix for the dynamic system. Then, we compute and analyze the evolutionary game EPs and ESS by using the Jacobian matrix. As the resulting evolutionary strategy, the MC chooses to non-cooperate, and the AC chooses to cooperate, or the MC chooses to cooperate, and the AC chooses not to work. The numerical analysis does verify and is consistent with the analytical results. Under the conditions of peak seasons and non-blockchain, the MC and AC cannot complete some long-distance transportation tasks, and the two populations betray each other and cannot form an effective cooperative alliance, which may cause malicious competition and damage the regional economy.

(2) In off-seasons and blockchain is not enabled.
In the off-seasons and when blockchain technology is not enabled, we set up the evolutionary game models to analyze the cooperative strategies for the MC and AC. As the resulting ESS, the MC chooses not to cooperate, and the AC chooses not to cooperate. The numerical analysis also verifies this result. In this case, there will be no cooperative relationship between the MC and AC. However, in the off-seasons, the container transportation tasks are mainly short-distance transportation, and the MC and AC have no strong desire for cooperation. So, they choose to complete the shipping task alone.

(3) In peak season and blockchain is enabled.
When in the peak seasons and the blockchain technology is enabled in container transport chains, the MC and AC will be subject to corresponding credit punishment in the event of betrayal. Accordingly, the carrier population that chooses to cooperate will receive credit compensation. In this case, the evolutionary equilibrium strategy is that both MC and AC choose long-term cooperation. Consistent with the numerical analysis, the carriers will form an effective cooperation alliance, accelerate the development of the regional container transport chain.

(4) In off-seasons and blockchain is enabled.
Similarly, we use evolutionary game modes to analyze the cooperative behavior strategies of the MC and AC. In this case, the ESS is that both the MC and AC choose long-term cooperation. The numerical analysis further verifies the analytical results. As indicated by the analytical and numerical results, the MC and AC will form an effective cooperative alliance.

Blockchain is a standard technology of information sharing and transparency, and secure transportation for container transport chains. Although we mainly use the term "blockchain", it mainly refers to a class of technologies with such functions and features. To sum up, when blockchain technology is not enabled, no effective cooperation alliance will be formed between carrier groups, and long-distance container transportation tasks cannot be completed. Malicious competition among carrier groups may also occur, which will impact the economy of the entire shipping region. However, after enabling blockchain technology, the MC and AC can form an effective cooperation alliance, which can efficiently complete all transportation tasks, promote the peaceful development of container transport chains, and promote regional economic progress.

6.2. *Conclusion*

The container transport chain is distributive and full of stakeholders, making the coordinations complicated in strategy development and technology innovation. Blockchain and similar information technologies enable secure information sharing and transparency feasible. Thus, the business and activities related to global logistics and supply chain can be seamlessly integrated and coordinated for improving efficiency and satisfaction. Considering the distinct features of the container transport chain, we categorize the stakeholders into two classes, MC and AC populations. The MCs represent the mega shipping companies and port authorities, which play essential roles in developing regulations and innovative technologies in the chain. In this study, we describe the interaction between carriers from the perspective of evolutionary game theory, enabling the MC to cooperate with AC and share information through sufficient penalty and incentive mechanisms. This study will be of significance to the operations of the container transport chains and the regional shipping industry. When the shipping enterprises in a specific region cannot effectively cooperate, they must use a platform to monitor the enterprise group's speculative behavior and set up a punishment mechanism. Moreover, the enterprise's active cooperation to give subsidies and incentives, and finally, make all shipping enterprises in the region committed to the development of the regional economy.

We devised the evolutionary game models to study the cooperative behaviors between the MC and AC in the container transport chain. Through theoretical and numerical studies, three conclusions are drawn, indicating that the cooperation between MC and AC in the shipping industry will be invalid without introducing blockchain technology for adequate supervision. In peak seasons, there is an evolutionary equilibrium between carrier groups of cooperation and non-cooperation, while in the low season, the evolutionary equilibrium between carrier groups is one in which both parties choose not to cooperate. However, when blockchain technology is enabled for adequate supervision, MC and AC will cooperate in peak and off-seasons for shipping. Besides, through numerical analysis, this paper conducts a numerical analysis of the established cooperation model. The results show that the introduction of blockchain technology as a regulatory model can enable carriers to form cooperative alliances, improve the previous inefficient operation, and achieve a long-term stable equilibrium strategy.

The yield matrix in this paper has many limitations. In a further study, the conditions can be further broadened, and some random variables can be added to improve the model's feasibility. At the same time, information asymmetry between carrier groups can also be considered. We classify the market status of container transportation demands into peak and off-seasons. However, this classification is intuitive and may be adjusted for considered different stakeholders and logistics scenarios. Besides, the risk preference factors of the carrier group can also be considered, such as risk aversion, risk neutrality, and risk-taking. Different risk preferences will bring different strategic choices, which are all parts that can be discussed and studied in detail in the future.

Acknowledgments

The authors gratefully acknowledge the editors and anonymous reviewers for their valuable comments that helped improve this paper. This study is partially supported by the National Nature Science of China (71871136).

References

Abd, MA, SF Al Rubeaai, S Salimpour and A Azab (2019). Evolutionary game theoretical approach for equilibrium of cross-border traffic. *Transportmetrica B*, 7(1), 1611–1626.

Bavassano, G, C Ferrari and A Tei (2020). Blockchain: How shipping industry is dealing with the ultimate technological leap. *Research in Transportation Business & Management*, 34, 100428.

Deja, A, M Kaup and R Strulak-Wójcikiewicz (2019). The concept of transport organization model in container logistics chains using inland waterway transport. In *Sustainable Design and Manufacturing*, pp. 521–531. Singapore: Springer.

Feng, F, C Liu and J Zhang (2020). China's railway transportation safety regulation system based on evolutionary game theory and system dynamics. *Risk Analysis*, 40, 1944–1966.

Franc, P and M Van der Horst (2010). Understanding hinterland service integration by shipping lines and terminal operators: A theoretical and empirical analysis. *Journal of Transport Geography*, 18(4), 557–566.

Frémont, A and P Franc (2010). Hinterland transportation in Europe: Combined transport versus road transport. *Journal of Transport Geography*, 18(4), 548–556.

García, J, JE Florez, Á Torralba, D Borrajo, CL López, Á García-Olaya and J Sáenz (2013). Combining linear programming and automated planning to solve intermodal transportation problems. *European Journal of Operational Research*, 227(1), 216–226.

Ghannadpour, SF and F Zandiyeh (2020). A new game-theoretical multi-objective evolutionary approach for cash-in-transit vehicle routing problem with time windows (a real life case). *Applied Soft Computing Journal*, 93, 106378.

Gu, L, L Xi and S Wen (2017). Exploration on the low-carbon strategy based on the evolutionary game between the government and highway logistics enterprises. *Agro Food Industry Hi-Tech*, 28(1), 1796–1800.

Hasan, H, E AlHadhrami, A AlDhaheri, K Salah and R Jayaraman (2019). Smart contract-based approach for efficient shipment management. *Computers and Industrial Engineering*, 136, 149–159.

Hernández, R, C Cárdenas and D Muñoz (2018). Game theory applied to transportation systems in smart cities: Analysis of evolutionary stable strategies in a generic car pooling system. *International Journal on Interactive Design and Manufacturing*, 12(1), 179–185.

Hilmola, OP and V Henttu (2015). Border-crossing constraints, railways and transit transports in Estonia. *Research in Transportation Business and Management*, 14, 72–79.

Jeong, Y, S Saha, D Chatterjee and I Moon (2018). Direct shipping service routes with an empty container management strategy. *Transportation Research Part E: Logistics and Transportation Review*, 118, 123–142.

Jiang, X, EP Chew and LH Lee (2015). Innovative container terminals to improve global container transport chains. In *Handbook of Ocean Container Transport Logistics*, International Series in Operations Research and Management Science, pp. 3–41. Cham: Springer.

Jović, M, M Filipović, E Tijan and M Jardas (2019). A review of blockchain technology implementation in shipping industry. *Pomorstvo*, 33(2), 140–148.

Lam, JSL (2015). Designing a sustainable maritime supply chain: A hybrid QFD-ANP approach. *Transportation Research Part E: Logistics and Transportation Review*, 78, 70–81.

Lee, CY and DP Song (2017). Ocean container transport in global supply chains: Overview and research opportunities. *Transportation Research Part B: Methodological*, 95, 442–474.

Lei, L and S Gao (2018). Evolutionary game analysis of ride sourcing industry between transportation network companies and passengers under new policies of ride sourcing. *IEEE Access*, 6, 71918–71931.

Lei, LC, S Gao and EY Zeng (2020). Regulation strategies of ride-hailing market in China: An evolutionary game theoretic perspective. *Electronic Commerce Research*, 20(3), 535–563.

Lin, N (2019). CO_2 emissions mitigation potential of buyer consolidation and rail-based intermodal transport in the China-Europe container supply chains. *Journal of Cleaner Production*, 240, 118121.

Lorenc, A and M Kuźnar (2017). The impact of cargo monitoring systems usage on intermodal transport risk and costs. *World Review of Intermodal Transportation Research*, 6(4), 336–351.

Martínez-López, A, J Kronbak and L Jiang (2015). Cost and time models for the evaluation of intermodal chains by using short sea shipping in the north sea region: The

Rosyth–Zeebrugge route. *International Journal of Shipping and Transport Logistics*, 7(4), 494–520.

Nguyen, S, PSL Chen and Y Du (2020). Risk identification and modeling for blockchain-enabled container shipping. *International Journal of Physical Distribution and Logistics Management*, 51, 126–148.

Papathanasiou, A, R Cole and P Murray (2020). The (non-) application of blockchain technology in the Greek shipping industry. *European Management Journal*, 38, 927–938.

Parola, F and A Sciomachen (2005). Intermodal container flows in a port system network: Analysis of possible growths via simulation models. *International Journal of Production Economics*, 97(1), 75–88.

Pu, S and JSL Lam (2020). Blockchain adoptions in the maritime industry: A conceptual framework. *Maritime Policy and Management*, DOI: 10.1080/03088839.2020.1825855.

Pu, D, F Xie and G Yuan (2020). Active supervision strategies of online ride-hailing based on the tripartite evolutionary game model. *IEEE Access*, 8, 149052–149064.

Song, DP, A Lyons, D Li and H Sharifi (2016). Modeling port competition from a transport chain perspective. *Transportation Research Part E: Logistics and Transportation Review*, 87, 75–96.

Tan, WKA and B Sundarakani (2020). Assessing blockchain technology application for freight booking business: A case study from technology acceptance model perspective. *Journal of Global Operations and Strategic Sourcing*, 14, 202–223.

Tsiulin, S, KH Reinau, OP Hilmola, N Goryaev and A Karam (2020). Blockchain-based applications in shipping and port management: A literature review towards defining key conceptual frameworks. *Review of International Business and Strategy*, 30(2), 201–224.

Yang, CS (2019). Maritime shipping digitalization: Blockchain-based technology applications, future improvements, and intention to use. *Transportation Research Part E: Logistics and Transportation Review*, 131, 108–117.

Yi, Z, C Xiang, L Li and H Jiang (2020). Evolutionary game analysis and simulation with system dynamics for behavioral strategies of participants in crowd logistics. *Transportation Letters*, DOI: 10.1080/19427867.2020.1783609.

Zhang, R and L Zhu (2019). Threshold incorporating freight choice modeling for hinterland leg transportation chain of export containers. *Transportation Research Part A: Policy and Practice*, 130, 858–872.

Zhang, L, R Long, Z Huang, W Li and J Wei (2020). Evolutionary game analysis on the implementation of subsidy policy for sustainable transportation development. *Journal of Cleaner Production*, 267, 122159.

Zhou, Y, YS Soh, HS Loh and KF Yuen (2020). The key challenges and critical success factors of blockchain implementation: Policy implications for Singapore's maritime industry. *Marine Policy*, 122, 104265.

Biography

Zhi-Hua Hu is currently a Professor at the Logistics Research Center, Shanghai Maritime University. He received his PhD degree in control theory and engineering from the Donghua University in 2009. He was a postdoctoral research fellow at the Tongji University. His research interests include logistics operations research, optimization and decision-making, and artificial intelligence. His research works has been published by many journals, such as Transportation Research Part B, European Journal of Operational Research, Decision Support Systems, and so on.

Ya-Jing Dong is currently a postgraduate student at the Logistics Research Center of Shanghai Maritime University. Her research interests include supply chain management, and blockchain-enabled transport systems.

https://doi.org/10.1142/9789819808588_0008

Chapter 8

How to Escape Supply Chain Dilemmas? Manufacturer Encroachment and Supplier Cost-Reduction Investment†

Qijun Wang

School of Economics and Management
Southwest Jiaotong University, Chengdu, P. R. China
wangqijun_yx@163.com

Jiajia Nie*

School of Economics and Management
Southwest Jiaotong University, Chengdu, P. R. China
nie_jia@126.com

Senmao Xia

Business School, Coventry University
Coventry CV15FB, UK
Senmao.Xia@coventry.ac.uk

Component suppliers and manufacturers in a supply chain have long faced different dilemmas. The component supplier intends to adopt new technologies to reduce production costs, but the new technologies usually require significant investment costs. The encroachment into retailing can bring more revenue to manufacturers, but the significant costs of establishing and maintaining direct channels and the potential conflicting interests with the retailer might discourage the manufacturer's encroachment. This study aims to address these dilemmas facing the component supplier and manufacturer by investigating an interesting scenario in which they both can obtain benefits. Within the given context, the manufacturer's encroachment increases the order of the components, which motivates the supplier to make more technological investments to reduce production costs. The reduction of component costs enables suppliers and manufacturers to reduce the wholesale prices of components and final products. In this case, the manufacturer's encroachment can benefit both the manufacturer and the retailer. This study is one of the first to investigate how the interaction between the manufacturer and supplier helps solve their respective dilemmas and provide benefits to the whole supply chain. Additionally, we extend the literature on manufacturer encroachment on retailers by considering supplier investment in cost-reduction production.

Keywords: Supply chain management; manufacturer encroachment; supplier investment; game theory.

*Corresponding author.
†To cite this article, please refer to its earlier version published in the Asia-Pacific Journal of Operational Research, Vol. 39, No. 1, (February 2022), DOI: 10.1142/S0217595921400303. Reprinted with permission from World Scientific Publishing Co. Pte. Ltd.

1. Introduction

In the manufacturing industry, especially in technology-intensive industries, manufacturers usually rely on upstream suppliers to supply key components that are used to manufacture final products (Liker and Choi, 2004). For example, chips for computers and mobile phones are produced by suppliers, such as Intel and Qualcomm; and batteries for electric vehicles are produced by suppliers, such as Panasonic and CATL. The production of these components often requires high cost and complex production processes. In Industry 4.0, many component suppliers, such as Intel,[a] Infineon,[b] and Jabil,[c] are investing in advanced technologies, such as additive manufacturing, the Internet of Things (IOT), big data analytics, artificial intelligence, and automation simulations. These technologies can effectively improve production efficiency and reduce production costs. For example, additive manufacturing can help firms quickly generate prototypes for automated testing, thus reducing engineering costs. Real-time production monitoring and predictive maintenance of industrial IOT equipment may prevent 70% of manufacturing failures and thus reduce costly equipment repair and downtime.[d] According to PwC's Global Industry 4.0 Survey on Building Digital Enterprises in 2016, surveyed companies that successfully implement Industry 4.0 are estimated to achieve an average annual cost reduction of 3.6%.[e]

However, investing in these advanced technologies is costly for most companies. Suppliers have long been facing a dilemma regarding cost-reduction investments. Underinvestment in cost reduction can not only undermine the earnings of supply chain members but also weaken the competitiveness of products and decrease the success rates of new products in the long term (Dahan and Srinivasan, 2011). Improving the investment in reducing components' cost is an issue that must be addressed by the whole chain. Measures to enhance investment have been proposed, such as investment cost sharing (Bernstein and Gürhan Kök, 2009) and collaborative innovation (Kim and Netessine, 2013). However, due to the negative effects of cooperation, such as opportunistic behaviors, managerial complexity of joint activities, and inequal resources, investment in cost reduction is often discouraged (Wu *et al.*, 2020). Thus, both academics and business managers have been looking for an appropriate incentive mechanism to enhance cost-reduction investment in the supply chain.

In addition to the production of key components, another crucial issue associated with supply chains is the distribution of the final products. Higher production

[a] https://www.nexteratechs.com/use-cases/usecase-manufacturing-electronics/.
[b] https://www.edb.gov.sg/en/our-industries/company-highlights/infineon-technologies-e.html.
[c] https://www.jabil.com/news/jabil-realizes-distributed-manufacturing-vision-with-new-additive-manufacturing-network.html.
[d] https://eagletechnologies.com/2020/05/12/how-industry-4-0-technologies-save-costs-for-manufacturers/.
[e] https://jbcole.co.uk/blog/the-financial-benefits-of-industry-4-0-cost-reductions-and-increased-productivity.

efficiency upstream requires a higher distribution efficiency downstream. In recent years, manufacturers have established direct channels and competed with retailers in the consumer market, which is referred to as manufacturer encroachment (Huang *et al.*, 2018). Compared with traditional single retailer channels, dual channels with manufacturer encroachment tend to sell more products (Sun *et al.*, 2019). However, although the rapid development of e-commerce in recent decades has made it easier for manufacturers to encroach, many manufacturers still choose to sell their products only through retailers. There are many reasons that prevent a manufacturer from establishing a direct channel. The first reason is associated with the high costs of channel establishment operations. These costs include the cost of maintaining online websites, training and enrolling a salesforce, or the cost of inventory and transportation of products (Huang *et al.*, 2018; Tian *et al.*, 2018). The second is that manufacturer encroachment may cause a rupture in its relationship with the retailer (Yoon, 2016). If the manufacturer encroaches, the conventional wisdom suggests that the competition between the two channels hurts the retailer and thereby threatens existing channel relationships (Huang *et al.*, 2018). Faced with these obstacles, many manufacturers abandon encroachment, which results in a situation in which product sales are still limited by the single traditional channel. Although previous studies have claimed that manufacturer encroachment is profitable, few studies have explored how to motivate manufacturers to encroach. In practice, manufacturers in industry with extensive investment often encroach (Yoon, 2016). For instance, smart phone manufacturers, such as Huawei, OPPO, and Vivo, sell their phones to consumers not only through retailers but also through established direct channels, including company-owned franchises and online retail websites. This finding indicates that the investment can enable the manufacturer to obtain extra profits from the encroachment, thereby making the manufacturer more likely to encroach. Since suppliers are extensively engaged in cost-reduction investment in Industry 4.0, we seek answers to the following questions. First, how does manufacturer encroachment affect the supplier's cost-reduction investment? Second, how does the supplier's cost-reduction investment influence the manufacturer encroachment? Third, can the interaction between the manufacturer's encroachment and the supplier's cost-reduction investment help each other relieve the dilemma facing them?

To answer these questions, we establish a three-level supply chain consisting of a supplier, a manufacturer, and a retailer. The supplier produces key components that the manufacturer uses to manufacture final products. The encroachment of the manufacturer creates a higher order for components. Therefore, the supplier is better off with the manufacturer's encroachment decision. Regarding the retailer, our analysis shows that if the supplier does not make cost-reduction investment, the manufacturer's encroachment always hurts the retailer.

Compared with the benchmark case, the supplier's cost-reduction investment allows for a reduction in the wholesale price to induce the manufacturer to order more components. Second, because of more component orders, the supplier is willing to invest more when the manufacturer encroaches. The profit of cost reduction spills over to the manufacturer and the retailer through the wholesale price of components and final products. Consequently, when the supplier invests to reduce production costs, the manufacturer is more likely to encroach. Additionally, different from the previous literature, e.g., Arya *et al.* (2007) and Xiong *et al.* (2012), this study finds that a manufacturer's encroachment benefits the retailer by encouraging the supplier to invest more in cost-reduction technologies. From this, we can conclude that the interaction between the manufacturer and supplier helps solve supply chain dilemmas. There exists a condition in which investment and encroachment can create a Pareto gain.

This paper makes a few significant contributions. First, this research is one of the first to consider the impacts of the supplier investment strategy on the manufacturer's encroachment decision, which enriches the literature on manufacturer encroachment. Second, this study adds new insights into suppliers' strategy of cost-reduction investments in the supply chain. Third, this study extends the literature on manufacturer encroachment by identifying a new interesting condition in which the manufacturer's encroachment might benefit the retailer.

The rest of the paper is organized as follows. Section 2 reviews the relevant literature on manufacturer encroachment and supplier investment. Section 3 develops the model using game theory. Section 4 analyzes the equilibrium of the model and discusses the impacts of manufacturer encroachment and supplier investment. Section 5 summarizes this study and indicates future research directions. All proofs are included in Appendix A.

2. Relevant Literature

This paper related to manufacturer encroachment. Earlier studies in this stream focus on the negative effects of manufacturer encroachment. For example, Frazier and Lassar (1996) show that manufacturer encroachment reduces system efficiency because it weakens brand image. Park and Keh (2003) and Liu and Zhang (2006) demonstrate that encroachment hurts the profit of the retailer due to intensified market competition. Li *et al.* (2014) study the impact of information asymmetry on supplier encroachment and find that demand information asymmetry can amplify the double marginalization of wholesale prices. However, the following literature mostly argues that encroachment can create a win–win outcome for manufacturers and retailers. For example, Arya *et al.* (2007) demonstrate that an encroaching manufacturer reduces the wholesale price to support the retailer's demand and that the particularly efficient retailer may benefit from the encroachment. This viewpoint is robust by considering durable (Xiong *et al.*, 2012) nonlinear pricing (Li *et al.*, 2015), quality differentiation (Ha *et al.*, 2016), channel power (Niu *et al.*, 2017), and a retailer's incentive to share demand information (Huang *et al.*, 2018). Although some of these studies demonstrate that manufacturer encroachment can create a win–win outcome, few of them have explored how to help manufacturers encroach. In addition, the change in the production efficiency of upstream members has not been considered in their research. If the supplier invests in reducing production costs, it is not known whether the original distribution channel strategy can still adapt to the improved production efficiency. Thus, we examine the manufacturer encroachment strategy by considering that the component supplier is investing in cost reduction and exploring whether the investment helps the manufacturer to encroach and the impact of the encroachment on the supply chain members in our setting.

In the stream related to cost-reduction investment, a number of papers focus on the manufacturer's cost-reduction investment, e.g., Gupta (2008) and Ha *et al.* (2017), retailer innovation, e.g., Arya and Mittendorf (2013) and Hu *et al.* (2019), or collaboration innovation, e.g., Kim and Netessine (2013) and Wang and Liu (2016). However, it is difficult to reduce the cost of the final product if the production cost of the component is high. Thus, it is important to study how manufacturers motivate component suppliers to reduce the production cost. The existing literature has explored this topic. For example, in the researches of Kim and Netessine (2013) and Wang and Liu (2016), the manufacturer and the supplier collaboratively reduce components' production cost. Bernstein and Gürhan Kök (2009) show that buyers of components can subsidize a fraction of the investment cost. Hu *et al.* (2017) prove that the technology opening can induce suppliers to invest in cost reduction. However, these methods may be inefficient or unworkable in some situations (Wu *et al.*, 2020). In fact, if the orders of components are limited by the poor sales of the final product, it will be difficult to incentivize the supplier to improve the investment level. Manufacturer encroachment is considered to increase the total sales volume of products (Sun *et al.*, 2019). Therefore, we investigate the interaction between supplier investment and manufacturer encroachment and examine the effect of manufacturer encroachment on improving the investment level.

Several papers have investigated manufacturer encroachment that incorporates investment. For example, Arya and Mittendorf (2013) investigate the manufacturer's encroachment when the retailer can invest to alter its own and the rival's market demand. In their research, the investment serves to enlarge the market demand, thus they does not examine how downstream sales activities interact with upstream production activities. In contrast, the investment discussed in our work is implemented by the component supplier to reduce its production cost and examine how manufacturer encroachment should interact with the supplier's investment. In addition, Yoon (2016) and Sun *et al.* (2019) consider that the manufacturer can make cost-reducing investments. In their research, both investment and encroachment are conducted by the manufacturer. In contrast, this paper investigates the manufacturer encroachment strategy based on the supplier's investment strategy.

3. Model

We consider the model of a three-level supply chain consisting of one supplier, one manufacturer, and one retailer. The retailer purchases the products from the manufacturer, and then resells to the end consumers. Each product produced by the manufacturer requires one unit of key component from the supplier. In addition, the manufacturer has opportunities to encroach on the retailer's business by establishing its own channel and selling products to consumers directly. For instance, computer manufacturers, such as Lenovo, HP, and ASUS, have established their own company-owned franchises and online retail websites in addition to selling through retailers, such as Suning.com. And, producing each of their computers requires one CPU from a supplier, such as Intel. Figure 1 illustrates the channel structure under encroachment.

3.1. *Market demand*

If the manufacturer does not encroach, the inverse demand is given by $p_r = a - q_r$. If the manufacturer establishes a direct channel, then the supplier and the retailer engage in competition by selling the same product in different channels. Note that two channels can be completely or incompletely substitutable in the market. Therefore, we utilize the Cournot model, which is widely used in the literature related to channel competition (Yoon, 2016; Huang *et al.*, 2018; Tian *et al.*, 2018; Dong *et al.*, 2020), to characterize the competition of two channels. The demand functions of each channel are, respectively, given by

$$p_r = a - q_r - bq_d, \quad p_d = a - q_d - bq_r, \tag{1}$$

where a represents the market size, and p_i and q_i refer to the selling price and quantities in the channel $i(i = r, d)$, respectively. Subscripts "r" and "d" denote

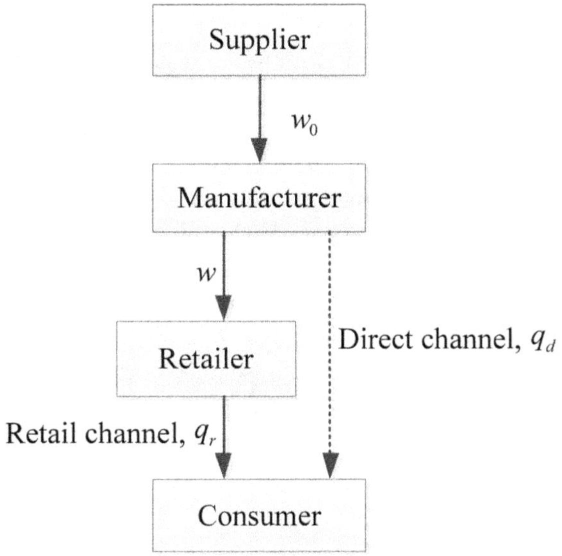

Fig. 1. Channel structure under manufacturer encroachment.

the retailer's channel and the direct channel, respectively. $b \in [0,1]$ captures the substitution degree of two channels. A higher b represents a greater competition between channels.

3.2. *Profit functions*

The supplier's production cost $c \in (0, a)$. The supplier can make cost-reduction efforts to reduce its production cost. Specifically, it can reduce its unit production cost to $c(1-x)$ with investment cost $\frac{1}{2}kx^2$, where $k \in (0,1)$ represents the supplier's efficiency in cost-reduction investment and x captures the cost investment level. A higher k means a lower efficiency of investment. This cost function is widely used in the literature (Ha *et al.*, 2017; Sun *et al.*, 2019). To avoid the trivial situation, we assume $k > k_0$ so that the supplier cannot always set x to 1 (Sun *et al.*, 2019), where $k_0 = \frac{ac(12-6b-b^2)}{4(8-3b^2)}$. We normalize the selling costs for the manufacturer and the retailer and the production cost for the manufacturer to zero (Dan *et al.*, 2014; Tian *et al.*, 2018). Thus, the profit functions of three firms are as follows:

$$\pi_S = (w_0 - c(1-x))(q_r + q_d) - \frac{1}{2}kx^2, \tag{2}$$

$$\pi_M = (w - w_0)q_r + (p_d - w_0)q_d - F, \tag{3}$$

$$\pi_R = (p_r - w)q_r, \tag{4}$$

where w_0 is the unit wholesale price of the key component set by the supplier and w is the unit wholesale price of the final product charged by the manufacturer. The term F captures the fixed cost of establishing the direct channel, which is common knowledge to all supply chain members. The fixed cost F includes the cost of maintaining an online website, training and enrolling a salesforce, or the cost of inventory and transportation of product (Huang *et al.*, 2018; Tian *et al.*, 2018).

The sequence of events and decisions is illustrated in Fig. 2. In stage 1, the supplier determines whether to invest to reduce the unit production cost. In stage 2, the manufacturer decides whether to encroach. In stage 3, the supplier sets the wholesale price of the key component. In stage 4, the manufacturer sets the wholesale price of the product. In stage 5, the retailer decides its order quantity, and the

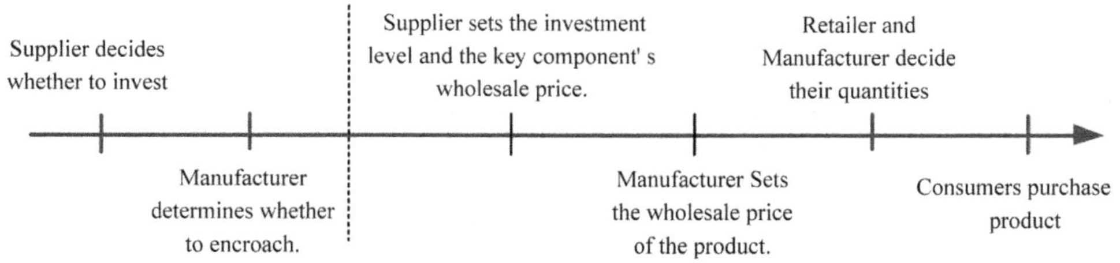

Fig. 2. Decision sequence.

manufacturer decides the direct channel quantity simultaneously (if necessary). In stage 6, the market clearing price is determined, and consumers buy the product.

4. Analysis

This section analyzes the interplay of manufacturer's encroachment and supplier's investment and its' impacts on the profits of members. Let superscripts NN, IN, NE, and IE denote the four possible scenarios, in which the first (second) letter refers to the supplier (manufacturer)'s choice; I denotes investment, E denotes encroachment, and N denotes no investment or no encroachment.

4.1. *Benchmark: No cost-reduction investment*

We first study the manufacturer's encroachment strategy if the supplier does not make investment to reduce its unit production cost. If the manufacturer does not encroach, the traditional retail channel is the only approach that the manufacturer uses to sell its product. In this setting, the retailer operates as a monopoly in the market. The problems of firms, respectively, are

$$\underset{q_r}{\text{Max}}\, q_r(a - q_r - w), \quad \underset{w}{\text{Max}}(w - w_0)q_r, \quad \pi_S = w_0 q_r. \tag{5}$$

Using backward induction, we obtain the optimal decision of each firm as

$$w_0^{NN} = \frac{a+c}{2}, \quad w^{NN} = \frac{3a+c}{4}, \quad q_r^{NN} = \frac{a-c}{8}, \tag{6}$$

and the equilibrium profits as

$$\pi_S^{NN} = \frac{(a-c)^2}{16}, \quad \pi_M^{NN} = \frac{(a-c)^2}{32}, \quad \pi_R^{NN} = \frac{(a-c)^2}{64}. \tag{7}$$

If the manufacturer encroaches, the retailer and the manufacturer compete with each other in the end market. Therefore, the retailer and the manufacturer maximize

$$\underset{q_r}{\text{Max}}\, q_r(a - q_r - bq_d - w), \quad \text{and} \tag{8}$$

$$\underset{q_d}{\text{Max}}[q_r(w - w_0) + q_d(a - q_d - bq_r - w_0) - F]. \tag{9}$$

Given the wholesale price w_0 of the component and the wholesale price w of the product, the retailer's and the manufacturer's quantities are given by

$$q_r^{NE}(w, w_0) = \frac{2(a-w) - b(a-w_0)}{4-b^2}, \quad q_d^{NE}(w, w_0) = \frac{2(a-w_0) - b(a-w)}{4-b^2}. \tag{10}$$

Substituting firms' quantities into the manufacturer's profit function, we can obtain that given w_0, its wholesale price is

$$w^{NE} = \frac{w_0(8 - 2b^2 - b^3) + a(2-b)(4+2b-b^2)}{2(8-3b^2)}. \tag{11}$$

Solving the maximized problem of the supplier yields the optimal key component's wholesale price as $w_0^{NE} = \frac{a+c}{2}$. Consequently, the wholesale price of the product and the optimal quantities are

$$w^{NE} = \frac{(24 - 10b^2 + b^3)a + c(8 - 2b^2 + b^3)}{4(8 - 3b^2)}, \tag{12}$$

$$q_r^{NE} = \frac{(a-c)(1-t)}{8 - 3b^2}, \quad q_d^{NE} = \frac{(a-c)(2-b)(4+b)}{4(8-3b^2)}. \tag{13}$$

Substituting all the decisions into firms' profit functions, we have firms' profits as

$$\pi_S^{NE} = \frac{(12 - 6b - b^2)(a-c)^2}{8(8-3b^2)}, \quad \pi_M^{NE} = \frac{(2-b)(6-b)(a-c)^2}{16(8-3b^2)} - F, \tag{14}$$

$$\pi_R^{NE} = \frac{(1-b)^2(a-c)^2}{(8-3b^2)^2}. \tag{15}$$

Comparing the manufacturer's profit with and without encroachment, we obtain the manufacturer's encroachment strategy under no cost-reduction investment.

Lemma 1. *Without investment, the manufacturer encroaches if* $F \leq F_N$*, in which* F_N *is strictly decreasing in the supplier's production cost* c*.*

Given that the supplier does not invest to reduce production costs, the manufacturer encroaches only when the entry cost is lower than F_N. If the supplier's production cost is low, it can charge a low wholesale price for the component. The low w_0^{NE} allows the manufacturer to earn more profits in the direct channel to cover the entry cost. Therefore, F_N is strictly decreasing in the supplier's production cost c. That is, the manufacturer is more likely to encroach in a lower c.

Lemma 2. *Without investment, the manufacturer's encroachment increases the supplier's profit, but it hurts the retailer's profit.*

The direct channel and the retailer channel are not perfectly substitutable if $b < 1$. Therefore, encroachment increases the total market size from a to $\frac{2a}{1+b}$. In addition, encroachment creates channel competition, which results in a higher total retail quantity even if the two channels are perfectly substitutable. The manufacturer needs to procure more components from the supplier to fulfill the demand. Therefore, the supplier always benefits from manufacturer encroachment. Regarding the retailer, the encroachment is detrimental to the retailer. The manufacturer's direct channel shares the market that originally belongs to the retailer. Unlike Arya *et al.* (2007), the retailer has no retail efficiency advantage in our setting, and even if the encroachment lowers the wholesale price of the product, it is not enough to make up the loss for a cut of sales of the retailer.

4.2. *Investment*

If the manufacturer does not encroach, the analysis is the same as in case *NN*, the retailer's quantity decision is $q_r^{IN}(w) = \frac{a-w}{2}$ and the manufacturer's product wholesale price decision is $w^{IN}(w_O) = \frac{a+w_O}{2}$. Anticipating downstream members' response, the supplier maximizes its profit

$$\operatorname*{Max}_{w_O,x}\left[(w_O - c(1-x))q_r^{IN}(w_O) - \frac{1}{2}kx^2\right], \tag{16}$$

which yields the optimal investment level $x^{IN} = \frac{c(a-c)}{8k-c^2}$ and the supplier's wholesale price $w_O^{IN} = \frac{4k(a+c)-ac^2}{8k-c^2}$. Consequently, the wholesale price of the product and the optimal order quantity of the retailer are

$$w^{IN} = \frac{a(6k-c^2)+2ck}{8k-c^2}, \quad q_r^{IN} = \frac{k(a-c)}{8k-c^2}. \tag{17}$$

Firms' equilibrium profits are

$$\pi_S^{IN} = \frac{k(a-c)^2}{2(8k-c^2)}, \quad \pi_M^{IN} = \frac{2k^2(a-c)^2}{(8k-c^2)^2}, \quad \pi_R^{IN} = \frac{k^2(a-c)^2}{(8k-c^2)^2}. \tag{18}$$

If the manufacturer encroaches, the retailer's order quantity, the manufacturer's direct channel quantity and the wholesale price of the product are the same as in case *NE* for a given w_O. However, the supplier's problem becomes

$$\operatorname*{Max}_{w_O,x}\left[(w_O - c(1-x))(q_r^{IE}(w_O) + q_d^{IE}(w_O)) - \frac{1}{2}kx^2\right]. \tag{19}$$

Therefore, the supplier's investment level and the wholesale price of the component are

$$x^{IE} = \frac{c(12-6b-b^2)(a-c)}{4(8-3b^2)k - c^2(12-6b-b^2)}, \tag{20}$$

$$w_O^{IE} = \frac{2(8-3b^2)(1+c)k - c^2(12-6b-b^2)}{4(8-3b^2)k - c^2(12-6b-b^2)}. \tag{21}$$

Consequently, the wholesale price of the product and the optimal quantities are

$$w^{IE} = \frac{((24-10b^2+)b^3k - (12-6b-b^2)c^2)a + (8-2b^2-b^3)ck}{4(8-3b^2)k - c^2(12-6b-b^2)}, \tag{22}$$

$$q_r^{IE} = \frac{4k(1-b)(a-c)}{4(8-3b^2)k - c^2(12-6b-b^2)}, \quad q_d^{IE} = \frac{k(4+b)(2-b)(a-c)}{4(8-3b^2)k - c^2(12-6b-b^2)}. \tag{23}$$

Firms' equilibrium profits are

$$\pi_S^{IE} = \frac{(12-6b-b^2)(a-c)^2k}{2(4(8-3b^2)k - c^2(12-6b-b^2))}, \tag{24}$$

$$\pi_M^{IE} = \frac{k^2(2-b)(6-b)(8-3b^2)(a-c)^2}{(4(8-3b^2)k - c^2(12-6b-b^2))^2} - F, \tag{25}$$

$$\pi_R^{IE} = \frac{16k^2(1-b)^2(a-c)^2}{(4(8-3b^2)k - c^2(12-6b-b^2))^2}. \tag{26}$$

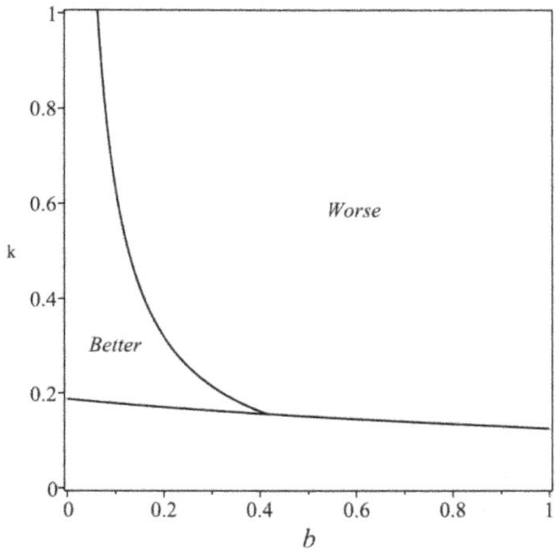

Fig. 3. Investment level under investment and no investment ($a = 1$, $c = 0.5$).

Obviously, the investment level in case *IE* is different from that in case *IN*. Comparing the investment levels in these two cases, we can obtain the following proposition.

Proposition 1. *The supplier's investment level with manufacturer encroachment is greater than that without manufacturer encroachment, that is,* $x^{IE} > x^{IN}$.

Proposition 1 indicates that the supplier invests more under encroachment than under no encroachment (see Fig. 3). The reason is that the total sales of final products with encroachment are higher than those without encroachment ($q_d^{IE} + q_r^{IE} > q_r^{IN}$). Since each unit product requires one unit component, the order quantities of the key components with encroachment are greater than those without encroachment. The increase in component orders makes it more profitable for the supplier to invest in reducing the unit production cost so that the supplier exerts a higher investment level if the manufacturer encroaches. In addition, x^{IE} is strictly decreasing in b because a higher substitution rate of two channels means a higher competition of these two channels. Intensified competition in the end market directly leads to a decrease in total sales, which thereby leads to a decrease in manufacturers' order for components and finally weakens the supplier's incentive to invest. This proposition reveals that manufacturer encroachment can help suppliers escape the dilemma of underinvestment.

Next, we present the manufacturer's encroachment strategy under supplier investment as Proposition 2.

Proposition 2. (a) *If the supplier invests to reduce the production cost of the key component, the manufacturer encroaches when* $F \leq F_I$, *where* F_I *decreases with* b.

(b) $F_I > F_N$, *compared with the case without investment, the region of manufacturer encroachment with investment is larger.*

Proposition 2 implies that the supplier's investment endows the manufacturer with more flexibility for encroaching. When the entry cost is low ($F \leq F_N$), the manufacturer should always encroach. When the entry cost is high ($F > F_I$), the manufacturer should never encroach. However, when the entry cost is moderate ($F_N < F \leq F_I$), the manufacturer's encroachment strategy relies on the supplier's investment strategy. Specifically, the manufacturer should encroach if the supplier invests, while he should not encroach if the supplier abandons to invest (see Fig. 4).

That is, the manufacturer is more likely to encroach when the supplier invests. The reason is as follows. The encroachment increases the sales of final products and thereby brings a higher order quantity of the component so that the supplier is willing to exert a higher investment level under encroachment than under no encroachment ($x^{IE} > x^{IN}$). The higher investment level allows the supplier to charge a lower components wholesale price, to induce the manufacturer order more components. Consequently, if the manufacturer encroaches, it can order the component at a much lower wholesale price ($w_0^{IE} < w_0^{IN}$). This dynamic implies that the supplier's investment can make the manufacturer's encroachment more profitable and relieve the pressure of the manufacturer's entry cost.

Furthermore, F_I decreases with b, which means that the effect of investment on the manufacturer increases with the substitution rate because a higher substitution results in lower sales of final products and lower orders of components, which consequently weakens the investment level of the supplier.

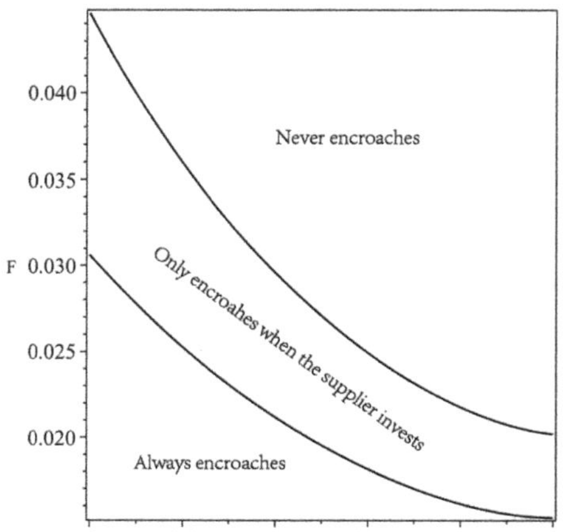

Fig. 4. Manufacturer's encroachment strategy under investment and no investment ($a = 1$, $c = 0.3$, $k = 0.25$).

In Lemma 2, we present that encroachment is always detrimental to the retailer. Proposition 3 shows that how it affects the retailer with supplier investment.

Proposition 3. *Under investment, manufacturer encroachment is beneficial to the retailer when* $k \leq k_1$ *and detrimental otherwise, where* $k_1 = \frac{(8-2b-b^2)c^2}{4b(8-3b)}$.

Proposition 3 shows that the manufacturer's encroachment is beneficial to the retailer when investment efficiency is high (see Fig. 4), because the interplay of encroachment and investment can induce an additional reduction in the wholesale price of the final product. Comparing the wholesale prices of the product under each case yields

$$w^{IN} - w^{IE} > w^{NN} - w^{NE}, \tag{27}$$

which confirms that the reduction of the wholesale price of the product with the supplier's investment is greater than that without the supplier's investment. Additionally, $w^{IN} - w^{IE}$ is decreasing in investment efficiency k as the investment level is increasing in k. That is, a higher investment efficiency means a greater reduction in the product's wholesale price induced by the encroachment. When the investment efficiency is high enough, w^{IE} is much lower than w^{IN}, so the retailer benefits from the manufacturer encroachment. However, if investment efficiency is low, the reduction in the wholesale price is weak, so manufacturer encroachment is still detrimental to the retailer.

Furthermore, k_1 decreases with the substitution rate b, which means that a lower channel substitution rate increases the likelihood that the retailer will benefit from the encroachment. On the one hand, the lower substitution rate, the retailer suffers less competition from the manufacturer's direct channel. On the other hand, a lower substitution rate will induce a higher investment level of the supplier.

Actually, manufacturer encroachment has two effects on the retailer: a negative effect in which the direct channel shares the consumer market and a positive effect in which encroachment can further reduce the wholesale price of the final product by attracting more investment of the supplier. When the positive effect dominates, the encroachment is beneficial to the retailer. Accordingly, supplier investment can not only allow the manufacturer to obtain more profits from encroachment but may also enable the manufacturer no need to worry about conflicts of interest with the retailer.

4.3. *Impacts of supplier investment*

In Sec. 4.2, we discuss the manufacturer's encroachment strategy under supplier investment. One might wonder the optimal investment strategy of the supplier. The answer is present in Proposition 4.

Proposition 4. *The supplier would always choose to invest in reducing production costs, and the best investment is* (a) x^{IE} *if* $F \leq F_I$ *and* (b) x^{IN} *if* $F > F_I$.

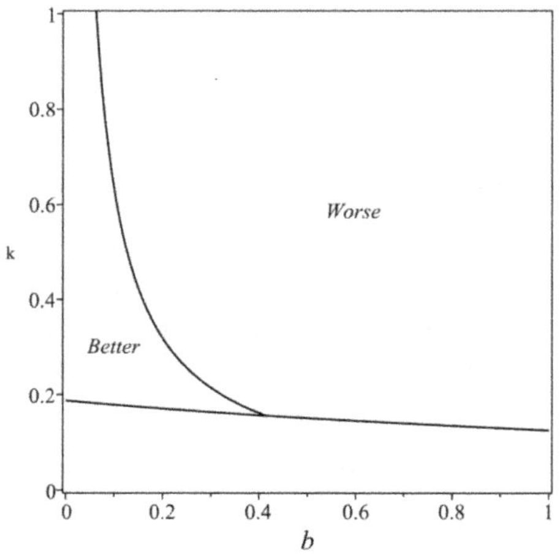

Fig. 5. Impact of manufacturer encroachment on the retailer's profit without investment ($a = 1$, $c = 0.5$).

When the entry cost is low ($F \leq F_N$), the manufacturer always encroaches, regardless of the supplier's investment decision. Anticipating the manufacturer's response, the supplier's best investment level is x^{IE}. When the entry cost is high ($F > F_I$), the manufacturer never encroaches regardless of whether the supplier invests. Anticipating the manufacturer's response, the supplier's best investment level is x^{IN}. When $F_N < F \leq F_I$, the manufacturer encroaches only if the supplier invests to reduce production costs. Owing to the increased sales of the product created by the dual channel, the supplier would like to exert a higher investment x^{IE}. In this case, in addition to the direct profits from the investment, the supplier also gains indirect profits from the encroachment. Consequently, the supplier is rewarded by investing in reducing production costs.

Of course, cost-reduction investment can enhance supply chain profits

$$\pi_S^{Ij} + \pi_M^{Ij} + \pi_R^{Ij} > [\pi_S^{Nj} + \pi_M^{Nj} + \pi_R^{Nj}](j = E, N). \tag{28}$$

However, for each supply chain member, the effect of supplier investment is not always positive owing to the existence of manufacturer encroachment. Proposition 5 presents the condition of Pareto gain.

Proposition 5. *Given* $k_2 = \frac{(12-6b-b^2)c^2}{4b(8-3b)}$, *investment and encroachment create a Pareto gain when* $F \leq F_N$ *and* $k < k_1$, $F_N < F \leq F_I$ *and* $k \leq k_2$, *or* $F > F_I$.

When $F \leq F_N$ and $F > F_I$, the manufacturer's encroachment strategy is independent of the supplier investment strategy. The manufacturer benefits from supplier investment. When $F_N < F \leq F_I$, the manufacturer maintains a dual channel only if the supplier invests. Supplier investment helps the manufacturer encroaches. In this case, the manufacturer benefits from both the encroachment and a lower component's wholesale price. As to the retailer, when $F \leq F_N$, the manufacturer always encroaches, which improves the retailer's profit only if $k < k_1$. When $F_N < F \leq F_I$, we have

$$\pi_R^{IE} - \pi_R^{NN} = -\frac{(a-c)^2\left(\frac{4(b+4)(3-3b)k}{(12-6b-b^2)} - c^2\right)\left(\frac{4(8-3b)bk}{(12-6b-b^2)} - c^2\right)}{64\left(\frac{4(8-3b^2)k}{(12-6b-b^2)} - c^2\right)^2}. \quad (29)$$

$\pi_R^{IE} \geq \pi_R^{NN}$ only when $k \leq k_2$. When $F > F_I$, the manufacturer never encroaches. Furthermore, both investment and encroachment are always profitable to the supplier. Consequently, investment and encroachment create a Pareto gain when $F \leq F_N$ and $k < k_1$, $F_N < F \leq F_I$ and $k \leq k_2$, or $F < F_I$, in which the supplier and manufacturer can both overcome their dilemmas (see Fig. 5).

5. Conclusions

This paper explores the interaction of component supplier cost-reduction investment and manufacturer encroachment to explore how to escape supply chain dilemmas. We demonstrate that when the manufacturer's entry cost is low or high, its encroachment strategy is independent to the supplier's investment decision. When the entry cost is moderate, the manufacturer should encroach if the supplier invests but should not encroach if the supplier does not invest. This proves that supplier investment can help the manufacturer encroach. Regarding the supplier, manufacturer encroachment is beneficial to the supplier regardless of whether the supplier invests. The supplier should exert a higher investment level if it anticipates that the manufacturer will encroach, while it should exert a lower investment level otherwise.

In addition, we examine the impact of manufacturer encroachment on the retailer. Without supplier investments, manufacturer encroachment always hurts the retailer. In contrast, when the supplier starts the investing, the profit of the cost reduction spills over to the manufacturer and retailer through the wholesale prices of components and products. The retailer may benefit from the encroachment since the encroachment encourages the supplier to invest more. That is, the supplier's cost-reduction investment can reduce potential interest conflicts between the manufacturer and the retailer. Accordingly, the manufacturer and supplier can help each other escape their dilemmas by applying encroachment and investment, respectively, thereby creating a Pareto gain.

This study makes theoretical contributions in three aspects. First, this research is one of the first to consider the impacts of the supplier investment on the manufacturer's encroachment decision, which extends the literature on manufacturer encroachment. The majority of past studies do not alleviate the manufacturer's dilemma regarding its encroachment primarily because these studies normally investigate the interaction between the manufacturer and retailer but do not consider the impacts of the component supplier, who is not involved in product distribution. This study finds that the supplier's cost-reduction investment can motivate the manufacturer to encroach on retail channels.

Second, this study adds new insights to the suppliers' strategy of cost-reduction investments in the supply chain. Although previous studies attempted to explore how cooperation between the manufacturer and supplier motivates the supplier to improve its investment level, they usually ignored the side effects, such as opportunistic behaviors, managerial complexity of joint activities, which can lead to the failure of cooperation or investment enhancement (Wu *et al.*, 2020). Our work abandons the traditional perspective, which limits itself to cooperation between firms, and investigates how the manufacturer encroachment can boost the supplier's investment in cost reduction.

Third, this study enriches the literature on the impact of manufacturer encroachment by identifying a new interesting condition in which the supplier's investments in cost-reduction production can help the manufacturer's encroachment benefit the retailer. Traditional studies usually argue that manufacturer encroachment is detrimental to retailers (Park and Keh, 2003; Liu and Zhang, 2006). Unfortunately, many of those studies have not reflected the business reality because they ignore the impacts of the component supplier. Compared with these previous views, we find that manufacturer encroachment may create a Pareto gain to the supply chain by considering the supplier's cost-reduction investment. Further, a few extreme conditions, e.g., efficient retailer, nonlinear pricing, channel power, have been previously reported in which the manufacturer's encroachment may benefit the retailer (Arya *et al.*, 2007; Li *et al.*, 2015; Niu *et al.*, 2017). Our work goes beyond those studies and argues that the benefits of the manufacturer encroachment still hold in common three-tier supply chains.

The practical implications of this work are as follows. First, for manufacturers with moderate entry costs, they should encroach when the supplier invests. Due to the concern of direct selling costs and possible conflicts with retailers, many manufacturers have abandoned direct selling channels in the past. However, in the era of Industry 4.0, suppliers are engaged in investing in new technologies to build smart factories, which can effectively reduce production costs. According to our studies, encroachment can benefit both the manufacturer and retailer when the supplier invests in cost-reduction technologies, thus providing opportunities for manufacturers to encroach.

Second, the supplier should maintain a relatively low investment level if the manufacturer does not encroach on retailing. However, if the manufacturer encroaches, then suppliers should exert a relatively high investment in cost-reduction technologies. If the manufacturer encroaches after the supplier starts to invest, then the supplier can raise its investment, which has a positive effect on the whole supply chain.

Third, the retailer should be more optimistic about manufacturer encroachment when the component supplier is committed to investing in cost-reduction technologies because the manufacturer's encroachment can be beneficial to the retailer when the supplier's investment efficiency is high. In this case, the retailer does not need to prevent the manufacturer from encroaching.

Our research has some limitations. First, demand uncertainty, information asymmetry and general cost structures are not considered in our model. These factors can be expanded in future research. In addition, it could be interesting to examine manufacturer encroachment and supplier investment in the competitive supply chain.

Appendix A

Proof of Proposition 2. Given that the supplier invests to reduce production costs, we compare the profit of the manufacturer under encroachment with no encroachment.

$$\pi_M^{IE} - \pi_M^{IN} = \frac{k^2(a-c)^2\begin{pmatrix}32k(8-3b^2)((16-16b+5b^2)k+(1-b)bc^2)\\ -(192-224b+52b^2+5b^4)c^4\end{pmatrix}}{(4(8-3b^2)k-(12-6b-b^2)c^2)^2(8k-c^2)^2} - F.$$

Let

$$F_I = \frac{k^2(a-c)^2\begin{pmatrix}32k(8-3b^2)((16-16b+5b^2)k+(1-b)bc^2)\\ -(192-224b+52b^2+5b^4)c^4\end{pmatrix}}{(4(8-3b^2)k-(12-6b-b^2)c^2)^2(8k-c^2)^2}.$$

$\pi_M^{IE} \geq \pi_M^{IN}$ only if $F \geq F_I$. Differentiating F_I with regard to k and b, we obtain $\frac{\partial F_I}{k} < 0$ and $\frac{\partial F_I}{b} < 0$. Therefore, F_I decreases with k and b.

Given no investment, we compare the profit of the manufacturer under encroachment with no encroachment.

$$\pi_M^{NE} - \pi_M^{NN} = \frac{(a-c)^2(16-16b+5b^2)}{32(8-3b^2)} - F.$$

Let $F_N = \frac{(a-c)^2(16-16b+5b^2)}{32(8-3b^2)}$. $\pi_M^{NE} \geq \pi_M^{NN}$ only if $F \geq F_N$. Comparing thresholds F_I and F_N, we have $F_I > F_N$. □

Proof of Proposition 3. Given that the supplier invests to reduce production costs, we compare the profit of the retailer under encroachment with no encroachment.

$$\pi_R^{IE} - \pi_R^{IN} = \frac{(a-c)^2k^2f_1(k)}{(4(8-3b^2)k-(12-6b-b^2)c^2)^2(8k-c^2)^2},$$

where $f_1(k) = -(4(8-3b)kb-(4+b)(2-b)c^2)(4(b+4)(4-3b)k-(16-10b-b^2)c^2)$. Solving $f_1(k) = 0$, we obtain two roots k_1 and k_1', where

$$k_1 = \frac{(8-2b-b^2)c^2}{4b(8-3b)}, \quad k_1' = \frac{(16-10b-b^2)c^2}{4(16-8b-3b^2)}.$$

Obviously, $k_1' < k_0 < k_1$ if $c > c'$, and $k_1' < k_1 < k_0$ if $c < c'$. Hence, $f_1(k) \geq 0$ and $\pi_R^{IE} \geq \pi_R^{IN}$ when $k_0 < k \leq k_1$, and $f_1(k) < 0$ and $\pi_R^{IE} < \pi_R^{IN}$ when $k > k_1$. □

Proof of Proposition 4. As $F_I > F_N$, we get the following results:

(a) When $F \leq F_N$, the manufacturer always encroaches regardless of whether the supplier invests. Anticipated manufacturer's response, the supplier determines its investment strategy by comparing its profit under the case of *IE* with that under the case of *NE*.

$$\pi_S^{IE} - \pi_S^{NE} = \frac{(12-6b-b^2)^2(a-c)^2c^2}{8(4(8-3b^2)k-(12-6b-b^2)c^2)(8-3b^2)}.$$

Thus, we have $\pi_S^{IE} > \pi_S^{NE}$ in the feasible region. Therefore, the supplier chooses to invest with the investment level $x = x^{IE}$.

(b) When $F > F_I$, the manufacturer always encroaches regardless of whether the supplier invests. Anticipated manufacturer's response, the supplier determines its investment strategy by comparing its profit under the case of *IN* with that under the case of *NN*.

$$\pi_S^{IN} - \pi_S^{NN} = \frac{(a-c)^2c^2}{16(8k-c^2)}.$$

Obviously, we have $\pi_S^{IN} > \pi_S^{NN}$ in the feasible region. Thus, the supplier chooses to invest with the investment level $x = x^{IN}$.

(c) When $F_N < F \leq F_I$, the manufacturer encroaches if the supplier invests, while the manufacturer does not encroach if the supplier does not invest. Anticipated manufacturer's response, the supplier determines its investment strategy by comparing its profit under the case of *IE* with that under the case of *NN*.

$$\pi_S^{IE} - \pi_S^{NN} = \frac{(a-c)^2(4k(b^2-12b+16)+(12-6b-b^2)c^2)}{16(4(8-3b^2)k-(12-6b-b^2)c^2)}. \quad \square$$

Proof of Proposition 5. (a) When $F \leq F_N$, we compare the manufacturer's profit and the retailer's profit under the case of *IE* with that under the case of *NE*.

$$\pi_M^{IE} - \pi_M^{NE} = \frac{(6-b)(2-b)(a-c)^2c^2(12-6b-b^2)(8(8-3b^2)k-(12-6b-b^2)c^2)}{(4(8-3b^2)k-(12-6b-b^2)c^2)^2(3b^2-8)}$$

and

$$\pi_R^{IE} - \pi_R^{NE} = \frac{(1-b)^2(a-c)^2c^2(12-6b-b^2)(8(8-3b^2)k-(12-6b-b^2)c^2)}{(4(8-3b^2)k-(12-6b-b^2)c^2)^2(3b^2-8)^2}.$$

Thus, $\pi_M^{IE} > \pi_M^{NE}$ and $\pi_R^{IE} > \pi_R^{NE}$ if $k > \frac{(12-6b-b^2)c^2}{8(8-3b^2)k}$. Since $\frac{(12-6b-b^2)c^2}{8(8-3b^2)k} < k_0$, we always have $\pi_M^{IE} > \pi_M^{NE}$ and $\pi_R^{IE} > \pi_R^{NE}$.

(b) When $F > F_I$, we compare the manufacturer's profit and the retailer's profit under the case of *IN* with that under the case of *NN*.

$$\pi_M^{IN} - \pi_M^{NN} = \frac{(a-c)^2c^2(16k-c^2)}{32(8k-c^2)^2} \quad \text{and} \quad \pi_R^{IN} - \pi_R^{NN} = \frac{(a-c)^2c^2(16k-c^2)}{64(8k-c^2)^2}.$$

Obviously, $\pi_M^{IN} > \pi_M^{NN}$ and $\pi_R^{IN} > \pi_R^{NN}$.

(c) When $F_N < F \leq F_I$, we compare the retailer's profit under the case of *IE* with that under the case of *NN*.

$$\pi_M^{IE} - \pi_M^{NN} = \frac{(a-c)^2 \begin{pmatrix} c^4(12-6t-t^2)^2 + 8c^2(12-6t-t^2)(8-3t^2)k \\ +16(8-3t^2)(5t^2-16t+16)k^2 \end{pmatrix}}{32(4(8-3b^2)k-(12-6b-b^2)c^2)^2} - F$$

and

$$\pi_R^{IE} - \pi_R^{NN} = -\frac{(a-c)^2 \begin{pmatrix} 4(b+4)(3-3b)k \\ -c^2(12-6b-b^2) \end{pmatrix} \begin{pmatrix} 4(8-3b)bk \\ -c^2(12-6b-b^2) \end{pmatrix}}{64(4(8-3b^2)k-(12-6b-b^2)c^2)^2}.$$

We proof that $\pi_M^{IE} > \pi_M^{NN}$ is hold when $F_N < F \leq F_I$. Solving $\pi_R^{IE} - \pi_R^{NN} = 0$, we obtain two roots k_2 and k_2', where

$$k_2 = \frac{(12-6b-b^2)c^2}{4b(8-3b)}, \quad k_2' = \frac{(12-6b-b^2)c^2}{4(16-8b-3b^2)}.$$

Obviously, $k_2' < k_0 < k_2$ if $c > c''$, and $k_2' < k_2 < k_0$ if $c < c''$. Hence, $\pi_R^{IE} \geq \pi_R^{NN}$ when $k_0 < k \leq k_2$, and $\pi_R^{IE} < \pi_R^{IN}$ when $k > k_2$. □

Appendix B

In the main model, we assume that the production cost of the manufacturer is normalized to zero. One might be concerned if the insights of the base model still hold considering that the cost is not equal to zero. We analyze this case in detail in the following.

First, we assume that the production cost of the manufacturer is $m > 0$. The equilibrium profits of firms under such cases can be solved and represented as $\tilde{\pi}_M^j = \frac{\pi_M^j(a-m-c)^2+Fm(m-2(a-c))}{(a-c)^2}$ and $\tilde{\pi}_i^j = \frac{\pi_i^j(a-m-c)^2}{(a-c)^2}$, where $i = S, R$ and $j = NN, NE, IN, IE$. Let $\tilde{F}_N = \tilde{\pi}_M^{NE} - \tilde{\pi}_M^{NN}$ and $\tilde{F}_I = \tilde{\pi}_M^{IE} - \tilde{\pi}_M^{IN}$. Then, if the supplier does not invest in cost reduction, the manufacturer encroaches when $F < \tilde{F}_N$, where $\tilde{F}_N = \frac{(a-m-c)^2(16-16b+5b^2)}{256-96b^2}$. If the supplier invests to reduce the production cost of the key component, the manufacturer encroaches when $F \leq \tilde{F}_I$, where

$$\tilde{F}_I = \frac{k^2(a-m-c)^2 \begin{pmatrix} 32k(8-3b^2)((16-16b+5b^2)k+(1-b)bc^2) \\ -(192-224b+52b^2+5b^4)c^4 \end{pmatrix}}{(4(8-3b^2)k-(12-6b-b^2)c^2)^2(8k-c^2)^2}$$

and $\tilde{F}_I$ decreases with b. (b) $\tilde{F}_I > \tilde{F}_N$, compared with the case without investment, the region of manufacturer encroachment with investment is larger. Accordingly, when $F \leq \tilde{F}_N$ ($F > \tilde{F}_I$), the manufacturer should (should not) encroach regardless of the investment strategy of the supplier. However, when $\tilde{F}_N < F \leq \tilde{F}_I$, the manufacturer should encroach if the supplier invests, and it should not encroach if the supplier does not invest. Thus, Proposition 2 still holds when the production cost is not equal to zero.

Second, given that the supplier does not invest to reduce production costs, we compare the profits of the retailer and the supplier under encroachment with no encroachment and obtain

$$\tilde{\pi}_R^{NE} - \tilde{\pi}_R^{NN} = -\frac{(a-m-c)^2 b(4-3b)(b+4)(8-3b)}{64(8-3b^2)^2} \quad \text{and}$$

$$\tilde{\pi}_S^{NE} - \tilde{\pi}_S^{NN} = \frac{(a-m-c)^2(16-12b+b^2)}{16(8-3b^2)}.$$

Given that the supplier invests to reduce production cost, we compare the profit of the retailer and the supplier under encroachment with no encroachment and obtain

$$\tilde{\pi}_R^{IE} - \tilde{\pi}_R^{IN} = \frac{(a-m-c)^2 k^2 f_1(k)}{(4(8-3b^2)k-(12-6b-b^2)c^2)^2(8k-c^2)^2} \quad \text{and}$$

$$\tilde{\pi}_S^{IE} - \tilde{\pi}_S^{IN} = \frac{2k^2(a-m-c)^2(16-12b+b^2)}{(4(8-3b^2)k-(12-6b-b^2)c^2)^2(8k-c^2)^2}.$$

Obviously, $\tilde{\pi}_R^{NE} < \tilde{\pi}_R^{NN}$, $\tilde{\pi}_S^{NE} > \tilde{\pi}_S^{NN}$, $\tilde{\pi}_S^{IE} > \tilde{\pi}_S^{IN}$. Also, $\tilde{\pi}_R^{IE} > \tilde{\pi}_R^{IN}$ if $k \leq k_1$. Therefore, Proposition 3 still holds under the condition of $m > 0$.

Third, we examine the investment strategy of the supplier. The supplier will always invest, and if the entry cost of the manufacturer is low ($F \leq \tilde{F}_I$), the supplier should exert a higher investment level $\tilde{x}^{IE}$; and if the entry cost is high ($F > \tilde{F}_I$), the supplier should exert a lower investment level $\tilde{x}^{IN}$, where $\tilde{x}^{IE} > \tilde{x}^{IN}$, $\tilde{x}^{IN} = \frac{c(a-c)}{8k-c^2}$, and $\tilde{x}^{IE} = \frac{c(12-6b-b^2)(a-c)}{4(8-3b^2)k-c^2(12-6b-b^2)}$. Investment and encroachment create a Pareto gain when $F \leq \tilde{F}_N$ and $k < k_1$, $\tilde{F}_N < F \leq \tilde{F}_I$ and $k \leq k_2$, or $F > \tilde{F}_I$. Therefore, Propositions 1, 4, and 5 can also hold when the production cost of the manufacturer is not equal to 1.

Acknowledgments

The authors thank the editors and the review team for their valuable comments that have significantly improved the quality of this work. This work was supported by the National Natural Science Foundation of China (Grant Number 71672153).

References

Arya, A and B Mittendorf (2013). The changing face of distribution channels: Partial forward integration and strategic investments. *Production and Operations Management*, 22(5), 1077–1088.

Arya, A, B Mittendorf and DEM Sappington (2007). The bright side of supplier encroachment. *Marketing Science*, 26(5), 651–659.

Bernstein, F and A Gürhan Kök (2009). Dynamic cost reduction through process improvement in assembly networks. *Management Science*, 55(4), 552–567.

Dahan, E and V Srinivasan (2011). The impact of unit cost reductions on gross profit: Increasing or decreasing returns? *IIMB Management Review*, 23(3), 131–139.

Dan, B, C Liu, G Xu and X Zhang (2014). Pareto improvement strategy for service-based free-riding in a dual-channel supply chain. *Asia-Pacific Journal of Operational Research*, 31(6), 339–340.

Dong, C, L Yang and CT Ng (2020). Quantity leadership for a dual-channel supply chain with retail service. *Asia-Pacific Journal of Operational Research*, 37(2), 1–32.

Frazier, GL and WM Lassar (1996). Determinants of distribution intensity. *Journal of Marketing*, 60(4), 39–51.

Gupta, S (2008). Research note-channel structure with knowledge spillovers. *Marketing Science*, 27(2), 247–261.

Ha, A, X Long and J Nasiry (2016). Quality in supply chain encroachment. *Manufacturing & Service Operations Management*, 18(2), 280–298.

Ha, AY, Q Tian and S Tong (2017). Information sharing in competing supply chains with production cost reduction. *Manufacturing & Service Operations Management*, 19(2), 246–262.

Hu, B, M Hu and Y Yang (2017). Open or closed? Technology sharing, supplier investment, and competition. *Manufacturing & Service Operations Management*, 19(1), 132–149.

Hu, J, Q Hu and Y Xia (2019). Who should invest in cost reduction in supply chains? *International Journal of Production Economics*, 207, 1–18.

Huang, S, X Guan and YJ Chen (2018). Retailer information sharing with supplier encroachment. *Production and Operations Management*, 27(6), 1133–1147.

Kim, SH and S Netessine (2013). Collaborative cost-reduction and component procurement under information asymmetry. *Management Science*, 59(1), 189–206.

Li, T, J Xie and X Zhao (2015). Supplier encroachment in competitive supply chains. *International Journal of Production Economics*, 165, 120–131.

Li, Z, SM Gilbert and G Lai (2014). Supplier encroachment under asymmetric information. *Management Science*, 60(2), 449–462.

Liker, JK and TY Choi (2004). Building deep supplier relationships. *Harvard Business Review*, 82(12), 295–310.

Liu, Y and ZJ Zhang (2006). Research note — The benefits of personalized pricing in a channel. *Marketing Science*, 25(1), 97–105.

Niu, B, Q Cui and J Zhang (2017). Impact of channel power and fairness concern on supplier's market entry decision. *Journal of the Operational Research Society*, 68(12), 1570–1581.

Park, SY and HT Keh (2003). Modeling hybrid distribution channels: A game-theoretic analysis. *Journal of Retailing and Consumer Services*, 10(3), 155–167.

Sun, X, W Tang, J Chen, S Li and J Zhang (2019). Manufacturer encroachment with production cost reduction under asymmetric information. *Transportation Research Part E: Logistics and Transportation Review*, 128, 191–211.

Tian, L, AJ Vakharia, YR Tan and Y Xu (2018). Marketplace, reseller, or hybrid: Strategic analysis of an emerging e-commerce model. *Production and Operations Management*, 27(8), 1595–1610.

Wang, S and F Liu (2016). Cooperative innovation in a supply chain with different market power structures. *American Journal of Operations Research*, 6(2), 173–198.

Wu, Y, F Gu, Y Ji, J Guo and Y Fan (2020). Technological capability, eco-innovation performance, and cooperative R&D strategy in new energy vehicle industry: Evidence from listed companies in China. *Journal of Cleaner Production*, 261, 121157.

Xiong, Y, W Yan, K Fernandes, ZK Xiong and N Guo (2012). "Bricks versus Clicks": The impact of manufacturer encroachment with a dealer leasing and selling of durable goods. *European Journal of Operational Research*, 217(1), 75–83.

Yoon, DH (2016). Supplier encroachment and investment spillovers. *Production and Operations Management*, 25(11), 1839–1854.

Biography

Qijun Wang is a PhD student of Southwest Jiaotong University, China. She is interested in supply chain management. One of her work has been published in the journal JORS.

Jiajia Nie is working as a professor and vice dean of the School of Economics and Management, Southwest Jiaotong University, China. He specializes in logistics and supply chain management. His research literatures have been published in journals such as IJPE, IJPR, JORS, CIE, and JCP.

Senmao Xia is an Associate Professor at International Center for Transformational Entrepreneurship and Center for Business in Society, Coventry University, UK. He served as the chair of the 31st Chinese Economic Association (UK/Europe) Annual Conference. Senmao acts as the Managing Editor for International Journal of Chinese Culture and Management and Journal of Chinese Economic and Business Studies. He is the guest editor for Technovation and International Journal of Technology Management. Senmao is the Senior Fellow of Higher Education Academy (UK).

https://doi.org/10.1142/9789819808588_0009

Chapter 9

Equilibrium Pricing, Advertising, and Quality Strategies in a Platform Service Supply Chain†

Yong He*

School of Economics and Management
Southeast University, Nanjing 210096, P. R. China
hy@seu.edu.cn

Yanan Yu

School of Economics and Management
Southeast University, Nanjing 210096, P. R. China
1543775224@qq.com

Zhongyuan Wang

School of Economics and Management
Southeast University, Nanjing 210096, P. R. China
313058838@qq.com

Henry Xu

UQ Business School
The University of Queensland, Brisbane
QLD 4072, Australia
h.xu@business.uq.edu.au

Online-to-Offline service platforms are rising with the development of e-commerce and the increasing need for service. Taking the hospitality and tourism industries as typical examples, this paper considers a platform service supply chain, where a leading hotel is responsible for offline service, and a following platform is in charge of pricing, online service, and advertising investment. Three decision modes (i.e., decentralized, cost-sharing, and integrated) for the platform service supply chain are investigated. We derive the optimal service levels for the hotel and the platform, advertising investment, and retail price in each mode. Our analyses indicate that perceived service quality and brand image vary over time, and they gradually converge to a steady-state. The cost-sharing mode can be achieved if the hotel can obtain enough profit per unit. Once the cost-sharing mode is achieved, it can help improve perceived service quality and brand image, which

*Corresponding author.
†To cite this article, please refer to its earlier version published in the Asia-Pacific Journal of Operational Research, Vol. 39, No. 1, (February 2022), DOI: 10.1142/S0217595921400315. Reprinted with permission from World Scientific Publishing Co. Pte. Ltd.

further increases both the hotel and the platform's profits. However, the integrated mode generates the best-perceived service quality, brand image, supply chain performance, and the lowest price.

Keywords: Pricing; advertising; quality strategy; platform service supply chain.

1. Introduction

Industry 4.0 can give personalized attention and fast service to customers via artificial intelligence.[a] Meanwhile, the Internet has played an important role in providing services, some of which are provided fully online (Marimon *et al.*, 2019). With the advancement of Industry 4.0, the Internet of Things and more diverse business models, companies can reinvent the way they run their business and serve their B2B and B2C customers.[b] For example, with the rapid development of e-commerce, Online-to-Offline (O2O) platforms have gained increasing popularity in recent years. Particularly supported by technologies such as digitization and artificial intelligence, the service platform (SP) as a new business model has developed rapidly (Liu *et al.*, 2021). More and more companies, especially in the service industry (e.g., hospitality and tourism), have distributed their services and products through online platforms to expand their markets. Online travel as one typical service industry has gained wide recognition of its importance with growing sales all over the world during the past years. Platform service supply chain, e.g., travel platform, provides online and offline services simultaneously, which both affect customer-perceived value. Wilkins *et al.* (2007) concluded that hotel service quality includes physical product factors (e.g., stylish comfort, room quality, added extras) and service experience factors (e.g., quality staff, speedy service, and personalization). Online service includes website design (Hahn *et al.*, 2017) and interface interactivity (Ku and Chen, 2015). These services can affect the perceived customer service quality through interaction and feedback. Meanwhile, prior research suggests that the perceived value presents a dynamic nature (Eid, 2015; Tsai *et al.*, 2015). Facing changing customer satisfaction, companies in travel supply chains should take on continuous service improvement. Therefore, traditional models considering customer-perceived quality in a static and short-term situation do not hold in reality.

In addition to perceived service quality, brand image also plays a critical role in demand. Researchers have recognized that brand equity results from long-term interactions between brands and relevant customers (Davcik *et al.*, 2015). Brand value is also crucial in the hotel industry, which can greatly affect consumer behavior through a long-run marketing strategy (Xu and Chan, 2010). In an O2O travel, hotels can establish and keep vigorous brand values via virtual interactions when customers browse their websites. Therefore, the platform's online advertisement can help build the hotel's brand. Liu and Mattila (2017) also demonstrated that

[a]https://global.hitachi-solutions.com/blog/industry-4-0-technologies-outcomes-and-the-future-of-manufacturing.
[b]https://atos.net/en/solutions/industry-4-0-the-industrial-internet-of-things.

online and dynamic advertising is crucial in building a good brand since consumers have become more dependent on social media in purchasing services. In fact, more and more advertising expenditure has been invested in the service industry. The cooperative advertising program has proven to be a vital tool for the hotel industry to promote their businesses and take full advantage of all available cost-saving opportunities.[c] Inspired by the real business problems, we formulate the function of brand image, and further study the mode of cooperative advertising in a platform service supply chain.

Jena and Meena (2019) pointed out that market demand is always sensitive to price and service. Consequently, the perceived quality, brand image, and the price will jointly affect customer demand. Against this background, this paper studies the platform service supply chain made up of a leading hotel and a following travel agency platform. A hotel, such as Hilton, may play a more dominant role than its SP. To simplify the exposition, we use SS to denote the hotel and SP to represent the service platform. Since perceived service quality and brand image are dynamic in the long term, this paper uses differential game models to study SS's offline service effort, SP's online service effort, pricing as well as advertising decisions. People can book hotel rooms on Hilton's official website, which can be considered as the integrated mode where SS and SP cooperate in advertising investment through an integrated way to maximize the profit of a supply chain. The online travel agency, such as Booking.com, can also provide Hilton's booking service, which is the decentralized mode as SP and SS make their own decisions such as pricing, service effort, or advertising investment, respectively. The third mode is the cost-sharing mode, which is commonly seen between a tour operator and an online travel agency, where the hotel shares a portion of the advertising costs with the platform. Cooperative advertising in a tourism supply chain can exist across different levels (e.g., between a hotel and a tour operator) or at the same level (e.g., between hotels). In this paper, we compare three modes (decentralized, cost-sharing, and integrated) from different aspects and mainly address the following research questions:

(1) How do the brand image and the perceived service quality change over time?
(2) What are the equilibrium outcomes in a decentralized, cost-sharing, and integrated mode, respectively?
(3) Which mode suits best for a particular member of the platform service supply chain?

The main contributions of this paper are as follows. (1) This paper provides a modified function of perceived quality related to online and offline service efforts and depicts the change process of perceived quality in a dynamic environment. Besides, we construct a demand function affected negatively by the retail price and positively by perceived service quality and brand image. (2) This paper compares three modes in dealing with advertising costs, namely, decentralized, cost-sharing, and

[c]https://www.sunny.org/partners/co-op-advertising/.

integrated modes. We also confirm that the hotel sharing a portion of advertising costs can improve its brand image under a cost-sharing contract and achieve Pareto improvement. Moreover, if the hotel and the SP act as an integrated unit, the platform service supply chain can achieve the best-perceived service quality and the best brand image, and the lowest price.

This paper is arranged as follows. In Sec. 2, the related literature is reviewed. Section 3 presents the assumptions and notations. In Sec. 4, three modes are formulated and the optimal decisions are determined. Section 5 presents a comparison of different modes. Simulations and sensitivity analysis are conducted in Sec. 6, and conclusions and further study are presented in Sec. 7.

2. Literature Review

2.1. *Platform service supply chain*

The service supply chain has received much attention in the operations research literature in recent years. Wang *et al.* (2015) provided a detailed review on this topic. Some researchers have started to focus on the SP's value co-creation. For example, Smedlund (2012) explored value co-creation by platforms based on different business models and illustrated the arguments using the video game industry. Barrett *et al.* (2016) explored the process of value creation in an online community over time and found participants engaged in the online community and evolving technology affect value creation. Ma *et al.* (2019) conceptualized the value co-creation between governments, sharing business firms and consumers in the sharing economy. Some researchers focused on the platform's pricing decisions. Radhi and Zhang (2018) investigated optimal pricing policies considering same- and cross-channel returns in a centralized or decentralized dual-channel. Liu *et al.* (2019) studied the pricing decision considering the provider's threshold participating quantity, value-added service, and matching ability by profit maximization. Some researchers focused on the platform's advertising decisions. Hao *et al.* (2017) studied the co-app advertising and agency pricing strategy between a platform and an app developer with an advertising revenue-sharing contract. Li *et al.* (2019) investigated cooperative advertising strategies in an O2O supply chain consisting of a seller and an online platform agent, and compared the integration model, unilateral co-op advertising model, and bilateral co-op advertising model. Xiang and Xu (2019) studied research and development, advertising, and big data marketing strategy in a platform service supply chain consisting of a manufacturer, a retailer, and an Internet SP.

The above-reviewed research works mainly focused on value co-creation and pricing policies in the SP. Some researchers such as Barrett *et al.* (2016) also considered the long-term process of value creation. However, they have neglected the time-varying perceived service quality in the platform, which constitutes one of the main contributions of this paper. Our paper examines the co-creation of perceived service quality in a dynamic and long-term environment.

2.2. *Perceived service quality*

Parasuraman *et al.* (1988) stated that service quality can be described through reliability, assurance, tangibles, empathy, and responsiveness. Furthermore, in defining online service quality, researchers suggested that e-service quality consists of the following aspects: website design (Hahn *et al.*, 2017), information quality (Xu *et al.*, 2013), and interface interactivity (Ku and Chen, 2015). Collier and Bienstock (2006) concluded that e-service quality includes the delivery of the desired product or service, online process quality (including functionality, information accuracy, design, privacy, and ease of use), and service failure recovery. Tsao *et al.* (2016) used the case of online shopping experience in Taiwan to study the effect of e-service quality on online loyalty. They indicated that system quality and electronic service quality play important roles in customer-perceived value, which further affects online loyalty. Cheng *et al.* (2018) investigated the factors affecting online and offline service quality in a sharing economy-driven car-hailing commerce. Anwar *et al.* (2019) studied the case of the Chinese banking industry and pointed out that organizations should provide good service quality at a fair price and create a good brand image to satisfy customers. The above literature is based on empirical studies. Some researchers also studied the problem of service and pricing from the perspective of operations management in the hospitality and tourism industries. García and Tugores (2006) developed a vertical differentiation model where hotels compete in both quality and prices. Jena and Meena (2019) studied a tourism supply chain consisting of a common local operator and two tour operators competing on price and service. Furthermore, a decentralized scenario, an integrated channel scenario and a global scenario were comparatively analyzed.

Although research indicates that perceived value shows dynamic nature (Eid, 2015; Tsai *et al.*, 2015), there are currently few papers that investigate long-term and dynamic perceived quality from the perspective of operations management, which is another research gap that is addressed by this study. Furthermore, we also study the value of cooperation in creating brand value.

2.3. *Dynamic cooperative advertising*

Jørgensen and Zaccour (2014) surveyed research on cooperative advertising with game-theoretic methods and found that it transforms to dynamic decisions. Some researchers have concentrated on the supply chain structure and supply chain members' decision behavior. Chutani and Sethi (2018) studied a Stackelberg differential game with multiple leading manufacturers and multiple following retailers. The manufacturers are in a Nash game to determine the subsidy rate, and the retailers are also in a Nash game to determine their optimal advertising efforts. Sigué and Chintagunta (2009) studied a franchise system made up of a franchisor and two competing franchisees considering a cooperative advertising problem. Chutani and Sethi (2012b) studied dynamic cooperative advertising strategy in a supply chain consisting of a manufacturer and N competing retailers.

Jørgensen *et al.* (2000, 2001) studied a model where both channel members make long-term or short-term advertising decisions to enhance sales and consumer goodwill. Zhang *et al.* (2013) studied the effect of reference price effect in a manufacturer–retailer supply chain through a dynamic cooperative advertising model. Zhang *et al.* (2017) combined the participation rate and the accrual rate in a dynamic cooperative advertising model. Shen *et al.* (2019) studied the optimal advertising and pricing decisions for new green products in the circular economy.

Some papers considered the negative effects of promotion on brand image. Jørgensen *et al.* (2003) found that cooperative advertising still works if the retailer's advertisement could damage the brand image. Huang *et al.* (2018) considered the cooperative advertisement in a supply chain made up of a manufacturer and two competing retailers. It was found that the retailer's promotion efforts positively affected the demand, but negatively affected the manufacturer's brand image.

Although some empirical research has found that perceived value shows dynamic nature, little research takes into account the dynamic perceived value and brand image simultaneously. As advertising can improve the product's brand image, research on advertising strategy in the context of a platform service supply chain is gradually emerging. Therefore, we focus on exploring the joint, long-term and steady decisions on optimal offline and online service levels, advertising efforts, and pricing where the dynamic perceived service quality can be affected by offline and online service levels, and brand image can be influenced by offline service level and advertising investment. We further analyze the advantage of cooperative advertising strategies by comparing three modes (i.e., decentralized, cost-sharing, and integrated).

3. Model Descriptions, Notations, and Assumptions

We study an O2O platform service supply chain with an online SP such as Booking.com and an offline hotel (SS) such as Hilton, which both provide customer service. As the leader in a Stackelberg game, SS supplies a product to the platform through a wholesale price contract. SP is in charge of online advertisement and online service activities. SS is responsible for offline service activities such as room quality and speedy service. As discussed in the Introduction, we suppose that SS shares a portion of advertising costs with SP to improve its brand image under a cost-sharing contract. Let the superscripts N, S, and C represent three modes (i.e., decentralized, cost-sharing, and integrated), respectively. All notations are summarized in Table 1.

The following assumptions apply to the study.

Assumption 1. In consistence with previous papers (He *et al.*, 2020; Zhang *et al.*, 2013), we use the quadratic functions to express the effort costs. Hence, advertising and service costs can be presented as the following quadratic form: $C(S_1(t)) = \frac{u_1}{2}S_1(t)^2$, $C(S_2(t)) = \frac{u_2}{2}S_2(t)^2$, and $C(A(t)) = \frac{u_3}{2}A(t)^2$, where $u_i > 0, i = 1, 2, 3$ are positive cost parameters towards SS's offline service effort $S_1(t)$, SP's online service effort $S_2(t)$, and SP's advertising effort $A(t)$, respectively.

Table 1. Notations and definitions.

Notations	Definitions
$S_1(t)$	SS's offline service effort
$S_2(t)$	SP's online service effort
$A(t)$	SP's advertising effort
$\phi(t)$	SS's cost-sharing rate on SP's advertising effort, $0 \leq \phi(t) \leq 1$
$p(t)$	Retail price
$S(t)$	Perceived service quality at time t with initial perceived quality $S(t)\|_{t=0} = S_0 \geq 0$
$G(t)$	SS's brand image at time t with an initial brand image $G(t)\|_{t=0} = G_0 \geq 0$
u_i	Cost parameters towards SS's offline service effort, SP's online service effort, and SP's advertising effort, $i = 1, 2, 3$
σ	The decay rate of perceived service quality over time
δ	The decay rate of brand image over time
ε, λ	The coefficient associated with SS's offline service effort and SP's online service effort in the function of perceived service quality
α, β	The coefficient associated with SP's advertising investment and SS's offline service effort in the function of SS's brand image
$D(t)$	Demand at time t
a	Potential market
b, η, γ	The coefficient associated with retail price, perceived service quality and brand image in the demand function
ρ	Discount rate
w	Wholesale price
S_1^{i*}	The optimal offline service level under mode i, $i = N, S, C$
S_2^{i*}	The optimal online service level under mode i, $i = N, S, C$
A^{i*}	The optimal advertising effort under mode i, $i = N, S, C$
p^{i*}	The optimal retail price under mode i, $i = N, S, C$
$V_j^i(t)$	Net value function of j with mode i, $i = N, S, C$, $j = ss, sp, sc$
J_j^i	The optimal steady-state present value of j with mode i, $i = N, S, C$, $j = ss, sp, sc$

Assumption 2. We first describe the dynamics of perceived service quality. Let $S(t) > 0$ represent the perceived service quality at time t for the service, which is related to online and offline service efforts and evolves over time based on the following differential equation:

$$\begin{cases} \dot{S(t)} = \varepsilon S_1(t) + \lambda S_2(t) - \sigma S(t), \\ S(0) = S_0 \geq 0. \end{cases} \tag{1}$$

Parameters $\varepsilon > 0$ and $\lambda > 0$ are the sensitivity coefficients towards SS's offline service effort and SP's online service effort on perceived service quality. Parameter $\sigma > 0$ represents the decay rate of perceived service quality over time, and S_0 is the initial perceived service quality.

Assumption 3. According to Nerlove and Arrow (1962), let $G(t) > 0$ represent SS's brand image at time t, which is related to SS's service effort and SP's advertising investment and evolves over time based on the following differential equation:

$$\begin{cases} \dot{G(t)} = \alpha A(t) + \beta S_1(t) - \delta G(t), \\ G(0) = G_0 \geq 0. \end{cases} \tag{2}$$

Parameters $\alpha > 0$ and $\beta > 0$ are the sensitivity coefficients towards SP's advertising investment and SS's offline service effort on SS's brand image. Parameter $\delta > 0$ represents the decay rate of brand image over time, and G_0 is the initial brand image.

Assumption 4. Market demand is affected negatively by the retail price and positively by perceived service quality and brand image. Following El Ouardighi (2014), we assume market demand is expressed by multiplicative function: $D(t) = (a - bp(t))(\eta S(t) + \gamma G(t))$, there would be no sales when perceived service quality and brand images were zero. b represents a price-sensitive coefficient. We also assume $a - bp(t) \geq 0$ to ensure demand non-negativity. $\eta > 0$ and $\gamma > 0$ represent perceived service quality-sensitive coefficient and brand image-sensitive coefficient, respectively.

Assumption 5. Since standard hotel rates generally remain steady for months,[d] we assume the wholesale price is fixed at value.

4. Optimal Decisions in Different Modes

In this part, we develop differential game models in three modes and determine the optimal decisions, respectively. Since the game is played over an infinite time horizon, it is rational to seek a steady-state feedback Stackelberg equilibrium, which is proved to be more meaningful than the open-loop control strategy (He *et al.*, 2020; Cellini and Lambertini, 2004).

4.1. *Decentralized mode*

In the decentralized mode, both SS and SP will independently decide their offline service effort, online service effort, advertising effort, and price to maximize their own profit. SS first decides offline service effort, and then SP decides online service effort, advertising effort, and price.

In this situation, the objective functions (net profit) of SS and SP in an infinite time horizon with a positive discount rate ρ can be presented as follows:

$$\Pi_{ss} = \int_0^{\infty} e^{-\rho t}\{\omega D(t) - C(S_1(t))\}dt, \tag{3}$$

$$\Pi_{sp} = \int_0^{\infty} e^{-\rho t}\{(p(t) - \omega)D(t) - C(S_2(t)) - C(A(t))\}dt. \tag{4}$$

For convenience in writing and ease of understanding, time t is omitted in the following analysis. We henceforth employ a notation $V_{ss}^N(S,G)$ ($V_{sp}^N(S,G)$) to represent the present value function of the SS (SP) after time t in the Hamilton–Jacobi–Bellman (HJB) equation. J_{ss}^N and J_{sp}^N represent the optimal steady-state

[d] https://marketbusinessnews.com/financial-glossary/sticky-prices-definition-meaning/.

present value of the hotel and the platform in the decentralized mode, respectively. $V_{ss}^{N}(S,G)$ ($V_{sp}^{N}(S,G)$) should satisfy the following equations:

$$\rho V_{sp}^{N}(S,G) = \max_{s_2,p,A}\Big\{(p-\omega)(a-bp)(\eta S+\gamma G) - \frac{u_2}{2}s_2^2 - \frac{u_3}{2}A^2 + V_{spS}^{N'}(S,G) \times (\varepsilon S_1 + \lambda S_2 - \sigma S) + V_{spG}^{N'}(S,G)(\alpha A + \beta S_1 - \delta G)\Big\}, \tag{5}$$

$$\rho V_{ss}^{N}(S,G) = \max_{s_1}\Big\{w(a-bp)(\eta S+\gamma G) - \frac{u_1}{2}s_1^2 + V_{ssS}^{N'}(S,G) \times (\varepsilon S_1 + \lambda S_2 - \sigma S) + V_{ssG}^{N'}(S,G)(\alpha A + \beta S_1 - \delta G)\Big\}. \tag{6}$$

Taking derivatives of the HJB equations regarding S_1, S_2, A, and p, we can obtain the optimal online service level, offline service level, advertising investment, and the retail price, which are shown as follows:

$$\begin{cases} S_1 = \dfrac{\varepsilon V_{ssS}^{N'}(S,G) + \beta V_{ssG}^{N'}(S,G)}{u_1}, \\ S_2 = \dfrac{\lambda V_{spS}^{N'}(S,G)}{u_2}, \\ A = \dfrac{\alpha V_{spG}^{N'}(S,G)}{u_3}, \\ p = \dfrac{a+b\omega}{2b}. \end{cases} \tag{7}$$

After inserting Eq. (7) into Eqs. (5) and (6), we set the general forms of these functions as linear expressions: $V_{ss}^{N}(S,G) = r_{11}S + r_{21}G + r_{31}$ and $V_{sp}^{N}(S,G) = t_{11}S + t_{21}G + t_{31}$, where r_{11}, r_{21}, r_{31}, t_{11}, t_{21}, and t_{31} are the constants to be solved. Taking a partial derivative of $V_{ss}^{N}(S,G)$ and $V_{sp}^{N}(S,G)$ with respect to S and G, respectively, it leads to

$$\begin{aligned} V_{spS}^{N'}(S,G) &= t_{11}, \\ V_{spG}^{N'}(S,G) &= t_{21}, \\ V_{ssG}^{N'}(S,G) &= r_{21}, \\ V_{ssS}^{N'}(S,G) &= r_{11}. \end{aligned} \tag{8}$$

By inserting Eqs. (7) and (8) into Eqs. (5) and (6), we can obtain the optimum feedback equilibrium decisions in a decentralized mode as presented in Lemma 1.

Lemma 1. *In the decentralized mode, the feedback equilibrium solutions are*

$$\begin{cases} S_1^{N*} = \omega(a - b\omega)\left(\dfrac{\varepsilon\eta}{2u_1(\rho+\sigma)} + \dfrac{\beta\gamma}{2u_1(\rho+\delta)}\right), \\ S_2^{N*} = \dfrac{\lambda\eta(a-b\omega)^2}{4bu_2(\rho+\sigma)}, \\ A^{N*} = \dfrac{\alpha\gamma(a-b\omega)^2}{4bu_3(\rho+\delta)}, \\ p^{N*} = \dfrac{a+b\omega}{2b}. \end{cases} \tag{9}$$

All proofs, if not provided in the paper, are in Appendix A.

Lemma 1 shows that the condition $\omega \leq \frac{a}{b}$ must be satisfied to ensure non-negative demand. If $\omega > \frac{a}{b}$, the demand in the decentralized mode will be zero, and it is beyond the scope of this paper. Consequently, the following of this paper assumes that $\omega \leq \frac{a}{b}$. This assumption of ensuring positive demand is common in previous research such as El Ouardighi (2014).

Proposition 1. *The optimal online service level, offline service level, advertising efforts, and the retail price in the decentralized mode have the following properties:*

(1) $\frac{\partial S_1^{N*}}{\partial \gamma} > 0$; $\frac{\partial S_2^{N*}}{\partial \gamma} = 0$; $\frac{\partial A^{N*}}{\partial \gamma} > 0$.

(2) $\frac{\partial S_1^{N*}}{\partial \eta} > 0$; $\frac{\partial S_2^{N*}}{\partial \eta} > 0$; $\frac{\partial A^{N*}}{\partial \eta} = 0$.

(3) *When* $\frac{a}{2b} < \omega < \frac{a}{b}$, $\frac{\partial S_1^{N*}}{\partial w} < 0$, *otherwise,* $\frac{\partial S_1^{N*}}{\partial w} > 0$; $\frac{\partial S_2^{N*}}{\partial w} < 0$; $\frac{\partial A^{N*}}{\partial w} < 0$.

Proposition 1(1) shows that the optimal online service effort is independent of brand image preference because online platform service such as web design does not affect the hotel's brand image. Similarly, the optimal advertising investment is irrespective of perceived service quality preference. The optimal offline service efforts and advertising investment increase in brand image preference γ because more consumers can be attracted as γ increases. Similarly, the optimal offline and online service efforts increase with the rise of perceived service quality preference η. The optimal online service level and advertising investment decrease in w as a higher wholesale price results in a lower marginal profit of the platform, which discourages the platform from investing in the corresponding efforts. However, the effect of w on the optimal offline service level is non-monotonic. A higher w will increase the hotel's marginal profit, whereas it also decreases the online service level and advertising investment. When w is relatively low, the optimal offline service level increases in w as a higher w brings the hotel a higher marginal profit. Thus, the hotel is inclined to invest more in offline service efforts. When w is high, the hotel will invest less in offline service efforts as w increases due to the low customer demand caused by the high retail price, low online service efforts, and advertising investments.

According to the dynamic function of Eq. (1), we can obtain the time trajectory of perceived service quality as follows:

$$\dot{S(t)} = \varepsilon\omega(a - b\omega)\left(\frac{\varepsilon\eta}{2u_1(\rho+\sigma)} + \frac{\beta\gamma}{2u_1(\rho+\delta)}\right) + \frac{\lambda^2\eta(a-b\omega)^2}{4bu_2(\rho+\sigma)} - \sigma S(t). \tag{10}$$

According to Eq. (10), we can obtain the time trajectory of accumulated perceived service quality as follows:

$$S(t)^N = S_\infty^N + (S_0 - S_\infty^N)e^{-\sigma t}. \tag{11}$$

S_∞^N represents the steady-state perceived service quality, which can be calculated by $S_\infty^N = \frac{\varepsilon S_1^{N*} + \lambda S_2^{N*}}{\sigma}$, and satisfies

$$S_\infty^N = \frac{\varepsilon\omega(a-b\omega)}{\sigma}\left(\frac{\varepsilon\eta}{2u_1(\rho+\sigma)} + \frac{\beta\gamma}{2u_1(\rho+\delta)}\right) + \frac{\lambda^2\eta(a-b\omega)^2}{4\sigma bu_2(\rho+\sigma)}. \tag{12}$$

According to the dynamic function of Eq. (2), we can obtain the time trajectory of the brand image as follows:

$$\dot{G(t)} = \frac{\alpha^2\gamma(a-b\omega)^2}{4bu_3(\rho+\delta)} + \beta\omega(a-b\omega)\left(\frac{\varepsilon\eta}{2u_1(\rho+\sigma)} + \frac{\beta\gamma}{2u_1(\rho+\delta)}\right) - \delta G(t). \tag{13}$$

According to Eq. (13), we can obtain the time trajectory of accumulated brand image as follows:

$$G(t)^N = G_\infty^N + (G_0 - G_\infty^N)e^{-\delta t}. \tag{14}$$

G_∞^N represents the steady-state brand image, which can be calculated by $G_\infty^N = \frac{\alpha A^{N*} + \beta S_1^{N*}}{\delta}$, and satisfies

$$G_\infty^N = \frac{\alpha^2\gamma(a-b\omega)^2}{4\delta bu_3(\rho+\delta)} + \frac{\beta}{\delta}\omega(a-b\omega)\left(\frac{\varepsilon\eta}{2u_1(\rho+\sigma)} + \frac{\beta\gamma}{2u_1(\rho+\delta)}\right). \tag{15}$$

D_∞^N represents the steady-state customer demand, and satisfies

$$D_\infty^N = \frac{(a-b\omega)^2\left(\begin{array}{c}2b(\delta\varepsilon\eta+\beta\gamma\sigma)(\varepsilon\eta(\delta+\rho)+\beta\gamma(\rho+\sigma))\omega u_2u_3\\ +(a-b\omega)u_1(\alpha^2\gamma^2\sigma(\rho+\sigma)u_2+\delta\eta^2\lambda^2(\delta+\rho)u_3)\end{array}\right)}{8b\delta(\delta+\rho)\sigma(\rho+\sigma)u_1u_2u_3}. \tag{16}$$

After substituting the optimal decisions into Eqs. (5) and (6), we can obtain the optimal present values of SP and SS as follows:

$$V_{ss}^{N}(S,G)=\frac{\eta\omega(a-b\omega)}{2(\rho+\sigma)}S+\frac{\gamma\omega(a-b\omega)}{2(\rho+\delta)}G+\frac{(\varepsilon r_{11}+\beta r_{21})^{2}}{2\rho u_{1}}+\frac{\lambda^{2}r_{11}t_{11}}{\rho u_{2}}+\frac{\alpha^{2}r_{21}t_{21}}{\rho u_{3}},\quad(17)$$

$$V_{sp}^{N}(S,G)=\frac{\eta(a-b\omega)^{2}}{4b(\rho+\sigma)}S+\frac{\gamma(a-b\omega)^{2}}{4b(\rho+\delta)}G+\frac{(\varepsilon t_{11}+\beta t_{21})(\varepsilon r_{11}+\beta r_{21})}{\rho u_{1}}+\frac{\lambda^{2}t_{11}^{2}}{2\rho u_{2}}+\frac{\alpha^{2}t_{21}^{2}}{2\rho u_{3}},\quad(18)$$

and the optimal present value of the supply chain satisfies

$$V_{sc}^{N}(S,G)=\frac{\eta(a^{2}-b^{2}\omega^{2})}{4b(\rho+\sigma)}S+\frac{\gamma(a^{2}-b^{2}\omega^{2})}{4b(\rho+\sigma)}G+\frac{a(\varepsilon\eta(\delta+\rho)+\beta\gamma(\rho+\sigma))^{2}\omega(a-b\omega)^{2}}{8b\rho(\delta+\rho)^{2}(\rho+\sigma)^{2}u_{1}}+\frac{\eta^{2}\lambda^{2}(a-b\omega)^{3}(a+3b\omega)}{32b^{2}\rho(\rho+\sigma)^{2}u_{2}}+\frac{\alpha^{2}\gamma^{2}(a-b\omega)^{3}(a+3b\omega)}{32b^{2}\rho(\delta+\rho)^{2}u_{3}}.\quad(19)$$

Proposition 2. *The steady perceived service quality and brand image in the decentralized mode satisfy*

(1) *If* $\eta\lambda^{2}(\delta+\rho)u_{1}<\varepsilon(\varepsilon\eta(\delta+\rho)+\beta\gamma(\rho+\sigma))u_{2}$, *when*

$$w<\frac{a\eta\lambda^{2}(\delta+\rho)u_{1}-a\varepsilon(\varepsilon\eta(\delta+\rho)+\beta\gamma(\rho+\sigma))u_{2}}{b\eta\lambda^{2}(\delta+\rho)u_{1}-2b\varepsilon(\varepsilon\eta(\delta+\rho)+\beta\gamma(\rho+\sigma))u_{2}},\quad\frac{\partial S_{\infty}^{N}}{\partial w}>0,$$

else, $\frac{\partial S_{\infty}^{N}}{\partial w}<0$. *If* $\eta\lambda^{2}(\delta+\rho)u_{1}>\varepsilon(\varepsilon\eta(\delta+\rho)+\beta\gamma(\rho+\sigma))u_{2}$, $\frac{\partial S_{\infty}^{N}}{\partial w}<0$.

(2) *If* $\alpha^{2}\gamma(\rho+\sigma)u_{1}<\beta(\varepsilon\eta(\delta+\rho)+\beta\gamma(\rho+\sigma))u_{3}$, *when*

$$w<\frac{a\alpha^{2}\gamma(\rho+\sigma)u_{1}-a\beta(\varepsilon\eta(\delta+\rho)+\beta\gamma(\rho+\sigma))u_{3}}{b\alpha^{2}\gamma(\rho+\sigma)u_{1}-2b\beta(\varepsilon\eta(\delta+\rho)+\beta\gamma(\rho+\sigma))u_{3}},\quad\frac{\partial G_{\infty}^{N}}{\partial w}>0,$$

else, $\frac{\partial G_{\infty}^{N}}{\partial w}<0$. *If* $\alpha^{2}\gamma(\rho+\sigma)u_{1}>2\beta(\varepsilon\eta(\delta+\rho)+\beta\gamma(\rho+\sigma))u_{3}$, $\frac{\partial G_{\infty}^{N}}{\partial w}<0$.

Proposition 2 shows that a higher wholesale price does not always damage the perceived service quality and brand image. When ε or β is large, offline service can greatly improve perceived service quality or brand image. We have confirmed in Proposition 1 that the optimal offline service level increases in w when w is relatively low, increasing perceived service quality and brand image. However, a higher wholesale price also leads to a reduction of online service level and advertising efforts and the increase of the retail price, reducing perceived service quality and brand image. When w is relatively low and ε or β is large, the former dominates the latter, and consequently the perceived service quality and brand image increase in w. Otherwise, perceived service quality and brand image always decrease in w since a higher w discourages two members from investing in more efforts.

4.2. *Cost-sharing mode*

In a cost-sharing mode, the hotel shares a portion of the advertising costs with the platform. The game is played according to the following sequence: first, SS determines the cost-sharing rate and offline service level. Then, SP determines the optimal online service level, advertising investment, and price. The profits of the two members can be presented as follows:

$$\Pi_{ss} = \int_0^{\infty} e^{-\rho t}\{\omega D(t) - C(S_1(t)) - \phi(t)C(A(t))\}dt, \tag{20}$$

$$\Pi_{sp} = \int_0^{\infty} e^{-\rho t}\{(p(t) - \omega)D(t) - C(S_2(t)) - (1 - \phi(t))C(A(t))\}dt. \tag{21}$$

Similarly, we employ a notation $V_{ss}^S(S,G)$ ($V_{sp}^S(S,G)$) to represent the present value function of the SS (SP) after time t in the HJB equation. J_{ss}^S and J_{sp}^S represent the optimal steady-state present value of the hotel and the platform in the cost-sharing mode, respectively. $V_{ss}^S(S,G)$ ($V_{sp}^S(S,G)$) should satisfy the following equations:

$$\begin{aligned}\rho V_{ss}^S(S,G) = \max_{S_1,\emptyset}\Big\{&w(a-bp)(\eta S+\gamma G) - \frac{u_1}{2}S_1^2 - \phi\frac{u_3}{2}A^2 + r_{12}(\varepsilon S_1 + \lambda S_2 - \sigma S)\\ &+ r_{22}(\alpha A + \beta S_1 - \delta G)\Big\},\end{aligned} \tag{22}$$

$$\begin{aligned}\rho V_{sp}^S(S,G) = \max_{A,S_2,p}\Big\{&(p-\omega)(a-bp)(\eta S+\gamma G) - \frac{u_2}{2}S_2^2 - (1-\phi)\frac{u_3}{2}A^2\\ &+ t_{12}(\varepsilon S_1 + \lambda S_2 - \sigma S) + t_{22}(\alpha A + \beta S_1 - \delta G)\Big\}.\end{aligned} \tag{23}$$

Taking derivatives of the HJB equation with respect to ϕ, S_1, S_2, A, and p, we can obtain the optimal cost-sharing rate, online service level, offline service level, and advertising efforts as well as the retail price, which are expressed as follows:

$$\begin{cases} S_2 = \dfrac{\lambda V_{spS}^{S'}(S,G)}{u_2}, \\ A = \dfrac{\alpha(2V_{ssG}^{S'}(S,G) + V_{spG}^{S'}(S,G))}{2u_3}, \\ p = \dfrac{a+b\omega}{2b}, \\ S_1 = \dfrac{\varepsilon V_{ssS}^{S'}(S,G) + \beta V_{ssG}^{S'}(S,G)}{u_1}, \\ \phi = \dfrac{2V_{ssG}^{S'}(S,G) - V_{spG}^{S'}(S,G)}{2V_{ssG}^{S'}(S,G) + V_{spG}^{S'}(S,G)}. \end{cases} \tag{24}$$

After substituting Eq. (24) into Eqs. (22) and (23), we can get the stationary feedback Stackelberg equilibrium as presented in Lemma 2.

Lemma 2. *In the cost-sharing mode, the feedback equilibrium solutions are as follows*:

$$\begin{cases} S_1^{S*} = \omega(a-b\omega)\left(\dfrac{\varepsilon\eta}{2u_1(\rho+\sigma)} + \dfrac{\beta\gamma}{2u_1(\rho+\delta)}\right), \\ S_2^{S*} = \dfrac{\lambda\eta(a-b\omega)^2}{4bu_2(\rho+\sigma)}, \\ A^{S*} = \dfrac{\alpha\gamma(a-b\omega)(3b\omega+a)}{8bu_3(\rho+\delta)}, \\ p^{S*} = \dfrac{a+b\omega}{2b}, \\ \phi = \dfrac{5b\omega-a}{3b\omega+a}. \end{cases} \tag{25}$$

Similar to Lemma 1, to avoid the negative cost-sharing rate, the condition $\omega \geq \frac{a}{5b}$ must be satisfied; otherwise, the hotel will not share the advertisement cost, which means that a cost-sharing contract can be achieved if ω is larger than a critical threshold. In other words, the hotel is willing to share the advertising cost if it can obtain sufficient profit per unit.

Proposition 3. *The optimal cost-sharing rate, online service level, offline service level, advertising efforts, and the retail price in the cost-sharing mode have the following properties*:

(1) $\frac{\partial S_1^{S*}}{\partial\gamma} > 0$; $\frac{\partial S_2^{S*}}{\partial\gamma} = 0$; $\frac{\partial A^{S*}}{\partial\gamma} > 0$.

(2) $\frac{\partial S_1^{S*}}{\partial\eta} > 0$; $\frac{\partial S_2^{S*}}{\partial\eta} > 0$; $\frac{\partial A^{S*}}{\partial\eta} = 0$.

(3) *When* $\frac{a}{2b} < \omega < \frac{a}{b}$, $\frac{\partial S_1^{S*}}{\partial w} < 0$, *otherwise,* $\frac{\partial S_1^{S*}}{\partial w} > 0$; $\frac{\partial S_2^{S*}}{\partial w} < 0$; *when* $\frac{a}{3b} < \omega < \frac{a}{b}$, $\frac{\partial A^{S*}}{\partial w} < 0$, *otherwise,* $\frac{\partial A^{S*}}{\partial w} > 0$; $\frac{\partial \phi}{\partial w} > 0$.

It can be explained that the optimal online service level is independent of the brand image coefficient; similarly, the optimal advertising effort is independent of the perceived service quality coefficient. From Proposition 3(3), we find that the hotel has a greater incentive to share with the platform more of advertising expenditure as w increases, which leads to the non-monotonic effect of w on the optimal advertising investment. The optimal advertising investment increases in w if w is relatively low ($\omega < \frac{a}{3b}$), and this result differs from that in Proposition 1. The marginal profit of the product can be defined as $\frac{a-bw}{2b}$, which decreases in w. However, the shared cost which increases in w, makes up for the profit loss from a lower marginal profit. As a result, the platform is prone to invest in more advertisements with the increase of w.

Similarly, we obtain the time trajectory of accumulated perceived service quality as follows:

$$S(t)^S = S_\infty^S + (S_0 - S_\infty^S)e^{-\sigma t}. \tag{26}$$

S_∞^S represents the steady-state perceived service quality, and can be calculated by $S_\infty^S = \frac{\varepsilon S_1^{S*} + \lambda S_2^{S*}}{\sigma}$, and satisfies

$$S_\infty^S = \frac{\varepsilon\omega(a-b\omega)}{\sigma}\left(\frac{\varepsilon\eta}{2u_1(\rho+\sigma)} + \frac{\beta\gamma}{2u_1(\rho+\delta)}\right) + \frac{\lambda^2\eta(a-b\omega)^2}{4\sigma b u_2(\rho+\sigma)}. \tag{27}$$

The time trajectory of accumulated brand image is

$$G(t)^S = G_\infty^S + (G_0 - G_\infty^S)e^{-\delta t}, \tag{28}$$

G_∞^S represents the steady-state brand image, and can be calculated by $G_\infty^S = \frac{\alpha A^{S*} + \beta S_1^{S*}}{\delta}$, and satisfies

$$G_\infty^S = \frac{\alpha^2\gamma(a-b\omega)(3b\omega+a)}{8\delta b u_3(\rho+\delta)} + \frac{\beta}{\delta}\omega(a-b\omega)\left(\frac{\varepsilon\eta}{2u_1(\rho+\sigma)} + \frac{\beta\gamma}{2u_1(\rho+\delta)}\right), \tag{29}$$

D_∞^S refers to the steady-state customer demand, and satisfies

$$D_\infty^S = \frac{(a-b\omega)^2\left(\begin{array}{l} 4b(\delta\varepsilon\eta+\beta\gamma\sigma)(\varepsilon\eta(\delta+\rho)+\beta\gamma(\rho+\sigma))\omega u_2 u_3 + u_1 \\ \quad\times(\alpha^2\gamma^2\sigma(\rho+\sigma)(a+3b\omega)u_2 + 2\delta\eta^2\lambda^2(\delta+\rho)(a-b\omega)u_3)\end{array}\right)}{16b\delta(\delta+\rho)\sigma(\rho+\sigma)u_1u_2u_3}. \tag{30}$$

After substituting the optimal decisions into Eqs. (22) and (23), we can obtain the optimal present values of SP and SS as follows:

$$V_{sp}^S(S,G) = \frac{\eta(a-b\omega)^2}{4b(\rho+\sigma)}S + \frac{\gamma(a-b\omega)^2}{4b(\rho+\delta)}G + \frac{(\varepsilon t_{12}+\beta t_{22})(\varepsilon r_{12}+\beta r_{22})}{\rho u_1} + \frac{\lambda^2 t_{12}^2}{2\rho u_2} + \frac{\alpha^2 t_{22}(2r_{22}+t_{22})}{4\rho u_3}, \tag{31}$$

$$V_{ss}^S(S,G) = \frac{\eta\omega(a-b\omega)}{2(\rho+\sigma)}S + \frac{\gamma\omega(a-b\omega)}{2(\rho+\delta)}G + \frac{(\varepsilon r_{12}+\beta r_{22})^2}{2\rho u_1} + \frac{\lambda^2 r_{12} t_{12}}{\rho u_2} + \frac{\alpha^2 (2r_{22}+t_{22})^2}{8\rho u_3}, \tag{32}$$

and the present value of the supply chain is

$$V_{sc}^S(S,G) = \frac{\eta(a^2-b^2\omega^2)}{4b(\rho+\sigma)}S + \frac{\gamma(a^2-b^2\omega^2)}{4b(\rho+\delta)}G + \frac{a(\varepsilon\eta(\delta+\rho)+\beta\gamma(\rho+\sigma))^2\omega(a-b\omega)^2}{8b\rho u_1(\delta+\rho)^2(\rho+\sigma)^2} + \frac{\alpha^2\gamma^2(a-b\omega)^2(3a+b\omega)(a+3b\omega)}{128b^2\rho u_3(\delta+\rho)^2} + \frac{\lambda^2\eta^2(a-b\omega)^3(a+3b\omega)}{32b^2\rho u_2(\rho+\sigma)^2}. \tag{33}$$

Proposition 4. (1) *If* $\eta\lambda^2(\delta+\rho)u_1 < \varepsilon(\varepsilon\eta(\delta+\rho)+\beta\gamma(\rho+\sigma))u_2$, *when* $w < \frac{a\eta\lambda^2(\delta+\rho)u_1 - a\varepsilon(\varepsilon\eta(\delta+\rho)+\beta\gamma(\rho+\sigma))u_2}{b\eta\lambda^2(\delta+\rho)u_1 - 2b\varepsilon(\varepsilon\eta(\delta+\rho)+\beta\gamma(\rho+\sigma))u_2}$, $\frac{\partial S_\infty^S}{\partial w} > 0$, *else,* $\frac{\partial S_\infty^S}{\partial w} < 0$. *If* $\eta\lambda^2(\delta+\rho)u_1 > \varepsilon(\varepsilon\eta(\delta+\rho)+\beta\gamma(\rho+\sigma))u_2$, $\frac{\partial S_\infty^S}{\partial w} < 0$.

(2) *If* $\frac{a}{5b} < w < \frac{a\alpha^2\gamma(\rho+\sigma)u_1 + 2a\beta(\varepsilon\eta(\delta+\rho)+\beta\gamma(\rho+\sigma))u_3}{3b\alpha^2\gamma(\rho+\sigma)u_1 + 4b\beta(\varepsilon\eta(\delta+\rho)+\beta\gamma(\rho+\sigma))u_3}$, $\frac{\partial G_\infty^S}{\partial w} > 0$; *else,* $\frac{\partial G_\infty^S}{\partial w} < 0$.

By comparing Proposition 4(2) with Proposition 2(2), we find the brand image is more inclined to increase in w in the cost-sharing mode. In Proposition 2(2), $\frac{\partial G_\infty^N}{\partial w} > 0$ when two conditions ($\alpha^2\gamma(\rho+\sigma)u_1 < 2\beta(\varepsilon\eta(\delta+\rho)+\beta\gamma(\rho+\sigma))u_3$ and $w < \frac{a\alpha^2\gamma(\rho+\sigma)u_1 - a\beta(\varepsilon\eta(\delta+\rho)+\beta\gamma(\rho+\sigma))u_3}{b\alpha^2\gamma(\rho+\sigma)u_1 - 2b\beta(\varepsilon\eta(\delta+\rho)+\beta\gamma(\rho+\sigma))u_3}$) are simultaneously satisfied. However, $\frac{\partial G_\infty^S}{\partial w} > 0$ when $\frac{a}{5b} < w < \frac{a\alpha^2\gamma(\rho+\sigma)u_1 + 2a\beta(\varepsilon\eta(\delta+\rho)+\beta\gamma(\rho+\sigma))u_3}{3b\alpha^2\gamma(\rho+\sigma)u_1 + 4b\beta(\varepsilon\eta(\delta+\rho)+\beta\gamma(\rho+\sigma))u_3}$ in the cost-sharing mode, and $w > \frac{a}{5b}$ is the precondition of the cost-sharing contract.

Proposition 5. (1) *If* $2(\delta\varepsilon\eta+\beta\gamma\sigma)(\varepsilon\eta(\delta+\rho)+\beta\gamma(\rho+\sigma))u_2u_3 > 3u_1(\alpha^2\gamma^2\sigma(\rho+\sigma)u_2 + \delta\eta^2\lambda^2(\delta+\rho)u_3)$ *and* $w < w_1$, $\frac{\partial D_\infty^N}{\partial w} > 0$, *else,* $\frac{\partial D_\infty^N}{\partial w} < 0$;

(2) *if* $2(\delta\varepsilon\eta+\beta\gamma\sigma)(\varepsilon\eta(\delta+\rho)+\beta\gamma(\rho+\sigma))u_2u_3 > u_1(\alpha^2\gamma^2\sigma(\rho+\sigma)u_2+6\delta\eta^2\lambda^2(\delta+\rho)u_3)$ *and* $w < w_2$, $\frac{\partial D^S_\infty}{\partial w} > 0$, *else*, $\frac{\partial D^S_\infty}{\partial w} < 0$; *where*

$$w_1 = \frac{3au_1(\alpha^2\gamma^2\sigma(\rho+\sigma)u_2+\delta\eta^2\lambda^2(\delta+\rho)u_3)-2a(\delta\varepsilon\eta+\beta\gamma\sigma) \times(\varepsilon\eta(\delta+\rho)+\beta\gamma(\rho+\sigma))u_2u_3}{3bu_1(\alpha^2\gamma^2\sigma(\rho+\sigma)u_2+\delta\eta^2\lambda^2(\delta+\rho)u_3)-6b(\delta\varepsilon\eta+\beta\gamma\sigma) \times(\varepsilon\eta(\delta+\rho)+\beta\gamma(\rho+\sigma))u_2u_3},$$

$$w_2 = \frac{a(-4(\delta\varepsilon\eta+\beta\gamma\sigma)(\varepsilon\eta(\delta+\rho)+\beta\gamma(\rho+\sigma))u_2u_3+u_1 \times(6\delta\eta^2\lambda^2(\delta+\rho)u_3-\alpha^2\gamma^2\sigma(\rho+\sigma)u_2))}{3b(-4(\delta\varepsilon\eta+\beta\gamma\sigma)(\varepsilon\eta(\delta+\rho)+\beta\gamma(\rho+\sigma))u_2u_3 +u_1(-3\alpha^2\gamma^2\sigma(\rho+\sigma)u_2+2\delta\eta^2\lambda^2(\delta+\rho)u_3))}.$$

Proposition 5 shows that a higher wholesale price can be effective in boosting market demand. This phenomenon can be attributed to the influences of w on the retail price, perceived service quality, and brand image altogether. We have confirmed in Propositions 2 and 4 that if w is lower than a threshold, then the hotel is willing to invest more in offline service efforts in both the decentralized and cost-sharing modes. Besides, as the platform increases the advertisement level in the cost-sharing mode, it enhances perceived service quality (in the above two modes) and brand image (in the cost-sharing mode). Although the retail price increases in w, along with demand reduction, it shows that the former dominates the latter, which results in higher demand with an increase of the wholesale price.

4.3. *Integrated mode*

In the integrated mode, the optimal decisions are determined centrally by a decision-maker, who maximizes the profit of the entire channel given by

$$\Pi_{sc} = \int_0^\infty e^{-\rho t}\{pD(t) - C(S_1(t)) - C(S_2(t)) - C(A(t))\}dt. \tag{34}$$

Similarly, we employ a notation $V^C_{sc}(S,G)$ to represent the present value function of the decision-maker after time t in the HJB equation. J^C_{sc} stands for the optimal steady-state present value of a decision-maker. $V^C_{sc}(S,G)$ should satisfy the following equations:

$$\rho V^C_{sc}(S,G) = \max_{A,S_1,S_2,p}\Big\{p(a-bp)(\eta S+\gamma G) - \frac{u_1}{2}S_1^2 - \frac{u_2}{2}S_2^2 - \frac{u_3}{2}A^2 + V^{C'}_{scS}(S,G) \times(\varepsilon S_1+\lambda S_2-\sigma S) + V^{C'}_{scG}(S,G)(\alpha A+\beta S_1-\delta G)\Big\}. \tag{35}$$

Taking derivatives of the HJB equation regarding S_1, S_2, A, and p, we can obtain the optimal online service level, offline service level, advertising efforts, and the retail price as follows:

$$\begin{cases} S_1^C = \dfrac{\varepsilon V_{scS}^{C'}(S,G) + \beta V_{scG}^{C'}(S,G)}{u_1}, \\ S_2^C = \dfrac{\lambda V_{scS}^{C'}(S,G)}{u_2}, \\ A^C = \dfrac{\alpha V_{scG}^{C'}(S,G)}{u_3}, \\ p^C = \dfrac{a}{2b}. \end{cases} \tag{36}$$

Substituting Eq. (36) into Eq. (35), we can get the stationary feedback Stackelberg equilibrium, as presented in Lemma 3.

Lemma 3. *In the integrated mode, the feedback equilibrium solutions are*

$$\begin{cases} S_1^{C*} = \dfrac{\varepsilon\eta a^2}{4bu_1(\rho+\sigma)} + \dfrac{\beta\gamma a^2}{4bu_1(\rho+\delta)}, \\ S_2^{C*} = \dfrac{\lambda\eta a^2}{4bu_2(\rho+\sigma)}, \\ A^{C*} = \dfrac{\alpha\gamma a^2}{4bu_3(\rho+\delta)}, \\ p^{C*} = \dfrac{a}{2b}. \end{cases} \tag{37}$$

After substituting Eq. (37) into Eq. (35), we can obtain the present value of the supply chain in the following equation:

$$V_{sc}^C(S,G) = \frac{\eta a^2}{4b(\rho+\sigma)}S + \frac{\gamma a^2}{4b(\rho+\delta)}G + \frac{(\varepsilon r_{13} + \beta r_{23})^2}{2u_1} + \frac{\lambda^2 r_{13}^2}{2u_2} + \frac{\alpha^2 r_{23}^2}{2u_3}. \tag{38}$$

S_∞^C represents the steady-state perceived service quality, and can be calculated by $S_\infty^C = \frac{\varepsilon S_1^{C*} + \lambda S_2^{C*}}{\sigma}$, and satisfies

$$S_\infty^C = \frac{\varepsilon}{\sigma}\left(\frac{\varepsilon\eta a^2}{4bu_1(\rho+\sigma)} + \frac{\beta\gamma a^2}{4bu_1(\rho+\delta)}\right) + \frac{\lambda^2\eta a^2}{4\sigma bu_2(\rho+\sigma)}. \tag{39}$$

The time trajectory of accumulated brand image can be expressed as follows:

$$G(t)^C = G_\infty^C + (G_0 - G_\infty^C)e^{-\delta t}, \tag{40}$$

G_∞^C represents the steady-state brand image, and can be calculated by $G_\infty^C = \frac{\alpha A^{C*} + \beta S_1^{C*}}{\delta}$, and satisfies

$$G_\infty^C = \frac{\alpha^2\gamma a^2}{4b\delta u_3(\rho+\delta)} + \frac{\beta}{\delta}\left(\frac{\varepsilon\eta a^2}{4bu_1(\rho+\sigma)} + \frac{\beta\gamma a^2}{4bu_1(\rho+\delta)}\right). \tag{41}$$

Proposition 6. *The optimal online service level, offline service level, advertising efforts, and the retail price in the integrated mode have the following properties*:

(1) $\frac{\partial S_1^{C*}}{\partial \gamma} > 0$; $\frac{\partial S_2^{C*}}{\partial \gamma} = 0$; $\frac{\partial A^{C*}}{\partial \gamma} > 0$,
(2) $\frac{\partial S_1^{C*}}{\partial \eta} > 0$; $\frac{\partial S_2^{C*}}{\partial \eta} > 0$; $\frac{\partial A^{C*}}{\partial \eta} = 0$,
(3) $\frac{\partial S_1^{C*}}{\partial w} = \frac{\partial S_2^{C*}}{\partial w} = \frac{\partial A^{C*}}{\partial w} = \frac{\partial p^{C*}}{\partial w} = 0$.

When the supply chain serves as a decision-maker, we find that all the optimal decision variables are irrespective of the wholesale price. Propositions 6(1) and 6(2) are similar to Propositions 3(1) and 3(2), and the corresponding explanations are omitted here.

5. A Comparison of Different Modes

In this section, we first compare the optimal online service level, offline service level, retail price, and advertising investment in the three modes. Then, the time trajectory and the steady-state of perceived service quality and brand image are analyzed. Finally, we compare the steady-state present values of the supply chain and its two members in the three modes.

Proposition 7. *The optimal service efforts, retail price, and advertising investment satisfy the following properties*:

(1) $S_1^{N*} = S_1^{S*} < S_1^{C*}$;
(2) $S_2^{N*} = S_2^{S*} < S_2^{C*}$;
(3) $p^{N*} = p^{S*} > p^{C*}$;
(4) $A^{N*} < A^{S*} < A^{C*}$.

Proposition 7 shows that integrated mode generates the highest service effort, advertising investment, and the lowest retail price, which indicates the advantage of channel integration. The optimal service level in a decentralized mode equals that in the cost-sharing mode. Since the cost-sharing mode is designed to share advertisement costs, cost-sharing mode always leads to a higher advertising level than the decentralized mode. This implies the hotel should share with the platform a portion of the advertising costs so that it can motivate the platform to invest more in advertisement. However, if the hotel and the platform act as an integrated channel, the supply chain will invest in the highest efforts and set the lowest price.

Proposition 8. *The perceived service quality and brand image satisfy the following properties*:

(1) $S(t)^N = S(t)^S < S(t)^C$, $S_\infty^N = S_\infty^S < S_\infty^C$;
(2) $G(t)^N < G(t)^S < G(t)^C$, $G_\infty^N < G_\infty^S < G_\infty^C$.

When two supply chain members are in an integrated mode, both their perceived service quality and brand image perform best which can be directly attributed to the fact that the service effort and the advertising level are at their highest in an integrated mode. The perceived service quality in the decentralized mode equals that in the cost-sharing mode because both the online and offline service efforts are the same in the two modes. The brand image in the cost-sharing mode is higher than that in the decentralized mode because the platform tends to invest more in advertising efforts with cost-sharing.

Proposition 9. *The optimal steady-state present values of the hotel, the platform, and the platform service supply chain satisfy the following properties*:

(1) $J_{ss}^{N} < J_{ss}^{S}$;
(2) $J_{sp}^{N} < J_{sp}^{S}$;
(3) $J_{sc}^{N} < J_{sc}^{S} < J_{sc}^{C}$.

Proposition 9 shows that the cost-sharing mode can help improve both the hotel and the platform's present value, which means that Pareto improvement can be achieved if the hotel shares the advertising cost with the platform. However, when the hotel and the platform serve as a central decision-maker, the overall supply chain owns the highest present value. Proposition 8(1) shows that the steady-state perceived service quality in the decentralized mode is the same as in the cost-sharing mode. However, the steady-state brand image in the cost-sharing mode is higher than that in the decentralized mode. Both the brand image and perceived service quality have a positive impact on consumer demand, positively affecting steady-state present values. However, Proposition 7(4) shows that $A^{N*} < A^{S*} < A^{C*}$, which means that the cost of advertising efforts in the integrated mode exceeds that in the cost-sharing mode, and further exceeds that in the decentralized mode. The positive effects from the brand image and perceived service quality dominates the cost of advertising effort, thus, we can get $J_{sc}^{N} < J_{sc}^{S} < J_{sc}^{C}$.

6. Numerical Simulation

In this part, we employ numerical examples to illustrate the effects of some parameters on the optimal decisions and present value. Following El Ouardighi (2014), we assume $\alpha = 1$, $S_0 = 10$, $G_0 = 10$, and following Chutani and Sethi (2012a), we assume $u_1 = u_2 = u_3 = 1$. Other parameters are set as follows: $a = 5$, $b = 1$, $\omega = 2$, $\rho = 0.3$, $\gamma = 0.5$, $\eta = 0.5$, $\varepsilon = 0.8$, $\lambda = 0.4$, $\sigma = 0.2$, $\beta = 0.5$, $\delta = 0.3$.

In Fig. 1, we aim to study the dynamic trajectory of perceived service quality and brand image with t varying from 0 to 20. Figure 1 shows that they gradually converge to a steady-state with the increase of t. When two members are in an integrated mode, both their perceived service quality and brand image perform best. This result validates Proposition 8. However, since advertising investment does not affect perceived service quality, Fig. 1(a) shows that the optimal perceived

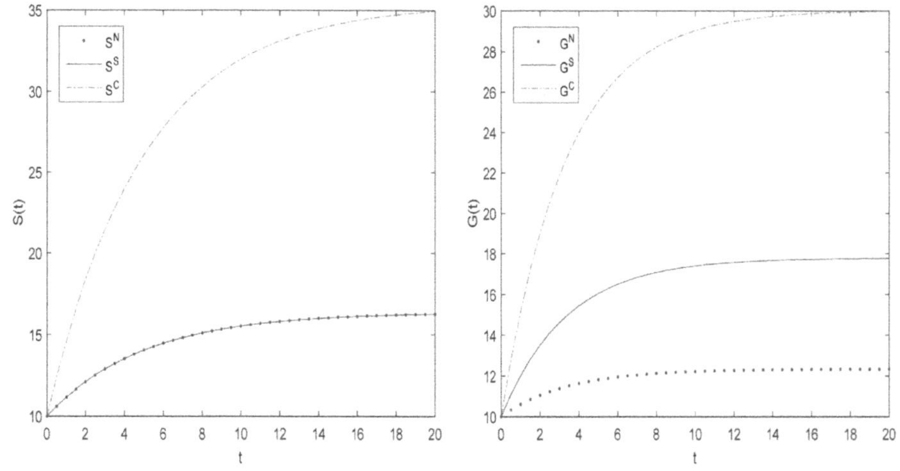

(a) (b)

Fig. 1. The time trajectory of perceived service quality and brand image.

service quality in the decentralized mode equals that in the cost-sharing mode. The optimal brand image in the cost-sharing mode outperforms that in the decentralized mode.

To further examine the effects of ω on the steady-state present value of the supply chain and its members in three modes, we conduct a sensitivity analysis with respect to ω in Fig. 2. Figure 2(a) shows that the platform's present value in a decentralized and cost-sharing mode both decreases in ω, whereas the hotel's steady-state present value firstly increases in ω and then decreases in ω. We have confirmed in Proposition 4 that the optimal and steady perceived service quality and brand image increase in w if w is relatively low, which further boosts customer demand. The profit increase from higher demand outweighs the decrease from more shared costs, which leads to the phenomenon that the hotel's present value will firstly increase in ω in the cost-sharing mode. Figure 2(a) shows that both the hotel and the platform can benefit from cost-sharing, thus, Pareto improvements can be achieved. Figure 2(b) shows that the present value of the supply chain is irrelevant to ω in the integrated mode, whereas it may increase in ω if ω is relatively low in the decentralized mode. Figure 2(b) also illustrates that the present value of the supply chain in the integrated mode is higher than that in the decentralized or the cost-sharing mode. This result validates Proposition 9.

Table 2 shows the variations of different decisions when keeping other parameters fixed, but changing a given parameter from -50%, -25%, $+25\%$ to $+50\%$, respectively. When the customer price sensitivity b increases, it decreases the optimal online and offline service effort, advertising investment, steady perceived service quality, brand image, as well as the present value of the two supply chain members. The initial demand of the market a has a contrary effect on the above-mentioned

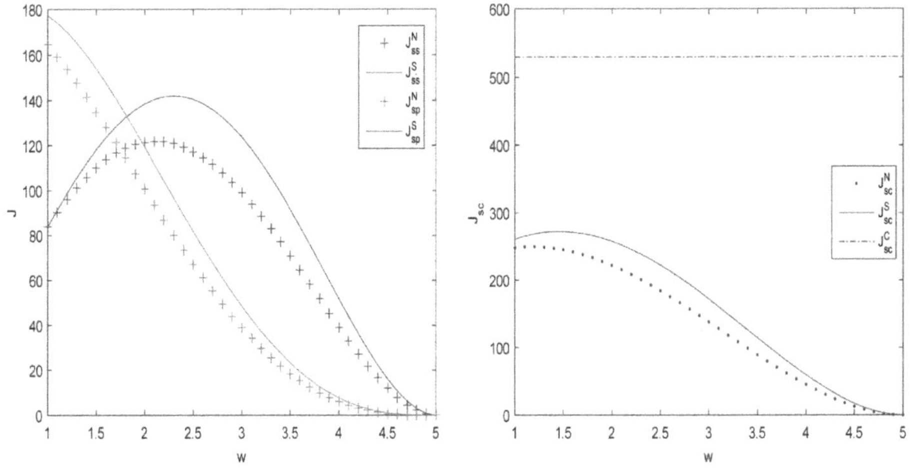

(a) (b)

Fig. 2. The effects of ω on the steady-state present value.

performance. Interestingly, we find the optimal cost-sharing rate $\emptyset$ increases in price sensitivity b (i.e., $\frac{\partial \emptyset}{\partial b} = \frac{8a\omega}{(a+3b\omega)^2} > 0$). This is because customer demand decreases in price sensitivity b, and the hotel needs to share a higher portion of the platform's advertising costs to incentivize the platform to invest more in advertising. The optimal cost-sharing rate $\emptyset$ decreases in initial demand a (i.e., $\frac{\partial \emptyset}{\partial a} = -\frac{8b\omega}{(a+3b\omega)^2} < 0$). This is because the platform will invest more in advertisements with a higher marginal profit caused by higher initial demand. Therefore, the hotel will reduce the cost-sharing rate.

As ε and β increase, the hotel tends to invest more in offline efforts, which further increases customer demand by improving perceived service quality and brand image. Similar explanations can be used to illustrate the effects of λ and α on the supply chain. However, the offline service cost coefficient μ_1 will negatively affect the entire chain. As μ_1 increases, the optimal offline effort investment decreases, resulting in

Table 2. Sensitivity analysis towards the optimal decisions ($i = N, S, C$).

Parameters	a	b	ρ	γ	η	ε	λ	σ	μ_1	μ_2	μ_3	α	β	δ
S_1^{i*}	↑	↓	↓	↑	↑	↑	—	↓	↓	—	—	—	↑	↓
S_2^{i*}	↑	↓	↓	—	↑	—	↑	↓	—	↓	—	—	—	↓
A^{i*}	↑	↓	↓	↑	—	—	—	↓	—	—	↓	↑	—	↓
S_∞^i	↑	↓	↓	↑	↑	↑	↑	↓	↓	↓	—	—	↑	↓
G_∞^i	↑	↓	↓	↑	↑	↑	—	↓	↓	—	↓	↑	↑	↓
J^i	↑	↓	↓	↑	↑	↑	↑	↓	↓	↓	↓	↑	↑	↓

lower perceived service quality and brand image as well as lower demand. These factors hurt profits. Similar phenomena can be found about the effects of μ_2, μ_3 on the entire chain.

7. Conclusions

7.1. *Summary of findings*

This paper investigates the strategy of service effort, advertising investment, and pricing in a platform service supply chain. The service supply chain comprises a leading hotel in charge of offline service, and the following platform responsible for online service, advertising investment, and pricing. The online and offline service efforts affect the perceived service quality. Similarly, offline service effort and advertising investment affect the brand image in a dynamic environment. We aim at solving the long-term and steady decisions in a decentralized, advertisement-cost-sharing mode, and integrated mode, respectively. By using HJB equations, we determine the optimal decisions based on profit maximization and further compare different decisions in three modes (i.e., decentralized, cost-sharing, and integrated). The main results of this paper are as follows.

First, this paper suggests when the hotel and the platform operate independently, the hotel should share a portion of the platform's advertising costs if the hotel can obtain enough profit per unit. However, the wholesale price must be less than a certain threshold to ensure non-negative demand.

Second, with the improvement of both perceived service quality and brand image over time, they gradually converge to a steady-state. Besides, they can increase with the rise of the wholesale price when the wholesale price is low and customers are more sensitive towards SS's offline service effort in the decentralized mode. The cost-sharing mode further relaxes the constraint condition for this increasing tendency since the optimal advertising investment will also increase with the rise of the wholesale price when it is relatively low.

Third, the cost-sharing mode can help improve perceived service quality and brand image by means of higher online and offline service effort and advertising investment, which increases both the hotel and the platform's present value. However, only in the integrated mode, the perceived service quality, brand image, as well as supply chain performance can reach the optimal, and the retail price can be the lowest.

7.2. *Management implications*

Based on the above findings, we provide the following managerial implications to guide various stakeholders in the platform service supply chain. When choosing tourism products and partners, hotels should consider the relationship among the exogenous wholesale price, their own service improvement ability, parameters influencing market demand and other relevant factors, so as to maximize their own profits. In the tourism service supply chain, both the hotel and the platform need to set different levels of service quality and advertising effort as well as different pricing strategies so as to achieve the "double Pareto optimization" of their own profits and the overall profit. It is suggested that the hotel should share a portion of the platform's advertising costs so that the latter is motivated to invest more in advertisement, leading to improved brand image and increased profits. However, if the hotel and the platform agree to operate like one single virtual enterprise, the supply chain can obtain the highest profit.

7.3. *Future studies*

When visitors buy tourism products, they cannot measure the quality of the travel service supplier, therefore, past experience and information for service quality from other sources can be considered as a subjective reference point. Further study can consider reference quality that is based on previous experiences. Besides, it would be interesting to analyze the influence of reference quality on optimal service quality, brand image and profits, and the present value of supply chain members. Furthermore, the wholesale price in this paper is regarded as a constant, further study can consider the endogenous wholesale price and its effects on service quality, brand image, profits, and the choice of cooperation mode.

Appendix A

Proof of Lemma 1. By inserting Eqs. (7) and (8) into Eqs. (5) and (6), we get

$$\begin{aligned}\rho(t_{11}S+t_{21}G+t_{31})&=\left(\frac{\eta(a-b\omega)^2}{4b}-\sigma t_{11}\right)S+\left(\frac{\gamma(a-b\omega)^2}{4b}-\delta t_{21}\right)G\\&\quad+\frac{\varepsilon^2 t_{11}r_{11}+\beta\varepsilon t_{21}r_{11}}{u_1}+\frac{\beta^2 t_{21}r_{21}+\beta\varepsilon t_{11}r_{21}}{u_1}+\frac{\lambda^2 t_{11}^2}{2u_2}\\&\quad+\frac{\alpha^2 t_{21}^2}{2u_3},\end{aligned}$$

$$\begin{aligned}\rho(r_{11}S+r_{21}G+r_{31})&=\left(\frac{\eta\omega(a-b\omega)}{2}-r_{11}\sigma\right)S+\left(\frac{\gamma\omega(a-b\omega)}{2}-r_{21}\delta\right)G\\&\quad+\frac{(\varepsilon r_{11}+\beta r_{21})^2}{2u_1}+\frac{\lambda^2 r_{11}t_{11}}{u_2}+\frac{\alpha^2 r_{21}t_{21}}{u_3}.\end{aligned}$$

Solving the above equations, we obtain the values of $r_{11}, r_{21}, r_{31}, t_{11}, t_{21}, t_{31}$ as follows:

$$\begin{cases} r_{11} = \dfrac{\eta\omega(a-b\omega)}{2(\rho+\sigma)}, \\ r_{21} = \dfrac{\gamma\omega(a-b\omega)}{2(\delta+\rho)}, \\ r_{31} = \omega(a-b\omega)^2 \\ \quad \times \left(\dfrac{(\varepsilon\eta(\delta+\rho)+\beta\gamma(\rho+\sigma))^2\omega}{(\delta+\rho)^2(\rho+\sigma)^2 8\rho u_1} + \dfrac{(a-b\omega)(\frac{\eta^2\lambda^2}{(\rho+\sigma)^2 u_2} + \frac{\alpha^2\gamma^2}{(\delta+\rho)^2 u_3})}{8\rho b} \right), \\ t_{11} = \dfrac{\eta(a-b\omega)^2}{4b(\rho+\sigma)}, \\ t_{21} = \dfrac{\gamma(a-b\omega)^2}{4b(\delta+\rho)}, \\ t_{31} = \dfrac{(a-b\omega)^3(u_1(a-b\omega)(\alpha^2\gamma^2u_2(\rho+\sigma)^2+\eta^2\lambda^2u_3(\delta+\rho)^2) + 4bu_2u_3\omega(\beta\gamma(\rho+\sigma)+\varepsilon\eta(\delta+\rho))^2)}{32b^2\rho u_1u_2u_3(\delta+\rho)^2(\rho+\sigma)^2}. \end{cases}$$

After substituting the above equations into Eq. (7), we can get Lemma 1. □

Proof of Proposition 1. (1) $\frac{\partial S_1^{N*}}{\partial\gamma} = \frac{\beta\omega(a-b\omega)}{2u_1(\rho+\delta)} > 0$, $\frac{\partial S_2^{N*}}{\partial\gamma} = 0$, $\frac{\partial A^{N*}}{\partial\gamma} = \frac{\alpha(a-b\omega)^2}{4bu_3(\rho+\delta)} > 0$;

(2) $\frac{\partial S_1^{N*}}{\partial\eta} = \frac{\varepsilon\omega(a-b\omega)}{2u_1(\rho+\sigma)} > 0$, $\frac{\partial S_2^{N*}}{\partial\eta} = \frac{\lambda(a-b\omega)^2}{4bu_2(\rho+\sigma)} > 0$, $\frac{\partial A^{N*}}{\partial\eta} = 0$;

(3) $\frac{\partial S_1^{N*}}{\partial w} = (a-2b\omega)(\frac{\varepsilon\eta}{2u_1(\rho+\sigma)} + \frac{\beta\gamma}{2u_1(\rho+\delta)})$, when $\frac{a}{2b} < \omega < \frac{a}{b}$, $\frac{\partial S_1^{N*}}{\partial w} < 0$, otherwise, $\frac{\partial S_1^{N*}}{\partial w} > 0$; $\frac{\partial S_2^{N*}}{\partial w} = \frac{-\lambda\eta(a-b\omega)}{2u_2(\rho+\sigma)} < 0$; $\frac{\partial A^{N*}}{\partial w} = -\frac{\alpha\gamma(a-b\omega)}{2(\delta+\rho)u_3} < 0$. □

Proof of Proposition 2.

(1) $$\frac{\partial S_\infty^N}{\partial w} = \frac{-\eta\lambda^2(\delta+\rho)(a-b\omega)u_1 + \varepsilon(\varepsilon\eta(\delta+\rho)+\beta\gamma(\rho+\sigma))(a-2b\omega)u_2}{2(\delta+\rho)\sigma(\rho+\sigma)u_1u_2},$$

$$\frac{\partial^2 S_\infty^N}{\partial w^2} = \frac{b\eta\lambda^2(\delta+\rho)u_1 - 2b\varepsilon(\varepsilon\eta(\delta+\rho)+\beta\gamma(\rho+\sigma))u_2}{2(\delta+\rho)\sigma(\rho+\sigma)u_1u_2},$$

if $\eta\lambda^2(\delta+\rho)u_1 < 2\varepsilon(\varepsilon\eta(\delta+\rho)+\beta\gamma(\rho+\sigma))u_2$, $\frac{\partial^2 S_\infty^N}{\partial w^2} < 0$, $S_\infty^N(w=0) = \frac{\lambda^2\eta a^2}{4\sigma bu_2(\rho+\sigma)} > 0$, $S_\infty^N(w=\frac{a}{b}) = 0$, let $w^{N1} = \frac{a\eta\lambda^2(\delta+\rho)u_1 - a\varepsilon(\varepsilon\eta(\delta+\rho)+\beta\gamma(\rho+\sigma))u_2}{b\eta\lambda^2(\delta+\rho)u_1 - 2b\varepsilon(\varepsilon\eta(\delta+\rho)+\beta\gamma(\rho+\sigma))u_2}$. If $\eta\lambda^2(\delta+\rho)u_1 > \varepsilon(\varepsilon\eta(\delta+\rho)+\beta\gamma(\rho+\sigma))u_2$, $w^{N1} < 0$, $\frac{\partial S_\infty^N}{\partial w} < 0$; else, if $w < w^{N1}$, $\frac{\partial S_\infty^N}{\partial w} > 0$, else,

$\frac{\partial S_\infty^N}{\partial w} < 0$. If $\eta\lambda^2(\delta+\rho)u_1 > 2\varepsilon(\varepsilon\eta(\delta+\rho)+\beta\gamma(\rho+\sigma))u_2$, $\frac{\partial^2 S_\infty^N}{\partial w^2} > 0$, $w^{N1} > 0$, $\frac{\partial S_\infty^N}{\partial w} < 0$.

(2) $$\frac{\partial G_\infty^N}{\partial w} = \frac{-\alpha^2\gamma(\rho+\sigma)(a-b\omega)u_1 + \beta(\varepsilon\eta(\delta+\rho)+\beta\gamma(\rho+\sigma))(a-2b\omega)u_3}{2\delta(\delta+\rho)(\rho+\sigma)u_1u_3},$$

$$\frac{\partial^2 G_\infty^N}{\partial w^2} = \frac{b\alpha^2\gamma(\rho+\sigma)u_1 - 2b\beta(\varepsilon\eta(\delta+\rho)+\beta\gamma(\rho+\sigma))u_3}{2\delta(\delta+\rho)(\rho+\sigma)u_1u_3},$$

if $\alpha^2\gamma(\rho+\sigma)u_1 < 2\beta(\varepsilon\eta(\delta+\rho)+\beta\gamma(\rho+\sigma))u_3$, $\frac{\partial^2 G_\infty^N}{\partial w^2} < 0$, $G_\infty^N(w=0) = \frac{\alpha^2\gamma a^2}{4\delta b u_3(\rho+\delta)} > 0$, $G_\infty^N(w=\frac{a}{b}) = 0$, let $w^{N2} = \frac{a\alpha^2\gamma(\rho+\sigma)u_1 - a\beta(\varepsilon\eta(\delta+\rho)+\beta\gamma(\rho+\sigma))u_3}{b\alpha^2\gamma(\rho+\sigma)u_1 - 2b\beta(\varepsilon\eta(\delta+\rho)+\beta\gamma(\rho+\sigma))u_3}$, if $\alpha^2\gamma(\rho+\sigma)u_1 > \beta(\varepsilon\eta(\delta+\rho)+\beta\gamma(\rho+\sigma))u_3$, $w^{N2} < 0$, $\frac{\partial G_\infty^N}{\partial w} < 0$; else, if $w < w^{N2}$, $\frac{\partial G_\infty^N}{\partial w} > 0$, else, $\frac{\partial G_\infty^N}{\partial w} < 0$. If $\alpha^2\gamma(\rho+\sigma)u_1 > 2\beta(\varepsilon\eta(\delta+\rho)+\beta\gamma(\rho+\sigma))u_3$, $\frac{\partial^2 G_\infty^N}{\partial w^2} > 0$, $w^{N2} > 0$, $\frac{\partial G_\infty^N}{\partial w} < 0$. □

Proof of Lemma 2. The proof here is similar to Lemma 1, we set $V_{ss}^S(S,G) = r_{12}S + r_{22}G + r_{32}$ and $V_{sp}^S(S,G) = t_{12}S + t_{22}G + t_{32}$, we can get r_{12}, r_{22}, r_{32}, t_{12}, t_{22}, t_{32} as follows:

$$\begin{cases} r_{12} = \dfrac{\eta\omega(a-b\omega)}{2(\rho+\sigma)}, \\ r_{22} = \dfrac{\gamma\omega(a-b\omega)}{2(\delta+\rho)}, \\ r_{32} = (a-b\omega)^2 \\ \quad\times\left(\dfrac{(\varepsilon\eta(\delta+\rho)+\beta\gamma(\rho+\sigma))^2\omega^2}{8\rho(\delta+\rho)^2(\rho+\sigma)^2u_1} + \dfrac{\eta^2\lambda^2\omega(a-b\omega)}{8\rho b(\rho+\sigma)^2u_2} + \dfrac{\alpha^2\gamma^2(a+3b\omega)^2}{128\rho b^2(\delta+\rho)^2u_3}\right), \\ t_{12} = \dfrac{\eta(a-b\omega)^2}{4b(\rho+\sigma)}, \\ t_{22} = \dfrac{\gamma(a-b\omega)^2}{4b(\delta+\rho)}, \\ t_{32} = \dfrac{(a-b\omega)^3\begin{pmatrix} u_1(\alpha^2\gamma^2u_2(\rho+\sigma)^2(a+3b\omega)+2\eta^2\lambda^2u_3(\delta+\rho)^2(a-b\omega)) \\ +8bu_2u_3\omega(\beta\gamma(\rho+\sigma)+\varepsilon\eta(\delta+\rho))^2\end{pmatrix}}{64b^2\rho u_1u_2u_3(\delta+\rho)^2(\rho+\sigma)^2}. \end{cases}$$

After substituting the above equations into Eq. (24), we can get Lemma 2. □

Proof of Proposition 3. (1) $\frac{\partial S_1^{S*}}{\partial\gamma} = \omega(a-b\omega)(\frac{\beta}{2u_1(\rho+\delta)}) > 0$, $\frac{\partial S_2^{S*}}{\partial\gamma} = 0$, $\frac{\partial A^{S*}}{\partial\gamma} = \frac{\alpha(a-b\omega)(3b\omega+a)}{8bu_3(\rho+\delta)} > 0$.

(2) $\frac{\partial S_1^{S*}}{\partial\eta} = \omega(a-b\omega)(\frac{\varepsilon}{2u_1(\rho+\sigma)}) > 0$, $\frac{\partial S_2^{S*}}{\partial\eta} = \frac{\lambda(a-b\omega)^2}{4bu_2(\rho+\sigma)} > 0$, $\frac{\partial A^{S*}}{\partial\eta} = 0$.

(3) $\frac{\partial S_1^{S*}}{\partial w} = (a-2b\omega)(\frac{\varepsilon\eta}{2u_1(\rho+\sigma)} + \frac{\beta\gamma}{2u_1(\rho+\delta)})$, when $\frac{a}{2b} < \omega < \frac{a}{b}$, $\frac{\partial S_1^{S*}}{\partial w} < 0$, otherwise, $\frac{\partial S_1^{S*}}{\partial w} > 0$; $\frac{\partial S_2^{S*}}{\partial w} = \frac{-2\lambda\eta b(a-b\omega)}{4bu_2(\rho+\sigma)} < 0$; $\frac{\partial A^{S*}}{\partial w} = \frac{\alpha\gamma(a-3b\omega)}{4(\delta+\rho)u_3}$, when $\frac{a}{3b} < \omega < \frac{a}{b}$, $\frac{\partial A^{S*}}{\partial w} < 0$, otherwise, $\frac{\partial A^{S*}}{\partial w} > 0$; $\frac{\partial \phi}{\partial w} = \frac{8ab}{(a+3b\omega)^2} > 0$. □

Proof of Proposition 4. (1) The same as Proposition 2(1);

(2)
$$\frac{\partial G_\infty^S}{\partial w} = \frac{\alpha^2\gamma(\rho+\sigma)(a-3b\omega)u_1 + 2\beta(\varepsilon\eta(\delta+\rho)+\beta\gamma(\rho+\sigma))(a-2b\omega)u_3}{4\delta(\delta+\rho)(\rho+\sigma)u_1u_3},$$

$$\frac{\partial^2 G_\infty^S}{\partial w^2} = -\frac{3b\alpha^2\gamma(\rho+\sigma)u_1 + 4b\beta(\varepsilon\eta(\delta+\rho)+\beta\gamma(\rho+\sigma))u_3}{4\delta(\delta+\rho)(\rho+\sigma)u_1u_3} < 0,$$

$$G_\infty^S\left(w=\frac{a}{5b}\right) = \frac{2a^2(2\alpha^2\gamma(\rho+\sigma)u_1 + \beta(\varepsilon\eta(\delta+\rho)+\beta\gamma(\rho+\sigma))u_3)}{25b\delta(\delta+\rho)(\rho+\sigma)u_1u_3} > 0,$$

$$G_\infty^S\left(w=\frac{a}{b}\right) = 0,$$

let

$$w^{N3} = \frac{a\alpha^2\gamma(\rho+\sigma)u_1 + 2a\beta(\varepsilon\eta(\delta+\rho)+\beta\gamma(\rho+\sigma))u_3}{3b\alpha^2\gamma(\rho+\sigma)u_1 + 4b\beta(\varepsilon\eta(\delta+\rho)+\beta\gamma(\rho+\sigma))u_3},$$

since $\frac{a}{5b} < w^{N3} < \frac{a}{b}$, we get if $\frac{a}{5b} < w < w^{N3}$, $\frac{\partial G_\infty^S}{\partial w} > 0$; else, $\frac{\partial G_\infty^S}{\partial w} < 0$. □

Proof of Proposition 5.

(1)
$$\frac{\partial D_\infty^N}{\partial w} = \frac{(a-b\omega)F_1(w)}{8\delta(\delta+\rho)\sigma(\rho+\sigma)u_1u_2u_3},$$

$$\begin{aligned} F_1(w) &= 2(\delta\varepsilon\eta+\beta\gamma\sigma)(\varepsilon\eta(\delta+\rho)+\beta\gamma(\rho+\sigma))(a-3b\omega)u_2u_3 \\ &\quad - 3(a-b\omega)u_1(\alpha^2\gamma^2\sigma(\rho+\sigma)u_2 + \delta\eta^2\lambda^2(\delta+\rho)u_3), \\ F_1(w=0) &= 2a(\delta\varepsilon\eta+\beta\gamma\sigma)(\varepsilon\eta(\delta+\rho)+\beta\gamma(\rho+\sigma))u_2u_3 \\ &\quad - 3au_1(\alpha^2\gamma^2\sigma(\rho+\sigma)u_2 + \delta\eta^2\lambda^2(\delta+\rho)u_3), \\ F_1\left(w=\frac{a}{b}\right) &= -4a(\delta\varepsilon\eta+\beta\gamma\sigma)(\varepsilon\eta(\delta+\rho)+\beta\gamma(\rho+\sigma))u_2u_3 < 0. \\ \frac{\partial F_1(w)}{\partial w} &= 3bu_1(\alpha^2\gamma^2\sigma(\rho+\sigma)u_2 + \delta\eta^2\lambda^2(\delta+\rho)u_3) \\ &\quad - 6b(\delta\varepsilon\eta+\beta\gamma\sigma)(\varepsilon\eta(\delta+\rho)+\beta\gamma(\rho+\sigma))u_2u_3. \end{aligned}$$

If $u_1(\alpha^2\gamma^2\sigma(\rho+\sigma)u_2 + \delta\eta^2\lambda^2(\delta+\rho)u_3) > 2(\delta\varepsilon\eta+\beta\gamma\sigma)(\varepsilon\eta(\delta+\rho)+\beta\gamma(\rho+\sigma))u_2u_3$, $\frac{\partial F_1(w)}{\partial w} > 0$, $F_1(w=0) < 0$, $\frac{\partial D_\infty^N}{\partial w} < 0$.

If $u_1(\alpha^2\gamma^2\sigma(\rho+\sigma)u_2+\delta\eta^2\lambda^2(\delta+\rho)u_3) < 2(\delta\varepsilon\eta+\beta\gamma\sigma)(\varepsilon\eta(\delta+\rho)+\beta\gamma(\rho+\sigma))u_2u_3$, $\frac{\partial F_1(w)}{\partial w} < 0$, $F_1(w=0) > 0$ if $2(\delta\varepsilon\eta+\beta\gamma\sigma)(\varepsilon\eta(\delta+\rho)+\beta\gamma(\rho+\sigma))u_2u_3 > 3u_1(\alpha^2\gamma^2\sigma(\rho+\sigma)u_2+\delta\eta^2\lambda^2(\delta+\rho)u_3)$, we let $F_1(w=w_1)=0$, therefore, if $w<w_1$, $\frac{\partial D_\infty^N}{\partial w} > 0$, else, $\frac{\partial D_\infty^N}{\partial w} < 0$; else $F_1(w=0) < 0$, $\frac{\partial D_\infty^N}{\partial w} < 0$.

(2)
$$\frac{\partial D_\infty^S}{\partial w} = \frac{(a-b\omega)F_2(w)}{16\delta(\delta+\rho)\sigma(\rho+\sigma)u_1u_2u_3},$$
$$F_2(w) = 4(\delta\varepsilon\eta+\beta\gamma\sigma)(\varepsilon\eta(\delta+\rho)+\beta\gamma(\rho+\sigma))(a-3b\omega)u_2u_3$$
$$+u_1(\alpha^2\gamma^2\sigma(\rho+\sigma)(a-9b\omega)u_2-6\delta\eta^2\lambda^2(\delta+\rho)(a-b\omega)u_3),$$
$$F_2\left(w=\frac{a}{5b}\right) = \frac{4}{5}a(2(\delta\varepsilon\eta+\beta\gamma\sigma)(\varepsilon\eta(\delta+\rho)+\beta\gamma(\rho+\sigma))u_2u_3$$
$$-u_1(\alpha^2\gamma^2\sigma(\rho+\sigma)u_2+6\delta\eta^2\lambda^2(\delta+\rho)u_3)),$$
$$F_2\left(w=\frac{a}{b}\right) = 8au_2(-\alpha^2\gamma^2\sigma(\rho+\sigma)u_1-(\delta\varepsilon\eta+\beta\gamma\sigma)(\varepsilon\eta(\delta+\rho)$$
$$+\beta\gamma(\rho+\sigma))u_3) < 0.$$
$$\frac{\partial F_2(w)}{\partial w} = 3b(-4(\delta\varepsilon\eta+\beta\gamma\sigma)(\varepsilon\eta(\delta+\rho)+\beta\gamma(\rho+\sigma))u_2u_3$$
$$+u_1(-3\alpha^2\gamma^2\sigma(\rho+\sigma)u_2+2\delta\eta^2\lambda^2(\delta+\rho)u_3)).$$

If $u_1(2\delta\eta^2\lambda^2(\delta+\rho)u_3-3\alpha^2\gamma^2\sigma(\rho+\sigma)u_2) > 4(\delta\varepsilon\eta+\beta\gamma\sigma)(\varepsilon\eta(\delta+\rho)+\beta\gamma(\rho+\sigma))u_2u_3$, $\frac{\partial F_2(w)}{\partial w} > 0$, $F_2(w=\frac{a}{5b}) < 0$, $\frac{\partial D_\infty^S}{\partial w} < 0$.

If $u_1(2\delta\eta^2\lambda^2(\delta+\rho)u_3-3\alpha^2\gamma^2\sigma(\rho+\sigma)u_2) < 4(\delta\varepsilon\eta+\beta\gamma\sigma)(\varepsilon\eta(\delta+\rho)+\beta\gamma(\rho+\sigma))u_2u_3$, $\frac{\partial F_2(w)}{\partial w} < 0$, $F_2(w=\frac{a}{5b}) > 0$ if $2(\delta\varepsilon\eta+\beta\gamma\sigma)(\varepsilon\eta(\delta+\rho)+\beta\gamma(\rho+\sigma))u_2u_3 > u_1(\alpha^2\gamma^2\sigma(\rho+\sigma)u_2+6\delta\eta^2\lambda^2(\delta+\rho)u_3)$, we let $F_2(w=w_2)=0$, therefore, if $w<w_2$, $\frac{\partial D_\infty^S}{\partial w} > 0$, else, $\frac{\partial D_\infty^S}{\partial w} < 0$; else $F_2(w=\frac{a}{5b}) < 0$, $\frac{\partial D_\infty^S}{\partial w} < 0$. □

Proof of Lemma 3. After substituting Eq. (36) into Eq. (35), we get

$$\rho V_{SC}^C(S,G) = \left(\frac{\eta a^2}{4b} - V_{scS}^{C'}(S,G)\sigma\right)S + \left(\frac{\gamma a^2}{4b} - V_{scG}^{C'}(S,G)\delta\right)G$$
$$+\frac{(\varepsilon V_{scS}^{C'}(S,G)+\beta V_{scG}^{C'}(S,G))^2}{2u_1}+\frac{\lambda^2(V_{scS}^{C'}(S,G))^2}{2u_2}$$
$$+\frac{\alpha^2(V_{scG}^{C'}(S,G))^2}{2u_3}.$$

Then, we set $V_{SC}^{C}(S,G) = r_{13}S + r_{23}G + r_{33}$, where r_{13}, r_{23}, r_{33} are the constants to be solved. By inserting $V_{SC}^{C}(S,G)$ into the above equation, we get

$$\rho(r_{13}S + r_{23}G + r_{33}) = \left(\frac{\eta a^2}{4b} - r_{13}\sigma\right)S + \left(\frac{\gamma a^2}{4b} - r_{23}\delta\right)G + \frac{a^4(\varepsilon\eta(\delta+\rho) + \beta\gamma(\rho+\sigma))^2}{32u_1b^2(\delta+\rho)^2(\rho+\sigma)^2} + \frac{\lambda^2 r_{13}^2}{2u_2} + \frac{\alpha^2 r_{23}^2}{2u_3}.$$

Solving the above equations regarding r_{13}, r_{23}, r_{33}, we get

$$\begin{cases} r_{13} = \dfrac{\eta a^2}{4b(\rho+\sigma)}, \\ r_{23} = \dfrac{\gamma a^2}{4b(\rho+\delta)}, \\ r_{33} = \dfrac{(\varepsilon r_{13} + \beta r_{23})^2}{2\rho u_1} + \dfrac{\lambda^2 r_{13}^2}{2\rho u_2} + \dfrac{\alpha^2 r_{23}^2}{2\rho u_3}. \end{cases}$$

After substituting the above equations into Eq. (36), we can get Lemma 3. □

Proof of Proposition 6. (1) $\frac{\partial S_1^{C*}}{\partial\gamma} = \frac{\beta a^2}{4bu_1(\rho+\delta)} > 0$, $\frac{\partial A^{C*}}{\partial\gamma} = \frac{\alpha a^2}{4bu_3(\rho+\delta)} > 0$;
(2) $\frac{\partial S_1^{C*}}{\partial\eta} = \frac{\varepsilon a^2}{4bu_1(\rho+\sigma)} > 0$, $\frac{\partial S_2^{C*}}{\partial\eta} = \frac{\lambda a^2}{4bu_2(\rho+\sigma)} > 0$. □

Proof of Proposition 7. (1) $S_1^{C*} - S_1^{S*} = \left(\frac{\varepsilon\eta}{2u_1(\rho+\sigma)} + \frac{\beta\gamma}{2u_1(\rho+\delta)}\right)\left(\frac{a^2-2b\omega(a-b\omega)}{2b}\right) > 0$;
(2) $S_2^{C*} - S_2^{S*} = \frac{b\eta\lambda\omega(2a-b\omega)}{4bu_2(\rho+\sigma)} > 0$;
(3) $p^{S*} - p^{C*} = \frac{b\omega}{2b} > 0$;
(4) $A^{S*} - A^{N*} = \frac{\alpha\gamma(a-b\omega)(5b\omega-a)}{8bu_3(\rho+\delta)} > 0$, $A^{C*} - A^{N*} = \frac{\alpha\gamma(a^2-(a-b\omega)^2)}{4bu_3(\rho+\delta)} > 0$, $A^{C*} - A^{S*} = \frac{\alpha\gamma b(a-b\omega)^2+2b^2\omega^2}{8bu_3(\rho+\delta)} > 0$. Thus, we get $A^{N*} < A^{S*} < A^{C*}$. □

Proof of Proposition 8.

(1)
$$S_\infty^S - S_\infty^C = \frac{\varepsilon(S_1^{S*} - S_1^{C*}) + \lambda(S_2^{S*} - S_2^{C*})}{\sigma} < 0,$$

$$S(t)^S - S(t)^C = (S_\infty^S - S_\infty^C)(1 - e^{-\sigma t}) < 0.$$

(2)
$$G_\infty^N - G_\infty^S = \frac{\alpha(A^{N*} - A^{S*}) + \beta(S_1^{N*} - S_1^{S*})}{\delta} < 0,$$

$$G_\infty^S - G_\infty^C = \frac{\alpha(A^{S*} - A^{C*}) + \beta(S_1^{S*} - S_1^{C*})}{\delta} < 0,$$

$$G(t)^S - G(t)^C = (G_\infty^S - G_\infty^C)(1 - e^{-\delta t}) < 0,$$

$$G(t)^N - G(t)^S = (G_\infty^N - G_\infty^S)(1 - e^{-\delta t}) < 0.$$ □

Proof of Proposition 9.

(1) $$J_{ss}^{N}(S,G) - J_{ss}^{S}(S,G) = \frac{(5bw-a)(a-bw)^2\alpha^2\gamma^2(a\delta - bw(5\delta+8\rho))}{128b^2\delta\rho(\delta+\rho)^2\mu_3} < 0;$$

(2) $$J_{sp}^{N}(S,G) - J_{sp}^{S}(S,G) = \frac{\alpha^2\gamma^2(\delta+2\rho)(a-5b\omega)(a-b\omega)^3}{64b^2\delta\rho(\delta+\rho)^2u_3} < 0;$$

(3) we let $\Delta = \frac{a}{bw}, 1 < \Delta < 5$, $J_{SC}^{C}(S,G) - J_{SC}^{S}(S,G) = \frac{\eta a^2}{4b(\rho+\sigma)}S_{\infty}^{C} + \frac{\gamma a^2}{4b(\rho+\delta)}G_{\infty}^{C} - \frac{\eta(a^2-b^2\omega^2)}{4b(\rho+\sigma)}S_{\infty}^{S} - \frac{\gamma(a^2-b^2\omega^2)}{4b(\rho+\delta)}G_{\infty}^{S} + \frac{b^2w^3}{4}(\frac{a(\varepsilon\eta(\delta+\rho)+\beta\gamma(\rho+\sigma))^2}{8b\rho u_1(\delta+\rho)^2(\rho+\sigma)^2})(\Delta^3 - 4(\Delta-1)^2) + \frac{\lambda^2\eta^2b^4\omega^4}{32b^2\rho u_2(\rho+\sigma)^2}(\Delta^4 - (\Delta-1)^3(\Delta+3)) + \frac{\alpha^2\gamma^2b^4\omega^4}{32\rho u_3 b^2(\rho+\delta)^2}(\Delta^4 - \frac{(\Delta-1)^2(3\Delta+1)(\Delta+3)}{4}) > 0.$

$$\begin{aligned} &J_{SC}^{S}(S,G) - J_{SC}^{N}(S,G) \\ &= \frac{\eta b^2\omega^2(\Delta^2-1)}{4b(\rho+\sigma)}(S_{\infty}^{S} - S_{\infty}^{N}) + \frac{\gamma b^2\omega^2(\Delta^2-1)}{4b(\rho+\delta)}(G_{\infty}^{S} - G_{\infty}^{N}) \\ &- \frac{\alpha^2\gamma^2b^4\omega^4(\Delta-5)(\Delta-1)^2(\Delta+3)}{128b^2\rho(\delta+\rho)^2u_3} > 0. \end{aligned}$$ □

Acknowledgments

The research is supported by the National Natural Science Foundation of China (Nos. 71771053 and 71371003), the Key Research and Development Plan (Modern Agriculture) of Jiangsu Province (No. BE2018385), the Key Research Project of Culture and Tourism in Jiangsu Province (20ZD02), the Key Project of Jiangsu Social Science Application Research Project (20SYA-049), and the Natural Science Foundation of Jiangsu Province (No. BK20201144).

References

Anwar, S, L Min and G Dastagir (2019). Effect of service quality, brand image, perceived value on customer satisfaction and loyalty in the Chinese banking industry. *International Journal of Business, Economics and Management Works*, 6(3), 24–30.

Barrett, M, E Oborn and W Orlikowski (2016). Creating value in online communities: The sociomaterial configuring of strategy, platform, and stakeholder engagement. *Information Systems Research*, 27(4), 704–723.

Cellini, R and L Lambertini (2004). Dynamic oligopoly with sticky prices: Closed-loop, feedback, and open-loop solutions. *Journal of Dynamical and Control Systems*, 10(3), 303–314.

Cheng, X, S Fu and GJ de Vreede (2018). A mixed method investigation of sharing economy driven car-hailing services: Online and offline perspectives. *International Journal of Information Management*, 41, 57–64.

Chutani, A and SP Sethi (2012a). Optimal advertising and pricing in a dynamic durable goods supply chain. *Journal of Optimization Theory & Applications*, 154(2), 615–643.

Chutani, A and SP Sethi (2012b). Cooperative advertising in a dynamic retail market oligopoly. *Dynamic Games and Applications*, 2(4), 347–375.

Chutani, A and SP Sethi (2018). Dynamic cooperative advertising under manufacturer and retailer level competition. *European Journal of Operational Research*, 268(2), 635–652.

Collier, JE and CC Bienstock (2006). Measuring service quality in e-retailing. *Journal of Service Research*, 8(3), 260–275.

Davcik, NS, R Vinhas da Silva and JF Hair (2015). Towards a unified theory of brand equity: Conceptualizations, taxonomy and avenues for future research. *Journal of Product & Brand Management*, 24(1), 3–17.

Eid, R (2015). Integrating muslim customer perceived value, satisfaction, loyalty and retention in the tourism industry: An empirical study. *International Journal of Tourism Research*, 17(3), 249–260.

El Ouardighi, F (2014). Supply quality management with optimal wholesale price and revenue sharing contracts: A two-stage game approach. *International Journal of Production Economics*, 156, 260–268.

García, D and M Tugores (2006). Optimal choice of quality in hotel services. *Annals of Tourism Research*, 33(2), 456–469.

Hahn, SE, B Sparks, H Wilkins and X Jin (2017). E-service quality management of a hotel website: A scale and implications for management. *Journal of Hospitality Marketing & Management*, 26(7), 694–716.

Hao, L, H Guo and RF Easley (2017). A mobile platform's in-app advertising contract under agency pricing for app sales. *Production and Operations Management*, 26(2), 189–202.

He, P, Y He, CV Shi, H Xu and L Zhou (2020). Cost-sharing contract design in a low-carbon service supply chain. *Computers & Industrial Engineering*, 139, 106160. https://doi.org/10.1016/j.cie.2019.106160.

Huang, Z, J Nie and J Zhang (2018). Dynamic cooperative promotion models with competing retailers and negative promotional effects on brand image. *Computers & Industrial Engineering*, 118, 291–308.

Jena, SK and PL Meena (2019). Price and service competition in a tourism supply chain. *Service Science*, 11(4), 279–291.

Jørgensen, S, SP Sigue and G Zaccour (2000). Dynamic cooperative advertising in a channel. *Journal of Retailing*, 76(1), 71–92.

Jørgensen, S, S Taboubi and G Zaccour (2001). Cooperative advertising in a marketing channel. *Journal of Optimization Theory and Applications*, 110(1), 145–158.

Jørgensen, S, S Taboubi and G Zaccour (2003). Retail promotions with negative brand image effects: Is cooperation possible? *European Journal of Operational Research*, 150(2), 395–405.

Jørgensen, S and G Zaccour (2014). A survey of game-theoretic models of cooperative advertising. *European Journal of Operational Research*, 237(1), 1–14.

Ku, EC and CD Chen (2015). Cultivating travellers' revisit intention to e-tourism service: The moderating effect of website interactivity. *Behaviour & Information Technology*, 34(5), 465–478.

Li, X, Y Li and W Cao (2019). Cooperative advertising models in O2O supply chains. *International Journal of Production Economics*, 215, 144–152.

Liu, SQ and AS Mattila (2017). Airbnb: Online targeted advertising, sense of power, and consumer decisions. *International Journal of Hospitality Management*, 60, 33–41.

Liu, W, X Yan, W Wei and D Xie (2019). Pricing decisions for service platform with provider's threshold participating quantity, value-added service and matching ability.

Transportation Research Part E: Logistics and Transportation Review, 122, 410–432.

Liu, W, S Long, D Xie, Y Liang and J Wang (2021). How to govern the big data discriminatory pricing behavior in the platform service supply chain? An examination with a three-party evolutionary game model. *International Journal of Production Economics*, 231, 107910.

Marimon, F, J Llach, M Alonso-Almeida and M Mas-Machuca (2019). CC-Qual: A holistic scale to assess customer perceptions of service quality of collaborative consumption services. *International Journal of Information Management*, 49, 130–141.

Ma, Y, K Rong, Y Luo, Y Wang, D Mangalagiu and TF Thornton (2019). Value co-creation for sustainable consumption and production in the sharing economy in China. *Journal of Cleaner Production*, 208, 1148–1158.

Nerlove, M and KJ Arrow (1962). Optimal advertising policy under dynamic conditions. *Economica*, 29(114), 129–142.

Parasuraman, A, VA Zeithaml and LL Berry (1988). SERVQUAL: A multiple-item scale for measuring consumer perceptions of service quality. *Journal of Retailing*, 64(1), 12–40.

Radhi, M and G Zhang (2018). Pricing policies for a dual-channel retailer with cross-channel returns. *Computers & Industrial Engineering*, 119, 63–75.

Shen, B, SY Liu, T Zhang and TM Choi (2019). Optimal advertising and pricing for new green products in the circular economy. *Journal of Cleaner Production*, 233, 314–327.

Sigué, SP and P Chintagunta (2009). Advertising strategies in a franchise system. *European Journal of Operational Research*, 198(2), 655–665.

Smedlund, A (2012). Value cocreation in service platform business models. *Service Science*, 4(1), 79–88.

Tsai, CY, JS Horng, CH Liu and DC Hu (2015). Work environment and atmosphere: The role of organizational support in the creativity performance of tourism and hospitality organizations. *International Journal of Hospitality Management*, 46, 26–35.

Tsao, WC, MT Hsieh and TM Lin (2016). Intensifying online loyalty! The power of website quality and the perceived value of consumer/seller relationship. *Industrial Management & Data Systems*, 116(9), 1987–2010.

Wang, Y, SW Wallace, B Shen and TM Choi (2015). Service supply chain management: A review of operational models. *European Journal of Operational Research*, 247(3), 685–698.

Wilkins, H, B Merrilees and C Herington (2007). Towards an understanding of total service quality in hotels. *International Journal of Hospitality Management*, 26(4), 840–853.

Xiang, Z and M Xu (2019). Dynamic cooperation strategies of the closed-loop supply chain involving the internet service platform. *Journal of Cleaner Production*, 220, 1180–1193.

Xu, J, I Benbasat and RT Cenfetelli (2013). Integrating service quality with system and information quality: An empirical test in the e-service context. *MIS Quarterly*, 37(3), 777–794.

Xu, JB and A Chan (2010). A conceptual framework of hotel experience and customer-based brand equity: Some research questions and implications. *International Journal of Contemporary Hospitality Management*, 22(2), 174–193.

Zhang, J, Q Gou, L Liang and Z Huang (2013). Supply chain coordination through cooperative advertising with reference price effect. *Omega*, 41(2), 345–353.

Zhang, J, Q Gou, S Li and Z Huang (2017). Cooperative advertising with accrual rate in a dynamic supply chain. *Dynamic Games and Applications*, 7(1), 112–130.

Biography

Yong He is a professor at School of Economics and Management, Southeast University, China. His research interests include supply chain management, logistics management, marketing/OM interfaces, food supply chain, and service science. His research has been published in many reputable international journals such as *Naval Research Logistics*, *Annals of Tourism Research*, *Omega-International Journal of Management Science*, *European Journal of Operational Research*, *International Journal of Production Economics*, *International Journal of Production Research*, *Transportation Research Part E* and so on.

Yanan Yu received the Bachelor's degree in Management from Southwest Jiaotong University, China, in 2015. She is currently working toward the PhD degree at Southeast University, China. Her current research interests include agricultural supply chain management, organic certification and information disclosure. Her research has been published in *Annals of Operations Research and Journal of Cleaner Production.*

Zhongyuan Wang received his Master's degree in Management Science and Engineering from Southeast University, China, in 2019. Now he is engaged in work related to community group purchase.

Henry Xu graduated from Imperial College London with a PhD in supply chain management. Currently, he is teaching and doing research in the area of operations/logistics/supply chain management in the Business School of the University of Queensland, Australia. His research interests include supply chain integration and coordination, risk/disruption management, and sustainable supply chains. He has published in a number of reputable international journals such as *International Journal of Production Economics*, *International Journal of Production Research*, *International Journal of Physical Distribution & Logistics Management*, *IEEE Transaction on Engineering Management*, *Transportation Research Part E: Logistics and Transportation Review*, among others.

https://doi.org/10.1142/9789819808588_0010

Chapter 10

Online Pricing Strategy with Considering Consumers' Fairness Concerns†

Liu Yang
Business School, University of International Business and Economics, Beijing, P. R. China
yangliu@uibe.edu.cn

Yuanyuan Zheng
Business School, University of International Business and Economics, Beijing, P. R. China
Angers Joint Institute, Ningbo University Ningbo, P. R. China
zhengyuanyuan@nbu.edu.cn

Jiasi Fan
Business School, University of International Business and Economics, Beijing, P. R. China
j.fan@uibe.edu.cn

Shaozeng Dong*
School of Business, Jiangsu Ocean University Lianyungang, P. R. China
**szdong@jou.edu.cn*

The development of emerging technologies, such as advanced information system, social media, and blockchain, has significantly changed consumers' behaviors in relation to online purchase. Having access to the historical price information, consumers are able to compare the current price with the historical prices and may raise fairness concerns in the comparison process. We investigate the impacts of consumers' fairness concerns on retailers' pricing strategies in a two-stage model. We show that when the retailer uses uniform pricing strategy, consumers' fairness concerns induce the retailer to decrease product price. As a consequence, the market demand expands and the retailer's profit reduces. When the retailer adopts multi-stage pricing strategy, we find that consumers' fairness concerns are not always harmful to the retailer's profit. Under certain conditions,

*Corresponding author.
†To cite this article, please refer to its earlier version published in the Asia-Pacific Journal of Operational Research, Vol. 39, No. 1, (February 2022), DOI: 10.1142/S0217595921400327. Reprinted with permission from World Scientific Publishing Co. Pte. Ltd.

the retailer can benefit from consumers' fairness concerns. Particularly, the product price in the first period increases, but the price in the second period and the market demand could be increased or decreased, depending on the situations.

Keywords: Fairness concern; online shopping; pricing; two-stage.

1. Introduction

Nowadays, with the development of advanced information technologies, such as big data and social media, consumers can easily access abundant information online, including historical prices, promotions, and online reviews offered by consumers who have used the product (Fu *et al.*, 2020). Moreover, blockchain technology adopted by e-commerce platform enables consumers to trace the source of a product. When a customer purchases a product on an e-commerce platform, a record is generated including the purchase date, the order time, and the amount of purchase (Zhao and O'Mahony, 2020). Social media has been widely used to assist consumers in communicating with sellers and other consumers on a frequent basis. The development of these emerging technologies has significantly changed the consumers' behaviors and considerations when they purchase online, which in turn affects sellers' price decisions.

Historical price data affects consumers' purchasing decisions. This price information is also known as the reference price (Mazumdar *et al.*, 2005; Moon *et al.*, 2006). Comparisons made between the market prices and the reference prices influence consumers' product evaluations and in turn their purchase decisions, especially in a market with repeated interactions (Popescu and Wu, 2005). Such issue has been addressed extensively in previous research, including both empirical and modeling studies (Fibich *et al.*, 2005; Popescu and Wu, 2007; Nasiry and Popescu, 2011; Cao *et al.*, 2019). One of the classic models is the memory-based reference price model which argues that information such as prices observed and historical purchasing prices forms reference prices and sets anchors in consumers' minds. Consumers will recall the reference prices when they make purchase decisions. Since consumers often forget the prices observed, the reference prices are more likely to be estimated as the most recent prices paid, or the weighted mean of the logarithms of the past prices, or an exponential smoothing of the past prices. Nevertheless, consumers' behaviors of recalling historical prices may be reshaped in the context of online shopping, as all the historical transaction information including product prices is recorded by online stores and platforms.

With the development of e-commerce, online shopping has become increasingly popular. There are more than three million companies engaged in e-commerce around the world, including Amazon, eBay, Alibaba, and JD (Goolsbee and Klenow, 2018). Competitions among online stores are quite fierce. In order to attract consumers, many online stores adopt promotions frequently. There are also many festivals around the world which cause peaks in e-commerce, such as Singles' Day, Black Friday, Cyber Monday, and the Christmas Sales. Meanwhile, consumers who purchase online become more sensitive to product prices. With the assistance of different types of apps (e.g., Price Tag and Price reader), consumers can access the historical information of product prices. In other words, it is convenient for consumers who purchase online to make price comparisons between the current product price and the historical prices. Consumers who purchase offline, on the contrary, will find it difficult to recall the historical product prices when making purchase decisions. Once a reference point has been evoked, consumers' decisions will be affected by the difference between the current price and the reference price. This comparison process drives consumers' fairness concerns. Prior research provides evidence that perceptions of fairness in turn will influence consumer satisfaction and behavioral intentions (Goldfarb *et al.*, 2012). It implies that consumers' fairness concerns will affect the market demands, and in turn influence the online stores' product price decisions. Therefore, the stores need to consider not only the profit of a selling season, but also the impact of the product price on future selling seasons.

In this paper, we study the impact of consumers' fairness concerns on the retailer's pricing strategies. We consider a retailer selling a new consumption product in a two-stage pricing model setting with considering consumers' fairness concerns. In the first period, consumers are not sure about their preferences to the product and make their decisions solely based on the expectation of utilities from buying the product. In the second period, consumers are aware of their preferences. By observing the product price and the historical price information (including price and discount rate in the first period) in the second period, consumers may raise fairness concerns. They make their purchase decisions based on the consumer utilities. To investigate the impacts of consumers' fairness concerns on the retailer's pricing strategies and profits, we consider four cases, namely, uniform pricing without fairness concerns, uniform pricing with fairness concerns, multi-stage pricing without fairness concerns, and multi-stage pricing with fairness concerns.

Our study reveals some interesting findings. First, when the retailer adopts the uniform pricing strategy, consumers' fairness concerns induce the retailer to decrease the price, resulting in a market expansion. Jointly affected by the reduced profit margin and the increased demand effect, the retailer's profit falls. Second, when the retailer chooses the multi-stage pricing strategy, consumers' fairness concerns have multiple effects on the retailer's price decisions. Differing from the uniform pricing case, the retailer sets a higher product price in the first period. In the second period, however, the product price could be increased or decreased, depending on the situations. Third, we find that consumers' fairness concerns can benefit the retailer under some situations.

The remainder of the paper is organized as follows. Section 2 reviews previous literature and shows the research gap that this paper attempts to fill in. In Sec. 3, we describe the basic model setting. Section 4 formulates the retailer's uniform pricing strategies with and without consumers' fairness concerns. In Sec. 5, we formulate the retailer's multi-stage pricing strategies with and without consumers' fairness concerns. In Sec. 6, we offer conclusions and directions for future research.

2. Literature Review

Our paper relates to three streams of literature: dynamic pricing with reference price effects, consumers' fairness concerns, and presale.

Consumers develop price expectations based on historical prices and use them to examine the current prices. Plenty of experimental and empirical studies have confirmed that the reference prices affect consumers' purchase behavior and sellers' profits (e.g., Fibich *et al.*, 2005; Popescu and Wu, 2007; Nasiry and Popescu, 2011). Accordingly, reference price effect in a dynamic pricing decision has attracted extensive studies in the fields of behavioral economic, marketing, and operations management. Mazumdar *et al.* (2005) and Arslan and Kachani (2010) have offered comprehensive reviews of studies on reference price effect. One classical behavioral pricing model is the memory-based reference price model. Studies based on this model have shown that there exists a base setting where consumers are loss-averse, and reference prices are updated via an exponential smoothing mechanism (Fibich *et al.*, 2003; Popescu and Wu, 2007; Nasiry and Popescu, 2011; Chen *et al.*, 2017b).

Recently, dynamic pricing with reference price effects has been studied in various contexts. For example, Hu *et al.* (2016) consider a firm facing gain-seeking demand with reference price effects. They show that the optimal pricing strategies may not admit any simple characterizations and the dynamic price can be very complicated. Nasiry and Popescu (2011) claim that the representative peak-end moments in reference price formation are associated with the lowest and latest price. Cao *et al.* (2019) introduce uncertainty by considering a seller who knows neither the underlying demand function nor the parameters of the reference price updating mechanism. Chen *et al.* (2019) investigate a two-stage dynamic pricing strategy in the presence of strategic consumers who consider the first-stage price as the reference price. They find that the seller's profit will increase (decrease) with the reference price effect if consumer strategic behavior is low (high). Zhang *et al.* (2014) address a supply chain consisting of a manufacturer and a retailer in a bilateral monopoly setting in the presence of consumers' reference price effects. Zhang *et al.* (2015) develop an advertising model in which goodwill affected by advertising effort has a positive effect on reference price and market demand. However, with few exceptions, such as Wang *et al.* (2020a) who investigate the online–offline competition pricing strategy by taking into account the reference price effect, little research has been focused on pricing strategies with reference price effects in the context of online shopping. We seek to address the gap in this paper by exploring the reference price effect and the impacts of consumers' fairness concerns on retailers' pricing strategies with a two-stage model.

In behavioral economics area, both experimental and empirical studies have suggested that people are averse to inequity between their own and others' monetary payoff. The emerging fairness concerns in turn affect market demands and firms' profits. A significant body of research further investigates fairness concerns in decision-making models from various areas, such as economics, marketing, and supply chain management. For example, in the realm of supply chain management, Cui *et al.* (2007) first use the inequality aversion to characterize fairness concerns in a manufacturer–retailer model and show that a designed wholesale-price contract can eliminate the double marginalization and achieve coordination. Afterwards, much research has focused on fairness concerns between suppliers and retailers in different contexts, such as Ho *et al.* (2014), Chen *et al.* (2017a), Yang *et al.* (2013), and Yi *et al.* (2018), just to name a few. These studies indicate that channel members' fairness concerns have important impacts on their coordination strategies, pricing policies, and maintaining channel relationships.

There are a few studies exploring the effects of consumers' fairness concerns on sellers' decision-making. Consumers with fairness concerns will get lower product utilities if any inequality is perceived in a transaction. As Goldfarb *et al.* (2012) illustrate, consumers' fairness concerns can significantly affect firms' optimal pricing strategies. Guo (2015) examines sellers' optimal selling strategies in the context under which buyers care about distributional fairness and seller's variable cost is *ex ante* uncertain. He shows that inequity aversion may benefit an efficient firm while hurt an inefficient one. Guo and Jiang (2016) extend the model of Guo's (2015) and examine a firm's quality and pricing decisions in the case where consumers have distributional fairness concerns and are uncertain about the firm's costs. Li and Jain (2015) take customers' fairness concerns into account in a two-period competition model. They show that when fairness concerns are sufficiently strong, practicing behavior-based pricing is more profitable than that without customer recognition. Although consumers do not always have explicit knowledge about a seller's cost and profit, they are often sensitive to changes in the price (Bolton *et al.*, 2003). Previous studies have shown that a normative reference price conceptualized by consumers may be the price that consumers consider fair (Bolton *et al.*, 2003; Kahneman *et al.*, 1986; Xia *et al.*, 2004). These reference prices may be historical prices, competitors' prices, or other consumers' paying prices. Consumers will anchor a reference price and evoke a sense of fairness when they make purchase decisions. In the context of online shopping, the product price information is complete, including the historical prices in different selling stages. Chen and Cui (2013) investigate the impacts of consumers' fairness concerns on a firm's uniform pricing decisions and show that uniform pricing induced by consumers' fairness concerns can actually help mitigate price competition and hence increase firms' profits if the demand of the product category is expandable. Yang *et al.* (2019) investigate the effect of consumers' fairness concerns on the optimal pricing strategies for service firm in the context of dual channels and show that the firm is induced to lower product price in the store. In the two papers above, the reference points are either competing brand's price, or the product price in other channels. In this paper, we consider the historical product prices as reference points.

Our paper also relates to the research on presale. The presale strategy has been argued to be beneficial to sellers through reducing market demand uncertainty and risks of inventory (Tang *et al.*, 2004; Li and Zhang, 2013).

Cachon and Feldman (2017) find that presale can improve the profit of the monopolist retailer. The presale of new products has been used by online sellers such as Amazon.com and TMall.com to increase sales in recent years (Wu *et al.*, 2019; Zhang *et al.*, 2020). Focusing on new products' presale, Prasad *et al.* (2011) demonstrate that although presale can help the retailer reduce demand uncertainty, customers are still not sure to purchase in advance because of valuation uncertainty of the new product.

Presale usually divides the traditional selling period into two stages: presale stage and spot selling stage. A two-stage pricing model has been widely used in the literature. Zhang *et al.* (2020) establish a two-period Stackelberg game model in which a manufacturer cooperates with an e-retailer to perform advance selling to consumers. They show that advance selling activities consistently benefit the manufacturer while being averse to the e-retailer. Wang *et al.* (2020b) investigate a seller's optimal presale strategy by taking into account the consumers' preference reversal or inconsistency. Cachon and Feldman (2017) argue that competition in the spot period can lower product prices during spot sales which should thus force sellers to lower product prices during presales. Zeng (2018) studies the retailer's optimal advance selling price and production quantity in a two-period model where the demand uncertainty comes from both the market size and the distribution of consumer valuations. Zhang and He (2019) examine the advance selling decisions over two periods and suggest that future-oriented consumers who are concerned more about the product quality rather than the price discount. They further find that the retailer can announce a higher advance selling price if consumers are moderately risk averse. These papers do not consider consumers' fairness concerns in the model. In this paper, we combine the consumers' fairness concerns with a two-stage pricing model in the context of online selling. In our model, selling the new product in the first period can be seen as presale.

3. Model Description

We consider a retailer selling a new consumption product which consumers will purchase repeatedly through an online store in an e-commerce platform. Denoted by $q(q > 0)$ as the product quality. Product cost is normalized to zero. Denoted by θ, as consumers' willingness to pay for the product quality, which is assumed follow a uniform distribution between 0 and 1, i.e., $\theta \sim U(0, 1)$. The total market demand is normalized to 1. Each consumer makes her purchase decision based on her expected utility.

We consider a two-period model. Define t as the period index, where $t = 1, 2$. In the first period, the retailer needs to join in some promotions issued by the e-commerce platform. The retailer introduces the product into the market and joins in some promotions issued by the e-commerce platform. The retailer charges the price of the product p_1, and claims a discount rate δ, $\frac{1}{2} < \delta < 1$. Such rate would be jointly determined by the e-commerce platform. There are some shopping days on the e-commerce platform, such as 11th November, 18th June, in each year. The e-commerce platform often claims big promotions in advance of these shopping days. For example, JD.com will offer 10% discount if a consumer buys two units of product, and 20% discount for three units of products. The value of δ presents the average discount of promotions. Therefore, consumers actually need to pay δp_1 for each unit product in the first period. Consumers observe the promotion information. Consumers are not sure if they like the product in the first period, because they cannot examine this new product in person. There would be a disutility effect if they do not like the product after receiving the product. The probability that the consumers like this product is γ, $0 \leq \gamma \leq 1$. When a consumer buys the product, she will receive a utility $u_{1a} = \theta q - \delta p_1$, if she likes the product; and get a utility $u_{1b} = \theta q - \delta p_1 - e$, if she does not like the product. The expected utility is $u_1 = \gamma u_{1a} + (1-\gamma)u_{1b} = \theta q - \delta p_1 - (1-\gamma)e$. When the consumer gets a non-negative expected utility $u_1 \geq 0$, she will buy the product from the online store.

In the second period, all consumers are aware of their preferences. Consumers who purchase in the first period know surely whether they like the product or not. Consumers who do not buy the product in the first period also know the attributions of the product through extensive online reviews offered by other consumers. Therefore, in the second period, only consumers who like the product may consider to buy it. In other words, a γ portion of the market will consider whether to buy the product.

The retailer determines the product price p_2. Consumers observe the price p_2, and are reminded by the e-commerce platform or some apps the historical price information, including p_1 and discount rate δ in the first period. The reminder of the historical price information is widely used in the e-commerce platform, like JD.com and Taobao.com. Knowing the current product price p_2 and the historical price information, consumers may have fairness concerns when comparing the prices in the two periods. When p_2 is greater than the reference price δp_1, consumers will perceive losses. When p_2 is less than the reference price δp_1, consumers will perceive gains. We use $\omega, 0 \leq \omega \leq 1$ to represent consumers' sensitivity to fairness. Specially, consumers do not have fairness concerns when $\omega = 0$. A consumer who buys the product in the second period, she will receive utility $u_2 = \theta q - p_2 - \omega(p_2 - \delta p_1)$. Consumers who receive non-negative expected utilities $u_2 \geq 0$ will buy the product in the second periods. Further, we assume that the product quality is large enough, i.e., $q \geq \frac{(1-\gamma)e}{1-\delta}$.

The planning horizon includes two periods. Another alternative pricing strategy is uniform pricing strategy. With adoption of the uniform pricing strategy, the retailer sets a same price in the two periods. Some researchers have shown that the uniform pricing strategy can be more profitable than the price differentiation or discrimination strategy in some circumstances (Cai *et al.*, 2019; Chen and Cui, 2013). Cai *et al.* (2019) show that the uniform pricing strategy can be better than the price differentiation strategy when the cost saving and demand increasing are large enough or consumers' acceptance of online channel lies in a certain interval.

Table 1. Summary of notations.

q	The quality of the product
p_1	The price of the product in the period $t = 1$
p_2	The price of the product in the period $t = 2$
δ	The discount rate in the period $t = 1$
γ	The probability that the consumer likes the product
θ	The consumers' willingness-to-pay for quality
e	Utility loss if consumer does not like the product in the period $t = 1$
ω	The coefficient of the sensitivity to fairness
u_1	Utility the consumer received in the period $t = 1$
u_2	Utility the consumer received in the period $t = 2$
d_1	The demand in the period $t = 1$
d_1	The demand in the period $t = 2$
π	The total profit of the firm

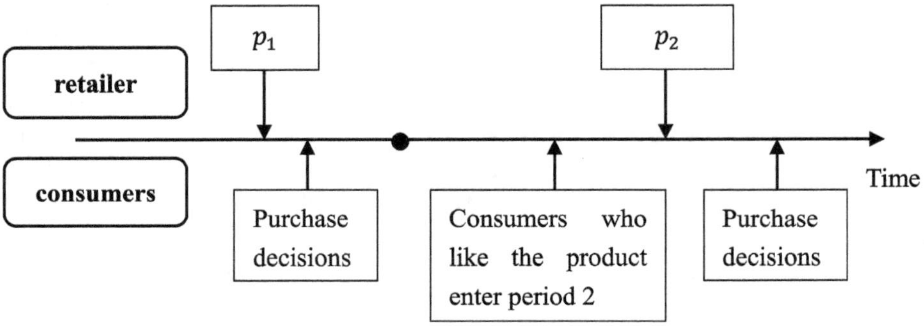

Fig. 1. The sequential events.

Chen and Cui (2013) show that the uniform pricing strategy of branded variants resulting from peer-induced consumers' fairness concerns can lead to higher profits for firms, compared with nonuniform pricing in the absence of consumers' fairness concerns.

To investigate the impacts of fairness concerns on retailers' pricing strategies, we consider four cases in this paper: uniform pricing without fairness concerns, uniform pricing with fairness concerns, multi-stage pricing without fairness concerns, and multi-stage pricing with fairness concerns. We use superscripts "UN", "UF", "MN", and "MF" to represent these four cases, respectively. We summarize the notations in Table 1. The decision order is shown in Fig. 1. All proofs are provided in Appendix A.

4. Uniform Pricing

4.1. *Uniform pricing without fairness concerns* (UN)

The retailer sets a uniform price p^{UN} in two stages. Without fairness concerns, consumers do not compare prices in the two periods and will make their purchase decisions only based on the selling price in each period. In the first period, a consumer gets utility $u_1^{\mathrm{UN}} = \theta q - \delta p^{\mathrm{UN}} - (1-\gamma)e$ if she buys the product. In the first period, we solve indifference point of θ between buying and not buying the product, and obtain the market demand in this period $d_1^{\mathrm{UN}} = 1 - \frac{\delta p^{\mathrm{UN}} + (1-\gamma)e}{q}$. In the second period, a consumer gets the utility $u_2^{\mathrm{UN}} = \theta q - p^{\mathrm{UN}}$ from buying the product. We derive the market demand $d_2^{\mathrm{UN}} = \gamma(1 - \frac{p^{\mathrm{UN}}}{q})$ in the second period. The retailer sets the price p^{UN} to maximize its profit, which is formulated as follows:

$$\mathrm{Max}\ \pi^{\mathrm{UN}}(p^{\mathrm{UN}}) = \delta p^{\mathrm{UN}} d_1^{\mathrm{UN}} + p^{\mathrm{UN}} d_2^{\mathrm{UN}}$$

$$\text{s.t.} \begin{cases} d_1^{\mathrm{UN}} \geq 0, \\ d_2^{\mathrm{UN}} \geq 0. \end{cases} \tag{1}$$

We solve the retailer's optimal price in case UN as presented in Lemma 1. The corresponding demand in case UN is listed in Table 2.

Lemma 1. *In case* UN, *the retailer's optimal price is* $p^{\mathrm{UN}} = \frac{q(\gamma+\delta) - \delta e(1-\gamma)}{2(\gamma+\delta^2)}$, *and the retailer's profit is* $\pi^{\mathrm{UN}} = \frac{(q(\gamma+\delta) - \delta e(1-\gamma))^2}{4q(\gamma+\delta^2)}$.

4.2. *Uniform pricing with fairness concern* (UF)

In this case, the retailer adopts uniform pricing in two periods and consumers have fairness concerns. Similar to situation UN, in the first period, a consumer gets a utility $u_1^{\mathrm{UF}} = \theta q - \delta p^{\mathrm{UF}} - (1-\gamma)e$ from buying the product. The market demand in the first period can be represented as $d_1^{\mathrm{UF}} = 1 - \frac{\delta p^{\mathrm{UF}} + (1-\gamma)e}{q}$. In the second period, consumers will have fairness concerns and they will compare the current price p^{UF} and the discounted price δp^{UF}. A consumer will obtain utility as $u_2^{\mathrm{UF}} = \theta q - p^{\mathrm{UF}} - \omega(p^{\mathrm{UF}} - \delta p^{\mathrm{UF}})$ if she buys the product in the second period. The market demand in the second period is $d_2^{\mathrm{UF}} = \gamma(1 - \frac{[1+\omega(1-\delta)]p^{\mathrm{UF}}}{q})$. The retailer's profit optimization problem is formulated as follows:

$$\mathrm{Max}\ \pi^{\mathrm{UF}}(p^{\mathrm{UF}}) = \delta p^{\mathrm{UF}} d_1^{\mathrm{UF}} + p^{\mathrm{UF}} d_2^{\mathrm{UF}}$$

$$\text{s.t.} \begin{cases} d_1^{\mathrm{UF}} \geq 0, \\ d_2^{\mathrm{UF}} \geq 0. \end{cases} \tag{2}$$

Table 2. The corresponding demands in case UN.

Demands
$d_1^{\mathrm{UN}} = 1 - \frac{e - e\gamma + \frac{\delta((\gamma+\delta)q - (1-\gamma)e\delta)}{2(\gamma+\delta^2)}}{q}$
$d_2^{\mathrm{UN}} = \gamma - \frac{\gamma((\gamma+\delta)q - (1-\gamma)\delta e)}{2q(\gamma+\delta^2)}$

Table 3. The corresponding demands in case UF.

Demands
$d_1^{\mathrm{UF}} = 1 - \frac{q\delta(\gamma+\delta)+e(1-\gamma)(2\gamma(1+\omega(1-\delta))+\delta^2)}{2q(\gamma(1+\omega(1-\delta))+\delta^2)}$
$d_2^{\mathrm{UF}} = \gamma + \frac{\gamma(1+\omega(1-\delta))(q(\gamma+\delta)-e\delta(1-\gamma))}{2q(\gamma(1+\omega(1-\delta))+\delta^2)}$

We solve the retailer's optimal price decision in case UF in Lemma 2. The corresponding demands in case UF are listed in Table 3.

Lemma 2. *In case* UF, *the retailer's optimal price is* $p^{\mathrm{UF}} = \frac{q(\gamma+\delta)-e\delta(1-\gamma)}{2\gamma(1+\omega(1-\delta))+2\delta^2}$, *and the retailer's profit is* $\pi^{\mathrm{UF}} = \frac{(q(\gamma+\delta)-e\delta(1-\gamma))^2}{4q(\gamma(1+\omega(1-\delta))+\delta^2)}$.

Proposition 1. *In case* UF, *we have:*

(i) *The product price is decreasing in consumers' sensitivity to fairness, i.e.,* $\frac{dp^{\mathrm{UF}}}{d\omega} < 0$.
(ii) *The total market demand is increasing in consumers' sensitivity to fairness, i.e.,* $\frac{dd^{\mathrm{UF}}}{d\omega} > 0$.
(iii) *The retailer's profit is decreasing in consumers' sensitivity to fairness, i.e.,* $\frac{d\pi^{\mathrm{UF}}}{d\omega} < 0$.

Proposition 1 demonstrates the impacts of the consumers' fairness concerns on the retailer's price decision and the corresponding profit. As consumers become more sensitive to fairness, they are reluctant to buy the product in the second period. As a result, the retailer has to lower the product price in order to attract more consumers to buy the product in the second period. We suggest that consumers' fairness concerns can affect the market demand. On the one hand, consumers feel a loss in the second period and are less willing to buy the product. On the other hand, the retailer lowers the product price in order to attract more consumers in both periods. As a result, the total market demand is increasing in the consumers' sensitivity to fairness. From the retailer's perspective, its profit margin reduces and the market demand increases. Proposition 1 indicates that the effect of profit margin reduction dominates, and the retailer' profit is reduced as consumers are more sensitive to fairness.

Proposition 2. *Comparing case* UN *and case* UF, *we have:*

(i) *The product price in case* UF *is lower than in case* UN, *i.e.,* $p^{\mathrm{UF}} < p^{\mathrm{UN}}$.
(ii) *The total market demand in case* UF *is higher than in case* UN, *i.e.,* $d^{\mathrm{UF}} > d^{\mathrm{UN}}$.
(iii) *The retailer's profit in case* UF *is lower than in case* UN, *i.e.,* $\pi^{\mathrm{UF}} < \pi^{\mathrm{UN}}$.

Proposition 2 compares cases UN and UF, which explains the impacts of consumers' fairness concerns on the retailer's decision when uniform pricing strategy is adopted. It shows that consumers' fairness concerns will lower the product price but increase the market demand. This is because consumers in the second period will feel a loss when comparing the current price and the discounted price in the first period. To make up the consumers' utility losses, the retailer is forced to lower the price. As a result, consumers will have an increase in utilities in both periods. The total market demand will increase. Affected by the demand effect and the profit margin effect, the retailer's profit will be decreased.

5. Multi-Stage Pricing

5.1. *Multi-stage pricing without fairness concern* MN

In this case, the retailer sets product price in each period. Consumers do not have fairness concerns. In the first period, the retailer sets the product price at p_1^{MN}. A consumer receives an expected utility $u_1^{\mathrm{MN}} = \theta q - \delta p_1^{\mathrm{MN}} - (1-\gamma)e$ from buying the product. We derive the market demand in the first period as $d_1^{\mathrm{MN}} = 1 - \frac{\delta p_1^{\mathrm{MN}} + (1-\gamma)e}{q}$. In the second period, the retailer sets the product price at p_2^{MN}. A consumer receives utility $u_2^{\mathrm{MN}} = \theta q - p_2^{\mathrm{MN}}$ from buying the product. Market demand in the second period is represented as $d_2^{\mathrm{MN}} = \gamma(1 - \frac{p_2^{\mathrm{MN}}}{q})$. We formulate the problems as follows.

In the second period, the retailer's profit maximization problem is

$$\begin{aligned} &\mathrm{Max}\ \pi_2^{\mathrm{MN}}(p_2^{\mathrm{MN}}) = p_2^{\mathrm{MN}} d_2^{\mathrm{MN}} \\ &\text{s.t. } d_2^{\mathrm{MN}} \geq 0. \end{aligned} \tag{3}$$

In the first period, the retailer sets the product price at p_1^{MN} to maximize the total profit.

$$\begin{aligned} &\mathrm{Max}\ \pi^{\mathrm{MN}}(p_1^{\mathrm{MN}}) = \delta p_1^{\mathrm{MN}} d_1^{\mathrm{MN}} + \pi_2^{\mathrm{MN}} \\ &\text{s.t. } d_1^{\mathrm{MN}} \geq 0. \end{aligned} \tag{4}$$

We solve the retailer's optimal price decisions in case MN in Lemma 3. The corresponding demands in case MN is listed in Table 4.

Lemma 3. *In case* MN, *the retailer's optimal product prices in the two periods are* $p_1^{\mathrm{MN}} = \frac{q - e(1-\gamma)}{2\delta}$ *and* $p_2^{\mathrm{MN}} = \frac{q}{2}$, *respectively*; *the retailer's profit is* $\pi^{\mathrm{MN}} = \frac{e^2(1-\gamma)^2 + q^2(1+\gamma) - 2eq(1-\gamma)}{4q}$.

Lemma 3 shows that without considering the consumers' fairness concerns, the product price in the two periods are independent to each other. The product price in the first period is affected by the product quality, the discount rate, and the disutility parameter. The product price in the second period is affected only by the product quality.

Table 4. The corresponding demands in case MN.

Demands
$d_1^{\mathrm{MN}} = \frac{q-e(1-\gamma)}{2q}$
$d_2^{\mathrm{MN}} = \frac{\gamma}{2}$

5.2. *Multi-stage pricing with fairness concerns* MF

In this case, the retailer sets the product price in each period with considering consumers' fairness concerns. Similar to case MN, the retailer determines p_1^{MF} in the first period. We solve the market demand in the first period as $d_1^{\mathrm{MF}} = 1 - \frac{\delta p_1^{\mathrm{MF}}+(1-\gamma)e}{q}$. In the second period, the retailer sets the product price as p_2^{MF}. Observing the product price p_2^{MF}, consumers will compare p_2^{MF} with the discounted price in the first period. When a consumer buys the product, she will get utility as $u_2^{\mathrm{MF}} = \theta q - p_2^{\mathrm{MF}} - \omega(p_2^{\mathrm{MF}} - \delta p_1^{\mathrm{MF}})$. The market demand in the second period is $d_2^{\mathrm{MF}} = \gamma(1 - \frac{p_2^{\mathrm{MF}}+\omega(p_2^{\mathrm{MF}}-\delta p_1^{\mathrm{MF}})}{q})$.

In the second period, the retailer decides p_2^{MF} to maximize the profit.

$$\begin{aligned} &\text{Max } \pi_2^{\mathrm{MF}}(p_2^{\mathrm{MF}}) = p_2^{\mathrm{MF}} d_2^{\mathrm{MF}} \\ &\text{s.t. } d_2^{\mathrm{MF}} \geq 0. \end{aligned} \tag{5}$$

In the first period, the retailer sets the product price at p_1^{MF} to maximize the total profit in the two periods. The retailer's total profit maximize problem can be formulated as follows:

$$\begin{aligned} &\text{Max } \pi^{\mathrm{MF}}(p_1^{\mathrm{MF}}) = \delta p_1^{\mathrm{MF}} d_1^{\mathrm{MF}} + \pi_2^{\mathrm{MF}} \\ &\text{s.t. } d_1^{\mathrm{MF}} \geq 0. \end{aligned} \tag{6}$$

The retailer's price decisions are given in Lemma 4. The corresponding demands in situation MF is listed in Table 5.

Lemma 4. *In case* MF, *the retailer's optiaml product prices in the two periods are* $p_1^{\mathrm{MF}} = \frac{q(2+\omega(2+\gamma))-2e(1+\omega)(1-\gamma)}{(4+4\omega-\omega^2\gamma)\delta}$ *and* $p_2^{\mathrm{MF}} = \frac{q(2+\omega)-e\omega(1-\gamma)}{4+4\omega-\omega^2\gamma}$, *respectively. The retailer's profit is* $\pi^{\mathrm{MF}} = \frac{e^2(1+\omega)(1-\gamma)^2+q^2(1+\omega)(1+\gamma)-eq(1-\gamma)(2+\omega(2+\gamma))}{q(4+4\omega-\omega^2\gamma)}$.

Proposition 3. *In case* MF, *the product price in the first period is increasing in consumers' sensitivity to fairness, i.e.,* $\frac{dp_1^{\mathrm{MF}}}{d\omega} > 0$.

Proposition 3 shows that as consumers become more sensitive for fairness, the retailer will set a higher product price in the first period. This is quite different from the impact of ω on the retailer's price decision in the uniform pricing case. It is because with higher sensitivity to fairness, consumers perceive a larger loss in

Table 5. The corresponding demands in case MF.

Demands
$d_1^{\text{MF}} = \frac{q(1+\omega)(2-\omega\gamma)+e(1-\gamma)(2+2\omega-\omega^2\gamma)}{q(4+4\omega-\omega^2\gamma)}$
$d_2^{\text{MF}} = \frac{(1+\omega)(q(2+\omega)-e\omega(1-\gamma))\gamma}{q(4+4\omega-\omega^2\gamma)}$

the second period by comparing the current price and the discounted price in the first period. Thus, consumers' utilities decline. To make up the losses of consumers' utilities, the retailer is motivated to increase the product price in the first period so that the price difference between the current price and the discounted price in the first period can be reduced.

Proposition 4. *In case* MF, *the impact of consumers' sensitivity to fairness on the product price in the second period is not monotonic. Specifically, we have*:

(i) *When* $\omega^2\gamma + 4\omega\gamma - 4 \leq 0$, *the product price in the second period is decreasing in consumers' sensitivity fo fairness, i.e.,* $\frac{dp_2^{\text{MF}}}{d\omega} < 0$.
(ii) *When* $\omega^2\gamma + 4\omega\gamma - 4 > 0$, *there exists a threshold of* $q^a = \frac{e(1-\gamma)(4+\omega^2\gamma)}{\omega^2\gamma+4\omega\gamma-4}$.
   (ii-a) *When* $q > q^a$, *the product price in the second period is increasing in consumers' sensitivity to fairness, i.e.,* $\frac{dp_2^{\text{MF}}}{d\omega} > 0$.
   (ii-b) *When* $q < q^a$, *the product price in the second period is decreasing in consumers' sensitivity to fairness, i.e.,* $\frac{dp_2^{\text{MF}}}{d\omega} < 0$.

Proposition 4 shows that the impact of the consumers' sensitivity to fairness on product price in the second period is not monotonic. Particularly, when ω, γ, and product quality q are very large, the product price in the second period increases as consumers become more sensitive to fairness. Under this situation, most consumers like the product and prefer to buy the product in the second period. As shown in Proposition 3, the product price in the first period will increase as ω increases. Because of the fairness concerns, consumers will perceive less loss. Therefore, the retailer could take this chance to increase the product price in the second period to gain a higher profit margin. In other situations, the retailer will lower the product price to attract more consumers.

Proposition 5. *In case* MF, *there exists a threshold* $q^b = \frac{e(1-\gamma)(4+4\omega+2\omega^2+\omega^2\gamma)}{2\omega(2+\omega)(1+\gamma)}$. *Regarding the impacts of* ω *on the total market demand, we have*:

(i) *When* $q > q^b$, *the total market demand is increasing in consumers' sensitivity to fairness, i.e.,* $\frac{dd^{\text{MF}}}{d\omega} > 0$.
(ii) *When* $q < q^b$, *the total market demand is decreasing in consumers' sensitivity to fairness, i.e.,* $\frac{dd^{\text{MF}}}{d\omega} < 0$.

Proposition 5 illustrates that the impact of ω on the total market demand could be positive or negaitve. It is because as consumers become more sensitive to fairness, two effects exist. On the one hand, consumers may feel larger loss and their utilities can be reduced. On the other hand, the retailer will adjust the product prices in two periods. Jointly affected by these two effects, the total market demand is increasing in ω when product quality is very high; otherwise, the total market demand is decreasing in ω.

Proposition 6. *In case* MF, *there exists a threshold* $\omega^a = \frac{2(1-\gamma)e}{(1+\gamma)q-(1-\gamma)e}$. *Regarding the impacts of* ω *on the retailer's profit, we have*:

(i) *When* $\omega > \omega^a$, *the retailer's profit is increasing in consumers' sensitivity to fairness, i.e.,* $\frac{d\pi^{\mathrm{UF}}}{d\omega} > 0$.
(ii) *When* $\omega < \omega^a$, *the retailer's profit is decreasing in consumers' sensitivity to fairness, i.e.,* $\frac{d\pi^{\mathrm{UF}}}{d\omega} < 0$.

Proposition 6 demonstrates that consumers' fairness concerns are not always harmful to the retailer's profit. Intuitively, it is believed that consumers' fairness concerns will reduce the customers' utilities and harm the retailer's profit. Proposition 6 shows that this is not always the case. Particularly, there exists a threshold of consumers' sensitive to fairness ω^a. When ω is higher than the threshold, the retailer' profit increases when ω becomes larger. Otherwise, the retailer's profit reduces as consumers becomes more sensitive to fairness. This is because the retailer's profit is jointly determined by the profit margin and the market demand.

Proposition 7. *Comparing the product prices in case* MF *and* MN, *we have*:

(i) *The product price in the first period in case* MF *is higher than that in case* MN, *i.e.,* $p_1^{\mathrm{MF}} > p_1^{\mathrm{MN}}$.
(ii) *The product price in the second period in case* MF *is lower than that in case* MN, *i.e.,* $p_2^{\mathrm{MF}} < p_2^{\mathrm{MN}}$.

Proposition 7 compares the product prices in cases MF and MN. It shows that consumers' fairness concerns increase the product price in the first period but lower the product price in the second period. This is because consumers' fairness concerns occur in the second period as they are able to compare the current price and the discounted price in the first period. Such fairness concerns cause losses of customers' utilities. To attract the consumers in the second period, the retailer will lower the product price in the second period. Meanwhile, to reduce the consumers' fairness concerns, the retailer will increase the product price in the first period, so that the price difference becomes smaller.

Proposition 8. *Let* $\omega^a = \frac{2(1-\gamma)e}{(1+\gamma)q-(1-\gamma)e}$, *by comparing the total market demands in cases* MF *and* MN, *we have*:

(i) *When* $\omega > \omega^a$, *the total market demand in case* MF *is higher than that in case* MN, *i.e.,* $d^{\mathrm{MF}} > d^{\mathrm{MN}}$.

(ii) *When* $\omega < \omega^a$, *the total market demand in case* MF *is lower than that in case* MN, *i.e.*, $d^{\mathrm{MF}} < d^{\mathrm{MN}}$.

Proposition 8 compares the total market demands in cases MF and MN. Consumers' fairness concerns could expand or reduce the total market demand, depending on the situations. When consumers are not very sensitive to fairness, the total market demand in case MF is lower than that in case MN. When consumers are very sensitive to fairness, their fairness concerns encourage more consumers to buy the product, rather than prevent people from buying the product. It is contrary to our intuition that fairness concerns always prevent consumers form buying products. Rather, under some situations the retailer will reduce the product price to attract more consumers.

Proposition 9. *Let* $q^c = \frac{(2+\omega+\sqrt{4+4\omega-\omega^2\gamma})(1-\gamma)e}{\omega(1+\gamma)}$, *by comparing the retailer's profits in cases* MF *and* MN, *we have*:

(i) *When* $q^c \leq \frac{(1-\gamma)e}{1-\delta}$, *the retaier's profit in case* MF *is higher than that in case* MN, *i.e.*, $\pi^{\mathrm{MF}} > \pi^{\mathrm{MN}}$.
(ii) *When* $q^c > \frac{(1-\gamma)e}{1-\delta}$, *there exist two scenarios*:

 (ii-a) *When* $q < q^c$, *the retaier's profit in case* MF *is lower than that in case* MN, *i.e.*, $\pi^{\mathrm{MF}} < \pi^{\mathrm{MN}}$.
 (ii-b) *When* $q > q^c$, *the retailer's profit in case* MF *is higher than that in case* MN, *i.e.*, $\pi^{\mathrm{MF}} > \pi^{\mathrm{MN}}$.

Intuitively, it is believed that consumers' fairness concerns are harmful to the retailer. However, Proposition 9 demonstrates that this is not always true. Under some conditions, the retailer can benefit from consumer's fairness concerns. Such situation is more likely to happen when the value of γ is very large or the product quality is very high. The possible reasons are as follows. First, when the value of γ is vary large, more people are willing to purchase the product in the second period. The retaielr will set a pricing strategy to attract consumers in the second period. Therefore, the retailer balances the gains and losses between the two periods. Second, when the quality of the product is very high, the retailer will set a price not very high in the first price. So the consumers in the second period may have some positive utility gains due to fairness concerns.

By comparing the uniform pricing with the multi-stage pricing, we find that the consumers' fairness concerns have different impacts on the retailer's profit. Particularly, using uniform pricing strategy, the retailer always gets hurt when consumers have fairness concerns. However, when the retailer adopts the multi-stage pricing strategy, consumers' fairness concerns can be beneficial or harmful to the retailer. This is because the retailer could adjust product price in different stages in response to consumers' fairness concerns.

6. Conclusion

This paper investigates the impacts of consumers' fairness concerns on a retailer's pricing decisions in the context of online shopping. We consider a two-stage model. In the first period, consumers make their purchase decisions based on their expected utilities, as they do not know whether they like the product or not. In the second period, consumers may raise fairness concerns by comparing the product price in the second period with the discounted price in the first period. We consider four cases: uniform pricing without fairness concerns, uniform pricing with fairness concerns, multi-stage pricing without fairness concerns, and multi-stage pricing with fairness concerns. We derive the optimal price decisions and the corresponding profits in each case. We conduct sensitivity analysis of system parameters.

We show that the retailer's price decision will be affected by consumers' fairness concerns under different pricing strategies. When the retailer adopts the uniform pricing strategy, the consumers' fairness concerns force the retailer to decrease the product price in order to attract more consumers. Interestingly, while the retailer's profit will be harmed by consumers' fairness concerns, the total market demand can be expanded when consumers are more sensitive to fairness. This result quite contradicts to our intuitive understanding. As we have explained earlier, the price reduction makes up for the consumers' utility losses due to fairness concerns. Therefore, more consumers are going to buy the product when they care about fairness.

We also address the consumers' fairness concerns effect in the case where the retailer uses the multi-stage pricing strategy. We find that the retailer will set a higher product price in the first period when consumers are more sensitive to fairness. This is because the retailer tries to relieve consumers' fairness concerns in the second period. However, the product price in the second period could be increasing or decreasing with the increasing consumers' sensitivity to fairness, depending on the situations. Our results show that the total market demand could be reduced or expanded as consumers become more sensitive to fairness. Intuitively, it is believed that consumers' fairness concerns are harmful to the retailer's profit. However, our results show that this is not always true. Under some situations, the retailer can benefit from consumers' fairness concerns.

There are two extensions deserving further investigations. First, we consider a monopoly model in our paper. When there are competitive retailers, consumers' fairness concerns will be surely affected by the competition. Integrating competition into the model would bring new managerial insights. Second, we assume that all consumers are aware of their preferences to the product in the second period. However, there are still some uncertainties due to the attributions of e-commerce. Further study could also address information asymmetry and investigate the issue of consumers' fairness concerns from a new perspective.

Appendix A

Proof of Lemma 1. From the constraint conditions of formula (1), we get

$$\begin{cases} 0 < p^{\mathrm{UN}} \leq \dfrac{q-(1-\gamma)e}{\delta} \\ 0 < p^{\mathrm{UN}} \leq q \end{cases}.$$

Because $q \geq \frac{(1-\gamma)e}{1-\delta}$, we have $0 < p^{\mathrm{UN}} \leq q$. By solving the second derivative of $\pi^{\mathrm{UN}}(p^{\mathrm{UN}})$ with respect to p^{UN}, we have $\frac{d^2\pi^{\mathrm{UN}}}{dp^{\mathrm{UN}2}} = -\frac{2\gamma}{q} - \frac{2\delta^2}{q} < 0$. By solving the first derivative of $\pi^{\mathrm{UN}}(p^{\mathrm{UN}})$ with respect to p^{UN}, we have $\frac{d\pi^{\mathrm{UN}}}{dp^{\mathrm{UN}}} = \frac{e(-1+\gamma)\delta+q(\gamma+\delta)-2p(\gamma+\delta^2)}{q}$. Because $\frac{d\pi^{\mathrm{UN}}}{dp^{\mathrm{UN}}}(p^{\mathrm{UN}}=0) = \gamma+\delta+\frac{e(-1+\gamma)\delta}{q} \geq \gamma+\delta^2 > 0$ and $\frac{d\pi^{\mathrm{UN}}}{dp^{\mathrm{UN}}}(p^{\mathrm{UN}}=q) = \gamma+\delta+\frac{e(-1+\gamma)\delta}{q} - 2(\gamma+\delta^2) < 0$, by solving the first condition of $\pi^{\mathrm{UN}}(p^{\mathrm{UN}})$ with respect to p^{UN} and get $p^{\mathrm{UN}} = \frac{e(-1+\gamma)\delta+q(\gamma+\delta)}{2(\gamma+\delta^2)}$. We can calculate the first market demand, the second period market demand and the retailer's optimal profit as $d_1^{\mathrm{UN}} = 1 - \frac{e-e\gamma+\frac{\delta(e(-1+\gamma)\delta+q(\gamma+\delta))}{2(\gamma+\delta^2)}}{q}$, $d_2^{\mathrm{UN}} = \gamma - \frac{\gamma(e(-1+\gamma)\delta+q(\gamma+\delta))}{2q(\gamma+\delta^2)}$, $d^{\mathrm{UN}} = \frac{q(\gamma^2+\delta^2+2\gamma(1-\delta+\delta^2))+e(-\gamma^2(-2+\delta)-\delta^2+\gamma(-2+\delta+\delta^2))}{2q(\gamma+\delta^2)}$, and $\pi^{\mathrm{UN}} = \frac{(e(-1+\gamma)\delta+q(\gamma+\delta))^2}{4q(\gamma+\delta^2)}$, respectively.

Sorting out of these results, we get Lemma 1. □

Proof of Lemma 2. By solving the second derivative of $\pi^{\mathrm{UF}}(p^{\mathrm{UF}})$ with respect to p^{UF}, we have $\frac{d^2\pi^{\mathrm{UF}}}{dp^{\mathrm{UF}2}} = -\frac{2\gamma(1+\omega(1-\delta))}{q} - \frac{2\delta^2}{q} < 0$. By solving the first derivative of $\pi^{\mathrm{UF}}(p^{\mathrm{UF}})$ with respect to p^{UF}, we have $\frac{d\pi^{\mathrm{UF}}}{dp^{\mathrm{UF}}} = \frac{2p^{\mathrm{UF}}\gamma(-1+\omega(-1+\delta))+e(-1+\gamma)\delta-2p^{\mathrm{UF}}\delta^2+q(\gamma+\delta)}{q}$. According to the constraint conditions of formula (2), we have

$$\begin{cases} 0 \leq p^{\mathrm{UF}} \leq \dfrac{q-(1-\gamma)e}{\delta} \\ 0 \leq p^{\mathrm{UF}} \leq \dfrac{q}{1+\omega(1-\delta)} \end{cases}.$$

Because $q \geq \frac{(1-\gamma)e}{1-\delta}$, we have $\frac{q-(1-\gamma)e}{\delta} > \frac{q}{1+\omega(1-\delta)}$ and $0 \leq p^{\mathrm{UF}} \leq \frac{q}{1+\omega(1-\delta)}$. Because $\frac{d\pi^{\mathrm{UF}}}{dp^{\mathrm{UF}}}(p^{\mathrm{UF}}=0) = \gamma+\delta+\frac{e(-1+\gamma)\delta}{q} > 0$ and $\frac{d\pi^{\mathrm{UF}}}{dp^{\mathrm{UF}}}(p^{\mathrm{UF}} = \frac{q}{1+\omega(1-\delta)}) = \frac{e(-1+\gamma)\delta}{q} + \frac{\delta(-1+\omega(-1+\delta)+2\delta)+\gamma(1+\omega-\omega\delta)}{-1+\omega(-1+\delta)} < 0$, by solving the first-order condition of $\pi^{\mathrm{UF}}(p^{\mathrm{UF}})$ with respect to p^{UF}, we get $p^{\mathrm{UF}} = -\frac{e(-1+\gamma)\delta+q(\gamma+\delta)}{2\gamma(-1+\omega(-1+\delta))-2\delta^2}$. We can calculate the first period market demand, the second period market demand, the total market demand and the retailer's profit as $d_1^{\mathrm{UF}} = 1 + \frac{q\delta(\gamma+\delta)+e(-1+\gamma)(2\gamma(-1+\omega(-1+\delta))-\delta^2)}{2q(\gamma(-1+\omega(-1+\delta))-\delta^2)}$, $d_2^{\mathrm{UF}} = \gamma - \frac{\gamma(-1+\omega(-1+\delta))(e(-1+\gamma)\delta+q(\gamma+\delta))}{2q(\gamma(-1+\omega(-1+\delta))-\delta^2)}$, $d^{\mathrm{UF}} = 1+r-\frac{q(\gamma(-1+\omega(-1+\delta))-\delta)(\gamma+\delta)+e(-1+\gamma)(\gamma(-1+\omega(-1+\delta))(-2+\delta)+\delta^2)}{2q(\gamma(-1+\omega(-1+\delta))-\delta^2)}$, and $\pi^{\mathrm{UF}} = -\frac{(e(-1+\gamma)\delta+q(\gamma+\delta))^2}{4q(\gamma(-1+\omega(-1+\delta))-\delta^2)}$, respectively.

Sorting out of these results, we get Lemma 2. □

Proof of Proposition 1. According to Lemma 2, we can calculate $\frac{dp^{\mathrm{UF}}}{dw} = \frac{\gamma(-1+\delta)(e(-1+\gamma)\delta+q(\gamma+\delta))}{2(\delta^2+\gamma(1+\omega-\omega\delta))^2} < 0$; $\frac{dd^{\mathrm{UF}}}{dw} = \frac{\gamma(-1+\delta)^2\delta(e(-1+\gamma)\delta+q(\gamma+\delta))}{2q(\delta^2+\gamma(1+\omega-\omega\delta))^2} > 0$ and $\frac{d\pi^{\mathrm{UF}}}{dw} = \frac{\gamma(-1+\delta)(e(-1+\gamma)\delta+q(\gamma+\delta))^2}{4q(\gamma(-1+\omega(-1+\delta))-\delta^2)^2} < 0$. □

Proof of Proposition 2. According to Lemmas 1 and 2, we can calculate $p^{\mathrm{UF}} - p^{\mathrm{UN}} = -\frac{\omega\gamma(-1+\delta)(e(-1+\gamma)\delta+q(\gamma+\delta))}{2(\gamma(-1+\omega(-1+\delta))-\delta^2)(\gamma+\delta^2)} < 0$; $d^{\mathrm{UF}} - d^{\mathrm{UN}} = -\frac{\omega\gamma(-1+\delta)^2\delta(e(-1+\gamma)\delta+q(\gamma+\delta))}{2q(\gamma(-1+\omega(-1+\delta))-\delta^2)(\gamma+\delta^2)} > 0$ and $\pi^{\mathrm{UF}} - \pi^{\mathrm{UN}} = -\frac{\omega\gamma(-1+\delta)(e(-1+\gamma)\delta+q(\gamma+\delta))^2}{4q(\gamma(-1+\omega(-1+\delta))-\delta^2)(\gamma+\delta^2)} < 0$.
□

Proof of Lemma 3. We use backward induction to solve this problem. In the second period, the retailer's profit is formulated as $\pi_2^{\mathrm{MN}}(p_2^{\mathrm{MN}}) = p_2^{\mathrm{MN}}\gamma(1-\frac{p_2^{\mathrm{MN}}}{q})$. By solving the second derivative of $\pi_2^{\mathrm{MN}}(p_2^{\mathrm{MN}})$ with respect to p_2^{MN}, we get $\frac{d^2\pi_2^{\mathrm{MN}}}{dp_2^{\mathrm{MN}2}} = -\frac{2\gamma}{q} < 0$. By solving the first derivative of $\pi_2^{\mathrm{MN}}(p_2^{\mathrm{MN}})$ with respect to p_2^{MN}, we get $\frac{d\pi_2^{\mathrm{MN}}}{dp_2^{\mathrm{MN}}} = \gamma - \frac{2p_2^{\mathrm{MN}}\gamma}{q}$. Because $\frac{d\pi_2^{\mathrm{MN}}}{dp_2^{\mathrm{MN}}}(p_2^{\mathrm{MN}}=0) = \gamma > 0$ and $\frac{d\pi_2^{\mathrm{MN}}}{dp_2^{\mathrm{MN}}}(p_2^{\mathrm{MN}}=q) = -\gamma < 0$, by solving the first-order condition of $\pi_2^{\mathrm{MN}}(p_2^{\mathrm{MN}})$ with respect to p_2^{MN}, we get $p_2^{\mathrm{MN}} = \frac{q}{2}$. We can calculate the second period market demand and the retailer's profit in the second period as $d_2^{\mathrm{MN}} = \frac{\gamma}{2}$ and $\pi_2^{\mathrm{MN}} = \frac{q\gamma}{4}$. □

In the first period, the retailer decides the product price p_1^{MN} to maximize the total profit. The retailer's total profit is formulated as $\pi^{\mathrm{MN}}(p_1^{\mathrm{MN}}) = \delta p_1^{\mathrm{MN}}[1 - \frac{\delta p_1^{\mathrm{MN}}+(1-\gamma)e}{q}] + \frac{q\gamma}{4}$. By solving the second derivative of $\pi^{\mathrm{MN}}(p_1^{\mathrm{MN}})$ with respect to p_1^{MN}, we get $\frac{d^2\pi^{\mathrm{MN}}(p_1^{\mathrm{MN}})}{dp_1^{\mathrm{MN}2}} = -\frac{2\delta^2}{q} < 0$. By solving the first derivative of $\pi^{\mathrm{MN}}(p_1^{\mathrm{MN}})$ with respect to p_1^{MN}, we get $\frac{d\pi^{\mathrm{MN}}(p_1^{\mathrm{MN}})}{dp_1^{\mathrm{MN}}} = \frac{\delta(q+e(-1+\gamma)-2\delta p_1)}{q}$. Because $\frac{d\pi^{\mathrm{MN}}(p_1^{\mathrm{MN}})}{dp_1^{\mathrm{MN}}}(p_1^{\mathrm{MN}}=0) = \delta + \frac{e(-1+\gamma)\delta}{q} > 0$ and $\frac{d\pi^{\mathrm{MN}}(p_1^{\mathrm{MN}})}{dp_1^{\mathrm{MN}}}(p_1^{\mathrm{MN}} = \frac{q-(1-\gamma)e}{\delta}) = -\frac{(q+e(-1+\gamma))\delta}{q} < 0$, by sovling the first-order condition for $\pi^{\mathrm{MN}}(p_1^{\mathrm{MN}})$ with respect to p_1^{MN}, we get $p_1^{\mathrm{MN}} = \frac{q+e(-1+\gamma)}{2\delta}$. We can calculate the first market demand and the retailer's total profit as $d_1^{\mathrm{MN}} = \frac{q+e(-1+\gamma)}{2q}$ and $\pi^{\mathrm{MN}} = \frac{2eq(-1+\gamma)+e^2(-1+\gamma)^2+q^2(1+\gamma)}{4q}$, respectively.

Proof of Lemma 4. The retailer decides the second period product price p_2^{MF} to maximize his profit in the second period. The retailer's profit in the second period is formulated as $\pi_2^{\mathrm{MF}}(p_2^{\mathrm{MF}}) = p_2^{\mathrm{MF}}\gamma(1-\frac{p_2^{\mathrm{MF}}+\omega(p_2^{\mathrm{MF}}-\delta p_1^{\mathrm{MF}})}{q})$. By solving the second derivative of $\pi_2^{\mathrm{MF}}(p_2^{\mathrm{MF}})$ with respect to p_2^{MF}, we have $\frac{d^2\pi_2^{\mathrm{MF}}(p_2^{\mathrm{MF}})}{dp_2^{\mathrm{MF}2}} = -\frac{2(1+\omega)\gamma}{q} < 0$. By solving the first derivative of $\pi_2^{\mathrm{MF}}(p_2^{\mathrm{MF}})$ with respect to p_2^{MF}, we have $\frac{d\pi_2^{\mathrm{MF}}}{dp_2^{\mathrm{MF}}} = \frac{\gamma(q+\omega\delta p_1^{\mathrm{MF}}-2(1+\omega)p_2^{\mathrm{MF}})}{q}$. Because $\frac{d\pi_2^{\mathrm{MF}}}{dp_2^{\mathrm{MF}}}(p_2^{\mathrm{MF}}=0) = \frac{\gamma(q+\omega\delta p_1^{\mathrm{MF}})}{q} > 0$ and $\frac{d\pi_2^{\mathrm{MF}}}{dp_2^{\mathrm{MF}}}(p_2^{\mathrm{MF}} = \frac{q+\delta\omega p_1^{\mathrm{MF}}}{1+\omega}) = -\frac{\gamma(q+\omega\delta p_1)}{q} < 0$, by solving the first-order condition of $\pi_2^{\mathrm{MF}}(p_2^{\mathrm{MF}})$ with respect to p_2^{MF}, we get $p_2^{\mathrm{MF}} = \frac{q+\omega\delta p_1^{\mathrm{MF}}}{2(1+\omega)}$. We can calculate $\pi_2^{\mathrm{MF}} = \frac{\gamma(q+\omega\delta p_1^{\mathrm{MF}})^2}{4q(1+\omega)}$.

In the first period, the retailer decides the first period price to maximize his total profit. The retailer's total profit is formulated as $\pi^{\mathrm{MF}}(p_1^{\mathrm{MF}}) = \delta p_1^{\mathrm{MF}}(1 - \frac{\delta p_1^{\mathrm{MF}}+(1-\gamma)e}{q}) + \frac{\gamma(q+\omega\delta p_1^{\mathrm{MF}})^2}{4q(1+\omega)}$. By solving the second derivative of $\pi^{\mathrm{MF}}(p_1^{\mathrm{MF}})$ with respect to p_1^{MF}, we get $\frac{d^2\pi^{\mathrm{MF}}(p_1^{\mathrm{MF}})}{dp_1^{\mathrm{MF}2}} = \frac{(-4-4\omega+\omega^2\gamma)\delta^2}{2q(1+\omega)} < 0$. By solving the first derivative of $\pi^{\mathrm{MF}}(p_1^{\mathrm{MF}})$ with respect to p_1^{MF}, we get $\frac{d\pi^{\mathrm{MF}}(p_1^{\mathrm{MF}})}{dp_1^{\mathrm{MF}}} = \frac{\delta(2e(1+\omega)(-1+\gamma)+q(2+\omega(2+\gamma))+(-4-4\omega+\omega^2\gamma)\delta p_1)}{2q(1+\omega)}$. Because $\frac{d\pi^{\mathrm{MF}}(p_1^{\mathrm{MF}})}{dp_1^{\mathrm{MF}}}(p_1^{\mathrm{MF}} = 0) = \frac{e(-1+\gamma)\delta}{q} + \frac{(2+\omega(2+\gamma))\delta}{2(1+\omega)} > 0$ and $\frac{d\pi^{\mathrm{MF}}(p_1^{\mathrm{MF}})}{dp_1^{\mathrm{MF}}}(p_1^{\mathrm{MF}} = \frac{q-(1-\gamma)e}{\delta}) = \frac{1}{2}(-2 + \omega\gamma + \frac{e(-1+\gamma)(-2-2\omega+\omega^2\gamma)}{q(1+\omega)})\delta < 0$, by solving the first-order condition of $\pi^{\mathrm{MF}}(p_1^{\mathrm{MF}})$ with respect to p_1^{MF}, we have $p_1^{\mathrm{MF}} = -\frac{2e(1+\omega)(-1+\gamma)+q(2+\omega(2+\gamma))}{(-4-4\omega+\omega^2\gamma)\delta}$. We can calculate the first period market demand, the second period market demand, the total market demand, the second period product price and the retailer's profit as $d_1^{\mathrm{MF}} = \frac{q(1+\omega)(-2+\omega\gamma)+e(-1+\gamma)(-2-2\omega+\omega^2\gamma)}{q(-4-4\omega+\omega^2\gamma)}$, $d_2^{\mathrm{MF}} = -\frac{(1+\omega)(q(2+\omega)+e\omega(-1+\gamma))\gamma}{q(-4-4\omega+\omega^2\gamma)}$, $d^{\mathrm{MF}} = -\frac{2q(1+\omega)(1+\gamma)+e(-1+\gamma)(2+\omega(2+\gamma))}{q(-4-4\omega+\omega^2\gamma)}$, $p_2^{\mathrm{MF}} = -\frac{q(2+\omega)+e\omega(-1+\gamma)}{-4-4\omega+\omega^2\gamma}$, and $\pi^{\mathrm{MF}} = -\frac{e^2(1+\omega)(-1+\gamma)^2+q^2(1+\omega)(1+\gamma)+eq(-1+\gamma)(2+\omega(2+\gamma))}{q(-4-4\omega+\omega^2\gamma)}$, respectively.

Sorting out of these results, we get Lemma 4. □

Proof of Proposition 3. According to Lemma 4, we can calculate $\frac{dp_1^{\mathrm{MF}}}{d\omega} = \frac{\gamma(2e\omega(2+\omega)(-1+\gamma)+q(4+4\omega+\omega^2(2+\gamma)))}{(4+4\omega-\omega^2\gamma)^2\delta} > 0$. □

Proof of Proposition 4. According to Lemma 4, we can calculate $\frac{dp_2^{\mathrm{MF}}}{d\omega} = \frac{e(-1+\gamma)(4+\omega^2\gamma)+q(-4+4\omega\gamma+\omega^2\gamma)}{(4+4\omega-\omega^2\gamma)^2}$. We consider this question in two scenarios:

(i) When $-4+4\omega\gamma+\omega^2\gamma > 0$, we have: when $q \geq \frac{e(1-\gamma)(4+\omega^2\gamma)}{-4+4\omega\gamma+\omega^2\gamma}$, we have $\frac{dp_2^{\mathrm{MF}}}{d\omega} \geq 0$; when $q < \frac{e(1-\gamma)(4+\omega^2\gamma)}{-4+4\omega\gamma+\omega^2\gamma}$, we have $\frac{dp_2^{\mathrm{MF}}}{d\omega} < 0$.

(ii) When $-4+4\omega\gamma+\omega^2\gamma \leq 0$, we have $\frac{dp_2^{\mathrm{MF}}}{d\omega} < 0$.

Sorting out of these results, we get Proposition 4. □

Proof of Proposition 5. According to Lemma 4, we can calculate $\frac{dd^{\mathrm{MF}}}{d\omega} = \frac{\gamma(2q\omega(2+\omega)(1+\gamma)+e(-1+\gamma)(4+4\omega+\omega^2(2+\gamma)))}{q(4+4\omega-\omega^2\gamma)^2}$. We consider this question in two scenarios:

(i) When $q \geq -\frac{e(-1+\gamma)(4+4\omega+2\omega^2+\omega^2\gamma)}{2\omega(2+\omega)(1+\gamma)}$, we have $\frac{dd^{\mathrm{MF}}}{d\omega} \geq 0$.

(ii) When $q < -\frac{e(-1+\gamma)(4+4\omega+2\omega^2+\omega^2\gamma)}{2\omega(2+\omega)(1+\gamma)}$, we have $\frac{dd^{\mathrm{MF}}}{d\omega} < 0$.

Sorting out of these results, we have Proposition 5. □

Proof of Proposition 6. According to Lemma 4, we can calculate

$$\frac{d\pi^{MF}}{d\omega} = \frac{\gamma(e^2\omega(2+\omega)(-1+\gamma)^2 + q^2\omega(2+\omega)(1+\gamma) + eq(-1+\gamma)(4+4\omega+\omega^2(2+\gamma)))}{q(4+4\omega-\omega^2\gamma)^2}$$

$$= \frac{\gamma[(2+\omega)q - \omega(1-\gamma)e][\omega(1+\gamma)q - (2+\omega)(1-\gamma)e]}{q(4+4\omega-\omega^2\gamma)^2}.$$

Because $[(2+\omega)q - \omega(1-\gamma)e] > 0$, we consider this question in two scenarios:

(i) When $\omega(1+\gamma)q - (2+\omega)(1-\gamma)e \geq 0$, i.e., $q \geq \frac{(2+\omega)(1-\gamma)e}{\omega(1+\gamma)}$, we have $\frac{d\pi^{MF}}{d\omega} \geq 0$.
(ii) When $\omega(1+\gamma)q - (2+\omega)(1-\gamma)e < 0$, i.e., $q < \frac{(2+\omega)(1-\gamma)e}{\omega(1+\gamma)}$, we have $\frac{d\pi^{MF}}{d\omega} < 0$.

Sorting out of these results, we get Proposition 6. □

Proof of Proposition 7. According to Lemmas 3 and 4, we can calculate $p_1^{MF} - p_1^{MN} = -\frac{2e(1+\omega)(-1+\gamma)+q(2+\omega(2+\gamma))}{(-4-4\omega+\omega^2\gamma)\delta} - \frac{q+e(-1+\gamma)}{2\delta} = -\frac{\omega(q(2+\omega)+e\omega(-1+\gamma))\gamma}{2(-4-4\omega+\omega^2\gamma)\delta} > 0$ and $p_2^{MF} - p_2^{MN} = -\frac{q*(2+\omega)+e*\omega*(-1+\gamma)}{-4-4*\omega+\omega^2*\gamma} - \frac{q}{2} = \frac{\omega(-2e(-1+\gamma)+q(2-\omega\gamma))}{-8-8\omega+2\omega^2\gamma} < 0$. □

Proof of Proposition 8. According to Lemmas 3 and 4, we can calculate the difference of the total market demand between case MF and case MN as $d^{MF} - d^{MN} = -\frac{\omega\gamma(e(2+w)(-1+\gamma)+q\omega(1+\gamma))}{2q(-4-4\omega+\omega^2\gamma)}$. When $q \geq \frac{(2+\omega)(1-\gamma)e}{\omega(1+\gamma)}$, we have $d^{MF} - d^{MN} \geq 0$; when $q < \frac{(2+\omega)(1-\gamma)e}{\omega(1+\gamma)}$, we have $d^{MF} - d^{MN} < 0$. □

Proof of Proposition 9. According to Lemmas 3 and 4, we can calculate the difference of retailer's profit between case MF and case MN as $\pi^{MF} - \pi^{MN} = -\frac{\omega\gamma(2eq(2+\omega)(-1+\gamma)+e^2\omega(-1+\gamma)^2+q^2\omega(1+\gamma))}{4q(-4-4\omega+\omega^2\gamma)}$. Let $g(q) = 2eq(2+\omega)(-1+\gamma)+e^2\omega(-1+\gamma)^2+q^2\omega(1+\gamma) = 0$, we can calculate $q = \frac{(2+\omega\pm\sqrt{4+4\omega-\omega^2\gamma})(1-\gamma)e}{\omega(1+\gamma)}$. Because $\frac{(1-\gamma)e}{1-\delta} > \frac{(2+\omega-\sqrt{4+4\omega-\omega^2\gamma})(1-\gamma)e}{\omega(1+\gamma)}$, we consider this question in two scenarios:

(i) When $\frac{(1-\gamma)e}{1-\delta} \geq \frac{(2+\omega+\sqrt{4+4\omega-\omega^2\gamma})(1-\gamma)e}{\omega(1+\gamma)}$, we have $\pi^{MF} > \pi^{MN}$.
(ii) When $\frac{(1-\gamma)e}{1-\delta} < \frac{(2+\omega+\sqrt{4+4\omega-\omega^2\gamma})(1-\gamma)e}{\omega(1+\gamma)}$, there exists two situations: when $\frac{(1-\gamma)e}{1-\delta} \leq q \leq \frac{(2+\omega+\sqrt{4+4\omega-\omega^2\gamma})(1-\gamma)e}{\omega(1+\gamma)}$, we have $\pi^{MF} < \pi^{MN}$; when $q > \frac{(2+\omega+\sqrt{4+4\omega-\omega^2\gamma})(1-\gamma)e}{\omega(1+\gamma)}$, we have $\pi^{MF} > \pi^{MN}$. □

Acknowledgments

This paper was supported in part by the National Natural Science Foundation of China (No. 71571043), the Humanities and Social Sciences Foundation of the Ministry of Education in China (No. 15YJC630172), Social Science Program of Beijing (No. 18GLB040), the University of International Business and Economics

(No. 17JQ06), and the Fundamental Research Funds for the Central Universities in UIBE (No. CXTD11-04).

References

Arslan, H and S Kachani (2010). Dynamic pricing under consumer reference-price effects. *Wiley Encyclopedia of Operations Research and Management Science*. New York: Wiley, doi:10.1002/9780470400531.

Bolton, LE, L Warlop and JW Alba (2003). Consumer perceptions of price (un)fairness. *Journal of Consumer Research*, 29, 474–491.

Cachon, GP and P Feldman (2017). Is advance selling desirable with competition? *Marketing Science*, 36, 214–231, doi:10.1287/mksc.2016.1006.

Cai, Q, C Luo, X Tian and S Wang (2019). Uniform pricing strategy versus price differentiation strategy in the presence of cost saving and demand increasing. *Journal of Systems Science and Complexity*, 32, 932–946.

Cao, P, N Zhao and J Wu (2019). Dynamic pricing with Bayesian demand learning and reference price effect. *European Journal of Operational Research*, 279, 540–556.

Chen, J, YW Zhou and Y Zhong (2017a). A pricing/ordering model for a dyadic supply chain with buyback guarantee financing and fairness concerns. *International Journal of Production Research*, 55, 5287–5304.

Chen, K, Y Zha, LC Alwan and L Zhang (2019). Dynamic pricing in the presence of reference price effect and consumer strategic behavior. *International Journal of Production Research*, 58, 546–561, doi:10.1080/00207543.2019.1598592.

Chen, X, P Hu and Z Hu (2017b). Efficient algorithms for dynamic pricing problem with reference price effect. *Management Science*, 63, 4389–4408.

Chen, Y and TH Cui (2013). The benefit of uniform price for branded variants. *Marketing Science*, 32, 36–50.

Cui, T, S Jagmohan, Z Raju and J Zhang (2007). Fairness and channel coordination. *Management Science*, 53, 1303–1314.

Fibich, G, A Gavious and O Lowengart (2003). Explicit solutions of optimization models and differential games with nonsmooth (asymmetric) reference-price effects. *Operations Research*, 51, 721–734.

Fibich, G, A Gavious and O Lowengart (2005). The dynamics of price elasticity of demand in the presence of reference price effects. *Journal of the Academy of Marketing Science*, 33, 66–78.

Fu, HL, G Manogaran, K Wu, M Cao, S Jiang and A Yang (2020). Intelligent decision-making of online shopping behavior based on internet of things. *International Journal of Information Management*, 50, 515–525.

Goldfarb, A, TH Ho, W Amaldoss, AL Brown, Y Chen, TH Cui, A Galasso, T Hossain, MH Su and N Lim (2012). Behavioral models of managerial decision-making. *Marketing Letters*, 23, 405–421.

Goolsbee, A and PJ Klenow (2018). Internet rising, prices falling: Measuring inflation in a world of e-commerce. *AEA Papers and Proceedings*, 108, 488–492.

Guo, L (2015). Inequity aversion and fair selling. *Journal of Marketing Research*, 52, 77–89.

Guo, X and B Jiang (2016). Signaling through price and quality to consumers with fairness concerns. *Journal of Marketing Research*, 53, 988–1000.

Ho, TH, X Su and Y Wu (2014). Distributional and peer-induced fairness in supply chain contract design. *Production and Operations Management*, 23, 161–175.

Hu, Z, X Chen and P Hu (2016). Dynamic pricing with gain-seeking reference price effects. *Operations Research*, 64, 150–157.

Kahneman, D, JL Knetsch and R Thaler (1986). Fairness as a constraint on profit seeking: Entitlements in the market. *The American Economic Review*, 76, 728–741.
Li, C and F Zhang (2013). Advance demand information, price discrimination, and pre-order strategies. *Manufacturing & Service Operations Management*, 15, 57–71.
Li, KJ and S Jain (2015). Behavior-based pricing: An analysis of the impact of peer-induced fairness. *Management Science*, 62, 2705–2721.
Mazumdar, T, SP Raj and I Sinha (2005). Reference price research: Review and propositions. *Journal of Marketing*, 69, 84–102.
Moon, S, GJ Russell and SD Duvvuri (2006). Profiling the reference price consumer. *Journal of Retailing*, 82, 1–11.
Nasiry, J and I Popescu (2011). Dynamic pricing with peak-end consumer anchoring. *Operations Research*, 59, 1361–1368.
Popescu, I and Y Wu (2005). Dynamic pricing strategies under repeated interactions. https://flora.insead.edu/fichiersti_wp/inseadwp2005/2005-11.pdf (access on July 19, 2021).
Popescu, I and Y Wu (2007). Dynamic pricing strategies with reference effects. *Operations Research*, 55, 413–429.
Prasad, A, KE Stecke and XY Zhao (2011). Advance selling by a newsvendor retailer. *Production and Operations Management*, 20, 129–142.
Tang, CS, K Rajaram, A Alptekinoğlu and JH Ou (2004). The benefits of advance booking discount programs: Model and analysis. *Management Science*, 50, 465–478.
Wang, N, T Zhang, X Zhu and P Li (2020a). Online-offline competitive pricing with reference price effect. *Journal of the Operational Research Society*, 72, 642–653, doi: 10.1080/01605682.2019.1696154.
Wang, X, J Tian and ZP Fan (2020b). Optimal presale strategy considering consumers' preference reversal or inconsistency. *Computers & Industrial Engineering*, 146, 106581, doi:10.1016/j.cie.2020.106581.
Wu, M, RH Teunter and SX Zhu (2019). Online marketing: When to offer a refund for advanced sales. *International Journal of Research in Marketing*, 36, 471–491.
Xia, L, KB Monroe and JL Cox (2004). The price is unfair! A conceptual framework of price fairness perceptions. *Journal of Marketing*, 68, 1–15.
Yang, J, J Xie, X Deng and H Xiong (2013). Cooperative advertising in a distribution channel with fairness concerns. *European Journal of Operational Research*, 227, 401–407.
Yang, L, YY Zheng, CH Wu, SZ Dong, XF Shao and W Liu (2019). Deciding online and offline sales strategies when service industry customers express fairness concerns. *Enterprise Information Systems*, 1–18, doi:10.1080/17517575.2019.1709665.
Yi, Z, Y Wang, Y Liu and YJ Chen (2018). The impact of consumer fairness seeking on distribution channel selection: Direct selling versus agent selling. *Production and Operations Management*, 27, 1148–1167.
Zeng, C (2018). Advance selling of new products considering retailers' learning. *International Journal of Economic Theory*, 16, 306–328.
Zhang, J, WK Chiang and L Liang (2014). Strategic pricing with reference effects in a competitive supply chain. *Omega*, 44, 126–135.
Zhang, Q, JX Zhang and WS Tang (2015). A dynamic advertising model with reference price effect. *Operations Research*, 49, 669–688.
Zhang, W and Y He (2019). Optimal advance selling discount strategy with future-oriented consumers. *Managerial and Decision Economics*, 41, 308–320, doi:10.1002/mde.3101.

Zhang, Y, B Li, X Chen and S Wu (2020). Online advance selling or not: Pricing strategy of new product entry in a supply chain. *Managerial and Decision Economics*, 41, 1446–1461.

Zhao, SJ and D O'Mahony (2020). Applying blockchain layer2 technology to mass e-commerce. *IACR Cryptol. ePrint Arch.*, 2020, 502.

Biography

Liu Yang is a Professor in Business School, University of International Business and Economics, Beijing, China. She received her PhD from The Hongkong Polytechnic University. Her current research interests include Supply Chain management, Operation management, interface between marketing and operations management. She has published over 20 research articles in international journals, such as *Decision Sciences*, *Naval Research Logistics*, *European Journal of Operational Research*, *International Journal of Production and Economics*, *Annals of Operations Research*, *Enterprise Information Systems*, etc.

Yuanyuan Zheng is a PhD student in Business School, University of International Business and Economics, China. She is also a lecturer in Angers Joint Institute, Ningbo University, China. Her current research interests are in Operations management and Marketing. She has published an article in *Enterprise Information Systems.*

Jiasi Fan is an Assistant Professor in Business School, University of International Business and Economics, Beijing, China. She received her PhD from the University of Groningen, the Netherlands. Her current research interests lie in international business and management, especially the corporate social responsibility in global supply chain management. She has published in various international journals, such as *Applied Mechanics and Materials*, *International Journal of Computer Network, and Information Security*, etc., and also a chapter in the book *Entrepreneurship and Behavioral Strategy.*

Shaozeng Dong is a Lecturer in School of Business, Jiangsu Ocean University in China. He received his PhD from University of International Business and Economics. His current research interests are Supply Chain management and Operation management. He is the author or coauthor of articles published in *International Journal of Production and Economics*, *Enterprise Information Systems*, *Sustainability*, etc.

https://doi.org/10.1142/9789819808588_0011

Chapter 11

Impact of RFID Technology on Coordination of a Three-Tier Fresh Product Supply Chain†

Qi Zheng

School of Management, Shanghai University of Engineering Science Shanghai 201620, P. R. China
zhengqi.zq@163.com

Bin Hu

School of Management, Shanghai University of Engineering Science Shanghai 201620, P. R. China
hubinlyj@163.com

Tijun Fan*

School of Business, East China University of Science and Technology Shanghai 200237, P. R. China
tjfan@ecust.edu.cn

Chang Xu

School of Business, East China University of Science and Technology Shanghai 200237, P. R. China
cxu@mail.ecust.edu.cn

Xiaolong Li

School of Business, East China University of Science and Technology Shanghai 200237, P. R. China
820652787@qq.com

*Corresponding author.

†To cite this article, please refer to its earlier version published in the Asia-Pacific Journal of Operational Research, Vol. 39, No. 1, (February 2022), DOI: 10.1142/S0217595921400339. Reprinted with permission from World Scientific Publishing Co. Pte. Ltd.

This paper focuses on the impact of radio-frequency identification (RFID) technology adoption on supply chain coordination. We consider a three-tier supply chain consisting of one supplier, one transporter and one retailer with centralized and decentralized decision-making. Considering the factors of RFID tag cost and product freshness, two scenarios — with RFID and without RFID — are analyzed. In the decentralized supply chain, a revenue-sharing contract is established to explore each partner's decisions on ordering quantity, wholesale price and profits. The results show that (1) the tag cost of RFID has different effects on the pricing decisions, ordering quantity and profit of an FPSC, and if the amount of transportation time compression increases, the range of the tag cost's boundary value will be wider when adopting RFID technology; (2) when the members of an FPSC choose the optimal wholesale price, optimal initial fare and appropriate revenue-sharing coefficient, the FPSC can achieve a win–win result; and (3) the amount of transportation time compression has a positive correlation with the expected profit of the supplier, transporter and retailer but has a negative correlation with loss of the product.

Keywords: RFID; fresh product; contracting coordination; three-tier supply chain.

1. Introduction

With advanced technologies growing rapidly in the Industrial 4.0 era, the operation of the supply chain has ushered in new opportunities (Luo and Choi, 2020). Rapid changes in consumer demand and increasingly fierce market competition require higher agility and lower costs from supply chains. The complexity of supply chain management has increased significantly; thus, enterprises need to apply new technology to build a more efficient supply chain (Shen and Chan, 2017). However, global supply chains for fresh products have put forward higher requirements for rapid response to customer demand and market changes. Therefore, it is very important to improve the operational efficiency of the supply chains for fresh products.

Fresh products are necessary in people's daily lives and are also an essential part of the food industry. However, as sellers of special perishable products, grocery retailers often suffer massive losses due to damage and spoilage of fresh products (Zheng *et al.*, 2017). In Europe, the attrition rate of fresh products in retail stores is as high as 15%, causing billions of dollars in losses each year (Fan *et al.*, 2020). In the USA, the losses in the fresh product industry are up to $30 billion annually (Chen *et al.*, 2018). In China, more than 25% of fresh products decay during circulation, which causes a loss of more than ¥150 billion every year (Wang and Chen, 2017). Hence, massive losses of fresh products have become a critical issue that many retailers must confront.

What causes these losses of fresh products? According to the operations processes of the fresh product supply chain, the losses mainly arise from transportation, delivery, and retail. During fresh product transportation and delivery to the grocery, if distribution is inadequately handled, such as keeping the fresh product at improper places and temperatures on the shelves, spoilage will increase greatly. Additionally, if fresh products are misplaced during retailing, consumer buying choices will be affected, and the losses of fresh products will also increase.

How can the loss rate of product be reduced? To date, the most prospective technology-based solution is radio-frequency identification (RFID) implementation. Using the technology, automatic identification and information capture technology can shorten the transportation time of produce, improve the efficiency of produce circulation (Mejjaouli and Babiceanu, 2018), and reduce losses (Keizer *et al.*, 2017). Moreover, RFID is considered an effective way to solve the problem of misplacement because it enables the tracking of produce and access to real-time inventory information (Zhang *et al.*, 2018). In addition, the retailer will not miss sales opportunities since the application of RFID makes replenishment more timely (Grunow and Piramuthu, 2013). However, RFID implementation will influence the benefits and costs of the different members of FPSCs. If there is a lack of effective revenue sharing and cost sharing among the members of the supply chain, RFID implementation will lead to inefficient cooperation in the FPSC, which will greatly aggravate the losses of fresh products. Therefore, an increasing number of researchers and practitioners are paying attention to the application of RFID.

Since RFID adoption may shorten the transportation time and may decrease the misplacement of fresh products during retailing, losses of fresh products can be reduced. In fact, several retail chains have urged their suppliers to apply RFID. For example, Walmart supermarkets implemented a pallet-level and box-level tracking system based on RFID that procures fruits from many different farms, and all of the fresh product is transported by third-party logistics companies. In reality, modern supply chains, including suppliers, transporters and retailers, are called three-tier supply chains (Heydari *et al.*, 2019). Although the three-tier supply chain is important and common in modern businesses, academic research in the field of FPSC coordination has paid less attention to it than two-tier FPSCs. This is an important gap that is addressed in this study. Accordingly, enhanced solutions need to be devised to coordinate the three-tier FPSC.

In three-tier FPSC management, the application of RFID technology increases costs to the supplier, improves the performance of the transporter, and reduces the misplacement rate of the retailer. Free-rider behavior by the retailer and the transporter causes them to share the benefits of the supplier and affects the operation of the FPSC. Therefore, how to coordinate the FPSC in centralized and decentralized decisions with RFID technology has become a question worth considering. Another major challenge is to maintain a low loss rate for fresh products. RFID technology has been verified to significantly improve efficiency in different stages of the supply chain, and the related effects on costs are by no means negligible (Fan *et al.*, 2015).

Consequently, we aim to address four questions in this paper: (1) What are the key factors that affect the profits of the supply chain and each partner with RFID technology in a three-tier FPSC? (2) What conditions does transportation time compression need to satisfy to improve the profit of FPSCs? (3) How will the RFID tag cost for contract coordination impact the profits of the FPSC? (4) How can the FPSC be coordinated by contract after adopting RFID technology?

To answer these questions, we investigate RFID investment in both centralized and decentralized FPSCs based on a mathematical model, in which the threshold values of tag cost and freshness are determined to identify the ordering strategies and revenue. In a decentralized FPSC, the effect of RFID application on supply chain decisions is discussed with a revenue-sharing contract among the supplier, transporter, and retailer. This is a worthy scientific problem for study.

It is interesting to find that transporter and retailer revenues are much more dependent on the RFID tag cost than those of the supplier, although RFID technology can benefit supply chain partners. The main reason is that the supplier is the Stackelberg leader, who determines the wholesale price, while the retailer is the follower. Therefore, if revenue is not shared appropriately among supply chain partners after adopting RFID, the supply chain will perform poorly even with a coordinated contract.

The novelty of our work relies on three main contributions. First, it is meaningful to investigate RFID tag cost-effectiveness in contract coordination and identify the threshold values analytically for both centralized and decentralized FPSCs, which can improve the efficiency of the supply chain. Second, the difficulty of the study is the modelling complexity of the decentralized FPSC, including stochastic behaviors such as demand, freshness, stocking factor and the proportion of product that has not suffered a quality loss. Finally, we apply the revenue-sharing contract to address the three-tier FPSC coordination with RFID technology, which leads to all the partners achieving a win–win result.

The remainder of the paper is organized as follows. In Sec. 2, we review the related literature and position our work before describing the model and assumptions in Sec. 3. In Sec. 4, we study a coordination model without RFID technology. In Sec. 5, we present a coordination model with RFID technology. In Sec. 6, we investigate the effect of RFID technology on supply chain decisions under different scenarios. In Sec. 7, we use numerical examples to illustrate the model before drawing our conclusions in Sec. 8.

2. Literature Review

Our research builds on existing work in three distinct areas. First, we investigate FPSC issues in operations management. This review primarily covers the recent analytical work addressing the various aspects of inventory management, pricing, and ordering policies. Second, we explore the work related to the coordination of the supply chain by contract. Third, we discuss RFID technology as applied to operations management.

2.1. *Related research on operations management of FPSCs*

In recent years, there have been a large number of quantitative studies on FPSCs. These studies have mainly focused on inventory management, pricing, and ordering strategies. Haijema and Minner (2019) proposed an overview of existing stock-age-dependent order strategies and provided new stock-age-dependent order strategies. Zheng *et al.* (2019) developed a fault tree model to discuss uncertain factors affecting the FPSC distribution system and evaluated the reliability of the FPSC distribution system for fresh products. Some studies have combined these three factors. For instance, Li *et al.* (2015) and Herbon (2018) analyzed the policies of joint dynamic pricing and inventory control for perishable produce in a stochastic inventory system. Wu *et al.* (2017) developed a mathematical model by taking pricing into consideration, exploring the deterioration rate linked to the expiration date and adding an appropriate nonconstant purchasing cost. Maihami *et al.* (2017) developed a model for pricing and inventory control of noninstantaneous deteriorating produce under two-echelon trade credit in which the supplier provided a credit period to the retailer and the retailer in turn offered a delay in payment to the consumer. Fan *et al.* (2020) examined the coexistence of a multi-age fresh product supply chain and investigated the corresponding joint pricing and replenishment strategy for fresh products. However, none of these studies considered ways of coordinating FPSCs with a contract.

2.2. *Related studies on contracting coordination*

The application of contracts in supply chain coordination has attracted the attention of practitioners and scholars. Contract management and coordination are essential in FPSCs. It is important to note that supply chain members usually have different coordination policies, and contracts are an alternative policy to coordinate supply chains. Wu *et al.* (2015) investigated an outsourcing logistics channel in which a distributor purchased a certain amount of fresh product and outsourced his or her logistics business to a third-party logistics service provider and developed two novel incentive mechanisms to coordinate the decentralized channel considering the risk preference. Zhang *et al.* (2015) established a cooperative investment and revenue-sharing contract to coordinate all the partners involved in an FPSC; all participants jointly invested in technology to reduce deterioration. Wang and Chen (2017) examined an FPSC composed of one supplier and one retailer. They investigated the option pricing policy in the newsvendor framework with wholesale price and call option portfolio contracts. Zheng *et al.* (2019) studied a fresh product supply chain consisting of one supplier and multiple retailers and discussed how to coordinate the supply chain with a quantity discount contract under joint procurement. The above papers mainly focused on the coordination mechanisms in a two-tier supply chain with one supplier and one retailer. These studies did not consider how to coordinate a supply chain with RFID technology in a three-tier system.

2.3. *Related research on RFID applications in supply chains*

In the Industry 4.0 era, an increasing number of researchers and entrepreneurs realize the importance of RFID technology for reducing operational costs and improving supply chain efficiency. There is some research on coordinating a supply chain with RFID technology. Fan *et al.* (2015) researched the impact of RFID technology application on supply chain decisions, which involves the problems of shrinkage and misplacement in the Internet of Things. Gautam *et al.* (2017) studied a case in the kiwifruit supply chain to reduce liability costs and analyzed the impact of RFID adoption on traceability. However, their models did not consider the characteristics of fresh products in a three-tier supply chain. Additionally, some studies presented a stochastic mathematical method to optimize supply chain profit and determine the optimal granularity level of perishable produce when an RFID solution is applied (Aiello *et al.*, 2015). George *et al.* (2019) investigated the main methods of food traceability and established a restaurant prototype that could achieve more reliable food traceability by using blockchain and product identifiers. However, these studies did not investigate the impact of RFID technology in a three-tier supply chain for fresh products.

In our work, the supply chain needs to address the highly perishable nature of the products. The tag cost of RFID technology is considered, and the supply chain partners are allowed to share the tag cost. We investigate the effect of RFID application on both centralized and decentralized supply chains, where the centralized supply chain means that there is a central planner who is responsible for decision-making, and the decentralized supply chain means that individual entities in the supply chain make their own decisions separately.

The differences between the abovementioned papers and our research lie in the following: (1) rather than focusing on the inventory management, pricing, and ordering strategies of FPSCs, we specifically analyze contract coordination of the supply chain; and (2) rather than considering the coordination of a two-tier supply chain, we investigate how to coordinate a three-tier supply chain for fresh products. Additionally, we consider RFID tag cost-effectiveness in coordination policy and identify the threshold values analytically for both centralized and decentralized supply chains.

3. Problem Description

We consider a three-tier fresh product supply chain in which a supplier sells a single type of fresh product to a retailer through one transporter in a single-period setting. To be consistent with most of the supply chain literature, in the following, we refer to the transporter exclusively as the distributor. The fresh product in this paper is a specific type of perishable product.

In an FPSC, the retailer determines his or her own ordering quantity according to actual market demand and procures an amount of fresh product at a wholesale price, which is set by the supplier. Then, the supplier needs to choose a transporter to transport the fresh product to a long-distance market. Thus, the transporter first develops a transportation cost function, including an initial fare and a penalty cost. The supplier determines his or her own delivery quantity of fresh product by considering the transportation cost and the retailer's ordering quantity. Finally, when

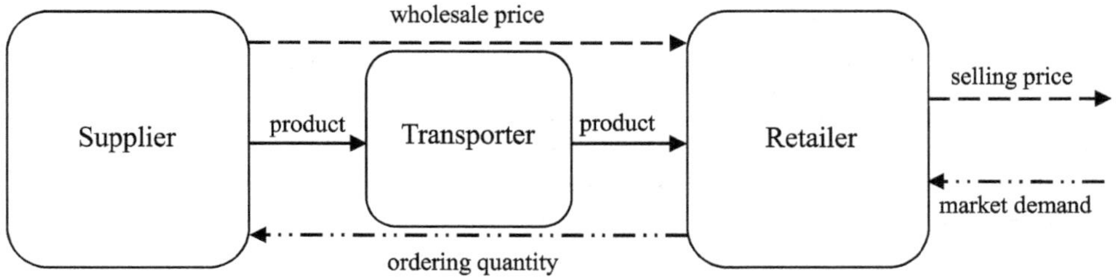

Fig. 1. The relationship of events in the three-tier FPSC.

the fresh product is transported to the market, the retailer determines the selling price according to the freshness and the loss of the product and then sells them to the consumers. The relationship of events in the three-tier FPSC is displayed in Fig. 1.

To simplify the mathematical model without losing generality, we assume the following:

- The supplier acts as the leader, and the retailer is the follower.
- The salvage value of unsold products is zero at the end of the sales period.
- Stock-out is not allowed.

We adopt the demand function developed by Cai *et al.* (2010), $D(P, \theta(t)) = M \cdot P^{-k} \cdot \theta(t) \cdot \varepsilon$, where M denotes the random factor, $f(x)$ and $F(x)$ denote the probability density function and distribution function, respectively. M denotes the constant of market size, k denotes the elasticity index of the selling price, P is the product's selling price, and $\theta(t)$ is the freshness function of the product. The product's freshness decreases with time and decreases with market demand.

In fact, we know that fresh products will suffer from a loss of quality and freshness during transportation. Let $m(t)$ represent the proportion of product that has not suffered a quality loss during transportation. If the transport time is longer, the proportion of fresh product lost will be greater. In this paper, $m(t) \in [0, 1]$, $\partial m(t)/\partial t \leq 0$, and $\partial^2 m(t)/\partial t^2 \leq 0$. It is positively correlated with $\theta(t)$. The lower the product's freshness, the smaller the proportion of product that has not suffered a quality loss.

The transporter's penalty function is $S = S_0 - \lambda \cdot (t - T_0)^+$, where S_0 is the transporter's initial fare, t is the transportation time, and λ is the coefficient of the penalty cost. T_0 is the maximum transportation time specified in the contract. When the transportation time exceeds T_0, the transporter must pay the penalty cost.

When the supply chain adopts RFID technology, the radio frequency reader can provide real-time information updates and improve products' traceability and visibility among FPSC, reducing the time of manual operations, and increasing

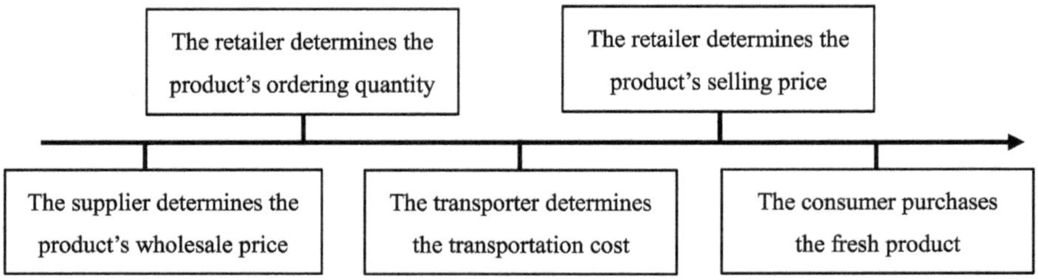

Fig. 2. Game sequence in a three-tier FPSC with RFID.

Table 1. Notation for mathematical models.

Parameters	Brief description
c_1	The production cost of fresh product
w	The wholesale price of the supplier
c_2	The transportation cost of the transporter
c_t	The tag cost of RFID technology
P	The selling price of the product
Q_R	The ordering quantity of the retailer
Q_S	The delivery quantity of the supplier
S_0	The initial fare of the transporter
c	The elasticity index of the selling price
t	The transportation time of the product
Δt	The amount of transportation time compression
$\theta(t)$	The freshness of the product
$m(t)$	The proportion of product that has not suffered a quality loss
π_R	The profit of the retailer
π_S	The profit of the supplier
π_L	The profit of the transporter
π	The total profit of the whole supply chain

the operation efficiency of supply chain, so it can increase the transportation time compression Δt, and reduce lead-time in the FPSC. In addition, it needs to invest in the tag cost of RFID technology to improve the product's freshness. In this paper, we examine the impact of the application of RFID technology on circulation efficiency and decision-making in supply chains. The game sequence in a three-tier FPSC is presented in Fig. 2.

Table 1 provides the notations used in the proposed problem modelling.

4. A Coordination Model without RFID

In this section, we examine the optimal decisions for retail pricing in a centralized FPSC and a decentralized FPSC without RFID.

4.1. *Decisions in a decentralized FPSC*

In this subsection, we consider a decentralized supply chain in which the supplier, transporter and retailer make their decisions independently. This section aims to determine the retailer's optimal ordering quantity, the supplier's optimal delivery quantity and the transporter's optimal initial fare to maximize expected individual profit.

4.1.1. *The optimal decisions of the retailer*

In the decentralized FPSC, the retailer makes optimal decisions according to wholesale price w^D and transportation time t, which are given by the supplier and transporter, respectively. Thus, the profit function of a fresh product retailer is

$$\pi_R^D(P^D, Q_R^D/t) = P^D \cdot E_\varepsilon[\min(D(P^D, \theta(t)), Q_R^D)] - w^D \cdot Q_R^D. \tag{1}$$

where $P^D \cdot E_\varepsilon[\min(D(P^D, \theta(t)), Q_R^D)]$ represents the revenue of the retailer, and $w^A \cdot Q_R^D$ represents the cost to the retailer. We adopt the stocking factor Z developed by Nicholas and Petruzzi (1999), $Z = Q_R^D/[M \cdot (P^D)^{-k} \cdot \theta(t)]$. Hence, the selling price is$P^D = [Z \cdot M \cdot \theta(t)]^{1/k} \cdot (Q_R^D)^{-1/k}$.

Substituting P^D into Eq. (1), we obtain

$$\pi_R^D(Z, Q_R^D) = [Z \cdot M \cdot \theta(t)]^{1/k} \cdot (Q_R^D)^{1-1/k} \times \left[1 - \int_0^Z \left(1 - \frac{x}{Z}\right) \cdot f(x)dx\right] - w^D \cdot Q_R^D. \tag{2}$$

Lemma 1. *If $xf(x)/F(x)$ is increasing with x and $\lim_{x\to\infty} xF(x) = 0$, the optimal stocking factor has a unique expression, $\int_0^Z (k-1)xf(x)dx = Z[1 - F(Z)]$.*

From Lemma 1, we know that Z^* is not affected by the ordering quantity. Substituting Z^* into Eq. (1), we obtain the profit of the retailer:

$$\pi_R^D(Q_R^D) = \frac{k}{k-1}[1 - F(Z^*)][Z^* \cdot M \cdot \theta(t)]^{1/k}(Q_R^D)^{1-1/k} - w^D \cdot Q_R^D. \tag{3}$$

Taking the second derivative of Eq. (3) with respect to Q_R^D, we have

$$\frac{\partial^2 \pi_R^D}{\partial (Q_R^D)^2} = -\frac{1}{k}[(Z^* M\theta(t))^{1/k_1} \cdot (Q_R^D)^{-(1+1/k_1)} \cdot [1 - F(Z^*)]] < 0. \tag{4}$$

From Eq. (4), we know that the retailer's profit function is strictly concave in its ordering quantity. Thus, there exists a maximum value.

Taking the first derivative of Eq. (3) with respect to Q_R^D, we have

$$\frac{\partial \pi_R^D}{\partial Q_R^D} = [(Z^* M\theta(t))^{1/k_1} \cdot Q_R^{D-1/k_1} \cdot [1 - F(Z^*)] - w^D = 0. \tag{5}$$

Therefore, the optimal ordering quantity of the retailer is

$$Q_R^{*D}(t, w) = Z^* \cdot M \cdot \theta(t) \cdot [(1 - F(Z^*))/w^D]^k. \tag{6}$$

Proposition 1. *For a given wholesale price w^D and transportation time t, the optimal selling price of the retailer is $P^{*D} = [Z^* \cdot M/Q_R^{*D}]^{1/k}$, where $Q_R^{*D} = \min[Q_R^{*D}(t, w^D), Q_S^D m(t)]$.*

It is interesting to analyze the relationship between the optimal selling price and the proportion of product that has not suffered a quality loss. Simple intuition may suggest that a higher proportion of products that have not suffered a quality loss should lead to a lower selling price since the product delivered to the target market is plenty. It emphasizes the impact of the remaining quantity of fresh product on the selling price but ignores the influence of the stocking factor on the selling price. Proposition 1 states that the selling price depends on the product's quantity and the stocking factor, which means that the selling price will be lower with decreasing stocking factor due to the inverse relationship between the product's freshness and the stocking factor. In addition, when the ordering quantity is more or less than the remaining quantity of fresh product, the optimal selling price is different, and the retailer can choose the most suitable one according to the actual situation.

4.1.2. *The optimal decision of the supplier*

In this subsection, the optimal decision of the supplier is a two-stage problem. Here, we solve the problem through backward induction. In the second stage, the ordering quantity of the retailer Q_R^D and the transportation time t are known conditions. The supplier needs to determine the optimal wholesale price to maximize its expected profit. In the first stage, the supplier considers the initial fare and transportation time to determine the optimal delivery quantity.

From Proposition 1, we know that the maximum ordering quantity of the retailer is $\min(Q_R^{*D}(t, w^D), Q_S^D m(t))$. Therefore, in the second stage, the profit function of the supplier is

$$\pi_S^D(w(t, Q_S^D)) = w^D \cdot \min(Q_R^{*D}(t, w), Q_S^D m(t)) - (c_1 + S(S_0^D, t))Q_S^D. \tag{7}$$

where $w^D \cdot \min(Q_R^{*D}(t, w), Q_S^D m(t))$ represents the revenue of the supplier, and $(c_1 + S(S_0^D, t))Q_S^D$ represents the cost to the supplier.

Proposition 2. *If the optimal wholesale price satisfies* $w^{*D}(t, Q_S^D) = [Z^* \cdot M \cdot \theta(t)/Q_S^D \cdot m(t)]^{1/k} \cdot [1 - F(Z^*)]$, *the supplier can obtain a larger profit.*

In the first stage, the supplier determines the optimal delivery quantity by considering the freshness of the product and the transportation cost. Here, we assume that the range of the transportation time is $[\overline{T}, \underline{T}]$. Thus, the profit of the supplier is

$$\begin{aligned}\pi_S^D(Q_S^D) &= E_t[w^{*D}(t, Q_S^D) \cdot Q_S^D m(t)] - E_t[c_1 + S_0^D - \gamma(t - T_0)^+] \cdot Q_S^D \\ &= \int_{\underline{T}}^{\overline{T}} [Z^* \cdot M \cdot \theta(t)]^{1/k} [Q_S m(t)]^{1-1/k} \cdot g(t) \cdot [1 - F(Z^*)] dt \\ &\quad + \int_{T_0}^{\overline{T}} \lambda(t - T_0) \cdot Q_S \cdot g(t) dt - (c_1 + S_0^D) \cdot Q_S.\end{aligned} \tag{8}$$

Similarly, solving the first- and second-order derivatives, we obtain the optimal delivery quantity of the supplier as follows:

$$Q_S^{*D} = Z^* \cdot M \cdot \left(\frac{k-1}{k}\right)^k \left(\frac{[1-F(Z^*)]\int_{\underline{T}}^{\overline{T}} \cdot \theta(t)^{1/k} m(t)^{1-1/k} \cdot g(t)dt}{c_1 + S_0 - \int_{T_0}^{\overline{T}} \lambda(t-T_0)\cdot g(t)dt}\right)^k. \quad (9)$$

Proposition 2 indicates that the supplier can obtain greater profit when the wholesale price reaches the optimal level. Therefore, the supplier can determine the wholesale price according to the results. It is clear that a higher proportion of products that have not suffered a quality loss should lead to a lower wholesale price. The wholesale price will be lower with a decrease in the stocking factor due to the inverse relationship between the product's freshness and the stocking factor. Therefore, the supplier can set the optimal wholesale price to maximize his or her own profit.

4.1.3. *The optimal decisions of the transporter*

In the first stage, the transporter needs to determine the optimal initial fare to maximize his or her profit. Therefore, the objective function of the transporter is

$$\begin{aligned}\pi_L^D(Q_S^D, S_0^D) &= E_t[S_0^D - \lambda(t-T_0)^+]\cdot Q_S^D - c_2 \cdot Q_S^D \\ &= [(S_0 - c_2) - \int_{T_0}^{\overline{T}} \lambda\cdot(t-T_0)\cdot g(t)dt]\cdot Q_S^D. \end{aligned} \quad (10)$$

where $E_t[S_0^D - \lambda(t-T_0)^+]\cdot Q_S^D$ represents the revenue of the transporter, and $c_2 \cdot Q_S^D$ represents the total cost during transportation. Solving the first- and second-order derivatives, we obtain the optimal initial fare of the transporter as follows:

$$S_0^{*D} = \frac{c_1 + k\cdot c_2 + (k-1)\int_{T_0}^{\overline{T}} \lambda(t-T_0)\cdot g(t)dt}{k-1}. \quad (11)$$

Substituting Eqs. (6), (7), (9), and (11) into (1), we can obtain the expected profit of the retailer:

$$\pi_R^{*D} = \frac{k^2}{(k-1)^3}\cdot(Z^*M)\cdot(c_1+c_2)\cdot\left(\left(\frac{k-1}{k}\right)^2\cdot\frac{[1-F(Z^*)]X}{(c_1+c_2)}\right)^k. \quad (12)$$

Substituting Eqs. (6), (7), (9), and (11) into (8), we can obtain the expected profit of the supplier:

$$\pi_S^{*D} = \frac{(2k-1)k}{(k-1)^2}\cdot(Z^*M)\cdot(c_1+c_2)\cdot\left(\left(\frac{k-1}{k}\right)^2\cdot\frac{[1-F(Z^*)]X}{(c_1+c_2)}\right)^k. \quad (13)$$

Substituting Eqs. (6), (7), (9) and (11) into (10), we can obtain the expected profit of the transporter

$$\pi_L^{*D} = \frac{1}{k-1} \cdot (Z^* M) \cdot (c_1 + c_2) \cdot \left(\left(\frac{k-1}{k} \right)^2 \cdot \frac{[1 - F(Z^*)]X}{(c_1 + c_2)} \right)^k, \tag{14}$$

where $X = \int_{\underline{T}}^{\overline{T}} \theta(t)^{1/k} m(t)^{1-1/k} \cdot g(t)dt$.

4.2. *Decisions in a centralized FPSC*

In a centralized FPSC, the supplier, transporter and retailer are treated as one entity. They make optimal decisions to maximize their total profit. Therefore, the profit of the whole FPSC is

$$\pi^C(Q^C) = E_t\{P^C \cdot E_\varepsilon[\min(Q^C m(t), D(P^C, t))]\} - (c_1 + c_2) \cdot Q^C. \tag{15}$$

Similarly, solving the first- and second-order derivatives, we obtain the optimal ordering quantity as follows:

$$Q^{*C} = \left[\frac{\int_{\underline{T}}^{\overline{T}} (Z^* \cdot M \cdot \theta(t))^{1/k} m(t)^{1-1/k} \cdot [1 - F(Z^*)] \cdot g(t)dt}{c_1 + c_2} \right]^k. \tag{16}$$

Substituting Eqs. (16) into (15), we can obtain the profit of the FPSC:

$$\pi^{*C} = (1/k - 1)(Z^* M)(c_1 + c_2)$$
$$\times \left[\int_{\underline{T}}^{\overline{T}} \theta(t)^{1/k} m(t)^{1-1/k} g(t)dt [1 - F(Z^*)]/(c_1 + c_2) \right]^k. \tag{17}$$

We highlight that a decision to centralize may achieve maximum profit. In the following sections, we adopt contracting to facilitate coordination; that is, the retailer, supplier and transporter intend to achieve individual maximized profit while also maximizing total profit in the FPSC.

4.3. *Contracting to facilitate coordination*

In this subsection, we investigate the best way to coordinate the FPSC by contract. That is, the goal of the FPSC members is to achieve the maximum profit as a centralized FPSC. When they agree on the contract, the retailer agrees to purchase all remaining fresh product that the supplier transports to the market. The supplier will supply the product to the retailer at a corresponding wholesale price. Here, let α_0 denote the revenue-sharing coefficient of the retailer, let β_0 denote the revenue-sharing coefficient of the transporter and let the superscript RS denote the case of revenue-sharing contracting coordination.

Proposition 3. *When the revenue-sharing coefficient satisfies* $(1 - \alpha_0)\beta_0 > (k-1)^{2k-1}/k^{2k}$, $(1 - \alpha_0)(1 - \beta_0) > (2k-1)(k-1)^{2k-2}/k^{2k-1}$ *and* $\alpha_0 > [(k-1)/k]^{2k-2}$, *then* $\pi_L^{*RS} + \pi_S^{*RS} + \pi_R^{*RS} = \pi^{*C}$ *is achieved.*

The proposition shows that coordination requires the wholesale price, the initial fare and the revenue-sharing coefficient to meet certain conditions. From Proposition 3, it can be seen that the revenue-sharing coefficient has important significance for achieving a win–win situation in the FPSC. The value of α_0, β_0 depends on the retailer's, supplier's and transporter's positions in the FPSC and their bargaining ability. If the supplier, the transporter and the retailer agree on such a contract and implement them, they can achieve more profit than in the case without a contract. This implies that a revenue-sharing contract plays an important role in resolving similar problems in practice.

Due to the highly perishable nature of the fresh product, the supplier needs to endure high risks of product losses during the transportation process. Thus, the supplier will have a strong incentive to improve the transportation service level to reduce product losses and increase revenue. Hence, it is necessary to adopt certain technical measures in the FPSC to shorten the transportation time and reduce the product losses.

5. A Coordination Model with RFID

It is always optimal to improve the efficiency of the FPSC, shorten the circulation time, reduce losses and maintain the freshness of the product when adopting RFID technology. In reality, many suppliers implement RFID technology to monitor the products' freshness and decrease loss. Therefore, we assume that the supplier bears the cost of RFID technology c_t. Then, a revenue sharing contract is used to make the supplier share part of the retailer's profit to avoid the free riding phenomenon in the FPSC. In this section, we specify that transportation time Δt can be reduced after adopting RFID. Therefore, the threshold value of the transportation time for the supplier to transport the product to the market can be shortened to $[\overline{T}-\Delta t, \underline{T}-\Delta t]$. The loss of product will be reduced, that is, $m(t) > m(t-\Delta t)$. The freshness of the product will be improved because of the shorter transportation time, that is, $\theta(t) < \theta(t-\Delta t)$. Therefore, the retailer will obtain greater profit due to higher-quality fresh products. Here, let $w^{\Delta t}$ denote the wholesale price and let $S_0^{\Delta t}$ denote the initial fare with RFID technology.

5.1. *Decisions in a decentralized FPSC*

In this subsection, we consider a decentralized FPSC in which the supplier, transporter and retailer make their decisions independently when RFID technology is adopted. Here, we aim to determine the optimal decisions to maximize expected individual profit.

In the decentralized FPSC with RFID, the expected profit of the retailer is

$$\begin{aligned}\pi_R^{D\Delta t}(P^{D\Delta t}, Q_R^{D\Delta t}/t) = P^{D\Delta t} \cdot E_\varepsilon[\min(D(P^{D\Delta t}, \theta(t)), Q_R^{D\Delta t})] \\ - w^{D\Delta t} \cdot Q_R^{D\Delta t}. \qquad (18)\end{aligned}$$

In the first stage, the expected profit of the supplier is,

$$\pi_S^{D\Delta t}(w(t, Q_S^{D\Delta t})) = w^{D\Delta t} \cdot \min(Q_R^{D\Delta t}(t, w), Q_s^{D\Delta t} m(t)) \\ - (c_1 + S(S_0^{D\Delta t}, t))Q_s^{D\Delta t}. \tag{19}$$

In the second stage, the expected profit of the supplier is

$$\pi_S^{D\Delta t}(Q_S^{D\Delta t}) = E_t[w^{D\Delta t}(t, Q_s^{D\Delta t}) \cdot Q_s^{D\Delta t} m(t)] - E_t[c_t + c_1 + S_0^{D\Delta t} \\ - \gamma(t - T_0)^+]Q_s^{D\Delta t}. \tag{20}$$

The expected profit of the transporter is,

$$\pi_L^{D\Delta t}(Q_S^{D\Delta t}, S_0^{D\Delta t}) = \left[(S_0 - c_2) - \int_{T_0}^{\overline{T}} \lambda \cdot (t - T_0) \cdot g(t)dt\right] \cdot Q_s^{D\Delta t}. \tag{21}$$

Similarly, solving the first- and second-order derivatives, we obtain the optimal ordering quantity as follows:

$$Q_R^{*D\Delta t}(t, w^{*D\Delta t}) = Z^* \cdot M \cdot \theta(t) \cdot [(1 - F(Z^*))/w^{*D\Delta t}]^k. \tag{22}$$

The optimal wholesale price is

$$w^{*D\Delta t}(t, Q_S^{*D\Delta t}) = \left[\frac{Z^* \cdot M \cdot \theta(t)}{Q_S^{*D\Delta t} \cdot m(t)}\right]^{1/k} [1 - F(Z^*)]. \tag{23}$$

The optimal delivery quantity of the supplier is

$$Q_S^{*D\Delta t} = Z^* \cdot M \cdot \left(\frac{k-1}{k}\right)^k \left(\frac{[1 - F(Z^*)] \int_{\underline{T}-\Delta t}^{\overline{T}-\Delta t} \cdot \theta(t)^{1/k} m(t)^{1-1/k} \cdot g(t)dt}{c_1 + c_t + S_0 - \int_{T_0}^{\overline{T}-\Delta t} \lambda(t - T_0) \cdot g(t)dt}\right)^k. \tag{24}$$

The optimal initial fare of the transporter is

$$S_0^{*D\Delta t} = \frac{c_1 + c_t + k \cdot c_2 + (k-1) \int_{T_0}^{\overline{T}-\Delta t} \lambda(t - T_0) \cdot g(t)dt}{k-1}. \tag{25}$$

Substituting Eqs. (22), (23), (24), and (25) into Eqs. (18), (19), (20), and (21), we can obtain the expected profit of the retailer:

$$\pi_R^{*D\Delta t} = \frac{k^2}{(k-1)^3} \cdot (Z^* M) \cdot (c_1 + c_2 + c_t) \\ \cdot \left(\left(\frac{k-1}{k}\right)^2 \cdot \frac{[1 - F(Z^*)]Y}{(c_1 + c_2 + c_t)}\right)^k. \tag{26}$$

The expected profit of the supplier is

$$\pi_S^{*D\Delta t} = \frac{(2k-1)k}{(k-1)^2} \cdot (Z^* M) \cdot (c_1 + c_2 + c_t) \cdot \left(\left(\frac{k-1}{k} \right)^2 \cdot \frac{[1 - F(Z^*)]Y}{(c_1 + c_2 + c_t)} \right)^k. \tag{27}$$

The expected profit of the transporter is

$$\pi_L^{*D\Delta t} = \frac{1}{k-1} \cdot (Z^* M) \cdot (c_1 + c_2 + c_t) \cdot \left(\left(\frac{k-1}{k} \right)^2 \cdot \frac{[1 - F(Z^*)]Y}{(c_1 + c_2 + c_t)} \right)^k. \tag{28}$$

where $Y = \int_{\underline{T}-\Delta t}^{\overline{T}-\Delta t} \cdot \theta(t)^{1/k} m(t)^{1-1/k} \cdot g(t)dt$.

5.2. *Decisions in a centralized FPSC*

Here, we investigate the optimal decisions in a centralized FPSC with RFID.

The total profit of the whole FPSC is

$$\pi^{C\Delta t}(Q^{C\Delta t}) = E_t\{P^{C\Delta t} \cdot E_\varepsilon[\min(Q^{C\Delta t} m(t), D(P^{C\Delta t}, t))]\} - (c_1 + c_2 + c_t) \cdot Q^{C\Delta t}. \tag{29}$$

Similarly, solving the first- and second-order derivatives, we obtain the optimal ordering quantity as follows:

$$Q^{*C\Delta t} = \left[\frac{\int_{\underline{T}-\Delta t}^{\overline{T}-\Delta t} [Z^* M \cdot \theta(t)]^{1/k} m(t)^{1-1/k} \cdot [1 - F(Z^*)] \cdot g(t)dt}{c_1 + c_2 + c_t} \right]^k. \tag{30}$$

Substituting Eqs. (30) into (29), we can obtain the optimal total profit of the whole FPSC:

$$\pi^{*C\Delta t} = \left(\frac{1}{k} - 1 \right) \cdot (Z^* M) \cdot (c_1 + c_2 + c_t) \cdot \left[\frac{\int_{\underline{T}-\Delta t}^{\overline{T}-\Delta t} \theta(t)^{1/k} m(t)^{1-1/k} g(t)dt [1 - F(Z^*)]}{c_1 + c_2 + c_t} \right]^k. \tag{31}$$

5.3. *Contracting to facilitate coordination*

In this subsection, we consider the supply chain partners' decisions in the RFID case. Here, let α_1 denote the revenue-sharing coefficient of the retailer and let β_1 denote the revenue-sharing coefficient of the transporter.

Proposition 4. *When the revenue-sharing coefficient satisfies* $(1-\alpha_1)\beta_1 > (k-1)^{2k-1}/k^{2k}$, $(1-\alpha_1)(1-\beta_1) > (2k-1)(k-1)^{2k-2}/k^{2k-1}$ *and* $\alpha_1 > [(k-1)/k]^{2k-2}$, $\pi_L^{*RS\Delta t} + \pi_S^{*RS\Delta t} + \pi_R^{*RS\Delta t} = \pi^{*C\Delta t}$ *is achieved, and the FPSC can be coordinated.*

Comparing Propositions 3 and 4, we find that the threshold value of the revenue-sharing coefficient is not affected by RFID technology. In practice, although the cost of the supplier increases by investing in RFID technology, RFID not only reduces the loss of the fresh product but also improves its freshness. The profit of the FPSC can be increased. Hence, the application of RFID technology does not affect the revenue-sharing coefficient. Proposition 4 indicates that the revenue-sharing coefficient has important significance for achieving a win–win situation in the FPSC. The revenue sharing contract can coordinate the FPSC and reasonably allocate profit. The profit split chosen likely depends on the firms' relative bargaining power. That is, the value of α_0, β_0 depends on the retailer's, supplier's and transporter's positions in the FPSC and their bargaining ability.

6. RFID Implementation Impact

As the variable tag cost of RFID investment increases, the new technology becomes a heavy fiscal burden. As a result, sharing the investment cost between supply chain parties is increasingly important.

6.1. *Impact on profit*

In this subsection, we compare the profit in a centralized FPSC when adopting RFID with the case without RFID, and then, we obtain the threshold value of the transportation time.

Corollary 1. *The profit of the FPSC does not always increase after adopting RFID technology. If the tag cost of RFID,* c_t *is in the range of the threshold value, the profit of the FPSC will increase; otherwise, the profit of the FPSC will decrease.*

When the tag cost of RFID is within the range of the threshold value, the profit of the FPSC can be increased after adopting RFID technology. When the tag cost of RFID increases beyond the threshold, the benefits of adopting RFID technology in the FPSC cannot compensate for the cost of the imported technology. Thus, the supplier will abandon the application of RFID in this situation.

Corollary 2. *For a given revenue-sharing coefficient* α_1, β_1, *when the amount of transportation time compression* Δt *is longer, the freshness of the product is larger,* *and the profit of the retailer will increase. For a given transportation time compression Δt, when the revenue-sharing coefficient α_1 increases, the profit of the retailer will increase.*

The amount of transportation time compression positively impacts the retailer's profit. Clearly, the retailer would like to participate in the FPSC where all the partners agree on the implementation of RFID technology. Additionally, the retailer's profit will be higher with the increasing revenue-sharing coefficient. Therefore, such reciprocal effects provide better opportunities for the supplier to persuade the retailer to apply RFID technology.

Corollary 3. *For a given revenue-sharing coefficient α_1, β_1, when the amount of transportation time compression Δt is longer, the profit of the supplier will increase. For a given saving transportation time Δt, when the revenue-sharing coefficient α_1 increases, the profit of the supplier will decrease, and when the revenue-sharing coefficient β_1 increases, the profit of the supplier will decrease.*

Corollary 3 suggests that if the retailer's revenue-sharing coefficient and the transporter's revenue-sharing coefficient are higher, the supplier's profit tends to be lower. More importantly, similar to Corollary 2, the amount of transportation time compression positively impacts the supplier's profit. Undoubtedly, the supplier will implement RFID technology to shorten the transportation time and reduce the product's losses.

Corollary 4. *The profit of the transporter is positively related to the amount of transportation time compression Δt. The profit of the transporter is negatively correlated with the revenue-sharing coefficient α_1, while it is positively related to the revenue-sharing coefficient β_1.*

In Corollary 3, we prove that the amount of transportation time compression also positively impacts the transporter's profit. The transporter's profit will be lower with an increase in the retailer's revenue-sharing coefficient. When they sign the contract, the transporter can argue with the supplier about the revenue-sharing coefficient. To obtain the benefits brought by the implementation of RFID technology, the supplier will agree to the sharing requirements put forward by the transporter.

6.2. *Impact on ordering quantity*

In this subsection, we first compare the ordering quantity in a centralized FPSC when adopting RFID with the case without RFID, and then, we can obtain the threshold value of the tag cost of RFID.

Proposition 5. *When the tag cost of RFID satisfies $c_t \in [0, ((\frac{G(\overline{T}-\Delta t)-G(\underline{T}-\Delta t)}{G(\overline{T})-G(\underline{T})}) - 1) \cdot (c_1 + c_2)]$, the optimal ordering quantity of the FPSC increases. When the tag cost of RFID satisfies $c_t \in [((\frac{G(\overline{T}-\Delta t)-G(\underline{T}-\Delta t)}{G(\overline{T})-G(\underline{T})}) - 1) \cdot (c_1 + c_2), +\infty]$, the optimal ordering quantity of the FPSC decreases.*

An interesting observation is prompted by Proposition 5. The optimal ordering quantity of the FPSC increases with respect to the tag cost of RFID when c_t is in a certain range but decreases with the tag cost of RFID when c_t is in another range. If the tag cost changes, the optimal ordering quantity does not always change in a trend, which first increases and then decreases. There exists a peak of the ordering quantity in one sale period. Thus, the supplier can arrange the supply quantity and make a reasonable plan for production according to the actual situation.

6.3. *Impact on wholesale price*

Proposition 6. *When the tag cost of RFID satisfies* $c_t \in [\frac{1}{k(k-\alpha_1)}(c_1 + c_2)(\alpha_1 - \alpha_0), +\infty]$, *the optimal wholesale price increases. When the tag cost of RFID satisfies* $c_t \in [0, \frac{1}{k(k-\alpha_1)}(c_1 + c_2)(\alpha_1 - \alpha_0)]$, *the optimal wholesale price decreases.*

The above relationships are derived through algebraic comparison. The result indicates that the optimal wholesale price does not always increase. How should the supplier set the wholesale price to improve his or her own profit and the whole supply chain's profit? According to Proposition 6, the supplier can set a suitable wholesale price to maximize the profit of the FPSC when considering the tag cost of RFID technology. The result closely relates to the industry observations. It is also a reminder to practitioners and policy makers to develop the optimal wholesale price strategy to support suppliers in markets where suppliers prefer to implement RFID technology.

6.4. *Impact on initial fare*

Proposition 7. *When the tag cost of RFID satisfies* $c_t \in [0, (1/\beta_1)m(t) \cdot [\beta_1 w^{*RS\Delta t}(Q^{*RS\Delta t}, t) - \beta_0 w^{*RS}(Q^{*RS}, t)] - (\beta_1 - \beta_0)(c_1 + c_2)]$, *the optimal initial fare of the transporter increases. When the tag cost of RFID satisfies* $c_t \in [(1/\beta_1)m(t) \cdot [\beta_1 w^{*RS\Delta t}(Q^{*RS\Delta t}, t) - \beta_0 w^{*RS}(Q^{*RS}, t)] - (\beta_1 - \beta_0)(c_1 + c_2), +\infty]$, *the optimal initial fare of the transporter decreases.*

From the perspective of the transporter, the optimal initial fare increases when compared with the case without RFID if the tag cost is in a certain range. Clearly, more initial fare means more profits for transporters. However, the optimal initial fare will decrease when the tag cost is in another range. The transporter can choose the optimal initial fare to maximize his or her own profit after adopting RFID technology. Thus, each partner can not only improve their own profits due to the optimal strategy but also obtain the benefits brought by RFID technology. The comparison of each partner and FPSC profits poses some degree of analytical complexity; hence, we resort to numerical experiments to analyze them.

7. Numerical Experiments

In this section, we present some numerical examples to illustrate the theoretical outcomes obtained in the previous section. Here, we set the production cost of the fresh product as $c_1 = 8$, the transportation cost as $c_2 = 5$, the market demand as $A = 3 \times 10^7$, the market demand random factor as $\varepsilon \in U[0, 2]$, the elasticity index as $k = 2$, the optimal stocking factor as $Z = 4/(k+1)$, the transportation time of fresh product as $t \in [5, 10]$, the probability density of transportation time as $g(t) = 0.2$, the maximum transportation penalty time of the transporter as $T_0 = 7$, the penalty coefficient as $\lambda = 0.5$, the quality loss function of fresh product as $m(t) = 1 - t^2/250$, and the freshness loss function as $\theta(t) = e^{-t/5}$.

7.1. *Effectiveness of RFID on the FPSC*

When the tag cost of RFID $c_t = 3$, the supply chain decisions and profit in both the non-RFID and RFID cases are as summarized in Table 2.

From Table 2, it can be seen that the ordering quantity declines when adopting RFID technology. However, the expected profit of the FPSC increases by more than 10%. In this case, to avoid the free-rider phenomenon in the FPSC, the supplier will increase the wholesale price, and the transporter will decrease the initial fare to offset the increase in RFID investment cost. Compared with decentralized decision-making, the efficiency of the FPSC can be improved in centralized decision-making. The profit of the FPSC under a revenue-sharing contract is the same as that of the centralized supply chain, which allows all partners to achieve a win–win situation.

The results in Table 3 verify Propositions 5 and 6. When the tag cost of RFID satisfies $c_t \in [0, 3.59]$, the profit of all partners in the FPSC can be increased after adopting RFID technology. When the tag cost of RFID satisfies $c_t \in [3.59, +\infty]$, the profit of all partners in the FPSC cannot be increased. Generally, when the tag cost of RFID is low, the supplier will pay the tag cost and then decrease the wholesale price to encourage the retailer to order more fresh products. Thus, the profit of the FPSC will be increased. When the tag cost of RFID increases, the supplier will still pay the tag cost of RFID alone, but the wholesale price will be increased. When the tag cost of RFID is further increased, the freshness of the product is increased, the loss of product is significantly reduced, and the ordering quantity of the FPSC begins to decrease, but at this time, the supply chain can still achieve a win–win

Table 2. The effect of RFID on the FPSC.

Parameters (CNY)	Without RFID			With RFID		
	Decentralized	Centralized	RS contract	Decentralized	Centralized	RS contract
Q_M	35.65	226.42	226.42	27.23	207.81	207.81
Q_R	35.65	226.42	226.42	27.23	207.81	207.81
w	31.63	—	22.75	36.66	—	25.73
S_0	11.95	—	10.36	10.11	—	9.82
π_L	129.2	—	154.53	145.95	—	174.56
π_S	969.03	—	1000.97	1094.62	—	1130.47
π_R	290.71	—	294.324	328.39	—	332.49
π	1388.75	1471.72	1471.72	1568.96	1662.46	1662.46

Table 3. The effect of the tag cost of RFID on the FPSC.

Parameters	The threshold value of the tag cost of RFID							
	[0, 0.78]	[0.78,1.36]	[1.36,2.55]	[2.55,3.59]	[3.59,4.01]	[4.01,4.84]	[4.84,4.88]	[4.88, +∞]
Q_R	↑	↑	↑	↓	↓	↓	↓	↓
w	↓	↑	↑	↑	↑	↑	↑	↑
S_0	↓	↓	↑	↑	↑	↑	↑	↑
π_L	↑	↑	↑	↑	↑	↑	↑	↓
π_S	↑	↑	↑	↑	↑	↑	↓	↓
π_R	↑	↑	↑	↑	↓	↓	↓	↓
π	↑	↑	↑	↑	↑	↓	↓	↓

situation. When the tag cost of RFID increases beyond the threshold, the benefits of the adoption of RFID technology in the FPSC cannot compensate for the cost of the imported technology. Thus, the supplier will abandon the application of RFID in this situation.

7.2. *Effectiveness of transportation time on the FPSC*

The effect of transportation time on the FPSC with RFID is shown in Figs. 2–4.

From Fig. 2, it can be clearly seen that the amount of transportation time compression is positively related to the tag cost of RFID. From Fig. 3, it can be seen that the expected profit difference of the FPSC increases with increasing transportation time compression. When $c_t \in [0, 1.18]$, the expected profit of the FPSC will decrease after adopting RFID technology. When $c_t \in [1.18, 3]$, the expected profit of the FPSC will be increased after adopting RFID technology, and all partners in the FPSC will realize a win–win situation.

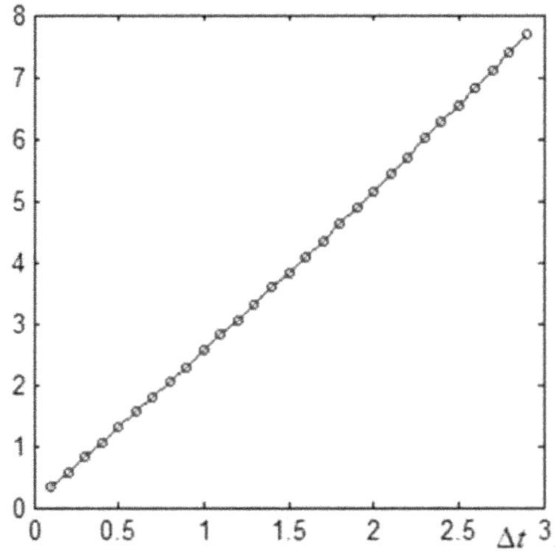

Fig. 3. The effect of transportation time compression on the tag cost of RFID.

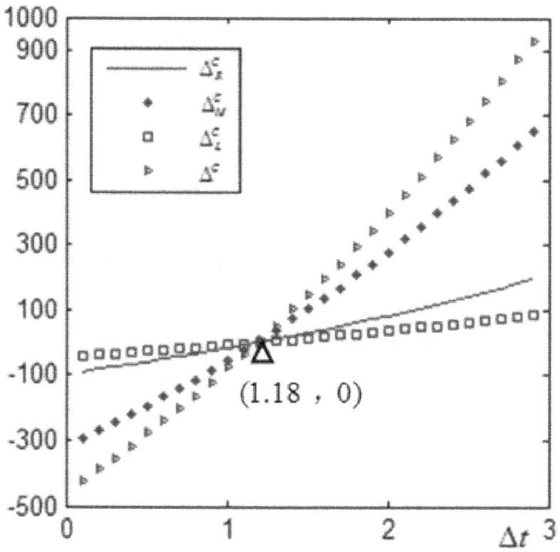

Fig. 4. The effect of transportation time compression on the expected profit difference of the FPSC.

When the amount of transportation time compression is larger within the threshold range, the expected profit of all partners in the FPSC can be increased; however, the expected profit difference of the supplier is more than that of the retailer and transporter. This is because the loss of fresh product is reduced significantly by adopting RFID, while the supplier will increase the wholesale price to transfer the tag cost of RFID to the retailer and the transporter. The transporter also reduces the penalty cost for shortening transportation time. The supplier will also require the transporter to reduce the initial fare to share the tag cost of RFID. Therefore, the supplier, a leader, becomes far more profitable than other members of the FPSC by adopting RFID technology.

From Fig. 4, we can see that the ordering quantity decreases with an increasing tag cost of RFID, and the ordering quantity increases with increasing transportation compression.

7.3. *Effectiveness of the revenue-sharing contract on the profit of the FPSC*

Figure 5 demonstrates the effect of the revenue-sharing coefficient on the profit of the FPSC.

Based on Proposition 4, we can obtain the threshold of the revenue-sharing coefficient as $0.197 \leq \alpha \leq 0.627$, $0.12 \leq \beta \leq 0.59$. Figure 6 reveals that when α increases, the expected profit of the retailer will increase, and the expected profit of the supplier and the transporter will decrease. When β increases, the expected profit of the retailer remains the same, the expected profit of the supplier will decrease, and the expected profit of the transporter will increase.

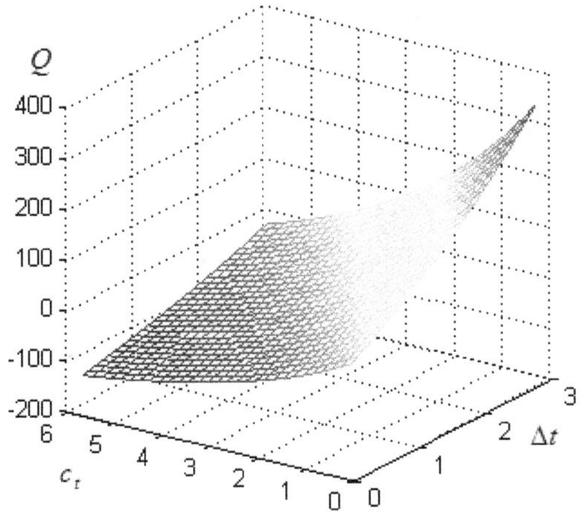

Fig. 5. The effect of tag cost of RFID and transportation time on the ordering quantity.

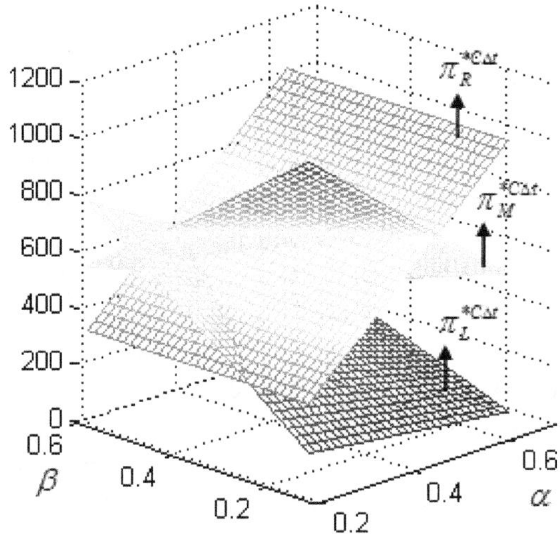

Fig. 6. The effect of the revenue-sharing coefficient on the profit of the FPSC.

8. Conclusions

In the Industry 4.0 era, RFID technology provides more accurate monitoring information about fresh products and provides many improvements for FPSC industries. In this paper, we examine coordination in a three-tier supply chain for fresh products. We focus on the effectiveness of RFID on the FPSC when the freshness of the product is considered in the model. Three cases are considered: a centralized FPSC, a decentralized FPSC and a revenue-sharing contract. In each case, we determine the amount of transportation time compression in FPSC and the threshold of the tag cost when adopting RFID technology as well as the range of the revenue-sharing coefficient for achieving a win–win situation in the FPSC. Then, we compare the parameters in the case without adopting RFID and the case with adopting RFID. The results are explained as follows:

- The optimal decisions and expected profit of the FPSC are mainly related to three factors: the transportation time, the revenue-sharing coefficient and the tag cost of RFID. The transportation time directly affects the quality and freshness of the product. In addition, the respective profits are closely related to the negotiation abilities of the FPSC members.
- When the amount of transportation time compression is longer and greater than a certain threshold, the profit of the FPSC will be increased after adopting RFID technology. Otherwise, the profit of the FPSC will be decreased. The amount of transportation time compression has a positive correlation with the expected profits of the supplier, transporter and retailer.
- The tag cost of RFID will have different effects on the pricing decisions, ordering quantity and profit of the FPSC. The boundary value of the tag cost is determined to achieve a win–win situation for each partner. Moreover, if the amount of transportation time compression increases, the range of the tag cost's boundary value will be wider when adopting RFID technology.
- When the supplier sets the optimal wholesale price, the transporter makes the optimal initial fare, the members of the FPSC choose the appropriate revenue-sharing coefficient, and the decentralized FPSC can obtain the same profit as that of a centralized FPSC. Moreover, this solution is far superior to the supply chain system without adopting RFID technology.

Our paper has important practical implications. In practice, cooperation among suppliers, transporters and retailers in the FPSC is the necessity of enterprise development through contract mechanisms. From our research results, we can infer two important managerial implications. On the one hand, the revenue sharing contract can lead to higher profits for FPSC partners in the supplier-led supply chain. This implies that supply chain members should know that the increase in FPSC profit is due to the implementation of RFID technology, and all partners can reach the revenue sharing contract to avoid the free-riding phenomenon in the FPSC. On the other hand, the supplier, the transporter and the retailer should make their own optimal strategy to support suppliers in markets where the suppliers prefer to implement RFID technology. This can further improve product freshness and profits.

There are several topics that merit further research. In this paper, we assume that the tag cost of RFID is borne by the supplier. In fact, the cost is often not paid by one partner alone. Hence, it could be an interesting topic to establish a cost-sharing contract after adopting RFID technology. In addition, governments can influence products' freshness-keeping measures through punishment and subsidy policies. Therefore, future research should incorporate governments into the FPSC and examine their effects.

Appendix A

A.1. *Proof of Lemma* 1

The optimal stocking factor must fulfil the following first-order condition: $\frac{\partial \pi_R^D(Z,Q_R^D)}{\partial Z} = \frac{[M\cdot\theta(t)]^{1/k_1}\cdot(Q_R^D)^{1-1/k_1}}{k\cdot Z^{1-1/k}}[1-\int_0^Z(1-\frac{x}{Z})\cdot f(x)dx]=0$.

Because $xf(x)/F(x)$ increases with x, the optimal stocking factor Z^* has a unique expression. That is, $\int_0^{Z^*}(k-1)xf(x)dx = Z^*[1-F(Z^*)]$.

A.2. *Proof of Proposition* 1

(1) When $Q_R^{*D}(t,w^D) \le Q_S^D m(t)$, the optimal ordering quantity, which depends on market demand, is less than the remaining quantity of fresh product that is transferred to the market by the supplier. According to the stocking factor $Z = Q_R^D/[M\cdot(P^D)^{-k}\cdot\theta(t)]$, we obtain the optimal selling price as $P^{*D} = [Z^*\cdot M/Q_R^{*D}(t,w^D)]^{1/k}$.

(2) When $Q_R^{*D}(t,w^D) \ge Q_S^D m(t)$, the optimal ordering quantity, which depends on market demand, is more than the remaining quantity of fresh product that is transferred to the market by the supplier. Thus, the maximum ordering quantity of fresh product for the retailer is $Q_S^D m(t)$; then, we can obtain the optimal selling price of the retailer as $P^{*D} = [Z^*\cdot M/Q_S^D m(t)]^{1/k}$.

Thus, $P^{*D} = [Z^*\cdot M/Q_R^{*D}]^{1/k}$ is verified. The proof of Proposition 1 is completed.

A.3. *Proof of Proposition* 2

(1) When $Q_R^{*D}(t,w^D) \le Q_S^D m(t)$, $w \ge w^D(t,Q_S^D)$, the maximum ordering quantity of fresh product is $Q_R^{*D}(t,w^D)$. The profit function of the supplier is

$$\pi_S^D = Q_R^{*D}(t,w^D)\cdot w^D = Z^*M\theta(t)[1-F(Z^*)]^k/(w^D)^{k-1}. \tag{A.1}$$

Taking the first derivative of Eq. (A.1) with respect to w^D, we have $\frac{\partial \pi_S^D}{\partial w^D} = -(k-1)(w^D)^{-k}(Z^*M\theta(t))[1-F(Z^*)]^k < 0$. It can be seen that the profit of the supplier decreases with the wholesale price. Therefore, the supplier will give a lower wholesale price, that is, $w = w^D(t,Q_S^D)$.

(2) When $Q_R^{*D}(t,w^D) \ge Q_S^D m(t)$, $w \le w^A(t,Q_S^A)$, the maximum ordering quantity of fresh product is $Q_S^D m(t)$. The profit function of the supplier is

$$\pi_S^D = Q_S^D m(t)\cdot w^D. \tag{A.2}$$

Taking the first derivative of Eq. (A.2) with respect to w^D, we have $\frac{\partial \pi_S^D}{\partial w^D} = Q_S^D m(t) > 0$. It can be seen that the profit of the supplier increases with the wholesale price. Therefore, the supplier will give a higher wholesale price, that is, $w = w^D(t,Q_S^D)$.

When $Q_R^{*D}(t, w^D) = Q_S^D \cdot m(t)$, we can obtain the optimal wholesale price. Therefore, the optimal wholesale price of the supplier is $w^{*D}(t, Q_S^D) = [Z^* \cdot M \cdot \theta(t)/(Q_S^D \cdot m(t))]^{1/k} \cdot [1 - F(Z^*)]$. The proof of Proposition 2 is completed.

A.4. *Proof of Proposition* 3

After signing the revenue sharing contract, the supplier's wholesale price is

$$w^{*RS}(t, Q^{*RS}) = (1-\alpha_0)\left[\frac{Z^* \cdot M \cdot \theta(t)}{Q^{*RS} \cdot m(t)}\right]^{1/k} \cdot E_\varepsilon\left\{\min\left(1, \frac{\varepsilon}{Z}\right)\right\} + \alpha_0 \frac{c_1 + c_2}{m(t)}. \tag{A.3}$$

The transporter's initial fare is

$$S_0^{*RS} = \lambda(t - T_0)^+ + c_2 + \beta_0[m(t) \cdot w^{*RS}(Q^{*RS}, t) - (c_1 + c_2)]. \tag{A.4}$$

Substituting Eqs. (A.3) and (A.4) into Eq. (1), (A.1) and (10), the profit of the transporter is

$$\pi_L^{*RS} = (1-\alpha_0)\beta_0 \pi^{*C}. \tag{A.5}$$

The profit of the supplier is

$$\pi_S^{*RS} = (1-\alpha_0)(1-\beta_0)\pi^{*C}. \tag{A.6}$$

The profit of the retailer is

$$\pi_R^{*RS} = \alpha_0 \pi^{*C}. \tag{A.7}$$

Thus, we can obtain $\pi^{*RS} = \pi_L^{*RS} + \pi_S^{*RS} + \pi_R^{*RS} = \pi^{*C}$.

If the FPSC can be coordinated by contract, each partner will obtain greater profit than in the decentralized FPSC. That is, $\pi_L^{*RS} = (1-\alpha_0)\beta_0\pi^{*C} > \pi_L^{*D}$, $\pi_S^{*RS} = (1-\alpha_0)(1-\beta_0)\pi^{*C} > \pi_S^{*D}$, and $\pi_R^{*RS} = \alpha_0\pi^{*C} > \pi_R^{*\mathrm{D}}$. Then, we can obtain $(1-\alpha_0)\beta_0 > (k-1)^{2k-1}/k^{2k}$, $(1-\alpha_0)(1-\beta_0) > (2k-1)(k-1)^{2k-2}/k^{2k-1}$, and $\alpha_0 > [(k-1)/k]^{2k-2}$. Therefore, the proof of Proposition 3 is completed.

A.5. *Proof of Proposition* 4

The wholesale price of the supplier is

$$w^{*RS\Delta t}(t, Q^{RS\Delta t}) = (1-\alpha_1)\left[\frac{Z^* \cdot M \cdot \theta(t)}{Q^{*RS\Delta t} \cdot m(t)}\right]^{1/k} \cdot E_\varepsilon\left\{\min\left(1, \frac{\varepsilon}{Z}\right)\right\} + \alpha_1 \frac{c_1 + c_2 + c_t}{m(t)}. \tag{A.8}$$

The initial fare of the transporter is

$$S_0^{*RS\Delta t} = \lambda(t - T_0)^+ + c_2 + \beta_1[m(t) \cdot w^{*RS\Delta t}(Q^{*RS\Delta t}, t) - (c_1 + c_2 + c_t)]. \tag{A.9}$$

Substituting Eqs. (A.8) and (A.9) into Eqs. (18), (20), and (21), we can obtain the expected profit of the transporter:

$$\pi_L^{*RS\Delta t} = (1-\alpha_1)\beta_1\pi^{*RS\Delta t}. \tag{A.10}$$

The expected profit of the supplier is

$$\pi_S^{*RS\Delta t} = (1-\alpha_1)(1-\beta_1)\pi^{*RS\Delta t}. \tag{A.11}$$

The expected profit of the retailer is

$$\pi_R^{*RS\Delta t} = \alpha_1\pi^{*RS\Delta t}. \tag{A.12}$$

The total profit of the FPSC is $\pi^{*RS\Delta t} = \pi_L^{*RS\Delta t} + \pi_S^{*RS\Delta t} + \pi_R^{*RS\Delta t} = \pi^{*C\Delta t}$.

If each partner under contract obtains greater profit than in the decentralized FPSC, the FPSC can be coordinated by contract. That is, $\pi_L^{*RS\Delta t} = (1-\alpha_1)\beta_1\pi^{*C\Delta t} > \pi_L^{*D\Delta t}$, $\pi_S^{*RS\Delta t} = (1-\alpha_1)(1-\beta_1)\pi^{*C\Delta t} > \pi_S^{*D\Delta t}$, and $\pi_R^{*RS\Delta t} = \alpha_1\pi^{*C\Delta t} > \pi_R^{*D\Delta t}$. Then, we can obtain $(1-\alpha_1)\beta_1 > (k-1)^{2k-1}/k^{2k}$, $(1-\alpha_1)(1-\beta_1) > (2k-1)(k-1)^{2k-2}/k^{2k-1}$, and $\alpha_1 > [(k-1)/k]^{2k-2}$. Therefore, the proof of Proposition 6 is completed.

A.6. *Proof of Corollary* 1

Let $\Delta^C = \pi^{*C\Delta t} - \pi^{*C} > 0$, that is

$$G(\overline{T}-\Delta t) - G(\underline{T}-\Delta t) > \left(1+\frac{c_t}{c_1+c_2}\right)^{\frac{k-1}{k}}[G(\overline{T}) - G(\underline{T})], \tag{A.13}$$

where $G(t) = \int_{\theta(t)}^{1/k} m(t)^{1-1/k}\cdot g(t)dt$.

Therefore, when the tag cost of RFID satisfies $c_t < [(\frac{G(\overline{T}-\Delta t)-G(\underline{T}-\Delta t)}{G(\overline{T})-G(\underline{T})})^{\frac{k}{k-1}} - 1]\cdot(c_1+c_2)$, the total profit of the FPSC can be increased when adopting RFID technology.

A.7. *Proof of Corollary* 2

We first compare the profit of the retailer when adopting RFID with the case that without RFID under a revenue-sharing contract; then, we can obtain as follows:

$$\Delta_R^{RS} = \alpha_1(1/k-1)\cdot(Z^*M)\cdot(c_1+c_2+c_t)$$
$$\cdot\left[\int_{\underline{T}-\Delta t}^{\overline{T}-\Delta t}\theta(t)^{1/k}m(t)^{1-1/k}g(t)dt[1-F(Z^*)]/(c_1+c_2+c_t)\right]^k - \pi_R^{*RS} > 0. \tag{A.14}$$

Therefore, when the tag cost of RFID satisfies $c_t < [(\frac{(1-\alpha_1)(1-\beta_1)}{(1-\alpha_0)(1-\beta_0)})^{\frac{1}{k-1}}(\frac{G(\overline{T}-\Delta t)-G(\underline{T}-\Delta t)}{G(\overline{T})-G(\underline{T})})^{\frac{k}{k-1}} - 1]\cdot(c_1+c_2)$, the profit of the retailer will increase after adopting RFID technology.

A.8. *Proof of Corollary* 3

We first compare the profit of the supplier when adopting RFID with the case that without RFID under a revenue-sharing contract; then, we can obtain as follows:

$$\Delta_S^{RS} = (1-\alpha_1)(1-\beta_1)(1/k-1)\cdot(Z^*M)\cdot(c_1+c_2+c_t)$$
$$\cdot\left[\int_{\underline{T}-\Delta t}^{\overline{T}-\Delta t}\theta(t)^{1/k}m(t)^{1-1/k}g(t)dt[1-F(Z^*)]/(c_1+c_2+c_t)\right]^k-\pi_S^{*RS}>0. \tag{A.15}$$

Therefore, when the tag cost of RFID satisfies $c_t < \left[\left(\frac{\alpha_1}{\alpha_0}\right)^{\frac{1}{k-1}}\left(\frac{G(\overline{T}-\Delta t)-G(\underline{T}-\Delta t)}{G(\overline{T})-G(\underline{T})}\right)^{\frac{k}{k-1}}-1\right]\cdot(c_1+c_2)$, the profit of the supplier will increase after adopting RFID technology.

A.9. *Proof of Corollary* 4

Comparing the profit of the transporter when adopting RFID with the case without RFID under a revenue-sharing contract, we can obtain as follows:

$$\Delta_L^{RS} = (1-\alpha_1)\beta_1(1/k-1)\cdot(Z^*M)\cdot(c_1+c_2+c_t)$$
$$\cdot\left[\int_{\underline{T}-\Delta t}^{\overline{T}-\Delta t}\theta(t)^{1/k}m(t)^{1-1/k}g(t)dt[1-F(Z^*)]/(c_1+c_2+c_t)\right]^k-\pi_L^{*RS}>0. \tag{A.16}$$

Therefore, when the tag cost of RFID satisfies $c_t < \left[\left(\frac{(1-\alpha_1)\beta_1}{(1-\alpha_0)\beta_0}\right)^{\frac{1}{k-1}}\left(\frac{G(\overline{T}-\Delta t)-G(\underline{T}-\Delta t)}{G(\overline{T})-G(\underline{T})}\right)^{\frac{k}{k-1}}-1\right]\cdot(c_1+c_2)$, the profit of the transporter will increase after adopting RFID technology.

A.10. *Proof of Proposition* 5

Comparing the optimal ordering quantity when adopting RFID with the case without RFID under a revenue-sharing contract, we can obtain as follows:

$$\Delta_Q = Z^*M\left\{\left[\frac{\int_{\underline{T}-\Delta t}^{\overline{T}-\Delta t}\theta(t)^{1/k}m(t)^{1-1/k}\cdot[1-F(Z^*)]g(t)dt}{c_1+c_2+c_t}\right]^k\right.$$
$$\left.-\left[\frac{\int_{\underline{T}}^{\overline{T}}\theta(t)^{1/k}m(t)^{1-1/k}\cdot[1-F(Z^*)]g(t)dt}{c_1+c_2}\right]^k\right\}.$$

Therefore, when $c_t < \left[\left(\frac{G(\overline{T}-\Delta t)-G(\underline{T}-\Delta t)}{G(\overline{T})-G(\underline{T})}\right)-1\right]\cdot(c_1+c_2)$, the optimal ordering quantity of the FPSC increases. When $c_t > \left[\left(\frac{G(\overline{T}-\Delta t)-G(\underline{T}-\Delta t)}{G(\overline{T})-G(\underline{T})}\right)-1\right]\cdot$

$(c_1 + c_2)$, the optimal ordering quantity of the FPSC decreases, where $G(x) = \int^x \theta(t)^{1/k} m(t)^{1-1/k} \cdot g(t)dt$.

A.11. *Proof of Proposition* 6

Comparing the optimal wholesale price when adopting RFID with the case without RFID under a revenue-sharing contract, we can obtain as follows:

$$\Delta_w = (1-\alpha_1)\left[\frac{Z^* \cdot M \cdot \theta(t)}{Q^{*RS\Delta t} \cdot m(t)}\right]^{1/k} \cdot E_\varepsilon \left\{\min\left(1, \frac{\varepsilon}{Z}\right)\right\} + \alpha_1 \frac{c_1 + c_2 + c_t}{m(t)} - w^{*RS}(t, Q^{*RS}).$$

Therefore, when $c_t > \frac{1}{k(k-\alpha_1)}(c_1 + c_2)(\alpha_1 - \alpha_0)$, the optimal wholesale price increases. When $c_t < \frac{1}{k(k-\alpha_1)}(c_1 + c_2)(\alpha_1 - \alpha_0)$, the optimal wholesale price decreases.

A.12. *Proof of Proposition* 7

Comparing the optimal initial fare when adopting RFID with the case without RFID under a revenue-sharing contract, we can obtain as follows:

$$\Delta_{S_0} = \lambda(t - T_0)^+ + c_2 + \beta_1[m(t) \cdot w^{*RS\Delta t}(Q^{*RS\Delta t}, t) - (c_1 + c_2 + c_t)] - S_0^{*RS}.$$

Therefore, when $c_t < (1/\beta_1)m(t) \cdot [\beta_1 w^{*RS\Delta t}(Q^{*RS\Delta t}, t) - \beta_0 w^{*RS}(Q^{*RS}, t)] - (\beta_1 - \beta_0)(c_1 + c_2)$, the optimal initial fare increases. When $c_t < \frac{1}{k(k-\alpha_1)}(c_1 + c_2)(\alpha_1 - \alpha_0)$, the optimal initial fare decreases.

Acknowledgments

This work is supported by the National Natural Science Foundation of China (72032001, 71972071 and 71901141), the Shanghai Planning Office of Philosophy and Social Science (2018EGL010), and the Humanities and Social Sciences Project of Ministry of Education in China (19YJA790028).

References

Aiello, G, M Enea and C Muriana (2015). The expected value of the traceability information. *European Journal of Operational Research*, 244(1), 176–186. http://doi.org/10.1016/j.ejor.2015.01.028.

Cai, X, J Chen, Y Xiao and X Xu (2010). Optimization and coordination of fresh product supply chains with freshness-keeping effort. *Production and Operations Management*, 19(3), 261–278.

Chen, J, M Dong, Y Rong and L Yang (2018). Dynamic pricing for deteriorating products with menu cost. *Omega*, 75, 13–26. http://doi.org/10.1016/j.omega.2017.02.001.

Fan, T, F Tao, S Deng and S Li (2015). Impact of RFID technology on supply chain decisions with inventory inaccuracies. *International Journal of Production Economics*, 159, 117–125.

Fan, T, C Xu and F Tao (2020). Dynamic pricing and replenishment policy for fresh produce. *Computers & Industrial Engineering*, 139, 106–127. http://doi.org/10.1016/j.cie.2019.106127.

Gautam, R, A Singh, K Karthik, S Pandey, F Scrimgeour and MK Tiwari (2017). Traceability using RFID and its formulation for a kiwifruit supply chain. *Computers & Industrial Engineering*, 103, 46–58. http://doi.org/10.1016/j.cie.2016.09.007.

George, RV, HO Harsh, P Ray and AK Babu (2019). Food quality traceability prototype for restaurants using blockchain and food quality data index. *Journal of Cleaner Production*, 240, 118021.

Grunow, M and S Piramuthu (2013). RFID in highly perishable food supply chains–Remaining shelf life to supplant expiry date? *International Journal of Production Economics*, 146(2), 717–727. http://doi.org/10.1016/j.ijpe.2013.08.028.

Haijema, R and S Minner (2019). Improved ordering of perishables: The value of stockage information. *International Journal of Production Economics*, 209, 316–324. http://doi.org/10.1016/j.ijpe.2018.03.008.

Herbon, A (2018). Optimal two-level piecewise-constant price discrimination for a storable perishable product. *International Journal of Production Research*, 56(5), 1738–1756. http://doi.org/10.1080/00207543.2015.1018451.

Heydari, J, K Govindan and A Aslani (2019). Pricing and greening decisions in a three-tier dual channel supply chain. *International Journal of Production Economics*, 217, 185–196. http://doi.org/10.1016/j.ijpe.2018.11.012.

Keizer, M De, R Akkerman, M Grunow, JM Bloemhof, R Haijema and J. G. A. J. Van Der Vorst (2017). Logistics network design for perishable products with heterogeneous quality decay. *European Journal of Operational Research*, 262(2), 535–549. http://doi.org/10.1016/j.ejor.2017.03.049.

Li, S, J Zhang and W Tang (2015). Joint dynamic pricing and inventory control policy for a stochastic inventory system with perishable products. *International Journal of Production Research*, 53(10), 2937–2950.

Luo, S and T Choi (2020). Operational research for technology-driven supply chains in the industry 4 era: Recent development and future studies. *Asia-Pacific Journal of Operational Research*, 37(4), 1–20. http://doi.org/10.1142/S0217595920400217.

Maihami, R, B Karimi, S Mohammad and T Fatemi (2017). Effect of two-echelon trade credit on pricing-inventory policy of non-instantaneous deteriorating products with probabilistic demand and deterioration functions. *Annals of Operations Research*, 257(1), 237–273. http://doi.org/10.1007/s10479-016-2195-3.

Mejjaouli, S and RF Babiceanu (2018). Cold supply chain logistics: System optimization for real-time rerouting transportation solutions. *Computers in Industry*, 95, 68–80. http://doi.org/10.1016/j.compind.2017.12.006.

Nicholas C and MD Petruzzi (1999). Pricing and the newsvendor problem: A review with extensions. *Operations Research*, 47(2), 183–194.

Shen, B and H Chan (2017). Forecast information sharing for managing supply chains in the big data era: Recent development and future research. *Asia-Pacific Journal of Operational Research*, 34(1), 1–26. http://doi.org/10.1142/S0217595917400012.

Wang, C and X Chen (2017). Option pricing and coordination in the fresh produce supply chain with portfolio contracts. *Annals of Operations Research*, 248(1), 471–491. http://doi.org/10.1007/s10479-016-2167-7.

Wu, J, C Chang, J Teng and K Lai (2017). Optimal order quantity and selling price over a product life cycle with deterioration rate linked to expiration date. *International Journal of Production Economics*, 193, 343–351. http://doi.org/10.1016/j.ijpe.2017.07.017.

Wu, Q, Y Mu and Y Feng (2015). Coordinating contracts for fresh product outsourcing logistics channels with power structures. *International Journal of Production Economics*, 160, 94–105. http://doi.org/10.1016/j.ijpe.2014.10.007.

Zhang, J, W Cao and M Park (2019). Reliability analysis and optimization of cold chain distribution system for fresh agricultural products. *Sustainability*, 11(13), 3618–3635.

Zhang, J, G Liu, Q Zhang and Z Bai (2015). Coordinating a supply chain for deteriorating items with a revenue sharing and cooperative investment contract. *Omega*, 56, 37–49. http://doi.org/10.1016/j.omega.2015.03.004.

Zhang, L, T Li and T Fan (2018). Radio-frequency identification (RFID) adoption with inventory misplacement under retail competition. *European Journal of Operational Research*, 270(3), 1028–1043. http://doi.org/10.1016/j.ejor.2018.04.038.

Zheng, Q, P Ieromonachou, T Fan and L Zhou (2017). Supply chain contracting coordination for fresh products with fresh-keeping effort. *Industrial Management & Data Systems*, 117(3), 538–559.

Zheng, Q, L Zhou, T Fan and P Ieromonachou (2019). Joint procurement and pricing of fresh produce for multiple retailers with a quantity discount contract. *Transportation Research Part E*, 130, 16–36. http://doi.org/10.1016/j.tre.2019.08.013.

Biography

Qi Zheng is Lecturer in the School of Management at the Shanghai University of Engineering Science, China. Her research interests include fresh product supply chain and operations management. She has published a number of papers in the international journals such as Transportation Research Part E, Industrial Management & Data Systems.

Bin Hu is Professor in the School of Management at the Shanghai University of Engineering Science, China. His research interests include industrial economics which focuses on innovation. He has published papers in journals such as Social Behavior and Personality, Complexity, etc.

Tijun Fan is Professor in the School of Business at the East China University of Science and Technology, China. His research interest lies on supply chain management and operations management. He has published papers in a number of international journals such as Production and Operations Management, International Journal of Production Economics, Omega, Transportation Research Part E, European Journal of Operational Research, International Journal of Production Research, etc. Dr Tijun Fan is the corresponding author and can be contacted at: tjfan@ecust.edu.cn

Chang Xu is currently Researcher in the School of Business at the East China University of Science and Technology, China. Her research interests include fresh product supply chain and operations management. She has published a number of papers in the international journals such as Computers & Industrial Engineering, International Journal of Production Research.

Xiaolong Li is currently Researcher in the School of Business at the East China University of Science and Technology, China. His research interests include fresh product supply chain and operations management. He has published a number of papers in journals and international conference proceedings.

https://doi.org/10.1142/9789819808588_bmatter

Author Index

www.ingramcontent.com/pod-product-compliance
Lightning Source LLC
Chambersburg PA
CBHW051050310325
24273CB00006B/86